Introduction to
Aristotle

Edited, with introductions, by
Richard McKeon

THE MODERN LIBRARY

NEW YORK

The numbers in the margin of this edition refer to the corresponding lines of the Greek text in the great modern edition of Aristotle's works published between 1831 and 1870 by the Berlin Academy. The pagination of the Berlin edition has become the customary means to locate a passage in Aristotle. A reference to, say, *Metaphysics* xii. 10. 1075^{a}25 would place the passage in question in Chapter 10 of Book 12 of the *Metaphysics*, on line 25 of the first column, i.e., column a, of page 1075 of the Berlin edition.

1992 Modern Library Edition

Copyright 1947 by Random House, Inc.

Jacket portrait courtesy of The Bettmann Archive

Printed on recycled, acid-free paper.

Library of Congress Cataloging-in-Publication Data
Aristotle.
    [Selections.   English.   1992]
    Introduction to Aristotle/edited by Richard McKeon.—1992 Modern Library ed.
        p.   cm.
    ISBN 0-679-60027-2 (alk. paper)
    1. Philosophy—Early works to 1800.   I. McKeon, Richard Peter, 1900–   .   II. Title
    B407.M22   1992   185 — dc20   92–50208

Manufactured in the United States of America

2 4 6 8 9 7 5 3

CONTENTS

PREFACE

It is true of Aristotle, as it is in the case of most philosophers, that the reading of his works is the only introduction to his philosophy. Yet some preliminaries to that introduction are needed, since his works are not easily accessible, and, when they are accessible, the place of any one work in the complex system of his philosophy is not discernible from reading it alone. The significance of what Aristotle says in development or support of a theory is usually clarified by the theories expounded in related sciences. This *Introduction to Aristotle* is a presentation in which Aristotle is permitted to speak for himself in the context of a sketched scheme of the relation of what he says in one treatise to what he says elsewhere. Four treatises are reproduced complete: the *Posterior Analytics, On the Soul,* the *Nicomachean Ethics,* and the *Poetics*; they are supplemented by complete books from three other treatises: one book from the *Physics,* two from the *Metaphysics,* and two from the *Politics.* The seven introductions which precede these seven works place them in their contexts by describing their relations to other works or parts of works, their place in the scheme of the Aristotelian sciences, and the fashion in which the subjects treated in the sciences they expound may be considered in the approaches proper to other sciences in the system. The General Introduction supplies the essential information concerning Aristotle, his times, and his influence, and fills in some of the background and interrelations of the special introductions.

Grateful acknowledgment is hereby extended to the Oxford University Press for permission to reprint the translation of the works of Aristotle prepared under the editorship of W. D. Ross.

R. McK.

GENERAL INTRODUCTION

by Richard McKeon

1. *The Life and Times of Aristotle*

ARISTOTLE was born in 384/3 B.C. in the little town of Stagira on the eastern coast of the peninsula of Chalcidice in Thrace. His father, Nicomachus, was court physician and, according to tradition, friend of Amyntas II, king of Macedon and father of Philip the Great. Nicomachus died while Aristotle was still a child, and he was raised by Proxenus of Atarneus, whose son Nicanor was later adopted, in turn, by Aristotle and was married to Aristotle's daughter. In 368/7, at the age of eighteen, Aristotle was sent to Athens, where he remained in close association with the Academy of Plato for twenty years, until the death of Plato in 348/7. After Plato's death he left Athens and, together with Xenocrates, visited the court of Hermias, a former member of the Academy who had become tyrant of Assos and Atarneus in Mysia in Asia Minor. Aristotle married Hermias' niece Pythias, and he probably taught at a kind of Academic center in Assos. Somewhat later he went to Mitylene in Lesbos, where he doubtless engaged in biological research. In 343/2, on the invitation of Philip of Macedon, he became tutor to Alexander. The instruction probably extended only to 340, when Alexander was appointed regent for his father, but his tutor did not return to Athens until 335/4, a year after the death of Philip.

The next twelve years Aristotle devoted with extraordinary industry to the establishment of a school, the Lyceum, to the institution and pursuit of a program of investigation, speculation, and teaching in almost every branch of knowledge, and to the composition of all, or most, or at least the more scientific portions, of those of his writings which are now extant. When Alexander died in 323, Aristotle's Macedonian connections brought him under suspicion and he fled Athens lest, as he is said to have remarked, the Athenians sin twice against philosophy. An accusation of impiety was brought against him, not unlike those which had been brought against Anaxagoras and Protagoras or that on which Socrates had been condemned. The specific charge was that he had instituted a private cult in the memory of his friend Hermias, since he had erected a statue to him at Delphi and had composed a poem, in what was alleged to be the manner of a paean, in his honor. He took refuge under the protection of Antipater, viceroy to Alexander, in Chalcis in Euboea, where he died in 322 a short time before the death of Demosthenes.

Most of the scant information that has come to us concerning the life of Aristotle is suggestive, but there is little positive evidence, in his works or in external sources, to support inferences concerning the formative forces that influenced his work. Since his father was a physician, he was a hereditary member of the guild of Asclepiads, and it is tempting to speculate on the youthful beginnings of his interest in biological investigations and his possible training in dissection, pharmacology, and medicine; but his

The life of Aristotle was thus spent in a period which has seemed confused and dim to historians who have learned from Demosthenes to see it as the time of the loss of Greek liberties and the decline of Greek ideals; it has seemed a period of stirring action which came close to the fulfillment of an ambitious hope to those who see in the growth of panhellenism preached by Isocrates the beginnings of more stable political organizations and in the exploits of Alexander the spread of Greek ideals. Aristotle spent a large part of his life as an alien in Athens, and he seems to have been unsympathetic with, if not unmindful of, the ambitions of Alexander. Contemporary political events and social changes left few marks on his political and moral philosophy, and the search for effects of social conditions in his metaphysics and in his contributions to science has led only to speculative generalizations concerning the influence of environment on thought: to the conclusion that the existence of classes in society suggested hierarchies in his conception of the universe, that slave labor led him to neglect the mechanical arts and prefer the theoretic to the practical sciences, that his theories were therefore verbal rather than based on the resources of experience, and that his physical principles reflected his conception of political rule. Apart from such speculations, it is clear that the peace which was forced on Athens by Macedonian domination permitted Aristotle to organize a course of studies and to initiate a vast scheme of research into the history of political organizations, of science, and philosophy—the study of constitutions of Greek states, of the history of mathematics and medicine, and of the opinions of philosophers—as well as into the natural history of minerals, plants, and animals, and to lay the foundations thereby for one of the first attempts at an encyclopedic organization of human knowledge.

2. Scientific Method in the Philosophy of Aristotle

Aristotle's philosophy consists in his contributions to the sciences and his reflections on the interrelations among the sciences, for even metaphysics, which he called "first philosophy," was one of the theoretic sciences, and its subject matter included the study of the principles of the other sciences. The interest in the structure and system of the sciences leads Aristotle into frequent inquiries into the origins of the sciences, both in the historical sense of tracing the development of particular doctrines or the course of investigation of particular problems and in the formal sense of setting forth the requirements of scientific inquiry and proof.

In many of his important works, as in the *Physics*, *On the Soul*, and the *Metaphysics*, he discusses other men's theories and conjectures as introduction to his own formulation of the problems and his determination of the principles of a given science. Among other such histories he traces the development of logical theory and scientific method. The history is short, since Aristotle was convinced that he had himself originated most of what was sound and precise in logic, and it is schematic, since the brief development of logic led to an opposition of devices and concepts that are reconciled in his own inquiry into method.

Some progress had been made in the use of scientific method by the scientific investigations of the atomists, Leucippus and Democritus, the definitions of the Pythagoreans, the logical inquiries of Socrates into the nature of definition and inductive arguments, and the dialectical devices and theories of Plato. These developments, however, illustrated two extremes of method: the atomists reduced scientific explanation to the discovery of the

material parts of the object to be explained and the dialecticians gave explanations which were inapplicable to the
changing things of experience. In both approaches the
true scientific method was distorted, and Aristotle's conception of scientific method is designed therefore to
provide both the treatment of first principles which was
inadequate in the practice of the atomists and the applica-
tions to motion and material things which were inaccurate
in the theory of the dialecticians. Its novelties center about
the treatment of causes, by which the application of principles to things is insured, and the analysis of terms and
propositions, by which the accuracy of statement and inference is ascertained.

This contrast suggests an opposition of kinds of causal
explanation, for the atomists had relied wholly on material
causes for their investigations and the dialecticians had
tended to an exclusive concern with formal causes. Yet to
explain natural substances and motions, consideration of
the efficient and final causes were of crucial importance,
and Aristotle found only little and confused evidence of
their use by his predecessors. He therefore used the four
causes to isolate particular processes and problems from
the continuum of nature, which he conceived to be unbroken from the functions of inorganic elements to the most
complex functions of the human organism and from the
center of the universe to the most distant heavenly body.
Discovery of the causes supplies the first principles of the
sciences and the connecting links of scientific demonstration, and the use of the causes therefore permitted him to
differentiate a scheme of distinct sciences with distinguishable subject matters, principles, and methods, where
Democritus and Plato had, according to Aristotle, only a
single, unified science. Moreover, since scientific method
depends on the discovery of principles which state causes,
scientific proof could be distinguished from dialectic

(which depends on the statement of opinions) and from eristic (which seeks only success in argument).

The peculiarities of words, thoughts, and things must therefore be separated in the interest of securing an adequate statement of causes in scientific proof, and once those distinctions have been made, the actual development of an argument can be stated formally, apart from consideration of the truth of the premises on which it depends. Aristotle was consequently able to construct the elaborate analysis of syllogisms as a relation among terms, of propositions as kinds of predication of terms, and of immediate inference among propositions, and of the categories as simple terms, that has formed the traditional ground of what has been called the "Aristotelian logic." The logic of syllogisms, propositions, and terms, however, depends not merely on the formal relations that are exemplified in the statement of proof but on the possibility of discovering causes, which can be stated as connectives among terms only because they are links among the phenomena of nature. For knowledge and inquiry depend both on the prior knowledge of the inquirer or learner and on the existent state of things.

3. Experience, Art, and Science

Aristotle was convinced that all knowledge is derived from sensation and that the mind in its knowledge becomes in a sense all things, without however reducing knowledge to the motion of material particles reacting to stimuli, as Democritus did, or transforming things into changeless ideas, as Plato did. The psychological functions and intellectual habits of man introduce differentiations which are essential to the sciences as we know them, for science itself, as something known, is a habit of the mind, and

Aristotle is therefore fond of tracing the steps of transition from sensation, to memory, to experience (which is developed from repeated memories), to art and science. So far as action is concerned, experience is not inferior to art, and men of experience succeed even better than those who have theory without experience, since experience is knowledge of individuals, art of universals, and actions and productions are concerned with the individual. But the man of experience knows only the fact, while art and science supply the causes, art for the processes of action and production, science for the understanding of being and natural change. The universal, which is first isolated in the recognition of the one in the many in experience, is thus the basis both of the skill of the artist and the knowledge of the scientist.

These distinctions are important since animals other than man live by appearances and memories and have but little of connected experience; but the human race lives also by art and reasoning. As possessions of the mind, art and practical wisdom, the virtues of making and doing, are distinguished by their concern with process and action from the other intellectual virtues—science, intuitive reason, and philosophic wisdom—which treat of the invariable. Psychological functions are likewise differentiated as they bear on practical or theoretic considerations: deliberation concerning actions to be taken is distinct from inquiry into the nature of things, and understanding of the affairs of men is distinct from opinion and scientific knowledge. But the possibility of knowledge of any kind, theoretic or practical, depends on the discovery of causes and on the transition from individual things perceived to universals understood. This is not a transition from things to constructs or inventions of the mind, but rather, as Aristotle likes to put it, from things prior and better known to us to things prior and better known in nature.

Our reason is related to things best known in nature as the eyes of bats are to the blaze of day, and we therefore do not perceive first principles immediately, nor are they innate in our souls, but we proceed from the half-light of sensation to the principles of science which, once grasped, are better known than the conclusions which flow from them or the experiences from which they were derived. We get to know first principles, therefore, by induction, but they are apprehended as principles by intuition. In an inchoate sense they are present in sensation, for though the act of sense-perception is of the particular, its content is universal, as for example, "man" rather than any particular man; and they are isolated in the repetitions of experience—in induction, abstraction, and analogy—until they are perceived as principles in intuition. Moreover, as the universal is present and is fixed in the experience of individuals, so too particulars emerge at each point at which thought processes deal with ultimates—not only in sense-perception and imagination which treat of particulars of existence, but in judgment, understanding, and practical wisdom which treat of the particulars of practical decisions, and finally in intuitive reason which is concerned with the ultimates in both directions, with first terms and last, for the intuitive reason presupposed by demonstrations grasps the unchangeable and first terms, while the intuitive reason involved in practical reasoning grasps the last and variable fact.

4. The Theoretic Sciences

The differentiation among the sciences which have as their end simply to know depends on differences found in the things which constitute their subject matter. One large class of things exists "by nature," and such natural or physical things are distinguished from the products of art by the possession of an internal principle of motion and rest. They move and remain stationary in place according to fixed principles; some of them grow and decrease in size; some change in the qualities they possess and are generated and pass away. These natural things include compound inorganic bodies and their constitutive elements, plants and their parts, animals and their parts: all such objects are studied in the sciences of physics, which are in turn differentiated into the various subdivisions of physics strictly conceived, including astronomy, chemistry, and meteorology, as well as biology, and psychology, according to kinds of natures and motions. In general the concern of physics with "natures" signifies that its subject matter is never purely formal, but always includes matter and motion, and that the principles of the physical sciences are arrived at by induction from the changing things of experience. The surfaces and volumes, lines, points, and numbers, which are the subject matter of mathematics, are contained, like the properties studied by the physicist, in physical bodies, and indeed they are treated, as physical properties, in the various branches of physics. The mathematician, however, treats them differently from the physicist, for although they cannot exist apart from matter and motion in fact, they can be abstracted in thought and treated separately in science. The possibility of mathematics depends on this peculiarity which adapts quantity alone among the properties of things to abstract treatment. Finally, those forms which not only can be known apart but also exist apart from matter and motion are studied in First Philosophy or metaphysics. The concern of metaphysics with being as such, therefore, involves inquiry not only into the ultimate principles of knowledge and the ultimate causes of existence and change, but also into those principles of order which determine the interrelations of the universe, among these prime movers, God being the supreme and unmoved mover, exempt from the mutability of which he is the source. The general differentiation of forms according to their existence and intelligibility in matter or apart from matter determines the three theoretic sciences, Physics, Mathematics, and Metaphysics.

Aristotle's conception of substance is intimately interwoven in both his scheme of the sciences and his projection of the methods proper to the sciences. The objects which are studied in the physical sciences "have natures" or internal principles of motion which determine inorganic, organic, and psychological change. Chance and art are both distinguished from nature as external principles of change, one with and the other without intelligent planning. The inquiries of physics are limited to the connections of things with the processes and properties consequent on their natures as distinguished from the chance interconnections in which they may become involved or the artful contrivances which may supplement or modify what is natural. Metaphysics is concerned with being as such, and the necessity of differentiating being from what is contributed by the mind and by the manner of speech in inquiry into being and of separating what is essential to the conception and statement of truth from what conception and statement are true of, leads to the conclusion that that which is most truly is substance. Aristotle begins his investigation of substances with the natural things studied in physics—animals and plants and their parts, the elements and their compounds—and grants that if these were the only beings, or if indeed these did not imply beings of another kind, there would be no need for a separate science of metaphysics, since this inquiry would be a branch of physics. He finds evidence for a third kind of substance in addition to the two kinds of sensible substances—eternal and perishable—exemplified in that list, and the peculiar mark of both his metaphysics and his physics is therefore to be found in the central place occupied in each by a non-sensible substance. Mathematics, finally, is distinct from both physics and metaphysics. It is not, as it has been conceived in the Platonic tradition, the basic theory on which physics is built, but rather the study of that one property of sensible things, quantity, which yields an order and matter for scientific inquiry abstracted from the natural connections and motions of things. It is not, again in distinction from the Platonic tradition, dependent on the supposition of mathematical entities existent somehow apart from the things of experience, but derives its subject matter by abstraction from sense-experience.

All three of the theoretic sciences treat, despite differences in their subject matters, of that which can not be other than it is, that is, of the necessary rather than the contingent. It is by virtue of this characteristic in their subject matter that their propositions are necessary and not merely probable. Necessity, however, may be either "simple" or "hypothetical." Only those broad and universal considerations which are treated in metaphysics or those properties that are involved in the essence or definition of a thing follow by simple or absolute necessity. Necessity is hypothetical in both mathematics and physics, but the manner in which hypothetical reasoning yields necessity is precisely opposite in the two sciences. In mathematics if the premisses are granted or are established, the argument can be shown to follow necessarily, but the premisses are not necessarily true if the conclusion which is shown to follow from them is known to be true. In physics if a process or motion has been completed, it can be shown that the antecedent steps must necessarily have occurred, but it does not follow from the existence of the antecedent stages that the effect must necessarily follow. Necessity in metaphysics must be sought in the essence, in mathematics in the postulates, in physics in the matter; in all three the problem of discovering the necessary is a problem of definition and of the causes.

5. *The Practical and Productive Sciences*

The practical sciences are differentiated from the theoretic by their purposes or ends, but differences may be detected in their subject matters as a consequence of this difference of purposes and in the scientific methods appropriate to their study. The end of the theoretic sciences is knowledge, and the subject matters which are investigated and the truths which are sought in them do not depend on our action or our volition. The end of the practical sciences, on the other hand, is not merely to know, but rather to act in the light of knowledge: it is not the purpose of political science, for example, to know the good, but to make men good. Aristotle sometimes isolates the practical sciences in general by this contrast to the theoretic sciences, and sometimes when his attention is turned to the differences among the ends of human purposes and operations, he differentiates the processes of making, which depend on an external matter, from those of doing, and thereby separates the arts from the virtues or the productive sciences from the practical sciences in the strict or narrow sense.

The differences between the subject matter and method of the practical sciences and those of the theoretic sciences may all be related to this difference of purpose. Since the end of the practical sciences is action, they have to do with potentialities, situations, and things which may be modified by human intelligence and volition. Their subject matter is things which may be other than they are, that is, contingent things as contrasted to necessary connections and to things which cannot be otherwise than they are found to be in the theoretic sciences. The inquirer in the practical sciences will therefore not seek the precision which is appropriate to mathematics or the other theoretic sciences. His definitions will be different, for his inquiries are not concerned with a "nature" or a "substance." The fashion in which a man grows, reproduces, nourishes himself, perceives or thinks may be studied as functions of his nature, but his virtues, the political and social institutions under which he lives, and the artificial objects he produces and appreciates depend on the habits induced by actions he has performed and influences he has suffered.

Yet each science is concerned with one class or genus of beings, and the practical and productive sciences may be related to their appropriate subject matter by contrasting their concern with action and production, or with doing and making, to the manner in which motion and change are investigated in physics. The physical sciences are confined to the study of substances which have the principles of their motion and rest present in themselves. The principle of action, on the other hand, is in the doer and the principle of production in the producer. Although the principles of the practical and productive sciences are both thus external as contrasted with the internal principles studied in physics, there is an important difference between them, for the principle of production is reason, or art, or some potency in the producer, while the principle of action is the will in the doer. Reason is therefore more important in art than in action, while the character of the agent is of crucial importance in the judgment of actions but irrelevant in art. The end of the practical sciences is to be found in the action itself and the state of character which produced it, while the end of the productive science is in the objects produced and the qualities discerned in those objects.

There are no sharp separations among the practical sciences. Ethics is a subdivision of Politics, and human conduct is studied in both, in ethics from the point of view of personal morality but with the recognition that the conduct of the individual is influenced by political institutions, in politics from the point of view of the associations and institutions of men but with the recognition that the character of communal institutions is determined by traits of the men who compose them. In both sciences, a natural foundation is sought for the ends of action and association. Ethics is concerned with the study of virtues, which are not natures or natural powers but habits; a natural basis is found for habits, however, in the potentialities of man which are influenced by repeated actions or passions. Politics is concerned with the study of constitutions or forms of human association, which likewise have no natural definitions or species, but a natural basis is found for habits in needs and interdependences of man for the ends of living and of living well, and in this sense the family, the village, and the state are natural and man is by nature a political animal.

The productive sciences are differentiated according to their products, and there are no sharply defined lines imposed by nature to separate the arts or to differentiate the kinds of artificial things. The Greeks did not differentiate the fine arts from the mechanical in the fashion that has been customary since the Renaissance, and they have therefore been criticized by humanists for confusing arts and trades, thereby degrading the artist, and by pragmatists for separating science and art, thereby reducing operations and mechanical contrivances to a servile level. The arts as conceived by Aristotle include not only such arts as painting, music, and poetry, but medicine, architecture, cobbling, and rhetoric. Since the arts imitate nature, they may be differentiated by consideration of the object, means, and manner of their imitation, and therefore, although he has no word for fine arts, Aristotle is able, in the opening chapter of the *Poetics*, to assemble the arts which we call fine by isolating their means of imitation and to differentiate tragedy from the other arts. Aristotle did, however, have a word by which to differentiate the liberal arts from the mechanical, and he sought their differentiation in educative influence of the arts in the formation of men for freedom.

The interrelations of the theoretic, practical, and productive sciences are thus far from simple: each group may be differentiated from the others by means of subject matter, end, and principle, yet each science is pertinent to all the others, and the subject matter of each may be treated incidentally from the point of view of the others and the principles of each may be employed incidentally in the others. The theoretic sciences are distinct from the practical and productive by their end or purpose. Yet the theoretic sciences appear among the subjects treated by the practical and productive sciences, since scientific knowledge is found among the intellectual virtues in ethics, the pursuit and teaching of science is a political problem, and the formulation of problems and presentation of conclusions is an artistic problem. Conversely the principles of the arts and of ethics and politics are studied in metaphysics; the proportions treated in mathematics supply a basis for the treatment of relations in the arts, virtues, and constitutions; and the psychological or intellectual processes involved in each are studied in psychology, which is a branch of physics. The practical sciences in like fashion are distinct from both the theoretic and the productive, yet the theoretic and productive sciences figure, not because of their proper problems but because of their practical implications, among the problems of ethics and politics, and the practical sciences derive basic distinctions from the theoretic sciences and are so involved in the problems of the arts that practical thinkers like the Sophists confused politics and rhetoric. The productive sciences, finally, are directed wholly to the artificial objects produced and they make their own materials, yet knowledge of the potentialities of materials, sensibilities of audiences, and formal interrelations may come from the theoretic and practical sciences, and the arts may in turn contribute to the construction of sciences, the formation of virtues, and the constitution of states.

The subtlety and clarity of the Aristotelian organization of the sciences depends on the discrimination of matter, purpose, and principle, which at once yields a sharp discrimination of artistic, moral, and theoretic considerations, and yet permits a single object or action, in its various circumstances or characteristics, to fall under the scrutiny of each mode of inquiry. The problem of the interrelations of the sciences has continued to be discussed in terms suggested by Aristotle, but without the functional variations he employed, with the result that the history of the discussion has been largely an alternation of efforts to reduce all sciences to theory or practice or art.

6. The Influence of Aristotle

The influence of Aristotle's writings on later philosophic speculation reflects in reverse the extremes between which he set his course: he has been reconciled with Democritus and reduced to a place among Plato's disciples, and he has been criticized for departing from the ideals set by the methods of both philosophers. The reputation which he has acquired and the turns which doctrines attributed to him have received in the context of other men's theories—and the influence of a philosopher is usually considered in some such manner—are difficult to explain by his works alone without consideration of the philosophic disputes which he sought to resolve and which served in turn as medium for the interpretation of his works. Aristotle's immediate influence seems to have bred scholars and specialists who seem quickly to have forgotten his scientific and philosophic principles and to have fixed philosophic terms and philosophic problems precisely but without holding to the meanings or solutions yielded by his philosophy. Theophrastus, his successor in the Lyceum, wrote on botany and on the history of the sciences of cosmology and physics; Eudemus of Rhodes, another of his disciples, wrote the first history of mathematics; Strato of Lampsacus, the third head of the Lyceum, undertook to reconcile the physics of Aristotle with the atomism of Democritus. During the Hellenistic period the discussion of problems of morals, logic, and physics reflects the impress of Aristotle's thought even in the far remove from Aristotle to which Stoics and Epicureans carried their discussions, but "peripatetic" apparently signified a scholar or a specialist in science rather than a philosopher, and Aristotle was thought of only as the most eminent of Plato's disciples.

This narrowly prescribed influence which Aristotle exercised in antiquity and continued to exercise in the early Middle Ages is explained in part by the slightness of the direct contact with his writings. According to an ancient legend, Aristotle's successor Theophrastus, fearful of the treatment and interpretation which Aristotle's works would receive in the Lyceum, presumably at the hands of his own successor, Strato, sold the manuscripts of Aristotle's works and his own to a pupil who took them to Asia

Minor where his heirs protected them by concealing them in a cellar for 150 years. They were edited by Andronicus of Rhodes in the first century B.C., probably much as they are still edited. There is no evidence that these works, as distinguished from the "published" works and dialogues which are now lost, were known during this time, but there is no need to suppose that the hidden manuscripts were the only extant copies of the works. During the period in which Aristotle's labors seem to have resulted chiefly in the production, not of theoretic philosophers, but of experts, technicians, scholars, and pedagogues, the teachings of Plato, whose writings were never lost or concealed by the Academy, were professed by "Academics" who argued for varieties of skepticism and confined themselves to practical moral problems, and still later, with the beginnings of "Neoplatonism," they inspired philosophers to mysticism and theological speculations.

The acquaintance with Aristotle in the West, after the knowledge of Greek had become a rare accomplishment, was even more narrowly restricted, and early Christian philosophy took a practical imprint from Roman thought, modified by successive infiltrations of Greek influence which were Neoplatonic rather than Aristotelian. Two or more of the six treatises on logic in Aristotle's *Organon* were translated into Latin by Boethius in the sixth century A.D., and the first two of these short works, together with the commentaries of Boethius and his essays on related logical subjects constituted the chief source of information concerning Aristotle's philosophy in Western Europe from the sixth to the middle of the twelfth century. During the next century all of the writings of Aristotle were translated into Latin, and were made the subject of intense study and voluminous commentary.

The tradition of commentaries, written in a half dozen languages, in which Aristotle appears as an "authority" and as The Philosopher, is the source of the impression that Aristotle ruled men's minds with dogmatic sway for centuries. The Greek commentators wrote from about 125 A.D., when Aspasius flourished, to 550 A.D., the time of Olympiodorus, continuing sporadically until the fourteenth century, when Sophonias was at work: they included the excellent works of Alexander of Aphrodisias, who was known as The Exegete, and the learned repositories of Simplicius, which are the source of much of our information about the earlier tradition. The remains of the labors of these commentators, considerably thinned by the accidents of history, fill twenty-three substantial volumes in the excellent edition published in Berlin from 1882 to 1909. No similar editions are available of the Syriac commentaries which began to appear in the fifth and continued to be produced until the twelfth century, or of the Arabic commentaries, which include such distinguished and influential works as those of Algazeli, Avicenna, and Averroes, the last of whom earned the name The Commentator from the numerous commentaries (written in Arabic, and soon translated or reported in Hebrew and Latin) which he prepared during the latter portion of the twelfth century. Hebrew philosophers continued the discussions initiated in these commentaries, and the long line of Latin commentaries which began to appear during the thirteenth century and continued into the seventeenth would, if all the manuscripts were assembled and published, probably exceed in bulk what survives of all the rest.

The commentaries on Aristotle assume a vast variety of forms and expound a vast variety of doctrines, exhibiting little tendency toward rigid adherence to the authority of a text or the dictate of a Master. Many of the Greek commentators were associated with the Academy or were avowed Neoplatonists or were, at least, in some manner

imbued with Platonic doctrines, and their works contain
ample indication of differences consequent on possible
resolutions of the question, still agitated, whether Aristotle should be read as a systematic opponent to Plato or
as one of his more or less inadequate and wrong-headed
followers. Many of the problems discussed by the Greek
commentators were early introduced into the Arabic and
Latin traditions, or arose independently from similar considerations, and the Christian commentators were faced
with the additional problem of reconciling Aristotle with
Christianity and therefore of freeing him from interpretations attached to his doctrines by the Arabic philosophers.
During the thirteenth century and increasingly during the
later Middle Ages, commentaries on Aristotle became the
major medium for philosophic disputation and independent scientific investigation. Albertus Magnus and
Thomas Aquinas constructed their interpretations in explicit opposition to, and in less obvious dependence on,
the Arabic interpretations, particularly those of the Averroists and the Avicennists. Even before the time of Pe-
trarch and even after the time of Galileo, the discussion of
the nature of the soul and its immortality was involved in a
dispute between the Alexandrians and the Averroists, that
is, between adherents of a third-century Greek commentator, The Exegete, and a twelfth-century Arab, The Commentator. Eventually commentaries were prepared to
interpret Aristotle "according to the mind of" Aquinas,
Scotus, Ockham, or Averroes. Disciples were won not so
much to the philosophy of Aristotle as to interpretations
of that philosophy, and the works of Aristotle have been
no more rigid in determining a unique interpretation, nor
less fertile in variety of intellectual inspiration, than the
Bible or nature itself.

The revolt of philosophers during the sixteenth and
seventeenth centuries was as much against this scholastic

mode of philosophic discussion as against Aristotle's doctrine, for much that was criticized as Aristotelian is found more easily in the commentaries than in Aristotle's works. The strictures against Aristotle which were part of the Renaissance reaction to him have been repeated since that time without adequate bases in Aristotle's doctrines or realization of how much of Aristotle was retained after the revolt. Yet during the period in which the direct influence of Aristotle has been slight in philosophy, the scholars have again been at work on the text of his writings. The great modern edition of his works, published by the Berlin Academy between 1831 and 1870, was the basis and beginning of a vast array of philological studies of the Aristotelian Corpus, its backgrounds, and tradition. His works are now available as they were never before and are accompanied by instruments and aids for their interpretation which make many of the old confusions even less plausible than they were. Moreover, Aristotle's name and doctrines are referred to increasingly in current philosophic discussions. In many cases the reference is only a reopening of old disputes and a repetition of old criticisms, but in some the citation of Aristotle is recognition that his terms and distinctions are embedded in our past intellectual traditions and our present habits of thought, and that an understanding of Aristotle may therefore shed light on the history of our problems and may suggest fruitful alternatives to the solutions that have become fashionable, or the subject of doubt. Such purposes—the understanding of strands of influence and discussion in Western civilization and the clarification of the basic problems of our philosophy—rather than the pursuit of historical or antiquarian curiosities, have led to new efforts to uncover the thought behind Aristotle's reputation and are reasons to return from what are alleged to have been his errors and his influences to an Introduction to Aristotle.

INTRODUCTION TO
ARISTOTLE

LOGIC

INTRODUCTION

The extant logical writings of Aristotle are six treatises, traditionally grouped under one name, the *Organon*. The *Categories* treats of simple terms and their peculiarities, differentiating ten most universal kinds or categories of terms as well as the simple relations—such as opposition, priority, simultaneity—which obtain between pairs of uncombined terms. *On Interpretation* treats of propositions, in which one term is asserted or denied of another and which therefore may be true or false, as well as the simple relations of immediate inference which obtain between pairs of propositions. The *Prior Analytics* treats of inferences and proofs or of syllogisms, which are combinations of three terms. Since all perfect inference may be reduced to a syllogism or a series of syllogisms, further logical differentiation of kinds of proofs is to be found in the premisses on which they are based. The *Posterior Analytics* treats of demonstration or scientific proof, which is reasoning based on true and primary premisses, that is, premisses which state the causes of the phenomena to be explained. *The Topics* treats of dialectical reasoning, which is based on opinions generally accepted, rather than on scientific premisses, which are believed on the strength not of something else but of themselves. *On Sophistical Refutations*, finally, treats of fallacious arguments which start from opinions that seem to be accepted generally, but are not really, or which seem to reason from opinions that are or seem to be accepted generally.

Aristotle's discussion of scientific knowledge in the *Posterior Analytics* is the source of many of the distinctions —and of most of the technical terms used in stating the distinctions—that have been important in the theories of scientific method developed by later logicians. Yet his formulation of the problems of scientific proof, although it involves the differentiation of induction and deduction, does not turn on the simple opposition of the inductive discovery of principles and their deductive use in demonstration. The problems of scientific proof, as he treated them, center about two processes, instruction and inquiry. All instruction by way of argument proceeds from pre-existent knowledge, whether the argument be deductive or inductive, and the problems of scientific proof, so viewed, are concerned with the principles of the sciences and the conditions of inference from the principles. The analysis of principles and proofs, in this approach, turns on the terms in which arguments are stated, and Aristotle undertook to prove that each science had first principles proper to it and that an infinite regress of premisses is impossible. Therefore predication must terminate in both the upward and the downward direction, that is, in ascent to generality and descent to particularity, and there must be a finite number of steps between the most universal and the most particular. Inquiry, on the other hand, is into facts and causes, and the problems of scientific proof, so viewed, are concerned with the relation between definition and proof. The analysis of principles and proofs, in this approach, turns on the relation of knowledge to facts, and Aristotle undertook to differentiate kinds of definition, some indemonstrable, some susceptible of demonstration, and to prove that causes are the middle terms in scientific demonstration.

Aristotle's conception of scientific method depends, thus, on analysis of both the structure of knowledge and the connections of things. He was fond of saying that we have scientific knowledge of something demonstrable when we possess a demonstration of it; and he was no less fond of repeating that we have scientific knowledge when we know the cause. In both formulations the problem of scientific proof centers on the middle term, both in the sense of the term which justifies the conclusion of a proof and in the sense of the cause which accounts for the connections in a situation. The problem of finding a middle term depends for its solution in the one formulation, as instruction, on the quick wit requisite for the discernment of middle terms and in the other, as inquiry, on that inductive process by which universals and primary premisses are derived from sense-perception and experience. The primary premisses of scientific demonstration, however, are not themselves subject to scientific proof, although they may be tested in indirect dialectical examination. In like manner, the resolution of difficulties and the discovery of principles are dialectical problems so long as they turn on the establishment and defense of propositions, and they become scientific only when they are related to the statement of a basic cause. Although Aristotle first formulated the distinctions and technical terms in which much of the later discussion of scientific method was conducted, his own distinctions have been used in criticism of his logic. He has seemed to writers who stress the development of inductive logic to have given inadequate development to the methods of interpreting the facts of observation and experimentation, while his treatment of principles and inference has seemed to symbolic logicians, who stress the methods of mathematics, too little concerned with the forms of validation and proof. Yet many of the problems which became central to these later discussions of scientific method are found in other contexts, treated as metaphysics or dialectic or sophistic, rather than scientific method, as is appropriate in Aristotle's conception of the sciences. Thus, the dialectical inquiry into first principles is found in Book Gamma of the *Metaphysics* and the formulation of the devices by which possible solutions to problems may be assembled and tests of possible positions may be constructed are detailed in the *Topics*.

ANALYTICA POSTERIORA

CONTENTS

BOOK I

ANALYTICA POSTERIORA

Posterior Analytics

Translated by G. R. G. Mure

BOOK I

1 All instruction given or received by way of argu- 71ª
ment proceeds from pre-existent knowledge. This
becomes evident upon a survey of all the species of
such instruction. The mathematical sciences and all other
speculative disciplines are acquired in this way, and so are 5
the two forms of dialectical reasoning, syllogistic and inductive; for each of these latter makes use of old knowledge to
impart new, the syllogism assuming an audience that
accepts its premisses, induction exhibiting the universal as
implicit in the clearly known particular. Again, the persuasion exerted by rhetorical arguments is in principle the
same, since they use either example, a kind of induction, or 10
enthymeme, a form of syllogism.

The pre-existent knowledge required is of two kinds.
In some cases admission of the fact must be assumed, in
others comprehension of the meaning of the term used, and
sometimes both assumptions are essential. Thus, we assume
that every predicate can be either truly affirmed or truly
denied of any subject, and that 'triangle' means so and so;
as regards 'unit' we have to make the double assumption of
the meaning of the word and the existence of the thing. The 15
reason is that these several objects are not equally obvious

to us. Recognition of a truth may in some cases contain as factors both previous knowledge and also knowledge acquired simultaneously with that recognition—knowledge, this latter, of the particulars actually falling under the universal and therein already virtually known. For example, the 20 student knew beforehand that the angles of every triangle are equal to two right angles; but it was only at the actual moment at which he was being led on to recognize this as true in the instance before him that he came to know 'this figure inscribed in the semicircle' to be a triangle. For some things (viz. the singulars finally reached which are not predicable of anything else as subject) are only learnt in this way, i. e. there is here no recognition through a middle of a minor term as subject to a major. Before he was led on to recognition or before he actually drew a conclusion, we 25 should perhaps say that in a manner he knew, in a manner not.

If he did not in an unqualified sense of the term *know* the existence of this triangle, how could he know without qualification that its angles were equal to two right angles? No: clearly he *knows* not without qualification but only in the sense that he *knows* universally. If this distinction is not drawn, we are faced with the dilemma in the *Meno*:[1] either a man will learn nothing or what he already knows; for we cannot accept the solution which some people offer. A man 30 is asked, 'Do you, or do you not, know that every pair is even?' He says he does know it. The questioner then produces a particular pair, of the existence, and so *a fortiori* of the evenness, of which he was unaware. The solution which some people offer is to assert that they do not know that every pair is even, but only that everything which they 71b know to be a pair is even: yet what they know to be even is that of which they have demonstrated evenness, i. e. what

[1] Plato, *Meno*, 80 E.

they made the subject of their premiss, viz. not merely every triangle or number which they know to be such, but any and every number or triangle without reservation. For no premiss is ever couched in the form 'every number which you know be such', or 'every rectilinear figure which you know to be such': the predicate is always construed as applicable to any and every instance of the thing. On the other hand, I imagine there is nothing to prevent a man in one sense 5 knowing what he is learning, in another not knowing it. The strange thing would be, not if in some sense he knew what he was learning, but if he were to know it in that precise sense and manner in which he was learning it.[2]

2 We suppose ourselves to possess unqualified scientific knowledge of a thing, as opposed to knowing it in the accidental way in which the sophist knows, when we think that we know the cause on 10 which the fact depends, as the cause of that fact and of no other, and, further, that the fact could not be other than it is. Now that scientific knowing is something of this sort is evident—witness both those who falsely claim it and those who actually possess it, since the former merely imagine themselves to be, while the latter are also actually, in the condition described. Consequently the proper object of unqualified scientific knowledge is something which cannot be other than it is.   15

There may be another manner of knowing as well—that will be discussed later.[3] What I now assert is that at all events we do know by demonstration. By demonstration I mean a syllogism productive of scientific knowledge, a syllogism, that is, the grasp of which is *eo ipso* such knowledge.

---

[2] Cf. *An. Pr.* ii, ch. 21.

[3] Cf. the following chapter and more particularly ii, ch. 19.

20 Assuming then that my thesis as to the nature of scientific
knowing is correct, the premisses of demonstrated knowledge must be true, primary, immediate, better known than
and prior to the conclusion, which is further related to them
as effect to cause. Unless these conditions are satisfied, the
basic truths will not be 'appropriate' to the conclusion. Syllogism there may indeed be without these conditions, but
such syllogism, not being productive of scientific knowledge, will not be demonstration. The premisses must be
25 true: for that which is non-existent cannot be known—we
cannot know, e. g., that the diagonal of a square is commensurate with its side. The premisses must be primary
and indemonstrable; otherwise they will require demonstration in order to be known, since to have knowledge, if it be
not accidental knowledge, of things which are demonstrable,
means precisely to have a demonstration of them. The premisses must be the causes of the conclusion, better known
30 than it, and prior to it; its causes, since we possess scientific knowledge of a thing only when we know its cause;
prior, in order to be causes; antecedently known, this
antecedent knowledge being not our mere understanding of
the meaning, but knowledge of the fact as well. Now 'prior'
and 'better known' are ambiguous terms, for there is a difference between what is prior and better known in the order
72ᵃ of being and what is prior and better known to man. I mean
that objects nearer to sense are prior and better known to
man; objects without qualification prior and better known
are those further from sense. Now the most universal causes
5 are furthest from sense and particular causes are nearest to
sense, and they are thus exactly opposed to one another. In
saying that the premisses of demonstrated knowledge must
be primary, I mean that they must be the 'appropriate' basic
truths, for I identify primary premiss and basic truth. A
'basic truth' in a demonstration is an immediate proposition. An immediate proposition is one which has no other

proposition prior to it. A proposition is either part of an enunciation, i. e. it predicates a single attribute of a single subject. If a proposition is dialectical, it assumes either part indifferently; if it is demonstrative, it lays down one part to the definite exclusion of the other because that part is true. The term 'enunciation' denotes either part of a contradiction indifferently. A contradiction is an opposition which of its own nature excludes a middle. The part of a contradiction which conjoins a predicate with a subject is an affirmation; the part disjoining them is a negation. I call an immediate basic truth of syllogism a 'thesis' when, though it is not susceptible of proof by the teacher, yet ignorance of it does not constitute a total bar to progress on the part of the pupil: one which the pupil must know if he is to learn anything whatever is an axiom. I call it an axiom because there are such truths and we give them the name of axioms *par excellence*. If a thesis assumes one part or the other of an enunciation, i. e. asserts either the existence or the non-existence of a subject, it is a hypothesis; if it does not so assert, it is a definition. Definition *is* a 'thesis' or a 'laying something down', since the arithmetician lays it down that to be a unit is to be quantitatively indivisible; but it is not a hypothesis, for to define what a unit is is not the same as to affirm its existence.

Now since the required ground of our knowledge—i. e. of our conviction—of a fact is the possession of such a syllogism as we call demonstration, and the ground of the syllogism is the facts constituting its premises, we must not only know the primary premises—some if not all of them—beforehand, but know them better than the conclusion: for the cause of an attribute's inherence in a subject always itself inheres in the subject more firmly than that attribute; e. g. the cause of our loving anything is dearer to us than the object of our love. So since the primary premises are the cause of our knowledge—i. e. of our

conviction—it follows that we know them better—that is, are more convinced of them—than their consequences, precisely because our knowledge of the latter is the effect of our knowledge of the premisses. Now a man cannot believe in anything more than in the things he knows, unless he has either actual knowledge of it or something better than actual knowledge. But we are faced with this paradox if a student
35 whose belief rests on demonstration has not prior knowledge; a man must believe in some, if not in all, of the basic truths more than in the conclusion. Moreover, if a man sets out to acquire the scientific knowledge that comes through demonstration, he must not only have a better knowledge of the basic truths and a firmer conviction of them than of the
72ᵇ connexion which is being demonstrated: more than this, nothing must be more certain or better known to him than these basic truths in their character as contradicting the fundamental premisses which lead to the opposed and erroneous conclusion. For indeed the conviction of pure science must be unshakable.

3 Some hold that, owing to the necessity of knowing
5 the primary premisses, there is no scientific knowledge. Others think there is, but that all truths are demonstrable. Neither doctrine is either true or a necessary deduction from the premisses. The first school, assuming that there is no way of knowing other than by demonstration, maintain that an infinite regress is involved, on the ground that if behind the prior stands no primary, we could
10 not know the posterior through the prior (wherein they are right, for one cannot traverse an infinite series): if on the other hand—they say—the series terminates and there are primary premisses, yet these are unknowable because incapable of demonstration, which according to them is the only form of knowledge. And since thus one cannot know the primary premisses, knowledge of the conclusions which fol-

low from them is not pure scientific knowledge nor properly knowing at all, but rests on the mere supposition that the premisses are true. The other party agree with them as regards knowing, holding that it is only possible by demonstration, but they see no difficulty in holding that all truths are demonstrated, on the ground that demonstration may be circular and reciprocal.

Our own doctrine is that not all knowledge is demonstrative: on the contrary, knowledge of the immediate premisses is independent of demonstration. (The necessity of this is obvious; for since we must know the prior premisses from which the demonstration is drawn, and since the regress must end in immediate truths, those truths must be indemonstrable.) Such, then, is our doctrine, and in addition we maintain that besides scientific knowledge there is its originative source which enables us to recognize the definitions.

Now demonstration must be based on premisses prior to and better known than the conclusion; and the same things cannot simultaneously be both prior and posterior to one another: so circular demonstration is clearly not possible in the unqualified sense of 'demonstration', but only possible if 'demonstration' be extended to include that other method of argument which rests on a distinction between truths prior to us and truths without qualification prior, i. e. the method by which induction produces knowledge. But if we accept this extension of its meaning, our definition of unqualified knowledge will prove faulty; for there seem to be two kinds of it. Perhaps, however, the second form of demonstration, that which proceeds from truths better known to us, is not demonstration in the unqualified sense of the term.

The advocates of circular demonstration are not only faced with the difficulty we have just stated: in addition their theory reduces to the mere statement that if a thing exists, then it does exist—an easy way of proving anything. That this is so can be clearly shown by taking three terms, for to constitute the circle it makes no difference whether many terms or few or even only two are taken. Thus by direct proof, if *A* is, *B* must be; if *B* is, C must be; therefore if *A* is, *C* must be. Since then—by the circular proof—if *A* is, *B* must be, and 73ª if *B* is, *A* must be, *A* may be substituted for *C* above. Then 'if *B* is, *A* must be' = 'if *B* is, *C* must be', which above gave the conclusion 'if *A* is, *C* must be': but *C* and *A* have been identified. Consequently the upholders of circular demonstration 5 are in the position of saying that if *A* is, *A* must be—a simple way of proving anything. Moreover, even such circular demonstration is impossible except in the case of attributes that imply one another, viz. 'peculiar' properties.

Now, it has been shown that the positing of one thing—be it one term or one premiss—never involves a necessary consequent:[4] two premisses constitute the first and 10 smallest foundation for drawing a conclusion at all and therefore *a fortiori* for the demonstrative syllogism of science. If, then, *A* is implied in *B* and *C*, and *B* and *C* are reciprocally implied in one another and in *A*, it is possible, as has been shown in my writings on the syllogism,[5] to prove all the assumptions on which the original conclusion rested, by circular demonstration in the first figure. But it 15 has also been shown that in the other figures either no conclusion is possible, or at least none which proves both the original premisses.[6] Propositions the terms of which are not convertible cannot be circularly demonstrated at all, and since convertible terms occur rarely in actual demonstrations, it is clearly frivolous and impossible to say that demonstration is reciprocal and that therefore everything 20 can be demonstrated.

[4] *An. Pr.* i, ch. 25.

[5] *Ibid.* ii, ch. 5.

[6] *Ibid.* ii, cc. 5 and 6.

4   Since the object of pure scientific knowledge cannot be other than it is, the truth obtained by demonstrative knowledge will be necessary. And since demonstrative knowledge is only present when we have a demonstration, it follows that demonstration is an inference from necessary premisses. So we must consider what are the premisses of demonstration—i. e. what is their character: and as a preliminary, let us define what we mean 25 by an attribute 'true in every instance of its subject', an 'essential' attribute, and a 'commensurate and universal' attribute. I call 'true in every instance' what is truly predicable of all instances—not of one to the exclusion of others—and at all times, not at this or that time only; e. g. if animal is truly predicable of every instance of man, then 30 if it be true to say 'this is a man', 'this is an animal' is also true, and if the one be true now the other is true now. A corresponding account holds if point is in every instance predicable as contained in line. There is evidence for this in the fact that the objection we raise against a proposition put to us as true in every instance is either an instance in which, or an occasion on which, it is not true. Essential attributes are (1) such as belong to their subject as elements 35 in its essential nature (e. g. line thus belongs to triangle, point to line; for the very being or 'substance' of triangle and line is composed of these elements, which are contained in the formulae defining triangle and line): (2) such that, while they belong to certain subjects, the subjects to which they belong are contained in the attribute's own defining formula. Thus straight and curved belong to line, odd and even, prime and compound, square and oblong, to number; 40 and also the formula defining any one of these attributes 73ᵇ contains its subject—e. g. line or number as the case may be.

Extending this classification to all other attributes, I distinguish those that answer the above description as belonging essentially to their respective subjects; whereas attributes related in neither of these two ways to their subjects I call accidents or 'coincidents'; e. g. musical or white is a 'coincident' of animal.

5   Further (a) that is essential which is not predicated of a subject other than itself: e. g. 'the walking [thing]' walks and is white in virtue of being something else besides; whereas substance, in the sense of whatever signifies a 'this somewhat', is not what it is in virtue of being something else besides. Things, then, not predicated of a subject I call essential; things predicated of a subject I call accidental or 'coincidental'.

10   In another sense again (b) a thing consequentially connected with anything is essential; one not so connected is 'coincidental'. An example of the latter is 'While he was walking it lightened': the lightning was not due to his walking; it was, we should say, a coincidence. If, on the other hand, there is a consequential connexion, the predication is essential; e. g. if a beast dies when its throat is being cut, then its death is also essentially connected with the cutting, 15 because the cutting was the cause of death, not death a 'coincident' of the cutting.

So far then as concerns the sphere of connexions scientifically known in the unqualified sense of that term, all attributes which (within that sphere) are essential either in the sense that their subjects are contained in them, or in the sense that they are contained in their subjects, are necessary as well as consequentially connected with their subjects. For it is impossible for them not to inhere in their subjects— 20 either simply or in the qualified sense that one or other of a pair of opposites must inhere in the subject; e. g. in line must be either straightness or curvature, in number either oddness or evenness. For within a single identical genus the contrary of a given attribute is either its privative or its contradictory; e. g. within number what is not odd is even,

inasmuch as within this sphere even is a necessary consequent of not-odd. So, since any given predicate must be
either affirmed or denied of any subject, essential attributes
must inhere in their subjects of necessity.

Thus, then, we have established the distinction between
the attribute which is 'true in every instance' and the 'essen-   25
tial' attribute.

I term 'commensurately universal' an attribute which
belongs to every instance of its subject, and to every
instance essentially and as such; from which it clearly follows that all commensurate universals inhere *necessarily* in
their subjects. The essential attribute, and the attribute that
belongs to its subject as such, are identical. E. g. point and
straight belong to line essentially, for they belong to line as   30
such; and triangle as such has two right angles, for it is
essentially equal to two right angles.

An attribute belongs commensurately and universally to
a subject when it can be shown to belong to any random
instance of that subject and when the subject is the first
thing to which it can be shown to belong. Thus, e. g., (1)
the equality of its angles to two right angles is not a commensurately universal attribute of figure. For though it is
possible to show that a figure has its angles equal to two
right angles, this attribute cannot be demonstrated of any   35
figure selected at haphazard, nor in demonstrating does one
take a figure at random—a square is a figure but its angles
are not equal to two right angles. On the other hand, any
isosceles triangle has its angles equal to two right angles, yet
isosceles triangle is not the primary subject of this attribute
but triangle is prior. So whatever can be shown to have its
angles equal to two right angles, or to possess any other
attribute, in any random instance of itself and primarily—   40
that is the first subject to which the predicate in question
belongs commensurately and universally, and the demon-   74ᵃ
stration, in the essential sense, of any predicate is the proof

of it as belonging to this first subject commensurately and universally: while the proof of it as belonging to the other subjects to which it attaches is demonstration only in a secondary and unessential sense. Nor again (2) is equality to two right angles a commensurately universal attribute of isosceles; it is of wider application.

5   We must not fail to observe that we often fall into error because our conclusion is not in fact primary and commensurately universal in the sense in which we think we prove it so. We make this mistake (1) when the subject is an individual or individuals above which there is no universal to be found: (2) when the subjects belong to different species and there is a higher universal, but it has no name: (3) when the subject which the demonstrator takes as a whole is really only a part of a larger whole; for then the demonstration will be true of the 10 individual instances within the part and will hold in every instance of it, yet the demonstration will not be true of this subject primarily and commensurately and universally. When a demonstration is true of a subject primarily and commensurately and universally, that is to be taken to mean that it is true of a given subject primarily and as such. Case (3) may be thus exemplified. If a proof were given that perpendiculars to the same line are parallel, it might be supposed that *lines thus perpendicular* were the proper sub- 15 ject of the demonstration because being parallel is true of every instance of them. But it is not so, for the parallelism depends not on these angles being equal to one another because each is a right angle, but simply on their being equal to one another. An example of (1) would be as follows: if isosceles were the only triangle, it would be thought to have its angles equal to two right angles *qua* isosceles. An instance of (2) would be the law that proportionals alternate. Alternation used to be demonstrated separately of numbers,

lines, solids, and durations, though it could have been 20
proved of them all by a single demonstration. Because there
was no single name to denote that in which numbers,
lengths, durations, and solids are identical, and because they
differed specifically from one another, this property was
proved of each of them separately. To-day, however, the
proof is commensurately universal, for they do not possess
this attribute *qua* lines or *qua* numbers, but *qua* manifest-
ing this generic character which they are postulated as 25
possessing universally. Hence, even if one prove of each
kind of triangle that its angles are equal to two right angles,
whether by means of the same or different proofs; still, as
long as one treats separately equilateral, scalene, and isosceles, one does not yet know, except sophistically, that triangle
has its angles equal to two right angles, nor does one yet
know that triangle has this property commensurately and
universally, even if there is no other species of triangle but 30
these. For one does not know that triangle as such has this
property, nor even that 'all' triangles have it—unless 'all'
means 'each taken singly': if 'all' means 'as a whole class',
then, though there be none in which one does not recognize
this property, one does not know it of 'all triangles'.

When, then, does our knowledge fail of commensurate
universality, and when is it unqualified knowledge? If triangle be identical in essence with equilateral, i. e. with each
or all equilaterals, then clearly we have unqualified knowledge: if on the other hand it be not, and the attribute
belongs to equilateral *qua* triangle; then our knowledge fails
of commensurate universality. 'But', it will be asked, 'does 35
this attribute belong to the subject of which it has been
demonstrated *qua* triangle or *qua* isosceles? What is the
point at which the subject to which it belongs is primary?
(i. e. to what subject can it be demonstrated as belonging
commensurately and universally?)' Clearly this point is the
first term in which it is found to inhere as the elimination of

inferior *differentiae* proceeds. Thus the angles of a brazen
isosceles triangle are equal to two right angles: but eliminate brazen and isosceles and the attribute remains. 'But'—
74b you may say—'eliminate figure or limit, and the attribute
vanishes'. True, but figure and limit are not the first *differentiae* whose elimination destroys the attribute. 'Then what
is the first?' If it is triangle, it will be in virtue of triangle
that the attribute belongs to all the other subjects of which
it is predicable, and triangle is the subject to which it can be
demonstrated as belonging commensurately and universally.

6 Demonstrative knowledge must rest on necessary
basic truths; for the object of scientific knowledge
cannot be other than it is. Now attributes attaching
essentially to their subjects attach necessarily to them: for
essential attributes are either elements in the essential nature
of their subjects, or contain their subjects as elements in
their own essential nature. (The pairs of opposites which the
latter class includes are necessary because one member or
the other necessarily inheres.) It follows from this that pre-
10 misses of the demonstrative syllogism must be connexions
essential in the sense explained: for all attributes must
inhere essentially or else be accidental, and accidental attributes are not necessary to their subjects.

We must either state the case thus, or else premise that
the conclusion of demonstration is necessary and that a
demonstrated conclusion cannot be other than it is, and then
15 infer that the conclusion must be developed from necessary
premisses. For though you may reason from true premisses
without demonstrating, yet if your premisses are necessary
you will assuredly demonstrate—in such necessity you have
at once a distinctive character of demonstration. That
demonstration proceeds from necessary premisses is also
indicated by the fact that the objection we raise against a
professed demonstration is that a premiss of it is not a nec-

essary truth—whether we think it altogether devoid of 20
necessity, or at any rate so far as our opponent's previous
argument goes. This shows how naïve it is to suppose one's
basic truths rightly chosen if one starts with a proposition
which is (1) popularly accepted and (2) true, such as the
sophists' assumption that to know is the same as to possess
knowledge.[7] For (1) popular acceptance or rejection is no
criterion of a basic truth, which can only be the primary law
of the genus constituting the subject matter of the demon- 25
stration; and (2) not *all* truth is 'appropriate'.

A further proof that the conclusion must be the development of necessary premisses is as follows. Where demonstration
is possible, one who can give no account which includes the
cause has no scientific knowledge. If, then, we suppose a
syllogism in which, though A necessarily inheres in C, yet
B, the middle term of the demonstration, is not necessarily
connected with A and C, then the man who argues thus has
no reasoned knowledge of the conclusion, since this conclu- 30
sion does not owe its necessity to the middle term; for
though the conclusion is necessary, the mediating link is a
contingent fact. Or again, if a man is without knowledge
now, though he still retains the steps of the argument,
though there is no change in himself or in the fact and no
lapse of memory on his part; then neither had he knowledge
previously. But the mediating link, not being necessary,
may have perished in the interval; and if so, though there be 35
no change in him nor in the fact, and though he will still
retain the steps of the argument, yet he has not knowledge,
and therefore had not knowledge before. Even if the link
has not actually perished but is liable to perish, this situation is possible and might occur. But such a condition
cannot be knowledge.

When the conclusion is necessary, the middle through 75a

[7] Plato, Euthydemus, 277 B.

which it was proved may yet quite easily be non-necessary.
You can in fact infer the necessary even from a non-necessary premiss, just as you can infer the true from the not
5 true. On the other hand, when the middle is necessary the
conclusion must be necessary; just as true premisses always
give a true conclusion. Thus, if A is necessarily predicated
of B and B of C, then A is necessarily predicated of C. But
when the conclusion is non-necessary the middle cannot be
10 necessary either. Thus: let A be predicated non-necessarily
of C but necessarily of B, and let B be a necessary predicate
of C; then A too will be a necessary predicate of C, which
by hypothesis it is not.

To sum up, then: demonstrative knowledge must be
knowledge of a necessary nexus, and therefore must clearly
be obtained through a necessary middle term; otherwise its
15 possessor will know neither the cause nor the fact that his
conclusion is a necessary connexion. Either he will mistake
the non-necessary for the necessary and believe the necessity of the conclusion without knowing it, or else he will
not even believe it—in which case he will be equally ignorant, whether he actually infers the mere fact through
middle terms or the reasoned fact and from immediate premisses.

Of accidents that are not essential according to our definition of essential there is no demonstrative knowledge; for
since an accident, in the sense in which I here speak of it,
20 may also not inhere, it is impossible to prove its inherence
as a necessary conclusion. A difficulty, however, might be
raised as to why in dialectic, if the conclusion is not a necessary connexion, such and such determinate premisses
should be proposed in order to deal with such and such
determinate problems. Would not the result be the same if
one asked any questions whatever and then merely stated
one's conclusion? The solution is that determinate questions
25 have to be put, not because the replies to them affirm facts

which necessitate facts affirmed by the conclusion, but because these answers are propositions which if the answerer affirm, he must affirm the conclusion—and affirm it with truth if they are true.

Since it is just those attributes within every genus which are essential and possessed by their respective subjects as such that are necessary, it is clear that both the conclusions and the premisses of demonstrations which produce scientific knowledge are essential. For accidents are not 30 necessary: and, further, since accidents are not necessary one does not necessarily have reasoned knowledge of a conclusion drawn from them (this is so even if the accidental premisses are invariable but not essential, as in proofs through signs; for though the conclusion be actually essential, one will not know it as essential nor know its reason); but to have reasoned knowledge of a conclusion is to know 35 it through its cause. We may conclude that the middle must be consequentially connected with the minor, and the major with the middle.

7 It follows that we cannot in demonstrating pass from one genus to another. We cannot, for instance, prove geometrical truths by arithmetic. For there are three elements in demonstration: (1) what is proved, the conclusion—an attribute inhering essentially in 40 a genus; (2) the axioms, i. e. axioms which are premisses of 75ᵇ demonstration; (3) the subject-genus whose attributes, i. e. essential properties, are revealed by the demonstration. The axioms which are premisses of demonstration may be identical in two or more sciences: but in the case of two different genera such as arithmetic and geometry you cannot apply arithmetical demonstration to the properties of magni- 5 tudes unless the magnitudes in question are numbers.[8]

---

[8] Cf. *Met.* 1039ª 9.

How in certain cases transference is possible I will explain later.[9]

Arithmetical demonstration and the other sciences likewise possess, each of them, their own genera; so that if the demonstration is to pass from one sphere to another, the genus must be either absolutely or to some extent the same. If this is not so, transference is clearly impossible, because the extreme and the middle terms must be drawn from the same genus: otherwise, as predicated, they will not be essential and will thus be accidents. That is why it cannot be proved by geometry that opposites fall under one science, nor even that the product of two cubes is a cube. Nor can the theorem of any one science be demonstrated by means of another science, unless these theorems are related as subordinate to superior (e. g. as optical theorems to geometry or harmonic theorems to arithmetic). Geometry again cannot prove of lines any property which they do not possess *qua* lines, i. e. in virtue of the fundamental truths of their peculiar genus: it cannot show, for example, that the straight line is the most beautiful of lines or the contrary of the circle; for these qualities do not belong to lines in virtue of their peculiar genus, but through some property which it shares with other genera.

8   It is also clear that if the premisses from which the syllogism proceeds are commensurately universal, the conclusion of such demonstration—demonstration, i. e, in the unqualified sense—must also be eternal. Therefore no attribute can be demonstrated nor known by strictly scientific knowledge to inhere in perishable things. The proof can only be accidental, because the attribute's connexion with its perishable subject is not commensurately universal but temporary and special. If such a demonstra-

[9] Cf. i, cc. 9 and 13.

tion is made, one premiss must be perishable and not commensurately universal (perishable because only if it is
perishable will the conclusion be perishable; not commensurately universal, because the predicate will be predicable of
some instances of the subject and not of others); so that the
conclusion can only be that a fact is true at the moment—
not commensurately and universally. The same is true of 30
definitions, since a definition is either a primary premiss or a
conclusion of a demonstration, or else only differs from a
demonstration in the order of its terms. Demonstration and
science of merely frequent occurrences—e. g. of eclipse as
happening to the moon—are, as such, clearly eternal:
whereas so far as they are not eternal they are not fully commensurate. Other subjects too have properties attaching to
them in the same way as eclipse attaches to the moon.   35

9   It is clear that if the conclusion is to show an
attribute inhering as such, nothing can be demonstrated except from its 'appropriate' basic truths.
Consequently a proof even from true, indemonstrable, and
immediate premisses does not constitute knowledge. Such 40
proofs are like Bryson's method of squaring the circle; for
they operate by taking as their middle a common character—a character, therefore, which the subject may share
with another—and consequently they apply equally to sub- 76ᵃ
jects different in kind. They therefore afford knowledge of
an attribute only as inhering accidentally, not as belonging
to its subject as such: otherwise they would not have been
applicable to another genus.

Our knowledge of any attribute's connexion with a subject is accidental unless we know that connexion through
the middle term in virtue of which it inheres, and as an
inference from basic premisses essential and 'appropriate' 5
to the subject—unless we know, e. g., the property of possessing angles equal to two right angles as belonging to that

subject in which it inheres essentially, and as inferred from
basic premises essential and 'appropriate' to that subject: so
that if that middle term also belongs essentially to the
minor, the middle must belong to the same kind as the
major and minor terms. The only exceptions to this rule are
such cases as theorems in harmonics which are demonstra-
10 ble by arithmetic. Such theorems are proved by the same
middle terms as arithmetical properties, but with a qualification—the fact falls under a separate science (for the
subject genus is separate), but the reasoned fact concerns
the superior science, to which the attributes essentially
belong. Thus, even these apparent exceptions show that no
attribute is strictly demonstrable except from its 'appropriate' basic truths, which, however, in the case of these
15 sciences have the requisite identity of character.

It is no less evident that the peculiar basic truths of
each inhering attribute are indemonstrable; for basic truths
from which they might be deduced would be basic truths
of all that is, and the science to which they belonged would
possess universal sovereignty. This is so because he knows
better whose knowledge is deduced from higher causes,
20 for his knowledge is from prior premises when it derives
from causes themselves uncaused: hence, if he knows better
than others or best of all, his knowledge would be science
in a higher or the highest degree. But, as things are, demonstration is not transferable to another genus, with such
exceptions as we have mentioned of the application of
25 geometrical demonstrations to theorems in mechanics or
optics, or of arithmetical demonstrations to those of harmonics.

It is hard to be sure whether one knows or not; for it is
hard to be sure whether one's knowledge is based on the
basic truths appropriate to each attribute—the differentia of
true knowledge We think we have scientific knowledge if
we have reasoned from true and primary premises. But

that is not so: the conclusion must be homogeneous with 30
the basic facts of the science.

10

I call the basic truths of every genus those elements in it the existence of which cannot be proved. As regards both these primary truths and the attributes dependent on them the meaning of the name is assumed. The fact of their existence as regards the primary truths must be assumed; but it has to be proved of the remainder, the attributes. Thus we assume the meaning alike of unity, straight, and triangular; but while as regards 35 unity and magnitude we assume also the fact of their existence, in the case of the remainder proof is required.

Of the basic truths used in the demonstrative sciences some are peculiar to each science, and some are common, but common only in the sense of analogous, being of use only in so far as they fall within the genus constituting the province of the science in question.

Peculiar truths are, e. g., the definitions of line and 40
straight; common truths are such as 'take equals from equals and equals remain'. Only so much of these common truths is required as falls within the genus in question: for 76^b
a truth of this kind will have the same force even if not used generally but applied by the geometer only to magnitudes, or by the arithmetician only to numbers. Also peculiar to a science are the subjects the existence as well as the meaning of which it assumes, and the essential attributes of which it investigates, e. g. in arithmetic units, in geometry 5
points and lines. Both the existence and the meaning of the subjects are assumed by these sciences; but of their essential attributes only the meaning is assumed. For example arithmetic assumes the meaning of odd and even, square and cube, geometry that of incommensurable, or of deflection or verging of lines, whereas the existence of these attributes is demonstrated by means of the axioms and from previous 10

conclusions as premisses. Astronomy too proceeds in the same way. For indeed every demonstrative science has three elements: (1) that which it posits, the subject genus whose essential attributes it examines; (2) the so-called axioms, 15 which are primary premisses of its demonstration; (3) the attributes, the meaning of which it assumes. Yet some sciences may very well pass over some of these elements; e. g. we might not expressly posit the existence of the genus if its existence were obvious (for instance, the existence of hot and cold is more evident than that of number); or we might omit to assume expressly the meaning of the attributes if it were well understood. In the same way the meaning of 20 axioms, such as 'Take equals from equals and equals remain', is well known and so not expressly assumed. Nevertheless in the nature of the case the essential elements of demonstration are three: the subject, the attributes, and the basic premisses.

That which expresses necessary self-grounded fact, and which we must necessarily believe,[10] is distinct both from the hypotheses of a science and from illegitimate postulate—I say 'must believe', because all syllogism, and therefore *a fortiori* demonstration, is addressed not to the 25 spoken word, but to the discourse within the soul,[11] and though we can always raise objections to the spoken word, to the inward discourse we cannot always object. That which is capable of proof but assumed by the teacher without proof is, if the pupil believes and accepts it, hypothesis, though only in a limited sense hypothesis—that is, relatively 30 to the pupil; if the pupil has no opinion or a contrary opinion on the matter, the same assumption is an illegitimate postulate. Therein lies the distinction between hypothesis and illegitimate postulate: the latter is the contrary of the

[10] *sc.* axioms.

[11] Cf. Plato, *Theaetetus,* 189 E ff.

pupil's opinion, demonstrable, but assumed and used without demonstration.

The definitions—viz. those which are not expressed as 35 statements that anything is or is not—are not hypotheses: but it is in the premises of a science that its hypotheses are contained. Definitions require only to be understood, and this is not hypothesis—unless it be contended that the pupil's hearing is also an hypothesis required by the teacher. Hypotheses, on the contrary, postulate facts on the being of which depends the being of the fact inferred. Nor are the geometer's hypotheses false, as some have held, urging that one must not employ falsehood and that the geometer is 40 uttering falsehood in stating that the line which he draws is a foot long or straight, when it is actually neither. The truth is that the geometer does not draw any conclusion from the 77a being of the particular line of which he speaks, but from what his diagrams symbolize. A further distinction is that all hypotheses and illegitimate postulates are either universal or particular, whereas a definition is neither.

11 So demonstration does not necessarily imply the being of Forms nor a One beside a Many, but it 5 does necessarily imply the possibility of truly predicating one of many; since without this possibility we cannot save the universal, and if the universal goes, the middle term goes with it, and so demonstration becomes impossible. We conclude, then, that there must be a single identical term unequivocally predicable of a number of individuals.

The law that it is impossible to affirm and deny simul- 10 taneously the same predicate of the same subject is not expressly posited by any demonstration except when the conclusion also has to be expressed in that form; in which case the proof lays down as its major premiss that the major is truly affirmed of the middle but falsely denied. It makes

no difference, however, if we add to the middle, or again to
the minor term, the corresponding negative. For grant a
15 minor term of which it is true to predicate man—even if it
be also true to predicate not-man of it—still grant simply
that man is animal and not not-animal, and the conclusion
follows: for it will still be true to say that Callias—even if
it be also true to say that not-Callias—is animal and not
not-animal. The reason is that the major term is predicable
not only of the middle, but of something other than the
20 middle as well, being of wider application; so that the conclusion is not affected even if the middle is extended to
cover the original middle term and also what is not the original middle term.[12]

The law that every predicate can be either truly
affirmed or truly denied of every subject is posited by such
demonstration as uses *reductio ad impossibile,* and then not
always universally, but so far as it is requisite; within the
25 limits, that is, of the genus—the genus, I mean (as I have
already explained[13]), to which the man of science applies his
demonstrations. In virtue of the common elements of
demonstration—I mean the common axioms which are used
as premisses of demonstration, not the subjects or the
attributes demonstrated as belonging to them—all the sciences have communion with one another, and in communion
with them all is dialectic and any science which might
30 attempt a universal proof of axioms such as the law of
excluded middle, the law that the subtraction of equals from
equals leaves equal remainders, or other axioms of the same
kind. Dialectic has no definite sphere of this kind, not being
confined to a single genus. Otherwise its method would not

[12] Lit. 'even if the middle is itself and also what is not itself'; i. e. you may
pass from the middle term man to include not-man without affecting the
conclusion.

[13] Cf. 75[a] 42 ff. and 76[b] 13.

be interrogative; for the interrogative method is barred to the demonstrator, who cannot use the opposite facts to prove the same *nexus*. This was shown in my work on the syllogism.[14]

35

12 If a syllogistic question[15] is equivalent to a proposition embodying one of the two sides of a contradiction, and if each science has its peculiar propositions from which its peculiar conclusion is developed, then there is such a thing as a distinctively scientific question, and it is the interrogative form of the premises from which the 'appropriate' conclusion of each science is 40 developed. Hence it is clear that not every question will be relevant to geometry, nor to medicine, nor to any other science: only those questions will be geometrical which form premises for the proof of the theorems of geometry or of 77^b any other science, such as optics, which uses the same basic truths as geometry. Of the other sciences the like is true. Of these questions the geometer is bound to give his account, using the basic truths of geometry in conjunction with his previous conclusions; of the basic truths the geometer, as such, is not bound to give any account. The 5 like is true of the other sciences. There is a limit, then, to the questions which we may put to each man of science; nor is each man of science bound to answer all inquiries on each several subject, but only such as fall within the defined field of his own science. If, then, in controversy with a geometer *qua* geometer the disputant confines himself to geometry and proves anything from geometrical premises, he is

---

[14] *An. Pr.* i. 1. The 'opposite facts' are those which would be expressed in the alternatively possible answers to the dialectical question, the dialectician's aim being to refute his interlocutor whether the latter answers the question put to him affirmatively or in the negative.

[15] i. e. a premiss put in the form of a question.

10 clearly to be applauded; if he goes outside these he will be
at fault, and obviously cannot even refute the geometer
except accidentally. One should therefore not discuss geometry among those who are not geometers, for in such a
15 company an unsound argument will pass unnoticed. This
is correspondingly true in the other sciences.

Since there are 'geometrical' questions, does it follow
that there are also distinctively 'ungeometrical' questions?
Further, in each special science—geometry for instance—
what kind of error is it that may vitiate questions, and yet
not exclude them from that science? Again, is the erroneous
conclusion one constructed from premises opposite to the
20 true premises, or is it formal fallacy though drawn from
geometrical premises? Or, perhaps, the erroneous conclusion is due to the drawing of premises from another science;
e. g. in a geometrical controversy a musical question is distinctively ungeometrical, whereas the notion that parallels
meet is in one sense geometrical, being ungeometrical in a
different fashion: the reason being that 'ungeometrical', like
'unrhythmical,' is equivocal, meaning in the one case not
25 geometry at all, in the other bad geometry? It is this error,
i. e. error based on premises of this kind—'of' the science
but false—that is the contrary of science. In mathematics
the formal fallacy is not so common, because it is the middle term in which the ambiguity lies, since the major is
30 predicated of the whole of the middle and the middle of the
whole of the minor (the *predicate* of course never has the
prefix 'all'); and in mathematics one can, so to speak, see
these middle terms with an intellectual vision, while in
dialectic the ambiguity may escape detection. E. g. 'Is every
circle a figure?' A diagram shows that this is so, but the
minor premiss 'Are epics circles?' is shown by the diagram
to be false.

If a proof has an inductive minor premiss, one should
35 not bring an 'objection' against it. For since every premiss

must be applicable to a number of cases (otherwise it will
not be true in every instance, which, since the syllogism
proceeds from universals, it must be), then assuredly the
same is true of an 'objection'; since premisses and 'objections' are so far the same that anything which can be
validly advanced as an 'objection' must be such that it   40
could take the form of a premiss, either demonstrative or
dialectical. On the other hand arguments formally illogical
do sometimes occur through taking as middles mere
attributes of the major and minor terms. An instance of this   78a
is Caeneus' proof that fire increases in geometrical proportion: 'Fire', he argues, 'increases rapidly, and so does
geometrical proportion'. There is no syllogism so, but there
is a syllogism if the most rapidly increasing proportion
is geometrical and the most rapidly increasing proportion is   5
attributable to fire in its motion. Sometimes, no doubt, it
is impossible to reason from premisses predicating mere
attributes: but sometimes it is possible, though the possibility is overlooked. If false premisses could never give true
conclusions 'resolution' would be easy, for premisses and
conclusion would in that case inevitably reciprocate. I might
then argue thus: let A be an existing fact; let the existence of
A imply such and such facts actually known to me to exist,
which we may call B. I can now, since they reciprocate,
infer A from B.

Reciprocation of premisses and conclusion is more fre-   10
quent in mathematics, because mathematics takes definitions,
but never an accident, for its premisses—a second characteristic distinguishing mathematical reasoning from dialectical
disputations.

A science expands not by the interposition of fresh
middle terms, but by the apposition of fresh extreme terms.
E. g. A is predicated of B, B of C, C of D, and so indefinitely. Or the expansion may be lateral: e. g. one major, A,   15
may be proved of two minors, C and E. Thus let A repre-

sent number—a number or *number* taken indeterminately; B
determinate odd number; C any particular odd number. We
can then predicate A of C. Next let D represent determi-
20 nate even number, and E even number. Then A is
predicable of E.

13 Knowledge of the fact differs from knowledge of
the reasoned fact. To begin with, they differ
within the same science and in two ways: (1)
when the premisses of the syllogism are not immediate (for
25 then the proximate cause is not contained in them—a necessary condition of knowledge of the reasoned fact): (2)
when the premisses are immediate, but instead of the cause
the better known of the two reciprocals is taken as the middle; for of two reciprocally predicable terms the one which
is not the cause may quite easily be the better known and so
become the middle term of the demonstration. Thus (2) (a)
30 you might prove as follows that the planets are near because
they do not twinkle: let C be the planets, B not twinkling, A
proximity. Then B is predicable of C; for the planets do not
twinkle. But A is also predicable of B, since that which does
not twinkle is near—we must take this truth as having been
reached by induction or sense-perception. Therefore A is a
35 necessary predicate of C; so that we have demonstrated that
the planets are near. This syllogism, then, proves not the
reasoned fact but only the fact; since they are not near
because they do not twinkle, but, because they are near, do
not twinkle. The major and middle of the proof, however,
may be reversed, and then the demonstration will be of the
40 reasoned fact. Thus: let C be the planets, B proximity, A
78b not twinkling. Then B is an attribute of C, and A—not
twinkling—of B. Consequently A is predicable of C, and
the syllogism proves the reasoned fact, since its middle term
is the proximate cause. Another example is the inference
that the moon is spherical from its manner of waxing. Thus:

since that which so waxes is spherical, and since the moon
so waxes, clearly the moon is spherical. Put in this form, the 5
syllogism turns out to be proof of the fact, but if the middle
and major be reversed it is proof of the reasoned fact; since
the moon is not spherical because it waxes in a certain manner, but waxes in such a manner because it is spherical. (Let
C be the moon, B spherical, and A waxing.) Again (b), in
cases where the cause and the effect are not reciprocal and 10
the effect is the better known, the fact is demonstrated but
not the reasoned fact. This also occurs (1) when the middle
falls outside the major and minor, for here too the strict
cause is not given, and so the demonstration is of the fact,
not of the reasoned fact. For example, the question 'Why 15
does not a wall breathe?' might be answered, 'Because it is
not an animal'; but that answer would not give the strict
cause, because if not being an animal causes the absence of
respiration, then being an animal should be the cause of respiration, according to the rule that if the negation of x causes
the non-inherence of y, the affirmation of x causes the inher- 20
ence of y; e. g. if the disproportion of the hot and cold
elements is the cause of ill health, their proportion is the
cause of health; and conversely, if the assertion of x causes
the inherence of y, the negation of x must cause y's non-
inherence. But in the case given this consequence does not
result; for not every animal breathes. A syllogism with this
kind of cause takes place in the second figure. Thus: let A be
animal, B respiration, C wall. Then A is predicable of all B 25
(for all that breathes is animal), but of no C; and consequently B is predicable of no C; that is, the wall does not
breathe. Such causes are like far-fetched explanations, which
precisely consist in making the cause too remote, as in 30
Anacharsis' account of why the Scythians have no flute-players; namely because they have no vines.

Thus, then, do the syllogism of the fact and the syllogism of the reasoned fact differ within one science and

according to the position of the middle terms. But there is
another way too in which the fact and the reasoned fact dif-
35 fer, and that is when they are investigated respectively by
different sciences. This occurs in the case of problems
related to one another as subordinate and superior, as when
40 optical problems are subordinated to geometry, mechanical
problems to stereometry, harmonic problems to arithmetic,
79ᵃ the data of observation to astronomy. (Some of these sciences bear almost the same name; e. g. mathematical and
nautical astronomy, mathematical and acoustical harmonics.) Here it is the business of the empirical observers to
know the fact, of the mathematicians to know the reasoned
fact; for the latter are in possession of the demonstrations
5 giving the causes, and are often ignorant of the fact: just as
we have often a clear insight into a universal, but through
lack of observation are ignorant of some of its particular
instances. These connexions[16] have a perceptible existence
though they are manifestations of forms. For the mathematical sciences concern forms: they do not demonstrate
properties of a substratum, since, even though the geometrical subjects are predicable as properties of a perceptible
substratum, it is not as thus predicable that the mathematician demonstrates properties of them. As optics is related
10 to geometry, so another science is related to optics, namely
the theory of the rainbow. Here knowledge of the fact is
within the province of the natural philosopher, knowledge
of the reasoned fact within that of the optician, either *qua*
optician or *qua* mathematical optician. Many sciences not
standing in this mutual relation enter into it at points; e. g.
medicine and geometry: it is the physician's business to
know that circular wounds heal more slowly, the geometer's
15 to know the reason why.

---

[16] *sc.* 'which require two sciences for their proof.' Cf. 78ᵇ 35.

14

Of all the figures the most scientific is the first. Thus, it is the vehicle of the demonstrations of all the mathematical sciences, such as arithmetic, geometry, and optics, and practically of all sciences that investigate causes: for the syllogism of the reasoned fact is either exclusively or generally speaking and in most cases in this figure—a second proof that this figure is the most scientific; for grasp of a reasoned conclusion is the primary condition of knowledge. Thirdly, the first is the only figure which enables us to pursue knowledge of the essence of a thing. In the second figure no affirmative conclusion is possible, and knowledge of a thing's essence must be affirmative; while in the third figure the conclusion can be affirmative, but cannot be universal, and essence must have a universal character: e. g. man is not two-footed animal in any qualified sense, but universally. Finally, the first figure has no need of the others, while it is by means of the first that the other two figures are developed, and have their intervals close-packed until immediate premisses are reached. Clearly, therefore, the first figure is the primary condition of knowledge.

15

Just as an attribute *A* may (as we saw) be atomically connected with a subject *B*, so its disconnexion may be atomic. I call 'atomic' connexions or disconnexions which involve no intermediate term; since in that case the connexion or disconnexion will not be mediated by something other than the terms themselves. It follows that if either *A* or *B*, or both *A* and *B*, have a genus, their disconnexion cannot be primary. Thus: let *C* be the genus of *A*. Then, if *C* is not the genus of *B*—for *A* may well have a genus which is not the genus of *B*—there will be a syllogism proving *A*'s disconnexion from *B* thus:

$$\text{all } A \text{ is } C,$$
$$\text{no } B \text{ is } C,$$
$$\therefore \text{no } B \text{ is } A.$$

Or if it is B which has a genus D, we have

$$\text{all } B \text{ is } D,$$
$$\text{no } D \text{ is } A,$$
$$\therefore \text{no } B \text{ is } A, \text{ by syllogism;}$$

5 and the proof will be similar if both A and B have a genus.
That the genus of A need not be the genus of B and vice
versa, is shown by the existence of mutually exclusive coor-
dinate series of predication. If no term in the series ACD
. . . is predicable of any term in the series BEF. . ., and if
10 G—a term in the former series—is the genus of A, clearly G
will not be the genus of B; since, if it were, the series would
not be mutually exclusive. So also if B has a genus, it will
not be the genus of A. If, on the other hand, neither A nor
B has a genus and A does not inhere in B, this disconnexion
must be atomic. If there be a middle term, one or other of
15 them is bound to have a genus, for the syllogism will be
either in the first or the second figure. If it is in the first, B
will have a genus—for the premiss containing it must be
affirmative;[17] if in the second, either A or B indifferently,
since syllogism is possible if either is contained in a negative
20 premiss,[18] but not if both premisses are negative.

Hence it is clear that one thing may be atomically disconnected from another, and we have stated when and how
this is possible.

---

[17] i.e. in Celarent.

[18] i.e. in Cesare or Camestres.

16 Ignorance—defined not as the negation of knowledge but as a positive state of mind—is error produced by inference.

(1) Let us first consider propositions asserting a predi- 25 cate's immediate connexion with or disconnexion from a subject. Here, it is true, positive error may befall one in alternative ways; for it may arise where one directly believes a connexion or disconnexion as well as where one's belief is acquired by inference. The error, however, that consists in a direct belief is without complication; but the error resulting from inference—which here concerns us—takes many forms. Thus, let A be atomically disconnected from all B: then the conclusion inferred through a middle term C, that 30 all B is A, will be a case of error produced by syllogism. Now, two cases are possible. Either (a) both premisses, or (b) one premiss only, may be false. (a) If neither A is an attribute of any C nor C of any B, whereas the contrary was posited in both cases, both premisses will be false. (C may quite well be so related to A and B that C is neither subor- 35 dinate to A nor a universal attribute of B: for B, since A was said to be primarily disconnected from B, cannot have a genus, and A need not necessarily be a universal attribute of all things. Consequently both premisses may be false.) On the other hand, (b) one of the premisses may be true, 40 though not either indifferently but only the major A–C; since, B having no genus, the premiss C–B will always be false, while A–C may be true. This is the case if, for exam- 80ᵃ ple, A is related atomically to both C and B; because when the same term is related atomically to more terms than one, neither of those terms will belong to the other. It is, of course, equally the case if A–C is not atomic. 5

Error of attribution, then, occurs through these causes and in this form only—for we found that no syllogism of universal attribution was possible in any figure but the first. On the other hand, an error of non-attribution may occur

either in the first or in the second figure. Let us therefore
first explain the various forms it takes in the first figure and
10 the character of the premisses in each case.

(c) It may occur when both premisses are false; e. g.
supposing A atomically connected with both C and B, if it
be then assumed that no C is A, and all B is C, both premisses are false.

(d) It is also possible when one is false. This may be
either premiss indifferently. A–C may be true, C–B false—
15 A–C true because A is not an attribute of all things, C–B
false because C, which never has the attribute A, cannot be
an attribute of B; for if C–B were true, the premiss A–C
would no longer be true, and besides if both premisses were
true, the conclusion would be true. Or again, C–B may be
20 true and A–C false; e. g. both C and A contain B as genera,
one of them must be subordinate to the other, so that if the
premiss takes the form No C is A, it will be false. This
25 makes it clear that whether either or both premisses are
false, the conclusion will equally be false.

In the second figure the premisses cannot both be
wholly false; for if all B is A, no middle term can be with
truth universally affirmed of one extreme and universally
30 denied of the other: but premisses in which the middle is
affirmed of one extreme and denied of the other are the necessary condition if one is to get a valid inference at all.
Therefore if, taken in this way, they are wholly false, their
contraries conversely should be wholly true. But this is
impossible. On the other hand, there is nothing to prevent
both premisses being partially false; e. g. if actually some A
35 is C and some B is C, then if it is premised that all A is C
and no B is C, both premisses are false, yet partially, not
wholly, false. The same is true if the major is made negative
instead of the minor. Or one premiss may be wholly false,
and it may be either of them. Thus, supposing that actu-
40 ally an attribute of all A must also be an attribute of all B,

then if C is yet taken to be a universal attribute of all A but   80b
universally non-attributable to B, C–A will be true but C–B
false. Again, actually that which is an attribute of no B will
not be an attribute of all A either, for if it be an attribute
of all A, it will also be an attribute of all B, which is contrary to supposition; but if C be nevertheless assumed to be   5
a universal attribute of A, but an attribute of no B, then the
premiss C–B is true but the major is false. The case is similar if the major is made the negative premiss. For in fact
what is an attribute of no A will not be an attribute of any
B either; and if it be yet assumed that C is universally non-
attributable to A, but a universal attribute of B, the premiss   10
C–A is true but the minor wholly false. Again, in fact it is
false to assume that that which is an attribute of all B is an
attribute of no A, for if it be an attribute of all B, it must
be an attribute of some A. If then C is nevertheless assumed
to be an attribute of all B but of no A, C–B will be true but
C–A false.

It is thus clear that in the case of atomic propositions
erroneous inference will be possible not only when both   15
premisses are false but also when only one is false.

17

(2) In the case of attributes not atomically connected with or disconnected from their subjects,
(a) (i) as long as the false conclusion is inferred
through the 'appropriate' middle, only the major and not   20
both premisses can be false. By 'appropriate middle' I mean
the middle term through which the contradictory—i. e. the
true—conclusion is inferrible. Thus, let A be attributable
to B through a middle term C: then, since to produce a
conclusion the premiss C–B must be taken affirmatively, it
is clear that this premiss must always be true, for its qual-   25
ity is not changed. But the major A–C is false, for it is by
a change in the quality of A–C that the conclusion becomes
its contradictory—i. e. true. Similarly (ii) if the middle is

taken from another series of predication; e. g. suppose D to
be not only contained within A as a part within its whole
but also predicable of all B. Then the premiss $D–B$ must
30 remain unchanged, but the quality of $A–D$ must be
changed; so that $D–B$ is always true, $A–D$ always false. Such
error is practically identical with that which is inferred
through the 'appropriate' middle. On the other hand, (b) if
the conclusion is not inferred through the 'appropriate' middle—(i) when the middle is subordinate to A but is
35 predicable of no B, both premisses must be false, because
if there is to be a conclusion both must be posited as asserting the contrary of what is actually the fact, and so posited
both become false: e. g. suppose that actually all D is A but
no B is D; then if these premisses are changed in quality, a
40 conclusion will follow and both of the new premisses will
80ᵃ be false. When, however, (ii) the middle D is not subordinate to A, $A–D$ will be true, $D–B$ false—$A–D$ true because
A was not subordinate to D, $D–B$ false because if it had
been true, the conclusion too would have been true; but it is
ex hypothesi false.

When the erroneous inference is in the second figure,
5 both premisses cannot be entirely false; since if B is subordinate to A, there can be no middle predicable of all of one
extreme and of none of the other as was stated before.[19]
One premiss, however, may be false, and it may be either of
them. Thus, if C is actually an attribute of both A and B,
10 but is assumed to be an attribute of A only and not of B,
$C–A$ will be true, $C–B$ false: or again if C be assumed to be
attributable to B but to no A, $C–B$ will be true, $C–A$ false.

We have stated when and through what kinds of prem-
15 isses error will result in cases where the erroneous
conclusion is negative. If the conclusion is affirmative, (a)
(i) it may be inferred through the 'appropriate' middle term.

---

[19] Cf. 80ᵃ 29.

In this case both premisses cannot be false since, as we said before,[20] C–B must remain unchanged if there is to be a conclusion, and consequently A–C, the quality of which is changed, will always be false. This is equally true if (ii) the middle is taken from another series of predication, as was 20 stated to be the case also with regard to negative error;[21] for D–B must remain unchanged, while the quality of A–D must be converted, and the type of error is the same as before.

(b) The middle may be inappropriate. Then (i) if D is subordinate to A, A–D will be true, but D–B false; since A 25 may quite well be predicable of several terms no one of which can be subordinated to another. If, however, (ii) D is not subordinate to A, obviously A–D, since it is affirmed, will always be false, while D–B may be either true or false; for A may very well be an attribute of no D, whereas all B 30 is D, e. g. no science is animal, all music is science. Equally well A may be an attribute of no D, and D of no B. It emerges, then, that if the middle term is not subordinate to the major, not only both premisses but either singly may be false.

Thus we have made it clear how many varieties of erroneous inference are liable to happen and through what kinds 35 of premisses they occur, in the case both of immediate and of demonstrable truths.

18 It is also clear that the loss of any one of the senses entails the loss of a corresponding portion of knowledge, and that, since we learn either by induction or by demonstration, this knowledge cannot be 40 acquired. Thus demonstration develops from universals, 81^b induction from particulars; but since it is possible to famil-

[20] Cf. 80^b 17–26.

[21] Cf. 80^a 26–32.

iarize the pupil with even the so-called mathematical abstractions only through induction—i. e. only because each subject genus possesses, in virtue of a determinate mathematical character, certain properties which can be treated as
5 separate even though they do not exist in isolation—it is consequently impossible to come to grasp universals except through induction. But induction is impossible for those who have not sense-perception. For it is sense-perception alone which is adequate for grasping the particulars: they cannot be objects of scientific knowledge, because neither can universals give us knowledge of them without induction, nor can we get it through induction without sense-perception.

10 **19** Every syllogism is effected by means of three terms. One kind of syllogism serves to prove that A inheres in C by showing that A inheres in B and B in C; the other is negative and one of its premisses asserts one term of another, while the other denies one
15 term of another. It is clear, then, that these are the fundamentals and so-called hypotheses of syllogism. Assume them as they have been stated, and proof is bound to follow—proof that A inheres in C through B, and again that A inheres in B through some other middle term, and similarly that B inheres in C. If our reasoning aims at gaining credence and so is merely dialectical, it is obvious that we have
20 only to see that our inference is based on premisses as credible as possible: so that if a middle term between A and B is credible though not real, one can reason through it and complete a dialectical syllogism. If, however, one is aiming at truth, one must be guided by the real connexions of subjects and attributes. Thus: since there are attributes which
25 are predicated of a subject essentially or naturally and not coincidentally—not, that is, in a sense in which we say 'That white (thing) is a man', which is not the same mode of predication as when we say 'The man is white': the man

is white not because he is something else but because he is
man, but the white is man because 'being white' coincides
with 'humanity' within one substratum—therefore there are
terms such as are naturally subjects of predicates. Suppose, 30
then, C such a term not itself attributable to anything else
as to a subject, but the proximate subject of the attribute
B—i. e. so that B–C is immediate; suppose further E related
immediately to F, and F to B. The first question is, must
this series terminate, or can it proceed to infinity? The second question is as follows: Suppose nothing is essentially
predicated of A, but A is predicated primarily of H and of 35
no intermediate prior term, and suppose H similarly related
to G and G to B; then must this series also terminate, or
can it too proceed to infinity? There is this much difference
between the questions: the first is, is it possible to start from
that which is not itself attributable to anything else but is
the subject of attributes, and ascend to infinity? The second is the problem whether one can start from that which is 40
a predicate but not itself a subject of predicates, and 82ª
descend to infinity? A third question is, if the extreme
terms are fixed, can there be an infinity of middles? I mean
this: suppose for example that A inheres in C and B is intermediate between them, but between B and A there are other
middles, and between these again fresh middles; can these 5
proceed to infinity or can they not? This is the equivalent of
inquiring, do demonstrations proceed to infinity, i. e. is
everything demonstrable? Or do ultimate subject and primary attribute limit one another?

I hold that the same questions arise with regard to negative conclusions and premisses: viz. if A is attributable to
no B, then either this predication will be primary, or there 10
will be an intermediate term prior to B to which A is not
attributable—G, let us say, which is attributable to all B—
and there may still be another term H prior to G, which is
attributable to all G. The same questions arise, I say,

because in these cases too either the series of prior terms to which *A* is not attributable is infinite or it terminates.

One cannot ask the same questions in the case of recip-
15 rocating terms, since when subject and predicate are convertible there is neither primary nor ultimate subject, seeing that all the reciprocals *qua* subjects stand in the same relation to one another, whether we say that the subject has an infinity of attributes or that both subjects and attributes —and we raised the question in both cases—are infinite in number. These questions then cannot be asked—unless, indeed, the terms can reciprocate by two different modes, by accidental predication in one relation and natural predi-
20 cation in the other.

20 Now, it is clear that if the predications termi-
nate in both the upward and the downward direction (by 'upward' I mean the ascent to the more universal, by 'downward' the descent to the more par-ticular), the middle terms cannot be infinite in number. For
25 suppose that *A* is predicated of *F*, and that the intermedi-ates—call them *BB' B''* . . .—are infinite, then clearly you might descend from *A* and find one term predicated of another *ad infinitum*, since you have an infinity of terms between you and *F*; and equally, if you ascend from *F*, there are infinite terms between you and *A*. It follows that if these processes are impossible there cannot be an infinity of
30 intermediates between *A* and *F*. Nor is it of any effect to urge that some terms of the series *AB* . . . *F* are contiguous so as to exclude intermediates, while others cannot be taken into the argument at all: whichever terms of the series *B* . . . I take, the number of intermediates in the direction either of *A* or of *F* must be finite or infinite: where the infinite series starts, whether from the first term or from a later one, is of
35 no moment, for the succeeding terms in any case are infinite in number.

21 Further, if in affirmative demonstration the series terminates in both directions, clearly it will terminate too in negative demonstration. Let us assume that we cannot proceed to infinity either by ascending from the ultimate term (by 'ultimate term' I mean a term such as F was, not itself attributable to a subject but itself the subject of attributes), or by descending towards an ultimate from the primary term (by 'primary term' I mean a term predicable of a subject but not itself a subject[22]). If this assumption is justified, the series will also terminate in the case of negation. For a negative conclusion can be proved in all three figures. In the first figure it is proved thus: no B is A, all C is B. In packing the interval B–C we must reach immediate propositions—as is always the case with the minor premiss—since B–C is affirmative. As regards the other premiss it is plain that if the major term is denied of a term D prior to B, D will have to be predicable of all B, and if the major is denied of yet another term prior to D, this term must be predicable of all D. Consequently, since the ascending series is finite, the descent will also terminate and there will be a subject of which A is primarily nonpredicable. In the second figure the syllogism is, all A is B, no C is B, $\therefore$ no C is A. If proof of this[23] is required, plainly it may be shown either in the first figure as above, in the second as here, or in the third. The first figure has been discussed, and we will proceed to display the second, proof by which will be as follows: all B is D, no C is D . . . , since it is required that B should be a subject of which a predicate is affirmed. Next, since D is to be proved not to belong to C, then D has a further predicate which is denied of C. Therefore, since the succession of predicate affirmed of an ever higher

82ᵇ is marked at line: 82^b

[22] *sc.* a predicate above which is no wider universal.

[23] *sc.* 'that no C is B'.

universal terminates,[24] the succession of predicates denied
terminates too.[25]

The third figure shows it as follows: all B is A, some
B is not C, $\therefore$ some A is not C. This premiss, i. e. C–B,
will be proved either in the same figure or in one of the two
25 figures discussed above. In the first and second figures the
series terminates. If we use the third figure, we shall take
as premisses, all E is B, some E is not C, and this premiss
again will be proved by a similar prosyllogism. But since it
is assumed that the series of descending subjects also terminates, plainly the series of more universal non-predicables
will terminate also. Even supposing that the proof is not
confined to one method, but employs them all and is now in
30 the first figure, now in the second or third—even so the
regress will terminate, for the methods are finite in number, and if finite things are combined in a finite number of
ways, the result must be finite.

Thus it is plain that the regress of middles terminates
in the case of negative demonstration, if it does so also in
the case of affirmative demonstration. That in fact the
regress terminates in both these cases may be made clear by
35 the following dialectical considerations.

[24] i.e. each of the successive prosyllogisms required to prove the negative
minors contains an affirmative major in which the middle is affirmed of a
subject successively 'higher' or more universal than the subject of the first
syllogism. Thus:

Syllogism:	All B is D	Prosyllogisms:	All D is E	All E is F
	No C is D		No C is E	No C is F
	$\therefore$No C is B		$\therefore$No C is D	$\therefore$No C is E

B, D, E, &c., are successively more universal subjects; and the series
of affirmative majors containing them must *ex hypothesi* terminate.

[25] Since the series of affirmative majors terminates and since an affirmative major is required for each prosyllogism, we shall eventually reach a
minor incapable of proof and therefore immediate.

22 In the case of predicates constituting the essential nature of a thing, it clearly terminates, seeing that if definition is possible, or in other words, if essential form is knowable, and an infinite series cannot be traversed, predicates constituting a thing's essential nature must be finite in number.[26] But as regards 83ª predicates generally we have the following prefatory remarks to make. (1) We can affirm without falsehood 'the white (thing) is walking', and 'that big (thing) is a log'; or again, 'the log is big', and 'the man walks'. But the affirmation differs in the two cases. When I affirm 'the white is a log', 5 I mean that something which happens to be white is a log— not that white is the substratum in which log inheres, for it was not *qua* white or *qua* a species of white that the white (thing) came to be a log, and the white (thing) is consequently not a log except incidentally. On the other hand, when I affirm 'the log is white', I do not mean that something else, which happens also to be a log, is white (as I 10 should if I said 'the musician is white', which would mean 'the man who happens also to be a musician is white'); on the contrary, log is here the substratum—the substratum which actually came to be white, and did so *qua* wood or *qua* a species of wood and *qua* nothing else.

If we must lay down a rule, let us entitle the latter kind of statement predication, and the former not predication at 15 all, or not strict but accidental predication. 'White' and 'log' will thus serve as types respectively of predicate and subject.

We shall assume, then, that the predicate is invariably predicated strictly and not accidentally of the subject, for on such predication demonstrations depend for their force. It follows from this that when a single attribute is predi-

[26] If the attributes in a series of prediction such as we are discussing are substantial, they must be finite in number, because they are then the elements constituting the definition of a substance.

cated of a single subject, the predicate must affirm of the subject either some element constituting its essential nature, or that it is in some way qualified, quantified, essentially related, active, passive, placed, or dated.[27]

(2) Predicates which signify substance signify that the subject is identical with the predicate or with a species of the predicate. Predicates not signifying substance which are predicated of a subject not identical with themselves or with a species of themselves are accidental or coincidental; e. g. white is a coincident of man, seeing that man *is* not identical with white or a species of white, but rather with animal, since man *is* identical with a species of animal. These predicates which do not signify substance must be predicates of some other subject, and nothing can be white which is not also other than white. The Forms we can dispense with, for they are mere sound without sense; and even if there are such things, they are not relevant to our discussion, since demonstrations are concerned with predicates such as we have defined.[28]

(3) If *A* is a quality of *B*, *B* cannot be a quality of *A*— a quality of a quality. Therefore *A* and *B* cannot be predicated reciprocally of one another in strict predication: they can be affirmed without falsehood of one another, but not

---

[27] The first of three statements preliminary to a proof that predicates which are accidental—other than substantial—cannot be unlimited in number: Accidental is to be distinguished from essential or natural predication [cf. i, ch. 4, 73^b 5 ff. and *An. Pr.* i, ch. 25, 43^a 25–6]. The former is alien to demonstration: hence, provided that a single attribute is predicated of a single subject, all genuine predicates fall either under the category of substance or under one of the adjectival categories.

[28] Second preliminary statement: The precise distinction of substantive from adjectival predication makes clear (implicitly) the two distinctions, (*a*) that between natural and accidental predication, (*b*) that between substantival and adjectival predication, which falls within natural predication. This enables us to reject the Platonic Forms.

genuinely predicated of each other.[29] For one alternative is
that they should be substantially predicated of one another,
i. e. B would become the genus or differentia of A—the
predicate now become subject. But it has been shown that   83ᵇ
in these substantial predications neither the ascending predicates nor the descending subjects form an infinite series;
e. g. neither the series, man is biped, biped is animal, &c.,
nor the series predicating animal of man, man of Callias,
Callias of a further subject as an element of its essential
nature, is infinite. For all such substance is definable, and
an infinite series cannot be traversed in thought: conse-   5
quently neither the ascent nor the descent is infinite, since a
substance whose predicates were infinite would not be
definable. Hence they will not be predicated each as the
genus of the other; for this would equate a genus with one
of its own species. Nor (the other alternative) can a *quale* be   10
reciprocally predicated of a *quale*, nor any term belonging to
an adjectival category of another such term, except by accidental predication; for all such predicates are coincidents
and are predicated of substances.[30] On the other hand—in
proof of the impossibility of an infinite ascending series—
every predication displays the subject as somehow qualified
or quantified or as characterized under one of the other
adjectival categories, or else is an element in its substantial
nature: these latter are limited in number, and the number   15

---

[29] Third preliminary statement merging into the beginning of the proof
proper: Reciprocal predication cannot produce an indefinite regress because
it is not natural predication.

[30] Expansion of third preliminary statement: Reciprocals A and B might be
predicated of one another (a) substantially; but it has been proved already
that because a definition cannot contain an infinity of elements substantial
predication cannot generate infinity; and it would disturb the relation of
genus and species: (b) as *qualia* or *quanta* &c.; but this would be unnatural predication, because all such predicates are adjectival, i.e. accidents, or
coincidents, of substances.

of the widest kinds under which predications fall is also limited, for every predication must exhibit its subject as
somehow qualified, quantified, essentially related, acting or
suffering, or in some place or at some time.[31]

I assume first that predication implies a single subject
and a single attribute, and secondly that predicates which are
not substantial are not predicated of one another. We
assume this because such predicates are all coincidents, and
20 though some are essential coincidents, others of a different
type, yet we maintain that all of them alike are predicated
of some substratum and that a coincident is never a substratum—since we do not class as a coincident anything which
does not owe its designation to its being something other
than itself, but always hold that any coincident is predicated
of some substratum other than itself, and that another group
of coincidents may have a different substratum. Subject to
25 these assumptions then, neither the ascending nor the
descending series of predication in which a single attribute is
predicated of a single subject is infinite.[32] For the subjects of
which coincidents are predicated are as many as the consti-

---

[31] The ascent of predicates is also finite; because all predicates fall under
one or other of the categories, and (a) the series of predicates under each
category terminates when the category is reached, and (b) the number of
the categories is limited. [(a) seems to mean that an attribute as well as a
substance is definable by genus and differentia, and the elements in its definition must terminate in an upward direction at the category, and can
therefore no more form an infinite series than can the elements constituting
the definition of a substance.]

[32] To reinforce this brief proof that descent and ascent are both finite we
may repeat the premises on which it depends. These are (1) the assumption that predication means the predication of one attribute of one subject,
and (2) our proof that accidents cannot be reciprocally predicated of one
another, because that would be unnatural predication. It follows from these
premises that both ascent and descent are finite. [Actually (2) only rein-
forces the proof that the descent terminates.]

tutive elements of each individual substance, and these we
have seen are not infinite in number, while in the ascending
series are contained those constitutive elements with their
coincidents—both of which are finite.[33] We conclude that
there is a given subject <D> of which some attribute <C> is
primarily predicable; that there must be an attribute <B>
primarily predicable of the first attribute, and that the series 30
must end with a term <A> not predicable of any term prior
to the last subject of which it was predicated <B>, and of
which no term prior to it is predicable.[34]

---

[33] To repeat again the proof that both ascent and descent are finite: The
subjects cannot be more in number than the constituents of a definable
form and these, we know, are not infinite in number: hence the descent is
finite. The series regarded as an ascent contains subjects and ever more universal accidents, and neither subjects nor accidents are infinite in number.

[34] Formal restatement of the last conclusion. [This is obscure: apparently
Aristotle here contemplates a hybrid series: category, accident, further specified accident . . . substantial genus, subgenus . . . *infima species*, individual
substance.

If this interpretation of the first portion of the chapter is at all correct, Aristotle's first proof that the first two questions of ch. 19 must be
answered in the negative is roughly as follows: The ultimate subject of all
judgement is an individual substance, a concrete singular. Of such concrete
singulars you can predicate substantially only the elements constituting their
infima species. These are limited in number because they form an intelligible
synthesis. So far, then, as substantial predicates are concerned, the questions are answered. But these elements are also the subjects of which
accidents, or coincidents, are predicated, and therefore as regards accidental predicates, at any rate, the descending series of subjects terminates. The
ascending series of attributes also terminates, (1) because each higher
attribute in the series can only be a higher genus of the accident predicated
of the ultimate subject of its genus, and therefore an element in the accident's definition; (2) because the number of the categories is limited.

We may note that the first argument seems to envisage a series which,
viewed as an ascent, starts with a concrete individual of which the elements
of its definition are predicated successively, specific differentia being followed
by proximate genus, which latter is the starting-point of a succession of ever
more universal attributes terminating in a category; and that the second
argument extends the scope of the dispute to the sum total of all the trains

The argument we have given is one of the so-called proofs; an alternative proof follows. Predicates so related to their subjects that there are other predicates prior to them predicable of those subjects are demonstrable; but of demonstrable propositions one cannot have something better than
35 knowledge, nor can one know them without demonstration. Secondly, if a consequent is only known through an antecedent (viz. premisses prior to it) and we neither know this antecedent nor have something better than knowledge of it, then we shall not have scientific knowledge of the consequent. Therefore, if it is possible through demonstration to know anything without qualification and not merely as dependent on the acceptance of certain premisses—i. e. hypothetically—the series of intermediate predications must terminate. If it does not terminate, and beyond any predicate
84a taken as higher than another there remains another still higher, then every predicate is demonstrable. Consequently, since these demonstrable predicates are infinite in number and therefore cannot be traversed, we shall not know them by demonstration. If, therefore, we have not something better
5 than knowledge of them, we cannot through demonstration have unqualified but only hypothetical science of anything.[35]

As dialectical proofs of our contention these may carry

of accidental predication which one concrete singular substance can beget. It is, as so often in Aristotle, difficult to be sure whether he is regarding the *infima species* or the concrete singular as the ultimate subject of judgement. I have assumed that he means the latter.]

[35] The former proof was dialectical. So is that which follows in this paragraph. If a predicate inheres in a subject but is subordinate to a higher predicate also predicable of that subject [i. e. not to a wider predicate but to a middle term giving logically prior premisses and in that sense higher], then the inherence can be known by demonstration and only by demonstration. But that means that it is known as the consequent of an antecedent. Therefore, if demonstration gives genuine knowledge, the series must terminate, i. e. every predicate is demonstrable and known only as a consequent and therefore hypothetically, unless an antecedent known *per se* is reached.

conviction, but an analytic process will show more briefly that neither the ascent nor the descent of predication can be infinite in the demonstrative sciences which are the object of our investigation. Demonstration proves the inherence of 10 essential attributes in things. Now attributes may be essential for two reasons: either because they are elements in the essential nature of their subjects, or because their subjects are elements in their essential nature. An example of the latter is odd as an attribute of number—though it is number's attribute, yet number itself is an element in the definition of 15 odd; of the former, multiplicity or the indivisible, which are elements in the definition of number. In neither kind of attribution can the terms be infinite. They are not infinite where each is related to the term below it as odd is to number, for this would mean the inherence in odd of another attribute of odd in whose nature odd was an essential ele- 20 ment: but then number will be an ultimate subject of the whole infinite chain of attributes, and be an element in the definition of each of them. Hence, since an infinity of attributes such as contain their subject in their definition cannot inhere in a single thing, the ascending series is equally finite.[36] Note, moreover, that all such attributes must so inhere in the ultimate subject—e. g. its attributes in number and number in them—as to be commensurate with the subject and not of wider extent. Attributes which are essential elements in the nature of their subjects are equally 25 finite: otherwise definition would be impossible. Hence, if all the attributes predicated are essential and these cannot be

[36] As regards type (2) [the opening of the chapter has disposed of type (1)]: in any series of such predicates any given term will contain in its definition all the lower terms, and the series will therefore terminate at the bottom in the ultimate subject. But since every term down to and including the ultimate subject is contained in the definition of any given term, if the series ascend infinitely there must be a term containing an infinity of terms in its definition. But this is impossible, and therefore the ascent terminates.

infinite, the ascending series will terminate, and consequently the descending series too.[37]

If this is so, it follows that the intermediates between
any two terms are also always limited in number.[38] An
immediately obvious consequence of this is that demonstrations necessarily involve basic truths, and that the
30 contention of some—referred to at the outset—that all
truths are demonstrable is mistaken. For if there are basic
truths, (a) not all truths are demonstrable, and (b) an infinite regress is impossible; since if either (a) or (b) were not a
fact, it would mean that no interval was immediate and
indivisible, but that all intervals were divisible. This is true
because a conclusion is demonstrated by the interposition,
not the apposition, of a fresh term. If such interposition
35 could continue to infinity there might be an infinite number
of terms between any two terms; but this is impossible if
both the ascending and descending series of predication
terminate; and of this fact, which before was shown dialec-
84b tically, analytic proof has now been given.[39]

[37] Note too that either type of essential attribute must be commensurate
with its subject, because the first defines, the second is defined by, its subject; and consequently no subject can possess an infinite number of essential
predicates of either type, or definition would be impossible. Hence if the
attributes predicated are all essential, the series terminates in both directions. [This passage merely displays the ground underlying the previous
argument that the ascent of attributes of type (2) is finite, and notes in passing its more obvious and already stated application to attributes of type (1).]

[38] It follows that the intermediates between a given subject and a given
attribute must also be limited in number.

[39] Corollary: (a) demonstrations necessarily involve basic truths and therefore (b) not all truths, as we saw [84a 32] that some maintain, are
demonstrable [cf. 72b 6]. If either (a) or (b) were not a fact, since conclusions are demonstrated by the interposition of a middle and not by the
apposition of an extreme term [cf. note on 78a 15], no premiss would be an
immediate indivisible interval. This closes the analytic argument.

23 It is an evident corollary of these conclusions that if the same attribute A inheres in two terms C and D predicable either not at all, or not of all instances, of one another, it does not always belong to them 5 in virtue of a common middle term. Isosceles and scalene possess the attribute of having their angles equal to two right angles in virtue of a common middle; for they possess it in so far as they are both a certain kind of figure, and not in so far as they differ from one another. But this is not always the case; for, were it so, if we take B as the common middle in virtue of which A inheres in C and D, clearly B would 10 inhere in C and D through a second common middle, and this in turn would inhere in C and D through a third, so that between two terms an infinity of intermediates would fall— an impossibility. Thus it need not always be in virtue of a common middle term that a single attribute inheres in several subjects, since there must be immediate intervals. Yet 15 if the attribute to be proved common to two subjects is to be one of their essential attributes, the middle terms involved must be within one subject genus and be derived from the same group of immediate premises; for we have seen that processes of proof cannot pass from one genus to another.[40]

It is also clear that when A inheres in B, this can be demonstrated if there is a middle term. Further, the 'ele- 20 ments' of such a conclusion are the premises containing the middle in question, and they are identical in number with the middle terms, seeing that the immediate propositions— or at least such immediate propositions as are universal—are the 'elements'. If, on the other hand, there is no middle term, demonstration ceases to be possible: we are on the way to the basic truths. Similarly if A does not inhere in B, this can be demonstrated if there is a middle term or a term 25 prior to B in which A does not inhere: otherwise there is no

[40] i, ch. 7.

demonstration and a basic truth is reached. There are, moreover, as many 'elements' of the demonstrated conclusion as there are middle terms, since it is propositions containing these middle terms that are the basic premisses on which the demonstration rests; and as there are some
30 indemonstrable basic truths asserting that 'this is that' or that 'this inheres in that', so there are others denying that 'this is that' or that 'this inheres in that'—in fact some basic truths will affirm and some will deny being.

When we are to prove a conclusion, we must take a primary essential predicate—suppose it C—of the subject B, and then suppose A similarly predicable of C. If we proceed in this manner, no proposition or attribute which falls beyond A is admitted in the proof: the interval is constantly con-
35 densed until subject and predicate become indivisible, i. e. one. We have our unit when the premiss becomes immediate, since the immediate premiss alone is a single premiss in the unqualified sense of 'single'. And as in other spheres the basic element is simple but not identical in all—in a system
85ᵃ of weight it is the mina, in music the quarter-tone, and so on—so in syllogism the unit is an immediate premiss, and in the knowledge that demonstration gives it is an intuition. In syllogisms, then, which prove the inherence of an attribute, nothing falls outside the major term. In the case of negative syllogisms on the other hand, (1) in the first figure nothing falls outside the major term whose inherence is in question; e. g. to prove through a middle C that A does not inhere in B
5 the premisses required are, all B is C, no C is A. Then if it has to be proved that no C is A, a middle must be found between A and C; and this procedure will never vary.

(2) If we have to show that E is not D by means of the premisses, all D is C; no E, or not all E[41] is C; then the

---

[41] Second figure, Camestres or Baroco.

middle will never fall beyond E, and E is the subject of which D is to be denied in the conclusion.

(3) In the third figure the middle will never fall beyond the limits of the subject and the attribute denied of it.   10

24 Since demonstrations may be either commensurately universal or particular,[42] and either affirmative or negative; the question arises, which form is the better? And the same question may be 15 put in regard to so-called 'direct' demonstration and *reductio ad impossibile*. Let us first examine the commensurately universal and the particular forms, and when we have cleared up this problem proceed to discuss 'direct' demonstration and *reductio ad impossibile*.

The following considerations might lead some minds to prefer particular demonstration.   20

(1) The superior demonstration is the demonstration which gives us greater knowledge (for this is the ideal of demonstration), and we have greater knowledge of a particular individual when we know it in itself than when we know it through something else; e. g. we know Coriscus the musician better when we know that Coriscus is musical 25 than when we know only that man is musical, and a like argument holds in all other cases. But commensurately universal demonstration, instead of proving that the subject itself actually is x, proves only that something else is x—e. g. in attempting to prove that isosceles is x, it proves not that isosceles but only that triangle is x—whereas particular demonstration proves that the subject itself is x. The demonstration, then, that a subject, as such, possesses an attribute is superior. If this is so, and if the particular rather

---

[42] The distinction is that of whole and part, genus and species; not that of universal and singular.

than the commensurately universal form so demonstrates,
30 particular demonstration is superior.

(2) The universal has not a separate being over against
groups of singulars. Demonstration nevertheless creates the
opinion that its function is conditioned by something like
this—some separate entity belonging to the real world; that,
35 for instance, of triangle or of figure or number, over against
particular triangles, figures, and numbers. But demonstration which touches the real and will not mislead is superior
to that which moves among unrealities and is delusory.
Now commensurately universal demonstration is of the latter kind: if we engage in it we find ourselves reasoning after
a fashion well illustrated by the argument that the proportionate is what answers to the definition of some entity
85b which is neither line, number, solid, nor plane, but a proportionate apart from all these. Since, then, such a proof is
characteristically commensurate and universal, and less
touches reality than does particular demonstration, and creates a false opinion, it will follow that commensurate and
universal is inferior to particular demonstration.

We may retort thus. (1) The first argument applies no
more to commensurate and universal than to particular
5 demonstration. If equality to two right angles is attributable
to its subject not *qua* isosceles but *qua* triangle, he who
knows that isosceles possesses that attribute knows the subject as *qua* itself possessing the attribute, to a less degree
than he who knows that triangle has that attribute. To sum
up the whole matter: if a subject is proved to possess *qua*
triangle an attribute which it does not in fact possess *qua*
triangle, that is not demonstration: but if it does possess it
qua triangle, the rule applies that the greater knowledge is
his who knows the subject as possessing its attribute *qua*
10 that in virtue of which it actually does possess it. Since,
then, triangle is the wider term, and there is one identical
definition of triangle—i. e. the term is not equivocal—and

since equality to two right angles belongs to all triangles, it is isosceles *qua* triangle and not triangle *qua* isosceles which has its angles so related. It follows that he who knows a connexion universally has greater knowledge of it as it in fact is than he who knows the particular; and the inference is that commensurate and universal is superior to particu- lar demonstration. (2) If there is a single identical definition—i. e. if the commensurate universal is unequiv- ocal—then the universal will possess being not less but more than some of the particulars, inasmuch as it is uni- versals which comprise the imperishable, particulars that tend to perish.

(3) Because the universal has a single meaning, we are not therefore compelled to suppose that in these examples it has being as a substance apart from its particulars—any more than we need make a similar supposition in the other cases of unequivocal universal predication, viz. where the predicate signifies not substance but quality, essential relat- edness, or action. If such a supposition is entertained, the blame rests not with the demonstration but with the hearer.

(4) Demonstration is syllogism that proves the cause, i. e. the reasoned fact, and it is rather the commensurate uni- versal than the particular which is causative (as may be shown thus: that which possesses an attribute through its own essential nature is itself the cause of the inherence, and the commensurate universal is primary;[43] hence the commen- surate universal is the cause). Consequently commensurately universal demonstration is superior as more especially prov- ing the cause, that is the reasoned fact.

(5) Our search for the reason ceases, and we think that we know, when the coming to be or existence of the fact before us is not due to the coming to be or existence of some other fact, for the last step of a search thus conducted is *eo*

---

[43] And therefore also essential; cf. i, ch. 4, 73^b 26 ff.

30 *ipso* the end and limit of the problem. Thus: 'Why did he come?' 'To get the money—wherewith to pay a debt—that he might thereby do what was right.' When in this regress we can no longer find an efficient or final cause, we regard the last step of it as the end of the coming—or being or coming to be—and we regard ourselves as then only having full knowledge of the reason why he came.

35 If, then, all causes and reasons are alike in this respect, and if this is the means to full knowledge in the case of final causes such as we have exemplified, it follows that in the case of the other causes also full knowledge is attained when an attribute no longer inheres because of something else. Thus, when we learn that exterior angles are equal to four right angles because they are the exterior angles of an isosceles, there still remains the question 'Why has isosceles this attribute?' and its answer 'Because it is a triangle, and a trian-
86a gle has it because a triangle is a rectilinear figure.' If rectilinear figure possesses the property for no further reason,[44] at this point we have full knowledge—but at this point our knowledge has become commensurately universal, and so we conclude that commensurately universal demonstration is superior.

(6) The more demonstration becomes particular the more it sinks into an indeterminate manifold, while universal demonstration tends to the simple and determinate. But
5 objects so far as they are an indeterminate manifold are unintelligible, so far as they are determinate, intelligible: they are therefore intelligible rather in so far as they are universal than in so far as they are particular. From this it follows that universals are more demonstrable: but since relative and correlative increase concomitantly, of the more demonstrable there will be fuller demonstration. Hence the
10 commensurate and universal form, being more truly demonstration, is the superior.

---

[44] i. e. for no reason other than its own nature.

(7) Demonstration which teaches two things is prefer-able to demonstration which teaches only one. He who possesses commensurately universal demonstration knows the particular as well, but he who possesses particular demonstration does not know the universal. So that this is an additional reason for preferring commensurately univer-sal demonstration. And there is yet this further argument:

(8) Proof becomes more and more proof of the com-mensurate universal as its middle term approaches nearer to the basic truth, and nothing is so near as the immediate premiss which is itself the basic truth. If, then, proof from the basic truth is more accurate than proof not so derived, demonstration which depends more closely on it is more accurate than demonstration which is less closely dependent. But commensurately universal demonstration is character-ized by this closer dependence, and is therefore superior. Thus, if *A* had to be proved to inhere in *D*, and the mid-dles were *B* and *C*, *B* being the higher term would render the demonstration which it mediated the more universal.

Some of these arguments, however, are dialectical. The clearest indication of the precedence of commensurately universal demonstration is as follows: if of two propositions, a prior and a posterior, we have a grasp of the prior, we have a kind of knowledge—a potential grasp—of the poste-rior as well. For example, if one knows that the angles of all triangles are equal to two right angles, one knows in a sense—potentially—that the isosceles' angles also are equal to two right angles, even if one does not know that the isosceles is a triangle; but to grasp this posterior proposi-tion is by no means to know the commensurate universal either potentially or actually. Moreover, commensurately universal demonstration is through and through intelligible; particular demonstration issues in sense-perception.

25 The preceding arguments constitute our defence of the superiority of commensurately universal to particular demonstration. That affirmative demonstration excels negative may be shown as follows.

(1) We may assume the superiority *ceteris paribus* of the demonstration which derives from fewer postulates or hypotheses—in short from fewer premisses; for, given that all these are equally well known, where they are fewer knowledge will be more speedily acquired, and that is a desideratum. The argument implied in our contention that demonstration from fewer assumptions is superior may be set out in universal form as follows. Assuming that in both cases alike the middle terms are known, and that middles which are prior are better known than such as are posterior, we may suppose two demonstrations of the inherence of A in E, the one proving it through the middles B, C and D, the other through F and G. Then A–D is known to the same degree as A–E (in the second proof), but A–D is better known than and prior to A–E (in the first proof); since A–E is proved through A–D, and the ground is more certain than the conclusion.

Hence demonstration by fewer premisses is *ceteris paribus* superior. Now both affirmative and negative demonstration operate through three terms and two premisses, but whereas the former assumes only that something is, the latter assumes both that something is and that something else is not, and thus operating through more kinds of premiss is inferior.

(2) It has been proved[45] that no conclusion follows if both premisses are negative, but that one must be negative, the other affirmative. So we are compelled to lay down the following additional rule: as the demonstration expands, the affirmative premisses must increase in number, but there

[45] *An Pr.* i ch. 7.

cannot be more than one negative premiss in each complete 15
proof.[46] Thus, suppose no *B* is *A*, and all *C* is *B*. Then, if
both the premisses are to be again expanded, a middle must
be interposed. Let us interpose *D* between *A* and *B*, and *E*
between *B* and *C*. Then clearly *E* is affirmatively related to
B and *C*, while *D* is affirmatively related to *B* but nega- 20
tively to *A*; for all *B* is *D*, but there must be no *D* which
is *A*. Thus there proves to be a single negative premiss,
A–D. In the further prosyllogisms too it is the same,
because in the terms of an affirmative syllogism the middle
is always related affirmatively to both extremes; in a negative syllogism it must be negatively related only to one of
them, and so this negation comes to be a single negative 25
premiss, the other premisses being affirmative. If, then, that
through which a truth is proved is a better known and more
certain truth, and if the negative proposition is proved
through the affirmative and not vice versa, affirmative
demonstration, being prior and better known and more certain, will be superior.

(3) The basic truth of demonstrative syllogism is the
universal immediate premiss, and the universal premiss 30
asserts in affirmative demonstration and in negative denies:
and the affirmative proposition is prior to and better known
than the negative (since affirmation explains denial and is 35
prior to denial, just as being is prior to not-being). It follows that the basic premiss of affirmative demonstration is
superior to that of negative demonstration, and the demonstration which uses superior basic premisses is superior.

(4) Affirmative demonstration is more of the nature of a
basic form of proof, because it is a *sine qua non* of negative
demonstration.

---

[46] i. e. in one syllogism and two prosyllogisms proving its premisses.

87ª

26

Since affirmative demonstration is superior to negative, it is clearly superior also to *reductio ad impossibile*. We must first make certain what is the difference between negative demonstration and *reductio* ad impossibile. Let us suppose that no *B* is *A*, and that all *C* is *B*: the conclusion necessarily follows that no *C* is *A*. If these premises are assumed, therefore, the negative demonstration that no *C* is *A* is direct. *Reductio ad impossibile*, on the other hand, proceeds as follows: Supposing we are to prove that *A* does not inhere in *B*, we have to assume that it does inhere, and further that *B* inheres in *C*, with the resulting inference that *A* inheres in *C*. This we have to suppose a known and admitted impossibility; and we then infer that *A* cannot inhere in *B*. Thus if the inherence of *B* in *C* is not questioned, *A*'s inherence in *B* is impossible.

The order of the terms is the same in both proofs: they differ according to which of the negative propositions is the better known, the one denying *A* of *B* or the one denying *A* of *C*. When the falsity of the conclusion[47] is the better known, we use *reductio ad impossibile;* when the major premiss of the syllogism is the more obvious, we use direct demonstration. All the same the proposition denying *A* of *B* is, in the order of being, prior to that denying *A* of *C;* for premisses are prior to the conclusion which follows from them, and 'no *C* is *A*' is the conclusion, 'no *B* is *A*' one of its premisses. For the destructive result of *reductio ad impossibile* is not a proper conclusion, nor are its antecedents proper premisses. On the contrary: the constituents of syllogism are premisses related to one another as whole to part or part to whole, whereas the premisses *A–C* and *A–B* are not thus related to one another. Now the superior demonstration is that which proceeds from better known and prior premisses, and while both these forms depend for credence

---

[47] i.e. the impossibility of *A–C*, the conclusion of the hypothetical syllogism.

on the not-being of something, yet the source of the one is prior to that of the other. Therefore negative demonstration will have an unqualified superiority to *reductio ad impossibile,* and affirmative demonstration, being superior to negative, will consequently be superior also to *reductio ad* 30 *impossibile.*

27 The science which is knowledge at once of the fact and of the reasoned fact, not of the fact by itself with out the reasoned fact, is the more exact and the prior science.

A science such as arithmetic, which is not a science of properties *qua* inhering in a substratum, is more exact than and prior to a science like harmonics, which is a science of properties inhering in a substratum; and similarly a science like arithmetic, which is constituted of fewer basic elements, is more exact than and prior to geometry, which requires additional elements. What I mean by 'additional elements' is this: a unit is substance without position, while a point 35 is substance with position; the latter contains an additional element.

28 A single science is one whose domain is a single genus, viz. all the subjects constituted out of the primary entities of the genus—i. e. the parts of this total subject—and their essential properties.

One science differs from another when their basic truths have neither a common source nor are derived those of the one science from those of the other. This is verified when we reach the indemonstrable premisses of a science, 87b for they must be within one genus with its conclusions: and this again is verified if the conclusions proved by means of them fall within one genus—i. e. are homogeneous.

5 **29** One can have several demonstrations of the same connexion not only by taking from the same series of predication middles which are other than the immediately cohering term—e. g. by taking C, D, and F severally to prove A-B—but also by taking a middle from another series. Thus let A be change, D alteration of a property, B feeling pleasure, and G relaxation. We can then without falsehood predicate D of B and A of 10 D, for he who is pleased suffers alteration of a property, and that which alters a property changes. Again, we can predicate A of G without falsehood, and G of B; for to feel pleasure is to relax, and to relax is to change. So the conclusion can be drawn through middles which are different, i. e. not in the same series—yet not so that neither of these middles is predicable of the other, for they must both be 15 attributable to some one subject.

A further point worth investigating is how many ways of proving the same conclusion can be obtained by varying the figure.

30 There is no knowledge by demonstration of chance conjunctions; for chance conjunctions 20 exist neither by necessity nor as general connexions but comprise what comes to be as something distinct from these. Now demonstration is concerned only with one or other of these two; for all reasoning proceeds from necessary or general premisses, the conclusion being necessary if 25 the premisses are necessary and general if the premisses are general. Consequently, if chance conjunctions are neither general nor necessary, they are not demonstrable.

31 Scientific knowledge is not possible through the act of perception. Even if perception as a faculty is of 'the such' and not merely of a 'this some-30 what', yet one must at any rate actually perceive a 'this

somewhat', and at a definite present place and time: but
that which is commensurately universal and true in all cases
one cannot perceive, since it is not 'this' and it is not 'now';
if it were, it would not be commensurately universal—the
term we apply to what is always and everywhere. Seeing,
therefore, that demonstrations are commensurately universal
and universals imperceptible, we clearly cannot obtain scientific knowledge by the act of perception: nay, it is obvious 35
that even if it were possible to perceive that a triangle has
its angles equal to two right angles, we should still be looking for a demonstration—we should not (as some[48] say)
possess knowledge of it; for perception must be of a particular, whereas scientific knowledge involves the recognition
of the commensurate universal. So if we were on the moon,
and saw the earth shutting out the sun's light, we should 40
not know the cause of the eclipse: we should perceive the
present fact of the eclipse, but not the reasoned fact at all, 88ᵃ
since the act of perception is not of the commensurate universal. I do not, of course, deny that by watching the
frequent recurrence of this event we might, after tracking
the commensurate universal, possess a demonstration, for
the commensurate universal is elicited from the several
groups of singulars.

The commensurate universal is precious because it 5
makes clear the cause; so that in the case of facts like these
which have a cause other than themselves universal knowledge[49] is more precious than sense-perceptions and than
intuition. (As regards primary truths there is of course a
different account to be given.[50]) Hence it is clear that
knowledge of things demonstrable cannot be acquired by 10

---

[48] Protagoras is perhaps referred to.

[49] i. e. demonstration through the commensurate universal.

[50] Cf. e. g. 100ᵇ 12.

perception, unless the term perception is applied to the possession of scientific knowledge through demonstration.
Nevertheless certain points do arise with regard to connexions to be proved which are referred for their explanation
to a failure in sense-perception: there are cases when an act
of vision would terminate our inquiry, not because in seeing
we should be knowing, but because we should have elicited
the universal from seeing; if, for example, we saw the pores
in the glass and the light passing through, the reason of the
15 kindling would be clear to us[51] because we should at the
same time see it in each instance and intuit that it must be
so in all instances.

32 All syllogisms cannot have the same basic
truths. This may be shown first of all by the following dialectical considerations. (1) Some
20 syllogisms are true and some false for though a true inference is possible from false premisses, yet this occurs once
only—I mean if A, for instance, is truly predicable of C,
but B, the middle, is false, both A–B and B–C being false;
nevertheless, if middles are taken to prove these premisses,
they will be false because every conclusion which is a false-
25 hood has false premisses, while true conclusions have true
premisses, and false and true differ in kind. Then again, (2)
falsehoods are not all derived from a single identical set of
principles: there are falsehoods which are the contraries of
one another and cannot coexist, e. g. 'justice is injustice',
and 'justice is cowardice'; 'man is horse', and 'man is ox';
'the equal is greater', and 'the equal is less'. From our
30 established principles we may argue the case as follows,
confining ourselves therefore to true conclusions. Not even
all these are inferred from the same basic truths; many of

[51] A theory of the concentration of rays through a burning-glass which was
not Aristotle's.

them in fact have basic truths which differ generically and are not transferable; units, for instance, which are without position, cannot take the place of points, which have position. The transferred terms could only fit in as middle terms or as major or minor terms, or else have some of the 35 other terms between them, others outside them.

Nor can any of the common axioms—such, I mean, as the law of excluded middle—serve as premisses for the proof of all conclusions. For the kinds of being are different, and some attributes attach to *quanta* and some to *qualia* 88ᵇ only; and proof is achieved by means of the common axioms taken in conjunction with these several kinds and their attributes.

Again, it is not true that the basic truths are much fewer than the conclusions, for the basic truths are the premisses, and the premisses are formed by the apposition of 5 a fresh extreme term or the interposition of a fresh middle. Moreover, the number of conclusions is indefinite, though the number of middle terms is finite; and lastly some of the basic truths are necessary, others variable.

Looking at it in this way we see that, since the number of conclusions is indefinite, the basic truth cannot be identical or limited in number. If, on the other hand, identity is 10 used in another sense, and it is said, e. g., 'these and no other are the fundamental truths of geometry, these the fundamentals of calculation, these again of medicine'; would the statement mean anything except that the sciences have basic truths? To call them identical because they are self-identical is absurd, since everything can be identified with everything in that sense of identity. Nor again can the con- 15 tention that all conclusions have the same basic truths mean that from the mass of all possible premisses any conclusion may be drawn. That would be exceedingly naïve, for it is not the case in the clearly evident mathematical sciences, nor is it possible in analysis, since it is the immediate prem-

isses which are the basic truths, and a fresh conclusion is
20 only formed by the addition of a new immediate premiss:
but if it be admitted that it is these primary immediate
premisses which are basic truths, each subject-genus will
provide one basic truth. If, however, it is not argued that
from the mass of all possible premisses any conclusion may
be proved, nor yet admitted that basic truths differ so as to
be generically different for each science, it remains to consider the possibility that, while the basic truths of all
knowledge are within one genus, special premisses are
required to prove special conclusions. But that this cannot
25 be the case has been shown by our proof that the basic
truths of things generically different themselves differ
generically. For fundamental truths are of two kinds, those
which are premisses of demonstration and the subject-
genus; and though the former are common, the latter—
number, for instance, and magnitude—are peculiar.

30 **33** Scientific knowledge and its object differ from
opinion, and the object of opinion in that scientific knowledge is commensurately universal and
proceeds by necessary connexions, and that which is necessary cannot be otherwise. So though there are things which
are true and real and yet can be otherwise, *scientific knowledge* clearly does not concern them: if it did, things which
35 can be otherwise would be incapable of being otherwise.
Nor are they any concern of *rational intuition*—by rational
intuition I mean an originative source of scientific knowl-
89ª edge—nor of indemonstrable knowledge, which is the
grasping of the immediate premiss. Since then rational intuition, science, and opinion, and what is revealed by these
terms, are the only things that can be 'true', it follows that
it is *opinion* that is concerned with that which may be true
or false, and can be otherwise: opinion in fact is the grasp of
a premiss which is immediate but not necessary. This view

also fits the observed facts, for opinion is unstable, and so is 5
the kind of being we have described as its object. Besides,
when a man thinks a truth incapable of being otherwise he
always thinks that he knows it, never that he opines it. He
thinks that he opines when he thinks that a connexion,
though actually so, may quite easily be otherwise; for he
believes that such is the proper object of opinion, while the
necessary is the object of knowledge.   10

In what sense, then, can the same thing be the object of
both opinion and knowledge? And if any one chooses to
maintain that all that he knows he can also opine, why
should not opinion be knowledge? For he that knows and he
that opines will follow the same train of thought through
the same middle terms until the immediate premisses are
reached; because it is possible to opine not only the fact but
also the reasoned fact, and the reason is the middle term; 15
so that, since the former knows, he that opines also has
knowledge.

The truth perhaps is that if a man grasp truths that
cannot be other than they are, in the way in which he grasps
the definitions through which demonstrations take place, he
will have not opinion but knowledge: if on the other hand
he apprehends these attributes as inhering in their subjects,
but not in virtue of the subjects' substance and essential
nature, he possesses opinion and not genuine knowledge;
and his opinion, if obtained through immediate premisses, 20
will be both of the fact and of the reasoned fact; if not so
obtained, of the fact alone. The object of opinion and
knowledge is not quite identical; it is only in a sense identical, just as the object of true and false opinion is in a sense
identical. The sense in which some maintain that true and 25
false opinion can have the same object leads them to
embrace many strange doctrines, particularly the doctrine
that what a man opines falsely he does not opine at all.
There are really many senses of 'identical', and in one sense

the object of true and false opinion can be the same, in another it cannot. Thus, to have a true opinion that the 30 diagonal is commensurate with the side would be absurd: but because the diagonal with which they are both concerned is the same, the two opinions have objects so far the same: on the other hand, as regards their essential definable nature these objects differ. The identity of the objects of knowledge and opinion is similar. Knowledge is the apprehension of, e. g. the attribute 'animal' as incapable of being otherwise, opinion the apprehension of 'animal' as capable 35 of being otherwise—e. g. the apprehension that animal is an element in the essential nature of man is knowledge; the apprehension of animal as predicable of man but not as an element in man's essential nature is opinion: man is the subject in both judgments, but the mode of inherence differs.

This also shows that one cannot opine and know the same thing simultaneously; for then one would apprehend the same thing as both capable and incapable of being oth- 89b erwise—an impossibility. Knowledge and opinion of the same thing can coexist in two different people in the sense we have explained, but not simultaneously in the same person. That would involve a man's simultaneously apprehending, e. g., (1) that man is essentially animal—i. e. cannot be other than animal—and (2) that man is not essentially ani- 5 mal, that is, we may assume, may be other than animal.

Further consideration of modes of thinking and their distribution under the heads of discursive thought, intuition, science, art, practical wisdom, and metaphysical thinking, belongs rather partly to natural science, partly to moral philosophy.

10 **34** Quick wit is a faculty of hitting upon the middle term instantaneously. It would be exemplified by a man who saw that the moon has her bright side always turned towards the sun, and quickly grasped the

cause of this, namely that she borrows her light from him;
or observed somebody in conversation with a man of wealth
and divined that he was borrowing money, or that the
friendship of these people sprang from a common enmity.
In all these instances he has seen the major and minor terms 15
and then grasped the causes, the middle terms. Let A represent 'bright side turned sunward', B 'lighted from the
sun', C the moon. Then B, 'lighted from the sun', is predicable of C, the moon, and A, 'having her bright side
towards the source of her light', is predicable of B. So A is 20
predicable of C through B.

BOOK II

1
The kinds of question we ask are as many as the
kinds of things which we know. They are in fact
four:—(1) whether the connexion of an attribute
with a thing is a fact, (2) what is the reason of the connex- 25
ion, (3) whether a thing exists, (4) what is the nature of the
thing. Thus, when our question concerns a complex of
thing and attribute and we ask whether the thing is thus or
otherwise qualified—whether, e. g., the sun suffers eclipse
or not—then we are asking as to the fact of a connexion.
That our inquiry ceases with the discovery that the sun
does suffer eclipse is an indication of this; and if we know
from the start that the sun suffers eclipse, we do not inquire
whether it does so or not. On the other hand, when we
know the fact we ask the reason; as, for example, when we
know that the sun is being eclipsed and that an earthquake
is in progress, it is the reason of eclipse or earthquake into 30
which we inquire.

Where a complex is concerned, then, those are the two

questions we ask; but for some objects of inquiry we have
a different kind of question to ask, such as whether there is
or is not a centaur or a God. (By 'is or is not' I mean 'is or
is not, without further qualification'; as opposed to 'is or is
not (e. g.) white'.) On the other hand, when we have ascertained the thing's existence, we inquire as to its nature,
35 asking, for instance, 'what, then, is God?' or 'what is man?'.

2 These, then, are the four kinds of question we ask,
and it is in the answers to these questions that our
knowledge consists.

Now when we ask whether a connexion is a fact, or
whether a thing without qualification *is,* we are really asking
whether the connexion or the thing has a 'middle'; and
when we have ascertained either that the connexion is a fact
or that the thing *is*—i. e. ascertained either the partial or the
90ᵃ unqualified being of the thing—and are proceeding to ask
the reason of the connexion or the nature of the thing, then
we are asking what the 'middle' is.

(By distinguishing the fact of the connexion and the
existence of the thing as respectively the partial and the
unqualified being of the thing, I mean that if we ask 'does
the moon suffer eclipse?', or 'does the moon wax?', the
question concerns a part of the thing's being; for what we
are asking in such questions is whether a thing is this or
that, i. e. has or has not this or that attribute: whereas, if
we ask whether the moon or night exists, the question concerns the unqualified being of a thing.)

We conclude that in all our inquiries we are asking
5 either whether there is a 'middle' or what the 'middle' is:
for the 'middle' here is precisely the cause, and it is the
cause that we seek in all our inquiries. Thus, 'Does the
moon suffer eclipse?' means 'Is there or is there not a cause
producing eclipse of the moon?', and when we have learnt
that there is, our next question is, 'What, then, is this

cause?'; for the cause through which a thing *is*—not *is this or that*, i. e. has this or that attribute, but without qualification *is* and the cause through which it is—not *is* without qualification, but *is this or that* as having some essential attribute or some accident—are both alike the 'middle'. By that which *is* without qualification I mean the subject, e. g. moon or earth or sun or triangle; by that which a subject *is* (in the partial sense) I mean a property, e. g. eclipse, equality or inequality, interposition or non-interposition. For in all these examples it is clear that the nature of the thing and the reason of the fact are identical: the question 'What is eclipse?' and its answer 'The privation of the moon's light by the interposition of the earth' are identical with the question 'What is the reason of eclipse?' or 'Why does the moon suffer eclipse?' and the reply 'Because of the failure of light through the earth's shutting it out'. Again, for 'What is a concord? A commensurate numerical ratio of a high and a low note', we may substitute 'What reason makes a high and a low note concordant? Their relation according to a commensurate numerical ratio.' 'Are the high and the low note concordant?' is equivalent to 'Is their ratio commensurate?'; and when we find that it is commensurate, we ask 'What, then, is their ratio?'.

Cases in which the 'middle' is sensible show that the object of our inquiry is always the 'middle': we inquire, because we have not perceived it, whether there is or is not a 'middle' causing e. g. an eclipse. On the other hand, if we were on the moon we should not be inquiring either as to the fact or the reason, but both fact and reason would be obvious simultaneously. For the act of perception would have enabled us to know the universal too; since, the present fact of an eclipse being evident, perception would then at the same time give us the present fact of the earth's screening the sun's light, and from this would arise the universal.

Thus, as we maintain, to know a thing's nature is to know the reason why it is; and this is equally true of things in so far as they are said without qualification to *be* as opposed to being possessed of some attribute, and in so far as they are said to be possessed of some attribute such as equal to two right angles, or greater or less.

35   It is clear, then, that all questions are a search for a 'middle'. Let us now state how essential nature is revealed, and in what way it can be reduced to demonstration;[1] what definition is, and what things are definable. And let us first discuss certain difficulties which 90b these questions raise, beginning what we have to say with a point most intimately connected with our immediately preceding remarks, namely the doubt that might be felt as to whether or not it is possible to know the same thing in the same relation, both by definition and by demonstration. It might, I mean, be urged that definition is held to concern 5 essential nature and is in every case universal and affirmative; whereas, on the other hand, some conclusions are negative and some are not universal; e. g. all in the second figure are negative, none in the third are universal. And again, not even all affirmative conclusions in the first figure are definable, e. g. 'every triangle has its angles equal to two right angles'. An argument proving this difference between demonstration and definition is that to have scientific 10 knowledge of the demonstrable is identical with possessing a demonstration of it: hence if demonstration of such conclusions as these is possible, there clearly cannot also be definition of them. If there could, one might know such a conclusion also in virtue of its definition without possessing the demonstration of it; for there is nothing to stop our having the one without the other.

[1] Cf. 94a 11–14.

Induction too will sufficiently convince us of this difference; for never yet by defining anything—essential attribute or accident—did we get knowledge of it. Again, if to define is to acquire knowledge of a substance, at any rate such attributes are not substances.

It is evident, then, that not everything demonstrable can be defined. What then? Can everything definable be demonstrated, or not? There is one of our previous arguments which covers this too. Of a single thing *qua* single there is a single scientific knowledge. Hence, since to know the demonstrable scientifically is to possess the demonstration of it, an impossible consequence will follow:—possession of its definition without its demonstration will give knowledge of the demonstrable.

Moreover, the basic premisses of demonstrations are definitions, and it has already been shown[2] that these will be found indemonstrable; either the basic premisses will be demonstrable and will depend on prior premisses, and the regress will be endless; or the primary truths will be indemonstrable definitions.

But if the definable and the demonstrable are not wholly the same, may they yet be partially the same? Or is that impossible, because there can be no demonstration of the definable? There can be none, because definition is of the essential nature or being of something, and all demonstrations evidently posit and assume the essential nature—mathematical demonstrations, for example, the nature of unity and the odd, and all the other sciences likewise. Moreover, every demonstration proves a predicate of a subject as attaching or as not attaching to it, but in definition one thing is not predicated of another; we do not, e. g., predicate animal of biped nor biped of animal, nor yet figure of plane—plane not being figure nor figure plane.

[2] Cf. 72^b 18–25 and 84^a 30–^{b} 2.

Again, to prove essential nature is not the same as to prove the fact of a connexion. Now definition reveals essential 91ª nature, demonstration reveals that a given attribute attaches or does not attach to a given subject; but different things require different demonstrations—unless the one demonstration is related to the other as part to whole. I add this because if all triangles have been proved to possess angles equal to two right angles, then this attribute has been proved to attach to isosceles; for isosceles is a part of which 5 all triangles constitute the whole. But in the case before us the fact and the essential nature are not so related to one another, since the one is not a part of the other.

So it emerges that not all the definable is demonstrable nor all the demonstrable definable; and we may draw the general conclusion that there is no identical object of which 10 it is possible to possess both a definition and a demonstration. It follows obviously that definition and demonstration are neither identical nor contained either within the other: if they were, their objects would be related either as identical or as whole and part.

4 So much, then, for the first stage of our problem. The next step is to raise the question whether syllogism—i. e. demonstration—of the definable nature is possible or, as our recent argument assumed, impossible.

We might argue it impossible on the following grounds:—(a) syllogism proves an attribute of a subject 15 through the middle term; on the other hand (b) its definable nature is both 'peculiar' to a subject and predicated of it as belonging to its essence. But in that case (1) the subject, its definition, and the middle term connecting them must be reciprocally predicable of one another; for if A is 'peculiar' to C, obviously A is 'peculiar' to B and B to C— in fact all three terms are 'peculiar' to one another: and

further (2) if *A* inheres in the essence of all *B* and *B* is predicated universally of all *C* as belonging to *C*'s essence, *A*   20
also must be predicated of *C* as belonging to its essence.

If one does not take this relation as thus duplicated—
if, that is, *A* is predicated as being of the essence of *B*, but
B is not of the essence of the subjects of which it is predicated—*A* will not necessarily be predicated of *C* as
belonging to its essence. So both premisses *will* predicate
essence, and consequently *B* also will be predicated of *C* as   25
its essence. Since, therefore, both premisses do predicate
essence—i. e. definable form—*C*'s definable form will
appear in the middle term before the conclusion is drawn.

We may generalize by supposing that it is possible to
prove the essential nature of man. Let *C* be man, *A* man's
essential nature—two-footed animal, or aught else it may
be. Then, if we are to syllogize, *A* must be predicated of all
B. But this premiss will be mediated by a fresh definition,
which consequently will also be the essential nature of   30
man.[3] Therefore the argument assumes what it has to prove,
since *B* too is the essential nature of man. It is, however,
the case in which there are only the two premisses—i. e. in
which the premisses are primary and immediate—which we
ought to investigate, because it best illustrates the point
under discussion.

Thus they who prove the essential nature of soul or
man or anything else through reciprocating terms beg the   35
question. It would be begging the question, for example, to
contend that the soul is that which causes its own life, and
that what causes its own life is a self-moving number; for
one would have to postulate that the soul is a self-moving

---

[3] *sc.* 'and an indefinite regress occurs'. This argument is a corollary of the
proof in 91ᵃ 15–26 that if the proposition predicating *A*—its definition—of
C can be a conclusion, there must be a middle term, *B*, and since *A*, *B*, and
C are reciprocally predicable, *B* too, as well as *A*, will be a definition of *C*.

91^b number in the sense of being identical with it. For if A is
predicable as a mere consequent of B and B of C, A will not
on that account be the definable form of C: A will merely
be what it was true to say of C. Even if A is predicated of
all B inasmuch as B is identical with a species of A, still it
will not follow: being an animal is predicated of being a
5 man—since it is true that in all instances to be human is to
be animal, just as it is also true that every man is an animal—but not as identical with being man.

We conclude, then, that unless one takes both the premisses as predicating essence, one cannot infer that A is the
definable form and essence of C: but if one does so take
them, in assuming B one will have assumed, before drawing
the conclusion, what the definable form of C is; so that there
10 has been no inference, for one has begged the question.

5 Nor, as was said in my formal logic, is the method
of division a process of inference at all, since at no
point does the characterization of the subject follow necessarily from the premising of certain other facts:
15 division demonstrates as little as does induction. For in a
genuine demonstration the conclusion must not be put as a
question nor depend on a concession, but must follow necessarily from its premises, even if the respondent deny it.
The definer asks 'Is man animal or inanimate?' and then
assumes—he has not inferred—that man is animal. Next,
when presented with an exhaustive division of animal into
20 terrestrial and aquatic, he assumes that man is terrestrial.
Moreover, that man is the complete formula, terrestrial-ani-
mal, does not follow necessarily from the premises: this too
is an assumption, and equally an assumption whether the
division comprises many differentiae or few. (Indeed as this
method of division is used by those who proceed by it, even
25 truths that can be inferred actually fail to appear as such.)
For why should not the whole of this formula be true of

man, and yet not exhibit his essential nature or definable form? Again, what guarantee is there against an unessential addition, or against the omission of the final or of an intermediate determinant of the substantial being?

The champion of division might here urge that though these lapses do occur, yet we can solve that difficulty if all the attributes we assume are constituents of the definable form, and if, postulating the genus, we produce by division the requisite uninterrupted sequence of terms, and omit 30 nothing; and that indeed we cannot fail to fulfil these conditions if what is to be divided falls whole into the division at each stage, and none of it is omitted; and that this—the dividendum—must without further question be (ultimately) incapable of fresh specific division. Nevertheless, we reply, division does not involve inference; if it gives knowledge, it gives it in another way. Nor is there any absurdity in this: induction, perhaps, is not demonstration any more than is division, yet it does make evident some truth. Yet to state a definition reached by division is not to state a conclusion: 35 as, when conclusions are drawn without their appropriate middles, the alleged necessity by which the inference follows from the premises is open to a question as to the reason for it, so definitions reached by division invite the same question. Thus to the question 'What is the essential 92ᵃ nature of man?' the divider replies 'Animal, mortal, footed, biped, wingless'; and when at each step he is asked 'Why?', he will say, and, as he thinks, prove by division, that all animal is mortal or immortal: but such a formula taken in its entirety is not definition; so that even if division does demonstrate its formula, definition at any rate does not turn 5 out to be a conclusion of inference.

6 Can we nevertheless actually demonstrate what a thing essentially and substantially is, but hypothetically, i. e. by premising (1) that its definable form

is constituted by the 'peculiar' attributes of its essential
nature; (2) that such and such are the only attributes of its
essential nature, and that the complete synthesis of them is
peculiar to the thing; and thus—since in this synthesis consists the being of the thing—obtaining our conclusion? Or is
10 the truth that, since proof must be through the middle
term, the definable form is once more assumed in this
minor premiss too?

Further, just as in syllogizing we do not premise what
syllogistic inference is (since the premises from which we
conclude must be related as whole and part),[4] so the definable form must not fall within the syllogism but remain
outside the premises posited. It is only against a doubt as
15 to its having been a syllogistic inference at all that we have
to defend our argument as conforming to the definition of
syllogism. It is only when some one doubts whether the
conclusion proved is the definable form that we have to
defend it as conforming to the definition of definable form
which we assumed. Hence syllogistic inference must be possible even without the express statement of what syllogism
is or what definable form is.

The following type of hypothetical proof also begs the
20 question. If evil is definable as the divisible, and the definition of a thing's contrary—if it has one—is the contrary of
the thing's definition; then, if good is the contrary of evil
and the indivisible of the divisible, we conclude that to be
good is essentially to be indivisible. The question is begged
because definable form is assumed as a premiss, and as a
premiss which is to prove definable form. 'But not the same
definable form', you may object. That I admit, for in
25 demonstrations also we premise that 'this' is predicable of

---

[4] A reminder of a necessary condition of syllogism. If the definition of syllogism is premised the conclusion would have to affirm some subject to
be of the nature of syllogism.

'that'; but in this premiss the term we assert of the minor
is neither the major itself nor a term identical in definition,
or convertible, with the major.

Again, both proof by division and the syllogism just
described are open to the question why man should be ani-
mal-biped-terrestrial and not merely animal *and* terrestrial,
since what they premise does not ensure that the predicates 30
shall constitute a genuine unity and not merely belong to a
single subject as do musical and grammatical when predicated of the same man.

7 How then by definition shall we *prove* substance or
essential nature? We cannot show it as a fresh fact
necessarily following from the assumption of prem- 35
isses admitted to be facts—the method of demonstration: we
may not proceed as by induction to establish a universal on
the evidence of groups of particulars which offer no exception, because induction proves not what the essential nature
of a thing is but that it has or has not some attribute.
Therefore, since presumably one cannot prove essential 92ᵇ
nature by an appeal to sense perception or by pointing with
the finger, what other method remains?

To put it another way: how shall we by definition
prove *essential nature*? He who knows what human—or any
other—nature is, must know also that man exists; for no 5
one knows the nature of what does not exist—one can know
the meaning of the phrase or name 'goat-stag' but not what
the essential nature of a goat-stag is. But further, if definition can prove what is the essential nature of a thing, can it
also prove that it exists? And how will it prove them both
by the same process, since definition exhibits one single
thing and demonstration another single thing, and what 10
human nature is and the fact that man exists are not the
same thing? Then too we hold that it is by *demonstration*
that the being of everything must be proved—unless indeed

to be were its essence; and, since being is not a genus, it is
not the essence of anything. Hence the being of anything as
15 fact is matter for demonstration; and this is the actual procedure of the sciences, for the geometer assumes the
meaning of the word triangle, but that it is possessed of
some attribute he proves. What is it, then, that we shall
prove in defining essential nature? Triangle? In that case a
man will know by definition what a thing's nature is without knowing whether it exists. But that is impossible.

Moreover it is clear, if we consider the methods of
defining actually in use, that definition does not prove that
20 the thing defined exists: since even if there does actually
exist something which is equidistant from a centre, yet *why*
should the thing named in the definition exist? Why, in
other words, should this be the formula defining circle? One
might equally well call it the definition of mountain cop-
per. For definitions do not carry a further guarantee that the
25 thing defined can exist or that it is what they claim to
define: one can always ask why.

Since, therefore, to define is to prove either a thing's
essential nature or the meaning of its name, we may conclude that definition, if it in no sense proves essential
nature, is a set of words signifying precisely what a name
signifies. But that were a strange consequence; for (1) both
what is not substance and what does not exist at all would
30 be definable, since even non-existents can be signified by a
name: (2) all sets of words or sentences would be definitions, since any kind of sentence could be given a name; so
that we should all be talking in definitions, and even the
Iliad would be a definition: (3) no demonstration can prove
that any particular name means any particular thing: neither, therefore, do definitions, in addition to revealing the
35 meaning of a name, also reveal that the name has *this* meaning. It appears then from these considerations that neither
definition and syllogism nor their objects are identical, and

further that definition neither demonstrates nor proves anything, and that knowledge of essential nature is not to be
obtained either by definition or by demonstration.

8 We must now start afresh and consider which of
these conclusions are sound and which are not, and   93ᵃ
what is the nature of definition, and whether essential
nature is in any sense demonstrable and definable or in none.

Now to know its essential nature is, as we said, the same
as to know the cause of a thing's existence, and the proof of
this depends on the fact that a thing must have a cause.   5
Moreover, this cause is either identical with the essential
nature of the thing or distinct from it;⁵ and if its cause is distinct from it, the essential nature of the thing is either
demonstrable or indemonstrable. Consequently, if the cause
is distinct from the thing's essential nature and demonstration is possible, the cause must be the middle term, and, the
conclusion proved being universal and affirmative, the proof
is in the first figure. So the method just examined of proving
it through another essential nature would be one way of
proving essential nature, because a conclusion containing   10
essential nature must be inferred through a middle which is
an essential nature just as a 'peculiar' property must be
inferred through a middle which is a 'peculiar' property; so
that of the two definable natures of a single thing this
method will prove one and not the other.⁶

⁵ 'distinct from it'; i. e. in the case of *properties*, with the definition of
which Aristotle is alone concerned in this chapter. The being of a property consists in its inherence in a substance through a middle which defines
it. Cf. the following chapter.

⁶Aristotle speaks of two moments of the definable form as two essential
natures. His argument amounts to this: that if the conclusion contains the
whole definition, the question has been begged in the premisses (cf. ii, ch.
4). Hence syllogism—and even so merely dialectical syllogism—is only
possible if premisses and conclusion each contain a part of the definition.

Now it was said before[7] that this method could not
amount to demonstration of essential nature—it is actually a
15 dialectical proof of it—so let us begin again and explain by
what method it can be demonstrated. When we are aware of
a fact we seek its reason, and though sometimes the fact and
the reason dawn on us simultaneously, yet we cannot apprehend the reason a moment sooner than the fact; and clearly
in just the same way we cannot apprehend a thing's definable form without apprehending that it exists, since while
we are ignorant whether it exists we cannot know its essen-
20 tial nature. Moreover we are aware whether a thing exists or
not sometimes through apprehending an element in its character, and sometimes accidentally,[8] as, for example, when we
are aware of thunder as a noise in the clouds, of eclipse as
a privation of light, or of man as some species of animal, or
of the soul as a self-moving thing. As often as we have acci-
25 dental knowledge that the thing exists, we must be in a
wholly negative state as regards awareness of its essential
nature; for we have not got genuine knowledge even of its
existence, and to search for a thing's essential nature when
we are unaware that it exists is to search for nothing. On
the other hand, whenever we apprehend an element in the
thing's character there is less difficulty. Thus it follows that
the degree of our knowledge of a thing's essential nature is
determined by the sense in which we are aware that it
exists. Let us then take the following as our first instance
30 of being aware of an element in the essential nature. Let A
be eclipse, C the moon, B the earth's acting as a screen.
Now to ask whether the moon is eclipsed or not is to ask
whether or not B has occurred. But that is precisely the

[7] ii, ch. 2.

[8] The distinction is that between genuine knowledge of a connexion
through its cause and accidental knowledge of it through a middle not the
cause.

same as asking whether A has a defining condition; and if this condition actually exists, we assert that A also actually exists. Or again we may ask which side of a contradiction the defining condition necessitates: does it make the angles of a triangle equal or not equal to two right angles? When we have found the answer, if the premisses are immediate, 35 we know fact and reason together; if they are not immediate, we know the fact without the reason, as in the following example: let C be the moon, A eclipse, B the fact that the moon fails to produce shadows[9] though she is full and though no visible body intervenes between us and her. Then if B, failure to 'produce shadows in spite of the 93^b absence of an intervening body, is attributable to C, and A, eclipse, is attributable to B, it is clear that the moon is eclipsed, but the reason why is not yet clear, and we know that eclipse exists, but we do not know what its essential nature is. But when it is clear that A is attributable to C and 5 we proceed to ask the reason of this fact, we are inquiring what is the nature of B: is it the earth's acting as a screen, or the moon's rotation or her extinction? But B is the definition of the other term, viz., in these examples, of the major term A; for eclipse is constituted by the earth acting as a screen. Thus, (1) 'What is thunder?' 'The quenching of fire in cloud', and (2) 'Why does it thunder?' 'Because fire is quenched in the cloud', are equivalent. Let C be cloud, A thunder, B the quenching of fire. Then B is attributable 10 to C, cloud, since fire is quenched in it; and A, noise, is attributable to B; and B is assuredly the definition of the major term A. If there be a further mediating cause of B, it will be one of the remaining partial definitions of A.

We have stated then how essential nature is discovered and becomes known, and we see that, while there is no 15

---

[9] i.e. that there is no moonlight casting shadows on the earth on a clear night at full moon.

syllogism—i. e. no demonstrative syllogism—of essential nature, yet it is through syllogism, viz. demonstrative syllogism, that essential nature is exhibited. So we conclude that neither can the essential nature of anything which has a cause distinct from itself be known without demonstration, nor can it be demonstrated; and this is what we contended 20 in our preliminary discussions.[10]

9 Now while some things have a cause distinct from themselves, others have not. Hence it is evident that there are essential natures which are immediate, that is, are basic premisses; and of these not only *that* they are but also *what* they are must be assumed or revealed in some other way. This too is the actual procedure of the arithmetician, who assumes both the nature and the exis-25 tence of unit. On the other hand, it is possible (in the manner explained) to exhibit through demonstration the essential nature of things which have a 'middle',[11] a cause of their substantial being other than that being itself; but we do not thereby demonstrate it.

10 Since definition is said to be the statement of a thing's nature, obviously one kind of definition will be a statement of the meaning of the name, 30 or of an equivalent nominal formula. A definition in this sense tells you, e. g. the meaning of the phrase 'triangular character'.[12] When we are aware that triangle exists, we inquire the reason why it exists. But it is difficult thus to learn the definition of things the existence of which we do not genuinely know—the cause of this difficulty being, as

[10] ii, ch. 3.

[11] Cf., however, ii, ch. 2.

[12] i. e. as treated by geometry; that is, as abstracted *a materia* and treated as a subject. Cf. 81^b 25.

we said before,[13] that we only know accidentally whether or not the thing exists. Moreover, a statement may be a unity 35 in either of two ways, by conjunction, like the *Iliad,* or because it exhibits a single predicate as inhering not accidentally in a single subject.[14]

That then is one way of defining definition. Another kind of definition is a formula exhibiting the cause of a thing's existence. Thus the former signifies without proving, 94a but the latter will clearly be a quasi-demonstration of essential nature, differing from demonstration in the arrangement of its terms. For there is a difference between stating why it thunders, and stating what is the essential nature of thunder; since the first statement will be 'Because fire is quenched in the clouds', while the statement of what the nature of thunder is will be 'The noise of fire being 5 quenched in the clouds'. Thus the same statement takes a different form: in one form it is continuous[15] demonstration, in the other definition. Again, thunder can be defined as noise in the clouds, which is the conclusion of the demonstration embodying essential nature. On the other hand the 10 definition of immediates is an indemonstrable positing of essential nature. We conclude then that definition is (*a*) an indemonstrable statement of essential nature, or (*b*) a syllogism of essential nature differing from demonstration in grammatical form, or (*c*) the conclusion of a demonstration giving essential nature.

Our discussion has therefore made plain (1) in what

---

[13] Cf. 93a 16–27.

[14] Presumably a reason for there being a kind of definition other than nominal. The reference is obviously to 92b 32.

[15] Demonstration, like a line, is continuous because its premisses are parts which are conterminous (as linked by middle terms), and there is a movement from premisses to conclusion. Definition resembles rather the indivisible simplicity of a point.

sense and of what things the essential nature is demonstra-
15 ble, and in what sense and of what things it is not; (2) what
are the various meanings of the term definition, and in what
sense and of what things it proves the essential nature, and
in what sense and of what things it does not; (3) what is the
relation of definition to demonstration, and how far the
same thing is both definable and demonstrable and how far
it is not.

20   **11** We think we have scientific knowledge when we
know the cause, and there are four causes: (1) the
definable form, (2) an antecedent which necessitates a consequent,[16] (3) the efficient cause, (4) the final
cause. Hence each of these can be the middle term of a
25 proof, for[17] (a) though the inference from antecedent to necessary consequent does not hold if only one premiss is
assumed—two is the minimum—still when there are two it
holds on condition that they have a single common middle
term. So it is from the assumption of this single middle term
that the conclusion follows necessarily. The following example will also show this.[18] Why is the angle in a semicircle a
right angle?—or from what assumption does it follow that it
is a right angle? Thus, let A be right angle, B the half of two
30 right angles, C the angle in a semicircle. Then B is the cause
in virtue of which A, right angle, is attributable to C, the
angle in a semicircle, since $B = A$ and the other, viz. C, $= B$,
for C is half of two right angles. Therefore it is the assumption of B, the half of two right angles, from which it follows
that A is attributable to C, i. e. that the angle in a semicir-

[16] By this Aristotle appears to mean the material cause; cf. *Physics* ii, 195ª
18, 19, where the premisses of a syllogism are said to be the material cause
of the conclusion.

[17] *sc.* 'lest you should suppose that (2) could not be a middle'.

[18] *sc.* 'that (2) can appear as a middle'.

cle is a right angle. Moreover, B is identical with (b) the
defining form of A, since it is what A's definition[19] signifies.
Moreover, the formal cause has already been shown to be
the middle.[20] (c) 'Why did the Athenians become involved   35
in the Persian war?' means 'What cause originated the wag-
ing of war against the Athenians?' and the answer is,
'Because they raided Sardis with the Eretrians', since this
originated the war. Let A be war, B unprovoked raiding, C 94b
the Athenians. Then B, unprovoked raiding, is true of C,
the Athenians, and A is true of B, since men make war on
the unjust aggressor. So A, having war waged upon them, is
true of B, the initial aggressors, and B is true of C, the   5
Athenians, who were the aggressors. Hence here too the
cause—in this case the efficient cause—is the middle term.
(d) This is no less true where the cause is the final cause.
E. g. why does one take a walk after supper? For the sake of
one's health. Why does a house exist? For the preservation
of one's goods. The end in view is in the one case health, in
the other preservation. To ask the reason why one must walk   10
after supper is precisely to ask to what end one must do it.
Let C be walking after supper, B the non-regurgitation of
food, A health. Then let walking after supper possess the
property of preventing food from rising to the orifice of the   15
stomach, and let this condition be healthy; since it seems
that B, the non-regurgitation of food, is attributable to C,
taking a walk, and that A, health, is attributable to B. What,
then, is the cause through which A, the final cause, inheres
in C? It is B, the non-regurgitation of food; but B is a kind

---

[19] Cf. Euclid, *Elem.* i, Def. x, but Aristotle may be referring to some earlier
definition. The proof here given that the angle in a semi-circle is a right
angle is not that of Euclid iii. 31; cf. Heath, *Greek Mathematics*, i. pp. 339,
340.

[20] The reference is to 93ª 3 ff., and other passages such as 94ª 5 ff. where
the middle is shown to define the major.

20 of definition of *A*, for *A* will be explained by it. Why is *B*
the cause of *A*'s belonging to *C*? Because to be in a condition
such as *B* is to be in health. The definitions must be trans-
posed, and then the detail will become clearer. Incidentally,
here the order of coming to be is the reverse of what it is in
proof through the efficient cause: in the efficient order the
25 middle term must come to be first, whereas in the teleologi-
cal order the minor, *C*, must first take place, and the end in
view comes last in time.

The same thing may exist for an end and be necessi-
tated as well. For example, light shines through a lantern
(1) because that which consists of relatively small particles
30 necessarily passes through pores larger than those particles—assuming that light does issue by penetration—and
(2) for an end, namely to save us from stumbling. If, then,
a thing can exist through two causes, can it come to be
through two causes—as for instance if thunder be a hiss and
a roar necessarily produced by the quenching of fire, and
also designed, as the Pythagoreans say, for a threat to terrify
35 those that lie in Tartarus? Indeed, there are very many such
cases, mostly among the processes and products of the natural world; for nature, in different senses of the term
'nature', produces now for an end, now by necessity.

Necessity too is of two kinds. It may work in accor-
95ª dance with a thing's natural tendency, or by constraint and
in opposition to it; as, for instance, by necessity a stone is
borne both upwards and downwards, but not by the same
necessity.

Of the products of man's intelligence some are never
due to chance or necessity but always to an end, as for
5 example a house or a statue; others, such as health or safety,
may result from chance as well.

It is mostly in cases where the issue is indeterminate
(though only where the production does not originate in
chance, and the end is consequently good), that a result is

due to an end, and this is true alike in nature or in art. By chance, on the other hand, nothing comes to be for an end.

12 The effect may be still coming to be, or its occurrence may be past or future, yet the cause will be the same as when it is actually existent—for it is the middle which is the cause—except that if the effect actually exists the cause is actually existent, if it is coming to be so is the cause, if its occurrence is past the cause is past, if future the cause is future. For example, the moon was eclipsed because the earth intervened, is becoming eclipsed because the earth is in process of intervening, will be eclipsed because the earth is will intervene, is eclipsed because the earth intervenes.

To take a second example: assuming that the definition of ice is solidified water, let C be water, A solidified, B the middle, which is the cause, namely total failure of heat. Then B is attributed to C, and A, solidification, to B: ice forms when B is occurring, has formed when B has occurred, and will form when B shall occur.

This sort of cause, then, and its effect come to be simultaneously when they are in process of becoming, and exist simultaneously when they actually exist; and the same holds good when they are past and when they are future. But what of cases where they are not simultaneous? Can causes and effects different from one another form, as they seem to us to form, a continuous succession, a past effect resulting from a past cause different from itself, a future effect from a future cause different from it, and an effect which is coming-to-be from a cause different from and prior to it? Now on this theory it is from the posterior event that we reason (and this though these later events actually have their source of origin in previous events—a fact which shows that also when the effect is coming-to-be we still reason from the posterior event), and from the prior event we

cannot reason (we cannot argue that because an event *A* has
30 occurred, therefore an event *B* has occurred subsequently
to *A* but still in the past—and the same holds good if the
occurrence is future)—cannot reason because, be the time
interval definite or indefinite, it will never be possible to
infer that because it is true to say that *A* occurred, therefore it is true to say that *B*, the subsequent event, occurred;
for in the interval between the events, though *A* has already
35 occurred, the latter statement will be false. And the same
argument applies also to future events; i. e. one cannot infer
from an event which occurred in the past that a future event
will occur. The reason of this is that the middle must be
homogeneous, past when the extremes are past, future when
they are future, coming to be when they are coming-to-be,
actually existent when they are actually existent; and there
cannot be a middle term homogeneous with extremes
respectively past and future. And it is a further difficulty
40 in this theory that the time interval can be neither indefinite
95ᵇ nor definite, since during it the inference will be false. We
have also to inquire what it is that holds events together so
that the coming-to-be now occurring in actual things follows upon a past event. It is evident, we may suggest, that a
past event and a present process cannot be 'contiguous', for
not even two past events can be 'contiguous'. For past
5 events are limits and atomic; so just as points are not 'contiguous' neither are past events, since both are indivisible.
For the same reason a past event and a present process cannot be 'contiguous', for the process is divisible, the event
indivisible. Thus the relation of present process to past
10 event is analogous to that of line to point, since a process
contains an infinity of past events. These questions, however, must receive a more explicit treatment in our general
theory of change.[21]

[21] Cf. *Physics* vi.

The following must suffice as an account of the manner in which the middle would be identical with the cause on the supposition that coming-to-be is a series of consecutive events: for[22] in the terms of such a series too the middle and major terms must form an immediate premiss; e. g. we argue that, since C has occurred, therefore A occurred: and C's occurrence was posterior, A's prior; but C is the source of the inference because it is nearer to the present moment, and the starting-point of time is the present. We next argue that, since D has occurred, therefore C occurred. Then we conclude that, since D has occurred, therefore A must have occurred; and the cause is C, for since D has occurred C must have occurred, and since C has occurred A must previously have occurred.

If we get our middle term in this way, will the series terminate in an immediate premiss, or since, as we said, no two events are 'contiguous', will a fresh term always intervene because there is an infinity of middles? No: though no two events are 'contiguous', yet we must start from a premiss consisting of a middle and the present event as major. The like is true of future events too, since if it is true to say that D will exist, it must be a prior truth to say that A will exist, and the cause of this conclusion is C; for if D will exist, C will exist prior to D, and if C will exist, A will exist prior to it. And here too the same infinite divisibility might be urged, since future events are not 'contiguous'. But here too an immediate basic premiss must be assumed. And in the world of fact this is so: if a house has been built, then

---

[22] i. e. Aristotle has had in this chapter to explain (1) how syllogisms concerning a process of events can be brought into line with other demonstrations equally derivable from immediate primary premisses, and (2) in what sense the middle term contains the cause. He has in fact had (1) to show that in these syllogisms inference must find its primary premiss in the effect, and (2) to imply that the 'cause' which appears as middle when cause and effect are not simultaneous is a *causa cognoscendi* and not *essendi*.

blocks must have been quarried and shaped. The reason is
that a house having been built necessitates a foundation
having been laid, and if a foundation has been laid blocks
35 must have been shaped beforehand. Again, if a house will
be built, blocks will similarly be shaped beforehand; and
proof is through the middle in the same way, for the foundation will exist before the house. Now we observe in
Nature a certain kind of circular process of coming-to-be;
and this is possible only if the middle and extreme terms
are reciprocal, since conversion is conditioned by reciprocity
40 in the terms of the proof. This—the convertibility of con-
96ᵃ clusions and premises—has been proved in our early
chapters,[23] and the circular process is an instance of this. In
actual fact it is exemplified thus: when the earth had been
moistened an exhalation was bound to rise, and when an
exhalation had risen cloud was bound to form, and from the
formation of cloud rain necessarily resulted, and by the fall
5 of rain the earth was necessarily moistened: but this was the
starting-point, so that a circle is completed; for posit any
one of the terms and another follows from it, and from that
another, and from that again the first.

Some occurrences are universal (for they are, or come-
to-be what they are, always and in every case); others again
are not always what they are but only as a general rule: for
10 instance, not every man can grow a beard, but it is the general rule. In the case of such connexions the middle term
too must be a general rule. For if A is predicted universally
of B and B of C, A too must be predicted always and in
every instance of C, since to hold in every instance and
always is of the nature of the universal. But we have
15 assumed a connexion which is a general rule; consequently
the middle term B must also be a general rule. So connex-

[23] i, ch. 3 and *An. Pr.* ii, cc. 3–5, 8–10.

ions which embody a general rule—i. e. which exist or come to be as a general rule—will also derive from immediate basic premisses.

13 [24] We have already explained how essential nature is set out in the terms of a demonstration, and 20 the sense in which it is or is not demonstrable or definable; so let us now discuss the method to be adopted in tracing the elements predicated as constituting the definable form.

Now of the attributes which inhere always in each several thing there are some which are wider in extent than it but not wider than its genus (by attributes of wider extent 25 I mean all such as are universal attributes of each several subject, but in their application are not confined to that subject). I. e. while an attribute may inhere in every triad, yet also in a subject not a triad—as being inheres in triad but also in subjects not numbers at all—odd on the other hand is an attribute inhering in every triad and of wider application (inhering as it does also in pentad), but which does not extend beyond the genus of triad; for pentad is a 30 number, but nothing outside number is odd. It is such attributes which we have to select, up to the exact point at which they are severally of wider extent than the subject but collectively coextensive with it; for this synthesis must be the substance of the thing. For example every triad possesses the attributes number, odd, and prime in both senses, 35 i. e. not only as possessing no divisors, but also as not being a sum of numbers. This, then, is precisely what triad is, viz. a number, odd, and prime in the former and also the latter sense of the term: for these attributes taken severally apply, the first two to all odd numbers, the last to the dyad also 96ᵇ

---

[24] This chapter treats only the definition of substances.

as well as to the triad, but, taken collectively, to no other
subject. Now since we have shown above[25] that attributes
predicated as belonging to the essential nature are necessary
and that universals are necessary, and since the attributes
which we select as inhering in triad, or in any other subject
5 whose attributes we select in this way, are predicated as
belonging to its essential nature, triad will thus possess
these attributes necessarily. Further, that the synthesis of
them constitutes the substance of triad is shown by the following argument. If it is not identical with the being of
triad, it must be related to triad as a genus named or nameless. It will then be of wider extent than triad—assuming
that wider potential extent is the character of a genus. If on
10 the other hand this synthesis is applicable to no subject
other than the individual triads, it will be identical with the
being of triad, because we make the further assumption that
the substance of each subject is the predication of elements
in its essential nature down to the last differentia characterizing the individuals. It follows that any other synthesis
thus exhibited will likewise be identical with the being of
the subject.

15   The author of a hand-book[26] on a subject that is a
generic whole should divide the genus into its first *infimae
species*—number e. g. into triad and dyad—and then endeavour to seize their definitions by the method we have
described—the definition, for example, of straight line or circle or right angle. After that, having established what the
category is to which the subaltern genus belongs—quantity
20 or quality, for instance—he should examine the properties
'peculiar' to the species, working through the proximate
common differentiae. He should proceed thus because the

---

[25] i, ch.4.

[26] With the remainder of the chapter compare *An. Pr.* i, ch. 25, where the
treatment covers all syllogism.

attributes of the genera compounded of the *infimae species* will be clearly given by the definitions of the species; since the basic element of them all[27] is the definition, i. e. the simple *infima species*, and the attributes inhere essentially in the simple *infimae species*, in the genera only in virtue of these.

Divisions according to differentiae are a useful accessory to this method. What force they have as proofs we did, indeed, explain above,[28] but that merely towards collecting the essential nature they may be of use we will proceed to show. They might, indeed, seem to be of no use at all, but rather to assume everything at the start and to be no better than an initial assumption made without division. But, in fact, the order in which the attributes are predicated does make a difference—it matters whether we say animal—tame—biped, or biped—animal—tame. For if every definable thing consists of two elements and 'animal-tame' forms a unity, and again out of this and the further differentia man (or whatever else is the unity under construction) is constituted, then the elements we assume have necessarily been reached by division. Again, division is the only possible method of avoiding the omission of any element of the essential nature. Thus, if the primary genus is assumed and we then take one of the lower divisions, the dividendum will not fall whole into this division: e. g. it is not all animal which is either whole-winged or split-winged but all winged animal, for it is winged animal to which this differentiation belongs. The primary differentiation of animal is that within which all animal falls. The like is true of every other genus, whether outside animal or a subaltern genus of animal; e. g. the primary differentiation of bird is that within which falls every bird, of fish that within which falls every fish. So, if we proceed in this way, we can be sure that nothing has

25

30

35

97a

5

[27] *sc.* genera and species.

[28] ii, ch. 5 and *An. Pr.* i, ch. 31.

been omitted: by any other method one is bound to omit something without knowing it.

To define and divide one need not know the whole of existence. Yet some hold it impossible to know the differentiae distinguishing each thing from every single other thing without knowing every single other thing; and one cannot, they say, know each thing without knowing its differentiae, since everything is identical with that from which it does not differ, and other than that from which it differs. Now first of all this is a fallacy: not every differentia precludes identity, since many differentiae inhere in things specifically identical, though not in the substance of these nor essentially. Secondly, when one has taken one's differing pair of opposites and assumed that the two sides exhaust the genus, and that the subject one seeks to define is present in one or other of them, and one has further verified its presence in one of them; then it does not matter whether or not one knows all the other subjects of which the differentiae are also predicated. For it is obvious that when by this process one reaches subjects incapable of further differentiation one will possess the formula defining the substance. Moreover, to postulate that the division exhausts the genus is not illegitimate if the opposites exclude a middle; since if it is the differentia of that genus, anything contained in the genus must lie on one of the two sides.

In establishing a definition by division one should keep three objects in view: (1) the admission only of elements in the definable form, (2) the arrangement of these in the right order, (3) the omission of no such elements. The first is feasible because one can establish genus and differentia through the topic of the genus,[29] just as one can conclude the inherence of an accident through the topic of the accident.[30] The

[29] Cf. *Topics* iv.

[30] Cf. *Topics* ii.

right order will be achieved if the right term is assumed as
primary, and this will be ensured if the term selected is
predicable of all the others but not all they of it; since there 30
must be one such term. Having assumed this we at once
proceed in the same way with the lower terms; for our second term will be the first of the remainder, our third the
first of those which follow the second in a 'contiguous'
series, since when the higher term is excluded, that term of
the remainder which is 'contiguous' to it will be primary,
and so on. Our procedure makes it clear that no elements in
the definable form have been omitted: we have taken the 35
differentia that comes first in the order of division, pointing out that animal e. g. is divisible exhaustively into A and
B, and that the subject accepts one of the two as its predicate. Next we have taken the differentia of the whole thus
reached, and shown that the whole we finally reach is not
further divisible—i. e. that as soon as we have taken the last
differentia to form the concrete totality, this totality admits
of no division into species. For it is clear that there is no 97^b
superfluous addition, since all these terms we have selected
are elements in the definable form; and nothing lacking,
since any omission would have to be a genus or a differentia. Now the primary term is a genus, and this term taken in
conjunction with its differentiae is a genus: moreover the
differentiae are all included, because there is now no further differentia; if there were, the final concrete would admit 5
of division into species, which, we said, is not the case.

   To resume our account of the right method of investigation: We must start by observing a set of similar—i. e.
specifically identical—individuals, and consider what element they have in common. We must then apply the same
process to another set of individuals which belong to one
species and are generically but not specifically identical with
the former set. When we have established what the common 10
element is in all members of this second species, and like-

wise in members of further species, we should again consider
whether the results established possess any identity, and per-
severe until we reach a single formula, since this will be the
definition of the thing. But if we reach not one formula but
two or more, evidently the *definiendum* cannot be one thing
but must be more than one. I may illustrate my meaning as
15 follows. If we were inquiring what the essential nature of
pride is, we should examine instances of proud men we
know of to see what, as such, they have in common; e. g. if
Alcibiades was proud, or Achilles and Ajax were proud, we
should find, on inquiring what they all had in common, that
it was intolerance of insult; it was this which drove Alcibi-
20 ades to war, Achilles to wrath, and Ajax to suicide. We
should next examine other cases, Lysander, for example, or
Socrates, and then if these have in common indifference alike
to good and ill fortune, I take these two results and inquire
what common element have equanimity amid the vicissi-
tudes of life and impatience of dishonour. If they have none,
25 there will be two genera of pride. Besides, every definition
is always universal and commensurate: the physician does
not prescribe what is healthy for a single eye, but for all eyes
or for a determinate species of eye. It is also easier by this
method to define the single species than the universal, and
that is why our procedure should be from the several species
to the universal genera—this for the further reason too that
30 equivocation is less readily detected in genera than in *infimae
species*. Indeed, perspicuity is essential in definitions, just as
inferential movement is the minimum required in demonstrations; and we shall attain perspicuity if we can collect
separately the definition of each species through the group of
singulars which we have established—e. g. the definition of
similarity not unqualified but restricted to colours and to fig-
35 ures; the definition of acuteness, but only of sound—and so
proceed to the common universal with a careful avoidance
of equivocation. We may add that if dialectical disputation

must not employ metaphors, clearly metaphors and metaphorical expressions are precluded in definition: otherwise dialectic would involve metaphors.

14 In order to formulate the connexions we wish to prove we have to select our analyses and divisions. The method of selection consists in laying down the common genus of all our subjects of investigation—if e. g. they are animals, we lay down what the properties are which inhere in every animal. These established, we next lay down the properties essentially connected with the first of the remaining classes—e. g. if this first subgenus is bird, the essential properties of every bird—and so on, always characterizing the proximate subgenus. This will clearly at once enable us to say in virtue of what character the subgenera—man, e. g., or horse—possess their properties. Let A be animal, B the properties of every animal, C, D, E, various species of animal. Then it is clear in virtue of what character B inheres in D—namely A—and that it inheres in C and E for the same reason: and throughout the remaining subgenera always the same rule applies.

We are now taking our examples from the traditional class-names, but we must not confine ourselves to considering these. We must collect any other common character which we observe, and then consider with what species it is connected and what properties belong to it. For example, as the common properties of horned animals we collect the possession of a third stomach and only one row of teeth. Then since it is clear in virtue of what character they possess these attributes—namely their horned character—the next question is, to what species does the possession of horns attach?

Yet a further method of selection is by analogy: for we cannot find a single identical name to give to a squid's pounce, a fish's spine, and an animal's bone, although these

too possess common properties as if there were a single osseous nature.

15 Some connexions that require proof are identical in that they possess an identical 'middle'—e. g. a whole group might be proved through 'recipro-
25 cal replacement'—and of these one class are identical in genus, namely all those whose difference consists in their concerning different subjects or in their mode of manifestation. This latter class may be exemplified by the questions as to the causes respectively of echo, of reflection, and of the rainbow: the connexions to be proved which these questions embody are identical generically, because all three are forms of repercussion; but specifically they are different.

Other connexions that require proof only differ in that
30 the 'middle' of the one is subordinate to the 'middle' of the other. For example: Why does the Nile rise towards the end of the month? Because towards its close the month is more stormy. Why is the month more stormy towards its close? Because the moon is waning. Here the one cause is subordinate to the other.

35 **16** The question might be raised with regard to cause and effect whether when the effect is present the cause also is present; whether, for instance, if a plant sheds its leaves or the moon is eclipsed, there is present also the cause of the eclipse or of the fall of the leaves—the possession of broad leaves, let us say, in the
98b latter case, in the former the earth's interposition. For, one might argue, if this cause is not present, these phenomena will have some other cause: if it *is* present, its effect will be at once implied by it—the eclipse by the earth's interposition, the fall of the leaves by the possession of broad leaves; but if so, they will be logically coincident and each capable
5 of proof through the other. Let me illustrate: Let A be

deciduous character, B the possession of broad leaves, C vine. Now if A inheres in B (for every broad-leaved plant is deciduous), and B in C (every vine possessing broad leaves); then A inheres in C (every vine is deciduous), and the middle term B is the cause. But we can also demonstrate that the vine has broad leaves because it is deciduous. Thus, let D be broad-leaved, E deciduous, F vine. Then E inheres in F (since every vine is deciduous), and D in E (for every deciduous plant has broad leaves): therefore every vine has broad leaves, and the cause is its deciduous character. If,[31] however, they cannot each be the cause of the other (for cause is prior to effect, and the earth's interposition is the cause of the moon's eclipse and not the eclipse of the interposition)—if, then, demonstration through the cause is of the reasoned fact and demonstration not through the cause is of the bare fact, one who knows it through the eclipse knows the fact of the earth's interposition but not the reasoned fact. Moreover, that the eclipse is not the cause of the interposition, but the interposition of the eclipse, is obvious because the interposition is an element in the definition of eclipse, which shows that the eclipse is known through the interposition and not vice versa.

On the other hand, can a single effect have more than one cause? One might argue as follows: if the same attribute is predicable of more than one thing as its primary subject, let B be a primary subject in which A inheres, and C another primary subject of A, and D and E primary subjects of B and C respectively. A will then inhere in D and E, and B will be the cause of A's inherence in D, C of A's inherence in E. The presence of the cause thus necessitates that of the effect, but the presence of the effect necessitates the presence not of all that may cause it but only of a cause which yet need not be the whole cause. We may, however,

---

[31] Here begins Aristotle's answer.

suggest[32] that if the connexion to be proved is always universal and commensurate, not only will the cause be a whole but also the effect will be universal and commensurate. For instance, deciduous character will belong exclusively to a subject which is a whole, and, if this whole has species, universally and commensurately to those species—i. e. either to
35 all species of plant or to a single species. So in these universal and commensurate connexions the 'middle' and its effect must reciprocate, i. e be convertible. Supposing, for example, that the reason why trees are deciduous is the coagulation of sap, then if a tree is deciduous, coagulation must be present, and if coagulation is present—not in *any* subject but in a tree—then that tree must be deciduous.

99ª
17
Can the cause of an identical effect be not identical in every instance of the effect but different? Or is that impossible? Perhaps it is impossible if the effect is demonstrated as essential and not as inhering in virtue of a symptom or an accident—because the middle is then the definition of the major term—though possible if the demonstration is not essential. Now it is possible to con-
5 sider the effect and its subject as an accidental conjunction, though such conjunctions would not be regarded as connexions demanding scientific proof. But if they are accepted as such, the middle will correspond to the extremes, and be equivocal if they are equivocal, generically one if they are generically one. Take the question why proportionals alternate. The cause when they are lines, and when they are
10 numbers, is both different and identical; different in so far as lines are lines and not numbers, identical as involving a given determinate increment. In all proportionals this is so. Again, the cause of likeness between colour and colour is other than that between figure and figure; for likeness here

---

[32] Here begins Aristotle's answer.

is equivocal, meaning perhaps in the latter case equality of
the ratios of the sides and equality of the angles, in the case
of colours identity of the act of perceiving them, or some- 15
thing else of the sort. Again, connexions requiring proof
which are identical by analogy have middles also analogous.

The truth is that cause, effect, and subject are reciprocally predicable in the following way. If the species are
taken severally, the effect is wider than the subject (e. g. the
possession of external angles equal to four right angles is an
attribute wider than triangle or square), but it is coexten- 20
sive with the species taken collectively (in this instance with
all figures whose external angles are equal to four right
angles). And the middle likewise reciprocates, for the middle is a definition of the major; which is incidentally the
reason why all the sciences are built up through definition.

We may illustrate as follows. Deciduous is a universal
attribute of vine, and is at the same time of wider extent than
vine; and of fig, and is of wider extent than fig: but it is not
wider than but coextensive with the totality of the species. 25
Then if you take the middle which is proximate, it is a definition of deciduous. I say that, because you will first reach a
middle[33] next the subject,[34] and a premiss asserting it of the
whole subject, and after that a middle—the coagulation of sap
or something of the sort—proving the connexion of the first
middle with the major:[35] but it is the coagulation of sap at the
junction of leaf-stalk and stem which defines deciduous.[36]

[33] *sc.* broad-leaved.

[34] vine, fig, &c.

[35] Broad-leaved with deciduous.

[36] Aristotle contemplates four terms: (1) deciduous, (2) coagulation, (3)
broad-leaved, (4) vine, fig, &c.

If we get the middle proximate to (1) it is a definition of (1). But in
investigating vines, figs, &c. according to the method of chapter 13, we
shall first find a common character of them in and taking this as a middle,

If an explanation in formal terms of the inter-relation of
30 cause and effect is demanded, we shall offer the following.
Let *A* be an attribute of all *B*, and *B* of every species of *D*,
but so that both *A* and *B* are wider than their respective
subjects. Then *B* will be a universal attribute of each species
of *D* (since I call such an attribute universal even if it is not
commensurate, and I call an attribute primary universal if it
is commensurate,[37] not with each species severally but with
their totality), and it extends beyond each of them taken
separately. Thus, *B* is the cause of *A*'s inherence in the
35 species of *D*: consequently *A* must be of wider extent than
B; otherwise why should *B* be the cause of *A*'s inherence in
D any more than *A* the cause of *B*'s inherence in *D*? Now
if *A* is an attribute of all the species of *E*, all the species of
E will be united by possessing some common cause other
than B: otherwise how shall we be able to say that *A* is
99b predicable of all of which *E* is predicable, while *E* is not
predicable of all of which *A* can be predicated? I mean how
can there fail to be some special cause of *A*'s inherence in *E*,
as there was of *A*'s inherence in all the species of *D*? Then
are the species of *E*, too, united by possessing some common cause? This cause we must look for. Let us call it *C*.[38]

we shall prove that vine, fig, &c., *qua* broad-leaved, are deciduous. But this
proof is not demonstration, because broad-leaved is not a definition of
deciduous. So our next step will be to find a middle—coagulation—mediating the major premiss of this proof, and demonstrate that broad-leaved
plants, *qua* liable to coagulation, are deciduous. This is strict demonstration, because coagulation defines deciduous.

[37] But cf. i, ch. 4, 73b 21–74a 3.

[38] The schema of Aristotle's argument in this paragraph is:

We conclude, then, that the same effect may have more than one cause, but not in subjects specifically identical. For instance, the cause of longevity in quadrupeds is lack of bile, in birds a dry constitution—or certainly something different.

18 If immediate premises are not reached at once, and there is not merely one middle but several middles, i. e. several causes; is the cause of the property's inherence in the several species the middle which is proximate to the primary universal,[39] or the middle which is proximate to the species?[40] Clearly the cause is that nearest to each species severally in which it is manifested, for that is the cause of the subject's falling under the universal. To illustrate formally: C is the cause of B's inherence in D; hence C is the cause of A's inherence in D, B of A's inherence in C, while the cause of A's inherence in B is B itself.

19 As regards syllogism and demonstration, the definition of, and the conditions required to produce each of them, are now clear, and with that also the definition of, and the conditions required to produce, demonstrative knowledge, since it is the same as demonstration. As to the basic premises, how they become known and what is the developed state of knowledge of them is made clear by raising some preliminary problems.

We have already said[41] that scientific knowledge through demonstration is impossible unless a man knows the primary immediate premises. But there are questions which might be raised in respect of the apprehension of these immediate premises: one might not only ask whether it is

[39] i. e. the property.

[40] the subject.

[41] i, ch. 2.

of the same kind as the apprehension of the conclusions, but
also whether there is or is not scientific knowledge of both;
or scientific knowledge of the latter, and of the former a different kind of knowledge; and, further, whether the
25 developed states of knowledge are not innate but come to be
in us, or are innate but at first unnoticed. Now it is strange
if we possess them from birth; for it means that we possess
apprehensions more accurate than demonstration and fail to
notice them. If on the other hand we acquire them and do
not previously possess them, how could we apprehend and
30 learn without a basis of pre-existent knowledge? For that is
impossible, as we used to find[42] in the case of demonstration.
So it emerges that neither can we possess them from birth,
nor can they come to be in us if we are without knowledge
of them to the extent of having no such developed state at
all. Therefore we must possess a capacity of some sort, but
not such as to rank higher in accuracy than these developed
states. And this at least is an obvious characteristic of all ani-
35 mals, for they possess a congenital discriminative capacity
which is called sense-perception. But though sense-perception is innate in all animals, in some the sense-impression
comes to persist, in others it does not. So animals in which
this persistence does not come to be have either no knowledge at all outside the act of perceiving, or no knowledge of
objects of which no impression persists; animals in which it
does come into being have perception and can continue to
100ᵃ retain the sense-impression in the soul: and when such persistence is frequently repeated a further distinction at once
arises between those which out of the persistence of such
sense-impressions develop a power of systematizing them
and those which do not. So out of sense-perception comes
to be what we call memory, and out of frequently repeated
5 memories of the same thing develops experience; for a num-

---

[42] i, ch. 1.

ber of memories constitute a single experience.[43] From experience again—i. e. from the universal now stabilized in its entirety within the soul, the one beside the many which is a single identity within them all—originate the skill of the craftsman and the knowledge of the man of science, skill in the sphere of coming to be and science in the sphere of being.

We conclude that these states of knowledge are neither innate in a determinate form, nor developed from other higher states of knowledge, but from sense-perception. It is 10 like a rout in battle stopped by first one man making a stand and then another, until the original formation has been restored. The soul is so constituted as to be capable of this process.

Let us now restate the account given already, though with insufficient clearness. When one of a number of logically indiscriminable particulars has made a stand, the 15 earliest universal is present in the soul: for though the act of sense-perception is of the particular, its content is universal—is man, for example, not the man Callias. A fresh stand 100b is made among these rudimentary universals, and the process does not cease until the indivisible concepts, the true universals, are established: e. g. such and such a species of animal is a step towards the genus animal, which by the same process is a step towards a further generalization.

Thus it is clear that we must get to know the primary premisses by induction; for the method by which even sense-perception implants the universal is inductive. Now of 5 the thinking states by which we grasp truth, some are unfailingly true, others admit of error—opinion, for instance, and calculation, whereas scientific knowing and intuition are always true: further, no other kind of thought except intuition is more accurate than scientific knowledge, whereas

---

[43] Cf. *Met.* A 980[a] 28. *Met.* A 1 should be compared with this chapter.

primary premisses are more knowable than demonstrations,
10 and all scientific knowledge is discursive. From these considerations it follows that there will be no scientific knowledge
of the primary premisses, and since except intuition nothing
can be truer than scientific knowledge, it will be intuition
that apprehends the primary premisses—a result which also
follows from the fact that demonstration cannot be the originative source of demonstration, nor, consequently, scientific
knowledge of scientific knowledge. If, therefore, it is the
only other kind of true thinking except scientific knowing,
15 intuition will be the originative source of scientific knowledge. And the originative source of science grasps the
original basic premiss, while science as a whole similarly
related as originative source to the whole body of fact.

PHYSICS

INTRODUCTION

Aristotle conceived physics—the science of natures and of natural changes—broadly to include not only inorganic processes such as those studied in astronomy, physics, chemistry, and meteorology, but also biological and psychological phenomena. Four of his treatises on physics in the narrow sense have survived. In the *Physics* he treats of the principles of natural bodies and of natural motions, analyzes the concepts implied in motion (such as continuity, infinity, place, void, time), sets forth the kinds and causes of motion, and relates them all by tracing the causes of motion back to an unmoved mover. In *On the Heavens* he treats of the local motions of bodies, differentiating the motions of the sublunar elements from the motions of the "primary element" of which the heavenly bodies are formed. In *On Generation and Corruption* he treats of the causes of changes other than local motion which terrestrial bodies undergo, such as generation and corruption (or change in substance), alteration (or change in quality), and growth and diminution (or change in size). Finally in the *Meteorology* he treats of the interplay of natural elements and of mixtures and compounds, seeking the causes of comets, rain, snow, dew, winds, earthquakes, thunder, lightning, storms, rainbows, studying the processes which affect mixed bodies like water, metals, clays, oils, wines, and finally, effecting a transition to organic bodies by differentiating (1) elements, (2) "homogeneous bodies" (like the metals among inanimate things, or the wood and bark of plants, or the tissues and bones of animals), which possess different qualities than the elements of which they are compounded, and (3) "heterogeneous bodies" (like organs and parts, hands and faces), which possess functions and purposes distinct from those of the homogeneous bodies of which they are compounded.

Aristotle sometimes refers to the first two books of the *Physics*, in which the principles of natural change are treated explicitly, as the *Physical Treatises*. The number and nature of the principles of change and motion are determined in Book I from a dialectical examination of the opinions of earlier physicists and of the requirements of the phenomena. By "principles of motion" Aristotle means, not propositions in a science, but the irreducible terms of the process, which may serve in the formation of propositions. Any change or motion must have an initial and terminating point (the quality, place, or quantity at which the process began and the quality, place, or quantity at which it ended) and it must have a continuing subject which undergoes the motion: these three principles are privation, form, and matter. "Nature" is a cause of motion, to be distinguished from art in that nature is a cause of motion internal to the thing moved whereas art is an externally imposed cause of motion; nature is to be distinguished from chance and spontaneity in that nature is related essentially to the motions it causes (as in the specific operations and functions of an inorganic body or an organism) whereas chance and spontaneity are accidental or incidental causes of effects which might have been caused by art or nature (as when a man digging a well finds a buried pot of gold).

Aristotle's treatment of the principles of motion reflects his conception of the organization of the sciences, the requirements of proof, and the analysis of being. Physics is sharply distinguished by its concern with nature and motion from mathematics which abstracts from matter and motion and from metaphysics which treats of being as such and of the existence and essence of "separable" forms. The various branches of physics are likewise distinguishable by consideration of the kind of change studied (change of substance, or generation and corruption; change of quality or alteration; change of quantity, or growth and diminution; and change of place or locomotionJ, the kind of cause sought (formal, material, final, or efficient), and the kind of substance or nature in which the change occurs. These same distinctions, moreover, relate the materials of physics to the requirement of logical proof, for the examination of substances yields definitions and propositions, and the examination of causes yields the middle terms of scientific proof. They are, finally, translated into the terms of metaphysical problems which turn on the examination of the principles of all sciences and of the being and causes of things.

PHYSICA

CONTENTS

BOOK II

PHYSICA[1]

Physics

Translated by R. P. Hardie and R. K. Gaye

BOOK II

192ᵇ

1 Of things that exist, some exist by nature, some from other causes. 'By nature' the animals and their parts exist, and the plants and the simple bodies (earth, fire, air water)—for we say that these and the like exist 'by nature'.

All the things mentioned present a feature in which they differ from things which are *not* constituted by nature. Each of them has *within itself* a principle of motion and of stationariness (in respect of place, or of growth and decrease, or by way of alteration). On the other hand, a bed and a coat and anything else of that sort, *qua* receiving these designations—i. e. in so far as they are products of art— have no innate impulse to change. But in so far as they happen to be composed of stone or of earth or of a mixture

---

[1] The present treatise, usually called the *Physics*, deals with natural body in general: the special kinds are discussed in Aristotle's other physical works, the *De Caelo*, &c. The first book is concerned with the elements of a natural body (matter and form): the second mainly with the different types of cause studied by the physicist. Books III–VII deal with movement, and the notions implied in it. The subject of VIII is the prime mover, which, though not itself a natural body, is the cause of movement in natural bodies.

of the two, they do have such an impulse, and just to that
extent—which seems to indicate that *nature is a source or
cause of being moved and of being at rest in that to which it
belongs primarily, in virtue of itself* and not in virtue of a
concomitant attribute.

I say 'not in virtue of a concomitant attribute', because
(for instance) a man who is a doctor might cure himself.
Nevertheless it is not in so far as he is a patient that he pos- 25
sesses the art of medicine: it merely has happened that the
same man is doctor and patient—and that is why these
attributes are not always found together. So it is with all
other artificial products. None of them has in itself the
source of its own production. But while in some cases (for
instance houses and the other products of manual labour)
that principle is in something else external to the thing, in 30
others—those which may cause a change in themselves in
virtue of a concomitant attribute—it lies in the things themselves (but not in virtue of what they are).

'Nature' then is what has been stated. Things 'have a
nature' which have a principle of this kind. Each of them is
a substance; for it is a subject, and nature always implies a
subject in which it inheres.

The term 'according to nature' is applied to all these 35
things and also to the attributes which belong to them in
virtue of what they are, for instance the property of fire to
be carried upwards—which is not a 'nature' nor 'has a
nature' but is 'by nature' or 'according to nature'.

What nature is, then, and the meaning of the terms 'by
nature' and 'according to nature', has been stated. *That* 193ᵃ
nature exists, it would be absurd to try to prove, for it is
obvious that there are many things of this kind, and to
prove what is obvious by what is not is the mark of a man 5
who is unable to distinguish what is self-evident from what
is not. (This state of mind is clearly possible. A man blind
from birth might reason about colours. Presumably there-

fore such persons must be talking about words without any thought to correspond.)

Some identify the nature or substance of a natural object with that immediate constituent of it which taken by 10 itself is without arrangement, e. g. the wood is the 'nature' of the bed, and the bronze the 'nature' of the statue.

As an indication of this Antiphon points out that if you planted a bed and the rotting wood acquired the power of sending up a shoot, it would not be a bed that would come up, but *wood*—which shows that the arrangement in accor- 15 dance with the rules of the art is merely an incidental attribute, whereas the real nature is the other, which, fur- ther, persists continuously through the process of making.

But if the material of each of these objects has itself the same relation to something else, say bronze (or gold) to water, bones (or wood) to earth and so on, *that* (they say) 20 would be their nature and essence. Consequently some assert earth, others fire or air or water or some or all of these, to be the nature of the things that are. For whatever any one of them supposed to have this character—whether one thing or more than one thing—this or these he declared 25 to be the whole of substance, all else being its affections, states, or dispositions. Every such thing they held to be eternal (for it could not pass into anything else), but other things to come into being and cease to be times without number.

This then is one account of 'nature', namely that it is the immediate material substratum of things which have in themselves a principle of motion or change.

Another account is that 'nature' is the shape or form 30 which is specified in the definition of the thing.

For the word 'nature' is applied to what is according to nature and the natural in the same way as 'art' is applied to what is artistic or a work of art. We should not say in the latter case that there is anything artistic about a thing, if it

is a bed only potentially, not yet having the form of a bed; 35
nor should we call it a work of art. The same is true of natural compounds. What is potentially flesh or bone has not
yet its own 'nature', and does not exist 'by nature', until it
receives the form specified in the definition, which we name 193^b
in defining what flesh or bone is. Thus in the second sense
of 'nature' it would be the shape or form (not separable
except in statement) of things which have in themselves a 5
source of motion. (The combination of the two, e. g. man,
is not 'nature' but 'by nature' or 'natural'.)

The form indeed is 'nature' rather than the matter; for
a thing is more properly said to be what it is when it has
attained to fulfilment than when it exists potentially. Again
man is born from man, but not bed from bed. That is why
people say that the figure is not the nature of a bed, but the 10
wood is—if the bed sprouted not a bed but wood would
come up. But even if the figure is art, then on the same
principle the shape of man is his nature. For man is born
from man.

We also speak of a thing's nature as being exhibited in
the process of growth by which its nature is attained. The
'nature' in this sense is not like 'doctoring', which leads not 15
to the art of doctoring but to health. Doctoring must start
from the art, not lead to it. But it is not in this way that
nature (in the one sense) is related to nature (in the other).
What grows *qua* growing grows from something into something. Into what then does it grow? Not into that from
which it arose but into that to which it tends. The shape
then is nature.

'Shape' and 'nature', it should be added, are used in
two senses. For the privation too is in a way form. But 20
whether in unqualified coming to be there is privation, i. e.
a contrary to what comes to be, we must consider later.[2]

---

[2] *De Gen. et Corr.* i. 3.

2   We have distinguished, then, the different ways in
    which the term 'nature' is used.
       The next point to consider is how the mathe-
matician differs from the physicist. Obviously physical
bodies contain surfaces and volumes, lines and points, and
these are the subject-matter of mathematics.

25   Further, is astronomy different from physics or a
department of it? It seems absurd that the physicist should
be supposed to know the nature of sun or moon, but not to
know any of their essential attributes, particularly as the
30 writers on physics obviously do discuss their shape also and
whether the earth and the world are spherical or not.

   Now the mathematician, though he too treats of these
things, nevertheless does not treat of them as the limits of
a physical body; nor does he consider the attributes indicated as the attributes of such bodies. That is why he
separates them; for in thought they are separable from
motion, and it makes no difference, nor does any falsity
result, if they are separated. The holders of the theory of
35 Forms do the same, though they are not aware of it; for
they separate the objects of physics, which are less separable
than those of mathematics. This becomes plain if one tries
194ª to state in each of the two cases the definitions of the things
and of their attributes. 'Odd' and 'even', 'straight' and
'curved', and likewise 'number', 'line', and 'figure', do not
5 involve motion; not so 'flesh' and 'bone' and 'man'—*these*
are defined like 'snub nose', not like 'curved'.

   Similar evidence is supplied by the more physical of the
branches of mathematics, such as optics, harmonics, and
astronomy. These are in a way the converse of geometry.
While geometry investigates physical lines but not *qua*
10 physical, optics investigates mathematical lines, but *qua*
physical, not *qua* mathematical.

   Since 'nature' has two senses, the form and the matter,
we must investigate its objects as we would the essence of

snubness. That is, such things are neither independent of matter nor can be defined in terms of matter only. Here too indeed one might raise a difficulty. Since there are two natures, with which is the physicist concerned? Or should he investigate the combination of the two? But if the combination of the two, then also each severally. Does it belong then to the same or to different sciences to know each severally?

If we look at the ancients, physics would seem to be concerned with the *matter*. (It was only very slightly that Empedocles and Democritus touched on the forms and the essence.)

But if on the other hand art imitates nature, and it is the part of the same discipline to know the form and the matter up to a point (e. g. the doctor has a knowledge of health and also of bile and phlegm, in which health is realized, and he builder both of the form of the house and of the matter, namely that it is bricks and beams, and so forth): if this is so, it would be the part of physics also to know nature in both its senses.

Again, 'that for the sake of which', or the end, belongs to the same department of knowledge as the means. But the nature is the end or 'that for the sake of which'. For if a thing undergoes a continuous change and there is a stage which is last, this stage is the end or 'that for the sake of which'. (That is why the poet was carried away into making an absurd statement when he said 'he has the end[3] for the sake of which he was born'. For not every stage that is last claims to be an end, but only that which is best.)

For the arts make their material (some simply 'make' it, others make it serviceable), and we use everything as if it was there for our sake. (We also are in a sense an end. 'That for the sake of which' has two senses: the distinction

---

[3] i. e. death.

is made in our work *On Philosophy*.[4]) The arts, therefore,
194b which govern the matter and have knowledge are two,
namely the art which uses the product and the art which
directs the production of it. That is why the using art also
is in a sense directive; but it differs in that it knows the
form, whereas the art which is directive as being concerned
5 with production knows the matter. For the helmsman
knows and prescribes what sort of form a helm should have,
the other from what wood it should be made and by means
of what operations. In the products of art, however, we
make the material with a view to the function, whereas in
the products of nature the matter is there all along.

Again, matter is a relative term: to each form there cor-
10 responds a special matter. How far then must the physicist
know the form or essence? Up to a point, perhaps, as the
doctor must know sinew or the smith bronze (i. e. until he
understands the purpose of each): and the physicist is concerned only with things whose forms are separable indeed,
but do not exist apart from matter. Man is begotten by man
and by the sun as well. The mode of existence and essence
15 of the separable it is the business of the primary type of
philosophy to define.

3 Now that we have established these distinctions,
we must proceed to consider causes, their character
and number. Knowledge is the object of our
20 inquiry, and men do not think they know a thing till they
have grasped the 'why' of it (which is to grasp its primary
cause) . So clearly we too must do this as regards both coming to be and passing away and every kind of physical
change, in order that, knowing their principles, we may try
to refer to these principles each of our problems.

In one sense, then, (1) that out of which a thing comes

---

[4] i. e. in the dialogue *De Philosophia*.

to be and which persists, is called 'cause', e. g. the bronze of the statue, the silver of the bowl, and the genera of which 25 the bronze and the silver are species.

In another sense (2) the form or the archetype, i.e. the statement of the essence, and its genera, are called 'causes' (e. g. of the octave the relation of 2:1, and generally number), and the parts in the definition.

Again (3) the primary source of the change or coming to rest; e. g. the man who gave advice is a cause, the father is cause of the child, and generally what makes of what is 30 made and what causes change of what is changed.

Again (4) in the sense of end or 'that for the sake of which' a thing is done, e. g. health is the cause of walking about. ('Why is he walking about?' we say. 'To be healthy', and, having said that, we think we have assigned the cause.) The same is true also of all the intermediate steps which are 35 brought about through the action of something else as means towards the end, e. g. reduction of flesh, purging, drugs, or surgical instruments are means towards health. All these things are 'for the sake of' the end, though they differ from **195**[a] one another in that some are activities, others instruments.

This then perhaps exhausts the number of ways in which the term 'cause' is used.

As the word has several senses, it follows that there are several causes of the same thing (not merely in virtue of a concomitant attribute), e. g. both the art of the sculptor and the bronze are causes of the statue. These are causes of the 5 statue *qua* statue, not in virtue of anything else that it may be—only not in the same way, the one being the material cause, the other the cause whence the motion comes. Some things cause each other reciprocally, e. g. hard work causes fitness and *vice versa*, but again not in the same way, but the one as end, the other as the origin of change. Further 10 the same thing is the cause of contrary results. For that which by its presence brings about one result is sometimes

blamed for bringing about the contrary by its absence.
Thus we ascribe the wreck of a ship to the absence of the
pilot whose presence was the cause of its safety.

   All the causes now mentioned fall into four familiar
15 divisions. The letters are the causes of syllables, the material of artificial products, fire, &c., of bodies, the parts of
the whole, and the premisses of the conclusion, in the sense
of 'that from which'. Of these pairs the one set are causes in
20 the sense of substratum, e. g. the parts, the other set in the
sense of essence—the whole and the combination and the
form. But the seed and the doctor and the adviser, and generally the maker, are all sources whence the change or
stationariness originates, while the others are causes in the
sense of the end or the good of the rest; for 'that for the
sake of which' means what is best and the end of the things
25 that lead up to it. (Whether we say the 'good itself' or the
'apparent good' makes no difference.)

   Such then is the number and nature of the kinds of
cause.

   Now the modes of causation are many, though when
brought under heads they too can be reduced in number. For
30 'cause' is used in many senses and even within the same kind
one may be prior to another (e. g. the doctor and the expert
are causes of health, the relation 2:1 and number of the
octave), and always what is inclusive to what is particular.
Another mode of causation is the incidental and its genera,
e. g. in one way 'Polyclitus', in another 'sculptor' is the cause
35 of a statue, because 'being Polyclitus' and 'sculptor' are incidentally conjoined. Also the classes in which the incidental
attribute is included; thus 'a man' could be said to be the
195^b cause of a statue or, generally, 'a living creature'. An incidental attribute too may be more or less remote, e. g. suppose
that 'a pale man' or 'a musical man' were said to be the cause
of the statue.

   All causes, both proper and incidental, may be spoken of

either as potential or as actual; e. g. the cause of a house being 5
built is either 'house-builder' or 'house-builder building'.

Similar distinctions can be made in the things of which
the causes are causes, e. g. of 'this statue' or of 'statue' or of
'image' generally, of 'this bronze' or of 'bronze' or of 'material' generally. So too with the incidental attributes. Again 10
we may use a complex expression for either and say, e. g.,
neither 'Polyclitus' nor 'sculptor' but 'Polyclitus, sculptor'.

All these various uses, however, come to six in number, under each of which again the usage is twofold. Cause
means either what is particular or a genus, or an incidental 15
attribute or a genus of that, and these either as a complex or
each by itself; and all six either as actual or as potential.
The difference is this much, that causes which are actually
at work and particular exist and cease to exist simultaneously with their effect, e. g. this healing person with this
being-healed person and that housebuilding man with that
being-built house; but this is not always true of potential 20
causes—the house and the housebuilder do not pass away
simultaneously.

In investigating the cause of each thing it is always necessary to seek what is most precise (as also in other things):
thus man builds because he is a builder, and a builder
builds in virtue of his art of building. This last cause then is
prior: and so generally.

Further, generic effects should be assigned to generic 25
causes, particular effects to particular causes, e. g. statue to
sculptor, this statue to this sculptor; and powers are relative to possible effects, actually operating causes to things
which are actually being effected.

This must suffice for our account of the number of
causes and the modes of causation.   30

4   But chance also and spontaneity are reckoned among causes: many things are said both to be and to come to be as a result of chance and spontaneity. We must inquire therefore in what manner chance and spontaneity are present among the causes enumerated, and whether they are the same or different, and generally what
35 chance and spontaneity are.

Some people[5] even question whether they are real or not. They say that nothing happens by chance, but that
196ᵃ everything which we ascribe to chance or spontaneity has some definite cause, e. g. coming 'by chance' into the market and finding there a man whom one wanted but did not expect to meet is due to one's wish to go and buy in the
5 market. Similarly in other cases of chance it is always possible, they maintain, to find something which is the cause; but not chance, for if chance were real, it would seem strange indeed, and the question might be raised, why on earth none of the wise men of old in speaking of the causes of generation and decay took account of chance; whence it
10 would seem that they too did not believe that anything is by chance. But there is a further circumstance that is surprising. Many things both come to be and are by chance and spontaneity, and although all know that each of them can be ascribed to some cause (as the old argument said
15 which denied chance), nevertheless they speak of some of these things as happening by chance and others not. For this reason also they ought to have at least referred to the matter in some way or other.

Certainly the early physicists found no place for chance among the causes which they recognized—love, strife, mind, fire, or the like. This is strange, whether they supposed that there is no such thing as chance or whether they thought
20 there is but omitted to mention it—and that too when they

---

[5] Apparently Democritus is meant.

sometimes used it, as Empedocles does when he says that the air is not always separated into the highest region, but 'as it may chance'. At any rate he says in his cosmogony that 'it happened to run that way at that time, but it often ran otherwise.' He tells us also that most of the parts of animals came to be by chance.

There are some[6] too who ascribe this heavenly sphere and all the worlds to spontaneity. They say that the vortex arose spontaneously, i. e. the motion that separated and arranged in its present order all that exists. This statement might well cause surprise. For they are asserting that chance is not responsible for the existence or generation of animals and plants, nature or mind or something of the kind being the cause of them (for it is not any chance thing that comes from a given seed but an olive from one kind and a man from another); and yet at the same time they assert that the heavenly sphere and the divinest of visible things arose spontaneously, having no such cause as is assigned to animals and plants. Yet if this is so, it is a fact which deserves to be dwelt upon, and something might well have been said about it. For besides the other absurdities of the statement, 196ᵇ it is the more absurd that people should make it when they see nothing coming to be spontaneously in the heavens, but much happening by chance among the things which as they say are not due to chance; whereas we should have expected exactly the opposite.

Others[7] there are who, indeed, believe that chance is a cause, but that it is inscrutable to human intelligence, as being a divine thing and full of mystery.

Thus we must inquire what chance and spontaneity are, whether they are the same or different, and how they fit into our division of causes.

[6] Apparently Democritus is meant.

[7] Democritus.

10   **5** First then we observe that some things always come
to pass in the same way, and others for the most
part. It is clearly of neither of these that chance is
said to be the cause, nor can the 'effect of chance' be identified with any of the things that come to pass by necessity
and always, or for the most part. But as there is a third class
of events besides these two—events which all say are 'by
chance'—it is plain that there is such a thing as chance and
15   spontaneity; for we know that things of this kind are due to
chance and that things due to chance are of this kind.

But, secondly, some events are for the sake of something, others not. Again, some of the former class are in
accordance with deliberate intention, others not, but both
20   are in the class of things which are for the sake of something. Hence it is clear that even among the things which
are outside the necessary and the normal, there are some in
connexion with which the phrase 'for the sake of something'
is applicable. (Events that are for the sake of something
include whatever may be done as a result of thought or of
nature.) Things of this kind, then, when they come to pass
25   incidentally are said to be 'by chance'. For just as a thing
is something either in virtue of itself or incidentally, so may
it be a cause. For instance, the housebuilding faculty is in
virtue of itself the cause of a house, whereas the pale or the
musical[8] is the incidental cause. That which is *per se* cause
of the effect is determinate, but the incidental cause is inde-
terminable, for the possible attributes of an individual are
innumerable. To resume then; when a thing of this kind
30   comes to pass among events which are for the sake of something, it is said to be spontaneous or by chance. (The
distinction between the two must be made later[9]—for the

---

[8] Incidental attributes of the housebuilder.

[9] In ch. 6.

present it is sufficient if it is plain that both are in the sphere of things done for the sake of something.)

Example: A man is engaged in collecting subscriptions for a feast. He would have gone to such and such a place for the purpose of getting the money, if he had known. He actually went there for another purpose, and it was only 35 incidentally that he got his money by going there; and this was not due to the fact that he went there as a rule or necessarily, nor is the end effected (getting the money) a cause 197ª present in himself—it belongs to the class of things that are intentional and the result of intelligent deliberation. It is when these conditions are satisfied that the man is said to have gone 'by chance'. If he had gone of deliberate purpose and for the sake of this—if he always or normally went there when he was collecting payments—he would not be said to have gone 'by chance'.

It is clear then that chance is an incidental cause in the sphere of those actions for the sake of something which 5 involve purpose. Intelligent reflection, then, and chance are in the same sphere, for purpose implies intelligent reflection.

It is necessary, no doubt, that the causes of what comes to pass by chance be indefinite; and that is why chance is supposed to belong to the class of the indefinite and to be inscrutable to man, and why it might be thought that, in a 10 way, nothing occurs by chance. For all these statements are correct, because they are well grounded. Things *do*, in a way, occur by chance, for they occur incidentally and chance is an *incidental cause*. But strictly it is not the *cause*—without qualification—of anything; for instance, a housebuilder is the cause of a house; incidentally, a flute-player may be so.

And the causes of the man's coming and getting the money (when he did not come for the sake of that) are 15 innumerable. He may have wished to see somebody or been

following somebody or avoiding somebody, or may have
gone to see a spectacle. Thus to say that chance is a thing
contrary to rule is correct. For 'rule' applies to what is
always true or true for the most part, whereas chance
belongs to a third type of event. Hence, to conclude, since
20 causes of this kind are indefinite, chance too is indefinite.
(Yet in some cases one might raise the question whether *any*
incidental fact might be the cause of the chance occurrence,
e. g. of health the fresh air or the sun's heat may be the
cause, but having had one's hair cut *cannot*; for some incidental causes are more relevant to the effect than others.)

25   Chance or fortune is called 'good' when the result is
good, 'evil' when it is evil. The terms 'good fortune' and
'ill fortune' are used when either result is of considerable
magnitude. Thus one who comes within an ace of some
great evil or great good is said to be fortunate or unfortunate. The mind affirms the presence of the attribute,
30 ignoring the hair's breadth of difference. Further, it is with
reason that good fortune is regarded as unstable; for chance
is unstable, as none of the things which result from it can be
invariable or normal.

Both are then, as I have said, incidental causes—both
chance and spontaneity—in the sphere of things which are
capable of coming to pass not necessarily, nor normally, and
35 with reference to such of these as might come to pass for
the sake of something.

6 They differ in that 'spontaneity' is the wider term.
Every result of chance is from what is spontaneous,
but not everything that is from what is spontaneous
is from chance.

197b   Chance and what results from chance are appropriate
to agents that are capable of good fortune and of moral
action generally. Therefore necessarily chance is in the
sphere of moral actions. This is indicated by the fact that

good fortune is thought to be the same, or nearly the same, as happiness, and happiness to be a kind of moral action, since it is well-doing. Hence what is not capable of moral action cannot do anything by chance. Thus an inanimate thing or a lower animal or a child cannot do anything by chance, because it is incapable of deliberate intention; nor can 'good fortune' or 'ill fortune' be ascribed to them, except metaphorically, as Protarchus, for example, said that the stones of which altars are made are fortunate because they are held in honour, while their fellows are trodden under foot. Even these things, however, can in a way be affected by chance, when one who is dealing with them does something to them by chance, but not otherwise.

The spontaneous on the other hand is found both in the lower animals and in many inanimate objects. We say, for example, that the horse came 'spontaneously', because, though his coming saved him, he did not come for the sake of safety. Again, the tripod fell 'of itself', because, though when it fell it stood on its feet so as to serve for a seat, it did not fall for the sake of that.

Hence it is clear that events which (1) belong to the general class of things that may come to pass for the sake of something, (2) do not come to pass for the sake of what actually results, and (3) have an external cause, may be described by the phrase 'from spontaneity'. These 'spontaneous' events are said to be 'from chance' if they have the further characteristics of being the objects of deliberate intention and due to agents capable of that mode of action. This is indicated by the phrase 'in vain', which is used when A, which is for the sake of B, does not result in B. For instance, taking a walk is for the sake of evacuation of the bowels; if this does not follow after walking, we say that we have walked 'in vain' and that the walking was 'vain'. This implies that what is naturally the means to an end is 'in vain', when it does not effect the end towards which it

was the natural means—for it would be absurd for a man to say that he had bathed in vain because the sun was not eclipsed, since the one was not done with a view to the other. Thus the spontaneous is even according to its derivation the case in which the thing itself happens in vain. The
30 stone that struck the man did not fall for the purpose of striking him; therefore it fell spontaneously, because it might have fallen by the action of an agent and for the purpose of striking. The difference between spontaneity and what results by chance is greatest in things that come to be by nature; for when anything comes to be contrary to nature, we do not say that it came to be by chance, but by
35 spontaneity. Yet strictly this too is different from the spontaneous proper; for the cause of the latter is external, that of the former internal.

198ᵃ   We have now explained what chance is and what spontaneity is, and in what they differ from each other. Both belong to the mode of causation 'source of change', for either some natural or some intelligent agent is always the cause; but in this sort of causation the number of possible causes is infinite.

Spontaneity and chance are causes of effects which,
5 though they might result from intelligence or nature, have in fact been caused by something *incidentally*. Now since nothing which is incidental is prior to what is *per se*, it is clear that no incidental cause can be prior to a cause *per se*. Spontaneity and chance, therefore, are posterior to intelli-
10 gence and nature. Hence, however true it may be that the heavens are due to spontaneity, it will still be true that intelligence and nature will be prior causes of this All and of many things in it besides.

7   It is clear then that there are causes, and that the number of them is what we have stated. The num-
15   ber is the same as that of the things comprehended

under the question 'why'. The 'why' is referred ultimately either (1), in things which do not involve motion, e. g. in mathematics, to the 'what' (to the definition of 'straight line' or 'commensurable', &c.), or (2) to what initiated a motion, e. g. 'why did they go to war?—because there had been a raid'; or (3) we are inquiring 'for the sake of what?'—'that they may rule'; or (4), in the case of things that come into being, we are looking for the matter. The causes, therefore, are these and so many in number.

Now, the causes being four, it is the business of the physicist to know about them all, and if he refers his problems back to all of them, he will assign the 'why' in the way proper to his science—the matter, the form, the mover, 'that for the sake of which'. The last three often coincide; for the 'what' and 'that for the sake of which' are one, while the primary source of motion is the same in species as these (for man generates man), and so too, in general, are all things which cause movement by being themselves moved; and such as are not of this kind are no longer inside the province of physics, for they cause motion not by possessing motion or a source of motion in themselves, but being themselves incapable of motion. Hence there are three branches of study, one of things which are incapable of motion, the second of things in motion, but indestructible, the third of destructible things.

The question 'why', then, is answered by reference to the matter, to the form, and to the primary moving cause. For in respect of coming to be it is mostly in this last way that causes are investigated—'what comes to be after what? what was the primary agent or patient?' and so at each step of the series.

Now the principles which cause motion in a physical way are two, of which one is not physical, as it has no principle of motion in itself. Of this kind is whatever causes movement, not being itself moved, such as (1) that which is completely unchangeable, the primary reality, and (2) the essence of that which is coming to be, i. e. the form; for this is the end or 'that for the sake of which'. Hence since nature is for the sake of something, we must know this cause also. We must explain 5 the 'why' in all the senses of the term, namely, (1) that from this that will necessarily result ('from this' either without qualification or in most cases); (2) that 'this must be so if that is to be so' (as the conclusion presupposes the premises); (3) that this was the essence of the thing; and (4) because it is better thus (not without qualification, but with reference to the essential nature in each case).

8 We must explain then (1) that Nature belongs to 10 the class of causes which act for the sake of something; (2) about the necessary and its place in physical problems, for all writers ascribe things to this cause, arguing that since the hot and the cold, &c., are of such and such a kind, therefore certain things *necessarily* are and come to be—and if they mention any other cause (one[10] 15 his 'friendship and strife', another[11] his 'mind'), it is only to touch on it, and then good-bye to it.

A difficulty presents itself: why should not nature work, not for the sake of something, nor because it is better so, but just as the sky rains, not in order to make the corn grow, but of necessity? What is drawn up must cool, 20 and what has been cooled must become water and descend, the result of this being that the corn grows. Similarly if a man's crop is spoiled on the threshing-floor, the rain did not fall for the sake of this—in order that the crop might be spoiled—but that result just followed. Why then should it not be the same with the parts in nature, e. g. that our teeth should come up of *necessity*—the front teeth sharp, fit-

[10] Empedocles.

[11] Anaxagoras.

ted for tearing, the molars broad and useful for grinding 25
down the food—since they did not arise for this end, but it
was merely a coincident result; and so with all other parts in
which we suppose that there is purpose? Wherever then all
the parts came about just what they would have been if they
had come to be for an end, such things survived, being 30
organized spontaneously in a fitting way; whereas those
which grew otherwise perished and continue to perish, as
Empedocles says his 'man-faced ox-progeny' did.

Such are the arguments (and others of the kind) which
may cause difficulty on this point. Yet it is impossible that
this should be the true view. For teeth and all other natural things either invariably or normally come about in a 35
given way; but of not one of the results of chance or spontaneity is this true. We do not ascribe to chance or mere
coincidence the frequency of rain in winter, but frequent 199a
rain in summer we do; nor heat in the dog-days, but only
if we have it in winter. If then, it is agreed that things are
either the result of coincidence or for an end, and these cannot be the result of coincidence or spontaneity, it follows
that they must be for an end; and that such things are all 5
due to nature even the champions of the theory which is
before us would agree. Therefore action for an end is present in things which come to be and are by nature.

Further, where a series has a completion, all the preceding steps are for the sake of that. Now surely as in
intelligent action, so in nature; and as in nature, so it is in 10
each action, if nothing interferes. Now intelligent action is
for the sake of an end; therefore the nature of things also is
so. Thus if a house, e. g., had been a thing made by nature,
it would have been made in the same way as it is now by
art; and if things made by nature were made also by art,
they would come to be in the same way as by nature. Each 15
step then in the series is for the sake of the next; and generally art partly completes what nature cannot bring to a

finish, and partly imitates her. If, therefore, artificial products are for the sake of an end, so clearly also are natural
products. The relation of the later to the earlier terms of the
series is the same in both.

20   This is most obvious in the animals other than man:
they make things neither by art nor after inquiry or deliberation. Wherefore people discuss whether it is by intelligence
or by some other faculty that these creatures work,—
spiders, ants, and the like. By gradual advance in this direc-
25 tion we come to see clearly that in plants too that is
produced which is conducive to the end—leaves, e. g. grow
to provide shade for the fruit. If then it is both by nature
and for an end that the swallow makes its nest and the spi-
der its web, and plants grow leaves for the sake of the fruit
and send their roots down (not up) for the sake of nourish-
30 ment, it is plain that this kind of cause is operative in things
which come to be and are by nature. And since 'nature'
means two things, the matter and the form, of which the
latter is the end, and since all the rest is for the sake of
the end, the form must be the cause in the sense of 'that
for the sake of which'.

Now mistakes come to pass even in the operations of
art: the grammarian makes a mistake in writing and the
35 doctor pours out the wrong dose. Hence clearly mistakes are
199ᵇ possible in the operations of nature also. If then in art there
are cases in which what is rightly produced serves a purpose, and if where mistakes occur there was a purpose in
what was attempted, only it was not attained, so must it be
also in natural products, and monstrosities will be failures in
5 the purposive effort. Thus in the original combinations the
'ox-progeny' if they failed to reach a determinate end must
have arisen through the corruption of some principle corresponding to what is now the seed.

Further, seed must have come into being first, and not

straightway the animals: the words 'whole-natured first . . .'[12] must have meant seed.

Again, in plants too we find the relation of means to end, though the degree of organization is less. Were there then in plants also 'olive-headed vine-progeny', like the 'man-headed ox-progeny', or not? An absurd suggestion; yet there must have been, if there were such things among animals.

Moreover, among the seeds anything must have come to be at random. But the person who asserts this entirely does away with 'nature' and what exists 'by nature'. For those things are natural which, by a continuous movement originated from an internal principle, arrive at some completion: the same completion is not reached from every principle; nor any chance completion, but always the tendency in each is towards the same end, if there is no impediment.

The end and the means towards it may come about by chance. We say, for instance, that a stranger has come by chance, paid the ransom, and gone away, when he does so as if he had come for that purpose, though it was not for that that he came. This is incidental, for chance is an incidental cause, as I remarked before.[13] But when an event takes place always or for the most part, it is not incidental or by chance. In natural products the sequence is invariable, if there is no impediment.

It is absurd to suppose that purpose is not present because we do not observe the agent deliberating. Art does not deliberate. If the ship-building art were in the wood, it would produce the same results *by nature*. If, therefore, purpose is present in art, it is present also in nature. The best illustration is a doctor doctoring himself: nature is like that.

[12] Empedocles, Fr. 62. 4.

[13] 196^b 23–7.

It is plain then that nature is a cause, a cause that oper-
ates for a purpose.

9 As regards what is 'of necessity', we must ask
whether the necessity is 'hypothetical', or 'simple'
as well. The current view places what is of necessity in the process of production, just as if one were to
suppose that the wall of a house necessarily comes to be
because what is heavy is naturally carried downwards and
what is light to the top, wherefore the stones and foundations take the lowest place, with earth above because it is
lighter, and wood at the top of all as being the lightest.
Whereas, though the wall does not come to be *without*
5 these, it is not *due* to these, except as its material cause: it
comes to be for the sake of sheltering and guarding certain
things. Similarly in all other things which involve production for an end; the product cannot come to be without
things which have a necessary nature, but it is not due to
these (except as its material); it comes to be for an end. For
10 instance, why is a saw such as it is? To effect so-and-so and
for the sake of so-and-so. This end, however, cannot be
realized unless the saw is made of iron. It is, therefore, necessary for it to be of iron, *if* we are to have a saw and
perform the operation of sawing. What is necessary then, is
necessary *on a hypothesis*; it is not a result necessarily determined by antecedents. Necessity is in the matter, while 'that
for the sake of which' is in the definition.

15 Necessity in mathematics is in a way similar to necessity in things which come to be through the operation of
nature. Since a straight line is what it is, it is necessary that
the angles of a triangle should equal two right angles. But
not conversely; though if the angles are *not* equal to two
right angles, then the straight line is not what it is either.
But in things which come to be for an end, the reverse is
20 true. If the end is to exist or does exist, that also which pre-

cedes it will exist or does exist; otherwise just as there, if
the conclusion is not true, the premiss will not be true, so
here the end or 'that for the sake of which' will not exist.
For this too is itself a starting-point, but of the reasoning,
not of the action; while in mathematics the starting-point is
the starting-point of the reasoning only, as there is no
action. If then there is to be a house, such-and-such things 25
must be made or be there already or exist, or generally the
matter relative to the end, bricks and stones if it is a house.
But the end is not due to these except as the matter, nor
will it come to exist because of them. Yet if they do not
exist at all, neither will the house, or the saw—the former in
the absence of stones, the latter in the absence of iron—just
as in the other case the premisses will not be true, if the
angles of the triangle are not equal to two right angles.

   The necessary in nature, then, is plainly what we call 30
by the name of matter, and the changes in it. Both causes
must be stated by the physicist, but especially the end; for
that is the cause of the matter, not *vice versa*; and the end
is 'that for the sake of which', and the beginning starts from 35
the definition or essence; as in artificial products, since a 200ᵇ
house is of such-and-such a kind, certain things must *necessarily* come to be or be there already, or since health is
this, these things must necessarily come to be or be there
already. Similarly if man is this, then these; if these, then
those. Perhaps the necessary is present also in the defini- 5
tion. For if one defines the operation of sawing as being a
certain kind of dividing, then this cannot come about unless
the saw has teeth of a certain kind; and these cannot be
unless it is of iron. For in the definition too there are some
parts that are, as it were, its matter.

PSYCHOLOGY
AND BIOLOGY

INTRODUCTION

The study of the soul is a part of physics, as conceived by Aristotle, since the soul is the form of a natural body; and all branches of biological inquiry are dependent on the study of the soul, since the soul is the form of those natural bodies which have life potentially within them. The functions which the soul explains include, therefore, nutrition, growth, and reproduction (which animals share with plants), sensation, emotions, memory, and local motion (which man shares with other animals), and thought (which is peculiar to man among animals, although God in a sense shares in thinking). The soul is related to the organic body as actuality is related to potentiality. It is the "substance" of the organic body, that is, it corresponds to the definition of the organic body's essence, in such fashion according to Aristotle's example, that if an axe were a natural rather than an artificial body, its soul would be "cutting," and if the eye were an animal rather than an organ, its soul would be "seeing."

In the treatise *On the Soul*, the soul is presented as the formal, efficient, and final cause of living, and the processes of sensation and thought are elaborated at considerable length. This analysis of the higher activities of human living is supplemented by inquiry, in the *Short Natural Treatises*, into the common characteristics of animal bodies and into the similar objects of animal activity in sense and sensibles, memory and reminiscence, length and brevity of life, youth and old age, life and death, and respiration. The remaining activities of the soul, which are touched on briefly in *On the Soul*, are investigated in Aristotle's four biological treatises, and both bodily organs and psychic qualities are examined in the context of the study of human functions, partly because we are more familiar with man than with any other animal, partly because man is more rounded and complete than other animals and the qualities and capacities investigated in biology are found in their perfection in him (Cf. *History of Animals* i. 6. 491^a 19–23 and ix. 1. 608^b 4–8). The *History of Animals* is a lengthy classification of animals on the basis of similarities and differences in their parts, organs, and functions, including reproduction, heredity, the development of the embryo, diet, diseases, the effects of environment and the struggle for means of subsistence, psychological differences, and intelligence. *On the Parts of Animals*, which contains an excellent statement of method in the biological sciences, treats of biological phenomena that are explained by the material parts and organs of animals. *On the Progression of Animals* differentiates the modes of their locomotion. *On the Generation of Animals* treats of their reproduction as an instance of the operation of the efficient cause.

Aristotle is at pains to differentiate the properties investigated in physics from those treated in the arts (like the arts of carpentry and medicine) and those proper to the other theoretic sciences, mathematics and metaphysics. He also differentiates the method of the "true physicist," who investigates the functions of the soul by considering both matter and form, from the method of the "dialectician," who neglects the matter, and that of the materialistic "physicist," who reduces all explanation to the enumeration of material parts. The various psychological activities are therefore investigated functionally in relation to their proper objects, and the faculties of the soul—nutritive, sensitive, and intellective—are defined in terms of their activities. In that inquiry the consideration of universal knowledge and truth gives the intellectual processes a peculiar character, since mind is what it is in one sense by becoming all things, and in another sense by making all things, in knowledge of them. All the faculties of the soul, finally, are considered in terms of their mutual relations and their fitness for the conditions of life. Psychological inquiries occupy an extremely important position in the philosophy of Aristotle, for the conception of the soul lays the foundation for the continuity of functions in nature, mounting continuously from the lifeless, to plants and animals; it provides an analysis of intellectual processes which would account for the character of the principles and materials employed in scientific inquiries and proofs; it lays the broad distinctions of potentialities in man which become by action and habituation the moral and intellectual virtues.

DE ANIMA

CONTENTS

BOOK I

BOOK II

BOOK III

DE ANIMA

On the Soul

Translated by J. A. Smith

BOOK I

1 Holding as we do that, while knowledge of any kind is a thing to be honoured and prized, one kind 402ᵃ of it may, either by reason of its greater exactness or of a higher dignity and greater wonderfulness in its objects, be more honourable and precious than another, on both accounts we should naturally be led to place in the front rank the study of the soul. The knowledge of the soul admittedly contributes greatly to the advance of truth in general, and, above all, to our understanding of Nature, for 5 the soul is in some sense the principle of animal life. Our aim is to grasp and understand, first its essential nature, and secondly its properties; of these some are thought to be affections proper to the soul itself, while others are considered to attach to the animal[1] owing to the presence within it of soul.

To attain any assured knowledge about the soul is one of the most difficult things in the world. As the form of 10 question which here presents itself, viz. the question 'What is it?', recurs in other fields, it might be supposed that there was some single method of inquiry applicable to all objects whose essential nature we are endeavouring to ascertain (as 15

[1] i. e. the complex of soul and body.

there *is* for derived properties the single method of demonstration); in that case what we should have to seek for would be this unique method. But if there is no such single and general method for solving the question of essence, our task becomes still more difficult; in the case of each different subject we shall have to determine the appropriate process of investigation. If to this there be a clear answer, e. g. that the process is demonstration or division, or some
20 other known method, difficulties and hesitations still beset us—with what facts shall we begin the inquiry? For the facts which form the starting-points in different subjects must be different, as e. g. in the case of numbers and surfaces.

First, no doubt, it is necessary to determine in which of the *summa genera* soul lies, what it *is;* is it 'a this-somewhat', a substance, or is it a quale or a quantum, or some
25 other of the remaining kinds of predicates which we have distinguished? Further, does soul belong to the class of potential existents, or is it not rather an actuality? Our answer to this question is of the greatest importance.

402ᵇ   We must consider also whether soul is divisible or is without parts, and whether it is everywhere homogeneous or not; and if not homogeneous, whether its various forms are different specifically or generically: up to the present time
5 those who have discussed and investigated soul seem to have confined themselves to the human soul. We must be careful not to ignore the question whether soul can be defined in a single unambiguous formula, as is the case with animal, or whether we must not give a separate formula for each sort of it, as we do for horse, dog, man, god (in the latter case the 'universal' animal—and so too every other 'common predicate'—being treated either as nothing at all or as a later product²).Further, if what exists is not a plu-

---

² i. e. as presupposing the various sorts instead of being presupposed by them.

rality of souls, but a plurality of parts of one soul, which
ought we to investigate first, the whole soul or its parts? (It 10
is also a difficult problem to decide which of these parts are
in nature distinct from one another.) Again, which ought we
to investigate first, these parts or their functions, mind or
thinking, the faculty or the act of sensation, and so on? If
the investigation of the functions precedes that of the parts,
the further question suggests itself: ought we not before
either to consider the correlative objects, e. g. of sense or 15
thought? It seems not only useful for the discovery of the
causes of the derived properties of substances to be
acquainted with the essential nature of those substances (as
in mathematics it is useful for the understanding of the
property of the equality of the interior angles of a triangle to
two right angles to know the essential nature of the straight 20
and the curved or of the line and the plane) but also conversely, for the knowledge of the essential nature of a
substance is largely promoted by an acquaintance with its
properties: for, when we are able to give an account con-
formable to experience of all or most of the properties of a
substance, we shall be in the most favourable position to say
something worth saying about the essential nature of that 25
subject; in all demonstration a definition of the essence is
required as a starting-point, so that definitions which do not 403a
enable us to discover the derived properties, or which fail to
facilitate even a conjecture about them, must obviously, one
and all, be dialectical and futile.

A further problem presented by the affections of soul is
this: are they all affections of the complex of body and soul,
or is there any one among them peculiar to the soul by
itself? To determine this is indispensable but difficult. If
we consider the majority of them, there seems to be no case 5
in which the soul can act or be acted upon without involving the body; e. g. anger, courage, appetite, and sensation
generally. Thinking seems the most probable exception; but

if this too proves to be a form of imagination or to be
impossible without imagination, it too requires a body as a
10 condition of its existence. If there is any way of acting or
being acted upon proper to soul, soul will be capable of separate existence; if there is none, its separate existence is
impossible. In the latter case, it will be like what is straight,
which has many properties arising from the straightness in
it, e. g. that of touching a bronze sphere at a point, though
straightness divorced from the other constituents of the
straight thing cannot touch it in this way; it cannot be so
15 divorced at all, since it is always found in a body. It therefore seems that all the affections of soul involve a body—
passion, gentleness, fear, pity, courage, joy, loving, and hating; in all these there is a concurrent affection of the body.
In support of this we may point to the fact that, while
sometimes on the occasion of violent and striking occur-
20 rences there is no excitement or fear felt, on others faint and
feeble stimulations produce these emotions, viz. when the
body is already in a state of tension resembling its condition when we are angry. Here is a still clearer case: in the
absence of any external cause of terror we find ourselves
experiencing the feelings of a man in terror. From all this
it is obvious that the affections of soul are enmattered formulable essences.

Consequently their definitions ought to correspond, e. g.
25 anger should be defined as a certain mode of movement of
such and such a body (or part or faculty of a body) by this
or that cause and for this or that end. That is precisely why
the study of the soul must fall within the science of Nature,
at least so far as in its affections it manifests this double
character. Hence a physicist would define an affection of
soul differently from a dialectician; the latter would define
30 e. g. anger as the appetite for returning pain for pain, or
something like that, while the former would define it as a
boiling of the blood or warm substance surrounding the

heart. The latter assigns the material conditions, the former 403b
the form or formulable essence; for what he states is the formulable essence of the fact, though for its actual existence
there must be embodiment of it in a material such as is
described by the other. Thus the essence of a house is
assigned in such a formula as 'a shelter against destruction
by wind, rain, and heat'; the physicist would describe it as 5
'stones, bricks, and timbers'; but there is a third possible
description which would say that it was that form in that
material with that purpose or end. Which, then, among
these is entitled to be regarded as the genuine physicist?
The one who confines himself to the material, or the one
who restricts himself to the formulable essence alone? Is it
not rather the one who combines both in a single formula?
If this is so, how are we to characterize the other two? Must
we not say that there is no type of thinker who concerns
himself with those qualities or attributes of the material
which are in fact inseparable from the material, and without
attempting even in thought to separate them? The physicist 10
is he who concerns himself with all the properties active and
passive of bodies or materials thus or thus defined;
attributes not considered as being of this character he leaves
to others, in certain cases it may be to a specialist, e. g. a
carpenter or a physician, in others (a) where they are inseparable in fact, but are separable from any particular kind of 15
body by an effort of abstraction, to the mathematician, (b)
where they are separate both in fact and in thought from
body altogether, to the First Philosopher or metaphysician.
But we must return from this digression, and repeat that the
affections of soul are inseparable from the material substratum of animal life, to which we have seen that such
affections, e. g. passion and fear, attach, and have not the
same mode of being as a line or a plane.

20   2   For our study of soul it is necessary, while formu-
           lating the problems of which in our further advance
           we are to find the solutions, to call into council the
views of those of our predecessors who have declared any
opinion on this subject, in order that we may profit by
whatever is sound in their suggestions and avoid their
errors.

The starting-point of our inquiry is an exposition of
those characteristics which have chiefly been held to belong
25 to soul in its very nature. Two characteristic marks have
above all others been recognized as distinguishing that
which has soul in it from that which has not—movement
and sensation. It may be said that these two are what our
predecessors have fixed upon as characteristic of soul.

Some say that what originates movement is both pre-
eminently and primarily soul; believing that what is not
30 itself moved cannot originate movement in another, they
arrived at the view that soul belongs to the class of things in
404ᵃ movement. This is what led Democritus to say that soul is
a sort of fire or hot substance; his 'forms' or atoms are infinite in number; those which are spherical he calls fire and
soul, and compares them to the motes in the air which we
see in shafts of light coming through windows; the mixture
of seeds of all sorts he calls the elements of the whole of
Nature (Leucippus gives a similar account); the spherical
5 atoms are identified with soul because atoms of that shape
are most adapted to permeate everywhere, and to set all the
others moving by being themselves in movement. This
implies the view that soul is identical with what produces
movement in animals. That is why, further, they regard respiration as the characteristic mark of life; as the environment
10 compresses the bodies of animals, and tends to extrude those
atoms which impart movement to them, because they themselves are never at rest, there must be a reinforcement of
these by similar atoms coming in from without in the act

of respiration; for they prevent the extrusion of those which
are already within by counteracting the compressing and
consolidating force of the environment; and animals con- 15
tinue to live only as long as they are able to maintain this
resistance.

The doctrine of the Pythagoreans seems to rest upon
the same ideas; some of them declared the motes in air,
others what moved them, to be soul. These motes were
referred to because they are seen always in movement, even
in a complete calm.

The same tendency is shown by those who define soul
as that which moves itself; all seem to hold the view that 20
movement is what is closest to the nature of soul, and that
while all else is moved by soul, it alone moves itself. This
belief arises from their never seeing anything originating
movement which is not first itself moved.

Similarly also Anaxagoras (and whoever agrees with
him in saying that mind set the whole in movement) declares 25
the moving cause of things to be soul. His position must,
however, be distinguished from that of Democritus. Democritus roundly identifies soul and mind, for he identifies
what appears with what is true—that is why he commends
Homer for the phrase 'Hector lay with thought distraught'[3];
he does not employ mind as a special faculty dealing with
truth, but identifies soul and mind. What Anaxagoras says 30
about them is more obscure; in many places he tells us that 404[b]
the cause of beauty and order is mind, elsewhere that it is
soul; it is found, he says, in all animals, great and small,
high and low, but mind (in the sense of intelligence) appears
not to belong alike to all animals, and indeed not even to 5
all human beings.

All those, then, who had special regard to the fact that
what has soul in it is moved, adopted the view that soul is

[3] *Il.* xxiii. 698.

to be identified with what is eminently originative of movement. All, on the other hand, who looked to the fact that
what has soul in it knows or perceives what is, identify soul
10 with the principle or principles of Nature, according as they
admit several such principles or one only. Thus Empedocles
declares that it is formed out of all his elements, each of
them also being soul; his words are:

> For 'tis by Earth we see Earth, by Water Water,
> By Ether Ether divine, by Fire destructive Fire,
15 > By Love Love, and Hate by cruel Hate.

In the same way Plato in the *Timaeus*[4] fashions the soul
out of his elements; for like, he holds, is known by like, and
things are formed out of the principles or elements, so
20 that soul must be so too. Similarly also in his lectures 'On
Philosophy' it was set forth that the Animal-itself is compounded of the Idea itself of the One together with the
primary length, breadth, and depth, everything else, the
objects of its perception, being similarly constituted. Again
he puts his view in yet other terms: Mind is the monad, science or knowledge the dyad (because[5] it goes undeviatingly
from one point to another), opinion the number of the
plane,[6] sensation the number of the solid[7]; the numbers are
by him expressly identified with the Forms themselves or
principles, and are formed out of the elements; now things
25 are apprehended either by mind or science or opinion or
sensation, and these same numbers are the Forms of things.
Some thinkers, accepting both premisses, viz. that the

---

[4] 35 A ff.

[5] Like the straight line, whose number is the dyad.

[6] The triad.

[7] The tetrad.

soul is both originative of movement and cognitive, have compounded it of both and declared the soul to be a self-moving number.

As to the nature and number of the first principles opin- 30 ions differ. The difference is greatest between those who regard them as corporeal and those who regard them as incorporeal, and from both dissent those who make a blend 405ᵃ and draw their principles from both sources. The number of principles is also in dispute; some admit one only, others assert several. There is a consequent diversity in their several accounts of soul; they assume, naturally enough, that what is in its own nature originative of movement must be among 5 what is primordial. That has led some to regard it as fire, for fire is the subtlest of the elements and nearest to incorporeality; further, in the most primary sense, fire both is moved and originates movement in all the others.

Democritus has expressed himself more ingeniously than the rest on the grounds for ascribing each of these two characters to soul; soul and mind are, he says, one and the 10 same thing, and this thing must be one of the primary and indivisible bodies, and its power of originating movement must be due to its fineness of grain and the shape of its atoms; he says that of all the shapes the spherical is the most mobile, and that this is the shape of the particles of both fire and mind.

Anaxagoras, as we said above,[8] seems to distinguish between soul and mind, but in practice he treats them as a single substance, except that it is mind that he specially posits as the principle of all things; at any rate what he says 15 is that mind alone of all that is is simple, unmixed, and pure. He assigns both characteristics, knowing and origination of movement, to the same principle, when he says that it was mind that set the whole in movement.

[8] 404ᵇ 1–6.

Thales, too, to judge from what is recorded about him,
20 seems to have held soul to be a motive force, since he said
that the magnet has a soul in it because it moves the iron.

Diogenes (and others) held the soul to be air because
he believed air to be finest in grain and a first principle;
therein lay the grounds of the soul's powers of knowing and
originating movement. As the primordial principle from
which all other things are derived, it is cognitive; as finest in
grain, it has the power to originate movement.

Heraclitus too says that the first principle—the 'warm
25 exhalation' of which, according to him, everything else is
composed—is soul; further, that this exhalation is most
incorporeal and in ceaseless flux; that what is in movement
requires that what knows it should be in movement; and
that all that is has its being essentially in movement (herein
agreeing with the majority).

Alcmaeon also seems to have held a similar view about
soul; he says that it is immortal because it resembles 'the
30 immortals', and that this immortality belongs to it in virtue
of its ceaseless movement; for all the 'things divine', moon,
sun, the planets, and the whole heavens, are in perpetual
movement.

Of more superficial writers, some, e. g. Hippo, have
405b pronounced it to be water; they seem to have argued from
the fact that the seed of all animals is fluid, for Hippo tries
to refute those who say that the soul is blood, on the ground
that the seed, which is the primordial soul, is not blood.

Another group (Critias, for example) did hold it to be
5 blood; they take perception to be the most characteristic
attribute of soul, and hold that perceptiveness is due to the
nature of blood.

Each of the elements has thus found its partisan, except
earth—earth has found no supporter unless we count as
such those who have declared soul to be, or to be com-
10 pounded of, *all* the elements. All, then, it may be said,

characterize the soul by three marks, Movement, Sensation, Incorporeality, and each of these is traced back to the first principles. That is why (with one exception) all those who define the soul by its power of knowing make it either an element or constructed out of the elements. The language they all use is similar; like, they say, is known by like; as 15 the soul knows everything, they construct it out of all the principles. Hence all those who admit but one cause or element, make the soul also one (e. g. fire or air), while those who admit a multiplicity of principles make the soul also multiple. The exception is Anaxagoras; he alone says that 20 mind is impassible and has nothing in common with anything else. But, if this is so, how or in virtue of what cause can it know? That Anaxagoras has not explained, nor can any answer be inferred from his words. All who acknowledge pairs of opposites among their principles, construct the soul also out of these contraries, while those who admit as principles only one contrary of each pair, e. g. either hot or cold, likewise make the soul some one of these. That is why, also, they allow themselves to be guided by the names; those who identify soul with the hot argue that *zen* (to live) is derived from *zein* (to boil), while those who identify it with the cold say that soul (*psyche*) is so called from the process of respiration and refrigeration (*katapsyxis*).

Such are the traditional opinions concerning soul, 30 together with the grounds on which they are maintained.

3 We must begin our examination with movement; for, doubtless, not only is it false that the essence of soul is correctly described by those who say that it is 406ᵃ what moves (or is capable of moving) itself, but it is an impossibility that movement should be even an attribute of it.

We have already⁹ pointed out that there is no necessity

---

⁹ *Phys.* viii. 5, esp. 257ᵃ 31–258ᵇ 9.

that what originates movement should itself be moved. There are two senses in which anything may be moved— either (a) indirectly, owing to something other than itself, or (b) directly, owing to itself. Things are 'indirectly moved' which are moved as being contained in something which is moved, e. g. sailors in a ship, for they are moved in a different sense from that in which the ship is moved; the ship is 'directly moved', they are 'indirectly moved', because they are in a moving vessel. This is clear if we consider their limbs; the movement proper to the legs (and so to man) is walking, and in this case the sailors are not walking. Recognizing the double sense of 'being moved', what we have to consider now is whether the soul is 'directly moved' and participates in such direct movement.

There are four species of movement—locomotion, alteration, diminution, growth; consequently if the soul is moved, it must be moved with one or several or all of these species of movement. Now if its movement is not incidental, there must be a movement natural to it, and, if so, as all the species enumerated involve place, place must be natural to it. But if the essence of soul be to move itself, its being moved cannot be incidental to it, as it is to what is white or three cubits long; they too can be moved, but only incidentally—what is moved is that of which 'white' and 'three cubits long' are the attributes, the body in which they inhere; hence *they* have no place: but if the soul naturally partakes in movement, it follows that it must have a place.

Further, if there be a movement natural to the soul, there must be a counter-movement unnatural to it, and conversely. The same applies to rest as well as to movement; for the *terminus ad quem* of a thing's natural movement is the place of its natural rest, and similarly the *terminus ad quem* of its enforced movement is the place of its enforced rest. But what meaning can be attached to enforced movements or rests of the soul, it is difficult even to imagine.

Further, if the natural movement of the soul be upward, the soul must be fire; if downward, it must be earth; for upward and downward movements are the definitory characteristics of these bodies. The same reasoning applies to the intermediate movements, *termini*, and bodies. Further, since the soul is observed to originate movement in 30 the body, it is reasonable to suppose that it transmits to the body the movements by which it itself is moved, and so, reversing the order, we may infer from the movements of the body back to similar movements of the soul. Now the body is moved from place to place with movements of loco- 406ᵇ motion. Hence it would follow that the soul too must in accordance with the body change either its place as a whole or the relative places of its parts. This carries with it the possibility that the soul might even quit its body and re-enter it, and with this would be involved the possibility of a resurrection of animals from the dead. But, it may be contended, the soul can be moved indirectly by something else; 5 for an animal can be pushed out of its course. Yes, but that to whose *essence* belongs the power of being moved by itself, cannot be moved by something else except incidentally,¹⁰ just as what is good by or in itself cannot owe its goodness to something external to it or to some end to which it is a means.

If the soul *is* moved, the most probable view is that 10 what moves it is sensible things.¹¹

We must note also that, if the soul moves itself, it must be the mover itself that is moved, so that it follows that if movement is in every case a displacement of that which is in movement, in that respect in which it is said to be

---

¹⁰ i. e. so that what is moved is not it but something which 'goes along with it', e. g. a vehicle in which it is contained.

¹¹ *sc.* in which case the movement can only be 'incidental'; for, as we shall see later, it is really the bodily organ of sensation that then is 'moved'.

moved, the movement of the soul must be a departure from its essential nature, at least if its self-movement is essential to it, not incidental.

Some go so far as to hold that the movements which the soul imparts to the body in which it is are the same in kind as those with which it itself is moved. An example of this is Democritus, who uses language like that of the comic dramatist Philippus, who accounts for the movements that Daedalus imparted to his wooden Aphrodite by saying that he poured quicksilver into it; similarly Dem-
20 ocritus says that the spherical atoms which according to him constitute soul, owing to their own ceaseless movements draw the whole body after them and so produce its movements. We must urge the question whether it is these very same atoms which produce rest also—how they could do so, it is difficult and even impossible to say. And, in
25 general, we may object that it is not in this way that the soul appears to originate movement in animals—it is through intention or process of thinking.

It is in the same fashion that the *Timaeus*[12] also tries to give a physical account of how the soul moves its body; the soul, it is here said, is in movement, and so owing to their mutual implication moves the body also. After compounding the soul-substance out of the elements and dividing it in accordance with the harmonic numbers, in order that it may
30 possess a connate sensibility for 'harmony' and that the whole may move in movements well attuned, the Demiurge bent the straight line into a circle; this single circle he
407a divided into two circles united at two common points; one of these he subdivided into seven circles. All this implies that the movements of the soul are identified with the local movements of the heavens.

Now, in the first place, it is a mistake to say that the

12 35 A ff.

soul is a spatial magnitude. It is evident that Plato means the soul of the whole to be like the sort of soul which is called mind—not like the sensitive or the desiderative soul, for the movements of neither of these are circular. Now mind is one and continuous in the sense in which the process of thinking is so, and thinking is identical with the thoughts which are its parts; these have a serial unity like that of number, not a unity like that of a spatial magnitude. Hence mind cannot have that kind of unity either; mind is either without parts or is continuous in some other way than that which characterizes a spatial magnitude. How, indeed, if it were a spatial magnitude, could mind possibly think? Will it think with any one indifferently of its parts? In this case, the 'part' must be understood, either in the sense of a spatial magnitude or in the sense of a point (if a point *can* be called a part of a spatial magnitude). If we accept the latter alternative, the points being infinite in number, obviously the mind can never exhaustively traverse them; if the former, the mind must think the same thing over and over again, indeed an infinite number of times (whereas it is manifestly possible to think a thing once only). If contact of any part whatsoever of itself with the object is all that is required, why need mind move in a circle, or indeed possess magnitude at all? On the other hand, if contact with the whole circle is necessary, what meaning can be given to the contact of the parts? Further, how could what has no parts think what has parts, or what has parts think what has none?[13] We must identify the circle referred to with mind; for it is mind whose movement is thinking, and it is the circle whose movement is revolution, so that if thinking is a movement of revolution, the circle which has this characteristic movement must be mind.

If the circular movement is eternal, there must be some-

[13] *sc.* but mind in fact thinks or cognizes both.

thing which mind is always thinking—what *can* this be? For all practical processes of thinking have limits—they all go on for the sake of something outside the process, and all theoretical processes come to a close in the same way as the phrases in speech which express processes and results of thinking. Every such linguistic phrase is either definitory or
25 demonstrative. Demonstration has both a starting-point and may be said to end in a conclusion or inferred result; even if the process never reaches final completion, at any rate it never returns upon itself again to its starting-point, it goes on assuming a fresh middle term or a fresh extreme, and moves straight forward, but circular movement returns to its
30 starting-point. Definitions, too, are closed groups of terms.

Further, if the same revolution is repeated, mind must repeatedly think the same object.

Further, thinking has more resemblance to a coming to rest or arrest than to a movement; the same may be said of inferring.

It might also be urged that what is difficult and
407ᵇ enforced is incompatible with blessedness; if the movement of the soul is not of its essence, movement of the soul must be contrary to its nature.[14] It must also be painful for the soul to be inextricably bound up with the body; nay more, if, as is frequently said and widely accepted, it is better for mind not to be embodied, the union must be for it undesirable.

5   Further, the cause of the revolution of the heavens is left obscure. It is not the essence of soul which is the cause of this circular movement—that movement is only incidental to soul—nor is, *a fortiori*, the body its cause. Again, it is not even asserted that it is better that soul should be so
10 moved; and yet the reason for which God caused the soul to move in a circle can only have been that movement was bet-

[14] *sc.* 'and so a hindrance to its bliss'.

ter for it than rest, and movement of this kind better than any other. But since this sort of consideration is more appropriate to another field of speculation, let us dismiss it for the present.

The view we have just been examining, in company with most theories about the soul, involves the following absurdity: they all join the soul to a body, or place it in a body, without adding any specification of the reason of their union, or of the bodily conditions required for it. Yet such explanation can scarcely be omitted; for some community of nature is presupposed by the fact that the one acts and the other is acted upon, the one moves and the other is moved; interaction always implies a *special* nature in the two inter-agents. All, however, that these thinkers do is to describe the specific characteristics of the soul; they do not try to determine anything about the body which is to contain it, as if it were possible, as in the Pythagorean myths, that any soul could be clothed upon with any body—an absurd view, for each body seems to have a form and shape of its own. It is as absurd as to say that the art of carpentry could embody itself in flutes; each art must use its tools, each soul its body.

4 There is yet another theory about soul, which has commended itself to many as no less probable than any of those we have hitherto mentioned, and has rendered public account of itself in the court of popular discussion. Its supporters say that the soul is a kind of harmony, for (*a*) harmony is a blend or composition of contraries, and (*b*) the body is compounded out of contraries. Harmony, however, is a certain proportion or composition of the constituents blended, and soul can be neither the one nor the other of these. Further, the power of originating movement cannot belong to a harmony, while almost all concur in regarding this as a principal attribute of soul. It

408ª is more appropriate to call health (or generally one of the good states of the body) a harmony than to predicate it of the soul. The absurdity becomes most apparent when we try to attribute the active and passive affections of the soul to a harmony; the necessary adjustment of their conceptions
5 is difficult. Further, in using the word 'harmony' we have one or other of two cases in our mind; the most proper sense is in relation to spatial magnitudes which have motion and position, where harmony means the disposition and cohesion of their parts in such a manner as to prevent the introduction into the whole of anything homogeneous with it, and the secondary sense, derived from the former, is that in which it means the ratio between the constituents so
10 blended; in neither of these senses is it plausible to predicate it of soul. That soul is a harmony in the sense of the mode of composition of the parts of the body is a view easily refutable; for there are many composite parts and those variously compounded; of what bodily part is mind or the sensitive or the appetitive faculty the mode of composition? And what *is* the mode of composition which constitutes each of them? It is equally absurd to identify the soul with the ratio of the mixture; for the mixture which makes flesh
15 has a different ratio between the elements from that which makes bone. The consequence of this view will therefore be that distributed throughout the whole body there will be many souls, since every one of the bodily parts is a different mixture of the elements, and the ratio of mixture is in each case a harmony, i. e. a soul.

From Empedocles at any rate we might demand an answer to the following question—for he says that each of the parts of the body is what it is in virtue of a ratio
20 between the elements: is the soul identical with this ratio, or is it not rather something over and above this which is formed in the parts? Is love the cause of any and every mixture, or only of those that are in the right ratio? Is love this

ratio itself, or is love something over and above this? Such
are the problems raised by this account. But, on the other
hand, if the soul is different from the mixture, why does it
disappear at one and the same moment with that relation   25
between the elements which constitutes flesh or the other
parts of the animal body? Further, if the soul is not identical with the ratio of mixture, and it is consequently not the
case that each of the parts has a soul, what is that which
perishes when the soul quits the body?

That the soul cannot either be a harmony, or be moved
in a circle, is clear from what we have said. Yet that it can
be moved incidentally is, as we said above,[15] possible, and   30
even that in a sense it can move itself, i. e. in the sense that
the vehicle in which it is can be moved, and moved by it; in
no other sense can the soul be moved in space. More legit-
imate doubts might remain as to its movement in view of
the following facts. We speak of the soul as being pained   408[b]
or pleased, being bold or fearful, being angry, perceiving,
thinking. All these are regarded as modes of movement,
and hence it might be inferred that the soul is moved.
This, however, does not necessarily follow. We may admit   5
to the full that being pained or pleased, or thinking, are
movements (each of them a 'being moved'), and that the
movement is originated by the soul. For example we may
regard anger or fear as such and such movements of the
heart, and thinking as such and such another movement of
that organ, or of some other; these modifications may arise
either from changes of place in certain parts or from qualitative alterations (the special nature of the parts and the   10
special modes of their changes being for our present purpose irrelevant). Yet to say that it is *the soul* which is angry
is as inexact as it would be to say that it is the soul that
weaves webs or builds houses. It is doubtless better to avoid

[15] 406[a] 30 ff., [b]5–8.

saying that the soul pities or learns or thinks, and rather to
15 say that it is the man who does this with his soul. What we
mean is not that the movement is in the soul, but that
sometimes it terminates in the soul and sometimes starts
from it, sensation e. g. coming from without inwards, and
reminiscence starting from the soul and terminating with
the movements, actual or residual, in the sense organs.

The case of mind is different; it seems to be an independent substance implanted within the soul and to be
incapable of being destroyed. If it could be destroyed at all,
20 it would be under the blunting influence of old age. What
really happens in respect of mind in old age is, however,
exactly parallel to what happens in the case of the sense
organs; if the old man could recover the proper kind of eye,
he would see just as well as the young man. The incapacity
of old age is due to an affection not of the soul but of its
vehicle, as occurs in drunkenness or disease. Thus it is that
in old age the activity of mind or intellectual apprehension
25 declines only through the decay of some other inward part;
mind itself is impassible. Thinking, loving, and hating are
affections not of mind, but of that which has mind, so far as
it has it. That is why, when this vehicle decays, memory and
love cease; they were activities not of mind, but of the composite which has perished; mind is, no doubt, something
30 more divine and impassible. That the soul cannot be moved
is therefore clear from what we have said, and if it cannot
be moved at all, manifestly it cannot be moved by itself.

Of all the opinions we have enumerated, by far the most
unreasonable is that which declares the soul to be a self-
moving number; it involves in the first place all the
impossibilities which follow from regarding the soul as
409ᵃ moved, and in the second special absurdities which follow
from calling it a number. How are we to imagine a unit
being moved? By what agency? What sort of movement can
be attributed to what is without parts or internal differences?

If the unit is both originative of movement and itself capable of being moved, it must contain difference.[16]

Further, since they say a moving line generates a surface and a moving point a line, the movements of the psychic units must be lines (for a point is a unit having position, and the number of the soul is, of course, somewhere and has position).

Again, if from a number a number or a unit is subtracted, the remainder is another number; but plants and many animals when divided continue to live, and each segment is thought to retain the same kind of soul.

It must be all the same whether we speak of units or corpuscles; for if the spherical atoms of Democritus became points, nothing being retained but their being a quantum, there must remain in each a moving and a moved part, just as there is in what is continuous; what happens has nothing to do with the size of the atoms, it depends solely upon their being a quantum. That is why there must be something to originate movement in the units. If in the animal what originates movement is the soul, so also must it be in the case of the number, so that not the mover and the moved together, but the mover only, will be the soul. But how is it possible for one of the units to fulfil this function of originating movement? There must be *some* difference between such a unit and all the other units, and what difference can there be between one placed unit and another except a difference of position? If then, on the other hand, these psychic units within the body are different from the points *of* the body, there will be two sets of units both occupying the same place; for each unit will occupy a point. And yet, if there can be two, why cannot there be an infinite number? For if things can occupy an indivisible place, they must themselves be indivisible. If, on the other hand, the

16 *sc.* 'and so, be no unit'.

25 points of the body are identical with the units whose number is the soul, or if the number of the points in the body
is the soul, why have not all bodies souls? For all bodies
contain points or an infinity of points.

Further, how is it possible for these points to be isolated or separated from their bodies, seeing that lines cannot
30 be resolved into points?

5 The result is, as we have said,[17] that this view, while
on the one side identical with that of those who
maintain that soul is a subtle kind of body,[18] is on
409b the other entangled in the absurdity peculiar to Democritus'
way of describing the manner in which movement is originated by soul. For if the soul is present throughout the whole
percipient body, there must, if the soul be a kind of body, be
two bodies in the same place; and for those who call it a
5 number, there must be many points at one point, or every
body must have a soul, unless the soul be a different sort of
number—other, that is, than the sum of the points existing in
a body. Another consequence that follows is that the animal
must be moved by its number precisely in the way that
Democritus explained its being moved by his spherical psychic atoms. What difference does it make whether we speak
of small spheres or of large[19] units, or, quite simply, of units
10 in movement? One way or another, the movements of the
animal must be due to their movements. Hence those who
combine movement and number in the same subject lay
themselves open to these and many other similar absurdities.
It is impossible not only that these characters should give the
definition of soul—it is impossible that they should even be

[17] 408b 33 ff.

[18] e. g. Heraclitus, and Diogenes of Apollonia.

[19] i. e. extended.

attributes of it. The point is clear if the attempt be made to 15
start from this as the account of soul and explain from it the
affections and actions of the soul, e. g. reasoning, sensation,
pleasure, pain, &c. For, to repeat what we have said earlier,[20]
movement and number do not facilitate even conjecture
about the derivative properties of soul.

Such are the three ways in which soul has traditionally
been defined; one group of thinkers declared it to be that
which is most originative of movement because it moves 20
itself, another group to be the subtlest and most nearly
incorporeal of all kinds of body. We have now sufficiently
set forth the difficulties and inconsistencies to which these
theories are exposed. It remains now to examine the doctrine that soul is composed of the elements.

The reason assigned for this doctrine is that thus the
soul may perceive or come to know everything that is, but
the theory necessarily involves itself in many impossibilities. 25
Its upholders assume that like is known only by like, and
imagine that by declaring the soul to be composed of the elements they succeed in identifying the soul with all the things
it is capable of apprehending. But the elements are not the
only things it knows; there are many others, or, more
exactly, an infinite number of others, formed out of the elements. Let us admit that the soul knows or perceives the 30
elements out of which each of these composites is made up;
but by what means will it know or perceive the composite
whole, e. g. what God, man, flesh, bone (or any other compound) is? For each *is*, not merely the elements of which it 410ᵃ
is composed, but those elements combined in a determinate
mode or ratio, as Empedocles himself says of bone,

The kindly Earth in its broad-bosomed moulds

[20] 402ᵇ 25–403ᵃ 2.

5   Won of clear Water two parts out of eight
           And four of Fire; and so white bones were formed.

Nothing, therefore, will be gained by the presence of
the elements in the soul, unless there be also present there
the various formulae of proportion and the various compo-
sitions in accordance with them. Each element will indeed
know its fellow outside, but there will be no knowledge of
bone or man, unless they too are present in the constitution
of the soul. The impossibility of this needs no pointing out;
10 for who would suggest that stone or man could enter into
the constitution of the soul? The same applies to 'the good'
and 'the not-good', and so on.

Further, the word 'is' has many meanings: it may be
used of a 'this' or substance, or of a quantum, or of a quale,
or of any other of the kinds of predicates we have distinguished. Does the soul consist of all of these or not? It does
15 not appear that all have common elements. Is the soul
formed out of those elements alone which enter into substances? If so, how will it be able to know each of the other
kinds of thing? Will it be said that each kind of thing has
elements or principles of its own, and that the soul is
formed out of the whole of these? In that case, the soul
20 must be a quantum *and* a quale *and* a substance. But all
that can be made out of the elements of a quantum is a
quantum, not a substance. These (and others like them) are
the consequences of the view that the soul is composed of
all the elements.

It is absurd, also, to say both (*a*) that like is not capable
of being affected by like, and (*b*) that like is perceived or
known by like, for perceiving, and also both thinking and
25 knowing, are, on their own assumption, ways of being
affected or moved.

There are many puzzles and difficulties raised by saying, as Empedocles does, that each set of things is known

by means of its corporeal elements and by reference to
something in soul which is like them, and additional testi-
mony is furnished by this new consideration; for all the 30
parts of the animal body which consist wholly of earth such
as bones, sinews, and hair seem to be wholly insensitive and
consequently not perceptive even of objects earthy like 410b
themselves, as they ought to have been.

Further, each of the principles will have far more ignorance than knowledge, for though each of them will know
one thing, there will be many of which it will be ignorant.
Empedocles at any rate must conclude that his God is the 5
least intelligent of all beings, for of him alone is it true that
there is one thing, Strife, which he does not know, while
there is nothing which mortal beings do not know, for there
is nothing which does not enter into their composition.

In general, we may ask, Why has not everything a soul,
since everything either is an element, or is formed out of
one or several or all of the elements? Each must certainly
know one or several or all.

The problem might also be raised, What is that which 10
unifies the elements into a soul? The elements correspond,
it would appear, to the matter; what unites them, whatever
it is, is the supremely important factor. But it is impossible
that there should be something superior to, and dominant
over, the soul (and *a fortiori* over the mind); it is reasonable
to hold that mind is by nature most primordial and domi- 15
nant, while their statement is that it is the elements which
are first of all that is.

All, both those who assert that the soul, because of its
knowledge or perception of what is, is compounded out of
the elements, and those who assert that it is of all things the
most originative of movement, fail to take into consideration
all kinds of soul. In fact (1) not all beings that perceive can
originate movement; there appear to be certain animals 20
which are stationary, and yet local movement is the only

one, so it seems, which the soul originates in animals. And (2) the same objection holds against all those who construct mind and the perceptive faculty out of the elements; for it appears that plants live, and yet are not endowed with loco-motion or perception, while a large number of animals are without discourse of reason. Even if these points were waived and mind admitted to be a part of the soul (and so
25 too the perceptive faculty), still, even so, there would be kinds and parts of soul of which they had failed to give any account.

The same objection lies against the view expressed in the 'Orphic' poems: there it is said that the soul comes
30 in from the whole when breathing takes place, being borne in upon the winds. Now this cannot take place in the case of
411ᵃ plants, nor indeed in the case of certain classes of animal, for not all classes of animal breathe. This fact has escaped the notice of the holders of this view.

If we must construct the soul out of the elements, there is no necessity to suppose that *all* the elements enter into its construction; one element in each pair of contraries will suffice to enable it to know both that element itself and its contrary. By means of the straight line we know both itself
5 and the curved—the carpenter's rule enables us to test both—but what is curved does not enable us to distinguish either itself or the straight.

Certain thinkers say that soul is intermingled in the whole universe, and it is perhaps for that reason that Thales came to the opinion that all things are full of gods. This presents some difficulties: Why does the soul when it
10 resides in air or fire not form an animal, while it does so when it resides in mixtures of the elements, and that although it is held to be of higher quality when contained in the former? (One might add the question, why the soul in air is maintained to be higher and more immortal than that in animals.) Both possible ways of replying to the former

question lead to absurdity or paradox; for it is beyond paradox to say that fire or air is an animal, and it is absurd to   15
refuse the name of animal to what has soul in it. The opinion that the elements have soul in them seems to have
arisen from the doctrine that a whole must be homogeneous
with its parts. If it is true that animals become animate by
drawing into themselves a portion of what surrounds them,
the partisans of this view are bound to say that the soul of
the Whole too is homogeneous with all its parts. If the air
sucked in is homogeneous, but soul heterogeneous, clearly
while some part of soul will exist in the in-breathed air,   20
some other part will not. The soul must either be homogeneous, or such that there are some parts of the Whole in
which it is not to be found.

From what has been said it is now clear that knowing
as an attribute of soul cannot be explained by soul's being
composed of the elements, and that it is neither sound nor
true to speak of soul as moved. But since (a) knowing, per-   25
ceiving, opining, and further (b) desiring, wishing, and
generally all other modes of appetition, belong to soul, and
(c) the local movements of animals, and (d) growth, matu-   30
rity, and decay are produced by the soul, we must ask
whether each of these is an attribute of the soul as a whole,
i.e. whether it is with the whole soul we think, perceive,   411b
move ourselves, act or are acted upon, or whether each of
them requires a different part of the soul? So too with
regard to life. Does it depend on one of the parts of soul?
Or is it dependent on more than one? Or on all? Or has it
some quite other cause?

Some hold that the soul is divisible, and that one part
thinks, another desires. If, then, its nature admits of its   5
being divided, what can it be that holds the parts together?
Surely not the body, on the contrary it seems rather to be
the soul that holds the body together; at any rate when the
soul departs the body disintegrates and decays. If, then,

there is something else which makes the soul one, this uni-
10 fying agency would have the best right to the name of soul,
and we shall have to repeat for it the question: Is *it* one or
multipartite? If it is one, why not at once admit that 'the
soul' is one? If it has parts, once more the question must be
put: What holds *its* parts together, and so *ad infinitum*?

The question might also be raised about the parts of
the soul: What is the separate rôle of each in relation to the
15 body? For, if the whole soul holds together the whole body,
we should expect each part of the soul to hold together a
part of the body. But this seems an impossibility; it is difficult even to imagine what sort of bodily part mind will
hold together, or how it will do this.

It is a fact of observation that plants and certain insects
20 go on living when divided into segments; this means that
each of the segments has a soul in it identical in species,
though not numerically identical in the different segments,
for both of the segments for a time possess the power of
sensation and local movement. That this does not last is not
surprising, for they no longer possess the organs necessary
for self-maintenance. But, all the same, in each of the bod-
25 ily parts there are present all the parts of soul, and the souls
so present are homogeneous with one another and with the
whole; this means that the several parts of the soul are
indisseverable from one another, although the whole soul
is[21] divisible. It seems also that the principle found in plants
is also a kind of soul; for this is the only principle which is
common to both animals and plants; and this exists in iso-
30 lation from the principle of sensation, though there is
nothing which has the latter without the former.

---

[21] *sc.* 'in a sense, i. e. so as to preserve its homogeneity in even its smallest part'.

BOOK II

1 Let the foregoing suffice as our account of the 412ᵃ
views concerning the soul which have been handed
on by our predecessors; let us now dismiss them
and make as it were a completely fresh start, endeavouring 5
to give a precise answer to the question, What is soul? i. e.
to formulate the most general possible definition of it.

We are in the habit of recognizing, as one determinate
kind of what is, substance, and that in several senses, (a) in
the sense of matter or that which in itself is not 'a this', and
(b) in the sense of form or essence, which is that precisely in
virtue of which a thing is called 'a this', and thirdly (c) in
the sense of that which is compounded of both (a) and (b).
Now matter is potentiality, form actuality; of the latter there 10
are two grades related to one another as e. g. knowledge to
the exercise of knowledge.

Among substances are by general consent reckoned
bodies and especially natural bodies; for they are the principles of all other bodies. Of natural bodies some have life
in them, others not; by life we mean self-nutrition and
growth (with its correlative decay). It follows that every nat- 15
ural body which has life in it is a substance in the sense of a
composite.

But since it is also a *body* of such and such a kind, viz.
having life, the *body* cannot be soul; the body is the subject
or matter, not what is attributed to it. Hence the soul must
be a substance in the sense of the form of a natural body 20
having life potentially within it. But substance[1] is actuality,
and thus soul is the actuality of a body as above character-

---

[1] *sc.* in the sense of form.

ized. Now the word actuality has two senses corresponding respectively to the possession of knowledge and the actual exercise of knowledge. It is obvious that the soul is actuality in the first sense, viz. that of knowledge as possessed, for both sleeping and waking presuppose the existence of soul, 25 and of these waking corresponds to actual knowing, sleeping to knowledge possessed but not employed, and, in the history of the individual, knowledge comes before its employment or exercise.

That is why the soul is the first grade of actuality of a natural body having life potentially in it. The body so described is a body which is organized. The parts of plants 412ᵇ in spite of their extreme simplicity are 'organs'; e. g. the leaf serves to shelter the pericarp, the pericarp to shelter the fruit, while the roots of plants are analogous to the mouth of animals, both serving for the absorption of food. If, then, we have to give a general formula applicable to all kinds of 5 soul, we must describe it as the first grade of actuality of a natural organized body. That is why we can wholly dismiss as unnecessary the question whether the soul and the body are one: it is as meaningless as to ask whether the wax and the shape given to it by the stamp are one, or generally the matter of a thing and that of which it is the matter. Unity has many senses (as many as 'is' has), but the most proper and fundamental sense of both is the relation of an actuality to that of which it is the actuality.

We have now given an answer to the question, What 10 is soul?—an answer which applies to it in its full extent. It is substance in the sense which corresponds to the definitive formula of a thing's essence. That means that it is 'the essential whatness' of a body of the character just assigned.[2] Suppose that what is literally an 'organ',[3] like an axe, were

---

[2] viz. organized, or possessed potentially of life.

[3] i. e. instrument.

a natural body, its 'essential whatness', would have been its essence, and so its soul; if this disappeared from it, it would have ceased to be an axe, except in name. As it is,[4] it is just 15 an axe; it wants the character which is required to make its whatness or formulable essence a soul; for that, it would have had to be a *natural* body of a particular kind, viz. one having *in itself* the power of setting itself in movement and arresting itself. Next, apply this doctrine in the case of the 'parts' of the living body. Suppose that the eye were an animal—sight would have been its soul, for sight is the substance or essence of the eye which corresponds to the 20 formula,[5] the eye being merely the matter of seeing; when seeing is removed the eye is no longer an eye, except in name—it is no more a real eye than the eye of a statue or of a painted figure. We must now extend our consideration from the 'parts' to the whole living body; for what the departmental sense is to the bodily part which is its organ, that the whole faculty of sense is to the whole sensitive body as such.

We must not understand by that which is 'potentially 25 capable of living' what has lost the soul it had, but only what still retains it; but seeds and fruits are bodies which possess the qualification.[6] Consequently, while waking is 413a actuality in a sense corresponding to the cutting and the seeing,[7] the soul is actuality in the sense corresponding to the power of sight and the power in the tool;[8] the body corresponds to what exists in potentiality; as the pupil *plus* the

[4] Being an artificial, not a natural, body.

[5] i. e. which states what it is to be an eye.

[6] Though only potentially, i. e. they are at a further remove from actuality than the fully formed and organized body.

[7] i. e. to the second grade of actuality.

[8] i. e. to the first grade of actuality.

power of sight constitutes the eye, so the soul *plus* the body constitutes the animal.

From this it indubitably follows that the soul is inseparable from its body, or at any rate that certain parts of it
5 are (if it has parts)—for the actuality of some of them is
nothing but the actualities of their bodily parts. Yet some
may be separable because they are not the actualities of any
body at all. Further, we have no light on the problem
whether the soul may not be the actuality of its body in the
sense in which the sailor is the actuality[9] of the ship.

This must suffice as our sketch or outline determina-
10 tion of the nature of soul.

2 Since what is clear or logically more evident
emerges from what in itself is confused but more
observable by us, we must reconsider our results
from this point of view. For it is not enough for a defini-
15 tive formula to express as most now do the mere fact; it
must include and exhibit the ground also. At present definitions are given in a form analogous to the conclusion of a
syllogism; e. g. What is squaring? The construction of an
equilateral rectangle equal to a given oblong rectangle. Such
a definition is in form equivalent to a conclusion.[10] One that
tells us that squaring is the discovery of a line which is a
mean proportional between the two unequal sides of the
given rectangle discloses the ground of what is defined.

We resume our inquiry from a fresh starting-point by
20 calling attention to the fact that what has soul in it differs
from what has not in that the former displays life. Now this
word has more than one sense, and provided any one alone
of these is found in a thing we say that thing is living. Living, that is, may mean thinking or perception or local

[9] i. e. actuator.

[10] i. e. it has nothing in it corresponding to a middle term.

movement and rest, or movement in the sense of nutrition, decay and growth. Hence we think of plants also as living, 25 for they are observed to possess in themselves an originative power through which they increase or decrease in all spatial directions; they grow up *and* down, and everything that grows increases its bulk alike in both directions or indeed in all, and continues to live so long as it can absorb nutriment. 30

This power of self-nutrition can be isolated from the other powers mentioned, but not they from it—in mortal beings at least. The fact is obvious in plants; for it is the only psychic power they possess.

This is the originative power the possession of which leads us to speak of things as *living* at all, but it is the pos- 413ᵇ session of sensation that leads us for the first time to speak of living things as animals; for even those beings which possess no power of local movement but do possess the power of sensation we call animals and not merely living things.

The primary form of sense is touch, which belongs to all animals. Just as the power of self-nutrition can be isolated from touch and sensation generally, so touch can be 5 isolated from all other forms of sense. (By the power of self-nutrition we mean that departmental power of the soul which is common to plants and animals: all animals whatsoever are observed to have the sense of touch.) What the explanation of these two facts is, we must discuss later.¹¹ At present we must confine ourselves to saying that soul is the 10 source of these phenomena and is characterized by them, viz. by the powers of self-nutrition, sensation, thinking, and motivity.

Is each of these a soul or a part of a soul? And if a part, a part in what sense? A part merely distinguishable by definition or a part distinct in local situation as well? In the 15 case of certain of these powers, the answers to these ques-

¹¹ iii, 12, esp. 434ᵃ 22–30, ᵇ10 ff.

tions are easy, in the case of others we are puzzled what to say. Just as in the case of plants which when divided are observed to continue to live though removed to a distance from one another (thus showing that in *their* case the soul of each individual plant before division was actually one, potentially many), so we notice a similar result in other
20 varieties of soul, i. e. in insects which have been cut in two; each of the segments possesses both sensation and local movement; and if sensation, necessarily also imagination and appetition; for, where there is sensation, there is also pleasure and pain, and, where these, necessarily also desire.

We have no evidence as yet about mind or the power to
25 think; it seems to be a widely different kind of soul, differing as what is eternal from what is perishable; it alone is capable of existence in isolation from all other psychic powers. All the other parts of soul, it is evident from what we have said, are, in spite of certain statements to the contrary, incapable of separate existence though, of course, distinguishable by definition. If opining is distinct from perceiving, to be
30 capable of opining and to be capable of perceiving must be distinct, and so with all the other forms of living above enumerated. Further, some animals possess all these parts of soul, some certain of them only, others one only (this is
414ᵃ what enables us to classify animals); the cause must be considered later.[12] A similar arrangement is found also within the field of the senses; some classes of animals have all the senses, some only certain of them, others only one, the most indispensable, touch.

Since the expression 'that whereby we live and perceive'
5 has two meanings, just like the expression 'that whereby we know'—that may mean either (a) knowledge or (b) the soul, for we can speak of knowing *by* or *with* either, and similarly that whereby we are in health may be either (a) health or (b)

12 iii. 12, 13.

the body or some part of the body; and since of the two
terms thus contrasted knowledge or health is the name of a
form, essence, or ratio, or if we so express it an actuality of
a recipient matter—knowledge of what is capable of know- 10
ing, health of what is capable of being made healthy (for the
operation of that which is capable of originating change terminates and has its seat in what is changed or altered);
further, since it is the soul by or with which primarily we
live, perceive, and think:—it follows that the soul must be a
ratio or formulable essence, not a matter or subject. For, as
we said,[13] the word substance has three meanings—form,
matter, and the complex of both—and of these three what
is called matter is potentiality, what is called form actuality. 15
Since then the complex here is the living thing, the body
cannot be the actuality of the soul; it is the soul which is the
actuality of a certain kind of body. Hence the rightness of
the view that the soul cannot be without a body, while it
cannot *be* a body; it is not a body but something relative to a
body. That is why it is *in* a body, and a body of a definite
kind. It was a mistake, therefore, to do as former thinkers
did, merely to fit it into a body without adding a definite
specification of the kind or character of that body. Reflection
confirms the observed fact; the actuality of any given thing 25
can only be realized in what is already potentially that thing,
i. e. in a matter of its own appropriate to it. From all this it
follows that soul is an actuality or formulable essence of
something that possesses a potentiality of being besouled.

3   Of the psychic powers above enumerated[14] some
kinds of living things, as we have said,[15] possess all,
some less than all, others one only. Those we have

[13] 412ᵃ 7.

[14] 413ᵃ 23–5, ᵇ11–13, 21–4.

[15] 413ᵇ 32–414ᵃ 1.

30 mentioned are the nutritive, the appetitive, the sensory, the
locomotive, and the power of thinking. Plants have none but
the first, the nutritive, while another order of living things
414ᵇ has this *plus* the sensory. If any order of living things has
the sensory, it must also have the appetitive; for appetite is
the genus of which desire, passion, and wish are the species;
now all animals have one sense at least, viz. touch, and
whatever has a sense has the capacity for pleasure and pain
and therefore has pleasant and painful objects present to it,
and wherever these are present, there is desire, for desire is
5 just appetition of what is pleasant. Further, all animals have
the sense for food (for touch is the sense for food); the food
of all living things consists of what is dry, moist, hot, cold,
and these are the qualities apprehended by touch; all other
sensible qualities are apprehended by touch only indirectly.
10 Sounds, colours, and odours contribute nothing to nutriment; flavours fall within the field of tangible qualities.
Hunger and thirst are forms of desire, hunger a desire for
what is dry and hot, thirst a desire for what is cold and
moist; flavour is a sort of seasoning added to both. We must
15 later[16] clear up these points, but at present it may be enough
to say that all animals that possess the sense of touch have
also appetition. The case of imagination is obscure; we must
examine it later.[17] Certain kinds of animals possess in addition the power of locomotion, and still another order of
20 animate beings, i. e. man and possibly another order like
man or superior to him, the power of thinking, i. e. mind.
It is now evident that a single definition can be given of soul
only in the same sense as one can be given of figure. For, as
in that case there is no figure distinguishable and apart from
triangle, &c., so here there is no soul apart from the forms of
soul just enumerated. It is true that a highly general defini-

[16] c. 11. iii. 12. 434ᵇ 18–21.

[17] iii. 3, 11. 433ᵇ 31–434ᵃ 7.

tion can be given for figure which will fit all figures without expressing the peculiar nature of any figure. So here in the case of soul and its specific forms. Hence it is absurd in 25 this and similar cases to demand an absolutely general definition, which will fail to express the peculiar nature of anything that *is*, or again, omitting this, to look for separate definitions corresponding to each *infima species*. The cases of figure and soul are exactly parallel; for the particulars subsumed under the common name in both cases—figures and 30 living beings—constitute a series, each successive term of which potentially contains its predecessor, e. g. the square the triangle, the sensory power the self-nutritive. Hence we must ask in the case of each order of living things, What is its soul, i. e. What is the soul of plant, animal, man? Why the terms are related in this serial way must form the subject 415ᵃ of later examination.[18] But the facts are that the power of perception is never found apart from the power of self-nutrition, while—in plants—the latter is found isolated from the former. Again, no sense is found apart from that of touch, while touch is found by itself; many animals have neither 5 sight, hearing, nor smell. Again, among living things that possess sense some have the power of locomotion, some not. Lastly, certain living beings—a small minority—possess calculation and thought, for (among mortal beings) those which possess calculation have all the other powers above mentioned, while the converse does not hold—indeed some live 10 by imagination alone, while others have not even imagination. The mind that knows with immediate intuition presents a different problem.[19]

It is evident that the way to give the most adequate definition of soul is to seek in the case of *each* of its forms for the most appropriate definition.

[18] iii. 12, 13.

[19] Cf. iii. 4–8.

15   4 It is necessary for the student of these forms of soul first to find a definition of each, expressive of what it is, and then to investigate its derivative properties, &c. But if we are to express what each is, viz. what the thinking power is, or the perceptive, or the nutritive, we must go farther back and first give an account of thinking or perceiving, for in the order of investigation the question of what an agent does precedes the question, what enables it to do what it does. If this is correct, we must on the same
20   ground go yet another step farther back and have some clear view of the objects of each; thus we must *start* with these objects, e. g. with food, with what is perceptible, or with what is intelligible.

It follows that first of all we must treat of nutrition and reproduction,[20] for the nutritive soul is found along with all the others and is the most primitive and widely distributed power of soul, being indeed that one in virtue of which all
25   are said to have life. The acts in which it manifests itself are reproduction and the use of food—reproduction, I say, because for any living thing that has reached its normal development and which is unmutilated, and whose mode of generation is not spontaneous, the most natural act is the production of another like itself, an animal producing an animal, a plant a plant, in order that, as far as its nature
415b   allows, it may partake in the eternal and divine. That is the goal towards which all things strive, that for the sake of which they do whatsoever their nature renders possible. The phrase 'for the sake of which' is ambiguous; it may mean either (*a*) the end to achieve which, or (*b*) the being in whose interest, the act is done. Since then no living thing is able to partake in what is eternal and divine by uninterrupted continuance (for nothing perishable can for ever
5   remain one and the same), it tries to achieve that end in the

---

[20] *sc.* 'which we shall see to be inseparable from nutrition'.

only way possible to it, and success is possible in varying degrees; so it remains not indeed as the self-same individual but continues its existence in something *like* itself—not numerically but specifically one.[21]

The soul is the cause or source of the living body. The terms cause and source have many senses. But the soul is the cause of its body alike in all three senses which we explicitly recognize. It is (*a*) the source or origin of movement, it is (*b*) the end, it is (*c*) the essence of the whole living body.

That it is the last, is clear; for in everything the essence is identical with the ground of its being, and here, in the case of living things, their being is to live, and of their being and their living the soul in them is the cause or source. Further, the actuality of whatever is potential is identical with its formulable essence.

It is manifest that the soul is also the final cause of its body. For Nature, like mind, always does whatever it does for the sake of something, which something is its end. To that something corresponds in the case of animals the soul and in this it follows the order of nature; all natural bodies are organs of the soul. This is true of those that enter into the constitution of plants as well as of those which enter into that of animals. This shows that that for the sake of which they are is soul. We must here recall the two senses of 'that for the sake of which', viz. (*a*) the end to achieve which, and (*b*) the being in whose interest, anything is or is done.

We must maintain, further, that the soul is also the cause of the living body as the original source of local movement. The power of locomotion is not found, however, in all living things. But change of quality and change of

---

[21] There is an unbroken current of the same specific life flowing through a discontinuous series of individual beings of the same species united by descent.

quantity are also due to the soul. Sensation is held to be a qualitative alteration, and nothing except what has soul in it
25 is capable of sensation. The same holds of the quantitative changes which constitute growth and decay; nothing grows or decays naturally[22] except what feeds itself, and nothing feeds itself except what has a share of soul in it.

Empedocles is wrong in adding that growth in plants is to be explained, the downward rooting by the natural ten-
416ᵃ dency of earth to travel downwards, and the upward branching by the similar natural tendency of fire to travel upwards. For he misinterprets up and down; up and down are not for all things what they are for the whole Cosmos:
5 if we are to distinguish and identify organs according to their *functions*, the roots of plants are analogous to the head in animals. Further, we must ask what is the force that holds together the earth and the fire which tend to travel in contrary directions; if there is no counteracting force, they will be torn asunder; if there is, this must be the soul and the cause of nutrition and growth. By some the element of
10 fire is held to be *the* cause of nutrition and growth, for it alone of the primary bodies or elements is observed to feed and increase *itself*. Hence the suggestion that in both plants and animals it is it which is the operative force. A concurrent cause in a sense it certainly is, but not the principal
15 cause; that is rather the soul; for while the growth of fire goes on without limit so long as there is a supply of fuel, in the case of all complex wholes formed in the course of nature there is a limit or ratio which determines their size and increase, and limit and ratio are marks of soul but not of fire, and belong to the side of formulable essence rather than that of matter.

Nutrition and reproduction are due to one and the same psychic power. It is necessary first to give precision to our

22 i. e. of itself.

account of food, for it is by this function of absorbing food 20
that this psychic power is distinguished from all the others.
The current view is that what serves as food to a living
thing is what is contrary to it—not that in every pair of contraries each is food to the other: to be food a contrary must
not only be transformable into the other and vice versa, it
must also in so doing increase the bulk of the other. Many a
contrary is transformed into its other and vice versa, where
neither is even a quantum and so cannot increase in bulk,
e. g. an invalid into a healthy subject. It is clear that not 25
even those contraries which satisfy both the conditions mentioned above are food to one another in precisely the same
sense; water may be said to feed fire, but not fire water.
Where the members of the pair are elementary bodies only
one of the contraries, it would appear, can be said to feed
the other. But there is a difficulty here. One set of thinkers 30
assert that like is fed, as well as increased in amount, by
like. Another set, as we have said, maintain the very
reverse, viz. that what feeds and what is fed are contrary to
one another; like, they argue, is incapable of being affected
by like; but food is changed in the process of digestion, and
change is always *to* what is opposite or to what is intermediate. Further, food is acted upon by what is nourished by 35
it, not the other way round, as timber is worked by a car- 416b
penter and not conversely; there is a change in the carpenter
but it is merely a change from not-working to working. In
answering this problem it makes all the difference whether
we mean by 'the food' the 'finished' or the 'raw' product.
If we use the word food of both, viz. of the completely
undigested and the completely digested matter, we can justify both the rival accounts of it; taking food in the sense of 5
undigested matter, it is the contrary of what is fed by it,
taking it as digested it is like what is fed by it. Consequently it is clear that in a certain sense we may say that
both parties are right, both wrong.

Since nothing except what is alive can be fed, what is fed is the besouled body and just because it has soul in it. Hence food is essentially related to what has soul in it. Food
10 has a power which is other than the power to increase the bulk of what is fed by it; so far forth as what has soul in it is a quantum, food may increase its quantity, but it is only so far as what has soul in it is a 'this-somewhat' or substance that food acts *as* food; in that case it maintains the being of what is fed, and that continues to be what it is so long as the process of nutrition continues. Further, it is the
15 agent in generation, i. e. not the generation of the individual fed but the reproduction of another like it; the substance of the individual fed is already in existence; the existence of no substance is a self-generation but only a self-maintenance.

Hence the psychic power which we are now studying may be described as that which tends to maintain whatever has this power in it of continuing such as it was, and food helps it to do its work. That is why, if deprived of food, it must cease to be.

20   The process of nutrition involves three factors, (*a*) what is fed, (*b*) that wherewith it is fed, (*c*) what does the feeding; of these (*c*) is the first soul,[23] (*a*) the body which has that soul in it, (*b*) the food. But since it is right to call things after the ends they realize, and the end of this soul is to
25 generate another being like that in which it is, the first soul ought to be named the reproductive soul. The expression (*b*) 'wherewith it is fed' is ambiguous just as is the expression 'wherewith the ship is steered'; that may mean either (i) the hand or (ii) the rudder, i. e. either (i) what is moved and sets in movement, or (ii) what is merely moved. We can apply this analogy here if we recall that all food must be capable of being digested, and that what produces digestion

23 i. e. the earliest and most indispensable kind of soul.

is warmth; that is why everything that has soul in it possesses warmth.

We have now given an outline account of the nature of food; further details must be given in the appropriate place.

5 Having made these distinctions let us now speak of sensation in the widest sense. Sensation depends, as we have said,[24] on a process of movement or affection from without, for it is held to be some sort of change of quality. Now some thinkers assert that like is affected only by like; in what sense this is possible and in what sense impossible, we have explained in our general discussion of acting and being acted upon.[25]

Here arises a problem: why do we not perceive the senses themselves as well as the external objects of sense, or why without the stimulation of external objects do they not produce sensation, seeing that they contain in themselves fire, earth, and all the other elements, which are the direct or indirect objects of sense? It is clear that what is sensitive is so only potentially, not actually. The power of sense is parallel to what is combustible, for that never ignites itself spontaneously, but requires an agent which has the power of starting ignition; otherwise it could have set itself on fire, and would not have needed actual fire to set it ablaze.

In reply we must recall that we use the word 'perceive' in two ways, for we say (a) that what has the power to hear or see, 'sees' or 'hears', even though it is at the moment asleep, and also (b) that what is actually seeing or hearing, 'sees' or 'hears'. Hence 'sense' too must have two meanings, sense potential, and sense actual. Similarly 'to be a sentient' means either (a) to have a certain power or (b) to manifest a

[24] 415[b] 24, cf. 410[a] 25.

[25] De Gen. et Corr. 323[b] 18 ff.

certain activity. To begin with, for a time, let us speak as if
there were no difference between (i) being moved or affected,
15 and (ii) being active, for movement is a kind of activity—an
imperfect kind, as has elsewhere been explained.[26] Everything that is acted upon or moved is acted upon by an agent
which is actually at work. Hence it is that in one sense, as
has already been stated,[27] what acts and what is acted upon
are like, in another unlike, i. e. prior to and during the
20 change the two factors are unlike, after it like.

But we must now distinguish not only *between* what is
potential and what is actual but also different senses in
which things can be said to be potential or actual; up to
now we have been speaking as if each of these phrases had
only one sense. We can speak of something as 'a knower'
either (*a*) as when we say that man is a knower, meaning
that man falls within the class of beings that know or have
knowledge, or (*b*) as when we are speaking of a man who
25 possesses a knowledge of grammar; each of these is so called
as having in him a certain potentiality, but there is a difference between their respective potentialities, the one (*a*)
being a potential knower, because his kind or matter is such
and such, the other (*b*), because he can in the absence of any
external counteracting cause realize his knowledge in actual
knowing at will. This implies a third meaning of 'a knower'
(*c*), one who is already realizing his knowledge—he is a
knower in actuality and in the most proper sense is know-
30 ing, e. g. this A. Both the former are potential knowers, who
realize their respective potentialities, the one (*a*) by change
of quality, i. e. repeated transitions from one state to its
opposite[28] under instruction, the other (*b*) by the transition

[26] *Phys.* 201[b] 31, 257[b] 8.

[27] 416[a] 29–[b]9.

[28] viz. from ignorance or error to knowledge or truth.

from the inactive possession of sense or grammar to their 417^b active exercise. The two kinds of transition are distinct.

Also the expression 'to be acted upon' has more than one meaning; it may mean either (a) the extinction of one of two contraries by the other, or (b) the maintenance of what is potential by the agency of what is actual and already like what is acted upon, with such likeness as is compatible with one's being actual and the other potential. For what pos- 5 sesses knowledge becomes an actual knower by a transition which is either not an alteration of it at all (being in reality a development into its true self or actuality) or at least an alteration in a quite different sense from the usual meaning.

Hence it is wrong to speak of a wise man as being 'altered' when he uses his wisdom, just as it would be absurd to speak of a builder as being altered when he is using his skill in building a house.

What in the case of knowing or understanding leads 10 from potentiality to actuality ought not to be called teaching but something else. That which starting with the power to know learns or acquires knowledge through the agency of one who actually knows and has the power of teaching either (a) ought not to be said 'to be acted upon' at all or 15 (b) we must recognize two senses of alteration, viz. (i) the substitution of one quality for another, the first being the contrary of the second, or (ii) the development of an exis- tent quality from potentiality in the direction of fixity or nature.

In the case of what is to possess sense, the first transi- tion is due to the action of the male parent and takes place before birth so that at birth the living thing is, in respect of sensation, at the stage which corresponds to the *possession* of knowledge. Actual sensation corresponds to the stage of the exercise of knowledge. But between the two cases compared 20 there is a difference; the objects that excite the sensory pow- ers to activity, the seen, the heard, &c., are outside. The ground of this difference is that what actual sensation apprehends is individuals, while what knowledge apprehends is universals, and these are in a sense within the soul. That is why a man can exercise his knowledge when he 25 wishes, but his sensation does not depend upon himself—a sensible object must be there. A similar statement must be made about our *knowledge* of what is sensible—on the same ground, viz. that the sensible objects are individual and external.

A later more appropriate occasion may be found[29] thor- 30 oughly to clear up all this. At present it must be enough to recognize the distinctions already drawn; a thing may be said to be potential in either of two senses, (a) in the sense in which we might say of a boy that he may become a general or (b) in the sense in which we might say the same of 418a an adult, and there are two corresponding senses of the term 'a potential sentient'. There are no separate names for the two stages of potentiality; we have pointed out that they are different and how they are different. We cannot help using the incorrect terms 'being acted upon or altered' of the two transitions involved. As we have said,[30] what has the power of sensation is potentially like what the perceived object is 5 actually; that is, while at the beginning of the process of its being acted upon the two interacting factors are dissimilar, at the end the one acted upon is assimilated to the other and is identical in quality with it.

6 In dealing with each of the senses we shall have first to speak of the objects which are perceptible by each. The term 'object of sense' covers three kinds of objects, two kinds of which are, in our language, directly perceptible, while the remaining one is only inci-

[29] iii. 4, 5.

[30] 417a 12–20.

dentally perceptible. Of the first two kinds one (*a*) consists of what is perceptible by a single sense, the other (*b*) of what is perceptible by any and all of the senses.[31] I call by 10 the name of special object of this or that sense that which cannot be perceived by any other sense than that one and in respect of which no error is possible; in this sense colour is the special object of sight, sound of hearing, flavour of taste. Touch, indeed, discriminates more than one set of different qualities. Each sense has one kind of object which it discerns, and never errs in reporting that what is before it is 15 colour or sound (though it may err as to what it is that is coloured or where that is, or what it is that is sounding or where that is). Such objects are what we propose to call the special objects of this or that sense.

'Common sensibles' are movement, rest, number, figure, magnitude; these are not peculiar to any one sense, but are common to all There are at any rate certain kinds of movement which are perceptible both by touch and by sight.

We speak of an incidental object of sense where e. g. the white object which we see is the son of Diares; here 20 because 'being the son of Diares' is incidental to the directly visible white patch we speak of the son of Diares as being (incidentally) perceived or seen by us. Because this is only incidentally an object of sense, it in no way as such affects the senses. Of the two former kinds, both of which are in their own nature perceptible by sense, the first kind—that of special objects of the several senses—constitute *the* objects of sense in the strictest sense of the term and it is to them that in the nature of things the structure of each 25 several sense is adapted.

[31] Really, it is enough if it is perceptible by more than one sense.

7 The object of sight is the visible, and what is visible is (a) colour and (b) a certain kind of object which can be described in words but which has no single name; what we mean by (b) will be abundantly clear as we proceed. Whatever is visible is colour and colour is
30 what lies upon what is in its own nature visible; 'in its own nature' here means not that visibility is involved in the definition of what thus underlies colour, but that that substratum contains in itself the cause of visibility. Every
418b colour has in it the power to set in movement what is actually transparent; that power constitutes its very nature. That is why it is not visible except with the help of light; it is only in light that the colour of a thing is seen. Hence our first task is to explain what light is.

Now there clearly is something which is transparent,
5 and by 'transparent' I mean what is visible, and yet not visible in itself, but rather owing its visibility to the colour of *something else*; of this character are air, water, and many solid bodies. Neither air nor water is transparent because it is air or water; they are transparent because each of them has contained in it a certain substance which is the same in both and is also found in the eternal body which constitutes the uppermost shell of the physical Cosmos. Of this substance light is the activity—the activity of what is transparent
10 so far forth as it has in it the determinate power of becoming transparent; where this power is present, there is also the potentiality of the contrary, viz. darkness. Light is as it were the proper colour of what is transparent, and exists whenever the potentially transparent is excited to actuality by the influence of fire or something resembling 'the uppermost body'; for fire too contains something which is one and the same with the substance in question.

We have now explained what the transparent is and what light is; light is neither fire nor any kind whatsoever of
15 body nor an efflux from any kind of body (if it were, it

would again itself be a kind of body)—it is the presence of
fire or something resembling fire in what is transparent. It is
certainly not a body, for two bodies cannot be present in the
same place. The opposite of light is darkness; darkness is
the absence from what is transparent of the corresponding
positive state above characterized; clearly therefore, light is
just the presence of that.

Empedocles (and with him all others who used the
same forms of expression) was wrong in speaking of light
as 'travelling' or being at a given moment between the earth
and its envelope, its movement being unobservable by us;
that view is contrary both to the clear evidence of argument
and to the observed facts; if the distance traversed were
short, the movement might have been unobservable, but
where the distance is from extreme East to extreme West,
the draught upon our powers of belief is too great.

What is capable of taking on colour is what in itself is
colourless, as what can take on sound is what is soundless;
what is colourless includes (a) what is transparent and (b)
what is invisible or scarcely visible, i. e. what is 'dark'. The
latter (b) is the same as what is transparent, when it is
potentially, not of course when it is actually transparent; it
is the same substance which is now darkness, now light.

Not everything that is visible depends upon light for its
visibility. This is only true of the 'proper' colour of things.
Some objects of sight which in light are invisible, in darkness stimulate the sense; that is, things that appear fiery or
shining. This class of objects has no simple common name,
but instances of it are fungi, flesh, heads, scales, and eyes of
fish. In none of these is what is seen their own 'proper'
colour. Why we see these at all is another question. At
present what is obvious is that what is seen in light is
always colour. That is why without the help of light colour
remains invisible. Its being colour at all means precisely its
having in it the power to set in movement what is already

actually transparent, and, as we have seen, the actuality of what is transparent is just light.

The following experiment makes the necessity of a medium clear. If what has colour is placed in immediate contact with the eye, it cannot be seen. Colour sets in movement not the sense organ but what is transparent, e. g. the air, and that, extending continuously from the object of the
15 organ, sets the latter in movement. Democritus misrepresents the facts when he expresses the opinion that if the interspace were empty one could distinctly see an ant on the vault of the sky; that is an impossibility. Seeing is due to an affection or change of what has the perceptive faculty, and it cannot be affected by the seen colour itself; it remains that it must be affected by what comes between. Hence it is indispensable that there be *something* in between—if there
20 were nothing, so far from seeing with greater distinctness, we should see nothing at all.

We have now explained the cause why colour cannot be seen otherwise than in light. Fire on the other hand is seen both in darkness and in light; this double possibility follows necessarily from our theory, for it is just fire that makes what is potentially transparent actually transparent.

The same account holds also of sound and smell; if the
25 object of either of these senses is in immediate contact with the organ no sensation is produced. In both cases the object sets in movement only what lies between, and this in turn sets the organ in movement: if what sounds or smells is brought into immediate contact with the organ, no sensation
30 will be produced. The same, in spite of all appearances, applies also to touch and taste; why there is this apparent difference will be clear later.[32] What comes between in the case of sounds is air; the corresponding medium in the case of smell has no name. But, corresponding to what is trans-

[32] 422b 34 ff.

parent in the case of colour, there is a quality found both
in air and water, which serves as a medium for what has 35
smell—I say 'in water' because animals that live in water as
well as those that live on land seem to possess the sense of
smell, and 'in air' because man and all other land animals 419ᵇ
that breathe, perceive smells only when they breathe air in.
The explanation of this too will be given later.³³

8 Now let us, to begin with, make certain distinctions
about sound and hearing.

Sound may mean either of two things—(a) 5
actual, and (b) potential, sound. There are certain things
which, as we say, 'have no sound', e. g. sponges or wool,
others which have, e. g. bronze and in general all things
which are smooth and solid—the latter are said to have a
sound because they can make a sound, i. e. can generate
actual sound between themselves and the organ of hearing.

Actual sound requires for its occurrence (i, ii) two such
bodies and (iii) a space between them; for it is generated by 10
an impact. Hence it is impossible for one body only to generate a sound—there must be a body impinging and a body
impinged upon; what sounds does so by striking against
something else, and this is impossible without a movement
from place to place.

As we have said, not all bodies can by impact on one
another produce sound; impact on wool makes no sound,
while the impact on bronze or any body which is smooth 15
and hollow does. Bronze gives out a sound when struck
because it is smooth; bodies which are hollow owing to
reflection repeat the original impact over and over again, the
body originally set in movement being unable to escape
from the concavity.

Further, we must remark that sound is heard both in

³³ 421ᵇ 13–422ª 6.

air and in water, though less distinctly in the latter. Yet nei-
20 ther air nor water is the principal cause of sound. What is
required for the production of sound is an impact of two
solids against one another and against the air. The latter
condition is satisfied when the air impinged upon does not
retreat before the blow, i. e. is not dissipated by it.

That is why it must be struck with a sudden sharp
blow, if it is to sound—the movement of the whip must
outrun the dispersion of the air, just as one might get in a
stroke at a heap or whirl of sand as it was travelling rapidly
past.

25   An echo occurs, when, a mass of air having been unified, bounded, and prevented from dissipation by the
containing walls of a vessel, the air originally struck by the
impinging body and set in movement by it rebounds from
this mass of air like a ball from a wall. It is probable that
in all generation of sound echo takes place, though it is frequently only indistinctly heard. What happens here must
be analogous to what happens in the case of light; light is
always reflected—otherwise it would not be diffused and
30 outside what was directly illuminated by the sun there would
be blank darkness; but this reflected light is not always
strong enough, as it *is* when it is reflected from water,
bronze, and other smooth bodies, to cast a shadow, which is
the distinguishing mark by which we recognize light.

It is rightly said that an empty space plays the chief
part in the production of hearing, for what people mean by
'the vacuum' is the air, which is what causes hearing, when
that air is set in movement as one continuous mass; but
35 owing to its friability it emits no sound, being dissipated by
420ᵃ impinging upon any surface which is not smooth. When the
surface on which it impinges is quite smooth, what is produced by the original impact is a united mass, a result due
to the smoothness of the surface with which the air is in
contact at the other end.

What has the power of producing sound is what has the power of setting in movement a single mass of air which is continuous from the impinging body up to the organ of hearing. The organ of hearing is physically united with air,[34] and because it is *in* air, the air inside is moved concurrently with the air outside. Hence animals do not hear with all parts 5 of their bodies, nor do all parts admit of the entrance of air; for even the part which can be moved and can sound has not air everywhere in it. Air in itself is, owing to its friability, quite soundless; only when its dissipation is prevented is its movement sound. The air in the ear is built into a chamber just to prevent this dissipating movement, in order that the animal may accurately apprehend all varieties of the move- 10 ments of the air outside. That is why we hear also in water, viz. because the water cannot get into the air chamber or even, owing to the spirals, into the outer ear. If this does happen, hearing ceases, as it also does if the tympanic membrane is damaged, just as sight ceases if the membrane covering the pupil is damaged. It is also a test of deafness 15 whether the ear does or does not reverberate like a horn; the air inside the ear has always a movement of its own, but the sound we hear is always the sounding of something else, not of the organ itself. That is why we say that we hear with what is empty and echoes, viz. because what we hear with is a chamber which contains a bounded mass of air.

Which is it that 'sounds', the striking body or the struck? Is not the answer 'it is both, but each in a different way'? Sound is a movement of what can rebound from a 20 smooth surface when struck against it. As we have explained[35] not everything sounds when it strikes or is struck, e. g. if one needle is struck against another, neither 25 emits any sound. In order, therefore, that sound may be

[34] i. e. it has air incorporated in its structure.

[35] 419^b 6, 13

generated, what is struck must be smooth, to enable the air to rebound and be shaken off from it in one piece.

The distinctions between different sounding bodies show themselves only in actual sound;[36] as without the help of light colours remain invisible, so without the help of actual sound the distinctions between acute and grave sounds remain inaudible. Acute and grave are here met-
30 aphors, transferred from their proper sphere, viz. that of touch, where they mean respectively (a) what moves the sense much in a short time, (b) what moves the sense little in a long time. Not that what is sharp really moves fast, and what is grave, slowly, but that the difference in the qualities
420ᵇ of the one and the other movement is due to their respective speeds. There seems to be a sort of parallelism between what is acute or grave to hearing and what is sharp or blunt to touch; what is sharp as it were stabs, while what is blunt pushes, the one producing its effect in a short, the other in a long time, so that the one is quick, the other slow.

5   Let the foregoing suffice as an analysis of sound. Voice is a kind of sound characteristic of what has soul in it; nothing that is without soul utters voice, it being only by a metaphor that we speak of the voice of the flute or the lyre or generally of what (being without soul) possesses the power of producing a succession of notes which differ in length and pitch and timbre. The metaphor is based on the fact that all these differences are found also in voice. Many animals are voiceless, e. g. all non-sanguineous animals and
10 among sanguineous animals fish. This is just what we should expect, since voice is a certain movement of air. The fish, like those in the Achelous, which are said to have voice, really make the sounds with their gills or some similar organ. Voice is the sound made by an animal, and that with a special organ. As we saw, everything that makes a

---

[36] i. e. when these bodies, e. g. the strings of a lyre, are actually sounding.

sound does so by the impact of something (*a*) against something else, (*b*) across a space, (*c*) filled with air; hence it is 15
only to be expected that no animals utter voice except those
which take in air. Once air is inbreathed, Nature uses it for
two different purposes, as the tongue is used both for tasting and for articulating; in that case of the two functions
tasting is necessary for the animal's existence (hence it is
found more widely distributed), while articulate speech is a
luxury subserving its possessor's well-being; similarly in the
former case Nature employs the breath both as an indis- 20
pensable means to the regulation of the inner temperature of
the living body and also as the matter of articulate voice, in
the interests of its possessor's well-being. Why its former
use is indispensable must be discussed elsewhere.[37]

The organ of respiration is the windpipe, and the organ
to which this is related as means to end is the lungs. The
latter is the part of the body by which the temperature of
land animals is raised above that of all others. But what primarily requires the air drawn in by respiration is not only 25
this but the region surrounding the heart. That is why when
animals breathe the air must penetrate inwards.

Voice then is the impact of the inbreathed air against the
'windpipe', and the agent that produces the impact is the
soul resident in these parts of the body. Not every sound, as
we said, made by an animal is voice (even with the tongue 30
we may merely make a sound which is not voice, or without
the tongue as in coughing); what produces the impact must
have soul in it and must be accompanied by an act of imagination, for voice is a sound *with a meaning*, and is not
merely the result of any impact of the breath as in coughing;
in voice the breath in the windpipe is used as an instrument
to knock with against the walls of the windpipe. This is con- 421ᵃ
firmed by our inability to speak when we are breathing

[37] *De Resp.* 478ᵃ 28; *P. A.* 642ᵃ 31–ᵇ4.

either out or in—we can only do so by holding our breath;
we make the movements with the breath so checked. It is
clear also why fish are voiceless; they have no windpipe. And
5 they have no windpipe because they do not breathe or take
in air. Why they do not is a question belonging to another
inquiry.[38]

9 Smell and its object are much less easy to determine than what we have hitherto discussed; the
distinguishing characteristic of the object of smell is
less obvious than those of sound or colour. The ground of
this is that our power of smell is less discriminating and in
10 general inferior to that of many species of animals; men
have a poor sense of smell and our apprehension of its
proper objects is inseparably bound up with and so confused by pleasure and pain, which shows that in us the
organ is inaccurate. It is probable that there is a parallel failure in the perception of colour by animals that have hard
eyes: probably they discriminate differences of colour only
15 by the presence or absence of what excites fear, and that it
is thus that human beings distinguish smells. It seems that
there is an analogy between smell and taste, and that the
species of tastes run parallel to those of smells—the only
difference being that our sense of taste is more discriminating than our sense of smell, because the former is a
20 modification of touch, which reaches in man the maximum
of discriminative accuracy. While in respect of all the other
senses we fall below many species of animals, in respect of
touch we far excel all other species in exactness of discrimination. That is why man is the most intelligent of all
animals. This is confirmed by the fact that it is to differences in the organ of touch and to nothing else that the
differences between man and man in respect of natural

[38] Cf. De Resp. 474[b] 25–9, 476[a] 6–15; P. A. 669[a] 2–5.

endowment are due; men whose flesh is hard are ill- 25
endowed by nature, men whose flesh is soft, well-endowed.

As flavours may be divided into (a) sweet, (b) bitter, so
with smells. In some things the flavour and the smell have
the same quality, i. e. both are sweet or both bitter, in others they diverge. Similarly a smell, like a flavour, may be 30
pungent, astringent, acid, or succulent. But, as we said,
because smells are much less easy to discriminate than
flavours, the names of these varieties are applied to smells
only metaphorically; for example 'sweet' is extended from 421b
the taste to the smell of saffron or honey, 'pungent' to that
of thyme, and so on.[39]

In the same sense in which hearing has for its object
both the audible and the inaudible, sight both the visible 5
and the invisible, smell has for its object both the odorous
and the inodorous. 'Inodorous' may be either (a) what has
no smell at all, or (b) what has a small or feeble smell. The
same ambiguity lurks in the word 'tasteless'.

Smelling, like the operation of the senses previously
examined, takes place through a medium, i. e. through air
or water—I add water, because water-animals too (both san- 10
guineous and non-sanguineous) seem to smell just as much
as land-animals; at any rate some of them make directly for
their food from a distance if it has any scent. That is why
the following facts constitute a problem for us. All animals
smell in the same way, but man smells only when he
inhales; if he exhales or holds his breath, he ceases to smell, 15
no difference being made whether the odorous object is distant or near, or even placed inside the nose and actually on
the wall of the nostril; it is a disability common to all the
senses not to perceive what is in immediate contact with the
organ of sense, but our failure to apprehend what is odorous

[39] Because of the felt likeness between the respective smells and the really
sweet or pungent tastes of the same herbs, &c.

without the help of inhalation is peculiar (the fact is obvious on making the experiment). Now since bloodless animals do
20 not breathe, they must, it might be argued, have some novel sense not reckoned among the usual five. Our reply must be that this is impossible, since it is scent that is perceived; a sense that apprehends what is odorous and what has a good or bad odour cannot be anything but smell. Further, they are observed to be deleteriously affected by the same
25 strong odours as man is, e. g. bitumen, sulphur, and the like. These animals must be able to smell without being able to breathe. The probable explanation is that in man the organ of smell has a certain superiority over that in all other animals just as his eyes have over those of hard-eyed animals. Man's eyes have in the eyelids a kind of shelter or envelope, which must be shifted or drawn back in order that
30 we may see, while hard-eyed animals have nothing of the kind, but at once see whatever presents itself in the transparent medium. Similarly in certain species of animals the organ of smell is like the eye of hard-eyed animals, uncur-
422ª tained, while in others which take in air it probably has a curtain over it, which is drawn back in inhalation, owing to the dilating of the veins or pores. That explains also why
5 such animals cannot smell under water; to smell they must first inhale, and that they cannot do under water.

Smells come from what is dry as flavours from what is moist. Consequently the organ of smell is potentially dry.

10 What can be tasted is always something that can be touched, and just for that reason it cannot be perceived *through* an interposed foreign body,
10 for touch means the absence of any intervening body. Further, the flavoured and tasteable body is suspended in a liquid matter, and this is tangible. Hence, if we lived in water, we should perceive a sweet object introduced into the water, but the water would not be the medium *through*

which we perceived; our perception would be due to the
solution of the sweet substance in what we imbibed, just as
if it were mixed with some drink. There is no parallel here
to the perception of colour, which is due neither to any
blending of anything with anything, nor to any efflux of
anything from anything. In the case of taste, there is nothing corresponding to the medium in the case of the senses 15
previously discussed; but as the object of sight is colour, so
the object of taste is flavour. But nothing excites a perception of flavour without the help of liquid; what acts upon
the sense of taste must be either actually or potentially liquid like what *is* saline; it must be both (*a*) itself easily
dissolved, and (*b*) capable of dissolving along with itself the 20
tongue. Taste apprehends both (*a*) what has taste and (*b*)
what has no taste, if we mean by (*b*) what has only a slight
or feeble flavour or what tends to destroy the sense of taste.
In this it is exactly parallel to sight, which apprehends both
what is visible and what is invisible (for darkness is invisible
and yet is discriminated by sight; so is, in a different way,
what is over-brilliant), and to hearing, which apprehends
both sound and silence, of which the one is audible and the 25
other inaudible, and also over-loud sound. This corresponds
in the case of hearing to over-bright light in the case of
sight. As a faint sound is 'inaudible', so in a sense is a loud
or violent sound. The word 'invisible' and similar privative
terms cover not only (*a*) what is simply without some
power, but also (*b*) what is adapted by nature to have it but
has not it or has it only in a very low degree, as when we
say that a species of swallow is 'footless' or that a variety of
fruit is 'stoneless'. So too taste has as its object both what
can be tasted and the tasteless—the latter in the sense of 30
what has little flavour or a bad flavour or one destructive
of taste. The difference between what is tasteless and what
is not seems to rest ultimately on that between what is
drinkable and what is undrinkable—both are tasteable, but

the latter is bad and tends to destroy taste, while the former is the normal stimulus of taste. What is drinkable is the
common object of both touch and taste.

422ᵇ   Since what can be tasted is liquid, the organ for its perception cannot be either (a) actually liquid or (b) incapable
of becoming liquid. Tasting means a being affected by[40]
what can be tasted as such; hence the organ of taste must be
liquefied, and so to start with must be non-liquid but capa-
5 ble of liquefaction without loss of its distinctive nature.
This is confirmed by the fact that the tongue cannot taste
either when it is too dry or when it is too moist; in the latter case what occurs is due to a contact with the pre-existent
moisture in the tongue itself, when after a foretaste of some
strong flavour we try to taste another flavour; it is in this
way that sick persons find everything they taste bitter, viz.
because, when they taste, their tongues are overflowing with
bitter moisture.

10   The species of flavour are, as in the case of colour, (a)
simple, i. e. the two contraries, the sweet and the bitter, (b)
secondary, viz. (i) on the side of the sweet, the succulent,
(ii) on the side of the bitter, the saline, (iii) between these
come the pungent, the harsh, the astringent, and the acid;
15 these pretty well exhaust the varieties of flavour. It follows
that what has the power of tasting is what is potentially of
that kind, and that what is tasteable is what has the power
of making it actually what it itself already is.

11   Whatever can be said of what is tangible, can be
said of touch, and vice versa; if touch is not a
single sense but a group of senses, there must be
several kinds of what is tangible. It is a problem whether
20 touch is a single sense or a group of senses. It is also a problem, what is the organ of touch; is it or is it not the flesh

---

[40] sc. 'and so, as we have seen, a being assimilated to'.

(including what in certain animals is homologous with flesh)? On the second view, flesh is 'the medium' of touch, the real organ being situated farther inward. The problem arises because the field of each sense is according to the accepted view determined as the range between a single pair of contraries, white and black for sight, acute and grave for hearing, bitter and sweet for taste; but in the field of what is 25 tangible we find several such pairs, hot cold, dry moist, hard soft, &c. This problem finds a partial solution, when it is recalled that in the case of the other senses more than one pair of contraries are to be met with, e. g. in sound not only acute and grave but loud and soft, smooth and rough, &c.; 30 there are similar contrasts in the field of colour. Nevertheless we are unable clearly to detect in the case of touch what the single subject is which underlies the contrasted qualities and corresponds to sound in the case of hearing.

To the question whether the organ of touch lies inward or not (i. e. whether we need look any farther than the flesh), no indication in favour of the second answer can be drawn from the fact that if the object comes into contact 423ᵃ with the flesh it is at once perceived. For even under present conditions if the experiment is made of making a web and stretching it tight over the flesh, as soon as this web is touched the sensation is reported in the same manner as before, yet it is clear that the organ is not in this membrane. If the membrane could be *grown* on to the flesh, the report would travel still quicker. The flesh plays in touch very 5 much the same part as would be played in the other senses by an air-envelope growing round our body; had we such an envelope attached to us we should have supposed that it was by a single organ that we perceived sounds, colours, and smells, and we should have taken sight, hearing, and smell to be a single sense. But as it is, because that through which the different movements are transmitted is not natu- 10 rally attached to our bodies, the difference of the various sense-organs is too plain to miss. But in the case of touch the obscurity remains.

There must be such a naturally attached 'medium' as flesh, for no living body could be constructed of air or water; it must be something solid. Consequently it must be composed of earth along with these, which is just what flesh
15 and its analogue in animals which have no true flesh tend to be. Hence of necessity the medium through which are transmitted the manifoldly contrasted tactual qualities must be a body naturally attached to the organism. That they are manifold is clear when we consider touching with the tongue; we apprehend at the tongue all tangible qualities as
20 well as flavour. Suppose all the rest of our flesh was, like the tongue, sensitive to flavour, we should have identified the sense of taste and the sense of touch; what saves us from this identification is the fact that touch and taste are not always found together in the same part of the body. The following problem might be raised. Let us assume that every body has depth, i. e. has three dimensions, and that if two bodies have a third body between them they cannot
25 be in contact with one another; let us remember that what is liquid is a body and must be or contain water, and that if two bodies touch one another under water, their touching surfaces cannot be dry, but must have water between, viz. the water which wets their bounding surfaces; from all this it follows that in water two bodies cannot be in contact with one another. The same holds of two bodies in air—air being
30 to bodies in air precisely what water is to bodies in water—but the facts are not so evident to our observation, because
423^b we live in air, just as animals that live in water would not notice that the things which touch one another in water have wet surfaces. The problem, then, is: does the perception of all objects of sense take place in the same way, or does it not, e. g. taste and touch requiring contact (as they are commonly thought to do), while all other senses perceive

over a distance? The distinction is unsound; we perceive 5
what is hard or soft, as well as the objects of hearing, sight,
and smell, through a 'medium', only that the latter are perceived over a *greater* distance than the former; that is why
the facts escape our notice. For we do perceive everything
through a medium; but in these cases the fact escapes us.
Yet, to repeat what we said before, if the medium for touch
were a membrane separating us from the object without our
observing its existence, we should be relatively to it in the 10
same condition as we are now to air or water in which we
are immersed; in their case we fancy we can touch objects,
nothing coming in between us and them. But there remains
this difference between what can be touched and what can
be seen or can sound; in the latter two cases we perceive
because the medium produces a certain effect upon us,
whereas in the perception of objects of touch we are affected 15
not *by* but *along with* the medium; it is as if a man were
struck through his shield, where the shock is not first given
to the shield and passed on to the man, but the concussion
of both is simultaneous.

In general, flesh and the tongue are related to the real
organs of touch and taste, as air and water are to those of
sight, hearing, and smell. Hence in neither the one case nor
the other can there be any perception of an object if it is 20
placed immediately upon the organ, e. g. if a white object
is placed on the surface of the eye. This again shows that
what has the power of perceiving the tangible is seated
inside. Only so would there be a complete analogy with all
the other senses. In their case if you place the object on the
organ it is not perceived, here if you place it on the flesh it
is perceived; therefore flesh is not the organ but the *medium* 25
of touch.

What can be touched are distinctive qualities of body
as body; by such differences I mean those which characterize the elements, viz. hot cold, dry moist, of which we have

spoken earlier in our treatise on the elements.[41] The organ
30 for the perception of these is that of touch—that part of the
body in which primarily the sense of touch resides. This is
that part which is potentially such as its object is actually:
for all sense-perception is a process of being so affected; so
that that which makes something such as it itself actually is
424ª makes the other such because the other is already potentially such. That is why when an object of touch is equally
hot and cold or hard and soft we cannot perceive; what we
perceive must have a degree of the sensible quality lying
beyond the neutral point. This implies that the sense itself
is a 'mean' between any two opposite qualities which determine the field of that sense. It is to this that it owes its
5 power of discerning the objects in that field. What is 'in the
middle' is fitted to discern; relatively to either extreme it
can put itself in the place of the other. As what is to perceive *both* white and black must, to begin with, be actually
neither but potentially either (and so with all the other
sense-organs), so the organ of touch must be neither hot nor
cold.

Further, as in a sense sight had[42] for its object both
10 what was visible and what was invisible (and there was a
parallel truth about all the other senses discussed),[43] so
touch has for its object both what is tangible and what is
intangible. Here by 'intangible' is meant (*a*) what like air
possesses some quality of tangible things in a very slight
degree and (*b*) what possesses it in an excessive degree, as
destructive things do.

We have now given an outline account of each of the
15 several senses.

[41] *De Gen. et Corr.* ii. 2, 3.

[42] 422ª 20 ff.

[43] 421ᵇ 3–6, 422ª 29.

12 The following results applying to any and every sense may now be formulated.

(A) By a 'sense' is meant what has the power of receiving into itself the sensible forms of things without the matter. This must be conceived of as taking place in the way in which a piece of wax takes on the impress of a signet-ring without the iron or gold; we say that what produces the impression is a signet of bronze or gold, but its particular metallic constitution makes no difference: in a similar way the sense is affected by what is coloured or flavoured or sounding, but it is indifferent what in each case the *substance* is; what alone matters is what *quality* it has, i. e. in what *ratio* its constituents are combined.

(B) By 'an organ of sense' is meant that in which ultimately such a power is seated.

The sense and its organ are the same in fact, but their essence is not the same. What perceives is, of course, a spatial magnitude, but we must not admit that either the having the power to perceive or the sense itself is a magnitude; what they are is a certain ratio or power *in* a magnitude. This enables us to explain why objects of sense which possess one of two opposite sensible qualities in a degree largely in excess of the other opposite destroy the organs of sense; if the movement set up by an object is too strong for the organ, the equipoise of contrary qualities in the organ, which just *is* its sensory power, is disturbed; it is precisely as concord and tone are destroyed by too violently twanging the strings of a lyre. This explains also why plants cannot perceive, in spite of their having a portion of soul in them and obviously being affected by tangible objects themselves; for undoubtedly their temperature can be lowered or raised. The explanation is that they have no mean of contrary qualities, and so no principle in them capable of taking on the forms of sensible objects without their matter; in the case of plants

the affection is an affection by form-and-matter together.
The problem might be raised: Can what cannot smell be
said to be affected by smells or what cannot see by colours,
and so on? It might be said that a smell is just what can be
smelt, and if it produces any effect it can only be so as to
make something smell it, and it might be argued that what
cannot smell cannot be affected by smells and further that
what can smell can be affected by it only in so far as it has
in it the power to smell (similarly with the proper objects
of all the other senses). Indeed that this *is so* is made quite
evident as follows. Light or darkness, sounds and smells
leave *bodies* quite unaffected; what does affect bodies is not
these but the bodies which are their vehicles, e. g. what
splits the trunk of a tree is not the sound of the thunder but
the air which accompanies thunder. Yes, but, it may be
objected, bodies are affected by what is tangible and by
flavours. If not, by what are things that are without soul
affected, i. e. altered in quality? Must we not, then, admit
that the objects of the other senses also may affect them? Is
not the true account this, that all bodies are capable of being
affected by smells and sounds, but that some on being acted
upon, having no boundaries of their own, disintegrate, as in
the instance of air, which does become odorous, showing
that *some* effect is produced on it by what is odorous? But
smelling is more than such an affection by what is odorous—*what* more? Is not the answer that, while the air owing
to the momentary duration of the action upon it of what is
odorous does itself become perceptible to the sense of smell,
smelling is an *observing* of the result produced?

BOOK III

1 That there is no sixth sense in addition to the five enumerated—sight, hearing, smell, taste, touch— 20 may be established by the following considerations:

If we have actually sensation of everything of which touch can give us sensation (for all the qualities of the tangible *qua* tangible are perceived by us through touch); and if 25 absence of a sense necessarily involves absence of a sense-organ; and if (1) all objects that we perceive by immediate contact with them are perceptible by touch, which sense we actually possess, and (2) all objects that we perceive through media, i. e. without immediate contact, are perceptible by or through the simple elements, e. g. air and water (and this 30 is so arranged that (*a*) if more than one kind of sensible object is perceivable through a single medium, the possessor of a sense-organ homogeneous with that medium has the power of perceiving both kinds of objects; for example, if the sense-organ is made of air, and air is a medium both for sound and for colour; and that (*b*) if more than one medium can transmit the same kind of sensible objects, as e. g. water as well as air can transmit colour, both being transparent, 425ᵃ then the possessor of either alone will be able to perceive the kind of objects transmissible through both); and if of the simple elements two only, air and water, go to form sense-organs (for the pupil is made of water, the organ of hearing is made of air, and the organ of smell of one or other of these two, while fire is found either in none or in all— warmth being an essential condition of all sensibility—and 5 earth either in none or, if anywhere, specially mingled with the components of the organ of touch; wherefore it would remain that there can be no sense-organ formed of anything

except water and air); and if these sense-organs are actually
found in certain animals;—then all the possible senses are
10 possessed by those animals that are not imperfect or mutilated (for even the mole is observed to have eyes beneath
its skin); so that, if there is no fifth element and no property
other than those which belong to the four elements of our
world, no sense can be wanting to such animals.

Further, there cannot be a special sense-organ for the
15 common sensibles either, i. e. the objects which we perceive
incidentally through this or that special sense, e. g. movement, rest, figure, magnitude, number, unity; for all these
we perceive by movement, e. g. magnitude by movement,
and therefore also figure (for figure is a species of magnitude), what is at rest by the absence of movement: number
is perceived by the negation of continuity, and by the special sensibles; for each sense perceives one class of sensible
20 objects. So that it is clearly impossible that there should be
a special sense for any one of the common sensibles, e. g.
movement; for, if that were so, our perception of it would
be exactly parallel to our present perception of what is sweet
by vision. *That* is so because we have a sense for each of the
two qualities, in virtue of which when they happen to meet
in one sensible object we are aware of both contemporane-
25 ously. If it were not like this our perception of the common
qualities would always be incidental, i. e. as is the perception of Cleon's son, where we perceive him not as Cleon's
son but as white, and the white thing which we really perceive happens to be Cleon's son.

But in the case of the common sensibles there is already
in us a general sensibility which enables us to perceive them
directly; there is therefore no special sense required for their
perception: if there were, our perception of them would
have been exactly like what has been above described.

30   The senses perceive each other's special objects incidentally; not because the percipient sense is this or that

special sense, but because all form a unity: this incidental
perception takes place whenever sense is directed at one and
the same moment to two disparate qualities in one and the   425^b
same object, e. g. to the bitterness and the yellowness of
bile; the assertion of the identity of both cannot be the act
of either of the senses; hence the illusion of sense, e. g. the
belief that if a thing is yellow it is bile.

It might be asked why we have more senses than one.
Is it to prevent a failure to apprehend the common sensi-   5
bles, e. g. movement, magnitude, and number, which go
along with the special sensibles? Had we no sense but sight,
and that sense no object but white, they would have tended
to escape our notice and everything would have merged for
us into an indistinguishable identity because of the concomitance of colour and magnitude. As it is, the fact that
the common sensibles are given in the objects of more than
one sense reveals their distinction from each and all of the
special sensibles.   10

2 Since it is through sense that we are aware that we
are seeing or hearing, it must be either by sight
that we are aware of seeing, or by some sense other
than sight. But the sense that gives us this new sensation
must perceive both sight and its object, viz. colour: so that
either (1) there will be two senses both percipient of the
same sensible object, or (2) the sense must be percipient of
itself. Further, even if the sense which perceives sight were   15
different from sight, we must either fall into an infinite
regress, or we must somewhere assume a sense which is
aware of itself. If so, we ought to do this in the first case.

This presents a difficulty: if to perceive by sight is just
to see, and what is seen is colour (or the coloured), then if
we are to see that which sees, that which sees originally
must be coloured. It is clear therefore that 'to perceive by
sight' has more than one meaning; for even when we are not   20

seeing, it is by sight that we discriminate darkness from light, though not in the same way as we distinguish one colour from another. Further, in a sense even that which sees *is* coloured; for in each case the sense-organ is capable of receiving the sensible object without its matter. That is why even when the sensible objects are gone the sensings 25 and imaginings continue to exist in the sense-organs.

The activity of the sensible object and that of the percipient sense is one and the same activity, and yet the distinction between their being remains. Take as illustration actual sound and actual hearing: a man may have hearing and yet not be hearing, and that which has a sound is not always sounding. But when that which can hear is 30 actively hearing and that which can sound is sounding, then the actual hearing and the actual sound are merged in one 426ᵃ (these one might call respectively hearkening and sounding).

If it is true that the movement, both the acting and the being acted upon, is to be found in that which is acted upon,[1] both the sound and the hearing so far as it is actual must be found in that which has the faculty of hearing; for it is in the passive factor that the actuality of the active or 5 motive factor is realized; that is why that which causes movement may be at rest. Now the actuality of that which can sound is just sound or sounding, and the actuality of that which can hear is hearing or hearkening; 'sound' and hearing' are both ambiguous. The same account applies to 10 the other senses and their objects. For as the-acting-and-being-acted-upon is to be found in the passive, not in the active factor, so also the actuality of the sensible object and that of the sensitive subject are both realized in the latter. But while in some cases each aspect of the total actuality has a distinct name, e. g. sounding and hearkening, in some one or other is nameless, e. g. the actuality of sight is called see-

[1] Cf. *Phys.* iii. 3.

ing, but the actuality of colour has no name: the actuality of
the faculty of taste is called tasting, but the actuality of 15
flavour has no name. Since the actualities of the sensible
object and of the sensitive faculty are *one* actuality in spite
of the difference between their modes of being, actual hearing and actual sounding appear and disappear from
existence at one and the same moment, and so actual savour
and actual tasting, &c., while as potentialities one of them 20
may exist without the other. The earlier students of nature
were mistaken in their view that without sight there was no
white or black, without taste no savour. This statement of
theirs is partly true, partly false: 'sense' and 'the sensible
object' are ambiguous terms, i. e. may denote either potentialities or actualities: the statement is true of the latter, false 25
of the former. This ambiguity they wholly failed to notice.

If voice always implies a concord, and if the voice and
the hearing of it are in one sense one and the same, and if
concord always implies a ratio, hearing as well as what is
heard must be a ratio. That is why the excess of either the 30
sharp or the flat destroys the hearing. (So also in the case
of savours excess destroys the sense of taste, and in the case 426^b
of colours excessive brightness or darkness destroys the
sight, and in the case of smell excess of strength whether in
the direction of sweetness or bitterness is destructive.) This
shows that the sense is a ratio.

That is also why the objects of sense are (1) pleasant
when the sensible extremes such as acid or sweet or salt
being pure and unmixed are brought into the proper ratio;[2] 5
then they are pleasant: and in general what is blended is
more pleasant than the sharp or the flat alone; or, to touch,
that which is capable of being either warmed or chilled: the
sense and the ratio are identical: while (2) in excess the sensible extremes are painful or destructive.

[2] i. e. that which is involved in the structure of the sense-organ.

Each sense then is relative to its particular group of sensible qualities: it is found in a sense-organ as such[3] and discriminates the differences which exist within that group; e. g. sight discriminates white and black, taste sweet and
10 bitter, and so in all cases. Since we also discriminate white from sweet, and indeed each sensible quality from every other, with what do we perceive that they are different? It must be by sense; for what is before us is sensible objects. (Hence it is also obvious that the flesh cannot be the ulti-
15 mate sense-organ: if it were, the discriminating power could not do its work without immediate contact with the object.)

Therefore (1) discrimination between white and sweet cannot be effected by two agencies which remain separate; both the qualities discriminated must be present to some-thing that is one and single. On any other supposition even if I perceived sweet and you perceived white, the difference
20 between them would be apparent. What says that two things are different must be one; for sweet is different from white. Therefore what asserts this difference must be self-identical, and as what asserts, so also what thinks or perceives. That it is not possible by means of two agencies which remain separate to discriminate two objects which are separate is therefore obvious; and that (2) it is not possible to do this in separate moments of time may be seen if we look at it as follows. For as what asserts the difference between the good and the bad is one and the same, so also
25 the time at which it asserts the one to be different and the other to be different is not accidental to the assertion (as it is for instance when I now assert a difference but do not assert that there is now a difference); it asserts thus—both now and that the objects are different now; the objects therefore must be present at one and the same moment.

---

[3] The qualification appears to mean that the sense-organ may in other respects have other qualities. Thus the tongue can touch as well as taste.

Both the discriminating power and the time of its exercise must be one and undivided.

But, it may be objected, it is impossible that what is self-identical should be moved at one and the same time with contrary movements in so far as it is undivided, and 30 in an undivided moment of time. For if what is sweet be the quality perceived, it moves the sense or thought in this determinate way, while what is bitter moves it in a contrary 427ᵃ way, and what is white in a different way. Is it the case then that what discriminates, though both numerically one and indivisible, is at the same time divided in its being? In one sense, it is what is divided that perceives two separate objects at once, but in another sense it does so *qua* undivided; for it is divisible in its being, but spatially and numerically undivided.

But is not this impossible? For while it is true that what 5 is self-identical and undivided may be both contraries at once *potentially*, it cannot be self-identical in its being—it must lose its unity by being put into activity. It is not possible to be at once white and black, and therefore it must also be impossible for a thing to be affected at one and the same moment by the forms of both, assuming it to be the case that sensation and thinking are properly so described.[4]

The answer is that just as what is called a 'point' is, as 10 being at once one and two, properly said to be divisible, so here, that which discriminates is *qua* undivided one, and active in a single moment of time, while so far forth as it is divisible it twice over uses the same dot at one and the same time. So far forth then as it takes the limit as two, it discriminates two separate objects with what in a sense is divided: while so far as it takes it as one, it does so with what is one and occupies in its activity a single moment of time.

[4] i. e. as the being affected by the forms of sensible qualities.

About the principle in virtue of which we say that ani-
15 mals are percipient, let this discussion suffice.

3   There are two distinctive peculiarities by reference
to which we characterize the soul—(l) local movement
and (2) thinking, discriminating, and perceiving.
Thinking, both speculative and practical, is regarded as akin to
20 a form of perceiving; for in the one as well as the other the
soul discriminates and is cognizant of something which is.
Indeed the ancients go so far as to identify thinking and
perceiving; e. g. Empedocles says 'For 'tis in respect of what
is present that man's wit is increased', and again 'whence it
befalls them from time to time to think diverse thoughts',
25 and Homer's phrase[5] 'For suchlike is man's mind' means
the same. They all look upon thinking as a bodily process
like perceiving, and hold that like is *known* as well as *perceived* by like, as I explained at the beginning of our
discussion.[6] Yet they ought at the same time to have
427ᵇ accounted for error also; for it is more intimately connected
with animal existence and the soul continues longer in the
state of error than in that of truth. They cannot escape the
dilemma: either (l) whatever seems is true (and there are
some who accept this) or (2) error is contact with the unlike:
for that is the opposite of the knowing of like by like.
5   But it is a received principle that error as well as knowledge in respect to contraries is one and the same.

That perceiving and practical thinking are not identical
is therefore obvious; for the former is universal in the animal world, the latter is found in only a small division of it.
Further, speculative thinking is also distinct from perceiving—I mean that in which we find rightness and
10 wrongness—rightness in prudence, knowledge, true opin-

[5] *Od.* xviii. 136.

[6] 404ᵇ 8–18.

ion, wrongness in their opposites; for perception of the special objects of sense is always free from error, and is found
in all animals, while it is possible to think falsely as well as
truly, and thought is found only where there is discourse of
reason as well as sensibility. For imagination is different
from either perceiving or discursive thinking, though it is 15
not found without sensation, or judgement without it. That
this activity is not the same kind of thinking as judgement
is obvious. For imagining lies within our own power whenever we wish (e. g. we can call up a picture, as in the
practice of mnemonics by the use of mental images), but in 20
forming opinions we are not free: we cannot escape the
alternative of falsehood or truth. Further, when we think
something to be fearful or threatening, emotion is immediately produced, and so too with what is encouraging; but
when we merely imagine we remain as unaffected as persons who are looking at a painting of some dreadful or
encouraging scene. Again within the field of judgement
itself we find varieties—knowledge, opinion, prudence, and
their opposites; of the differences between these I must
speak elsewhere.[7]

Thinking is different from perceiving and is held to be
in part imagination, in part judgement: we must therefore
first mark off the sphere of imagination and then speak of
judgement. If then imagination is that in virtue of which an 428ª
image arises for us, excluding metaphorical uses of the term,
is it a single faculty or disposition relative to images, in
virtue of which we discriminate and are either in error or
not? The faculties in virtue of which we do this are sense,
opinion, science, intelligence.

That imagination is not sense is clear from the following considerations: (1) Sense is either a faculty or an 5
activity, e. g. sight or seeing: imagination takes place in the

---

[7] The reference is perhaps to E.N. 1139ᵇ 15 ff.

absence of both, as e. g. in dreams. (2) Again, sense is always present, imagination not. If actual imagination and actual sensation were the same, imagination would be found in all the brutes: this is held not to be the case; e. g. it is
10 not found in ants or bees or grubs. (3) Again, sensations are always true, imaginations are for the most part false. (4) Once more, even in ordinary speech, we do not, when sense functions precisely with regard to its object, say that we imagine it to be a man, but rather when there is some fail-
15 ure of accuracy in its exercise. And (5), as we were saying before, visions appear to us even when our eyes are shut. Neither is imagination any of the things that are never in error: e. g. knowledge or intelligence; for imagination may be false.

It remains therefore to see if it is opinion, for opinion may be either true or false.

20 But opinion involves belief (for without belief in what we opine we cannot have an opinion), and in the brutes though we often find imagination we never find belief. Further, every opinion is accompanied by belief, belief by conviction, and conviction by discourse of reason: while there are some of the brutes in which we find imagination, without discourse of reason. It is clear then that imagina-
25 tion cannot, again, be (1) opinion *plus* sensation, or (2) opinion mediated by sensation, or (3) a blend of opinion and sensation;[8] this is impossible both for these reasons and because the content of the supposed opinion cannot be dif-ferent from that of the sensation (I mean that imagination
30 must be the blending of the perception of white with the opinion that it is white: it could scarcely be a blend of the opinion that it is good with the perception that it is white):
428b to imagine is therefore (on this view) identical with the thinking of exactly the same as what one in the strictest

[8] For these three views Cf. Pl. *Tim.* 52 A, *Soph.* A, B, *Phil.* 39 B.

sense perceives. But what we imagine is sometimes false though our contemporaneous judgement about it is true; e. g. we imagine the sun to be a foot in diameter though we are convinced that it is larger than the inhabited part of the earth, and the following dilemma presents itself. Either (a) while the fact has not changed and the observer has neither 5 forgotten nor lost belief in the true opinion which he had, that opinion has disappeared, or (b) if he retains it then his opinion is at once true and false. A true opinion, however, becomes false only when the fact alters without being noticed.

Imagination is therefore neither any one of the states enumerated, nor compounded out of them.

But since when one thing has been set in motion another thing may be moved by it, and imagination is held to be a movement and to be impossible without sensation, i. e. to occur in beings that are percipient and to have for its content what can be perceived, and since movement may be produced by actual sensation and that movement is necessarily similar in character to the sensation itself, this movement must be (1) necessarily (a) incapable of existing 15 apart from sensation, (b) incapable of existing except when we perceive, (2) such that in virtue of its possession that in which it is found may present various phenomena both active and passive, and (3) such that it may be either true or false.

The reason of the last characteristic is as follows. Perception (1) of the special objects of sense is never in error or admits the least possible amount of falsehood. (2) That of the concomitance of the objects concomitant with the sensible qualities comes next: in this case certainly we may be 20 deceived; for while the perception that there is white before us cannot be false, the perception that what is white is this or that may be false. (3) Third comes the perception of the universal attributes which accompany the concomitant

objects to which the special sensibles attach (I mean e. g. of
movement and magnitude); it is in respect of these that the
greatest amount of sense-illusion is possible.

The motion which is due to the activity of sense in
25 these three modes of its exercise will differ from the activity of sense; (1) the first kind of derived motion is free from
error while the sensation is present; (2) and (3) the others
may be erroneous whether it is present or absent, especially
30 when the object of perception is far off. If then imagination presents no other features than those enumerated and
is what we have described, then imagination must be a
429ᵃ movement resulting from an actual exercise of a power of
sense.

As sight is the most highly developed sense, the name
phantasia (imagination) has been formed from *phaos* (light)
because it is not possible to see without light.

And because imaginations remain in the organs of sense
and resemble sensations, animals in their actions are largely
5 guided by them, some (i. e. the brutes) because of the non-
existence in them of mind, others (i. e. men) because of the
temporary eclipse in them of mind by feeling or disease or
sleep.

About imagination, what it is and why it exists, let so
much suffice.

4 Turning now to the part of the soul with which the
10 soul knows and thinks (whether this is separable
from the others in definition only, or spatially as
well) we have to inquire (1) what differentiates this part,
and (2) how thinking can take place.

If thinking is like perceiving, it must be either a process in which the soul is acted upon by what is capable of
being thought, or a process different from but analogous to
that. The thinking part of the soul must therefore be, while
15 impassible, capable of receiving the form of an object; that

is, must be potentially identical in character with its object without being the object. Mind must be related to what is thinkable, as sense is to what is sensible.

Therefore, since everything is a possible object of thought, mind in order, as Anaxagoras says, to dominate, that is, to know, must be pure from all admixture; for the 20 co-presence of what is alien to its nature is a hindrance and a block: it follows that it too, like the sensitive part, can have no nature of its own, other than that of having a certain capacity. Thus that in the soul which is called mind (by mind I mean that whereby the soul thinks and judges) is, before it thinks, not actually any real thing. For this reason it cannot reasonably be regarded as blended with the body: 25 if so, it would acquire some quality, e. g. warmth or cold, or even have an organ like the sensitive faculty: as it is, it has none. It was a good idea to call the soul 'the place of forms', though (1) this description holds only of the intellective soul, and (2) even this is the forms only potentially, not actually.

Observation of the sense-organs and their employment reveals a distinction between the impassibility of the 30 sensitive and that of the intellective faculty. After strong stimulation of a sense we are less able to exercise it than 429b before, as e. g. in the case of a loud sound we cannot hear easily immediately after, or in the case of a bright colour or a powerful odour we cannot see or smell, but in the case of mind, thought about an object that is highly intelligible renders it more and not less able afterwards to think objects that are less intelligible: the reason is that while the faculty of sensation is dependent upon the body, mind is separable from it.

Once the mind has become each set of its possible 5 objects, as a man of science has, when this phrase is used of one who is actually a man of science (this happens when he is now able to exercise the power on his own initiative),

its condition is still one of potentiality, but in a different
sense from the potentiality which preceded the acquisition
of knowledge by learning or discovery: the mind too is then
able to think *itself*.

10   Since we can distinguish between a spatial magnitude
and what it is to be such, and between water and what it is
to be water, and so in many other cases (though not in all;
for in certain cases the thing and its form are identical),
flesh and what it is to be flesh are discriminated either by
different faculties, or by the same faculty in two different
states: for flesh necessarily involves matter and is like what
is snub-nosed, a *this* in a *this*.[9] Now it is by means of the
sensitive faculty that we discriminate the hot and the cold,
15 i. e. the factors which combined in a certain ratio constitute
flesh: the essential character of flesh is apprehended by
something different either wholly separate from the sensitive
faculty or related to it as a bent line to the same line when
it has been straightened out.

Again in the case of abstract objects what is straight is
analogous to what is snub-nosed; for it necessarily implies
a continuum as its matter: its constitutive essence is different, if we may distinguish between straightness and what is
20 straight: let us take it to be two-ness. It must be apprehended, therefore, by a different power or by the same
power in a different state. To sum up, in so far as the realities it knows are capable of being separated from their
matter, so it is also with the powers of mind.

The problem might be suggested: if thinking is a passive affection, then if mind is simple and impassible and has
nothing in common with anything else, as Anaxagoras says,
how can it come to think at all? For interaction between two
factors is held to require a precedent community of nature
between the factors. Again it might be asked, is mind a pos-

[9] i. e. a particular form in a particular matter.

sible object of thought to itself? For if mind is thinkable *per se* and what is thinkable is in kind one and the same, then either (*a*) mind will belong to everything, or (*b*) mind will contain some element common to it with all other realities which makes them all thinkable.

(1) Have not we already disposed of the difficulty about interaction involving a common element, when we said[10] that mind is in a sense potentially whatever is thinkable, 30 though actually it is nothing until it has thought? What it thinks must be in it just as characters may be said to be on a writing-tablet on which as yet nothing actually stands 430ᵃ written: this is exactly what happens with mind.

(2) Mind is itself thinkable in exactly the same way as its objects are. For (*a*) in the case of objects which involve no matter, what thinks and what is thought are identical; for speculative knowledge and its object are identical. (Why mind is not always thinking we must consider later.)[11] (*b*) In 5 the case of those which contain matter each of the objects of thought is only potentially present. It follows that while *they* will not have mind in them (for mind is a potentiality of them only in so far as they are capable of being disengaged from matter) mind may yet be thinkable.

5 Since in every class of things, as in nature as a whole, we find two factors involved, (1) a matter 10 which is potentially all the particulars included in the class, (2) a cause which is productive in the sense that it makes them all (the latter standing to the former, as e. g. an art to its material), these distinct elements must likewise be found within the soul.

And in fact mind as we have described it[12] is what it is

10 ᵃ15–24.

11 Ch. 5.

12 In ch. 4.

15 by virtue of becoming all things, while there is another
which is what it is by virtue of making all things: this is a
sort of positive state like light; for in a sense light makes
potential colours into actual colours.

Mind in this sense of it is separable, impassible,
unmixed, since it is in its essential nature activity (for
always the active is superior to the passive factor, the originating force to the matter which it forms).

20 Actual knowledge is identical with its object: in the
individual, potential knowledge is in time prior to actual
knowledge, but in the universe as a whole it is not prior
even in time. Mind is not at one time knowing and at
another not. When mind is set free from its present conditions it appears as just what it is and nothing more: this
alone is immortal and eternal (we do not, however, remember its former activity because, while mind in this sense is
25 impassible, mind as passive is destructible), and without it
nothing thinks.

6 The thinking then of the simple objects of thought
is found in those cases where falsehood is impossible: where the alternative of true or false applies,
there we always find a putting together of objects of thought
in a quasi-unity. As Empedocles said that 'where heads of
30 many a creature sprouted without necks' they afterwards by
Love's power were combined, so here too objects of thought
which were given separate are combined, e. g. 'incommen-
surate' and 'diagonal': if the combination be of objects past
or future the combination of thought includes in its content
430ᵇ the date. For falsehood always involves a synthesis; for even
if you assert that what is white is not white you have
included not-white in a synthesis. It is possible also to call
all these cases division as well as combination. However that
may be, there is not only the true or false assertion that
Cleon is white but also the true or false assertion that he

was or *will be* white. In each and every case that which unifies is mind.

Since the word 'simple' has two senses, i. e. may mean
either (*a*) 'not capable of being divided' or (*b*) 'not actually
divided', there is nothing to prevent mind from knowing
what is undivided, e. g. when it apprehends a length (which
is actually undivided) and that in an undivided time; for the
time is divided or undivided in the same manner as the line.
It is not possible, then, to tell what part of the line it was 10
apprehending in each half of the time: the object has no
actual parts until it has been divided: if in thought you
think each half separately, then by the same act you divide
the time also, the half-lines becoming as it were new wholes
of length. But if you think it as a whole consisting of these
two possible parts, then also you think it in a time which
corresponds to both parts together. (But what is not quantitatively but qualitatively simple is thought in a simple 15
time and by a simple act of the soul.)

But that which mind thinks and the time in which it
thinks are in this case divisible only incidentally and not as
such. For in them too there is something indivisible
(though, it may be, not isolable) which gives unity to the
time and the whole of length; and this is found equally in
every continuum whether temporal or spatial.

Points and similar instances of things that divide, themselves being indivisible, are realized in consciousness in the 20
same manner as privations.

A similar account may be given of all other cases, e. g.
how evil or black is cognized; they are cognized, in a sense,
by means of their contraries. That which cognizes must
have an element of potentiality in its being, and one of the
contraries must be in it.[13] But if there is anything that has

---

[13] i. e. it must be characterized actually by one and potentially by the other
of the contraries.

25 no contrary, then it knows itself and is actually and possesses independent existence.

Assertion is the saying of something concerning something, e. g. affirmation, and is in every case either true or false: this is not always the case with mind: the thinking of the definition in the sense of the constitutive essence is never in error nor is it the assertion of something concerning something, but, just as while the seeing of the special object of sight can never be in error, the belief that the white object seen is a man may be mistaken, so too in the
30 case of objects which are without matter.

7   Actual knowledge is identical with its object:
431ᵃ   potential knowledge in the individual is in time prior to actual knowledge but in the universe it has no priority even in time; for all things that come into being arise from what actually is. In the case of sense clearly the
5 sensitive faculty already was potentially what the object makes it to be actually; the faculty is not affected or altered. This must therefore be a different kind from movement; for movement is, as we saw,[14] an activity of what is imperfect, activity in the unqualified sense, i. e. that of what has been perfected, is different from movement.

To perceive then is like bare asserting or knowing; but when the object is pleasant or painful, the soul makes a quasi-affirmation or negation, and pursues or avoids the
10 object. To feel pleasure or pain is to act with the sensitive mean towards what is good or bad as such. Both avoidance and appetite when actual are identical with this: the faculty of appetite and avoidance are not different, either from one another or from the faculty of sense-perception; but their being *is* different.

To the thinking soul images serve as if they were con-

[14] Cf. 417ᵇ 2–16.

tents of perception (and when it asserts or denies them to be 15
good or bad it avoids or pursues them). That is why the
soul never thinks without an image. The process is like that
in which the air modifies the pupil in this or that way and
the pupil transmits the modification to some third thing
(and similarly in hearing), while the ultimate point of arrival
is one, a single mean, with different manners of being.

With what part of itself the soul discriminates sweet 20
from hot[15] I have explained before[16] and must now describe
again as follows: That with which it does so is a sort of
unity, but in the way just mentioned,[17] i. e. as a connecting
term. And the two faculties it connects,[18] being one by analogy and numerically, are each to each as the qualities
discerned are to one another (for what difference does it
make whether we raise the problem of discrimination
between disparates or between contraries, e. g. white and 25
black?). Let then C be to D as A is to B:[19] it follows *alternando* that $C:A::D:B$. If then C and D belong to one
subject, the case will be the same with them as with A and
B; A and B form a single identity with different modes of 431[b]
being; so too will the former pair. The same reasoning holds
if A be sweet and B white.

The faculty of thinking then thinks the forms in the
images, and as in the former case[20] what is to be pursued or
avoided is marked out for it, so where there is no sensation

[15] i. e. the sweetness and the heat in a sweet-hot object.

[16] 426[b] 12–427[a] 14.

[17] i. e. as one thing with two aspects; cf. 1.19.

[18] i. e. the faculty by which we discern sweet and that by which we discern
hot.

[19] i. e. let the faculty that discerns sweet be to that which discerns hot as
sweet is to hot.

[20] i. e. that of sense-data.

5 and it is engaged upon the images it is moved to pursuit or
avoidance. E. g. perceiving by sense that the beacon is fire,
it recognizes in virtue of the general faculty of sense that it
signifies an enemy, because it sees it moving; but sometimes
by means of the images or thoughts which are within the
soul, just as if it were seeing, it calculates and deliberates
what is to come by reference to what is present; and when it
makes a pronouncement, as in the case of sensation it pro-
nounces the object to be pleasant or painful, in this case it
avoids or pursues; and so generally in cases of action.

That too which involves no action, i. e. that which is
10 true or false, is in the same province with what is good or
bad: yet they differ in this, that the one set imply and the
other do not a reference to a particular person.

The so-called abstract objects the mind thinks just as, if
one had thought of the snub-nosed not as snub-nosed but
as hollow, one would have thought of an actuality without
15 the flesh in which it is embodied: it is thus that the mind
when it is thinking the objects of Mathematics thinks as
separate, elements which do not exist separate. In every case
the mind which is actively thinking is the objects which it
thinks. Whether it is possible for it while not existing separate from spatial conditions to think anything that is
separate, or not, we must consider later.[21]

8   Let us now summarize our results about soul, and
20   repeat that the soul is in a way all existing things;
     for existing things are either sensible or thinkable,
and knowledge is in a way what is knowable, and sensation
is in a way what is sensible: in *what* way we must inquire.

Knowledge and sensation are divided to correspond with
the realities, potential knowledge and sensation answering to
25 potentialities, actual knowledge and sensation to actualities.

---

[21] This promise does not seem to have been fulfilled.

Within the soul the faculties of knowledge and sensation are *potentially* these objects, the one what is knowable, the other what is sensible. They must be either the things themselves or their forms. The former alternative is of course impossible: it is not the stone which is present in the soul but its form.

It follows that the soul is analogous to the hand; for as the hand is a tool of tools,[22] so the mind is the form of 432ᵃ forms and sense the form of sensible things.

Since according to common agreement there is nothing outside and separate in existence from sensible spatial magnitudes, the objects of thought are in the sensible forms, viz. both the abstract objects and all the states and affections of 5 sensible things. Hence (1) no one can learn or understand anything in the absence of sense, and (2) when the mind is actively aware of anything it is necessarily aware of it along with an image; for images are like sensuous contents except in that they contain no matter.

Imagination is different from assertion and denial; for what is true or false involves a synthesis of concepts. In what will the primary concepts differ from images? Must 10 we not say that neither these nor even our other concepts are images, though they necessarily involve them?

9 The soul of animals is characterized by two facul- 15 ties, (*a*) the faculty of discrimination which is the work of thought and sense, and (*b*) the faculty of originating local movement. Sense and mind we have now sufficiently examined. Let us next consider what it is in the soul which originates movement. Is it a single part of the soul 20 separate either spatially or in definition? Or is it the soul as a whole? If it is a part, is that part different from those usually distinguished or already mentioned by us, or is it

---

[22] i. e. a tool for using tools.

one of them? The problem at once presents itself, in what
sense we are to speak of parts of the soul, or how many
25 we should distinguish. For in a sense there is an infinity of
parts: it is not enough to distinguish, with some thinkers,[23]
the calculative, the passionate, and the desiderative, or
with others[24] the rational and the irrational; for if we take
the dividing lines followed by these thinkers we shall find
parts far more distinctly separated from one another than
these, namely those we have just mentioned: (1) the nutri-
30 tive, which belongs both to plants and to all animals, and
(2) the sensitive, which cannot easily be classed as either
irrational or rational; further (3) the imaginative, which is,
432[b] in its being, different from all, while it is very hard to say
with which of the others it is the same or not the same,
supposing we determine to posit *separate* parts in the soul;
and lastly (4) the appetitive, which would seem to be distinct both in definition and in power from all hitherto
enumerated.

5   It is absurd to break up the last-mentioned faculty: as
these thinkers do, for wish is found in the calculative part
and desire and passion in the irrational;[25] and if the soul is
tripartite appetite will be found in all three parts. Turning
our attention to the present object of discussion, let us ask
what that is which originates local movement of the animal.

The movement of growth and decay, being found in all
10 living things, must be attributed to the faculty of reproduction and nutrition, which is common to all: inspiration and
expiration, sleep and waking, we must consider later:[26] these
too present much difficulty: at present we must consider

[23] Pl. *Rep.* 435–41.

[24] A popular view, Cf. *E. N.* 1102ª 26–28.

[25] All three being forms of appetite.

[26] Cf. *De Respiratione, De Somno.*

local movement, asking what it is that originates forward movement in the animal.

That it is not the nutritive faculty is obvious; for this kind of movement is always for an end and is accompanied 15 either by imagination or by appetite; for no animal moves except by compulsion unless it has an impulse towards or away from an object. Further, if it were the nutritive faculty, even plants would have been capable of originating such movement and would have possessed the organs necessary to carry it out. Similarly it cannot be the sensitive faculty either; for there are many animals which have sensibility but remain fast and immovable throughout their lives. 20

If then Nature never makes anything without a purpose and never leaves out what is necessary (except in the case of mutilated or imperfect growths; and that here we have neither mutilation nor imperfection may be argued from the facts that such animals (a) can reproduce their species and (b) rise to completeness of nature and decay to an end), it follows that, had they been capable of originating forward 25 movement, they would have possessed the organs necessary for that purpose. Further, neither can the calculative faculty or what is called 'mind' be the cause of such movement; for mind as speculative never thinks what is practicable, it never says anything about an object to be avoided or pursued, while this movement is always in something which is avoiding or pursuing an object. No, not even when it is aware of such an object does it at once enjoin pursuit or avoidance of it; e. g. the mind often thinks of something terrifying or pleasant without enjoying the emotion of fear. It is the heart that is moved (or in the case of a pleasant object some other part). Further, even when the mind does command and 433a thought bids us pursue or avoid something, sometimes no movement is produced; we act in accordance with desire, as in the case of moral weakness. And, generally, we observe

that the possessor of medical knowledge is not necessarily
healing, which shows that something else is required to pro-
5 duce action in accordance with knowledge; the knowledge
alone is not the cause. Lastly, appetite too is incompetent to
account fully for movement; for those who successfully
resist temptation have appetite and desire and yet follow
mind and refuse to enact that for which they have appetite.

10   These two at all events appear to be sources of
movement: appetite and mind (if one may ven-
ture to regard imagination as a kind of thinking;
for many men follow their imaginations contrary to knowledge, and in all animals other than man there is no thinking
or calculation but only imagination).

Both of these then are capable of originating local movement, mind and appetite: (1) mind, that is, which calculates
15 means to an end, i. e. mind practical (it differs from mind
speculative in the character of its end); while (2) appetite is
in every form of it relative to an end: for that which is the
object of appetite is the stimulant of mind practical; and that
which is last in the process of thinking is the beginning of
the action. It follows that there is a justification for regarding
these two as the sources of movement, i. e. appetite and
practical thought; for the object of appetite starts a move-
20 ment and as a result of that thought gives rise to movement,
the object of appetite being to it a source of stimulation. So
too when imagination originates movement, it necessarily
involves appetite.

That which moves therefore is a single faculty and the
faculty of appetite; for if there had been two sources of
movement—mind and appetite—they would have produced
movement in virtue of some common character. As it is,
mind is never found producing movement without appetite
(for wish is a form of appetite; and when movement is produced according to calculation it is also according to wish),

but appetite can originate movement contrary to calculation, 25
for desire is a form of appetite. Now mind is always right,
but appetite and imagination may be either right or wrong.
That is why, though in any case it is the object of appetite
which originates movement, this object may be either the
real or the apparent good. To produce movement the object
must be more than this: it must be good that can be brought
into being by action; and only what can be otherwise than as 30
it is can thus be brought into being. That then such a power
in the soul as has been described, i. e. that called appetite, 433b
originates movement is clear. Those who distinguish parts in
the soul, if they distinguish and divide in accordance with
differences of power, find themselves with a very large
number of parts, a nutritive, a sensitive, an intellective, a
deliberative, and now an appetitive part; for these are more
different from one another than the faculties of desire and
passion.

Since appetites run counter to one another, which happens when a principle of reason and a desire are contrary
and is possible only in beings with a sense of time (for while
mind bids us hold back because of what is future, desire is
influenced by what is just at hand: a pleasant object which
is just at hand presents itself as both pleasant and good,
without condition in either case, because of want of foresight into what is farther away in time), it follows that while 10
that which originates movement must be specifically one,
viz. the faculty of appetite as such (or rather farthest back of
all the object of that faculty; for it is it that itself remaining
unmoved originates the movement by being apprehended
in thought or imagination), the things that originate movement are numerically many.

All movement involves three factors, (1) that which
originates the movement, (2) that by means of which it originates it, and (3) that which is moved. The expression 'that
which originates the movement' is ambiguous: it may mean

either (a) something which itself is unmoved or (b) that
15 which at once moves and is moved. Here that which moves
without itself being moved is the realizable good, that which
at once moves and is moved is the faculty of appetite (for
that which is influenced by appetite so far as it is actually so
influenced is set in movement, and appetite in the sense of
actual appetite *is* a kind of movement), while that which is
in motion is the animal. The instrument which appetite
employs to produce movement is no longer psychical but
20 bodily: hence the examination of it falls within the province
of the functions common to body and soul.[27] To state the
matter summarily at present, that which is the instrument
in the production of movement is to be found where a
beginning and an end coincide as e. g. in a ball and socket
joint; for there the convex and the concave sides are respectively an end and a beginning (that is why while the one
remains at rest, the other is moved): they are separate in
definition but not separable spatially. For everything is
25 moved by pushing and pulling. Hence just as in the case of
a wheel, so here there must be a point which remains at
rest, and from that point the movement must originate.

To sum up, then, and repeat what I have said, inasmuch
as an animal is capable of appetite it is capable of self-movement; it is not capable of appetite without possessing
imagination; and all imagination is either (1) calculative or (2)
30 sensitive. In the latter all animals, and not only man, partake.

11 We must consider also in the case of imperfect
animals, *sc.* those which have no sense but touch,
what it is that in them originates movement. Can
434ᵃ they have imagination or not? or desire? Clearly they have
feelings of pleasure and pain, and if they have these they
must have desire. But how can they have imagination? Must

---

[27] Cf. *De Motu An.* 702ᵃ 21–703ᵃ 22.

not we say that, as their movements are indefinite, they have imagination and desire, but indefinitely?

Sensitive imagination, as we have said,[28] is found in all animals, deliberative imagination only in those that are cal-   5
culative: for whether this or that shall be enacted is already a task requiring calculation; and there must be a single standard to measure by, for that is pursued which is greater. It follows that what acts in this way must be able to make a unity out of several images.

This is the reason why imagination is held not to   10
involve opinion, in that it does not involve opinion based on inference, though opinion involves imagination. Hence appetite contains no deliberative element. Sometimes it overpowers wish and sets it in movement: at times wish acts thus upon appetite, like one sphere imparting its movement to another, or appetite acts thus upon appetite, i. e. in the condition of moral weakness (though by *nature* the higher faculty is always more authoritative and gives rise to movement). Thus *three* modes of movement are possible.   15

The faculty of knowing is never moved but remains at rest. Since the one premiss or judgement is universal and the other deals with the particular (for the first tells us that such and such a kind of man should do such and such a kind of act, and the second that *this* is an act of the kind meant, and I a person of the type intended), it is the latter   20
opinion that really originates movement, not the universal; or rather it is both, but the one does so while it remains in a state more like rest, while the other partakes in movement.

12 The nutritive soul then must be possessed by everything that is alive, and every such thing is endowed with soul from its birth to its death. For what has been born must grow, reach maturity, and decay—   25

[28] 433[b] 29.

all of which are impossible without nutrition. Therefore the nutritive faculty must be found in everything that grows and decays.

But sensation need not be found in all things that live. For it is impossible for touch to belong either (1) to those whose body is uncompounded or (2) to those which are incapable of taking in the forms without their matter.

30   But animals must be endowed with sensation, since Nature does nothing in vain. For all things that exist by Nature are means to an end, or will be concomitants of means to an end. Every body capable of forward movement

434b would, if unendowed with sensation, perish and fail to reach its end, which is the aim of Nature; for how could it obtain nutriment? Stationary living things, it is true, have as their nutriment that from which they have arisen; but it is not possible that a body which is not stationary but produced by generation should have a soul and a discerning mind without also having sensation. (Nor yet even if it were not produced by generation. Why should it not have sensation?

5 Because it were better so either for the body or for the soul? But clearly it would not be better for either: the absence of sensation will not enable the one to think better or the other to exist better.) Therefore no body which is not stationary has soul without sensation.

But if a body *has* sensation, it must be either simple or compound. And simple it cannot be; for then it could not

10 have touch, which is indispensable. This is clear from what follows. An animal is a body with soul in it: every body is tangible, i. e. perceptible by touch; hence necessarily, if an animal is to survive, its body must have tactual sensation.

15   All the other senses, e. g. smell, sight, hearing, apprehend through media; but where there is immediate contact the animal, if it has no sensation, will be unable to avoid some things and take others, and so will find it impossible to survive. That is why taste also is a sort of touch; it is rel-

ative to nutriment, which is just tangible body; whereas sound, colour, and odour are innutritious, and further neither grow nor decay. Hence it is that taste also must be a 20 sort of touch, because it is the sense for what is tangible and nutritious.

Both these senses, then, are indispensable to the animal, and it is clear that without touch it is impossible for an animal to be. All the other senses subserve well-being and for that very reason belong not to any and every kind of animal, but only to some, e. g. those capable of forward movement 25 must have them; for, if they are to survive, they must perceive not only by immediate contact but also at a distance from the object. This will be possible if they can perceive through a medium, the medium being affected and moved by the perceptible object, and the animal by the medium. Just as that which produces local movement causes a change extending to a certain point, and that which gave an impulse 30 causes another to produce a new impulse so that the movement traverses a medium—the first mover impelling without being impelled, the last moved being impelled without impelling, while the medium (or media, for there are many) is both—so is it also in the case of alteration, except that the 435ª agent produces it without the patient's changing its place. Thus if an object is dipped into wax, the movement goes on until submersion has taken place, and in stone it goes no distance at all, while in water the disturbance goes far beyond the object dipped: in air the disturbance is propagated farthest of all, the air acting and being acted upon, so long as it maintains an unbroken unity. That is why in the 5 case of reflection it is better, instead of saying that the sight issues from the eye and is reflected, to say that the air, so long as it remains one, is affected by the shape and colour. On a smooth surface the air possesses unity; hence it is that it in turn sets the sight in motion, just as if the impression 10 on the wax were transmitted as far as the wax extends.

13

It is clear that the body of an animal cannot be simple, i. e. consist of one element such as fire or air. For without touch it is impossible to have any other sense; for every body that has soul in it must, as we have said,[29] be capable of touch. All the other

15 elements with the exception of earth can constitute organs of sense, but all of them bring about perception only through something else, viz. through the media. Touch takes place by direct contact with its objects, whence also its name. All the other organs of sense, no doubt, perceive by contact, only the contact is mediate: touch alone perceives by immediate contact. Consequently no animal body can consist of these other elements.

20 Nor can it consist solely of earth. For touch is as it were a mean between all tangible qualities, and its organ is capable of receiving not only all the specific qualities which characterize earth, but also the hot and the cold and all

25 other tangible qualities whatsoever. That is why we have no

435b sensation by means of bones, hair, &c., because they consist of earth. So too plants, because they consist of earth, have no sensation. Without touch there can be no other sense, and the organ of touch cannot consist of earth or of any other single element.

It is evident, therefore, that the loss of this one sense

5 alone must bring about the death of an animal. For as on the one hand nothing which is not an animal can have this sense, so on the other it is the only one which is indispensably necessary to what is an animal. This explains, further, the following difference between the other senses and touch. In the case of all the others excess of intensity in the qualities which they apprehend, i. e. excess of intensity in colour, sound, and smell, destroys not the animal but only the

10 organs of the sense (except incidentally, as when the sound

29 434b 10–24.

is accompanied by an impact or shock, or where through the objects of sight or of smell certain other things are set in motion, which destroy by contact); flavour also destroys only in so far as it is at the same time tangible. But excess of intensity in tangible qualities, e. g. heat, cold, or hardness, destroys the animal itself. As in the case of every 15 sensible quality excess destroys the organ, so here what is tangible destroys touch, which is the essential mark of life; for it has been shown that without touch it is impossible for an animal to be. That is why excess in intensity of tangible qualities destroys not merely the organ, but the animal itself, because this is the only sense which it must have.

All the other senses are necessary to animals, as we have said,[30] not for their being, but for their well-being. Such, e. g., is sight, which, since it lives in air or water, or 20 generally in what is pellucid, it must have in order to see, and taste because of what is pleasant or painful to it, in order that it may perceive these qualities in its nutriment and so may desire to be set in motion, and hearing that it may have communication made to it, and a tongue that it 25 may communicate with its fellows.

[30] 434^b 24.

METAPHYSICS

INTRODUCTION

The term "metaphysics" was invented by one of the early editors of Aristotle's works to serve as a title for a group of treatises which he placed "after the physics," a place which the Metaphysics still occupies in modern editions, separating the physical and biological sciences from the practical and productive sciences. The inquiries to which the term was applied constitute an independent science in the system of Aristotle, variously designated by him as "First Philosophy," "Theology," or "Wisdom." For in a philosophy in which sciences are distinguished by their proper principles and their proper subject matter, the examination of the first principles of the sciences or of the being shared by the diverse genera of things investigated in the various sciences does not fall within the province of any one of those sciences but constitutes the field of inquiry of a separate science.

As the investigation of problems of proof in logic led back to the problem of the discovery of causes in scientific demonstration, and as inquiry in physics had been found to consist in the search for causes, metaphysics is concerned with causes as such, and it is described as the science of first principles and causes. Aristotle found that his predecessors had tended first to limit their attention to material causes, that is, to explain things by the matter or the elements of which they are composed, and then had turned to the formal causes, that is, essences and definitions which they separated from matter and constituted into independent and self-subsistent Forms. The efficient cause and the final cause, that is, the source of the change and what it is to eventuate in, which Aristotle conceived to be his own peculiar contribution to the discussion of causes, were touched on only sporadically and vaguely by a few philosophers like Empedocles and Anaxagoras.

The problem of the metaphysician in treating of causes is, in a sense, the converse of that of the physicist, for whereas the investigation of nature consists in seeking to know causes and to state them in scientific formulae, the investigation of being requires the careful separation of traits of being from traits peculiar to certain kinds of being and from traits that might be attributed to things because of our ways of knowing them or because of our ways of formulating our knowledge. Aristotle therefore argues that truth and falsity are not in things, but only in thoughts, and that the differentiation of essential and accidental traits, which is necessary in scientific inquiry, is irrelevant to the conditions of being. In like fashion he investigates carefully the sense in which the parts of a true formula or statement may be said to correspond to the parts of the existent situation of which it is true. Once considerations of how things are differentiated, how we think about things, and how we state what we think, have been excluded, the study of being is seen to be primarily the study of substance, which in turn is analyzed into form and matter, actuality and potentiality. The conception of actuality and potentiality and the analysis of their relations to each other carries the inquiry beyond natural or sensible substances, that is, beyond elements and their compounds, plants and their parts, animals and their parts, and the heavenly bodies. In addition to the two kinds of substance —perishable sensible and eternal sensible—which are studied in physics, there is a third kind, immovable and nonsensible, whose existence is established in the famous proof of the necessity of an unmoved mover as cause of existence and motion, and whose nature therefore constitutes the peculiar subject-matter of metaphysics. For if there were no separated substances, all sciences would be reduced to physics, while if forms and numbers were conceived to be separated all philosophy would be reduced to mathematics.

Book I (or Alpha) sets forth the preliminary statement of the characteristics of first philosophy and the criticism of earlier conceptions of the causes. Book XII (or Lambda) investigates the existence and properties of the eternal mover. In both, the consequences of the metaphysical analysis in the conception of the relation of the sciences are apparent, for metaphysics must be differentiated by its subject-matter from physics and mathematics among the theoretic sciences, while the theoretic sciences, which have the acquisition of knowledge as their end must be differentiated by their purpose from the practical sciences, which have the performance of actions as their end, and from the productive sciences, which are directed to the making of artificial objects.

METAPHYSICA

CONTENTS

A. (I)

Λ. (X I I)

mover, and one whose essence is actuality (actuality being prior to potency). To account for the uniform change in the universe, there must be one principle which acts always alike, and one whose action varies.

7. The eternal mover originates motion by being the primary object of desire (as it is of thought); being thoroughly actual, it cannot change or move; it is a living being, perfect, separate from sensible things, and without parts.

8. Besides the first mover there must be as many unmoved movers as there are simple motions involved in the motions of the planets. The number is probably either 55 or 47. As there is but one prime mover, there must be but one heaven.

9. The divine thought must be concerned with the most divine object, which is itself. Thought and the object of thought are never different when the object is immaterial.

10. How the good is present in the universe both as the order of the parts and (more primarily) as their ruler. Difficulties which attend the views of other philosophers.

METAPHYSICA

Metaphysics

Translated by W. D. Ross

BOOK A (1)

1 All men by nature desire to know. An indication
of this is the delight we take in our senses; for even 980ᵃ
apart from their usefulness they are loved for themselves; and above all others the sense of sight. For not only
with a view to action, but even when we are not going to 25
do anything, we prefer seeing (one might say) to everything
else. The reason is that this, most of all the senses, makes us
know and brings to light many differences between things.

By nature animals are born with the faculty of sensation, and from sensation memory is produced in some of
them, though not in others. And therefore the former are
more intelligent and apt at learning than those which cannot 980ᵇ
remember; those which are incapable of hearing sounds are
intelligent though they cannot be taught, e. g. the bee, and
any other race of animals that may be like it; and those
which besides memory have this sense of hearing can be
taught.

The animals other than man live by appearances and
memories, and have but little of connected experience; but 25
the human race lives also by art and reasonings. Now from
memory experience is produced in men; for the several
memories of the same thing produce finally the capacity for

981ª a single experience. And experience seems pretty much like
science and art, but really science and art come to men
through experience; for 'experience made art', as Polus says,[1]
'but inexperience luck'. Now art arises when from many
5 notions gained by experience one universal judgement about
a class of objects is produced. For to have a judgement that
when Callias was ill of this disease this did him good, and
similarly in the case of Socrates and in many individual
cases, is a matter of experience; but to judge that it has done
good to all persons of a certain constitution, marked off in
10 one class, when they were ill of this disease, e. g. to phleg-
matic or bilious people when burning with fever—this is a
matter of art.

   With a view to action experience seems in no respect
inferior to art, and men of experience succeed even better
15 than those who have theory without experience. (The reason
is that experience is knowledge of individuals, art of universals, and actions and productions are all concerned with
the individual; for the physician does not cure *man*, except
in an incidental way, but Callias or Socrates or some other
called by some such individual name, who happens to be a
20 man. If, then, a man has the theory without the experience,
and recognizes the universal but does not know the individual included in this, he will often fail to cure; for it is the
individual that is to be cured.) But yet we think that *knowl-*
25 *edge* and *understanding* belong to art rather than to
experience, and we suppose artists to be wiser than men of
experience (which implies that Wisdom depends in all cases
rather on knowledge); and this because the former know the
cause, but the latter do not. For men of experience know
30 that the thing is so, but do not know why, while the others
know the 'why' and the cause. Hence we think also that the
master-workers in each craft are more honourable and know

1 Cf. Pl. *Gorg.* 448 c, 462 bc.

in a truer sense and are wiser than the manual workers, 981^b
because they know the causes of the things that are done
(we think the manual workers are like certain lifeless things
which act indeed, but act without knowing what they do,
as fire burns—but while the lifeless things perform each of
their functions by a natural tendency, the labourers perform 5
them through habit); thus we view them as being wiser not
in virtue of being able to act, but of having the theory for
themselves and knowing the causes. And in general it is a
sign of the man who knows and of the man who does not
know, that the former can teach, and therefore we think art
more truly knowledge than experience is; for artists can
teach, and men of mere experience cannot.

Again, we do not regard any of the senses as Wisdom; 10
yet surely these give the most authoritative knowledge of
particulars. But they do not tell us the 'why' of anything—
e. g. why fire is hot; they only say *that* it is hot.

At first he who invented any art whatever that went
beyond the common perceptions of man was naturally
admired by men, not only because there was something use- 15
ful in the inventions, but because he was thought wise and
superior to the rest. But as more arts were invented, and
some were directed to the necessities of life, others to recreation, the inventors of the latter were naturally always
regarded as wiser than the inventors of the former, because
their branches of knowledge did not aim at utility. Hence
when all such inventions were already established, the sci- 20
ences which do not aim at giving pleasure or at the
necessities of life were discovered, and first in the places
where men first began to have leisure. This is why the
mathematical arts were founded in Egypt; for there the
priestly caste was allowed to be at leisure.

We have said in the *Ethics*^{2} what the difference is

^{2} 1139^b 14–1141^b 8.

25 between art and science and the other kindred faculties; but the point of our present discussion is this, that all men suppose what is called Wisdom to deal with the first causes and the principles of things; so that, as has been said before, the
30 man of experience is thought to be wiser than the possessors of any sense-perception whatever, the artist wiser than the men of experience, the master-worker than the mechanic, and the theoretical kinds of knowledge to be more of the
982ᵃ nature of Wisdom than the productive. Clearly then Wisdom is knowledge about certain principles and causes.

2 Since we are seeking this knowledge, we must
5 inquire of what kind are the causes and the principles, the knowledge of which is Wisdom. If one were to take the notions we have about the wise man, this might perhaps make the answer more evident. We suppose first, then, that the wise man knows all things, as far as
10 as possible, although he has not knowledge of each of them in detail; secondly, that he who can learn things that are difficult, and not easy for man to know, is wise (sense-perception is common to all, and therefore easy and no mark of Wisdom); again, that he who is more exact and more capable of teaching the causes is wiser, in every branch of
15 knowledge; and that of the sciences, also, that which is desirable on its own account and for the sake of knowing it is more of the nature of Wisdom than that which is desirable on account of its results, and the superior science is more of the nature of Wisdom than the ancillary; for the wise man must not be ordered but must order, and he must not obey another, but the less wise must obey *him*.

Such and so many are the notions, then, which we have
20 about Wisdom and the wise. Now of these characteristics that of knowing all things must belong to him who has in the highest degree universal knowledge; for he knows in a sense all the instances that fall under the universal. And

these things, the most universal, are on the whole the hardest for men to know; for they are farthest from the senses. And the most exact of the sciences are those which deal 25 most with first principles; for those which involve fewer principles are more exact than those which involve additional principles, e. g. arithmetic than geometry. But the science which investigates causes is also *instructive*, in a higher degree, for the people who instruct us are those who tell the causes of each thing. And understanding and knowl- 30 edge pursued for their own sake are found most in the knowledge of that which is most knowable (for he who chooses to know for the sake of knowing will choose most readily that which is most truly knowledge, and such is the 982b knowledge of that which is most knowable); and the first principles and the causes are most knowable; for by reason of these, and from these, all other things come to be known, and not these by means of the things subordinate to them. And the science which knows to what end each thing must be done is the most authoritative of the sciences, and more 5 authoritative than any ancillary science; and this end is the good of that thing, and in general the supreme good in the whole of nature. Judged by all the tests we have mentioned, then, the name in question falls to the same science; this must be a science that investigates the first principles and 10 causes; for the good, i. e. the end, is one of the causes.

That it is not a science of production is clear even from the history of the earliest philosophers. For it is owing to their wonder that men both now begin and at first began to philosophize; they wondered originally at the obvious difficulties, then advanced little by little and stated difficulties 15 about the greater matters, e. g. about the phenomena of the moon and those of the sun and of the stars, and about the genesis of the universe. And a man who is puzzled and wonders thinks himself ignorant (whence even the lover of myth is in a sense a lover of Wisdom, for the myth is com-

posed of wonders); therefore since they philosophized in order to escape from ignorance, evidently they were pursuing science in order to know, and not for any utilitarian end. And this is confirmed by the facts; for it was when almost all the necessities of life and the things that make for comfort and recreation had been secured, that such knowledge began to be sought. Evidently then we do not seek it for the
25 sake of any other advantage; but as the man is free, we say, who exists for his own sake and not for another's, so we pursue this as the only free science, for it alone exists for its own sake.

Hence also the possession of it might be justly regarded as beyond human power; for in many ways human nature is
30 in bondage, so that according to Simonides 'God alone can have this privilege', and it is unfitting that man should not be content to seek the knowledge that is suited to him. If,
983ᵃ then, there is something in what the poets say, and jealousy is natural to the divine power, it would probably occur in this case above all, and all who excelled in this knowledge would be unfortunate. But the divine power cannot be jealous (nay, according to the proverb, 'bards tell many a lie'),
5 nor should any other science be thought more honourable than one of this sort. For the most divine science is also most honourable; and this science alone must be, in two ways, most divine. For the science which it would be most meet for God to have is a divine science, and so is any science that deals with divine objects; and this science alone has both these qualities; for (1) God is thought to be among the causes of all things and to be a first principle, and (2)
10 such a science either God alone can have, or God above all others. All the sciences, indeed, are more necessary than this, but none is better.

Yet the acquisition of it must in a sense end in something which is the opposite of our original inquiries. For all men begin, as we said, by wondering that things are as they

are, as they do about self-moving marionettes, or about the 15
solstices or the incommensurability of the diagonal of a
square with the side; for it seems wonderful to all who have
not yet seen the reason, that there is a thing which cannot be
measured even by the smallest unit. But we must end in the
contrary and, according to the proverb, the better state, as
is the case in these instances too when men learn the cause;
for there is nothing which would surprise a geometer so
much as if the diagonal turned out to be commensurable.   20

We have stated, then, what is the nature of the science
we are searching for, and what is the mark which our search
and our whole investigation must reach.

3   Evidently we have to acquire knowledge of the
original causes (for we say we know each thing only
when we think we recognize its first cause), and 25
causes are spoken of in four senses. In one of these we mean
the substance, i. e. the essence (for the 'why' is reducible
finally to the definition, and the ultimate 'why' is a cause
and principle); in another the matter or substratum, in a
third the source of the change, and in a fourth the cause 30
opposed to this, the purpose and the good (for this is the
end of all generation and change). We have studied these 983ᵇ
causes sufficiently in our work on nature,[3] but yet let us call
to our aid those who have attacked the investigation of
being and philosophized about reality before us. For obviously they too speak of certain principles and causes; to go
over their views, then, will be of profit to the present
inquiry, for we shall either find another kind of cause, or 5
be more convinced of the correctness of those which we
now maintain.

Of the first philosophers, then, most thought the principles which were of the nature of matter were the only

[3] *Phys.* ii. 3, 7

principles of all things. That of which all things that are
consist, the first from which they come to be, the last into
10 which they are resolved (the substance remaining, but
changing in its modifications), this they say is the element
and this the principle of things, and therefore they think
nothing is either generated or destroyed, since this sort of
entity is always conserved, as we say Socrates neither comes
to be absolutely when he comes to be beautiful or musical,
15 nor ceases to be when he loses these characteristics, because
the substratum, Socrates himself, remains. Just so they say
nothing else comes to be or ceases to be; for there must be
some entity—either one or more than one—from which all
other things come to be, it being conserved.

Yet they do not all agree as to the number and the
20 nature of these principles. Thales, the founder of this type
of philosophy, says the principle is water (for which reason
he declared that the earth rests on water), getting the notion
perhaps from seeing that the nutriment of all things is
moist, and that heat itself is generated from the moist and
kept alive by it (and that from which they come to be is a
25 principle of all things). He got his notion from this fact, and
from the fact that the seeds of all things have a moist
nature, and that water is the origin of the nature of moist
things.

Some[4] think that even the ancients who lived long
before the present generation, and first framed accounts of
30 the gods, had a similar view of nature; for they made Ocean
and Tethys the parents of creation,[5] and described the oath
of the gods as being by water,[6] to which they give the name
of Styx; for what is oldest is most honourable, and the most

[4] The reference is probably to Plato (Crat. 402 B, Theaet. 152 E, 162 D,
180 C).

[5] Hom. Il. xiv. 201, 246.

[6] Ibid. ii. 755, xiv. 271, xv. 37.

honourable thing is that by which one swears. It may perhaps be uncertain whether this opinion about nature is 984ᵃ
primitive and ancient, but Thales at any rate is said to have
declared himself thus about the first cause. Hippo no one
would think fit to include among these thinkers, because of
the paltriness of his thought.

Anaximenes and Diogenes make air prior to water, and 5
the most primary of the simple bodies, while Hippasus of
Metapontium and Heraclitus of Ephesus say this of fire,
and Empedocles says it of the four elements (adding a
fourth—earth—to those which have been named); for these,
he says, always remain and do not come to be, except that 10
they come to be more or fewer, being aggregated into one
and segregated out of one.

Anaxagoras of Clazomenae, who, though older than
Empedocles, was later in his philosophical activity, says the
principles are infinite in number; for he says almost all the
things that are made of parts like themselves, in the manner of water or fire, are generated and destroyed in this way,
only by aggregation and segregation, and are not in any 15
other sense generated or destroyed, but remain eternally.

From these facts one might think that the only cause is
the so-called material cause; but as men thus advanced, the
very facts opened the way for them and joined in forcing
them to investigate the subject. However true it may be that
all generation and destruction proceed from some one or 20
(for that matter) from more elements, why does this happen and what is the cause? For at least the substratum itself
does not make itself change; e. g. neither the wood nor the
bronze causes the change of either of them, nor does the
wood manufacture a bed and the bronze a statue, but something else is the cause of the change. And to seek this is to 25
seek the second cause, as we should say—that from which
comes the beginning of the movement. Now those who at
the very beginning set themselves to this kind of inquiry,

and said the substratum was one,[7] were not at all dissatisfied
with themselves; but some at least of those who maintained
30 it to be one[8]—as though defeated by this search for the second
cause—say the one and nature as a whole is unchangeable
not only in respect of generation and destruction (for this
is a primitive belief, and all agreed in it), but also of all
other change; and this view is peculiar to them. Of those
984b who said the universe was one, then, none succeeded in discovering a cause of this sort, except perhaps Parmenides,
and he only inasmuch as he supposes that there is not only
one but also in some sense two causes. But for those who
5 make more elements[9] it is more possible to state the second
cause, e. g. for those who make hot and cold, or fire and
earth, the elements; for they treat fire as having a nature
which fits it to move things, and water and earth and such
things they treat in the contrary way.

When these men and the principles of this kind had
had their day, as the latter were found inadequate to generate the nature of things men were again forced by the truth
10 itself, as we said,[10] to inquire into the next kind of cause.
For it is not likely either that fire or earth or any such element should be the reason why things manifest goodness
and beauty both in their being and in their coming to be, or
that those thinkers should have supposed it was; nor again
could it be right to entrust so great a matter to spontaneity
and chance. When one man[11] said, then, that reason was
15 present—as in animals, so throughout nature—as the cause
of order and of all arrangement, he seemed like a sober man

[7] Thales, Anaximenes, and Heraclitus.

[8] The Eleatics.

[9] The reference is probably to Empedocles.

[10] a18.

[11] Anaxagoras.

in contrast with the random talk of his predecessors. We know that Anaxagoras certainly adopted these views, but Hermotimus of Clazomenae is credited with expressing them earlier. Those who thought thus stated that there is a 20 principle of things which is at the same time the cause of beauty, and that sort of cause from which things acquire movement.

4 One might suspect that Hesiod was the first to look for such a thing—or some one else who put love or desire among existing things as a principle, as Par- 25 menides, too, does; for he, in constructing the genesis of the universe, says:—

> Love first of all the Gods she planned.

And Hesiod says:—

> First of all things was chaos made, and then
> Broad-breasted earth, . . .
> And love, 'mid all the gods pre-eminent,

which implies that among existing things there must be from 30 the first a cause which will move things and bring them together. How these thinkers should be arranged with regard to priority of discovery let us be allowed to decide later;[12] but since the contraries of the various forms of good were also perceived to be present in nature—not only order and the beautiful, but also disorder and the ugly, and bad things in greater number than good, and ignoble things than beau- 985a tiful—therefore another thinker introduced friendship and strife, each of the two the cause of one of these two sets of qualities. For if we were to follow out the view of Emped- 5

---

[12] The promise is not fulfilled.

ocles, and interpret it according to its meaning and not to its
lisping expression, we should find that friendship is the cause
of good things, and strife of bad. Therefore, if we said that
Empedocles in a sense both mentions, and is the first to
mention, the bad and the good as principles, we should perhaps be right, since the cause of all goods is the good itself.

10   These thinkers, as we say, evidently grasped, and to
this extent, two of the causes which we distinguished in our
work on nature[13]—the matter and the source of the movement—vaguely, however, and with no clearness, but as
15 untrained men behave in fights; for they go round their
opponents and often strike fine blows, but they do not fight
on scientific principles, and so too these thinkers do not
seem to know what they say; for it is evident that, as a rule,
they make no use of their causes except to a small extent.
For Anaxagoras uses reason as a *deus ex machina* for the
making of the world, and when he is at a loss to tell from
20 what cause something necessarily is, then he drags reason
in, but in all other cases ascribes events to anything rather
than to reason.[14] And Empedocles, though he uses the
causes to a greater extent than this, neither does so sufficiently nor attains consistency in their use. At least, in
many cases he makes love segregate things, and strife aggre-
25 gate them. For whenever the universe is dissolved into its
elements by strife, fire is aggregated into one, and so is each
of the other elements; but whenever again under the influence of love they come together into one, the parts must
again be segregated out of each element.

Empedocles, then, in contrast with his predecessors,
was the first to introduce the dividing of this cause, not
30 positing one source of movement, but different and contrary
sources. Again, he was the first to speak of four material

[13] *Phys.* ii. 3, 7.

[14] Cf. Pl. *Phaedo,* 98 BC, *Laws,* 967 B–D.

elements; yet he does not *use* four, but treats them as two 985ᵇ
only; he treats fire by itself, and its opposites—earth, air,
and water—as one kind of thing. We may learn this by
study of his verses.

This philosopher then, as we say, has spoken of the
principles in this way, and made them of this number. Leucippus and his associate Democritus say that the full and
the empty are the elements, calling the one being and the 5
other non-being—the full and solid being being, the empty
non-being (whence they say being no more is than non-
being, because the solid no more is than the empty); and
they make these the material causes of things. And as those
who make the underlying substance one generate all other 10
things by its modifications, supposing the rare and the
dense to be the sources of the modifications, in the same
way these philosophers say the differences in the elements
are the causes of all other qualities. These differences, they
say, are three—shape and order and position. For they say
the real is differentiated only by 'rhythm' and 'inter-contact' 15
and 'turning'; and of these rhythm is shape, inter-contact is
order, and turning is position; for A differs from N in shape,
AN from NA in order, H from H in position. The question
of movement—whence or how it is to belong to things—
these thinkers, like the others, lazily neglected.

Regarding the two causes, then, as we say, the inquiry
seems to have been pushed thus far by the early philoso- 20
phers.

5 Contemporaneously with these philosophers and
before them, the so-called Pythagoreans, who were
the first to take up mathematics, not only advanced 25
this study, but also having been brought up in it they
thought its principles were the principles of all things. Since
of these principles numbers are by nature the first, and in
numbers they seemed to see many resemblances to the

things that exist and come into being—more than in fire
and earth and water (such and such a modification of num-
30 bers being justice, another being soul and reason, another
being opportunity—and similarly almost all other things
being numerically expressible); since, again, they saw that
the modifications and the ratios of the musical scales were
expressible in numbers;—since, then, all other things
seemed in their whole nature to be modelled on numbers,
986ᵃ and numbers seemed to be the first things in the whole of
nature, they supposed the elements of numbers to be the
elements of all things, and the whole heaven to be a musical
scale and a number. And all the properties of numbers and
scales which they could show to agree with the attributes
5 and parts and the whole arrangement of the heavens, they
collected and fitted into their scheme; and if there was a gap
anywhere, they readily made additions so as to make their
whole theory coherent. E. g. as the number 10 is thought
to be perfect and to comprise the whole nature of numbers,
10 they say that the bodies which move through the heavens
are ten, but as the visible bodies are only nine, to meet this
they invent a tenth—the 'counter-earth'. We have discussed
these matters more exactly elsewhere.[15]

But the object of our review is that we may learn from
these philosophers also what they suppose to be the princi-
15 ples and how these fall under the causes we have named.
Evidently, then, these thinkers also consider that number is
the principle both as matter for things and as forming both
their modifications and their permanent states, and hold
that the elements of number are the even and the odd, and
that of these the latter is limited, and the former unlimited;
and that the One proceeds from both of these (for it is both
20 even and odd), and number from the One; and that the
whole heaven, as has been said, is numbers.

[15] *De Caelo*, ii. 13.

Other members of this same school say there are ten
principles, which they arrange in two columns of cognates—
limit and unlimited, odd and even, one and plurality, right 25
and left, male and female, resting and moving, straight and
curved, light and darkness, good and bad, square and
oblong. In this way Alcmaeon of Croton seems also to have
conceived the matter, and either he got this view from them
or they got it from him; for he expressed himself similarly
to them. For he says most human affairs go in pairs, mean- 30
ing not definite contrarieties such as the Pythagoreans speak
of, but any chance contrarieties, e. g. white and black, sweet
and bitter, good and bad, great and small. He threw out
indefinite suggestions about the other contrarieties, but the
Pythagoreans declared both how many and which their con- 986b
trarieties are.

From both these schools, then, we can learn this much,
that the contraries are the principles of things; and how
many these principles are and which they are, we can learn
from one of the two schools. But how these principles can
be brought together under the causes we have named has 5
not been clearly and articulately stated by them; they seem,
however, to range the elements under the head of matter;
for out of these as immanent parts they say substance is
composed and moulded.

From these facts we may sufficiently perceive the
meaning of the ancients who said the elements of nature
were more than one; but there are some who spoke of the
universe as if it were one entity, though they were not all 10
alike either in the excellence of their statement or in its conformity to the facts of nature. The discussion of them is in
no way appropriate to our present investigation of causes,
for they do not, like some of the natural philosophers,
assume being to be one and yet generate it out of the one
as out of matter, but they speak in another way; those oth- 15
ers add change, since they generate the universe, but these

thinkers say the universe is unchangeable. Yet *this* much is germane to the present inquiry: Parmenides seems to fasten on that which is one in definition, Melissus on that which is one in matter, for which reason the former says that it is limited, the latter that it is unlimited; while Xenophanes, the first of these partisans of the One (for Parmenides is said to have been his pupil), gave no clear statement, nor does he seem to have grasped the nature of either of these causes, but with reference to the whole material universe he says the One is God. Now these thinkers, as we said, must be neglected for the purposes of the present inquiry—two of them entirely, as being a little too naïve, viz. Xenophanes and Melissus; but Parmenides seems in places to speak with more insight. For, claiming that, besides the existent, nothing non-existent exists, he thinks that of necessity one thing exists, viz. the existent and nothing else (on this we have spoken more clearly in our work on nature),[16] but being forced to follow the observed facts, and supposing the existence of that which is one in definition, but more than one according to our sensations, he now posits two causes and two principles, calling them hot and cold, i. e. fire and earth; and of these he ranges the hot with the existent, and the other with the non-existent.

From what has been said, then, and from the wise men who have now sat in council with us, we have got thus much—on the one hand from the earliest philosophers, who regard the first principle as corporeal (for water and fire and such things are bodies), and of whom some suppose that there is one corporeal principle, others that there are more than one, but both put these under the head of matter; and on the other hand from some who posit both this cause and besides this the source of movement, which we have got from some as single and from others as twofold.

16 *Phys.* i. 3.

Down to the Italian school, then, and apart from it, philosophers have treated these subjects rather obscurely, 10 except that, as we said, they have in fact used two kinds of cause, and one of these—the source of movement—some treat as one and others as two. But the Pythagoreans have said in the same way that there are two principles, but 15 added this much, which is peculiar to them, that they thought that finitude and infinity were not attributes of certain other things, e. g. of fire or earth or anything else of this kind, but that infinity itself and unity itself were the substance of the things of which they are predicated. This is why number was the substance of all things. On this sub- 20 ject, then, they expressed themselves thus; and regarding the question of essence they began to make statements and definitions, but treated the matter too simply. For they both defined superficially and thought that the first subject of which a given definition was predicable was the substance of the thing defined, as if one supposed that 'double' and '2' were the same, because 2 is the first thing of which 'dou- 25 ble' is predicable. But surely to be double and to be 2 are not the same; if they are, one thing will be many[17]—a consequence which they actually drew.[18] From the earlier philosophers, then, and from their successors we can learn thus much.

6 After the systems we have named came the philosophy of Plato, which in most respects followed 30 these thinkers, but had peculiarities that distinguished it from the philosophy of the Italians. For, having in his youth first become familiar with Cratylus and with the Heraclitean doctrines (that all sensible things are ever in a state of flux and there is no knowledge about them), these

[17] i. e. 2 will be each of several things whose definition is predicable of it.

[18] e. g. 2 was identified both with opinion and with daring.

987^b views he held even in later years. Socrates, however, was
busying himself about ethical matters and neglecting the
world of nature as a whole but seeking the universal in these
ethical matters, and fixed thought for the first time on definitions; Plato accepted his teaching, but held that the
5 problem applied not to sensible things but to entities of
another kind—for this reason, that the common definition
could not be a definition of any sensible thing, as they were
always changing. Things of this other sort, then, he called
Ideas, and sensible things, he said, were all named after
these, and in virtue of a relation to these; for the many
existed by participation in the Ideas that have the same
10 name as they. Only the name 'participation' was new; for
the Pythagoreans say that things exist by 'imitation' of
numbers, and Plato says they exist by participation, changing the name. But what the participation or the imitation of
the Forms could be they left an open question.

Further, besides sensible things and Forms he says
there are the objects of mathematics, which occupy an inter-
15 mediate position, differing from sensible things in being
eternal and unchangeable, from Forms in that there are
many alike, while the Form itself is in each case unique.

Since the Forms were the causes of all other things, he
thought their elements were the elements of all things. As
20 matter, the great and the small were principles; as essential
reality, the One; for from the great and the small, by participation in the One, come the Numbers.

But he agreed with the Pythagoreans in saying that the
One is substance and not a predicate of something else; and
in saying that the Numbers are the causes of the reality of
25 other things he agreed with them; but positing a dyad and
constructing the infinite out of great and small, instead of
treating the infinite as one, is peculiar to him; and so is his
view that the Numbers exist apart from sensible things,
while *they* say that the things themselves are Numbers, and

do not place the objects of mathematics between Forms and sensible things. His divergence from the Pythagoreans in making the One and the Numbers separate from things, 30 and his introduction of the Forms, were due to his inquiries in the region of definitions (for the earlier thinkers had no tincture of dialectic), and his making the other entity besides the One a dyad was due to the belief that the numbers, except those which were prime, could be neatly produced out of the dyad as out of some plastic material.

Yet what *happens* is the contrary; the theory is not a reasonable one. For they make many things out of the mat- 988ᵃ ter, and the form generates only once, but what we observe is that one table is made from one matter, while the man who applies the form, though he is one, makes many tables. 5 And the relation of the male to the female is similar; for the latter is impregnated by one copulation, but the male impregnates many females; yet these are analogues of those first principles.

Plato, then, declared himself thus on the points in question; it is evident from what has been said that he has used only two causes, that of the essence and the material cause (for the Forms are the causes of the essence of all 10 other things, and the One is the cause of the essence of the Forms); and it is evident what the underlying matter is, of which the Forms are predicated in the case of sensible things, and the One in the case of Forms, viz. that this is a dyad, the great and the small. Further, he has assigned the cause of good and that of evil to the elements, one to each of the two, as we say[19] some of his predecessors sought to 15 do, e. g. Empedocles and Anaxagoras.

---

[19] Cf. 984ᵇ 15–19, 32–ᵇ10.

7 Our review of those who have spoken about first
principles and reality and of the way in which they
20 have spoken, has been concise and summary; but
yet we have learnt *this* much from them, that of those who
speak about 'principle' and 'cause' no one has mentioned
any principle except those which have been distinguished
in our work on nature,[20] but all evidently have some inkling
of *them*, though only vaguely. For some speak of the first
principle as matter, whether they suppose one or more first
25 principles, and whether they suppose this to be a body or to
be incorporeal; e. g. Plato spoke of the great and the small,
the Italians of the infinite, Empedocles of fire, earth, water,
and air, Anaxagoras of the infinity of things composed of
similar parts. These, then, have all had a notion of this kind
30 of cause, and so have all who speak of air or fire or water, or
something denser than fire and rarer than air; for some have
said the prime element is of this kind.

These thinkers grasped this cause only; but certain others have mentioned the source of movement, e. g. those who
make friendship and strife, or reason, or love, a principle.

The essence, i. e. the substantial reality, no one has
35 expressed distinctly. It is hinted at chiefly by those who
988b believe in the Forms; for they do not suppose either that the
Forms are the matter of sensible things, and the One the
matter of the Forms, or that they are the source of movement (for they say these are causes rather of immobility and
of being at rest), but they furnish the Forms as the essence
of every other thing, and the One as the essence of the
5 Forms.

That for whose sake actions and changes and movements take place, they assert to be a cause in a way, but not
in this way, i. e. not in the way in which it is its *nature* to be
a cause. For those who speak of reason or friendship class

[20] *Phys.* ii. 3, 7.

these causes as goods; they do not speak, however, as if anything that exists either existed or came into being for the
sake of these, but as if movements started from these. In the
same way those who say the One or the existent is the good, 10
say that it is the cause of substance, but not that substance
either is or comes to be for the sake of this. Therefore it
turns out that in a sense they both say and do not say the
good is a cause; for they do not call it a cause *qua* good but 15
only incidentally.

All these thinkers, then, as they cannot pitch on
another cause, seem to testify that we have determined
rightly both how many and of what sort the causes are.
Besides this it is plain that when the causes are being looked
for, either all four must be sought thus or they must be
sought in one of these four ways. Let us next discuss the 20
possible difficulties with regard to the way in which each of
these thinkers has spoken, and with regard to his situation
relatively to the first principles.

8 Those, then, who say the universe is one and posit
one kind of thing as matter, and as corporeal matter which has spatial magnitude, evidently go
astray in many ways. For they posit the elements of bodies
only, not of incorporeal things, though there are also incor- 25
poreal things. And in trying to state the causes of generation
and destruction, and in giving a physical account of all
things, they do away with the cause of movement. Further,
they err in not positing the substance, i. e. the essence, as
the cause of anything, and besides this in lightly calling any
of the simple bodies except earth the first principle, with- 30
out inquiring how they are produced out of one another,—I
mean fire, water, earth, and air. For some things are produced out of each other by combination, others by
separation, and this makes the greatest difference to their
priority and posteriority. For (1) in a way the property of

35 being most elementary of all would seem to belong to the
first thing from which they are produced by combination,
989ª and *this* property would belong to the most fine-grained and
subtle of bodies. For this reason those who make fire the
principle would be most in agreement with this argument.
But each of the other thinkers agrees that the element of
5 corporeal things is of this sort. At least none of those who
named one element claimed that earth was the element, evidently because of the coarseness of its grain. (Of the other
three elements each has found some judge on its side; for
some maintain that fire, others that water, others that air is
the element. Yet why, after all, do they not name earth also,
as most men do? For people say all things are earth. And
10 Hesiod says earth was produced first of corporeal things; so
primitive and popular has the opinion been.) According to
this argument, then, no one would be right who either says
the first principle is any of the elements other than fire, or
15 supposes it to be denser than air but rarer than water. But
(2) if that which is later in generation is prior in nature, and
that which is concocted and compounded is later in generation, the contrary of what we have been saying must be
true—water must be prior to air, and earth to water.

So much, then, for those who posit one cause such as
20 we mentioned; but the same is true if one supposes more of
these, as Empedocles says the matter of things is four bodies. For he too is confronted by consequences some of
which are the same as have been mentioned, while others
are peculiar to him. For we see these bodies produced from
one another, which implies that the same body does not
always remain fire or earth (we have spoken about this in
25 our works on nature[21]); and regarding the cause of movement and the question whether we must posit one or two,
he must be thought to have spoken neither correctly nor

[21] *De Caelo*, iii. 7.

altogether plausibly. And in general, change of quality is
necessarily done away with for those who speak thus, for on
their view cold will not come from hot nor hot from cold.
For if it did there would be something that accepted the
contraries themselves, and there would be some one entity
that became fire and water, which Empedocles denies.

As regards Anaxagoras, if one were to suppose that he 30
said there were two elements, the supposition would accord
thoroughly with an argument which Anaxagoras himself did
not state articulately, but which he must have accepted if
any one had led him on to it. True, to say that in the beginning all things were mixed is absurd both on other grounds
and because it follows that they must have existed before in
an unmixed form, and because nature does not allow any 989b
chance thing to be mixed with any chance thing, and also
because on this view modifications and accidents could be
separated from substances (for the same things which are
mixed can be separated); yet if one were to follow him up,
piecing together what he means, he would perhaps be seen 5
to be somewhat modern in his views. For when nothing was
separated out, evidently nothing could be truly asserted of
the substance that then existed. I mean, e. g., that it was
neither white nor black, nor grey nor any other colour, but
of necessity colourless; for if it had been coloured, it would
have had one of these colours. And similarly, by this same 10
argument, it was flavourless, nor had it any similar attribute;
for it could not be either of any quality or of any size, nor
could it be any definite kind of thing. For if it were, one of
the particular forms would have belonged to it, and this is
impossible, since all were mixed together; for the particular
form would necessarily have been already separated out, but
he says all were mixed except reason, and this alone was 15
unmixed and pure. From this it follows, then, that he must
say the principles are the One (for this is simple and
unmixed) and the Other, which is of such a nature as we

suppose the indefinite to be before it is defined and partakes of some form. Therefore, while expressing himself
neither rightly nor clearly, he means something like what
the later thinkers say and what is now more clearly seen to
20 be the case.

But these thinkers are, after all, at home only in arguments about generation and destruction and movement; for
it is practically only of this sort of substance that they seek
the principles and the causes. But those who extend their
25 vision to all things that exist, and of existing things suppose
some to be perceptible and others not perceptible evidently
study both classes, which is all the more reason why one
should devote some time to seeing what is good in their
views and what bad from the standpoint of the inquiry we
have now before us.

The 'Pythagoreans' treat of principles and elements
stranger than those of the physical philosophers (the reason
30 is that they got the principles from non-sensible things, for
the objects of mathematics, except those of astronomy, are
of the class of things without movement); yet their discussions and investigations are all about nature; for they
generate the heavens, and with regard to their parts and
990ᵃ attributes and functions they observe the phenomena, and
use up the principles and the causes in explaining these,
which implies that they agree with the others, the physical
philosophers, that the *real* is just all that which is perceptible and contained by the so-called 'heavens'. But the causes
5 and the principles which they mention are, as we said, sufficient to act as steps even up to the higher realms of reality,
and are more suited to these than to theories about nature.
They do not tell us at all, however, how there can be movement if limit and unlimited and odd and even are the only
10 things assumed, or how without movement and change
there can be generation and destruction, or the bodies that
move through the heavens can do what they do.

Further, if one either granted them that spatial magnitude consists of these elements, or this were proved, still how would some bodies be light and others have weight? To judge from what they assume and maintain they are 15 speaking no more of mathematical bodies than of perceptible; hence they have said nothing whatever about fire or earth or the other bodies of this sort, I suppose because they have nothing to say which applies *peculiarly* to perceptible things.

Further, how are we to combine the beliefs that the attributes of number, and number itself, are causes of what 20 exists and happens in the heavens both from the beginning and now, and that there is no other number than this number out of which the world is composed? When in one particular region they place opinion and opportunity, and, a little above or below, injustice and decision or mixture, and allege, as proof, that each of these is a number, and that there happens to be already in this place a plurality of the 25 extended bodies composed of numbers, because these attributes of number attach to the various places—this being so, is this number, which we must suppose each of these abstractions to be, the same number which is exhibited in the material universe, or is it another than this? Plato says it is different; yet even he thinks that both these bodies 30 and their causes are numbers, but that the *intelligible* numbers are causes, while the others are *sensible*.

9 Let us leave the Pythagoreans for the present; for it is enough to have touched on them as much as we have done. But as for those who posit the Ideas as 990ᵇ causes, firstly, in seeking to grasp the causes of the things around us, they introduced others equal in number to these, as if a man who wanted to count things thought he would not be able to do it while they were few, but tried to count them when he had added to their number. For the Forms

5 are practically equal to—or not fewer than—the things, in
trying to explain which these thinkers proceeded from them
to the Forms. For to each thing there answers an entity
which has the same name and exists apart from the substances, and so also in the case of all other groups there is
a one over many, whether the many are in this world or are
eternal.

Further, of the ways in which we prove that the Forms
10 exist, none is convincing; for from some no inference necessarily follows, and from some arise Forms even of things
of which we think there are no Forms. For according to the
arguments from the existence of the sciences there will be
Forms of all things of which there are sciences, and according to the 'one over many' argument there will be Forms
even of negations, and according to the argument that there
is an object for thought even when the thing has perished,
there will be Forms of perishable things; for we have an
15 image of these. Further, of the more accurate arguments,
some lead to Ideas of relations, of which we say there is no
independent class, and others introduce the 'third man'.

And in general the arguments for the Forms destroy
the things for whose existence we are more zealous than for
the existence of the Ideas; for it follows that not the dyad
but number is first, i. e. that the relative is prior to the
20 absolute—besides all the other points on which certain people by following out the opinions held about the Ideas have
come into conflict with the principles of the theory.

Further, according to the assumption on which our
belief in the Ideas rests, there will be Forms not only of
substances but also of many other things (for the concept
25 is single not only in the case of substances but also in the
other cases, and there are sciences not only of substance but
also of other things, and a thousand other such difficulties
confront them). But according to the necessities of the case
and the opinions held about the Forms, if Forms can be

shared in there must be Ideas of substances only. For they
are not shared in incidentally, but a thing must share in its
Form as in something not predicated of a subject (by 'being 30
shared in incidentally' I mean that e. g. if a thing shares in
'double itself', it shares also in 'eternal', but incidentally;
for 'eternal' happens to be predicable of the 'double').
Therefore the Forms will be substance; but the same terms
indicate substance in this and in the ideal world (or what
will be the meaning of saying that there is something apart
from the particulars—the one over many?). And if the Ideas 991ᵃ
and the particulars that share in them have the same form,
there will be something common to these; for why should
'2' be one and the same in the perishable 2's or in those
which are many but eternal, and not the same in the '2
itself' as in the particular 2? But if they have not the same 5
form, they must have only the name in common, and it is
as if one were to call both Callias and a wooden image a
'man', without observing any community between them.[22]

Above all one might discuss the question what on earth
the Forms contribute to sensible things, either to those that
are eternal or to those that come into being and cease to be. 10
For they cause neither movement nor any change in them.
But again they help in no wise either towards the knowledge of the other things (for they are not even the substance
of these, else they would have been in them), or towards
their being, if they are not *in* the particulars which share in
them; though if they were, they might be thought to be
causes, as white causes whiteness in a white object by entering into its composition. But this argument, which first 15
Anaxagoras and later Eudoxus and certain others used, is
very easily upset; for it is not difficult to collect many insu-
perable objections to such a view.

But, further, all other things cannot come from the

[22] With 990ᵇ 2–991ᵃ 8 Cf. xiii. 1078ᵇ 34–1079ᵇ 3.

20 Forms in any of the usual senses of 'from'. And to say that
they are patterns and the other things share in them is to
use empty words and poetical metaphors. For what is it that
works, looking to the Ideas? And anything can either be, or
become, like another without being copied from it, so that
25 whether Socrates exists or not a man like Socrates might
come to be; and evidently this might be so even if Socrates
were eternal. And there will be several patterns of the same
thing, and therefore several Forms; e. g. 'animal' and 'two-
footed' and also 'man himself' will be Forms of man. Again,
30 the Forms are patterns not only of sensible things, but of
Forms themselves also; i. e. the genus, as genus of various
species, will be so; therefore the same thing will be pattern
and copy.

991ᵇ   Again, it would seem impossible that the substance and
that of which it is the substance should exist apart; how,
therefore, could the Ideas, being the substances of things,
exist apart? In the *Phaedo*[23] the case is stated in this way—
that the Forms are causes both of being and of becoming;
5 yet when the Forms exist, still the things that share in them
do not come into being, unless there is something to originate movement; and many other things come into being
(e. g. a house or a ring) of which we say there are no Forms.
Clearly, therefore, even the other things can both be and
come into being owing to such causes as produce the things
just mentioned.[24]

     Again, if the Forms are numbers, how can they be
10 causes? Is it because existing things are other numbers, e. g.
one number is man, another is Socrates, another Callias?
Why then are the one set of numbers causes of the other
set? It will not make any difference even if the former are
eternal and the latter are not. But if it is because things in

[23] 100 C–E.

[24] With 991ª 8–ᵇ 9 Cf. xiii. 1079ᵇ 12–1080ª 8.

this sensible world (e. g. harmony) are ratios of numbers, evidently the things between which they are ratios are some one class of things. If, then, this—the matter—is some def- inite thing, evidently the numbers themselves too will be ratios of something to something else. E. g. if Callias is a numerical ratio between fire and earth and water and air, his Idea also will be a number of certain other underlying things; and man-himself, whether it is a number in a sense or not, will still be a numerical ratio of certain things and not a number proper, nor will it be a kind of number merely because it is a numerical ratio.

Again, from many numbers one number is produced, but how can one Form come from many Forms? And if the number comes not from the many numbers themselves but from the units in them, e. g. in 10,000, how is it with the units? If they are specifically alike, numerous absurdities will follow, and also if they are not alike (neither the units in one number being themselves like one another nor those in other numbers being all like to all); for in what will they differ, as they are without quality? This is not a plausible view, nor is it consistent with our thought on the matter.

Further, they must set up a second kind of number (with which arithmetic deals), and all the objects which are called 'intermediate' by some thinkers; and how do these exist or from what principles do they proceed? Or why must they be intermediate between the things in this sensi- ble world and the things-themselves?

Further, the units in 2 must each come from a prior 2; but this is impossible.

Further, why is a number, when taken all together, one? Again, besides what has been said, if the units are *diverse* the Platonists should have spoken like those who say there are four, or two, elements; for each of these thinkers gives the name of element not to that which is common, e. g. to body, but to fire and earth, whether there is something

common to them, viz. body, or not. But in fact the Platonists speak as if the One were *homogeneous* like fire or water;
and if this is so, the numbers will not be substances. Evidently, if there is a One-itself and this is a first principle,
'one' is being used in more than one sense; for otherwise the
theory is impossible.

When we wish to reduce substances to their principles,
10 we state that lines come from the short and long (i. e. from
a kind of small and great), and the plane from the broad
and narrow, and body from the deep and shallow. Yet how
then can either the plane contain a line, or the solid a line or
a plane? For the broad and narrow is a different class from
15 the deep and shallow. Therefore, just as number is not present in these, because the many and few are different from
these, evidently no other of the higher classes will be present in the lower. But again the broad is not a genus which
includes the deep, for then the solid would have been a
species of plane.[25] Further, from what principle will the
presence of the *points* in the line be derived? Plato even used
20 to object to this class of things as being a geometrical fic-
tion. He gave the name of principle of the line—and this he
often posited—to the indivisible lines. Yet these must have
a limit; therefore the argument from which the existence of
the line follows proves also the existence of the point.

In general, though philosophy seeks the cause of per-
25 ceptible things, we have given this up (for we say nothing of
the cause from which change takes its start), but while we
fancy we are stating the substance of perceptible things, we
assert the existence of a second class of substances, while
our account of the way in which they are the substances of
perceptible things is empty talk; for 'sharing', as we said
before,[26] means nothing.

[25] With 992ª 10–19 Cf. xiii. 1085ª 9–19.

[26] 991ª 20–22.

Nor have the Forms any connexion with what we see to be the cause in the case of the arts, that for whose sake 30 both all mind and the whole of nature are operative[27]—with this cause which we assert to be one of the first principles; but mathematics has come to be identical with philosophy for modern thinkers, though they say that it should be studied for the sake of other things.[28]

Further, one might suppose that the substance which according to them underlies as matter is too mathematical, 992[b] and is a predicate and differentia of the substance, i. e. of the matter, rather than the matter itself; i. e. the great and the small are like the rare and the dense which the physical 5 philosophers speak of, calling these the primary differentiae of the substratum; for these are a kind of excess and defect. And regarding movement, if the great and the small are to *be* movement, evidently the Forms will be moved; but if they are not to be movement, whence did movement come? The whole study of nature has been annihilated.

And what is thought to be easy—to show that all things are one—is not done; for what is proved by the method of 10 setting out instances[29] is not that all things are one but that there is a One-itself,—if we grant all the assumptions. And not even this follows, if we do not grant that the universal is a genus; and this in some cases it cannot be.

Nor can it be explained either how the lines and planes and solids that come after the numbers exist or can exist, or what significance they have; for these can neither be 15 Forms (for they are not numbers), nor the intermediates (for those are the objects of mathematics), nor the perishable things. This is evidently a distinct fourth class.

In general, if we search for the elements of existing

---

[27] *sc.* the final cause.

[28] Cf. Plato, *Rep.* vii. 531 D, 533 B–E.

[29] For this Platonic method Cf. vii. 1031[b] 21, xiii. 1086[b] 9, xiv. 1090[a] 17.

things without distinguishing the many senses in which
things are said to exist, we cannot find them, especially if
the search for the elements of which things are made is con-
20 ducted in this manner. For it is surely impossible to
discover what 'acting' or 'being acted on', or 'the straight',
is made of, but if elements can be discovered at all, it is
only the elements of substances; therefore either to seek the
elements of all existing things or to think one has them is
incorrect.

And how could we *learn* the elements of all things? Evidently we cannot start by knowing anything before. For as
25 he who is learning geometry, though he may know other
things before, knows none of the things with which the science deals and about which he is to learn, so is it in all other
cases. Therefore if there is a science of all things, such as
some assert to exist, he who is learning this will know nothing before. Yet all learning is by means of premisses which
30 are (either all or some of them) known before—whether the
learning be by demonstration or by definitions; for the elements of the definition must be known before and be
familiar; and learning by induction proceeds similarly. But
993ª again, if the science were actually innate, it were strange that
we are unaware of our possession of the greatest of sciences.

Again, how is one to *come to know* what all things are
made of, and how is this to be made *evident*? This also
affords a difficulty; for there might be a conflict of opinion,
5 as there is about certain syllables; some say *za* is made out
of *s* and *d* and *a*, while others say it is a distinct sound and
none of those that are familiar.

Further, how could we know the objects of sense without having the sense in question? Yet we ought to, if the
elements of which all things consist, as complex sounds
10 consist of the elements proper to sound, are the same.

10 It is evident, then, even from what we have said before, that all men seem to seek the causes named in the *Physics*,[30] and that we cannot name any beyond these; but they seek these vaguely; and though in a sense they have all been described before, in a sense they have not been described at all. For the earliest philos- 15 ophy is, on all subjects, like one who lisps, since it is young and in its beginnings. For even Empedocles says bone exists by virtue of the ratio in it. Now this is the essence and the substance of the thing. But it is similarly necessary that flesh and each of the other tissues should be the ratio of its elements, or that not one of them should; for it is on account of this that both flesh and bone and everything else 20 will exist, and not on account of the matter, which *he* names —fire and earth and water and air. But while he would nec- essarily have agreed if another had said this, he has not said it clearly.

On these questions our views have been expressed before; but let us return to enumerate the difficulties that 25 might be raised on these same points;[31] for perhaps we may get from them some help toward our later difficulties.

BOOK Λ (XII)

1 The subject of our inquiry is substance; for the 1069ᵃ principles and the causes we are seeking are those of substances. For if the universe is of the nature of 20 a whole, substance is its first part; and if it coheres merely by virtue of serial succession, on this view also substance is first, and is succeeded by quality, and then by quantity. At the same time these latter are not even being in the full

[30] ii. 3, 7.

[31] The reference is to Bk. iii.

sense, but are qualities and movements of it—or else even
the not-white and the not-straight would be being; at least
25 we say even these *are*, e. g. 'there is a not-white'.[1] Further,
none of the categories other than substance can exist apart.
And the early philosophers also in practice testify to the pri-
macy of substance; for it was of substance that they sought
the principles and elements and causes. The thinkers of the
present[2] day tend to rank universals as substances (for genera are universals, and these they tend to describe as
principles and substances, owing to the abstract nature of
their inquiry); but the thinkers of old ranked particular
things as substances, e. g. fire and earth, not what is common to both, body.

30   There are three kinds of substance—one that is sensible
(of which one subdivision is eternal and another is perishable; the latter is recognized by all men, and includes e. g.
plants and animals), of which we must grasp the elements,
whether one or many; and another that is immovable, and
35 this certain thinkers assert to be capable of existing apart,
some dividing it into two, others identifying the Forms and
the objects of mathematics, and others positing, of these
two, only the objects of mathematics.[3] The former two kinds
1069ᵇ of substance are the subject of physics (for they imply
movement); but the third kind belongs to another science, if
there is no principle common to it and to the other kinds.

2   Sensible substance is changeable. Now if change
proceeds from opposites or from intermediates, and
5   not from all opposites (for the voice is not-white
[but it does not therefore change to white]), but from the

1 This is an implication of the ordinary type of judgement, '*x* is not white'.

2 The Platonists.

3 The three views appear to have been held respectively by Plato,
Xenocrates, and Speusippus.

contrary, there must be something underlying which changes into the contrary state; for the *contraries* do not change. Further, something persists, but the contrary does not persist; there is, then, some third thing besides the contraries, viz. the matter. Now since changes are of four kinds—either in respect of the 'what' or of the quality or of the quantity or of the place, and change in respect of 'this- 10 ness' is simple generation and destruction, and change in quantity is increase and diminution, and change in respect of an affection is alteration, and change of place is motion, changes will be from given states into those contrary to them in these several respects. The matter, then, which changes must be capable of both states. And since that which 'is' has two senses, we must say that everything 15 changes from that which is potentially to that which is actually, e. g. from potentially white to actually white, and similarly in the case of increase and diminution. Therefore not only can a thing come to be, incidentally, out of that which is not, but also all things come to be out of that which is, but is potentially, and is not actually. And this is the 'One' of Anaxagoras; for instead of 'all things were 20 together'—and the 'Mixture' of Empedocles and Anaximander and the account given by Democritus—it is better to say 'all things were together potentially but not actually'. Therefore these thinkers seem to have had some notion of matter. Now all things that change have matter, but different matter; and of eternal things those which are not 25 generable but are movable in space have matter—not matter for generation, however, but for motion from one place to another.

One might raise the question from what sort of nonbeing generation proceeds; for 'non-being' has three senses. If, then, one form of non-being exists potentially, still it is not by virtue of a potentiality for any and every thing, but different things come from different things; nor is it satis-

30 factory to say that 'all things were together'; for they differ
in their matter, since otherwise why did an infinity of things
come to be, and not one thing? For 'reason' is one, so that if
matter also were one, that must have come to be in actuality which the matter was in potency.[4] The causes and the
principles, then, are three, two being the pair of contraries
of which one is definition and form and the other is privation, and the third being the matter.

3 Note, next, that neither the matter nor the form
35 comes to be—and I mean the last matter and form.
For everything that chances is something and is
1070ᵃ changed by something and into something. That by which
it is changed is the immediate mover; that which is changed,
the matter; that into which it is changed, the form. The
process, then, will go on to infinity, if not only the bronze
comes to be round but also the round or the bronze comes
to be; therefore there must be a stop.

Note, next, that each substance comes into being out
of something that shares its name. (Natural objects and
5 other things both rank as substances.) For things come into
being either by art or by nature or by luck or by spontaneity. Now art is a principle of movement in something other
than the thing moved, nature is a principle in the thing
itself (for man begets man), and the other causes are privations of these two.

There are three kinds of substance—the matter, which
10 is a 'this' in appearance (for all things that are characterized
19 by contact and not by organic unity are matter and substratum, e. g. fire, flesh, head; for these are all matter, and the
11 last matter is the matter of that which is in the full sense
substance); the nature, which is a 'this' or positive state
towards which movement takes place; and again, thirdly,

---

[4] *sc.* an undifferentiated unity.

the particular substance which is composed of these two,
e. g. Socrates or Callias. Now in some cases the 'this' does
not exist apart from the composite substance, e. g. the form
of house does not so exist, unless the art of building exists 15
apart (nor is there generation and destruction of these
forms, but it is in another way that the house apart from its
matter, and health, and all ideals of art, exist and do not
exist); but if the 'this' exists apart from the concrete thing,
it is only in the case of natural objects. And so Plato was
not far wrong when he said that there are as many Forms as 21
there are kinds of natural object (if there *are* Forms distinct
from the things of this earth). The moving causes exist as
things preceding the effects, but causes in the sense of definitions are simultaneous with their effects. For when a man
is healthy, then health also exists; and the shape of a bronze
sphere exists at the same time as the bronze sphere. (But we 25
must examine whether any form also survives afterwards.
For in some cases there is nothing to prevent this; e. g. the
soul may be of this sort—not all soul but the reason; for
presumably it is impossible that *all* soul should survive.)
Evidently then there is no necessity, on this ground at least,
for the existence of the Ideas. For man is begotten by man,
a given man by an individual father; and similarly in the 30
arts; for the medical art is the formal cause of health.

4　　The causes and the principles of different things
are in a sense different, but in a sense, if one speaks
universally and analogically, they are the same for
all. For one might raise the question whether the principles
and elements are different or the same for substances and 35
for relative terms, and similarly in the case of each of the
categories. But it would be paradoxical if they were the
same for all. For then from the same elements will proceed
relative terms and substances. What then will this common 1070ᵇ
element be? For (1) (*a*) there is nothing common to and dis-

tinct from substance and the other categories, viz. those
which are predicated; but an element is prior to the things
of which it is an element. But again (b) substance is not an
element in relative terms, nor is any of these an element in
substance. Further, (2) how can all things have the same
elements? For none of the elements can be the same as that
5 which is composed of elements, e. g. b or a cannot be the
same as ba. (None, therefore, of the intelligibles, e. g. being
or unity, is an element; for these are predicable of each of
the compounds as well.) None of the elements, then, will
be either a substance or a relative term; but it must be one
or other. All things, then, have not the same elements.

Or, as we are wont to put it, in a sense they have and
10 in a sense they have not; e. g. perhaps the elements of perceptible bodies are, as *form*, the hot, and in another sense
the cold, which is the *privation*; and, as *matter*, that which
directly and of itself potentially has these attributes; and
substances comprise both these and the things composed of
these, of which these are the principles, or any unity which
is produced out of the hot and the cold, e. g. flesh or bone;
15 for the product must be different from the elements. These
things then have the same elements and principles (though
specifically different things have specifically different elements); but *all* things have not the same elements in this
sense, but only analogically; i. e. one might say that there
are three principles—the form, the privation, and the mat-
20 ter. But each of these is different for each class; e. g. in
colour they are white, black, and surface, and in day and
night they are light, darkness, and air.

Since not only the elements present in a thing are
causes, but also something external, i. e. the moving cause,
clearly while 'principle' and 'element' are different both are
causes, and 'principle' is divided into these two kinds[5] and

---

[5] i. e. the principles which are elements and those which are not.

that which acts as producing movement or rest is a principle
and a substance. Therefore analogically there are three ele-   25
ments, and four causes and principles; but the elements are
different in different things, and the proximate moving
cause is different for different things. Health, disease, body;
the moving cause is the medical art. Form, disorder of a
particular kind, bricks; the moving cause is the building art.
And since the moving cause in the case of natural things   30
is—for man, for instance, man, and in the products of
thought the form or its contrary, there will be in a sense
three causes, while in a sense there are four. For the medical art is in some sense health, and the building art is the
form of the house, and man begets man;[6] further, besides
these there is that which as first of all things moves all   35
things.

5 Some things can exist apart and some cannot, and
it is the former that are substances. And therefore   1071a
all things have the same causes,[7] because, without
substances, modifications and movements do not exist. Further, these causes will probably be soul and body, or reason
and desire and body.

And in yet another way, analogically identical things   5
are principles, i. e. actuality and potency; but these also are
not only different for different things but also apply in different ways to them. For in some cases the same thing exists
at one time actually and at another potentially, e. g. wine
or flesh or man does so. (And these two fall under the
above-named causes.[8] For the form exists actually, if it can
exist apart, and so does the complex of form and matter,   10

[6] i. e. the efficient cause is identical with the formal.

[7] i. e. the causes of substance are the causes of all things.

[8] i. e. the division into potency and actuality stands in a definite relation
to the previous division into matter, form, and privation.

and the privation, e. g. darkness or disease; but the matter exists potentially; for this is that which can become qualified either by the form or by the privation.) But the distinction of actuality and potentiality applies in another way to cases where the matter of cause and of effect is not the same, in some of which cases the form is not the same but different; e. g. the cause of man is (1) the elements in
15 man (viz. fire and earth as matter, and the peculiar form), and further (2) something else outside, i. e. the father, and (3) besides these the sun and its oblique course, which are neither matter nor form nor privation of man nor of the same species with him, but moving causes.

Further, one must observe that some causes can be expressed in universal terms, and some cannot. The proximate principles of all things are the 'this' which is proximate in actuality, and another which is proximate in
20 potentiality.[9] The universal causes, then, of which we spoke[10] do not *exist*. For it is the individual that is the originative principle of the individuals. For while man is the originative principle of man universally, there *is* no universal man, but Peleus is the originative principle of Achilles, and your father of you, and this particular *b* of this particular *ba*, though *b* in general is the originative principle of *ba* taken without qualification.

Further, if the causes of substances are the causes of all things, yet different things have different causes and ele-
25 ments, as was said[11]; the causes of things that are not in the same class, e. g. of colours and sounds, of substances and quantities, are different except in an analogical sense; and

[9] e. g. the proximate causes of a child are the individual father (who on Aristotle's view is the efficient and contains the formal cause) and the germ contained in the individual mother (which is the material cause).

[10] In l. 17.

[11] In 1070^b 17.

those of things in the same species are different, not in
species, but in the sense that the causes of different individuals are different, your matter and form and moving
cause being different from mine, while in their universal
definition they are the same. And if we inquire what are the
principles or elements of substances and relations and qual-   30
ities—whether they are the same or different—clearly when
the names of the causes are used in several senses the causes
of each are the same, but when the senses are distinguished
the causes are not the same but different, except that in the
following senses the causes of all are the same. They are (1)
the same or analogous in this sense, that matter, form, privation, and the moving cause are common to all things; and
(2) the causes of substances may be treated as causes of all
things in this sense, that when substances are removed all
things are removed; further, (3) that which is first in respect
of complete reality is the cause of all things. But in another   35
sense there are different first causes, viz. all the contraries
which are neither generic nor ambiguous terms; and, further, the matters of different things are different. We have   1071^b
stated, then, what are the principles of sensible things and
how many they are, and in what sense they are the same
and in what sense different.

6 Since there were[12] three kinds of substance, two of
them physical and one unmovable, regarding the
latter we must assert that it is necessary that there
should be an eternal unmovable substance. For substances
are the first of existing things, and if they are all destruc-   5
tible, all things are destructible. But it is impossible that
movement should either have come into being or cease to
be (for it must always have existed), or that time should.
For there could not be a before and an after if time did not

[12] Cf. 1069^a 30.

exist. Movement also is continuous, then, in the sense in which time is; for time is either the same thing as movement or an attribute of movement. And there is no 10 continuous movement except movement in place, and of this only that which is circular is continuous.

But if there is something which is capable of moving things or acting on them, but is not actually doing so, there will not necessarily be movement; for that which has a potency need not exercise it. Nothing, then, is gained even if we suppose eternal substances, as the believers in the Forms do, unless there is to be in them some principle 15 which can cause change; nay, even this is not enough, nor is another substance besides the Forms enough; for if it is not to *act*, there will be no movement. Further, even if it acts, this will not be enough, if its essence is potency; for there will not be *eternal* movement, since that which is potentially 20 may possibly not be. There must, then, be such a principle, whose very essence is actuality. Further, then, these substances must be without matter; for they must be eternal, if *anything* is eternal. Therefore they must be actuality.

Yet there is a difficulty, for it is thought that everything that acts is able to act, but that not everything that is able to 25 act acts, so that the potency is prior. But if this is so, nothing that is need be; for it is possible for all things to be capable of existing but not yet to exist.

Yet if we follow the theologians who generate the world from night, or the natural philosophers who say that 'all things were together',[13] the same impossible result ensues. For how will there be movement, if there is no actually 30 existing cause? Wood will surely not move itself—the carpenter's art must act on it; nor will the menstrual blood nor the earth set themselves in motion, but the seeds must act on the earth and the *semen* on the menstrual blood.

[13] Anaxagoras.

This is why some suppose eternal actuality—e. g. Leucippus[14] and Plato[15]; for they say there is always movement.
But why and what this movement is they do not say, nor,
if the world moves in this way or that, do they tell us the
cause of its doing so. Now nothing is moved at random, but
there must always be something present to move it; e. g. as
a matter of fact a thing moves in one way by nature, and in 35
another by force or through the influence of reason or something else. (Further, what sort of movement is primary?
This makes a vast difference.) But again for Plato, at least,
it is not permissible to name here that which he sometimes 1072ᵃ
supposes to be the source of movement—that which moves
itself;[16] for the soul is later, and coeval with the heavens,
according to his account.[17] To suppose potency prior to
actuality, then, is in a sense right, and in a sense not; and
we have specified these senses.[18] That actuality is prior is 5
testified by Anaxagoras (for his 'reason' is actuality) and by
Empedocles in his doctrine of love and strife, and by those
who say that there is always movement, e. g. Leucippus.
Therefore chaos or night did not exist for an infinite time,
but the same things have always existed (either passing
through a cycle of changes or obeying some other law),
since actuality is prior to potency. If, then, there is a constant cycle, something must always remain,[19] acting in the 10
same way. And if there is to be generation and destruction,
there must be something else[20] which is always acting in dif-

14 Cf. *De Caelo*, iii. 300ᵇ 8.

15 Cf. *Timaeus*, 30 A.

16 Cf. *Phaedrus*, 245 C; *Laws*, 894 E.

17 Cf. *Timaeus*, 34 B.

18 Cf. 1071ᵇ 22–26.

19 i. e. the sphere of the fixed stars.

20 i. e. the sun. Cf. *De Gen. et Corr.* ii. 336ᵃ 23 ff.

ferent ways. This must, then, act in one way in virtue of
itself, and in another in virtue of something else—either of
a third agent, therefore, or of the first. Now it must be in
virtue of the first. For otherwise this again causes the
motion both of the second agent and of the third. There-
15 fore it is better to say 'the first'. For it was the cause of
eternal uniformity; and something else is the cause of variety, and evidently both together are the cause of eternal
variety. This, accordingly, is the character which the
motions actually exhibit. What need then is there to seek
for other principles?

7 Since (1) this is a possible account of the matter,
and (2) if it were not true, the world would have
proceeded out of night and 'all things together' and
20 out of non-being, these difficulties may be taken as solved.
There is, then, something which is always moved with an
unceasing motion, which is motion in a circle; and this is
plain not in theory only but in fact. Therefore the first
heaven[21] must be eternal. There is therefore also something
which moves it. And since that which is moved and moves
is intermediate, there is something which moves without
25 being moved, being eternal, substance, and actuality. And
the object of desire and the object of thought move in this
way; they move without being moved. The primary objects
of desire and of thought are the same. For the apparent
good is the object of appetite, and the real good is the primary object of rational wish. But desire is consequent on
opinion rather than opinion on desire; for the thinking is the
30 starting-point. And thought is moved by the object of
thought, and one of the two columns of opposites is in itself
the object of thought; and in this, substance is first, and in
substance, that which is simple and exists actually. (The
one and the simple are not the same; for 'one' means a mea-

[21] i. e. the outer sphere of the universe, that in which the fixed stars are set.

sure, but 'simple' means that the thing itself has a certain nature.) But the beautiful, also, and that which is in itself desirable are in the same column; and the first in any class 35 is always best, or analogous to the best.

That a final cause may exist among unchangeable entities is shown by the distinction of its meanings. For the 1072ᵇ final cause is (a) some being for whose good an action is done, and (b) something at which the action aims; and of these the latter exists among unchangeable entities though the former does not. The final cause, then, produces motion as being loved, but all other things move by being moved.

Now if something is moved it is capable of being otherwise than as it is. Therefore if its actuality is the primary 5 form of spatial motion, then in so far as it is subject to change, in *this* respect it is capable of being otherwise—in place, even if not in substance. But since there is something which moves while itself unmoved, existing actually, this can in no way be otherwise than as it is. For motion in space is the first of the kinds of change, and motion in a circle the first kind of spatial motion; and this the first mover 10 produces²² The first mover, then, exists of necessity; and in so far as it exists by necessity, its mode of being is good, and it is in this sense a first principle. For the necessary has all these senses—that which is necessary perforce because it is contrary to the natural impulse, that without which the good is impossible, and that which cannot be otherwise but can exist only in a single way.

On such a principle, then, depend the heavens and the world of nature. And it is a life such as the best which we enjoy, and enjoy for but a short time (for it is ever in this 15 state, which we cannot be), since its actuality is also plea-

²² If it had any movement, it would have the first. But it produces this and therefore cannot share in it, for if it did, we should have to look for something that is prior to the first mover and imparts this motion to it.

sure. (And for this reason[23] are waking, perception, and thinking most pleasant, and hopes and memories are so on account of these.) And thinking in itself deals with that which is best in itself, and that which is thinking in the fullest sense with that which is best in the fullest sense. And
20 thought thinks on itself because it shares the nature of the object or thought; for it becomes an object of thought in coming into contact with and thinking its objects, so that thought and object of thought are the same. For that which is *capable* of receiving the object of thought, i. e. the essence, is thought. But it is *active* when it possesses this object. Therefore the possession rather than the receptivity is the divine element which thought seems to contain, and the act of contemplation is what is most pleasant and best. If, then, God is always in that good state in which we some-times are, this compels our wonder; and if in a better this
25 compels it yet more. And God *is* in a better state. And life also belongs to God; for the actuality of thought is life, and God is that actuality; and God's self-dependent actuality is life most good and eternal. We say therefore that God is a living being, eternal, most good, so that life and duration continuous and eternal belong to God; for this is God.

Those who suppose, as the Pythagoreans[24] and Speusip-
30 pus[25] do, that supreme beauty and goodness are not present in the beginning, because the beginnings both of plants and of animals are *causes*, but beauty and completeness are in the effects of these,[26] are wrong in their opinion. For the
35 seed comes from other individuals which are prior and com-plete, and the first thing is not seed but the complete being;

[23] *sc.* because they are activities or actualities.

[24] Cf 1075ª 36.

[25] Cf. vii 1028ᵇ 21, xiv 1091ª 34, 1092ª 11.

[26] i. e. the animal or plant is more beautiful and perfect than the seed.

e. g. we must say that before the seed there is a man—not the man produced from the seed, but another from whom 1073ᵃ the seed comes.

It is clear then from what has been said that there is a substance which is eternal and unmovable and separate from sensible things. It has been shown also that this substance cannot have any magnitude, but is without part and 5 indivisible (for it produces movement through infinite time, but nothing finite has infinite power; and, while every magnitude is either infinite or finite, it cannot, for the above reason, have finite magnitude, and it cannot have infinite magnitude because there is no infinite magnitude at all). But 10 it has also been shown that it is impassive and unalterable; for all the other changes are posterior to[27] change of place.

8 It is clear, then, why these things are as they are. But we must not ignore the question whether we have to suppose one such substance or more than one, and if the latter, how many; we must also mention, 15 regarding the opinions expressed by others, that they have said nothing about the number of the substances that can even be clearly stated. For the theory of Ideas has no special discussion of the subject; for those who speak of Ideas say the Ideas are numbers, and they speak of numbers now as unlimited, now[28] as limited by the number 10; but as for the reason why there should be just so many numbers, nothing 20 is said with any demonstrative exactness. We however must discuss the subject, starting from the presuppositions and distinctions we have mentioned. The first principle or primary being is not movable either in itself or accidentally, but produces the primary eternal and single movement. But 25 since that which is moved must be moved by something,

---

[27] i. e. impossible without.

[28] The reference is to Plato (Cf. *Phys.* 206ᵇ 32).

and the first mover must be in itself unmovable, and eternal movement must be produced by something eternal and a single movement by a single thing, and since we see that
30 besides the simple spatial movement of the universe, which we say the first and unmovable substance produces, there are other spatial movements—those of the planets—which are eternal (for a body which moves in a circle is eternal and unresting; we have proved these points in the physical treatises[29]), each of *these* movements also must be caused by a substance both unmovable in itself and eternal. For the nature of the stars[30] is eternal just because it is a certain kind
35 of substance, and the mover is eternal and prior to the moved, and then which is prior to a substance must be a substance. Evidently, then, there must be substances which are of the same number as the movements of the stars, and in their nature eternal, and in themselves unmovable, and without magnitude, for the reason before mentioned.[31]

1073[b]   That the movers are substances, then, and that one of these is first and another second according to the same order as the movements of the stars, is evident. But in the number of the movements we reach a problem which must be treated from the standpoint of that one of the mathematical sciences which is most akin to philosophy—viz. of astron
5 omy; for this science speculates about substance which is perceptible but eternal, but the other mathematical sciences, i. e. arithmetic and geometry, treat of no substance. That the movements are more numerous than the bodies that are moved is evident to those who have given even moderate attention to the matter; for each of the planets has more
10 than one movement. But as to the actual number of these

[29] Cf. *Phys.* viii. 8, 9; *De Caelo,* i. 2, ii. 3–8.

[30] This is to be understood as a general term including both fixed stars and planets.

[31] Cf. ll. 5–11.

movements, we now—to give some notion of the subject—
quote what some of the mathematicians say, that our
thought may have some definite number to grasp; but, for
the rest, we must partly investigate for ourselves, partly 15
learn from other investigators, and if those who study this
subject form an opinion contrary to what we have now
stated, we must esteem both parties indeed, but follow the
more accurate.

Eudoxus supposed that the motion of the sun or of the
moon involves, in either case, three spheres, of which the
first is the sphere of the fixed stars, and the second moves
in the circle which runs along the middle of the zodiac, and 20
the third in the circle which is inclined across the breadth of
the zodiac; but the circle in which the moon moves is
inclined at a greater angle than that in which the sun moves.
And the motion of the planets involves, in each case, four
spheres, and of these also the first and second are the same
as the first two mentioned above (for the sphere of the fixed 25
stars is that which moves all the other spheres, and that
which is placed beneath this and has its movement in the
circle which bisects the zodiac is common to all), but the
poles of the third sphere of each planet are in the circle
which bisects the zodiac, and the motion of the fourth
sphere is in the circle which is inclined at an angle to the
equator of the third sphere; and the poles of the third
sphere are different for each of the other planets, but those 30
of Venus and Mercury are the same.

Callippus made the position of the spheres the same as
Eudoxus did, but while he assigned the same number as
Eudoxus did to Jupiter and to Saturn, he thought two more
spheres should be added to the sun and two to the moon, 35
if one is to explain the observed facts; and one more to each
of the other planets.

But it is necessary, if all the spheres combined are to
explain the observed facts, that for each of the planets there

1074ᵃ should be other spheres (one fewer than those hitherto
assigned) which counteract those already mentioned and
bring back to the same position the outermost sphere of the
star which in each case is situated below[32] the star in ques-
5 tion; for only thus can all the forces at work produce the
observed motion of the planets. Since, then, the spheres
involved in the movement of the planets themselves are—
eight for Saturn and Jupiter and twenty-five for the others,
and of these only those involved in the movement of the
lowest-situated planet need not be counteracted, the spheres
which counteract those of the outermost two planets will be
six in number, and the spheres which counteract those of
the next four planets will be sixteen; therefore the number
10 of all the spheres—both those which move the planets and
those which counteract these—will be fifty-five. And if one
were not to add to the moon and to the sun the movements
we mentioned,[33] the whole set of spheres will be forty-seven
in number.

Let this, then, be taken as the number of the spheres,
so that the unmovable substances and principles also may
15 probably be taken as just so many; the assertion of necessity
must be left to more powerful thinkers. But if there can be
no spatial movement which does not conduce to the moving
of a star, and if further every being and every substance
which is immune from change and in virtue of itself has
attained to the best must be considered an end, there can
be no other being apart from these we have named, but this
20 must be the number of the substances. For if there are
others, they will cause change as being a final cause of
movement; but there cannot *be* other movements besides
those mentioned. And it is reasonable to infer this from a

[32] i. e. inwards from, the universe being thought of as a system of concen-
tric spheres encircling the earth.

[33] In 1073ᵇ 35, 38–1074ᵃ 4.

consideration of the bodies that are moved; for if everything 25
that moves is for the sake of that which is moved, and every
movement belongs to something that is moved, no movement can be for the sake of itself or of another movement,
but all the movements must be for the sake of the stars. For
if there is to be a movement for the sake of a movement,
this latter also will have to be for the sake of something else; 30
so that since there cannot be an infinite regress, the end of
every movement will be one of the divine bodies which
move through the heaven.

(Evidently there is but one heaven. For if there are
many heavens as there are many men, the moving principles,
of which each heaven will have one, will be one in form but
in *number* many. But all things that are many in number
have matter; for one and the same definition, e. g. that of 35
man, applies to many things, while Socrates is one. But the
primary essence has not matter; for it is complete reality. So
the unmovable first mover is one both in definition and in
number; so too, therefore, is that which is moved always and
continuously; therefore there is one heaven alone.)

Our forefathers in the most remote ages have handed 1074^b
down to their posterity a tradition, in the form of a myth,
that these bodies are gods and that the divine encloses the
whole of nature. The rest of the tradition has been added
later in mythical form with a view to the persuasion of the
multitude and to its legal and utilitarian expediency; they
say these gods are in the form of men or like some of the 5
other animals, and they say other things consequent on and
similar to these which we have mentioned. But if one were
to separate the first point from these additions and take it
alone—that they thought the first substances to be gods, 10
one must regard this as an inspired utterance, and reflect
that, while probably each art and each science has often
been developed as far as possible and has again perished,
these opinions, with others, have been preserved until the

present like relics of the ancient treasure. Only thus far, then, is the opinion of our ancestors and of our earliest predecessors clear to us.

15   **9** The nature of the divine thought involves certain problems; for while thought is held to be the most divine of things observed by us, the question how it must be situated in order to have that character involves difficulties. For if it thinks of nothing, what is there here of dignity? It is just like one who sleeps. And if it thinks, but this depends on something else, then (since that which is its substance is not the act of thinking, but a potency) it cannot

20 be the best substance; for it is through thinking that its value belongs to it. Further, whether its substance is the faculty of thought or the act of thinking, what does it think of? Either of itself or of something else; and if of something else, either of the same thing always or of something different. Does it matter, then, or not, whether it thinks of the good or of any chance thing? Are there not some things

25 about which it is incredible that it should think? Evidently, then, it thinks of that which is most divine and precious, and it does not change; for change would be change for the worse, and this would be already a movement. First, then, if 'thought' is not the act of thinking but a potency, it would be reasonable to suppose that the continuity of its thinking is wearisome to it. Secondly, there would evidently be something else more precious than thought, viz. that which is

30 thought of. For both thinking and the act of thought will belong even to one who thinks of the worst thing in the world, so that if this ought to be avoided (and it ought, for there are even some things which it is better not to see than to see), the act of thinking cannot be the best of things. Therefore it must be of itself that the divine thought thinks (since it is the most excellent of things), and its thinking is a thinking on thinking.

But evidently knowledge and perception and opinion and understanding have always something else as their 35 object, and themselves only by the way. Further, if thinking and being thought of are different, in respect of which does goodness belong to thought? For to *be* an act of thinking and to *be* an object of thought are not the same thing. We answer that in some cases the knowledge is the object. In the productive sciences it is the substance or essence of the 1075[a] object, matter omitted, and in the theoretical sciences the definition or the act of thinking is the object. Since, then, thought and the object of thought are not different in the case of things that have not matter, the divine thought and its object will be the same, i. e. the thinking will be one with the object of its thought.

A further question is left—whether the object of the divine thought is composite; for if it were, thought would 5 change in passing from part to part of the whole. We answer that everything which has not matter is indivisible— as human thought, or rather the thought of composite beings, is in a certain period of time (for it does not possess the good at this moment or at that, but its best, being some- thing *different* from it, is attained only in a whole period of time), so throughout eternity is the thought which has *itself* 10 for its object.

10 We must consider also in which of two ways the nature of the universe contains the good and the highest good, whether as something separate and by itself, or as the order of the parts. Probably in both ways, as an army does; for its good is found both in its 15 order and in its leader, and more in the latter; for he does not depend on the order but it depends on him. And all things are ordered together somehow, but not all alike— both fishes and fowls and plants; and the world is not such that one thing has nothing to do with another, but they are

20 connected. For all are ordered together to one end, but it is
as in a house, where the freemen are least at liberty to act at
random, but all things or most things are already ordained
for them, while the slaves and the animals do little for the
common good, and for the most part live at random; for
this is the sort of principle that constitutes the nature of
each. I mean, for instance, that all must at least come to be
dissolved into their elements,[34] and there are other functions
similarly in which all share for the good of the whole.

25   We must not fail to observe how many impossible or
paradoxical results confront those who hold different views
from our own, and what are the views of the subtler
thinkers, and which views are attended by fewest difficulties. All make all things out of contraries. But neither 'all
things' nor 'out of contraries' is right; nor do these thinkers
tell us how all the things in which the contraries are pres-
30 ent can be made out of the contraries; for contraries are not
affected by one another. Now for us this difficulty is solved
naturally by the fact that there is a third element.[35] These
thinkers however make one of the two contraries matter;
this is done for instance by those who make the unequal
matter for the equal, or the many matter for the one.[36] But
this also is refuted in the same way; for the one matter
which underlies any pair of contraries is contrary to nothing. Further, all things, except the one, will, on the view we
35 are criticizing, partake of evil; for the bad itself is one of the
two elements. But the other school[37] does not treat the good

---

[34] sc. in order that higher forms of being may be produced by new combinations of the elements.

[35] i. e. the substratum.

[36] The reference is to Platonists.

[37] The reference is to the Pythagoreans and Speusippus; Cf. xii. 1072^b 31.

and the bad even as principles; yet in all things the good is in the highest degree a principle. The school we first mentioned is right in saying that it is a principle, but *how* the good is a principle they do not say—whether as end or as mover or as form.

1075b

Empedocles[38] also has a paradoxical view; for he identifies the good with love, but this is a principle both as mover (for it brings things together) and as matter (for it is part of the mixture). Now even if it happens that the same thing is a principle both as matter and as mover, still the being, at least, of the two is not the same. In which respect then is love a principle? It is paradoxical also that strife should be imperishable; the nature of his 'evil' is just strife.

Anaxagoras makes the good a motive principle; for his 'reason' moves things. But it moves them for an end, which must be something other than it, except according to our way of stating the case; for, on our view, the medical art is in a sense health. It is paradoxical also not to suppose a contrary to the good, i. e. to reason. But all who speak of the contraries make no use of the contraries, unless we bring their views into shape. And why some things are perishable and others imperishable, no one tells us; for they make all existing things out of the same principles. Further, some make existing things out of the non-existent; and others to avoid the necessity of this make all things one.

Further, why should there always be becoming, and what is the cause of becoming?—this no one tells us. And those who suppose two principles must suppose another, a superior principle, and so must those who believe in the Forms; for why did things come to participate, or why do they participate, in the Forms? And all other thinkers[39] are

38 Cf. i. 985a 4.

39 The special reference is to Plato; Cf. *Rep.* 477.

confronted by the necessary consequence that there is something contrary to Wisdom, i. e. to the highest knowledge; but we are not. For there is nothing contrary to that which is primary; for all contraries have matter, and things that have matter exist only potentially; and the ignorance which is contrary to any knowledge leads to an object contrary to the object of the knowledge; but what is primary has no contrary.

Again, if besides sensible things no others exist, there
25 will be no first principle, no order, no becoming, no heavenly bodies, but each principle will have a principle before it, as in the accounts of the theologians and all the natural philosophers. But if the Forms or the numbers are to exist, they will be causes of nothing; or if not that, at least not of movement. Further, how is extension, i. e. a *continuum*, to be produced out of unextended parts? For number will not, either as mover or as form, produce a *continuum*. But again
30 there cannot be any *contrary* that is also essentially a productive or moving principle; or it would be possible not to be.[40] Or at least its action would be posterior to its potency. The world, then, would not be eternal. But it is; one of these premisses, then, must be denied. And we have said how this must be done.[41] Further, in virtue of what the
35 numbers, or the soul and the body, or in general the form and the thing, are one—of this no one tells us anything; nor can any one tell, unless he says, as we do, that the mover makes them one. And those who say[42] mathematical number is first and go on to generate one kind of substance after
1076ᵃ another and give different principles for each, make the substance of the universe a mere series of episodes (for one

[40] Since contraries must contain matter, and matter implies potentiality and contingency.

[41] Cf. 1071ᵇ 19, 20.

[42] Speusippus is meant, Cf. vii. 1028ᵇ 21, xiv. 1090ᵇ 13–20.

substance has no influence on another by its existence or non-existence), and they give us many governing principles; but the world refuses to be governed badly.

'The rule of many is not good; one ruler let there be.'[43]

[43] Cf. *Iliad*, ii. 204.

ETHICS

INTRODUCTION

Since every art, inquiry, and action is directed to some good, the investigation of moral problems takes its peculiar turn in the philosophy of Aristotle from his undertaking to treat that end as a principle and a cause relative to the potentialities of man. For although there is some verbal agreement among men identifying the good with happiness, there is no agreement concerning what happiness is, and Aristotle concludes that happiness must be defined, not in terms of something else with which it is identical, but in terms of activity of the soul in accordance with perfect virtue.

The study of ethics is therefore in good part a study of virtues, that is, a study of values and actions not in terms of ends in which the action terminates but in terms of habits from which it originates, and the inquiry is in that sense functional and determined by the peculiarities and potentialities of individual men. "Habit" is a source of action distinct from "nature," which is not altered as a principle of motion by prior actions or by the influence of a rational principle, and from "art," which is more dependent than virtue on knowledge. There is no virtue proper to the vegetative faculty of the soul, since its functions are not affected by reason, but there are two varieties of virtues, moral virtues proper to the appetitive soul which shares in a rational principle, and intellectual virtues proper to the intellective soul. In addition to the virtues, however, Aristotle considers continence and superhuman virtue (which are also moral states), pleasure (which some men think a good and which is a mark of the good in the virtuous man), friendship (which either is a virtue or implies virtue), and the influence of the state in the inculcation of virtue. The relativity of the moral virtues to the potentialities of the individual man and the peculiarities of his environment does not lead to a moral relativism, however, for political justice is in part natural, and moral virtue is in accordance with the rule of right reason or of practical wisdom. Practical wisdom is in turn so closely dependent on philosophic wisdom, that wisdom may be said to be the formal cause of happiness, and happiness in the highest sense is found in the contemplative life.

The ethics of Aristotle reflects in many ways the place which it occupies in the system of the Aristotelian sciences. It is itself a science, although it does not employ the same method as the theoretic sciences and it does not aim at the same precision. It depends on the nature of man and borrows dialectical distinctions therefore from psychology to differentiate moral from intellectual virtues. Yet it treats, among the intellectual virtues, of those habits of mind which are the source of discursive scientific proof, intuition of first principles, and wisdom itself which combines scientific proof and principles. Moreover, among the practical sciences, it is not distinct, strictly, from political science, but it is rather the other aspect of the analysis of human action by which the study of the associations of men (which are affected by the character of their members) is supplemented by the study of the virtues of men (which are affected by political institutions). Political science, finally, which as a science makes use of first principles treated properly in metaphysics, is itself an "architectonic science," and as science of action determines what sciences will be studied in the state and in what manner.

ETHICA NICOMACHEA

CONTENTS

BOOK I. THE GOOD FOR MAN

D. *Inner side of moral virtue: conditions of responsibility for action*

1. Praise and blame attach to voluntary actions, i. e. actions done (1) not under compulsion, and (2) with knowledge of the circumstances.
2. Moral virtue implies that the action is done (3) by choice; the object of choice is the result of previous deliberation.
3. The nature of deliberation and its objects: choice is deliberate desire of things in our own power.
4. The object of rational wish is the end, i. e. the good or the apparent good.
5. We are responsible for bad as well as for good actions.

III. 6-V. 11. THE VIRTUES AND VICES.

A. *Courage.*

6. Courage concerned with the feelings of fear and confidence—strictly speaking, with the fear of death in battle.
7. The motive of courage is the sense of honour: characteristics of the opposite vices, cowardice and rashness.
8. Five kinds of courage improperly so called.
9. Relation of courage to pain and pleasure.

B. *Temperance.*

10. Temperance is limited to certain pleasures of touch.
11. Characteristics of temperance and its opposites, self-indulgence and 'insensibility'.
12. Self-indulgence more voluntary than cowardice: comparison of the self-indulgent man to the spoilt child.

C. *Virtues concerned with money.*

1. Liberality, prodigality, meanness.
2. Magnificence, vulgarity, niggardliness.

D. *Virtues concerned with honour.*

3. Pride, vanity, humility.
4. Ambition, unambitiousness, and the mean between them.

E. *The virtue concerned with anger.*

5. Good temper, irascibility, inirascibility.

F. *Virtues of social intercourse.*

6. Friendliness, obsequiousness, churlishness.
7. Truthfulness, boastfulness, mock-modesty.
8. Ready wit, buffoonery, boorishness.

G. *A quasi-virtue.*

9. Shame, bashfulness, shamelessness.

H. *Justice.*

I. Its sphere and outer nature: in what sense it is a mean.

1. The just as the lawful (universal justice) and the just as the fair and equal (particular justice): the former considered.
2. The latter considered: divided into distributive and rectificatory justice.
3. Distributive justice, in accordance with geometrical proportion.
4. Rectificatory justice, in accordance with arithmetical progression.
5. Justice in exchange, reciprocity in accordance with proportion.
6. Political justice and analogous kinds of justice.
7. Natural and legal justice.

II. Its inner nature as involving choice.

8. The scale of degrees of wrongdoing.
9. Can a man be voluntarily treated unjustly? Is it the distrib-

utor or the recipient that is guilty of injustice in distribution? Justice not so easy as it might seem, because it is not
a way of acting but an inner disposition.
10. Equity, a corrective of legal justice.
11. Can a man treat himself unjustly?

BOOK VI. INTELLECTUAL VIRTUE

A. *Introduction.*

1. Reasons for studying intellectual virtue: intellect divided
into the contemplative and the calculative.
2. The object of the former is truth, that of the latter truth
corresponding with right desire.

B. *The chief intellectual virtues.*

3. Science—demonstrative knowledge of the necessary and
eternal.
4. Art—knowledge of how to make things.
5. Practical wisdom—knowledge of how to secure the ends of
human life.
6. Intuitive reason—knowledge of the principles from which
science proceeds.
7. Philosophic wisdom—the union of intuitive reason and science.
8. Relations between practical wisdom and political science.

C. *Minor intellectual virtues concerned with conduct.*

9. Goodness in deliberation, how related to practical wisdom.
10. Understanding—the critical quality answering to the imper-
ative quality practical wisdom.
11. Judgement—right discrimination of the equitable: the place
of intuition in morals.

D. *Relation of philosophic to practical wisdom.*

12. What is the use of philosophic and of practical wisdom?

BOOK VII. CONTINENCE AND INCONTINENCE. PLEASURE

A. *Continence and incontinence.*

B. *Pleasure.*

BOOKS VIII, IX. FRIENDSHIP

A. *Kinds of friendship.*

1. Friendship both necessary and noble: main questions about it.
2. Three objects of love: implications of friendship.
3. Three corresponding kinds of friendship: superiority of friendship whose motive is the good.
4. Contrast between the best and the inferior kinds.
5. The state of friendship distinguished from the activity of friendship and from the feeling of friendliness.
6. Various relations between the three kinds.

B. *Reciprocity of friendship.*

7. In unequal friendships a proportion must be maintained.
8. Loving is more of the essence of friendship than being loved.

C. *Relation of reciprocity in friendship to that involved in other forms of community.*

9. Parallelism of friendship and justice: the state comprehends all lesser communities.
10. Classification of constitutions: analogies with family relations.
11. Corresponding forms of friendship, and of justice.
12. Various forms of friendship between relations.

D. *Casuistry of friendship.*

13. Principles of interchange of services (*a*) in friendship between equals.
14. (*b*) In friendship between unequals.
    (*c*) In friendship in which the motives on the two sides are
1. different.
2. Conflict of obligations.
3. Occasions of breaking off friendship.

ETHICA NICOMACHEA

Nicomachean Ethics

Translated by W. D. Ross

BOOK I

1 Every art and every inquiry, and similarly every
action and pursuit, is thought to aim at some good; 1094ª
and for this reason the good has rightly been
declared[1] to be that at which all things aim. But a certain
difference is found among ends; some are activities, others
are products apart from the activities that produce them. 5
Where there are ends apart from the actions, it is the nature
of the products to be better than the activities. Now, as
there are many actions, arts, and sciences, their ends also
are many; the end of the medical art is health, that of ship-
building a vessel, that of strategy victory, that of economics
wealth. But where such arts fall under a single capacity—as 10
bridle-making and the other arts concerned with the equipment of horses fall under the art of riding, and this and
every military action under strategy, in the same way other
arts fall under yet others—in all of these the ends of the
master arts are to be preferred to all the subordinate ends;
for it is for the sake of the former that the latter are pur- 15
sued. It makes no difference whether the activities
themselves are the ends of the actions, or something else

---

[1] Perhaps by Eudoxus; Cf. 1172ᵇ 9.

apart from the activities, as in the case of the sciences just mentioned.

2 If, then, there is some end of the things we do, which we desire for its own sake (everything else being desired for the sake of this), and if we do not choose everything for the sake of something else (for at that 20 rate the process would go on to infinity, so that our desire would be empty and vain), clearly this must be the good and the chief good. Will not the knowledge of it, then, have a great influence on life? Shall we not, like archers who have a mark to aim at, be more likely to hit upon what is right? 25 If so, we must try, in outline at least to determine what it is, and of which of the sciences or capacities it is the object. It would seem to belong to the most authoritative art and that which is most truly the master art. And politics appears to be of this nature, for it is this that ordains which of the sci- 1094b ences should be studied in a state, and which each class of citizens should learn and up to what point they should learn them; and we see even the most highly esteemed of capaci- 5 ties to fall under this, e. g. strategy, economics, rhetoric; now, since politics uses the rest of the sciences, and since, again, it legislates as to what we are to do and what we are to abstain from, the end of this science must include those of the others, so that this end must be the good for man. For even if the end is the same for a single man and for a state, that of the state seems at all events something greater and more complete whether to attain or to preserve; though it is worth while to attain the end merely for one man, it is 10 finer and more godlike to attain it for a nation or for city-states. These, then, are the ends at which our inquiry aims, since it is political science, in one sense of that term.

3 Our discussion will be adequate if it has as much clearness as the subject-matter admits of, for precision is not to be sought for alike in all discussions, any more than in all the products of the crafts. Now fine 15 and just actions, which political science investigates, admit of much variety and fluctuation of opinion, so that they may be thought to exist only by convention, and not by nature. And goods also give rise to a similar fluctuation because they bring harm to many people; for before now men have been undone by reason of their wealth, and others by reason of their courage. We must be content, then, in 20 speaking of such subjects and with such premisses to indicate the truth roughly and in outline, and in speaking about things which are only for the most part true and with premisses of the same kind to reach conclusions that are no better. In the same spirit, therefore, should each type of statement be *received*; for it is the mark of an educated man 25 to look for precision in each class of things just so far as the nature of the subject admits; it is evidently equally foolish to accept probable reasoning from a mathematician and to demand from a rhetorician scientific proofs.

Now each man judges well the things he knows, and of these he is a good judge. And so the man who has been educated in a subject is a good judge of that subject, and 1095[a] the man who has received an all-round education is a good judge in general. Hence a young man is not a proper hearer of lectures on political science; for he is inexperienced in the actions that occur in life, but its discussions start from these and are about these; and, further, since he tends to follow his passions, his study will be vain and unprofitable, because the end aimed at is not knowledge but action. And it makes no difference whether he is young in years or 5 youthful in character; the defect does not depend on time, but on his living, and pursuing each successive object, as passion directs. For to such persons, as to the incontinent,

knowledge brings no profit; but to those who desire and act
10 in accordance with a rational principle knowledge about
such matters will be of great benefit.

These remarks about the student, the sort of treatment
to be expected, and the purpose of the inquiry, may be
taken as our preface.

4 Let us resume our inquiry and state, in view of the
fact that all knowledge and every pursuit aims at
some good, what it is that we say political science
15 aims at and what is the highest of all goods achievable by
action. Verbally there is very general agreement; for both
the general run of men and people of superior refinement
say that it is happiness, and identify living well and doing
well with being happy; but with regard to what happiness is
20 they differ, and the many do not give the same account as
the wise. For the former think it is some plain and obvious
thing, like pleasure, wealth, or honour; they differ, however,
from one another—and often even the same man identifies
it with different things, with health when he is ill, with
25 wealth when he is poor; but, conscious of their ignorance,
they admire those who proclaim some great ideal that is
above their comprehension. Now some[2] thought that apart
from these many goods there is another which is self-subsistent and causes the goodness of all these as well. To
examine all the opinions that have been held were perhaps
somewhat fruitless; enough to examine those that are most
prevalent or that seem to be arguable.

Let us not fail to notice, however, that there is a differ-
30 ence between arguments from and those to the first
principles. For Plato, too, was right in raising this question

---

[2] The Platonic School; Cf. ch. 6.

and asking, as he used to do, 'are we on the way from or to the first principles?'³ There is a difference, as there is in a race-course between the course from the judges to the turning-point and the way back. For, while we must begin with what is known, things are objects of knowledge in two senses—some to us, some without qualification. Presumably, then, we must begin with things known to us. Hence any one who is to listen intelligently to lectures about what is noble and just and, generally, about the subjects of political science must have been brought up in good habits. For the fact is the starting-point, and if this is sufficiently plain to him, he will not at the start need the reason as well; and the man who has been well brought up has or can easily get starting-points. And as for him who neither has nor can get them, let him hear the words of Hesiod:

> Far best is he who knows all things himself;
> Good, he that hearkens when men counsel right;
> But he who neither knows, nor lays to heart
> Another's wisdom, is a useless wight.

5   Let us, however, resume our discussion from the point at which we digressed. To judge from the lives that men lead, most men, and men of the most vulgar type; seem (not without some ground) to identify the good, or happiness, with pleasure; which is the reason why they love the life of enjoyment. For there are, we may say, three prominent types of life—that just mentioned, the political, and thirdly the contemplative life. Now the mass of mankind are evidently quite slavish in their tastes, preferring a life suitable to beasts, but they get some ground for their view from the fact that many of those in high

1095ᵇ (margin, at line "senses")

5 (margin)

10 (margin)

15 (margin)

20 (margin)

³ Cf. *Rep.* 511 B

places share the tastes of Sardanapallus. A consideration of
the prominent types of life shows that people of superior
refinement and of active disposition identify happiness with
honour; for this is, roughly speaking, the end of the political life. But it seems too superficial to be what we are
25 looking for, since it is thought to depend on those who
bestow honour rather than on him who receives it, but the
good we divine to be something proper to a man and not
easily taken from him. Further, men seem to pursue honour in order that they may be assured of their goodness; at
least it is by men of practical wisdom that they seek to be
honoured, and among those who know them, and on the
ground of their virtue; clearly, then, according to them, at
30 any rate, virtue is better. And perhaps one might even suppose this to be, rather than honour, the end of the political
life. But even this appears somewhat incomplete; for possession of virtue seems actually compatible with being
1096ᵃ asleep, or with lifelong inactivity, and, further, with the
greatest sufferings and misfortunes; but a man who was living so no one would call happy, unless he were maintaining
a thesis at all costs. But enough of this; for the subject has
been sufficiently treated even in the current discussions.
Third comes the contemplative life, which we shall consider later.[4]

The life of money-making is one undertaken under
5 compulsion, and wealth is evidently not the good we are
seeking; for it is merely useful and for the sake of something
else. And so one might rather take the aforenamed objects
to be ends; for they are loved for themselves. But it is evident that not even these are ends; yet many arguments have
been thrown away in support of them. Let us leave this
10 subject, then.

---

[4] 1177ᵃ 12–1178ᵃ 8, 1178ᵃ 22–1179ᵃ 32.

6 We had perhaps better consider the universal good and discuss thoroughly what is meant by it, although such an inquiry is made an uphill one by the fact that the Forms have been introduced by friends of our own. Yet it would perhaps be thought to be better, indeed to be our duty, for the sake of maintaining the truth even to destroy what touches us closely, especially as we are philosophers or lovers of wisdom; for, while both are dear, 15 piety requires us to honour truth above our friends.

The men who introduced this doctrine did not posit Ideas of classes within which they recognized priority and posteriority (which is the reason why they did not maintain the existence of an Idea embracing all numbers); but the term 'good' is used both in the category of substance and in that of quality and in that of relation, and that which is *per se*, i. e. substance, is prior in nature to the relative (for 20 the latter is like an offshoot and accident of being); so that there could not be a common Idea set over all these goods. Further, since 'good' has as many senses as 'being' (for it is predicated both in the category of substance, as of God and of reason, and in quality, i. e. of the virtues, and in quan- 25 tity, i. e. of that which is moderate, and in relation, i. e. of the useful, and in time, i. e. of the right opportunity, and in place, i. e. of the right locality and the like), clearly it cannot be something universally present in all cases and single; for then it could not have been predicated in all the categories but in one only. Further, since of the things answering to one Idea there is one science, there would have been one sci- ence of all the goods; but as it is there are many sciences 30 even of the things that fall under one category, e. g. of opportunity, for opportunity in war is studied by strategics and in disease by medicine, and the moderate in food is studied by medicine and in exercise by the science of gym- nastics. And one might ask the question, what in the world they *mean* by 'a thing itself', if (as is the case) in 'man him-

35 self' and in a particular man the account of man is one and
1096ᵇ the same. For in so far as they are man, they will in no
respect differ; and if this is so, neither will 'good itself' and
particular goods, in so far as they are good. But again it will
not be good any the more for being eternal, since that which
5 lasts long is no whiter than that which perishes in a day.
The Pythagoreans seem to give a more plausible account of
the good, when they place the one in the column of goods;
and it is they that Speusippus seems to have followed.

But let us discuss these matters elsewhere[5]; an objection to what we have said, however, may be discerned in the
10 fact that the Platonists have not been speaking about *all*
goods, and that the goods that are pursued and loved for
themselves are called good by reference to a single Form,
while those which tend to produce or to preserve these
somehow or to prevent their contraries are called so by reference to these, and in a secondary sense. Clearly, then,
goods must be spoken of in two ways, and some must be
good in themselves, the others by reason of these. Let us
15 separate, then, things good in themselves from things useful, and consider whether the former are called good by
reference to a single Idea. What sort of goods would one
call good in themselves? Is it those that are pursued even
when isolated from others, such as intelligence, sight, and
certain pleasures and honours? Certainly, if we pursue these
also for the sake of something else, yet one would place
20 them among things good in themselves. Or is nothing other
than the Idea of good good in itself? In that case the Form
will be empty. But if the things we have named are also
things good in themselves, the account of the good will have
to appear as something identical in them all, as that of
whiteness is identical in snow and in white lead. But of hon-

[5] Cf. *Met.* 986ᵃ 22–6, 1028ᵇ 21–4, 1072ᵇ 30–1073ᵃ 3, 1091ᵃ 29–ᵇ3,
ᵇ13–1092ᵃ 17.

our, wisdom, and pleasure, just in respect of their goodness, 25
the accounts are distinct and diverse. The good, therefore, is
not some common element answering to one Idea.

But what then do we mean by the good? It is surely not
like the things that only chance to have the same name. Are
goods one, then, by being derived from one good or by all
contributing to one good, or are they rather one by analogy?
Certainly as sight is in the body, so is reason in the soul, 30
and so on in other cases. But perhaps these subjects had
better be dismissed for the present; for perfect precision
about them would be more appropriate to another branch of
philosophy.[6] And similarly with regard to the Idea; even if
there is some one good which is universally predicable of
goods or is capable of separate and independent existence,
clearly it could not be achieved or attained by man; but we
are now seeking something attainable. Perhaps, however, 35
some one might think it worth while to recognize this with
a view to the goods that *are* attainable and achievable; for
having this as a sort of pattern we shall know better the 1097ª
goods that are good for us, and if we know them shall attain
them. This argument has some plausibility, but seems to
clash with the procedure of the sciences; for all of these,
though they aim at some good and seek to supply the defi- 5
ciency of it, leave on one side the knowledge of *the* good.
Yet that all the exponents of the arts should be ignorant of,
and should not even seek, so great an aid is not probable.
It is hard, too, to see how a weaver or a carpenter will be
benefited in regard to his own craft by knowing this 'good
itself', or how the man who has viewed the Idea itself will 10
be a better doctor or general thereby. For a doctor seems
not even to study health in this way, but the health of man,
or perhaps rather the health of a particular man; it is individuals that he is healing. But enough of these topics.

[6] Cf. *Met.* iv. 2.

7 Let us again return to the good we are seeking, and ask what it can be. It seems different in different actions and arts; it is different in medicine, in strategy, and in the other arts likewise. What then is the good of each? Surely that for whose sake everything else is done. In medicine this is health, in strategy victory, in architecture a house, in any other sphere something else, and in every action and pursuit the end; for it is for the sake of this that all men do whatever else they do. Therefore, if there is an end for all that we do, this will be the good achievable by action, and if there are more than one, these will be the goods achievable by action.

So the argument has by a different course reached the same point; but we must try to state this even more clearly. Since there are evidently more than one end, and we choose some of these (e. g. wealth, flutes, and in general instruments) for the sake of something else, clearly not all ends are final ends, but the chief good is evidently something final. Therefore, if there is only one final end, this will be what we are seeking, and if there are more than one, the most final of these will be what we are seeking. Now we call that which is in itself worthy of pursuit more final than that which is worthy of pursuit for the sake of something else, and that which is never desirable for the sake of something else more final than the things that are desirable both in themselves and for the sake of that other thing, and therefore we call final without qualification that which is always desirable in itself and never for the sake of something else.

Now such a thing happiness, above all else, is held to be; for this we choose always for itself and never for the sake of something else, but honour, pleasure, reason, and every virtue we choose indeed for themselves (for if nothing resulted from them we should still choose each of them), but we choose them also for the sake of happiness, judging that by means of them we shall be happy. Happiness, on the other hand, no one chooses for the sake of these, nor, in general, for anything other than itself.

From the point of view of self-sufficiency the same result seems to follow; for the final good is thought to be self-sufficient. Now by self-sufficient we do not mean that which is sufficient for a man by himself, for one who lives a 10 solitary life, but also for parents, children, wife, and in general for his friends and fellow citizens, since man is born for citizenship. But some limit must be set to this; for if we extend our requirement to ancestors and descendants and friends' friends we are in for an infinite series. Let us examine this question, however, on another occasion;[7] the self-sufficient we now define as that which when isolated 15 makes life desirable and lacking in nothing; and such we think happiness to be; and further we think it most desirable of all things, without being counted as one good thing among others—if it were so counted it would clearly be made more desirable by the addition of even the least of goods; for that which is added becomes an excess of goods, 20 and of goods the greater is always more desirable. Happiness, then, is something final and self-sufficient, and is the end of action.

Presumably, however, to say that happiness is the chief good seems a platitude, and a clearer account of what it is is still desired. This might perhaps be given, if we could first 25 ascertain the function of man. For just as for a flute-player, a sculptor, or any artist, and, in general, for all things that have a function or activity, the good and the 'well' is thought to reside in the function, so would it seem to be for man, if he has a function. Have the carpenter, then, and the tanner certain functions or activities, and has man none? Is 30 he born without a function? Or as eye, hand, foot, and in general each of the parts evidently has a function, may one

[7] i. 10, 11, ix. 10.

lay it down that man similarly has a function apart from all
these? What then can this be? Life seems to be common
even to plants, but we are seeking what is peculiar to man.
1098ᵃ Let us exclude, therefore, the life of nutrition and growth.
Next there would be a life of perception, but *it* also seems
to be common even to the horse, the ox, and every animal.
There remains, then, an active life of the element that has
a rational principle; of this, one part has such a principle in-
5 the sense of being obedient to one, the other in the sense of
possessing one and exercising thought. And, as 'life of the
rational element' also has two meanings, we must state that
life in the sense of activity is what we mean; for this seems
to be the more proper sense of the term. Now if the function of man is an activity of soul which follows or implies
a rational principle, and if we say 'a so-and-so' and 'a good
so-and-so' have a function which is the same in kind, e. g. a
lyre-player and a good lyre-player, and so without qualification in all cases, eminence in respect of goodness being
10 added to the name of the function (for the function of a
lyre-player is to play the lyre, and that of a good lyre-player
is to do so well): if this is the case, [and we state the function of man to be a certain kind of life, and this to be an
activity or actions of the soul implying a rational principle,
and the function of a good man to be the good and noble
performance of these, and if any action is well performed
15 when it is performed in accordance with the appropriate
excellence: if this is the case,] human good turns out to be
activity of soul in accordance with virtue, and if there are
more than one virtue, in accordance with the best and most
complete.

But we must add 'in a complete life'. For one swallow
does not make a summer, nor does one day; and so too one
day, or a short time, does not make a man blessed and happy.

Let this serve as an outline of the good; for we must
20 presumably first sketch it roughly, and then later fill in the

details. But it would seem that any one is capable of carrying on and articulating what has once been well outlined, and that time is a good discoverer or partner in such a work; to which facts the advances of the arts are due; for any one can add what is lacking. And we must also remember what has been said before,[8] and not look for precision in all things 25 alike, but in each class of things such precision as accords with the subject-matter, and so much as is appropriate to the inquiry. For a carpenter and a geometer investigate the right angle in different ways; the former does so in so far as the right angle is useful for his work, while the latter 30 inquires what it is or what sort of thing it is; for he is a spectator of the truth. We must act in the same way, then, in all other matters as well, that our main task may not be subordinated to minor questions. Nor must we demand the cause in all matters alike; it is enough in some cases that the *fact* be well established, as in the case of the first principles; 1098b the fact is the primary thing or first principle. Now of first principles we see some by induction, some by perception, some by a certain habituation, and others too in other ways. But each set of principles we must try to investigate in the natural way, and we must take pains to state them definitely, since they have a great influence on what follows. For 5 the beginning is thought to be more than half of the whole, and many of the questions we ask are cleared up by it.

8 We must consider it, however, in the light not only of our conclusion and our premisses, but also of what is commonly said about it; for with a true view all the data harmonize, but with a false one the facts soon clash. Now goods have been divided into three classes,[9] and some are described as external, others as relating to soul

8 1094b 11–27.

9 Pl. *Euthyd.* 279 AB, *Phil.* 48 E, *Laws,* 743 E.

or to body; we call those that relate to soul most properly
15 and truly goods, and psychical actions and activities we class
as relating to soul. Therefore our account must be sound, at
least according to this view, which is an old one and agreed
on by philosophers. It is correct also in that we identify the
end with certain actions and activities; for thus it falls
among goods of the soul and not among external goods.
20 Another belief which harmonizes with our account is that
the happy man lives well and does well; for we have practically defined happiness as a sort of good life and good
action. The characteristics that are looked for in happiness
seem also, all of them, to belong to what we have defined
happiness as being. For some identify happiness with
virtue, some with practical wisdom, others with a kind of
25 philosophic wisdom, others with these, or one of these,
accompanied by pleasure or not without pleasure; while others include also external prosperity. Now some of these
views have been held by many men and men of old, others
by a few eminent persons; and it is not probable that either
of these should be entirely mistaken, but rather that they
should be right in at least some one respect or even in most
respects.

30   With those who identify happiness with virtue or some
one virtue our account is in harmony; for to virtue belongs
virtuous activity. But it makes, perhaps, no small difference
whether we place the chief good in possession or in use, in
1099a state of mind or in activity. For the state of mind may exist
without producing any good result, as in a man who is
asleep or in some other way quite inactive, but the activity
cannot; for one who has the activity will of necessity be acting, and acting well. And as in the Olympic Games it is not
the most beautiful and the strongest that are crowned but
5 those who compete (for it is some of these that are victori-
ous), so those who act win, and rightly win, the noble and
good things in life.

Their life is also in itself pleasant. For pleasure is a state of *soul*, and to each man that which he is said to be a lover of is pleasant; e. g. not only is a horse pleasant to the lover of horses, and a spectacle to the lover of sights, but 10 also in the same way just acts are pleasant to the lover of justice and in general virtuous acts to the lover of virtue. Now for most men their pleasures are in conflict with one another because these are not by nature pleasant, but the lovers of what is noble find pleasant the things that are by nature pleasant; and virtuous actions are such, so that these are pleasant for such men as well as in their own nature. Their life, therefore, has no further need of pleasure as a 15 sort of adventitious charm, but has its pleasure in itself. For, besides what we have said, the man who does not rejoice in noble actions is not even good; since no one would call a man just who did not enjoy acting justly, nor any man liberal who did not enjoy liberal actions; and similarly in all other cases. If this is so, virtuous actions must be in them- 20 selves pleasant. But they are also *good* and *noble*, and have each of these attributes in the highest degree, since the good man judges well about these attributes; his judgement is such as we have described.[10] Happiness then is the best, noblest, and most pleasant thing in the world, and these attributes are not severed as in the inscription at Delos— 25

Most noble is that which is justest, and best is health;
But pleasantest is it to win what we love.

For all these properties belong to the best activities; and these, or one—the best—of these, we identify with happiness. 30 Yet evidently, as we said,[11] it needs the external goods

[10] i. e., he judges that virtuous actions are good and noble in the highest degree.

[11] 1098[b] 26–9.

as well; for it is impossible, or not easy, to do noble acts **1099^b** without the proper equipment. In many actions we use friends and riches and political power as instruments; and there are some things the lack of which takes the lustre from happiness, as good birth, goodly children, beauty; for the man who is very ugly in appearance or ill-born or solitary and childless is not very likely to be happy, and perhaps a 5 man would be still less likely if he had thoroughly bad children or friends or had lost good children or friends by death. As we said,[11] then, happiness seems to need this sort of prosperity in addition; for which reason some identify happiness with good fortune, though others identify it with virtue.

9 For this reason also the question is asked, whether happiness is to be acquired by learning or by habituation or some other sort of training, or comes in 10 virtue of some divine providence or again by chance. Now if there is *any* gift of the gods to men, it is reasonable that happiness should be god-given, and most surely god-given of all human things inasmuch as it is the best. But this question would perhaps be more appropriate to another 15 inquiry; happiness seems, however, even if it is not god-sent but comes as a result of virtue and some process of learning or training, to be among the most god-like things; for that which is the prize and end of virtue seems to be the best thing in the world, and something godlike and blessed.

It will also on this view be very generally shared; for all who are not maimed as regards their potentiality for virtue 20 may win it by a certain kind of study and care. But if it is better to be happy thus than by chance, it is reasonable that the facts should be so, since everything that depends on the action of nature is by nature as good as it can be, and similarly everything that depends on art or any rational cause, and especially if it depends on the best of all causes. To entrust to chance what is greatest and most noble would be a very defective arrangement.

The answer to the question we are asking is plain also from the definition of happiness; for it has been said[12] to be a virtuous activity of soul, of a certain kind. Of the remaining goods, some must necessarily pre-exist as conditions of happiness, and others are naturally co-operative and useful as instruments. And this will be found to agree with what we said at the outset;[13] for we stated the end of political science to the best end, and political science spends most of its pains on making the citizens to be of a certain character, viz. good and capable of noble acts.

It is natural, then, that we call neither ox nor horse nor any other of the animals happy: for none of them is capable of sharing in such activity. For this reason also a boy is not happy; for he is not yet capable of such acts, owing to his age; and boys who are called happy are being congratulated by reason of the hopes we have for them. For there is required, as we said,[14] not only complete virtue but also a complete life, since many changes occur in life, and all manner of chances, and the most prosperous may fall into great misfortunes in old age, as is told of Priam in the Trojan Cycle; and one who has experienced such chances and has ended wretchedly no one calls happy.

10 Must no one at all, then, be called happy while he lives; must we, as Solon says, see the end? Even if we are to lay down this doctrine, is it also the case that a man is happy when he is *dead*? Or is not this quite absurd, especially for us who say that happiness

25

30

1100ᵃ

5

10

15

[12] 1098ᵃ 16.

[13] 1094ᵃ 27.

[14] 1098ᵃ 16–18.

is an activity? But if we do not call the dead man happy,
and if Solon does not mean this, but that one can then
safely *call* a man blessed as being at last beyond evils and
misfortunes, this also affords matter for discussion; for both
evil and good are thought to exist for a dead man, as much
20 as for one who is alive but not aware of them; e. g. honours
aud dishonours and the good or bad fortunes of children
and in general of descendants. And this also presents a
problem; for though a man has lived happily up to old age
and has had a death worthy of his life, many reverses may
befall his descendants—some of them may be good and
25 attain the life they deserve, while with others the opposite
may be the case; and clearly too the degrees of relationship
between them and their ancestors may vary indefinitely. It
would be odd, then, if the dead man were to share in these
changes and become at one time happy, at another
wretched; while it would also be odd if the fortunes of the
30 descendants did not for *some* time have *some* effect on the
happiness of their ancestors.

But we must return to our first difficulty; for perhaps
by a consideration of it our present problem might be
solved. Now if we must see the end and only then call a
man happy, not as being happy but as having been so
35 before, surely this is a paradox, that when he is happy the
attribute that belongs to him is not to be truly predicated
of him because we do not wish to call living men happy,
1100^b on account of the changes that may befall them, and
because we have assumed happiness to be something permanent and by no means easily changed, while a single
man may suffer many turns of fortune's wheel. For clearly
5 if we were to keep pace with his fortunes, we should often
call the same man happy and again wretched, making the
happy man out to be a 'chameleon and insecurely based'.
Or is this keeping pace with his fortunes quite wrong?
Success or failure in life does not depend on these, but

human life, as we said,[15] needs these as mere additions,
while virtuous activities or their opposites are what constitute happiness or the reverse.   10

The question we have now discussed confirms our definition. For no function of man has so much permanence as
virtuous activities (these are thought to be more durable even
than knowledge of the sciences), and of these themselves the
most valuable are more durable because those who are happy   15
spend their life most readily and most continuously in these;
for this seems to be the reason why we do not forget them.
The attribute in question,[16] then, will belong to the happy
man, and he will be happy throughout his life; for always, or
by preference to everything else, he will be engaged in virtuous action and contemplation, and he will bear the chances
of life most nobly and altogether decorously, if he is 'truly   20
good' and 'foursquare beyond reproach'.[17]

Now many events happen by chance, and events differing in importance; small pieces of good fortune or of its
opposite clearly do not weigh down the scales of life one
way or the other, but a multitude of great events if they   25
turn out well will make life happier (for not only are they
themselves such as to add beauty to life, but the way a man
deals with them may be noble and good), while if they turn
out ill they crush and maim happiness; for they both bring
pain with them and hinder many activities. Yet even in   30
these nobility shines through, when a man bears with res-
ignation many great misfortunes, not through insensibility
to pain but through nobility and greatness of soul.

If activities are, as we said,[18] what gives life its charac-

15 1099[a] 31–[b] 7.

16 Durability.

17 Simonides.

18 1. 9.

ter, no happy man can become miserable; for he will never
35 do the acts that are hateful and mean. For the man who is
1101ᵃ truly good and wise, we think, bears all the chances of life
becomingly and always makes the best of circumstances, as
a good general makes the best military use of the army at
his command and a good shoemaker makes the best shoes
5 out of the hides that are given him; and so with all other
craftsmen. And if this is the case, the happy man can never
become miserable—though he will not reach *blessedness*, if
he meet with fortunes like those of Priam.

Nor, again, is he many-coloured and changeable; for
10 neither will he be moved from his happy state easily or by
any ordinary misadventures, but only by many great ones,
nor, if he has had many great misadventures, will he recover
his happiness in a short time, but if at all, only in a long
and complete one in which he has attained many splendid
successes.

Why then should we not say that he is happy who is
15 active in accordance with complete virtue and is sufficiently
equipped with external goods, not for some chance period
but throughout a complete life? Or must we add 'and who
is destined to live thus and die as befits his life'? Certainly
the future is obscure to us, while happiness, we claim, is an
end and something in every way final. If so, we shall call
happy those among living men in whom these conditions
20 are, and are to be, fulfilled—but happy *men*. So much for
these questions.

11 ¹⁹ That the fortunes of descendants and of all a
man's friends should not affect his happiness at
all seems a very unfriendly doctrine, and one
25 opposed to the opinions men hold; but since the events that
happen are numerous and admit of all sorts of difference,

¹⁹ Aristotle now returns to the question stated in 1100ᵃ 18–30.

and some come more near to us and others less so, it seems a long—nay, an infinite—task to discuss each in detail; a general outline will perhaps suffice. If, then, as some of a man's own misadventures have a certain weight and influence on life while others are, as it were, lighter, so too there are differences among the misadventures of our friends 30 taken as a whole, and it makes a difference whether the various sufferings befall the living or the dead (much more even than whether lawless and terrible deeds are presupposed in a tragedy or done on the stage), this difference also must be taken into account; or rather, perhaps, the fact that doubt is felt whether the dead share in any good or evil. For 35 it seems, from these considerations, that even if anything 1101^b whether good or evil penetrates to them, it must be something weak and negligible, either in itself or for them, or if not, at least it must be such in degree and kind as not to make happy those who are not happy nor to take away their blessedness from those who are. The good or bad fortunes of friends, then, seem to have some effects on the dead, but 5 effects of such a kind and degree as neither to make the happy unhappy nor to produce any other change of the kind.

12 These questions having been definitely answered, let us consider whether happiness is among the 10 things that are praised or rather among the things that are prized; for clearly it is not to be placed among *potentialities*.[20] Everything that is praised seems to be praised because it is of a certain kind and is related somehow to something else; for we praise the just or brave man and in general both the good man and virtue itself because of the actions and functions involved, and we praise the strong 15 man, the good runner, and so on, because he is of a certain

[20] Cf. *Top.* 126^b 4; *M.M.* 1183^b 20.

kind and is related in a certain way to something good and important. This is clear also from the praises of the gods; for it seems absurd that the gods should be referred to our standard, but this *is* done because praise involves a refer-
20 ence, as we said, to something else. But if praise is for things such as we have described, clearly what applies to the best things is not praise, but something greater and better, as is indeed obvious; for what we do to the gods and the most godlike of men is to call them blessed and happy. And
25 so too with good *things*; no one praises happiness as he does justice, but rather calls it blessed, as being something more divine and better.

Eudoxus also seems to have been right in his method of advocating the supremacy of pleasure; he thought that the fact that, though a good, it is not praised indicated it to be better than the things that are praised, and that this is
30 what God and the good are; for by reference to these all other things are judged. *Praise* is appropriate to virtue, for as a result of virtue men tend to do noble deeds; but *encomia* are bestowed on acts, whether of the body or of the
35 soul. But perhaps nicety in these matters is more proper to those who have made a study of encomia; to us it is clear
1102ª from what has been said that happiness is among the things that are prized and perfect. It seems to be so also from the fact that it is a first principle; for it is for the sake of this that we all do all that we do, and the first principle and cause of goods is, we claim, something prized and divine.

5 **13** Since happiness is an activity of soul in accordance with perfect virtue, we must consider the nature of virtue; for perhaps we shall thus see better the nature of happiness. The true student of politics, too, is thought to have studied virtue above all things; for
10 he wishes to make his fellow citizens good and obedient to the laws. As an example of this we have the lawgivers of the

Cretans and the Spartans, and any others of the kind that
there may have been. And if this inquiry belongs to political science, clearly the pursuit of it will be in accordance
with our original plan. But clearly the virtue we must study
is human virtue; for the good we were seeking was human
good and the happiness human happiness. By human virtue 15
we mean not that of the body but that of the soul; and happiness also we call an activity of soul. But if this is so,
clearly the student of politics must know somehow the facts
about soul, as the man who is to heal the eyes or the body
as a whole must know about the eyes or the body; and all
the more since politics is more prized and better than 20
medicine; but even among doctors the best educated spend
much labour on acquiring knowledge of the body. The student of politics, then, must study the soul, and must study
it with these objects in view, and do so just to the extent
which is sufficient for the questions we are discussing; for
further precision is perhaps something more laborious than 25
our purposes require.

Some things are said about it, adequately enough, even
in the discussions outside our school, and we must use
these; e. g. that one element in the soul is irrational and one
has a rational principle. Whether these are separated as the 30
parts of the body or of anything divisible are, or are distinct
by definition but by nature inseparable, like convex and
concave in the circumference of a circle, does not affect the
present question.

Of the irrational element one division seems to be
widely distributed, and vegetative in its nature, I mean that
which causes nutrition and growth; for it is this kind of
power of the soul that one must assign to all nurslings and 1102^{b}
to embryos, and this same power to full-grown creatures;
this is more reasonable than to assign some different power
to them. Now the excellence of this seems to be common
to all species and not specifically human; for this part or

5 faculty seems to function most in sleep, while goodness and badness are least manifest in sleep (whence comes the saying that the happy are no better off than the wretched for half their lives; and this happens naturally enough, since sleep is an inactivity of the soul in that respect in which it is called good or bad), unless perhaps to a small extent some
10 of the movements actually penetrate to the soul, and in this respect the dreams of good men are better than those of ordinary people. Enough of this subject, however; let us leave the nutritive faculty alone, since it has by its nature no share in human excellence.

There seems to be also another irrational element in the soul—one which in a sense, however, shares in a rational principle. For we praise the rational principle of the conti-
15 nent man and of the incontinent, and the part of their soul that has such a principle, since it urges them aright and towards the best objects; but there is found in them also another element naturally opposed to the rational principle, which fights against and resists that principle. For exactly as paralysed limbs when we intend to move them to the right
20 turn on the contrary to the left, so is it with the soul; the impulses of incontinent people move in contrary directions. But while in the body we see that which moves astray, in the soul we do not. No doubt, however, we must none the less suppose that in the soul too there is something contrary
25 to the rational principle, resisting and opposing it. In what sense it is distinct from the other elements does not concern us. Now even this seems to have a share in a rational principle, as we said; [21] at any rate in the continent man it obeys the rational principle—and presumably in the temperate and brave man it is still more obedient; for in him it speaks, on all matters, with the same voice as the rational principle.

Therefore the irrational element also appears to be

[21] 1. 13.

twofold. For the vegetative element in no way shares in a rational principle, but the appetitive, and in general the 30 desiring element in a sense shares in it, in so far as it listens to and obeys it; this is the sense in which we speak of 'taking account' of one's father or one's friends, not that in which we speak of 'accounting' for a mathematical property. That the irrational element is in some sense persuaded by a rational principle is indicated also by the giving of advice and by all reproof and exhortation. And if this element also 1103a must be said to have a rational principle, that which has a rational principle (as well as that which has not) will be twofold, one subdivision having it in the strict sense and in itself, and the other having a tendency to obey as one does one's father.

Virtue too is distinguished into kinds in accordance with this difference; for we say that some of the virtues are intellectual and others moral, philosophic wisdom and 5 understanding and practical wisdom being intellectual, liberality and temperance moral. For in speaking about a man's character we do not say that he is wise or has understanding but that he is good-tempered or temperate; yet we praise the wise man also with respect to his state of mind; and of states of mind we call those which merit praise virtues. 10

BOOK II

1 Virtue, then, being of two kinds, intellectual and moral, intellectual virtue in the main owes both its 15 birth and its growth to teaching (for which reason it requires experience and time), while moral virtue comes about as a result of habit, whence also its name *ethike* is one that is formed by a slight variation from the word *ethos*

(habit). From this it is also plain that none of the moral
20 virtues arises in us by nature; for nothing that exists by
nature can form a habit contrary to its nature. For instance
the stone which by nature moves downwards cannot be
habituated to move upwards, not even if one tries to train
it by throwing it up ten thousand times; nor can fire be
habituated to move downwards, nor can anything else that
by nature behaves in one way be trained to behave in
another. Neither by nature, then, nor contrary to nature do
the virtues arise in us; rather we are adapted by nature to
25 receive them, and are made perfect by habit.

Again, of all the things that come to us by nature we
first acquire the potentiality and later exhibit the activity
30 (this is plain in the case of the senses; for it was not by
often seeing or often hearing that we got these senses, but
on the contrary we had them before we used them, and did
not come to have them by using them); but the virtues we
get by first exercising them, as also happens in the case of
the arts as well. For the things we have to learn before we
can do them, we learn by doing them, e. g. men become
1103b builders by building and lyre-players by playing the lyre;
so too we become just by doing just acts, temperate by
doing temperate acts, brave by doing brave acts.

This is confirmed by what happens in states, for legislators make the citizens good by forming habits in them,
5 and this is the wish of every legislator, and those who do
not effect it miss their mark, and it is in this that a good
constitution differs from a bad one.

Again, it is from the same causes and by the same
means that every virtue is both produced and destroyed,
and similarly every art; for it is from playing the lyre that
both good and bad lyre-players are produced. And the corresponding statement is true of builders and of all the rest;
10 men will be good or bad builders as a result of building well
or badly. For if this were not so, there would have been no

need of a teacher, but all men would have been born good
or bad at their craft. This, then, is the case with the virtues
also; by doing the acts that we do in our transactions with
other men we become just or unjust, and by doing the acts   15
that we do in the presence of danger, and being habituated
to feel fear or confidence, we become brave or cowardly.
The same is true of appetites and feelings of anger; some
men become temperate and good-tempered, others self-
indulgent and irascible, by behaving in one way or the other
in the appropriate circumstances. Thus, in one word, states   20
of character arise out of like activities. This is why the
activities we exhibit must be of a certain kind; it is because
the states of character correspond to the differences between
these. It makes no small difference, then, whether we form
habits of one kind or of another from our very youth; it
make a very great difference, or rather *all* the difference.   25

2   Since, then, the present inquiry does not aim at
theoretical knowledge like the others (for we are
inquiring not in order to know what virtue is, but
in order to become good, since otherwise our inquiry would
have been of no use), we must examine the nature of
actions, namely how we ought to do them; for these deter-   30
mine also the nature of the states of character that are
produced, as we have said.[1] Now, that we must act according to the right rule is a common principle and must be
assumed—it will be discussed later,[2] i. e. both what the right
rule is, and how it is related to the other virtues. But this   1104a
must be agreed upon beforehand, that the whole account of
matters of conduct must be given in outline and not precisely, as we said at the very beginning [3] that the accounts

[1] a 31–b 25.

[2] vi. 13.

[3] 1094b 11–27.

we demand must be in accordance with the subject-matter;
matters concerned with conduct and questions of what is
5 good for us have no fixity, any more than matters of health.
The general account being of this nature, the account of
particular cases is yet more lacking in exactness; for they do
not fall under any art or precept but the agents themselves
must in each case consider what is appropriate to the occasion, as happens also in the art of medicine or of navigation.

But though our present account is of this nature we
10 must give what help we can. First, then, let us consider this,
that it is the nature of such things to be destroyed by defect
and excess, as we see in the case of strength and of health
(for to gain light on things imperceptible we must use the
evidence of sensible things); both excessive and defective
15 exercise destroys the strength, and similarly drink or food
which is above or below a certain amount destroys the
health, while that which is proportionate both produces and
20 increases and preserves it. So too is it, then, in the case of
temperance and courage and the other virtues. For the man
who flies from and fears everything and does not stand his
ground against anything becomes a coward, and the man
who fears nothing at all but goes to meet every danger
becomes rash; and similarly the man who indulges in every
pleasure and abstains from none becomes self-indulgent,
25 while the man who shuns every pleasure, as boors do,
becomes in a way insensible; temperance and courage, then,
are destroyed by excess and defect, and preserved by the
mean.

But not only are the sources and causes of their origination and growth the same as those of their destruction,
but also the sphere of their actualization will be the same;
30 for this is also true of the things which are more evident to
sense, e. g. of strength; it is produced by taking much food
and undergoing much exertion, and it is the strong man
that will be most able to do these things. So too is it with

the virtues; by abstaining from pleasures we become temperate, and it is when we have become so that we are most 35
able to abstain from them; and similarly too in the case of 1104^b
courage; for by being habituated to despise things that are
terrible and to stand our ground against them we become
brave, and it is when we have become so that we shall be
most able to stand our ground against them.

3 We must take as a sign of states of character the
pleasure or pain that ensues on acts; for the man 5
who abstains from bodily pleasures and delights in
this very fact is temperate, while the man who is annoyed at
it is self-indulgent, and he who stands his ground against
things that are terrible and delights in this or at least is not
pained is brave, while the man who is pained is a coward.
For moral excellence is concerned with pleasures and pains;
it is on account of the pleasure that we do bad things, and 10
on account of the pain that we abstain from noble ones.
Hence we ought to have been brought up in a particular
way from our very youth, as Plato says,[4] so as both to
delight in and to be pained by the things that we ought; for
this is the right education.

Again, if the virtues are concerned with actions and
passions, and every passion and every action is accompanied
by pleasure and pain, for this reason also virtue will be con- 15
cerned with pleasures and pains. This is indicated also by
the fact that punishment is inflicted by these means; for it is
a kind of cure, and it is the nature of cures to be effected
by contraries.

Again, as we said but lately,[5] every state of soul has a
nature relative to and concerned with the kind of things by
which it tends to be made worse or better; but it is by rea- 20

[4] *Laws*, 653 A ff., *Rep.* 401 E–402 A.

[5] a 27–b 3.

son of pleasures and pains that men become bad, by pursuing and avoiding these—either the pleasures and pains
they ought not or when they ought not or as they ought
not, or by going wrong in one of the other similar ways
that may be distinguished. Hence men[6] even define the
25 virtues as certain states of impassivity and rest; not well,
however, because they speak absolutely, and do not say 'as
one ought' and 'as one ought not' and 'when one ought or
ought not', and the other things that may be added. We
assume, then, that this kind of excellence tends to do what
is best with regard to pleasures and pains, and vice does the
contrary.

The following facts also may show us that virtue and
vice are concerned with these same things. There being
30 three objects of choice and three of avoidance, the noble, the
advantageous, the pleasant, and their contraries, the base,
the injurious, the painful, about all of these the good man
tends to go right and the bad man to go wrong, and especially about pleasure; for this is common to the animals, and
also it accompanies all objects of choice; for even the noble
35 and the advantageous appear pleasant.

Again, it has grown up with us all from our infancy;
1105ª this is why it is difficult to rub off this passion, engrained as
it is in our life. And we measure even our actions, some of
5 us more and others less, by the rule of pleasure and pain.
For this reason, then, our whole inquiry must be about
these; for to feel delight and pain rightly or wrongly has no
small effect on our actions.

Again, it is harder to fight with pleasure than with
anger, to use Heraclitus' phrase, but both art and virtue are
always concerned with what is harder; for even the good is
10 better when it is harder. Therefore for this reason also the
whole concern both of virtue and of political science is with

[6] Probably Speusippus is referred to.

pleasures and pains; for the man who uses these well will be good, he who uses them badly bad.

That virtue, then, is concerned with pleasures and pains, and that by the acts from which it arises it is both increased and, if they are done differently, destroyed, and that the acts from which it arose are those in which it actu- 15 alizes itself—let this be taken as said.

4 The question might be asked, what we mean by saying[7] that we must become just by doing just acts, and temperate by doing temperate acts; for if men do just and temperate acts, they are already just and 20 temperate, exactly as, if they do what is in accordance with the laws of grammar and of music, they are grammarians and musicians.

Or is this not true even of the arts? It is possible to do something that is in accordance with the laws of grammar, either by chance or at the suggestion of another. A man will be a grammarian, then, only when he has both done some- 25 thing grammatical and done it grammatically; and this means doing it in accordance with the grammatical knowledge in himself.

Again, the case of the arts and that of the virtues are not similar; for the products of the arts have their goodness in themselves, so that it is enough that they should have a certain character, but if the acts that are in accordance with the virtues have themselves a certain character it does not 30 follow that they are done justly or temperately. The agent also must be in a certain condition when he does them; in the first place he must have knowledge, secondly he must choose the acts, and choose them for their own sakes, and thirdly his action must proceed from a firm and unchangeable character. These are not reckoned in as conditions of

[7] 1103[a] 31–[b] 25, 1104[a] 27–[b] 3.

1105^b the possession of the arts, except the bare knowledge; but as a condition of the possession of the virtues knowledge has little or no weight, while the other conditions count not for a little but for everything, i. e. the very conditions which result from often doing just and temperate acts.

5   Actions, then, are called just and temperate when they are such as the just or the temperate man would do; but it is not the man who does these that is just and temperate, but the man who also does them *as* just and temperate men do

10 them. It is well said, then, that it is by doing just acts that the just man is produced, and by doing temperate acts the temperate man; without doing these no one would have even a prospect of becoming good.

But most people do not do these, but take refuge in theory and think they are being philosophers and will

15 become good in this way, behaving somewhat like patients who listen attentively to their doctors, but do none of the things they are ordered to do. As the latter will not be made well in body by such a course of treatment, the former will not be made well in soul by such a course of philosophy.

5 Next we must consider what virtue is. Since things

20 that are found in the soul are of three kinds—passions, faculties, states of character, virtue must be one of these. By passions I mean appetite, anger, fear, confidence, envy, joy, friendly feeling, hatred, longing, emulation, pity, and in general the feelings that are accompanied by pleasure or pain; by faculties the things in virtue of which we are said to be capable of feeling these, e. g. of becoming angry or being pained or feeling pity; by states of

25 character the things in virtue of which we stand well or badly with reference to the passions, e. g. with reference to anger we stand badly if we feel it violently or too weakly, and well if we feel it moderately; and similarly with reference to the other passions.

Now neither the virtues nor the vices are *passions*, because we are not called good or bad on the ground of our passions, but are so called on the ground of our virtues and our vices, and because we are neither praised nor blamed for our passions (for the man who feels fear or anger is not praised, nor is the man who simply feels anger blamed, but the man who feels it in a certain way), but for our virtues and our vices we *are* praised or blamed. 1106^a

Again, we feel anger and fear without choice, but the virtues are modes of choice or involve choice. Further, in respect of the passions we are said to be moved, but in respect of the virtues and the vices we are said not to be moved but to be disposed in a particular way.

For these reasons also they are not *faculties*; for we are neither called good nor bad, nor praised nor blamed, for the simple capacity of feeling the passions; again, we have the faculties by nature, but we are not made good or bad by nature; we have spoken of this before.[8]

If, then, the virtues are neither passions nor faculties, all that remains is that they should be *states of character*.

Thus we have stated what virtue is in respect of its genus.

6 We must, however, not only describe virtue as a state of character, but also say what sort of state it is. We may remark, then, that every virtue or excellence both brings into good condition the thing of which it is the excellence and makes the work of that thing be done well; e. g. the excellence of the eye makes both the eye and its work good; for it is by the excellence of the eye that we see well. Similarly the excellence of the horse makes a horse both good in itself and good at running and at carrying its rider and at awaiting the attack of the enemy.

[8] 1103^a 18–^{b} 2.

Therefore, if this is true in every case, the virtue of man also will be the state of character which makes a man good and which makes him do his own work well.

How this is to happen we have stated already,[9] but it will be made plain also by the following consideration of the

25 specific nature of virtue. In everything that is continuous and divisible it is possible to take more, less, or an equal amount, and that either in terms of the thing itself or relatively to us; and the equal is an intermediate between excess and defect. By the intermediate in the object I mean that

30 which is equidistant from each of the extremes, which is one and the same for all men; by the intermediate relatively to us that which is neither too much nor too little—and this is not one, nor the same for all. For instance, if ten is many and two is few, six is the intermediate, taken in terms of the object; for it exceeds and is exceeded by an equal amount;

35 this is intermediate according to arithmetical proportion. But the intermediate relatively to us is not to be taken so; if ten

1106ᵇ pounds are too much for a particular person to eat and two too little, it does not follow that the trainer will order six pounds; for this also is perhaps too much for the person who is to take it, or too little—too little for Milo,[10] too much for

5 the beginner in athletic exercises. The same is true of running and wrestling. Thus a master of any art avoids excess and defect, but seeks the intermediate and chooses this—the intermediate not in the object but relatively to us.

If it is thus, then, that every art does its work well—by looking to the intermediate and judging its works by this

10 standard (so that we often say of good works of art that it is not possible either to take away or to add anything, implying that excess and defect destroy the goodness of works of art, while the mean preserves it; and good artists, as we say, look

---

[9] 1104ᵃ 11–27.

[10] A famous wrestler.

to this in their work), and if, further, virtue is more exact
and better than any art, as nature also is, then virtue must
have the quality of aiming at the intermediate. I mean moral 15
virtue; for it is this that is concerned with passions and
actions, and in these there is excess, defect, and the intermediate. For instance, both fear and confidence and appetite
and anger and pity and in general pleasure and pain may
be felt both too much and too little, and in both cases not
well; but to feel them at the right times, with reference to 20
the right objects, towards the right people, with the right
motive, and in the right way, is what is both intermediate
and best, and this is characteristic of virtue. Similarly with
regard to actions also there is excess, defect, and the intermediate. Now virtue is concerned with passions and actions,
in which excess is a form of failure, and so is defect, while 25
the intermediate is praised and is a form of success; and
being praised and being successful are both characteristics
of virtue. Therefore virtue is a kind of mean, since, as we
have seen, it aims at what is intermediate.

Again, it is possible to fail in many ways (for evil
belongs to the class of the unlimited, as the Pythagoreans
conjectured, and good to that of the limited), while to suc- 30
ceed is possible only in one way (for which reason also one
is easy and the other difficult—to miss the mark easy, to hit
it difficult); for these reasons also, then, excess and defect
are characteristic of vice, and the mean of virtue;

For men are good in but one way, but bad in many.   35

Virtue, then, is a state of character concerned with
choice, lying in a mean, i. e. the mean relative to us, this
being determined by a rational principle, and by that prin- 1107ª
ciple by which the man of practical wisdom would determine
it. Now it is a mean between two vices, that which depends
on excess and that which depends on defect; and again it is

a mean because the vices respectively fall short of or exceed
what is right in both passions and actions, while virtue both
5 finds and chooses that which is intermediate. Hence in
respect of its substance and the definition which states its
essence virtue is a mean, with regard to what is best and
right an extreme.

But not every action nor every passion admits of a
mean; for some have names that already imply badness, e. g.
10 spite, shamelessness, envy, and in the case of actions adultery, theft, murder; for all of these and suchlike things
imply by their names that they are themselves bad, and not
the excesses or deficiencies of them. It is not possible, then,
ever to be right with regard to them; one must always be
wrong. Nor does goodness or badness with regard to such
15 things depend on committing adultery with the right
woman, at the right time, and in the right way, but simply
to do any of them is to go wrong. It would be equally
absurd, then, to expect that in unjust, cowardly, and volup-
tuous action there should be a mean, an excess, and a
20 deficiency; for at that rate there would be a mean of excess
and of deficiency, an excess of excess, and a deficiency of
deficiency. But as there is no excess and deficiency of temperance and courage because what is intermediate is in a
sense an extreme, so too of the actions we have mentioned
there is no mean nor any excess and deficiency, but however
they are done they are wrong; for in general there is neither
25 a mean of excess and deficiency, nor excess and deficiency
of a mean.

7 We must, however, not only make this general
statement, but also apply it to the individual facts.
For among statements about conduct those which
are general apply more widely, but those which are partic-
30 ular are more genuine, since conduct has to do with
individual cases, and our statements must harmonize with

the facts in these cases. We may take these cases from our table. With regard to feelings of fear and confidence courage is the mean; of the people who exceed, he who exceeds in fearlessness has no name (many of the states have no name), while the man who exceeds in confidence is rash, and he who exceeds in fear and falls short in confidence is a coward. With regard to pleasures and pains—not all of them, and not so much with regard to the pains—the mean is temperance, the excess self-indulgence. Persons deficient with regard to the pleasures are not often found; hence such persons also have received no name. But let us call them 'insensible'.

With regard to giving and taking of money the mean is liberality, the excess and the defect prodigality and meanness. In these actions people exceed and fall short in contrary ways; the prodigal exceeds in spending and falls short in taking, while the mean man exceeds in taking and falls short in spending. (At present we are giving a mere outline or summary, and are satisfied with this; later these states will be more exactly determined.[11]) With regard to money there are also other dispositions—a mean, magnificence (for the magnificent man differs from the liberal man; the former deals with large sums, the latter with small ones), and excess, tastelessness and vulgarity, and a deficiency, niggardliness; these differ from the states opposed to liberality, and the mode of their difference will be stated later.[12]

With regard to honour and dishonour the mean is proper pride, the excess is known as a sort of 'empty vanity', and the deficiency is undue humility; and as we said[13] liberality was related to magnificence, differing from it by

1107ᵇ

5

10

15

20

25

[11] iv. 1.

[12] 1122ᵃ 20–9, ᵇ10–18.

[13] ll. 17–19.

dealing with small sums, so there is a state similarly related
to proper pride, being concerned with small honours while
that is concerned with great. For it is possible to desire honour as one ought, and more than one ought, and less, and
the man who exceeds in his desires is called ambitious, the
30 man who falls short unambitious, while the intermediate
person has no name. The dispositions also are nameless,
except that that of the ambitious man is called ambition.
Hence the people who are at the extremes lay claim to the
middle place; and we ourselves sometimes call the intermediate person ambitious and sometimes unambitious, and
1108ᵃ sometimes praise the ambitious man and sometimes the
unambitious. The reason of our doing this will be stated in
what follows;[14] but now let us speak of the remaining states
according to the method which has been indicated.

With regard to anger also there is an excess, a defi-
5 ciency, and a mean. Although they can scarcely be said to
have names, yet since we call the intermediate person good-
tempered let us call the mean good temper; of the persons at
the extremes let the one who exceeds be called irascible, and
his vice irascibility, and the man who falls short an irasc-
cible sort of person, and the deficiency inirascibility.

There are also three other means, which have a certain
likeness to one another, but differ from one another: for they
10 are all concerned with intercourse in words and actions, but
differ in that one is concerned with truth in this sphere, the
other two with pleasantness; and of this one kind is exhibited in giving amusement, the other in all the circumstances
of life. We must therefore speak of these too, that we may
the better see that in all things the mean is praiseworthy,
15 and the extremes neither praiseworthy nor right, but worthy of blame. Now most of these states also have no names,

[14] b 11–26, 1125ᵇ 14–18.

but we must try, as in the other cases, to invent names ourselves so that we may be clear and easy to follow. With
regard to truth, then, the intermediate is a truthful sort of 20
person and the mean may be called truthfulness, while the
pretence which exaggerates is boastfulness and the person
characterized by it a boaster, and that which understates is
mock modesty and the person characterized by it mock-
modest. With regard to pleasantness in the giving of
amusement the intermediate person is ready-witted and the
disposition ready wit, the excess is buffoonery and the person characterized by it a buffoon, while the man who falls
short is a sort of boor and his state is boorishness. With 25
regard to the remaining kind of pleasantness, that which is
exhibited in life in general, the man who is pleasant in the
right way is friendly and the mean is friendliness, while the
man who exceeds is an obsequious person if he has no end
in view, a flatterer if he is aiming at his own advantage, and
the man who falls short and is unpleasant in all circumstances is a quarrelsome and surly sort of person.

There are also means in the passions and concerned
with the passions; since shame is not a virtue, and yet 30
praise is extended to the modest man. For even in these
matters one man is said to be intermediate, and another to
exceed, as for instance the bashful man who is ashamed of
everything; while he who falls short or is not ashamed of
anything at all is shameless, and the intermediate person is
modest. Righteous indignation is a mean between envy and
spite, and these states are concerned with the pain and 35
pleasures that are felt at the fortunes of our neighbours; the 1108ᵇ
man who is characterized by righteous indignation is
pained at undeserved good fortune, the envious man, going
beyond him, is pained at all good fortune, and the spiteful
man falls so far short of being pained that he even rejoices. 5
But these states there will be an opportunity of describing

elsewhere;[15] with regard to justice, since it has not one simple meaning, we shall, after describing the other states, distinguish its two kinds and say how each of them is a
10 mean;[16] and similarly we shall treat also of the rational virtues.[17]

8 There are three kinds of disposition, then, two of them vices, involving excess and deficiency respectively, and one a virtue, viz. the mean, and all are in a sense opposed to all; for the extreme states are contrary both to the intermediate state and to each other, and the
15 intermediate to the extremes; as the equal is greater relatively to the less, less relatively to the greater, so the middle states are excessive relatively to the deficiencies, deficient relatively to the excesses, both in passions and in actions.
20 For the brave man appears rash relatively to the coward, and cowardly relatively to the rash man; and similarly the temperate man appears self-indulgent relatively to the insensible man, insensible relatively to the self-indulgent, and the liberal man prodigal relatively to the mean man, mean relatively to the prodigal. Hence also the people at the extremes push the intermediate man each over to the other,
25 and the brave man is called rash by the coward, cowardly by the rash man, and correspondingly in the other cases.

These states being thus opposed to one another, the greatest contrariety is that of the extremes to each other, rather than to the intermediate; for these are further from

---

[15] The reference may be to the whole treatment of the moral virtues in iii. 6–iv. 9, or to the discussion of shame in iv. 9 and an intended corresponding discussion of righteous indignation, or to the discussion of these two states in *Rhet.* ii. 6, 9, 10.

[16] 1129ª 26–b 1, 1130ª 14–b 5, 1131b 9–15, 1132ª 24–30, 1133b 30–1134ª 1.

[17] Bk. vi.

each other than from the intermediate, as the great is further
from the small and the small from the great than both are   30
from the equal. Again, to the intermediate some extremes
show a certain likeness, as that of rashness to courage and
that of prodigality to liberality; but the extremes show the
greatest unlikeness to each other; now contraries are defined
as the things that are furthest from each other, so that things
that are further apart are more contrary.   35

To the mean in some cases the deficiency, in some the   1109a
excess is more opposed; e. g. it is not rashness, which is an
excess, but cowardice, which is a deficiency, that is more
opposed to courage, and not insensibility, which is a deficiency, but self-indulgence, which is an excess, that is more   5
opposed to temperance. This happens from two reasons,
one being drawn from the thing itself; for because one
extreme is nearer and liker to the intermediate, we oppose
not this but rather its contrary to the intermediate. E. g.,
since rashness is thought liker and nearer to courage, and
cowardice more unlike, we oppose rather the latter to   10
courage; for things that are further from the intermediate
are thought more contrary to it. This, then, is one cause,
drawn from the thing itself; another is drawn from ourselves; for the things to which we ourselves more naturally
tend seem more contrary to the intermediate. For instance,
we ourselves tend more naturally to pleasures, and hence are   15
more easily carried away towards self-indulgence than
towards propriety. We describe as contrary to the mean,
then, rather the directions in which we more often go to
great lengths; and therefore self-indulgence, which is an
excess, is the more contrary to temperance.

9 That moral virtue is a mean, then, and in what
sense it is so, and that it is a mean between two   20
vices, the one involving excess, the other deficiency, and that it is such because its character is to aim at

what is intermediate in passions and in actions, has been sufficiently stated. Hence also it is no easy task to be good. For in everything it is no easy task to find the middle, e. g. to find the middle of a circle is not for every one but for him who knows; so, too, any one can get angry—that is easy—or give or spend money; but to do this to the right person, to the right extent, at the right time, with the right motive, and in the right way, *that* is not for every one, nor is it easy; wherefore goodness is both rare and laudable and noble.

Hence he who aims at the intermediate must first depart from what is the more contrary to it, as Calypso advises—

Hold the ship out beyond that surf and spray.[18]

For of the extremes one is more erroneous, one less so; therefore, since to hit the mean is hard in the extreme, we must as a second best, as people say, take the least of the evils; and this will be done best in the way we describe.

But we must consider the things towards which we ourselves also are easily carried away; for some of us tend to one thing, some to another; and this will be recognizable from the pleasure and the pain we feel. We must drag ourselves away to the contrary extreme; for we shall get into the intermediate state by drawing well away from error, as people do in straightening sticks that are bent.

Now in everything the pleasant or pleasure is most to be guarded against; for we do not judge it impartially. We ought, then, to feel towards pleasure as the elders of the people felt towards Helen, and in all circumstances repeat

---

[18] *Od.* xii. 219 f. (Mackail's trans.). But it was Circe who gave the advice (xii. 108), and the actual quotation is from Odysseus' orders to his steersman.

their saying;[19] for if we dismiss pleasure thus we are less 10
likely to go astray. It is by doing this, then, (to sum the
matter up) that we shall best be able to hit the mean.

But this is no doubt difficult, and especially in individual cases; for it is not easy to determine both how and 15
with whom and on what provocation and how long one
should be angry; for we too sometimes praise those who fall
short and call them good-tempered, but sometimes we
praise those who get angry and call them manly. The man,
however, who deviates little from goodness is not blamed,
whether he do so in the direction of the more or of the less,
but only the man who deviates more widely; for *he* does
not fail to be noticed. But up to what point and to what 20
extent a man must deviate before he becomes blameworthy it is not easy to determine by reasoning, any more than
anything else that is perceived by the senses; such things
depend on particular facts, and the decision rests with perception. So much, then, is plain, that the intermediate state
is in all things to be praised, but that we must incline 25
sometimes towards the excess, sometimes towards the deficiency; for so shall we most easily hit the mean and what is
right.

BOOK III

1 Since virtue is concerned with passions and actions, 30
and on voluntary passions and actions praise and
blame are bestowed, on those that are involuntary
pardon, and sometimes also pity, to distinguish the voluntary and the involuntary is presumably necessary for those
who are studying the nature of virtue, and useful also for

[19] *Il.* iii. 156–60.

legislators with a view to the assigning both of honours and
of punishments.

35   Those things, then, are thought involuntary, which take
1110ª place under compulsion or owing to ignorance; and that is
compulsory of which the moving principle is outside, being
a principle in which nothing is contributed by the person
who is acting or is feeling the passion, e. g. if he were to be
carried somewhere by a wind, or by men who had him in
their power.

But with regard to the things that are done from fear
5   of greater evils or for some noble object (e. g. if a tyrant
were to order one to do something base, having one's parents and children in his power, and if one did the action
they were to be saved, but otherwise would be put to
death), it may be debated whether such actions are involuntary or voluntary. Something of the sort happens also with
regard to the throwing of goods overboard in a storm; for in
10   the abstract no one throws goods away voluntarily, but on
condition of its securing the safety of himself and his crew
any sensible man does so. Such actions, then, are mixed, but
are more like voluntary actions, for they are worthy of
choice at the time when they are done, and the end of an
action is relative to the occasion. Both the terms, then, 'voluntary' and 'involuntary', must be used with reference to
the moment of action. Now the man acts voluntarily; for the
principle that moves the instrumental parts of the body in
such actions is in him, and the things of which the moving
15   principle is in a man himself are in his power to do or not
to do. Such actions, therefore, are voluntary, but in the
abstract perhaps involuntary; for no one would choose any
such act in itself.

For such actions men are sometimes even praised, when
20   they endure something base or painful in return for great
and noble objects gained; in the opposite case they are
blamed, since to endure the greatest indignities for no noble

end or for a trifling end is the mark of an inferior person.
On some actions praise indeed is not bestowed, but pardon
is, when one does what he ought not under pressure which
overstrains human nature and which no one could with- 25
stand. But some acts, perhaps, we cannot be forced to do,
but ought rather to face death after the most fearful sufferings; for the things that 'forced' Euripides' Alcmaeon to
slay his mother seem absurd. It is difficult sometimes to
determine what should be chosen at what cost, and what
should be endured in return for what gain, and yet more
difficult to abide by our decisions; for as a rule what is 30
expected is painful, and what we are forced to do is base,
whence praise and blame are bestowed on those who have
been compelled or have not.

What sort of acts, then, should be called compulsory?
We answer that without qualification actions are so when 1110ᵇ
the cause is in the external circumstances and the agent contributes nothing. But the things that in themselves are
involuntary, but now and in return for these gains are worthy of choice, and whose moving principle is in the agent,
are in themselves involuntary, but now and in return for
these gains voluntary. They are more like voluntary acts; for 5
actions are in the class of particulars, and the particular acts
here are voluntary. What sort of things are to be chosen,
and in return for what, it is not easy to state; for there are
many differences in the particular cases.

But if some one were to say that pleasant and noble
objects have a compelling power, forcing us from without,
all acts would be for him compulsory; for it is for these
objects that all men do everything they do. And those who 10
act under compulsion and unwillingly act with pain, but
those who do acts for their pleasantness and nobility do
them with pleasure; it is absurd to make external circumstances responsible, and not oneself, as being easily caught
by such attractions, and to make oneself responsible for

noble acts but the pleasant objects responsible for base acts.
The compulsory, then, seems to be that whose moving principle is outside, the person compelled contributing nothing.

Everything that is done by reason of ignorance is *not*
voluntary; it is only what produces pain and repentance that
is *in*voluntary. For the man who has done something owing
20 to ignorance, and feels not the least vexation at his action,
has not acted voluntarily, since he did not know what he
was doing, nor yet involuntarily, since he is not pained. Of
people, then, who act by reason of ignorance he who repents
is thought an involuntary agent, and the man who does not
repent may, since he is different, be called a not voluntary
agent; for, since he differs from the other, it is better that he
should have a name of his own.

Acting by reason of ignorance seems also to be different
25 from acting *in* ignorance; for the man who is drunk or in a
rage is thought to act as a result not of ignorance but of one
of the causes mentioned, yet not knowingly but in ignorance.

Now every wicked man is ignorant of what he ought to
do and what he ought to abstain from, and it is by reason of
error of this kind that men become unjust and in general
30 bad; but the term 'involuntary' tends to be used not if a
man is ignorant of what is to his advantage—for it is not
mistaken purpose that causes involuntary action (it leads
rather to wickedness), nor ignorance of the universal (for
that men are *blamed*), but ignorance of particulars, i. e. of
the circumstances of the action and the objects with which
1111ᵃ it is concerned. For it is on these that both pity and pardon
depend, since the person who is ignorant of any of these
acts involuntarily.

Perhaps it is just as well, therefore, to determine their
nature and number. A man may be ignorant, then, of who
he is, what he is doing, what or whom he is acting on, and
5 sometimes also what (e. g. what instrument) he is doing it
with, and to what end (e. g. he may think his act will con-

duce to some one's safety), and how he is doing it (e. g.
whether gently or violently). Now of all of these no one
could be ignorant unless he were mad, and evidently also
he could not be ignorant of the agent; for how could he not
know himself? But of what he is doing a man might be
ignorant, as for instance people say 'it slipped out of their
mouths as they were speaking', or 'they did not know it was 10
a secret', as Aeschylus said of the mysteries, or a man might
say he 'let it go off when he merely wanted to show its
working', as the man did with the catapult. Again, one
might think one's son was an enemy, as Merope did, or that
a pointed spear had a button on it, or that a stone was
pumice-stone; or one might give a man a draught to save
him, and really kill him; or one might want to touch a man,
as people do in sparring, and really wound him. The igno- 15
rance may relate, then, to any of these things, i. e. of the
circumstances of the action, and the man who was ignorant
of any of these is thought to have acted involuntarily, and
especially if he was ignorant on the most important points;
and these are thought to be the circumstances of the action
and its end. Further, the doing of an act that is called involuntary in virtue of ignorance of this sort must be painful
and involve repentance.   20

   Since that which is done under compulsion or by reason
of ignorance is involuntary, the voluntary would seem to be
that of which the moving principle is in the agent himself,
he being aware of the particular circumstances of the action.
Presumably acts done by reason of anger or appetite are not
rightly called involuntary.[1] For in the first place, on that
showing none of the other animals will act voluntarily, nor 25
will children; and secondly, is it meant that we do not do
voluntarily *any* of the acts that are due to appetite or anger,

---

[1] A reference to Pl. *Laws* 863 B, ff., where anger and appetite are coupled
with ignorance as sources of wrong action.

or that we do the noble acts voluntarily and the base acts
involuntarily? Is not this absurd, when one and the same
thing is the cause? But it would surely be odd to describe as
30   involuntary the things one ought to desire; and we ought
both to be angry at certain things and to have an appetite
for certain things, e. g. for health and for learning. Also
what is involuntary is thought to be painful, but what is in
accordance with appetite is thought to be pleasant. Again,
what is the difference in respect of involuntariness between
errors committed upon calculation and those committed in
1111ᵇ anger? Both are to be avoided, but the irrational passions
are thought not less human than reason is, and therefore
also the actions which proceed from anger or appetite are
the man's actions. It would be odd, then, to treat them as
involuntary.

2   Both the voluntary and the involuntary having
been delimited, we must next discuss choice, for it
5   is thought to be most closely bound up with virtue
and to discriminate characters better than actions do.

Choice, then, seems to be voluntary, but not the same
thing as the voluntary; the latter extends more widely. For
both children and the lower animals share in voluntary
action, but not in choice, and acts done on the spur of the
moment we describe as voluntary, but not as chosen.

10   Those who say it is appetite or anger or wish or a kind
of opinion do not seem to be right. For choice is not common to irrational creatures as well, but appetite and anger
are. Again, the incontinent man acts with appetite, but not
15 with choice; while the continent man on the contrary acts
with choice, but not with appetite. Again, appetite is contrary to choice, but not appetite to appetite. Again, appetite
relates to the pleasant and the painful, choice neither to the
painful nor to the pleasant.

Still less is it anger; for acts due to anger are thought to be less than any others objects of choice.

But neither is it wish, though it seems near to it; for choice cannot relate to impossibles, and if any one said he chose them he would be thought silly; but there may be a wish even for impossibles, e. g. for immortality. And wish may relate to things that could in no way be brought about by one's own efforts, e. g. that a particular actor or athlete should win in a competition; but no one chooses such things, but only the things that he thinks could be brought about by his own efforts. Again, wish relates rather to the end, choice to the means; for instance, we wish to be healthy, but we choose the acts which will make us healthy, and we wish to be happy and say we do, but we cannot well say we choose to be so; for, in general, choice seems to relate to the things that are in our own power.

For this reason, too, it cannot be opinion; for opinion is thought to relate to all kinds of things, no less to eternal things and impossible things than to things in our own power; and it is distinguished by its falsity or truth, not by its badness or goodness, while choice is distinguished rather by these.

Now with opinion in general perhaps no one even says it is identical. But it is not identical even with any kind of opinion; for by choosing what is good or bad we are men of a certain character, which we are not by holding certain opinions. And we choose to get or avoid something good or bad, but we have opinions about what a thing is or whom it is good for or how it is good for him; we can hardly be said to opine to get or avoid anything. And choice is praised for being related to the right object rather than for being rightly related to it, opinion for being truly related to its object. And we choose what we best know to be good, but we opine what we do not quite know; and it is not the same

people that are thought to make the best choices and to have the best opinions, but some are thought to have fairly good opinions, but by reason of vice to choose what they
10 should not. If opinion precedes choice or accompanies it, that makes no difference; for it is not this that we are considering, but whether it is *identical* with some kind of opinion.

What, then, or what kind of thing is it, since it is none of the things we have mentioned? It seems to be voluntary, but not all that is voluntary to be an object of choice. Is it,
15 then, what has been decided on by previous deliberation? At any rate choice involves a rational principle and thought. Even the name seems to suggest that it is what is chosen before other things.

3 Do we deliberate about everything, and is everything a possible subject of deliberation, or is deliberation
20 impossible about some things? We ought presumably to call not what a fool or a madman would deliberate about, but what a sensible man would deliberate about, a subject of deliberation. Now about eternal things no one deliberates, e. g. about the material universe or the incommensurability of the diagonal and the side of a square. But no more do we deliberate about the things that involve momement but always happen in the same way, whether of
25 necessity or by nature or from any other cause, e. g. the solstices and the risings of the stars; nor about things that happen now in one way, now in another, e. g. droughts and rains; nor about chance events, like the finding of treasure. But we do not deliberate even about all human affairs; for instance, no Spartan deliberates about the best constitution for the Scythians. For none of these things can be brought about by our own efforts.

We deliberate about things that are in our power and

can be done; and these are in fact what is left. For nature, 30
necessity, and chance are thought to be causes, and also reason and everything that depends on man. Now every class
of men deliberates about the things that can be done by
their own efforts. And in the case of exact and self-con-
tained sciences there is no deliberation, e. g. about the
letters of the alphabet (for we have no doubt how they 1112ᵇ
should be written); but the things that are brought about
by our own efforts, but not always in the same way, are the
things about which we deliberate, e. g. questions of medical treatment or of money-making. And we do so more in
the case of the art of navigation than in that of gymnastics, 5
inasmuch as it has been less exactly worked out, and again
about other things in the same ratio, and more also in the
case of the arts than in that of the sciences; for we have
more doubt about the former. Deliberation is concerned
with things that happen in a certain way for the most part,
but in which the event is obscure, and with things in which 10
it is indeterminate. We call in others to aid us in deliberation on important questions, distrusting ourselves as not
being equal to deciding.

We deliberate not about ends but about means. For a
doctor does not deliberate whether he shall heal, nor an orator whether he shall persuade, nor a statesman whether he
shall produce law and order, nor does any one else deliber- 15
ate about his end. They assume the end and consider how
and by what means it is to be attained; and if it seems to
be produced by several means they consider by which it is
most easily and best produced, while if it is achieved by one
only they consider how it will be achieved by this and by
what means *this* will be achieved, till they come to the first
cause, which in the order of discovery is last. For the person 20
who deliberates seems to investigate and analyse in the way
described as though he were analysing a geometrical con-

struction[2] (not all investigation appears to be deliberation—for instance mathematical investigations—but all deliberation is investigation), and what is last in the order of analysis seems to be first in the order of becoming. And if
25 we come on an impossibility, we give up the search, e. g. if we need money and this cannot be got; but if a thing appears possible we try to do it. By 'possible' things I mean things that might be brought about by our own efforts, and these in a sense include things that can be brought about by the efforts of our friends, since the moving principle is in ourselves. The subject of investigation is sometimes the
30 instruments, sometimes the use of them; and similarly in the other cases—sometimes the means, sometimes the mode of using it or the means of bringing it about. It seems, then, as has been said, that man is a moving principle of actions; now deliberation is about the things to be done by the agent himself, and actions are for the sake of things other than themselves. For the end cannot be a subject of deliberation,
1113ᵃ but only the means; nor indeed can the particular facts be a subject of it, as whether this is bread or has been baked as it should; for these are matters of perception. If we are to be always deliberating, we shall have to go on to infinity.

The same thing is deliberated upon and is chosen, except that the object of choice is already determinate, since;
5 it is that which has been decided upon as a result of deliberation that is the object of choice. For every one ceases to inquire how he is to act when he has brought the moving principle back to himself and to the ruling part of himself; for this is what chooses. This is plain also from the ancient

---

[2] Aristotle has in mind the method of discovering the solution of a geometrical problem. The problem being to construct a figure of a certain kind, we suppose it constructed and then analyse it to see if there is some figure by constructing which we can construct the required figure, and so on till we come to a figure which our existing knowledge enables us to construct.

constitutions, which Homer represented; for the kings
announced their choices to the people. The object of choice
being one of the things in our own power which is desired   10
after deliberation, choice will be deliberate desire of things
in our own power; for when we have decided as a result of
deliberation we desire in accordance with our deliberation.

We may take it, then, that we have described choice in
outline, and stated the nature of its objects and the fact that
it is concerned with means.

4   That *wish* is for the end has already been stated;[3]
some think it is for the good, others for the appar-   15
ent good. Now those who say that the good is the
object of wish must admit in consequence that that which
the man who does not choose aright wishes for is not an
object of wish (for if it is to be so, it must also be good;
but it was, if it so happened, bad); while those who say the
apparent good is the object of wish must admit that there   20
is no natural object of wish, but only what seems good to
each man. Now different things appear good to different
people, and, if it so happens, even contrary things.

If these consequences are unpleasing, are we to say that
absolutely and in truth the good is the object of wish, but
for each person the apparent good; that that which is in   25
truth an object of wish is an object of wish to the good man,
while any chance thing may be so to the bad man, as in the
case of bodies also the things that are in truth wholesome
are wholesome for bodies which are in good condition,
while for those that are diseased other things are wholesome—or bitter or sweet or hot or heavy, and so on; since
the good man judges each class of things rightly, and in
each the truth appears to him? For each state of character   25
has its own ideas of the noble and the pleasant, and perhaps

[3] 1111^b 26.

the good man differs from others most by seeing the truth in each class of things, being as it were the norm and measure of them. In most things the error seems to be due to pleasure; for it appears a good when it is not. We therefore 1113ᵇ choose the pleasant as a good, and avoid pain as an evil.

5   The end, then, being what we wish for, the means what we deliberate about and choose, actions concerning means must be according to choice and voluntary. Now the exercise of the virtues is concerned with means. Therefore virtue also is in our own power, and so too vice. For where it is in our power to act it is also in our power not to act, and *vice versa*; so that, if to act, where this is noble, is in our power, not to act, which will be base, will 10 also be in our power, and it not to act, where this is noble, is in our power, to act, which will be base, will also be in our power. Now if it is in our power to do noble or base acts, and likewise in our power not to do them, and this was what being good or bad meant,⁴ then it is in our power to be virtuous or vicious.

The saying that 'no one is voluntarily wicked nor in-15 voluntarily happy' seems to be partly false and partly true; for no one is involuntarily happy, but wickedness *is* voluntary. Or else we shall have to dispute what has just been said, at any rate, and deny that man is a moving principle or begetter of his actions as of children. But if these facts are evident and we cannot refer actions to moving princi-20 ples other than those in ourselves, the acts whose moving principles are in us must themselves also be in our power and voluntary.

Witness seems to be borne to this both by individuals in their private capacity and by legislators themselves; for these punish and take vengeance on those who do wicked

⁴ 1112ᵃ 1 f.

acts (unless they have acted under compulsion or as a result of ignorance for which they are not themselves responsible), 25 while they honour those who do noble acts, as though they meant to encourage the latter and deter the former. But no one is encouraged to do the things that are neither in our power nor voluntary; it is assumed that there is no gain in being persuaded not to be hot or in pain or hungry or the like, since we shall experience these feelings none the less. 30 Indeed, we punish a man for his very ignorance, if he is thought responsible for the ignorance, as when penalties are doubled in the case of drunkenness; for the moving principle is in the man himself, since he had the power of not getting drunk and his getting drunk was the cause of his ignorance. And we punish those who are ignorant of anything in the laws that they ought to know and that is not 1114ᵃ difficult, and so too in the case of anything else that they are thought to be ignorant of through carelessness; we assume that it is in their power not to be ignorant, since they have the power of taking care.

But perhaps a man is the kind of man not to take care. Still they are themselves by their slack lives responsible for becoming men of that kind, and men make themselves 5 responsible for being unjust or self-indulgent, in the one case by cheating and in the other by spending their time in drinking bouts and the like; for it is activities exercised on particular objects that make the corresponding character. This is plain from the case of people training for any contest or action; they practice the activity the whole time. Now not to know that it is from the exercise of activities on particular objects that states of character are produced is the 10 mark of a thoroughly senseless person. Again, it is irrational to suppose that a man who acts unjustly does not wish to be unjust or a man who acts self-indulgently to be self-indulgent. But if *without* being ignorant a man does the things which will make him unjust, he will be unjust voluntarily.

Yet it does not follow that if he wishes he will cease to be unjust and will be just. For neither does the man who is ill
15 become well on those terms. We may suppose a case in which he is ill voluntarily, through living incontinently and disobeying his doctors. In that case it was *then* open to him not to be ill, but not now, when he has thrown away his chance, just as when you have let a stone go it is too late to recover it; but yet it was in your power to throw it, since the moving principle was in you. So, too, to the unjust and
20 to the self-indulgent man it was open at the beginning not to become men of this kind, and so they are unjust and self-indulgent voluntarily; but now that they have become so it is not possible for them not to be so.

But not only are the vices of the soul voluntary, but those of the body also for some men, whom we accordingly blame; while no one blames those who are ugly by nature, we blame those who are so owing to want of exercise and
25 care. So it is, too, with respect to weakness and infirmity; no one would reproach a man blind from birth or by disease or from a blow, but rather pity him, while every one would blame a man who was blind from drunkenness or some other form of self-indulgence. Of vices of the body, then, those in our own power are blamed, those not in our power
30 are not. And if this be so, in the other cases also the vices that are blamed must be in our own power.

Now some one may say that all men desire the apparent good, but have no control over the appearance, but the end appears to each man in a form answering to his character.
1114ᵇ We reply that if each man is somehow responsible for his state of mind, he will also be himself somehow responsible for the appearance; but if not, no one is responsible for his own evildoing, but every one does evil acts through ignorance of the end, thinking that by these he will get what is
5 best, and the aiming at the end is not self-chosen but one

must be born with an eye, as it were, by which to judge
rightly and choose what is truly good, and he is well
endowed by nature who is well endowed with this. For it is
what is greatest and most noble, and what we cannot get or
learn from another, but must have just such as it was when 10
given us at birth, and to be well and nobly endowed with
this will be perfect and true excellence of natural endowment. If this is true, then, how will virtue be more
voluntary than vice? To both men alike, the good and the
bad, the end appears and is fixed by nature or however it 15
may be, and it is by referring everything else to this that
men do whatever they do.

Whether, then, it is not by nature that the end appears
to each man such as it does appear, but something also
depends on him, or the end is natural but because the good
man adopts the means voluntarily virtue is voluntary, vice 20
also will be none the less voluntary; for in the case of the
bad man there is equally present that which depends on
himself in his actions even if not in his end. If, then, as is
asserted, the virtues are voluntary (for we are ourselves
somehow partly responsible for our states of character, and
it is by being persons of a certain kind that we assume the
end to be so and so), the vices also will be voluntary; for
the same is true of them.   25

With regard to the virtues in *general* we have stated
their genus in outline, viz. that they are means and that they
are states of character, and that they tend, and by their own
nature, to the doing of the acts by which they are produced,
and that they are in our power and voluntary, and act as the 30
right rule prescribes. But actions and states of character are
not voluntary in the same way; for we are masters of our
actions from the beginning right to the end, if we know the
particular facts, but though we control the beginning of our 1115ᵃ
states of character the gradual progress is not obvious, any

more than it is in illnesses; because it was in our power, however, to act in this way or not in this way, therefore the states are voluntary.

Let us take up the several virtues, however, and say which they are and what sort of things they are concerned 5 with and how they are concerned with them; at the same time it will become plain how many they are. And first let us speak of courage.

6 That it is a mean with regard to feelings of fear and confidence has already been made evident; [5] and plainly the things we fear are terrible things, and 10 these are, to speak without qualification, evils; for which reason people even define fear as expectation of evil. Now we fear all evils, e. g. disgrace, poverty, disease, friendlessness, death, but the brave man is not thought to be concerned with all; for to fear some things is even right and noble, and it is base not to fear them—e. g. disgrace; he who fears this is good and modest, and he who does not is shameless. He is, however, by some people called brave, by a transference of the word to a new meaning; for he has in 15 him something which is like the brave man, since the brave man also is a fearless person. Poverty and disease we perhaps ought not to fear, nor in general the things that do not proceed from vice and are not due to a man himself. But not even the man who is fearless of these is brave. Yet we apply 20 the word to him also in virtue of a similarity; for some who in the dangers of war are cowards are liberal and are confident in face of the loss of money. Nor is a man a coward if he fears insult to his wife and children or envy or anything of the kind; nor brave if he is confident when he is about to be flogged. With what sort of terrible things, then, is the brave man concerned? Surely with the greatest; for no one is

[5] 1107ᵃ 33–ᵇ 4.

more likely than he to stand his ground against what is awe- 25
inspiring. Now death is the most terrible of all things; for
it is the end, and nothing is thought to be any longer either
good or bad for the dead. But the brave man would not
seem to be concerned even with death in *all* circumstances,
e. g. at sea or in disease. In what circumstances, then?
Surely in the noblest. Now such deaths are those in battle;
for these take place in the greatest and noblest danger. And 30
these are correspondingly honoured in city-states and at the
courts of monarchs. Properly, then, he will be called brave
who is fearless in face of a noble death, and of all emergencies that involve death; and the emergencies of war are in
the highest degree of this kind. Yet at sea also, and in dis- 35
ease, the brave man is fearless, but not in the same way as 1115ᵇ
the seamen; for he has given up hope of safety, and is dis-
liking the thought of death in this shape, while they are
hopeful because of their experience. At the same time, we
show courage in situations where there is the opportunity
of showing prowess or where death is noble; but in these 5
forms of death neither of these conditions is fulfilled.

7 What is terrible is not the same for all men; but we
say there are things terrible even beyond human
strength. These, then, are terrible to every one—at
least to every sensible man; but the terrible things that are
not beyond human strength differ in magnitude and degree,
and so too do the things that inspire confidence. Now the
brave man is as dauntless as man may be. Therefore, while 10
he will fear even the things that are not beyond human
strength, he will face them as he ought and as the rule
directs, for honour's sake; for this is the end of virtue. But it
is possible to fear these more, or less, and again to fear
things that are not terrible as if they were. Of the faults that 15
are committed one consists in fearing what one should not,
another in fearing as we should not, another in fearing when

we should not, and so on; and so too with respect to the things that inspire confidence. The man, then, who faces and who fears the right things and from the right motive, in the right way and at the right time, and who feels confidence under the corresponding conditions, is brave; for the brave man feels and acts according to the merits of the case
20 and in whatever way the rule directs. Now the end of every activity is conformity to the corresponding state of character. This is true, therefore, of the brave man as well as of others. But courage is noble. Therefore the end also is noble; for each thing is defined by its end. Therefore it is for a noble end that the brave man endures and acts as courage directs.

Of those who go to excess he who exceeds in fearless-
25 ness has no name (we have said previously that many states of character have no names[6]), but he would be a sort of madman or insensible person if he feared nothing, neither earthquakes nor the waves, as they say the Celts do not; while the man who exceeds in confidence about what really is terrible is rash. The rash man, however, is also thought to
30 be boastful and only a pretender to courage; at all events, as the brave man *is* with regard to what is terrible, so the rash man wishes to *appear*; and so he imitates him in situations where he can. Hence also most of them are a mixture of rashness and cowardice; for, while in these situations they display confidence, they do not hold their ground against what is really terrible. The man who exceeds in fear is a
35 coward; for he fears both what he ought not and as he
1116a ought not, and all the similar characterizations attach to him. He is lacking also in confidence; but he is more conspicuous for his excess of fear in painful situations. The coward, then, is a despairing sort of person; for he fears everything. The brave man, on the other hand, has the

---

[6] 1107b 2, Cf. 1107b 29, 1108a 5.

opposite disposition; for confidence is the mark of a hopeful
disposition. The coward, the rash man, and the brave man
then, are concerned with the same objects but are differently 5
disposed towards them; for the first two exceed and fall
short, while the third holds the middle, which is the right,
position; and rash men are precipitate, and wish for dangers
beforehand but draw back when they are in them, while
brave men are keen in the moment of action, but quiet
beforehand.

As we have said, then, courage is a mean with respect 10
to things that inspire confidence or fear, in the circumstances that have been stated;[7] and it chooses or endures
things because it is noble to do so, or because it is base not
to do so.[8] But to die to escape from poverty or love or anything painful is not the mark of a brave man, but rather of
a coward; for it is softness to fly from what is troublesome,
and such a man endures death not because it is noble but to
fly from evil.

8 Courage, then, is something of this sort, but the
name is also applied to five other kinds. (1) First 15
comes the courage of the citizen-soldier; for this
is most like true courage. Citizen-soldiers seem to face
dangers because of the penalties imposed by the laws and
the reproaches they would otherwise incur, and because
of the honours they win by such action; and therefore
those peoples seem to be bravest among whom cowards 20
are held in dishonour and brave men in honour. This is
the kind of courage that Homer depicts, e. g. in Diomede
and in Hector:

[7] Ch. 6.

[8] 1115[b] 11–24.

First will Polydamas be to heap reproach on me then;[9]

and

25   For Hector one day 'mid the Trojans shall utter his
            vaulting harangue:
        "Afraid was Tydeides, and fled from my face."[10]

This kind of courage is most like to that which we described earlier,[11] because it is due to virtue; for it is due to shame and to desire of a noble object (i. e. honour) and avoidance of disgrace, which is ignoble. One might rank in the same
30 class even those who are compelled by their rulers; but they are inferior, inasmuch as they do what they do not from shame but from fear, and to avoid not what is disgraceful but what is painful; for their masters compel them, as Hector[12] does:

      But if I shall spy any dastard that cowers far from the fight,
35   Vainly will such an one hope to escape from the dogs.

And those who give them their posts, and beat them if they retreat, do the same, and so do those who draw them up
1116b with trenches or something of the sort behind them; all of these apply compulsion. But one ought to be brave not under compulsion but because it is noble to be so.

(2) Experience with regard to particular facts is also thought to be courage; this is indeed the reason why

[9] *Il.* xxii. 100.

[10] *Il.* viii. 148, 149.

[11] Chs. 6, 7.

[12] Aristotle's quotation is more like *Il.* ii. 391-3, where Agamemnon speaks, than xv. 348-51, where Hector speaks.

Socrates thought courage was knowledge. Other people
exhibit this quality in other dangers, and professional sol- 5
diers exhibit it in the dangers of war; for there seem to be
many empty alarms in war, of which these have had the
most comprehensive experience; therefore they seem brave,
because the others do not know the nature of the facts.
Again, their experience makes them most capable in attack 10
and in defence, since they can use their arms and have the
kind that are likely to be best both for attack and for defence;
therefore they fight like armed men against unarmed or like
trained athletes against amateurs; for in such contests too it is
not the bravest men that fight best, but those who are
strongest and have their bodies in the best condition. Pro- 15
fessional soldiers turn cowards, however, when the danger
puts too great a strain on them and they are inferior in
numbers and equipment; for they are the first to fly, while
citizen-forces die at their posts, as in fact happened at the
temple of Hermes.[13] For to the latter flight is disgraceful
and death is preferable to safety on those terms; while the 20
former from the very beginning faced the danger on the
assumption that they were stronger, and when they know
the facts they fly, fearing death more than disgrace; but the
brave man is not that sort of person.

(3) Passion also is sometimes reckoned as courage; those
who act from passion, like wild beasts rushing at those who
have wounded them, are thought to be brave, because brave 25
men also are passionate; for passion above all things is eager
to rush on danger, and hence Homer's 'put strength into his
passion'[14] and 'aroused their spirit and passion'[15] and 'hard

[13] The reference is to a battle at Coronea in the Sacred War, c. 353 B. C.,
in which the Phocians defeated the citizens of Coronea and some Boeotian
regulars.

[14] This is a conflation of *Il.* xi. 11 or xiv. 151 and xvi. 529.

[15] Cf. *Il.* v. 470, xv. 232, 594.

he breathed panting'[16] and 'his blood boiled'.[17] For all such
expressions seem to indicate the stirring and onset of pas-
30　sion. Now brave men act for honour's sake, but passion aids
them; while wild beasts act under the influence of pain; for
they attack because they have been wounded or because
they are afraid, since if they are in a forest they do not come
near one. Thus they are not brave because, driven by pain
35　and passion, they rush on danger without foreseeing any of
the perils, since at that rate even asses would be brave when
1117ᵃ　they are hungry; for blows will not drive them from their
food; and lust also makes adulterers do many daring things.
[Those creatures are not brave, then, which are driven on to
danger by pain or passion.] The 'courage' that is due to
passion seems to be the most natural, and to be courage if
choice and motive be added.

5　　　　Men, then, as well as beasts, suffer pain when they are
angry, and are pleased when they exact their revenge; those
who fight for these reasons, however, are pugnacious but
not brave; for they do not act for honour's sake nor as the
rule directs, but from strength of feeling; they have, however, something akin to courage.

　　　　(4) Nor are sanguine people brave; for they are confi-
10　dent in danger only because they have conquered often and
against many foes. Yet they closely resemble brave men,
because both are confident; but brave men are confident for
the reasons stated earlier,[18] while these are so because they
think they are the strongest and can suffer nothing.
(Drunken men also behave in this way; they become sanguine.) When their adventures do not succeed, however,
15　they run away; but it was [18] the mark of a brave man to face
things that are, and seem, terrible for a man, because it is

---

[16] Cf. *Od.* xxiv. 318 f.

[17] The phrase does not occur in Homer; it is found in Theocr. xx. 15.

[18] 1115ᵇ 11–24.

noble to do so and disgraceful not to do so. Hence also it is thought the mark of a braver man to be fearless and undisturbed in sudden alarms than to be so in those that are foreseen; for it must have proceeded more from a state of character, because less from preparation; acts that are foreseen may be chosen by calculation and rule, but sudden 20 actions must be in accordance with one's state of character.

(5) People who are ignorant of the danger also appear brave, and they are not far removed from those of a sanguine temper, but are inferior inasmuch as they have no self-reliance while these have. Hence also the sanguine hold their ground for a time; but those who have been deceived 25 about the facts fly if they know or suspect that these are different from what they supposed, as happened to the Argives when they fell in with the Spartans and took them for Sicyonians.[19]

9 We have, then, described the character both of brave men and of those who are thought to be brave.

Though courage is concerned with feelings of confidence and of fear, it is not concerned with both alike, but more with the things that inspire fear; for he who is undisturbed in face of these and bears himself as he should 30 towards these is more truly brave than the man who does so towards the things that inspire confidence. It is for facing what is painful, then, as has been said,[20] that men are called brave. Hence also courage involves pain, and is justly praised; for it is harder to face what is painful than to abstain from what is pleasant. Yet the end which courage sets before it would seem to be pleasant, but to be concealed 35 by the attending circumstances, as happens also in athletic 1117ᵇ

---

[19] At the Long Walls of Corinth, 392 B. C. Cf. Xen. Hell. iv. 4.10.

[20] 1115ᵇ 7–13.

contests; for the end at which boxers aim is pleasant—the
crown and the honours—but the blows they take are dis-
tressing to flesh and blood, and painful, and so is their
whole exertion; and because the blows and the exertions are
many the end, which is but small, appears to have nothing
pleasant in it. And so, if the case of courage is similar, death
and wounds will be painful to the brave man and against
his will, but he will face them because it is noble to do so or
because it is base not to do so. And the more he is possessed of virtue in its entirety and the happier he is, the
more he will be pained at the thought of death; for life is
best worth living for such a man, and he is knowingly losing the greatest goods, and this is painful. But he is none
the less brave, and perhaps all the more so, because he
chooses noble deeds of war at that cost. It is not the case,
then, with all the virtues that the exercise of them is pleasant, except in so far as it reaches its end. But it is quite
possible that the best soldiers may be not men of this sort
but those who are less brave but have no other good; for
these are ready to face danger, and they sell their life for trifling gains.

So much, then, for courage; it is not difficult to grasp
its nature in outline, at any rate, for what has been said.

After courage let us speak of temperance; for these
seem to be the virtues of the irrational parts.

10 We have said[21] that temperance is a mean with
regard to pleasures (for it is less, and not in the
same way, concerned with pains); self-indulgence also is manifested in the same sphere. Now, therefore,
let us determine with what sort of pleasures they are concerned. We may assume the distinction between bodily
pleasures and those of the soul, such as love of honour and

[21] 1107^b 4–6.

love of learning; for the lover of each of these delights in 30
that of which he is a lover, the body being in no way
affected, but rather the mind; but men who are concerned
with such pleasures are called neither temperate nor self-
indulgent. Nor, again, are those who are concerned with the
other pleasures that are not bodily; for those who are fond
of hearing and telling stories and who spend their days on 35
anything that turns up are called gossips, but not self-indulgent, nor are those who are pained at the loss of money or
of friends.

Temperance must be concerned with bodily pleasures, 1118ᵃ
but not all even of these; for those who delight in objects
of vision, such as colours and shapes and painting, are 5
called neither temperate nor self-indulgent; yet it would
seem possible to delight even in these either as one should
or to excess or to a deficient degree.

And so too is it with objects of hearing; no one calls
those who delight extravagantly in music or acting self-
indulgent, nor those who do so as they ought temperate.

Nor do we apply these names to those who delight in
odour, unless it be incidentally; we do not call those self-
indulgent who delight in the odour of apples or roses or
incense, but rather those who delight in the odour of 10
unguents or of dainty dishes; for self-indulgent people
delight in these because these remind them of the objects
of their appetite. And one may see even other people, when
they are hungry, delighting in the smell of food; but to
delight in this kind of thing is the mark of the self-indulgent 15
man; for these are objects of appetite to him.

Nor is there in animals other than man any pleasure
connected with these senses, except incidentally. For dogs
do not delight in the scent of hares, but in the eating of
them, but the scent told them the hares were there; nor does 20
the lion delight in the lowing of the ox, but in eating it; but
he perceived by the lowing that it was near, and therefore

appears to delight in the lowing; and similarly he does not
delight because he sees 'a stag or a wild goat',[22] but because
he is going to make a meal of it. Temperance and self-indulgence, however, are concerned with the kind of pleasures
25 that the other animals share in, which therefore appear slavish and brutish; these are touch and taste. But even of taste
they appear to make little or no use; for the business of taste
is the discriminating of flavours, which is done by wine-
tasters and people who season dishes; but they hardly take
pleasure in making these discriminations, or at least self-
30 indulgent people do not, but in the actual enjoyment, which
in all cases comes through touch, both in the case of food
and in that of drink and in that of sexual intercourse. This is
why a certain gourmand prayed that his throat might
become longer than a crane's, implying that it was the con-
1118ᵇ tact that he took pleasure in. Thus the sense with which
self-indulgence is connected is the most widely shared of the
senses; and self-indulgence would seem to be justly a matter of reproach, because it attaches to us not as men but as
animals. To delight in such things, then, and to love them
above all others, is brutish. For even of the pleasures of
touch the most liberal have been eliminated, e. g. those produced in the gymnasium by rubbing and by the consequent
5 heat; for the contact characteristic of the self-indulgent man
does not affect the whole body but only certain parts.

11 Of the appetites some seem to be common, others to be peculiar to individuals and acquired; e. g.
10 the appetite for food is natural, since every one
who is without it craves for food or drink, and sometimes
for both, and for love also (as Homer says)[23] if he is young
and lusty; but not every one craves for this or that kind of

[22] Il. iii. 24.

[23] Il. xxiv. 130.

nourishment or love, nor for the same things. Hence such craving appears to be our very own. Yet it has of course something natural about it; for different things are pleasant to different kinds of people, and some things are more 15 pleasant to every one than chance objects. Now in the natural appetites few go wrong, and only in one direction, that of excess; for to eat or drink whatever offers itself till one is surfeited is to exceed the natural amount, since natural appetite is the replenishment of one's deficiency. Hence these people are called belly-gods, this implying that they 20 fill their belly beyond what is right. It is people of entirely slavish character that become like this. But with regard to the pleasures peculiar to individuals many people go wrong and in many ways. For while the people who are 'fond of so and so' are so called because they delight either in the wrong things, or more than most people do, or in the wrong 25 way, the self-indulgent exceed in all three ways; they both delight in some things that they ought not to delight in (since they are hateful), and if one ought to delight in some of the things they delight in, they do so more than one ought and than most men do.

Plainly, then, excess with regard to pleasures is self-indulgence and is culpable; with regard to pains one is not, as in the case of courage, called temperate for facing them 30 or self-indulgent for not doing so, but the self-indulgent man is so called because he is pained more than he ought at not getting pleasant things (even his pain being caused by pleasure), and the temperate man is so called because he is not pained at the absence of what is pleasant and at his abstinence from it.

The self-indulgent man, then, craves for all pleasant 1119a things or those that are most pleasant, and is led by his appetite to choose these at the cost of everything else; hence he is pained both when he fails to get them and when he is merely craving for them (for appetite involves pain), but it

5 seems absurd to be pained for the sake of pleasure. People who fall short with regard to pleasures and delight in them less than they should are hardly found; for such insensibility is not human. Even the other animals distinguish different kinds of food and enjoy some and not others; and if there is any one who finds nothing pleasant and nothing more attractive than anything else, he must be something

10 quite different from a man; this sort of person has not received a name because he hardly occurs. The temperate man occupies a middle position with regard to these objects. For he neither enjoys the things that the self-indulgent man enjoys most—but rather dislikes them—nor in general the things that he should not, nor anything of this sort to excess, nor does he feel pain or craving when they are absent, or does so only to a moderate degree, and not more than he

15 should, nor when he should not, and so on; but the things that, being pleasant, make for health or for good condition, he will desire moderately and as he should, and also other pleasant things if they are not hindrances to these ends, or contrary to what is noble, or beyond his means. For he who neglects these conditions loves such pleasures more than they are worth, but the temperate man is not that sort of

20 person, but the sort of person that the right rule prescribes.

12 Self-indulgence is more like a voluntary state than cowardice. For the former is actuated by pleasure, the latter by pain, of which the one is to be chosen and the other to be avoided; and pain upsets and destroys the nature of the person who feels it, while pleasure does nothing of the sort. Therefore self-indulgence is more volun-

25 tary. Hence also it is more a matter of reproach; for it is easier to become accustomed to its objects, since there are many things of this sort in life, and the process of habituation to them is free from danger, while with terrible objects the reverse is the case. But cowardice would seem to be voluntary

in a different degree from its particular manifestations; for it is itself painless, but in these we are upset by pain, so that we even throw down our arms and disgrace ourselves in other ways; hence our acts are even thought to be done under com- 30 pulsion. For the self-indulgent man, on the other hand, the particular acts are voluntary (for he does them with craving and desire), but the whole state is less so; for no one craves to be self-indulgent.

The name self-indulgence is applied also to childish faults; for they bear a certain resemblance to what we have been considering. Which is called after which, makes no difference to our present purpose; plainly, however, the later 1119b is called after the earlier. The transference of the name seems not a bad one; for that which desires what is base and which develops quickly ought to be kept in a chastened condition, and these characteristics belong above all to appetite and to the child, since children in fact live at the beck and call of appetite, and it is in them that the desire for what is 5 pleasant is strongest. If, then, it is not going to be obedient and subject to the ruling principle, it will go to great lengths; for in an irrational being the desire for pleasure is insatiable even if it tries every source of gratification, and the exercise of appetite increases its innate force, and if 10 appetites are strong and violent they even expel the power of calculation. Hence they should be moderate and few, and should in no way oppose the rational principle—and this is what we call an obedient and chastened state—and as the child should live according to the direction of his tutor, so the appetitive element should live according to rational 15 principle. Hence the appetitive element in a temperate man should harmonize with the rational principle; for the noble is the mark at which both aim, and the temperate man craves for the things he ought, as he ought, and when he ought; and this is what rational principle directs.

Here we conclude our account of temperance.

BOOK IV

1 Let us speak next of liberality. It seems to be the mean with regard to wealth; for the liberal man is praised not in respect of military matters, nor of
25 those in respect of which the temperate man is praised, nor of judicial decisions, but with regard to the giving and taking of wealth, and especially in respect of giving. Now by 'wealth' we mean all the things whose value is measured by money. Further, prodigality and meanness are excesses and
30 defects with regard to wealth; and meanness we always impute to those who care more than they ought for wealth, but we sometimes apply the word 'prodigality' in a complex sense; for we call those men prodigals who are incontinent and spend money on self-indulgence. Hence also they are thought the poorest characters; for they combine more vices than one. Therefore the application of the word to them is
1120ᵃ not its proper use; for a 'prodigal' means a man who has a single evil quality, that of wasting his substance; since a prodigal is one who is being ruined by his own fault, and the wasting of substance is thought to be a sort of ruining of oneself, life being held to depend on possession of substance.

This, then, is the sense in which we take the word
5 'prodigality'. Now the things that have a use may be used either well or badly; and riches is a useful thing; and everything is used best by the man who has the virtue concerned with it; riches, therefore, will be used best by the man who has the virtue concerned with wealth; and this is the liberal man. Now spending and giving seem to be the using of wealth; taking and keeping rather the possession of it.
10 Hence it is more the mark of the liberal man to give to the right people than to take from the right sources and not to

take from the wrong. For it is more characteristic of virtue
to do good than to have good done to one, and more characteristic to do what is noble than not to do what is base;
and it is not hard to see that giving implies doing good and
doing what is noble, and taking implies having good done to
one or not acting basely. And gratitude is felt towards him   15
who gives, not towards him who does not take, and praise
also is bestowed more on him. It is easier, also, not to take
than to give; for men are apter to give away their own too
little than to take what is another's. Givers, too, are called
liberal; but those who do not take are not praised for liberality but rather for justice; while those who take are hardly   20
praised at all. And the liberal are almost the most loved of
all virtuous characters, since they are useful; and this
depends on their giving.

Now virtuous actions are noble and done for the sake of
the noble. Therefore the liberal man, like other virtuous
men, will give for the sake of the noble, and rightly; for he
will give to the right people, the right amounts, and at the   25
right time, with all the other qualifications that accompany
right giving; and that too with pleasure or without pain; for
that which is virtuous is pleasant or free from pain—least of
all will it be painful. But he who gives to the wrong people
or not for the sake of the noble but for some other cause,
will be called not liberal but by some other name. Nor is he
liberal who gives with pain; for he would prefer the wealth   30
to the noble act, and this is not characteristic of a liberal
man. But no more will the liberal man take from wrong
sources; for such taking is not characteristic of the man who
sets no store by wealth. Nor will he be a ready asker; for it
is not characteristic of a man who confers benefits to accept
them lightly. But he will take from the right sources, e. g.
from his own possessions, not as something noble but as a   1120^b
necessity, that he may have something to give. Nor will he
neglect his own property, since he wishes by means of this

to help others. And he will refrain from giving to anybody
and everybody, that he may have something to give to the
right people, at the right time, and where it is noble to do
so. It is highly characteristic of a liberal man also to go to
excess in giving, so that he leaves too little for himself; for it
5 is the nature of a liberal man not to look to himself. The
term 'liberality' is used relatively to a man's substance; for
liberality resides not in the multitude of the gifts but in
the state of character of the giver, and this is relative to
the giver's substance. There is therefore nothing to prevent the man who gives less from being the more liberal
man, if he has less to give. Those are thought to be more
10 liberal who have not made their wealth but inherited it; for
in the first place they have no experience of want, and secondly all men are fonder of their own productions, as are
15 parents and poets. It is not easy for the liberal man to be
rich, since he is not apt either at taking or at keeping, but at
giving away, and does not value wealth for its own sake but
as a means to giving. Hence comes the charge that is
brought against fortune, that those who deserve riches most
get it least. But it is not unreasonable that it should turn out
20 so; for he cannot have wealth, any more than anything else,
if he does not take pains to have it. Yet he will not give to
the wrong people nor at the wrong time, and so on; for he
would no longer be acting in accordance with liberality, and
if he spent on these objects he would have nothing to spend
on the right objects. For, as has been said, he is liberal who
25 spends according to his substance and on the right objects;
and he who exceeds is prodigal. Hence we do not call
despots prodigal; for it is thought not easy for them to give
and spend beyond the amount of their possessions. Liberality, then, being a mean with regard to giving and taking of
wealth, the liberal man will both give and spend the right
30 amounts and on the right objects, alike in small things and
in great, and that with pleasure; he will also take the right

amounts and from the right sources. For, the virtue being a mean with regard to both, he will do both as he ought; since this sort of taking accompanies proper giving, and that which is not of this sort is contrary to it, and accordingly the giving and taking that accompany each other are present together in the same man, while the contrary kinds evidently are not. But if he happens to spend in a manner contrary to what is right and noble, he will be pained, but moderately and as he ought; for it is the mark of virtue both to be pleased and to be pained at the right objects and in the right way. Further, the liberal man is easy to deal with in money matters; for he can be got the better of, since he sets no store by money, and is more annoyed if he has not spent something that he ought than pained if he has spent something that he ought not, and does not agree with the saying of Simonides.

The prodigal errs in these respects also; for he is neither pleased nor pained at the right things or in the right way; this will be more evident as we go on. We have said[1] that prodigality and meanness are excesses and deficiencies, and in two things, in giving and in taking; for we include spending under giving. Now prodigality exceeds in giving and not taking, and falls short in taking, while meanness falls short in giving, and exceeds in taking, except in small things.

The characteristics of prodigality are not often combined; for it is not easy to give to all if you take from none; private persons soon exhaust their substance with giving, and it is to these that the name of prodigals is applied—though a man of this sort would seem to be in no small degree better than a mean man. For he is easily cured both by age and by poverty, and thus he may move towards the middle state. For he has the characteristics of the liberal man, since he both gives and refrains from taking, though

1121ᵃ

5

10

15

20

---

[1] 1119ᵇ 27.

he does neither of these in the right manner or well. Therefore if he were brought to do so by habituation or in some
other way, he would be liberal; for he will then give to the
right people, and will not take from the wrong sources. This
25 is why he is thought to have not a bad character; it is not
the mark of a wicked or ignoble man to go to excess in giving and not taking, but only of a foolish one. The man who
is prodigal in this way is thought much better than the
mean man both for the aforesaid reasons and because he
benefits many while the other benefits no one, not even
himself.

But most prodigal people, as has been said,[2] also take
30 from the wrong sources, and are in this respect mean. They
become apt to take because they wish to spend and cannot
do this easily; for their possessions soon run short. Thus
they are forced to provide means from some other source.
1121ᵇ At the same time, because they care nothing for honour,
they take recklessly and from any source; for they have an
appetite for giving, and they do not mind how or from what
source. Hence also their giving is not liberal; for it is not
noble, nor does it aim at nobility, nor is it done in the right
5 way; sometimes they make rich those who should be poor,
and will give nothing to people of respectable character, and
much to flatterers or those who provide them with some
other pleasure. Hence also most of them are self-indulgent;
for they spend lightly and waste money on their indul-
gences, and incline towards pleasures because they do not
10 live with a view to what is noble.

The prodigal man, then, turns into what we have
described if he is left untutored, but if he is treated with
care he will arrive at the intermediate and right state. But
meanness is both incurable (for old age and every disability
15 is thought to make men mean) and more innate in men than

2 ll. 16–19.

prodigality; for most men are fonder of getting money than of giving. It also extends widely, and is multiform, since there seem to be many kinds of meanness.

For it consists in two things, deficiency in giving and excess is taking, and is not found complete in all men but is sometimes divided; some men go to excess in taking, others fall short in giving. Those who are called by such names 20 as 'miserly', 'close', 'stingy', all fall short in giving, but do not covet the possessions of others nor wish to get them. In some this is due to a sort of honesty and avoidance of what is disgraceful (for some seem, or at least profess, to hoard 25 their money for this reason, that they may not some day be forced to do something disgraceful; to this class belong the cheeseparer and every one of the sort; he is so called from his excess of unwillingness to give anything); while others again keep their hands off the property of others from fear, on the ground that it is not easy, if one takes the property of others oneself, to avoid having one's own taken by them; they are therefore content neither to take nor to give.

Others again exceed in respect of taking by taking any- 30 thing and from any source, e. g. those who ply sordid trades, pimps and all such people, and those who lend small sums and at high rates. For all of these take more than they 1122ª ought and from wrong sources. What is common to them is evidently sordid love of gain; they all put up with a bad name for the sake of gain, and little gain at that. For those who make great gains but from wrong sources, and not the right gains, e. g. despots when they sack cities and spoil 5 temples, we do not call mean but rather wicked, impious, and unjust. But the gamester and the footpad [and the high-wayman] belong to the class of the mean, since they have a sordid love of gain. For it is for gain that both of them ply their craft and endure the disgrace of it, and the one faces the greatest dangers for the sake of the booty, while the other makes gain from his friends, to whom he ought to be 10 giving. Both, then, since they are willing to make gain from wrong sources, are sordid lovers of gain; therefore all such forms of taking are mean.

And it is natural that meanness is described as the contrary of liberality; for not only is it a greater evil than prodigality, but men err more often in this direction than in the way of prodigality as we have described it.

So much, then, for liberality and the opposed vices.

2 It would seem proper to discuss magnificence next. For this also seems to be a virtue concerned with wealth; but it does not like liberality extend to all the actions that are concerned with wealth, but only to those that involve expenditure; and in these it surpasses liberality in scale. For, as the name itself suggests, it is a fitting expenditure involving largeness of scale. But the scale is relative; for the expense of equipping a trireme is not the same as that of heading a sacred embassy. It is what is fitting, then, in relation to the agent, and to the circumstances and the object. The man who in small or middling things spends according to the merits of the case is not called magnificent (e. g. the man who can say 'many a gift I gave the wanderer'),[3] but only the man who does so in great things. For the magnificent man is liberal, but the liberal man is not necessarily magnificent. The deficiency of this state of character is called niggardliness, the excess vulgarity, lack of taste, and the like, which do not go to excess in the amount spent on right objects, but by showy expenditure in the wrong circumstances and the wrong manner; we shall speak of these vices later.[4]

The magnificent man is like an artist; for he can see

[3] *Od.* xvii 420.

[4] 1123ᵃ 19–33.

what is fitting and spend large sums tastefully. For, as we
said at the beginning[5], a state of character is determined by   35
its activities and by its objects. Now the expenses of the   1122ᵇ
magnificent man are large and fitting. Such, therefore, are
also his results; for thus there will be a great expenditure and
one that is fitting to its result. Therefore the result should be
worthy of the expense, and the expense should be worthy of
the result, or should even exceed it. And the magnificent   5
man will spend such sums for honour's sake; for this is common to the virtues. And further he will do so gladly and
lavishly; for nice calculation is a niggardly thing. And he will
consider how the result can be made most beautiful and
most becoming rather than for how much it can be produced
and how it can be produced most cheaply. It is necessary,
then, that the magnificent man be also liberal. For the liberal   10
man also will spend what he ought and as he ought; and it is
in these matters that the greatness implied in the name of
the magnificent man—his bigness, as it were—is manifested,
since liberality is concerned with these matters; and at an
equal expense he will produce a more magnificent work of
art. For a possession and a work of art have not the same
excellence. The most valuable possession is that which is   15
worth most, e. g. gold, but the most valuable work of art is
that which is great and beautiful (for the contemplation of
such a work inspires admiration, and so does magnificence);
and a work has an excellence—viz. magnificence—which
involves magnitude. Magnificence is an attribute of expenditures of the kind which we call honourable, e. g. those
connected with the gods—votive offerings, buildings, and
sacrifices—and similarly with any form of religious worship,
and all those that are proper objects of public-spirited ambi-   20
tion, as when people think they ought to equip a chorus or

[5] Not in so many words, but Cf. 1103ᵇ 21–23, 1104ᵃ, 27–29.

a trireme, or entertain the city, in a brilliant way. But in all
cases, as has been said[6], we have regard to the agent as well
25 and ask who he is and what means he has; for the expenditure should be worthy of his means, and suit not only the
result but also the producer. Hence a poor man cannot be
magnificent, since he has not the means with which to spend
large sums fittingly; and he who tries is a fool, since he
spends beyond what can be expected of him and what is
proper, but it is *right* expenditure that is virtuous. But great
30 expenditure is becoming to those who have suitable means to
start with, acquired by their own efforts or from ancestors or
connexions, and to people of high birth or reputation, and so
on; for all these things bring with them greatness and pres-
35 tige. Primarily, then, the magnificent man is of this sort, and
magnificence is shown in expenditures of this sort, as has
been said;[7] for these are the greatest and most honourable.
Of *private* occasions of expenditure the most suitable are
those that take place once for all, e. g. a wedding or anything
1123ᵃ of the kind, or anything that interests the whole city or the
people of position in it, and also the receiving of foreign
guests and the sending of them on their way, and gifts and
5 counter-gifts; for the magnificent man spends not on himself but on public objects, and gifts bear some resemblance
to votive offerings. A magnificent man will also furnish his
house suitably to his wealth (for even a house is a sort of
public ornament), and will spend by preference on those
works that are lasting (for these are the most beautiful),
and on every class of things he will spend what is becoming;
10 for the same things are not suitable for gods and for men,
nor in a temple and in a tomb. And since each expenditure
may be great of its kind, and what is most magnificent
absolutely is great expenditure on a great object, but what is

6 ᵃ24–26.

7 ll. 19–23.

magnificent *here* is what is great in *these* circumstances, and greatness in the work differs from greatness in the expense (for the most beautiful ball or bottle is magnificent as a gift to a child, but the price of it is small and mean)—therefore it is characteristic of the magnificent man, whatever kind of result he is producing, to produce it magnificently (for such a result is not easily surpassed) and to make it worthy of the expenditure.

Such, then, is the magnificent man; the man who goes to excess and is vulgar exceeds, as has been said,[8] by spending beyond what is right. For on small objects of expenditure he spends much and displays a tasteless showiness; e. g. he gives a club dinner on the scale of a wedding banquet, and when he provides the chorus for a comedy he brings them on to the stage in purple, as they do at Megara. And all such things he will do not for honour's sake but to show off his wealth, and because he thinks he is admired for these things, and where he ought to spend much he spends little and where little, much. The niggardly man on the other hand will fall short in everything, and after spending the greatest sums will spoil the beauty of the result for a trifle, and whatever he is doing he will hesitate and consider how he may spend least, and lament even that, and think he is doing everything on a bigger scale than he ought.

These states of character, then, are vices; yet they do not bring *disgrace* because they are neither harmful to one's neighbour nor very unseemly.

3   Pride seems even from its name[9] to be concerned with great things; what sort of great things, is the first question we must try to answer. It makes no

---

[8] 1122ª 31–33.

[9] 'Pride' of course has not the etymological associations of *megalopsychia*, but seems in other respects the best translation.

35 difference whether we consider the state of character or the
man characterized by it. Now the man is thought to be
1123^b proud who thinks himself worthy of great things, being
worthy of them; for he who does so beyond his deserts is a
fool, but no virtuous man is foolish or silly. The proud
man, then, is the man we have described. For he who is
5 worthy of little and thinks himself worthy of little is temperate, but not proud; for pride implies greatness, as beauty
implies a good-sized body, and little people may be neat
and well-proportioned but cannot be beautiful. On the
other hand, he who thinks himself worthy of great things,
being unworthy of them, is vain; though not every one who
thinks himself worthy of more than he really is worthy of
is vain. The man who thinks himself worthy of less than he
is really worthy of is unduly humble, whether his deserts
10 be great or moderate, or his deserts be small but his claims
yet smaller. And the man whose deserts are great would
seem *most* unduly humble; for what would he have done if
they had been less? The proud man, then, is an extreme in
respect of the greatness of his claims, but a mean in respect
of the rightness of them; for he claims what is in accordance
with his merits, while the others go to excess or fall short.

If, then, he deserves and claims great things, and above
15 all the greatest things, he will be concerned with one thing
in particular. Desert is relative to external goods; and the
greatest of these, we should say, is that which we render to
the gods, and which people of position most aim at, and
20 which is the prize appointed for the noblest deeds; and this
is honour; that is surely the greatest of external goods. Honours and dishonours, therefore, are the objects with respect
to which the proud man is as he should be. And even apart
from argument it is with honour that proud men appear to
be concerned; for it is honour that they chiefly claim, but in
accordance with their deserts. The unduly humble man falls
short both in comparison with his own merits and in com-

parison with the proud man's claims. The vain man goes to 25
excess in comparison with his own merits, but does not
exceed the proud man's claims.

Now the proud man, since he deserves most, must be
good in the highest degree; for the better man always
deserves more, and the best man most. Therefore the truly 30
proud man must be good. And greatness in every virtue
would seem to be characteristic of a proud man. And it
would be most unbecoming for a proud man to fly from
danger, swinging his arms by his sides, or to wrong another,
for to what end should he do disgraceful acts, he to whom
nothing is great? If we consider him point by point, we shall
see the utter absurdity of a proud man who is not good.
Nor, again, would he be worthy of honour if he were bad, 35
for honour is the prize of virtue, and it is to the good that
it is rendered. Pride, then, seems to be a sort of crown of 1124ᵃ
the virtues; for it makes them greater, and it is not found
without them. Therefore it is hard to be truly proud; for it
is impossible without nobility and goodness of character. It
is chiefly with honours and dishonours, then, that the proud 5
man is concerned; and at honours that are great and conferred by good men he will be moderately pleased, thinking
that he is coming by his own or even less than his own; for
there can be no honour that is worthy of perfect virtue, yet
he will at any rate accept it since they have nothing greater 10
to bestow on him; but honour from casual people and on
trifling grounds he will utterly despise, since it is not this
that he deserves, and dishonour too, since in his case it cannot be just. In the first place, then, as has been said,[10] the
proud man is concerned with honours; yet he will also bear
himself with moderation towards wealth and power and all
good or evil fortune, whatever may befall him, and will be 15
neither over-joyed by good fortune nor over-pained by evil.

[10] 1123ᵇ 15–22.

For not even towards honour does he bear himself as if it were a very great thing. Power and wealth are desirable for the sake of honour (at least those who have them wish to get honour by means of them); and for him to whom even honour is a little thing the others must be so too. Hence proud men are thought to be disdainful.

20   The goods of fortune also are thought to contribute towards pride. For men who are well-born are thought worthy of honour, and so are those who enjoy power or wealth; for they are in a superior position, and everything that has a superiority in something good is held in greater honour. Hence even such things make men prouder; for they are honoured by some for having them; but in truth the good

25   man alone is to be honoured; he, however, who has both advantages is thought the more worthy of honour. But those who without virtue have such goods are neither justified in making great claims nor entitled to the name of 'proud'; for these things imply perfect virtue. Disdainful and insolent, however, even those who have such goods become. For without virtue it is not easy to bear gracefully the goods of

30   fortune; and, being unable to bear them, and thinking themselves superior to others, they despise others and them-

1124ᵇ   selves do what they please. They imitate the proud man without being like him, and this they do where they can; so they do not act virtuously, but they do despise others. For

5   the proud man despises justly (since he thinks truly), but the many do so at random.

He does not run into trifling dangers, nor is he fond of danger, because he honours few things; but he will face great dangers, and when he is in danger he is unsparing of his life, knowing that there are conditions on which life is not worth having. And he is the sort of man to confer benefits, but he is ashamed of receiving them; for the one is the

10   mark of a superior, the other of an inferior. And he is apt to confer greater benefits in return; for thus the original bene-

factor besides being paid will incur a debt to him, and will
be the gainer by the transaction. They seem also to remember any service they have done, but not those they have
received (for he who receives a service is inferior to him
who has done it, but the proud man wishes to be superior),
and to hear of the former with pleasure, of the latter with
displeasure; this, it seems, is why Thetis did not mention to 15
Zeus the services she had done him,[11] and why the Spartans
did not recount their services to the Athenians, but those
they had received. It is a mark of the proud man also to ask
for nothing or scarcely anything, but to give help readily,
and to be dignified towards people who enjoy high position
and good fortune, but unassuming towards those of the
middle class; for it is a difficult and lofty thing to be supe- 20
rior to the former, but easy to be so to the latter, and a lofty
bearing over the former is no mark of ill-breeding, but
among humble people it is as vulgar as a display of strength
against the weak. Again, it is characteristic of the proud
man not to aim at the things commonly held in honour, or
the things in which others excel; to be sluggish and to hold
back except where great honour or a great work is at stake, 25
and to be a man of few deeds, but of great and notable
ones. He must also be open in his hate and in his love (for
to conceal one's feelings, i. e. to care less for truth than for
what people will think, is a coward's part), and must speak
and act openly; for he is free of speech because he is con-
temptuous, and he is given to telling the truth, except when 30
he speaks in irony to the vulgar. He must be unable to
make his life revolve round another, unless it be a friend; 1125ᵃ
for this is slavish, and for this reason all flatterers are servile
and people lacking in self-respect are flatterers. Nor is he
given to admiration; for nothing to him is great. Nor is he
mindful of wrongs; for it is not the part of a proud man to

[11] In fact she did, *Il.* i. 503.

5 have a long memory, especially for wrongs, but rather to overlook them. Nor is he a gossip; for he will speak neither about himself nor about another, since he cares not to be praised nor for others to be blamed; nor again is he given to praise; and for the same reason he is not an evil-speaker, even about his enemies, except from haughtiness. With
10 regard to necessary or small matters he is least of all men given to lamentation or the asking of favours; for it is the part of one who takes such matters seriously to behave so with respect to them. He is one who will possess beautiful and profitless things rather than profitable and useful ones; for this is more proper to a character that suffices to itself.

Further, a slow step is thought proper to the proud man, a deep voice, and a level utterance; for the man who takes few things seriously is not likely to be hurried, nor the man
15 who thinks nothing great to be excited, while a shrill voice and a rapid gait are the results of hurry and excitement.

Such, then, is the proud man; the man who falls short of him is unduly humble, and the man who goes beyond him is vain. Now even these are not thought to be bad (for they are not malicious), but only mistaken. For the unduly
20 humble man, being worthy of good things, robs himself of what he deserves, and seems to have something bad about him from the fact that he does not think himself worthy of good things, and seems also not to know himself; else he would have desired the things he was worthy of, since these were good. Yet such people are not thought to be fools, but
25 rather unduly retiring. Such a reputation, however, seems actually to make them worse; for each class of people aims at what corresponds to its worth, and these people stand back even from noble actions and undertakings, deeming themselves unworthy, and from external goods no less. Vain people, on the other hand, are fools and ignorant of themselves, and that manifestly; for, not being worthy of them, they attempt honourable undertakings, and then are found

out; and they adorn themselves with clothing and outward 30
show and such things, and wish their strokes of good fortune to be made public, and speak about them as if they
would be honoured for them. But undue humility is more
opposed to pride than vanity is; for it is both commoner
and worse.

Pride, then, is concerned with honour on the grand
scale, as has been said.[12]   35

4   There seems to be in the sphere of honour also, as
was said in our first remarks on the subject,[13] a 1125[b]
virtue which would appear to be related to pride as
liberality is to magnificence. For neither of these has anything to do with the grand scale, but both dispose us as is 5
right with regard to middling and unimportant objects; as in
getting and giving of wealth there is a mean and an excess
and defect, so too honour may be desired more than is
right, or less, or from the right sources and in the right way.
We blame both the ambitious man as aiming at honour
more than is right and from wrong sources, and the unam- 10
bitious man as not willing to be honoured even for noble
reasons. But sometimes we praise the ambitious man as
being manly and a lover of what is noble, and the unambitious man as being moderate and self-controlled, as we said
in our first treatment of the subject.[14] Evidently, since 'fond
of such and such an object' has more than one meaning, we
do not assign the term 'ambition' or 'love of honour' always
to the same thing, but when we praise the quality we think
of the man who loves honour more than most people, and 15
when we blame it we think of him who loves it more than is
right. The mean being without a name, the extremes seem

[12] 1107[b] 26, 1123[a] 34–[b]22.

[13] Ib. 24–27.

[14] 1107[b] 33.

to dispute for its place as though that were vacant by
default. But where there is excess and defect, there is also an
intermediate; now men desire honour both more than they
should and less; therefore it is possible also to do so as one
20 should; at all events this is the state of character that is
praised, being an unnamed mean in respect of honour. Relatively to ambition it seems to be unambitiousness, and
relatively to unambitiousness it seems to be ambition, while
relatively to both severally it seems in a sense to be both
together. This appears to be true of the other virtues also.
But in this case the extremes seem to be contradictories
25 because the mean has not received a name.

5 Good temper is a mean with respect to anger; the
middle state being unnamed, and the extremes
almost without a name as well, we place good temper in the middle position, though it inclines towards the
30 deficiency, which is without a name. The excess might be
called a sort of 'irascibility'. For the passion is anger, while
its causes are many and diverse.

The man who is angry at the right things and with the
right people, and, further, as he ought, when he ought, and
as long as he ought, is praised. This will be the good-
tempered man, since good temper is praised. For the
35 good-tempered man tends to be unperturbed and not to be
1126ᵃ led by passion, but to be angry in the manner, at the things,
and for the length of time, that the rule dictates; but he is
thought to err rather in the direction of deficiency; for the
good-tempered man is not revengeful, but rather tends to
make allowances.

The deficiency, whether it is a sort of 'inirascibility' or
whatever it is, is blamed. For those who are not angry at the
5 things they should be angry at are thought to be fools, and
so are those who are not angry in the right way, at the right

time, or with the right persons; for such a man is thought
not to feel things nor to be pained by them, and, since he
does not get angry, he is thought unlikely to defend himself; and to endure being insulted and put up with insult to
one's friends is slavish.

The excess can be manifested in all the points that have
been named (for one can be angry with the wrong persons,
at the wrong things, more than is right, too quickly, or too
long); yet *all* are not found in the same person. Indeed they
could not; for evil destroys even itself, and if it is complete
becomes unbearable. Now *hot-tempered* people get angry
quickly and with the wrong persons and at the wrong things
and more than is right, but their anger ceases quickly—
which is the best point about them. This happens to them
because they do not restrain their anger but retaliate openly
owing to their quickness of temper, and then their anger
ceases. By reason of excess *choleric* people are quick-tem-
pered and ready to be angry with everything and on every
occasion; whence their name. *Sulky* people are hard to
appease, and retain their anger long; for they repress their
passion. But it ceases when they retaliate; for revenge
relieves them of their anger, producing in them pleasure
instead of pain. If this does not happen they retain their
burden; for owing to its not being obvious no one even reasons with them, and to digest one's anger in oneself takes
time. Such people are most troublesome to themselves and
to their dearest friends. We call *bad-tempered* those who are
angry at the wrong things, more than is right, and longer,
and cannot be appeased until they inflict vengeance or punishment.

To good temper we oppose the excess rather than the
defect; for not only is it commoner (since revenge is the
more human), but bad-tempered people are worse to live
with.

What we have said in our earlier treatment of the subject[15] is plain also from what we are now saying; viz. that it
is not easy to define how, with whom, at what, and how
long one should be angry, and at what point right action
35 ceases and wrong begins. For the man who strays a little
from the path, either towards the more or towards the less,
is not blamed; since sometimes we praise those who exhibit
the deficiency, and call them good-tempered, and some-
1126b times we call angry people manly, as being capable of
ruling. How far, therefore, and how a man must stray
before he becomes blameworthy, it is not easy to state in
words; for the decision depends on the particular facts and
on perception. But so much at least is plain, that the middle
5 state is praiseworthy—that in virtue of which we are angry
with the right people, at the right things, in the right way,
and so on, while the excesses and defects are blameworthy—slightly so if they are present in a low degree, more if
in a higher degree, and very much if in a high degree. Evidently, then, we must cling to the middle state.—Enough of
10 the states relative to anger.

6 In gatherings of men, in social life and the interchange of words and deeds, some men are thought
to be obsequious, viz. those who to give pleasure
praise everything and never oppose, but think it their duty
15 'to give no pain to the people they meet'; while those who,
on the contrary, oppose everything and care not a whit
about giving pain are called churlish and contentious. That
the states we have named are culpable is plain enough, and
that the middle state is laudable—that in virtue of which a
man will put up with, and will resent, the right things and
in the right way; but no name has been assigned to it,
20 though it most resembles friendship. For the man who corresponds to this middle state is very much what, with
affection added, we call a good friend. But the state in ques-

tion differs from friendship in that it implies no passion or affection for one's associates; since it is not by reason of loving or hating that such a man takes everything in the right way, but by being a man of a certain kind. For he will 25 behave so alike towards those he knows and those he does not know, towards intimates and those who are not so, except that in each of these cases he will behave as is befitting; for it is not proper to have the same care for intimates and for strangers, nor again is it the same conditions that make it right to give pain to them. Now we have said generally that he will associate with people in the right way; but it is by reference to what is honourable and expedient that he will aim at not giving pain or at contributing pleasure. 30 For he seems to be concerned with the pleasures and pains of social life; and wherever it is not honourable, or is harmful, for him to contribute pleasure, he will refuse, and will choose rather to give pain; also if his acquiescence in another's action would bring disgrace, and that in a high degree, or injury, *on that other*, while his opposition brings a 35 little pain, he will not acquiesce but will decline. He will associate differently with people in high station and with 1127ª ordinary people, with closer and more distant acquaintances, and so too with regard to all other differences, rendering to each class what is befitting, and while for its own sake he chooses to contribute pleasure, and avoids the giving of pain, he will be guided by the consequences, if these are 5 greater, i. e. honour and expediency. For the sake of a great future pleasure, too, he will inflict small pains.

The man who attains the mean, then, is such as we have described, but has not received a name; of those who contribute pleasure, the man who aims at being pleasant with no ulterior object is obsequious, but the man who does so in order that he may get some advantage in the direction 10 of money or the things that money buys is a flatterer; while the man who quarrels with everything is, as has been

said,[16] churlish and contentious. And the extremes seem to
be contradictory to each other because the mean is without
a name.

7 The mean opposed to boastfulness is found in
almost the same sphere; and this also is without a
15   name. It will be no bad plan to describe these
states as well; for we shall both know the facts about character better if we go through them in detail, and we shall
be convinced that the virtues are means if we see this to be
so in all cases. In the field of social life those who make the
giving of pleasure or pain their object in associating with
others have been described; [17] let us now describe those who
20 pursue truth or falsehood alike in words and deeds and in
the claims they put forward. The boastful man, then, is
thought to be apt to claim the things that bring glory, when
he has not got them, or to claim more of them than he has,
and the mock-modest man on the other hand to disclaim
what he has or belittle it, while the man who observes the
mean is one who calls a thing by its own name, being truth-
25 ful both in life and in word, owning to what he has, and
neither more nor less. Now each of these courses may be
adopted either with or without an object. But each man
speaks and acts and lives in accordance with his character, if
he is not acting for some ulterior object. And falsehood is *in
itself*[18] mean and culpable, and truth noble and worthy of
30 praise. Thus the truthful man is another case of a man who,
being in the mean, is worthy of praise, and both forms of
untruthful man are culpable, and particularly the boastful
man.

[16] 1125^b 14–16.

[17] Ch. 6.

[18] i. e. apart from any ulterior object it may serve.

Let us discuss them both, but first of all the truthful man. We are not speaking of the man who keeps faith in his agreements, i. e. in the things that pertain to justice or injustice (for this would belong to another virtue), but the man who in the matters in which nothing of this sort is at stake is true both in word and in life because his character is such. But such a man would seem to be as a matter of fact equitable. For the man who loves truth, and is truthful where nothing is at stake, will still more be truthful where something is at stake; he will avoid falsehood as something base, seeing that he avoided it even for its own sake; and such a man is worthy of praise. He inclines rather to understate the truth; for this seems in better taste because exaggerations are wearisome.

He who claims more than he has with no ulterior object is a contemptible sort of fellow (otherwise he would not have delighted in falsehood), but seems futile rather than bad; but if he does it for an object, he who does it for the sake of reputation or honour is (for a boaster) not very much to be blamed, but he who does it for money, or the things that lead to money, is an uglier character (it is not the capacity that makes the boaster, but the purpose; for it is in virtue of his state of character and by being a man of a certain kind that he is a boaster); as one man is a liar because he enjoys the lie itself, and another because he desires reputation or gain. Now those who boast for the sake of reputation claim such qualities as win praise or congratulation, but those whose object is gain claim qualities which are of value to one's neighbours and one's lack of which is not easily detected, e. g. the powers of a seer, a sage, or a physician. For this reason it is such things as these that most people claim and boast about; for in them the above-mentioned qualities are found.

Mock-modest people, who understate things, seem more attractive in character; for they are thought to speak

1127^b

5

10

15

20

not for gain but to avoid parade; and here too it is qualities
25 which bring reputation that they disclaim, as Socrates used
to do. Those who disclaim trifling and obvious qualities are
called humbugs and are more contemptible; and sometimes
this seems to be boastfulness, like the Spartan dress; for
both excess and great deficiency are boastful. But those who *
30 use understatement with moderation and understate about
matters that do not very much force themselves on our
notice seem attractive. And it is the boaster that seems to be
opposed to the truthful man; for he is the worse character.

8 Since life includes rest as well as activity, and in
this is included leisure and amusement, there seems
1128ᵃ here also to be a kind of intercourse which is tasteful; there is such a thing as saying—and again listening
to—what one should and as one should. The kind of people one is speaking or listening to will also make a difference.
Evidently here also there is both an excess and a deficiency
5 as compared with the mean. Those who carry humour to
excess are thought to be vulgar buffoons, striving after
humour at all costs, and aiming rather at raising a laugh
than at saying what is becoming and at avoiding pain to the
object of their fun; while those who can neither make a joke
themselves nor put up with those who do are thought to be
boorish and unpolished. But those who joke in a tasteful
10 way are called ready-witted, which implies a sort of readiness to turn this way and that; for such sallies are thought
to be movements of the character, and as bodies are discriminated by their movements, so too are characters. The
ridiculous side of things is not far to seek, however, and
most people delight more than they should in amusement
15 and in jesting, and so even buffoons are called ready-witted
because they are found attractive; but that they differ from
the ready-witted man, and to no small extent, is clear from
what has been said.

To the middle state belongs also tact; it is the mark of a tactful man to say and listen to such things as befit a good and well-bred man; for there are some things that it befits 20 such a man to say and to hear by way of jest, and the well-bred man's jesting differs from that of a vulgar man, and the joking of an educated man from that of an uneducated. One may see this even from the old and the new comedies; to the authors of the former indecency of language was amusing, to those of the latter innuendo is more so; and these differ in no small degree in respect of propriety. Now 25 should we define the man who jokes well by his saying what is not unbecoming to a well-bred man, or by his not giving pain, or even giving delight, to the hearer? Or is the latter definition, at any rate, itself indefinite, since different things are hateful or pleasant to different people? The kind of jokes he will listen to will be the same; for the kind he can put up with are also the kind he seems to make. There are, then, jokes he will not make; for the jest is a sort of abuse, and there are things that lawgivers forbid us to abuse; and 30 they should, perhaps, have forbidden us even to make a jest of such. The refined and well bred man, therefore, will be as we have described, being as it were a law to himself.

Such, then, is the man who observes the mean, whether he be called tactful or ready-witted. The buffoon, on the other hand, is the slave of his sense of humour, and spares neither himself nor others if he can raise a laugh, and says 35 things none of which a man of refinement would say, and to some of which he would not even listen. The boor, again, 1128^b is useless for such social intercourse; for he contributes nothing and finds fault with everything. But relaxation and amusement are thought to be a necessary element in life.

The means in life that have been described, then, are three in number, and are all concerned with an interchange of words and deeds of some kind. They differ, however, in 5 that one is concerned with truth, and the other two with pleasantness. Of those concerned with pleasure, one is displayed in jests, the other in the general social intercourse of life.

9 Shame should not be described as a virtue; for it is
10   more like a feeling than a state of character. It is
defined, at any rate, as a kind of fear of dishonour, and produces an effect similar to that produced by fear of danger; for people who feel disgraced blush, and those who fear death turn pale. Both, therefore, seem to be in a sense bodily conditions, which is thought to be characteristic of feeling rather than of a state of character.

The feeling is not becoming to every age, but only to
15 youth. For we think young people should be prone to the feeling of shame because they live by feeling and therefore commit many errors, but are restrained by shame; and we praise young people who are prone to this feeling, but an older person no one would praise for being prone to the sense of disgrace, since we think he should not do anything
20 that need cause this sense. For the sense of disgrace is not even characteristic of a good man,[19] since it is consequent on bad actions (for such actions should not be done; and if some actions are disgraceful in very truth and others only according to common opinion, this makes no difference; for neither class of actions should be done, so that no disgrace
25 should be felt); and it is a mark of a bad man even to be such as to do any disgraceful action. To be so constituted as to feel disgraced if one does such an action, and for this reason to think oneself good, is absurd; for it is for voluntary actions that shame is felt, and the good man will never vol-
30 untarily do bad actions. But shame may be said to be conditionally a good thing; if a good man does such actions, he will feel disgraced; but the virtues are not subject to such

---

[19] sc. still less is it itself a virtue.

a qualification. And if shamelessness—not to be ashamed of doing base actions—is bad, that does not make it good to be ashamed of doing such actions. Continence too is not virtue, but a mixed sort of state; this will be shown later.[20] 35 Now, however, let us discuss justice.

BOOK V

1 With regard to justice and injustice we must con- 1129ª sider (1) what kind of actions they are concerned with, (2) what sort of mean justice is, and (3) 5 between what extremes the just act is intermediate. Our investigation shall follow the same course as the preceding discussions.

We see that all men mean by justice that kind of state of character which makes people disposed to do what is just and makes them act justly and wish for what is just; and similarly by injustice that state which makes them act 10 unjustly and wish for what is unjust. Let us too, then, lay this down as a general basis. For the same is not true of the sciences and the faculties as of states of character. A faculty or a science which is one and the same is held to relate to contrary objects, but a state of character which is one of two contraries does *not* produce the contrary results; e. g. as a 15 result of health we do not do what is the opposite of healthy, but only what is healthy; for we say a man walks healthily, when he walks as a healthy man would.

Now often one contrary state is recognized from its contrary, and often states are recognized from the subjects that exhibit them; for (A) if good condition is known, bad 20 condition also becomes known, and (B) good condition is

known from the things that are in good condition, and they from it. If good condition is firmness of flesh, it is necessary both that bad condition should be flabbiness of flesh and that the wholesome should be that which causes firmness in flesh. And it follows for the most part that if one con-
25 trary is ambiguous the other also will be ambiguous; e. g. if 'just' is so, that 'unjust' will be so too.

Now 'justice' and 'injustice' seem to be ambiguous, but because their different meanings approach near to one another the ambiguity escapes notice and is not obvious as it is, comparatively, when the meanings are far apart, e. g. (for here the difference in outward form is great) as the
30 ambiguity in the use of *kleis* for the collar-bone of an animal and for that with which we lock a door. Let us take as a starting-point, then, the various meanings of 'an unjust man'. Both the lawless man and the grasping and unfair man are thought to be unjust, so that evidently both the law-abiding and the fair man will be just. The just, then, is the lawful and the fair, the unjust the unlawful and the unfair.

Since the unjust man is grasping, he must be concerned
1129b with goods—not all goods, but those with which prosperity and adversity have to do, which taken absolutely are always good, but for a particular person are not always good. Now
5 men pray for and pursue these things; but they should not, but should pray that the things that are good absolutely may also be good for them, and should choose the things that are good for them. The unjust man does not always choose the greater, but also the less—in the case of things bad absolutely; but because the lesser evil is itself thought to be in a sense good, and graspingness is directed at the
10 good, therefore he is thought to be grasping. And he is unfair; for this contains and is common to both.

Since the lawless man was seen to be unjust and the law-abiding man just, evidently all lawful acts are in a sense just acts; for the acts laid down by the legislative art are lawful, and each of these, we say, is just. Now the laws in their enactments on all subjects aim at the common advan- 15 tage either of all or of the best or of those who hold power, or something of the sort; so that in one sense we call those acts just that tend to produce and preserve happiness and its components for the political society. And the law bids us do both the acts of a brave man (e. g. not to desert our post 20 nor take to flight nor throw away our arms), and those of a temperate man (e. g. not to commit adultery nor to gratify one's lust), and those of a good-tempered man (e. g. not to strike another nor to speak evil), and similarly with regard to the other virtues and forms of wickedness, commanding some acts and forbidding others; and the rightly-framed law does this rightly, and the hastily conceived one less well.

This form of justice, then, is complete virtue, but not absolutely, but in relation to our neighbour. And therefore 25 justice is often thought to be the greatest of virtues, and 'neither evening nor morning star' is so wonderful; and proverbially 'in justice is every virtue comprehended'. And it is complete virtue in its fullest sense, because it is the 30 actual exercise of complete virtue. It is complete because he who possesses it can exercise his virtue not only in himself but towards his neighbour also; for many men can exercise virtue in their own affairs, but not in their relations to their 1130a neighbour. This is why the saying of Bias is thought to be true, that 'rule will show the man'; for a ruler is necessarily in relation to other men and a member of a society. For this same reason justice, alone of the virtues, is thought to be 'another's good',[1] because it is related to our neighbour; for it does what is advantageous to another, either a ruler or a 5 copartner. Now the worst man is he who exercises his

[1] Pl. *Rep.* 343 c.

wickedness both towards himself and towards his friends,
and the best man is not he who exercises his virtue towards
himself but he who exercises it towards another; for this is a
10 difficult task. Justice in this sense, then, is not part of virtue
but virtue entire, nor is the contrary injustice a part of vice
but vice entire. What the difference is between virtue and
justice in this sense is plain from what we have said; they
are the same but their essence is not the same; what, as a
relation to one's neighbour, is justice is, as a certain kind of
state without qualification, virtue.

2 But at all events what we are investigating is the
justice which is a *part* of virtue; for there is a jus-
15 tice of this kind, as we maintain. Similarly it is with
injustice in the particular sense that we are concerned.

That there is such a thing is indicated by the fact that
while the man who exhibits in action the other forms of
wickedness acts wrongly indeed, but not graspingly (e. g.
the man who throws away his shield through cowardice or
speaks harshly through bad temper or fails to help a friend
with money through meanness), when a man acts graspingly
20 he often exhibits none of these vices—no, nor all together,
but certainly wickedness of some kind (for we blame him)
and injustice. There is, then, another kind of injustice which
is a part of injustice in the wide sense, and a use of the word
'unjust' which answers to a part of what is unjust in the
wide sense of 'contrary to the law'. Again if one man commits adultery for the sake of gain and makes money by it,
25 while another does so at the bidding of appetite though he
loses money and is penalized for it, the latter would be held
to be self-indulgent rather than grasping, but the former is
unjust, but not self-indulgent; evidently, therefore, he is
unjust by reason of his making gain by his act. Again, all
other unjust acts are ascribed invariably to some particular
30 kind of wickedness, e. g. adultery to self-indulgence, the

desertion of a comrade in battle to cowardice, physical violence to anger; but if a man makes gain, his action is
ascribed to no form of wickedness but injustice. Evidently,
therefore, there is apart from injustice in the wide sense
another, 'particular', injustice which shares the name and
nature of the first, because its definition falls within the
same genus; for the significance of both consists in a relation to one's neighbour, but the one is concerned with   1130^b
honour or money or safety—or that which includes all
these, if we had a single name for it—and its motive is the
pleasure that arises from gain; while the other is concerned
with all the objects with which the good man is concerned. 5

It is clear, then, that there is more than one kind of justice, and that there is one which is distinct from virtue
entire; we must try to grasp its genus and differentia.

The unjust has been divided into the unlawful and the
unfair, and the just into the lawful and the fair. To the
unlawful answers the afore-mentioned sense of injustice.
But since the unfair and the unlawful are not the same, but
are different as a part is from its whole (for all that is unfair 10
is unlawful, but not all that is unlawful is unfair), the unjust
and injustice in the sense of the unfair are not the same as
but different from the former kind, as part from whole; for
injustice in this sense is a part of injustice in the wide sense,
and similarly justice in the one sense of justice in the other.
Therefore we must speak also about particular justice and 15
particular injustice, and similarly about the just and the
unjust. The justice, then, which answers to the whole of
virtue, and the corresponding injustice, one being the exercise of virtue as a whole, and the other that of vice as a
whole, towards one's neighbour, we may leave on one side.
And how the meanings of 'just' and 'unjust' which answer 20
to these are to be distinguished is evident; for practically the
majority of the acts commanded by the law are those which
are prescribed from the point of view of virtue taken as a

whole; for the law bids us practise every virtue and forbids
us to practise any vice. And the things that tend to produce
25 virtue taken as a whole are those of the acts prescribed by
the law which have been prescribed with a view to education for the common good. But with regard to the education
of the individual as such, which makes him without qualification a good *man*, we must determine later[2] whether this
is the function of the political art or of another; for perhaps
it is not the same to be a good man and a good citizen of
any state taken at random.

Of particular justice and that which is just in the cor-
30 responding sense, (A) one kind is that which is manifested
in distributions of honour or money or the other things that
fall to be divided among those who have a share in the constitution (for in these it is possible for one man to have a
share either unequal or equal to that of another), and (B)
one is that which plays a rectifying part in transactions
1131a between man and man. Of this there are two divisions; of
transactions (1) some are voluntary and (2) others involuntary—voluntary such transactions as sale, purchase, loan for
consumption, pledging, loan for use, depositing, letting
(they are called voluntary because the origin of these trans-
5 actions is voluntary), while of the involuntary (*a*) some are
clandestine, such as theft, adultery, poisoning, procuring,
enticement of slaves, assassination, false witness, and (*b*)
others are violent, such as assault, imprisonment, murder,
robbery with violence, mutilation, abuse, insult.

10   3   (A) We have shown that both the unjust man and
the unjust act are unfair or unequal; now it is clear
that there is also an intermediate between the two
unequals involved in either case. And this is the equal; for

---

2 1179b 20–1181b 12. *Pol.* 1276b 16–1277b 32, 1278a 40–b5, 1288a 32–b2,
1333a 11–16, 1337a 11–14.

in any kind of action in which there is a more and a less
there is also what is equal. If, then, the unjust is unequal,
the just is equal, as all men suppose it to be, even apart
from argument. And since the equal is intermediate, the just
will be an intermediate. Now equality implies at least two 15
things. The just, then, must be both intermediate and equal
and relative (i. e. for certain persons). And *qua* intermediate it must be between certain things (which are respectively
greater and less); *qua* equal, it involves *two* things; *qua* just,
it is for certain people. The just, therefore, involves at least
four terms; for the persons for whom it is in fact just are
two, and the things in which it is manifested, the objects 20
distributed, are two. And the same equality will exist
between the persons and between the things concerned; for
as the latter—the things concerned—are related, so are the
former; if they are not equal, they will not have what is
equal, but this is the origin of quarrels and complaints—
when either equals have and are awarded unequal shares, or
unequals equal shares. Further, this is plain from the fact
that awards should be 'according to merit'; for all men agree 25
that what is just in distribution must be according to merit
in some sense, though they do not all specify the same sort
of merit, but democrats identify it with the status of freeman, supporters of oligarchy with wealth (or with noble
birth), and supporters of aristocracy with excellence.

The just, then, is a species of the proportionate (propor- 30
tion being not a property only of the kind of number which
consists of abstract units, but of number in general). For
proportion is equality of ratios, and involves four terms at
least (that discrete proportion involves four terms is plain,
but so does continuous proportion, for it uses one term as
two and mentions it twice; e. g. 'as the line A is to the line
B, so is the line B to the line C'; the line B, then, has been 1131^b
mentioned twice, so that if the line B be assumed twice, the
proportional terms will be four); and the just, too, involves at

least four terms, and the ratio between one pair is the same as that between the other pair; for there is a similar distinction between the persons and between the things. As the
5 term A, then, is to B, so will C be to D, and therefore, *alternando*, as A is to C, B will be to D. Therefore also the whole is in the same ratio to the whole;[3] and this coupling the distribution effects, and, if the terms are so combined, effects justly. The conjunction, then, of the term A with C and of B with D is what is just in distribution,[4] and this species of the
10 just is intermediate, and the unjust is what violates the proportion; for the proportional is intermediate, and the just is proportional. (Mathematicians call this kind of proportion geometrical; for it is in geometrical proportion that it follows
15 that the whole is to the whole as either part is to the corresponding part.) This proportion is not continuous; for we cannot get a single term standing for a person and a thing.

This, then, is what the just is—the proportional; the unjust is what violates the proportion. Hence one term becomes too great, the other too small, as indeed happens in practice; for the man who acts unjustly has too much, and the man who is unjustly treated too little, of what is good.
20 In the case of evil the reverse is true; for the lesser evil is reckoned a good in comparison with the greater evil, since the lesser evil is rather to be chosen than the greater, and what is worthy of choice is good, and what is worthier of choice a greater good.

This, then, is one species of the just.

[3] Person A + thing C to person B + thing D.

[4] The problem of distributive justice is to divide the distributable honour or reward into parts which are to one another as are the merits of the persons who are to participate. If

A (first person) : B (second person) : : C (first portion) : D (second portion), then (*alternando*) A : C : : B : D,

and therefore (*componendo*) A + C: B + D : : A : B.

In other words the position established answers to the relative merits of the parties.

4 (B) The remaining one is the rectificatory, which arises in connexion with transactions both volun- 25 tary and involuntary. This form of the just has a different specific character from the former. For the justice which distributes common possessions is always in accordance with the kind of proportion mentioned above[5] (for in the case also in which the distribution is made from the common funds of a partnership it will be according to the same 30 ratio which the funds put into the business by the partners bear to one another); and the injustice opposed to this kind of justice is that which violates the proportion. But the justice in transactions between man and man is a sort of 1132[a] equality indeed, and the injustice a sort of inequality; not according to that kind of proportion, however, but according to arithmetical proportion.[6] For it makes no difference whether a good man has defrauded a bad man or a bad man a good one, nor whether it is a good or a bad man that has committed adultery; the law looks only to the distinctive character of the injury, and treats the parties as equal, 5 if one is in the wrong and the other is being wronged, and if one inflicted injury and the other has received it. Therefore, this kind of injustice being an inequality, the judge tries to equalize it; for in the case also in which one has

---

[5] l. 12 f.

[6] The problem of 'rectificatory justice' has nothing to do with punishment proper but is only that of rectifying a wrong that has been done, by awarding damages; i. e. rectificatory justice is that of the civil, not that of the criminal courts. The parties are treated by the court as equal (since a law court is not a court of morals), and the wrongful act is reckoned as having brought equal gain to the wrongdoer and loss to his victim; it brings A to the position $A + C$, and B to the position $B - C$. The judge's task is to find the arithmetical mean between these, and this he does by transferring C from A to B. Thus (A being treated as $= B$) we get the arithmetical 'proportion'

$$(A + C) - (A + C - C) = (A + C - C) - (B - C)$$
or $$(A + C) - (B - C + C) = (B - C + C) - (B - C).$$

received and the other has inflicted a wound, or one has
slain and the other been slain, the suffering and the action
have been unequally distributed; but the judge tries to
10 equalize things by means of the penalty, taking away from
the gain of the assailant. For the term 'gain' is applied generally to such cases, even if it be not a term appropriate to
certain cases, e. g. to the person who inflicts a wound—and
'loss' to the sufferer; at all events when the suffering has
15 been estimated, the one is called loss and the other gain.
Therefore the equal is intermediate between the greater and
the less, but the gain and the loss are respectively greater
and less in contrary ways; more of the good and less of the
evil are gain, and the contrary is loss; intermediate between
them is, as we saw,[7] the equal, which we say is just; there-
20 fore corrective justice will be the intermediate between loss
and gain. This is why, when people dispute, they take
refuge in the judge; and to go to the judge is to go to justice; for the nature of the judge is to be a sort of animate
justice; and they seek the judge as an intermediate, and in
some states they call judges mediators, on the assumption
that if they get what is intermediate they will get what is
just. The just, then, is an intermediate, since the judge is
so. Now the judge restores equality; it is as though there
25 were a line divided into unequal parts, and he took away
that by which the greater segment exceeds the half, and
added it to the smaller segment. And when the whole has
been equally divided, then they say they have 'their own'—
i. e. when they have got what is equal. The equal is
intermediate between the greater and the lesser line accord-
30 ing to arithmetical proportion. It is for this reason also that
it is called just (*dikaion*), because it is a division into two
equal parts (*dicha*), just as if one were to call it (*dichaion*);
and the judge (*dicastes*) is one who bisects (*dichastes*). For

[7] l. 14.

when something is subtracted from one of two equals and added to the other, the other is in excess by these two; since if what was taken from the one had not been added to the other, the latter would have been in excess by one only. It therefore exceeds the intermediate by one, and the inter- 1132^b mediate exceeds by one that from which something was taken. By this, then, we shall recognize both what we must subtract from that which has more, and what we must add to that which has less; we must add to the latter that by which the intermediate exceeds it, and subtract from the greatest that by which it exceeds the intermediate. Let the 5 lines AA', BB', CC' be equal to one another; from the line AA' let the segment AE have been subtracted, and to the line CC' let the segment CD[8] have been added, so that the whole line DCC' exceeds the line EA' by the segment CD and the segment CF; therefore it exceeds the line BB' by the segment CD.

$$
\begin{array}{lll}
A \qquad\quad E & & A' \\
\rule{2cm}{0.4pt}\rule{5cm}{0.4pt} \\
B & & B' \\
\rule{7cm}{0.4pt} \\
D \qquad C \qquad F & & C' \\
\rule{7cm}{0.4pt}
\end{array}
$$

These names, both loss and gain, have come from volun- tary exchange; for to have more than one's own is called 11 gaining, and to have less than one's original share is called losing, e. g. in buying and selling and in all other matters in 15 which the law has left people free to make their own terms; but when they get neither more nor less but just what belongs to themselves, they say that they have their own and that they neither lose nor gain.

Therefore the just is intermediate between a sort of gain

---

[8] *sc.* equal to AE.

and a sort of loss, viz. those which are involuntary;[9] it con-
20 sists in having an equal amount before and after the
transaction.

5 Some think that *reciprocity* is without qualification
just, as the Pythagoreans said; for they defined justice without qualification as reciprocity. Now
25 'reciprocity' fits neither distributive nor rectificatory justice—yet people *want* even the justice of Rhadamanthus to
mean this:

> Should a man suffer what he did, right justice would
> be done

—for in many cases reciprocity and rectificatory justice are
not in accord, e. g. (1) if an official has inflicted a wound,
he should not be wounded in return, and if some one has
30 wounded an official, he ought not to be wounded only but
punished in addition. Further (2) there is a great difference
between a voluntary and an involuntary act. But in associations for exchange this sort of justice does hold men
together—reciprocity in accordance with a proportion and
not on the basis of precisely equal return. For it is by proportionate requital that the city holds together. Men seek to
1133ᵃ return either evil for evil—and if they cannot do so, think
their position mere slavery—or good for good—and if they
cannot do so there is no exchange, but it is by exchange that
they hold together. This is why they give a prominent place
to the temple of the Graces—to promote the requital of services; for this is characteristic of grace—we should serve in
return one who has shown grace to us, and should another
time take the initiative in showing it.
5   Now proportionate return is secured by cross-conjunc-

9 i. e. for the loser.

tion. Let *A* be a builder, *B* a shoemaker, *C* a house, *D* a shoe. The builder, then, must get from the shoemaker the latter's work, and must himself give him in return his own. If, then, first there is proportionate equality of goods, and then reciprocal action takes place, the result we mention will be effected. If not, the bargain is not equal, and does not hold; for there is nothing to prevent the work of the one being better than that of the other; they must therefore be equated. (And this is true of the other arts also; for they would have been destroyed if what the patient suffered had not been just what the agent did, and of the same amount and kind.) For it is not two doctors that associate for exchange, but a doctor and a farmer, or in general people who are different and unequal; but these must be equated. This is why all things that are exchanged must be somehow comparable. It is for this end that money has been introduced, and it becomes in a sense an intermediate; for it measures all things, and therefore the excess and the defect—how many shoes are equal to a house or to a given amount of food. The number of shoes exchanged for a house [or for a given amount of food] must therefore correspond to the ratio of builder to shoemaker. For if this be not so, there will be no exchange and no intercourse. And this proportion will not be effected unless the goods are somehow equal. All goods must therefore be measured by some one thing, as we said before. Now this unit is in truth demand, which holds all things together (for if men did not need one another's goods at all, or did not need them equally, there would be either no exchange or not the same exchange); but money has become by convention a sort of representative of demand; and this is why it has the name 'money' (*nomisma*)—because it exists not by nature but by law (*nomos*) and it is in our power to change it and make it useless. There will, then, be reciprocity when the terms have been equated so that as farmer is to shoemaker, the

amount of the shoemaker's work is to that of the farmer's
1133^b work for which it exchanges. But we must not bring them
into a figure of proportion when they have already
exchanged (otherwise one extreme will have both excesses),
but when they still have their own goods. Thus they are
equals and associates just because this equality can be
5 effected in their case. Let A be a farmer, C food, B a shoemaker, D his product equated to C. If it had not been
possible for reciprocity to be thus effected, there would have
been no association of the parties. That demand holds
things together as a single unit is shown by the fact that
when men do not need one another, i. e. when neither needs
the other or one does not need the other, they do not
exchange, as we do when some one wants what one has oneself, e. g. when people permit the exportation of corn in
exchange for wine. This equation therefore must be estab-
10 lished. And for the future exchange—that if we do not need
a thing now we shall have it if ever we do need it—money
is as it were our surety; for it must be possible for us to get
what we want by bringing the money. Now the same thing
happens to money itself as to goods—it is not always worth
the same; yet it tends to be steadier. This is why all goods
15 must have a price set on them; for then there will always be
exchange, and if so, association of man with man. Money,
then, acting as a measure, makes goods commensurate and
equates them; for neither would there have been association
if there were not exchange, nor exchange if there were not
equality, nor equality if there were not commensurability.
Now in truth it is impossible that things differing so much
20 should become commensurate, but with reference to
demand they may become so sufficiently. There must, then,
be a unit, and that fixed by agreement (for which reason it
is called money); for it is this that makes all things commensurate, since all things are measured by money. Let A
be a house, B ten minae, C a bed. A is half of B, if the

house is worth five minae or equal to them; the bed, C, is 25
a tenth of B; it is plain, then, how many beds are equal to
a house, viz. five. That exchange took place thus before
there was money is plain; for it makes no difference whether
it is five beds that exchange for a house, or the money value
of five beds.

We have now defined the unjust and the just. These 30
having been marked off from each other, it is plain that just
action is intermediate between acting unjustly and being
unjustly treated; for the one is to have too much and the
other to have too little. Justice is a kind of mean, but not
in the same way as the other virtues, but because it relates
to an intermediate amount, while injustice relates to the
extremes. And justice is that in virtue of which the just man 1134ª
is said to be a doer, by choice, of that which is just, and one
who will distribute either between himself and another or
between two others not so as to give more of what is desirable to himself and less to his neighbour (and conversely
with what is harmful), but so as to give what is equal in 5
accordance with proportion; and similarly in distributing
between two other persons. Injustice on the other hand is
similarly related to the unjust, which is excess and defect,
contrary to proportion, of the useful or hurtful. For which
reason injustice is excess and defect, viz. because it is productive of excess and defect—in one's own case excess of
what is in its own nature useful and defect of what is hurt- 10
ful, while in the case of others it is as a whole like what it
is in one's own case, but proportion may be violated in
either direction. In the unjust act to have too little is to be
unjustly treated; to have too much is to act unjustly.

Let this be taken as our account of the nature of justice and injustice, and similarly of the just and the unjust 15
in general.

6 Since acting unjustly does not necessarily imply being unjust, we must ask what sort of unjust acts imply that the doer is unjust with respect to each type of injustice, e. g. a thief, an adulterer, or a brigand. Surely the answer does not turn on the difference between these types. For a man might even lie with a woman knowing who she was, but the origin of his act might be not 20 deliberate choice but passion. He acts unjustly, then, but is not unjust; e. g. a man is not a thief, yet he stole, nor an adulterer, yet he committed adultery, and similarly in all other cases.

Now we have previously stated how the reciprocal is related to the just;[10] but we must not forget that what we 25 are looking for is not only what is just without qualification but also political justice. This is found among men who share their life with a view to self-sufficiency, men who are free and either proportionately or arithmetically equal, so that between those who do not fulfil this condition there is no political justice but justice in a special sense and by analogy. For justice exists only between men whose mutual 30 relations are governed by law; and law exists for men between whom there is injustice; for legal justice is the discrimination of the just and the unjust. And between men between whom there is injustice there is also unjust action (though there is not injustice between all between whom there is unjust action), and this is assigning too much to oneself of things good in themselves and too little of things evil in themselves. This is why we do not allow a *man* to 35 rule, but *rational principle*, because a man behaves thus in his own interests and becomes a tyrant. The magistrate on 1134b the other hand is the guardian of justice, and, if of justice, then of equality also. And since he is assumed to have no more than his share, if he is just (for he does not assign to

10 1132b 21–1133b 28.

himself more of what is good in itself, unless such a share is
proportional to his merits—so that it is for others that he
labours, and it is for this reason that men, as we stated previously,[11] say that justice is 'another's good'), therefore a   5
reward must be given him, and this is honour and privilege;
but those for whom such things are not enough become
tyrants.

The justice of a master and that of a father are not the
same as the justice of citizens, though they are like it; for
there can be no injustice in the unqualified sense towards
things that are one's own, but a man's chattel,[12] and his
child until it reaches a certain age and sets up for itself, are   10
as it were part of himself, and no one chooses to hurt himself (for which reason there can be no injustice towards
oneself). Therefore the justice or injustice of citizens is not
manifested in these relations; for it was as we saw[13] according to law, and between people naturally subject to law, and
these as we saw[14] are people who have an equal share in ruling and being ruled. Hence justice can more truly be   15
manifested towards a wife than towards children and chat-
tels, for the former is household justice; but even this is
different from political justice.

7 Of political justice part is natural, part legal—natural, that which everywhere has the same force and
does not exist by people's thinking this or that;   20
legal, that which is originally indifferent, but when it has
been laid down is not indifferent, e. g. that a prisoner's ransom shall be a mina, or that a goat and not two sheep shall

[11] 1130ª 3.

[12] i. e. his slave.

[13] a 30.

[14] a 26–8.

be sacrificed, and again all the laws that are passed for particular cases, e. g. that sacrifice shall be made in honour of
25 Brasidas, and the provisions of decrees. Now some think
that all justice is of this sort, because that which is by
nature is unchangeable and has everywhere the same force
(as fire burns both here and in Persia), while they see
change in the things recognized as just. This, however, is
not true in this unqualified way, but is true in a sense; or
rather, with the gods it is perhaps not true at all, while with
us there is something that is just even by nature, yet all of it
30 is changeable; but still some is by nature, some not by
nature. It is evident which sort of thing, among things capable of being otherwise, is by nature; and which is not but
is legal and conventional, assuming that both are equally
changeable. And in all other things the same distinction will
apply; by nature the right hand is stronger, yet it is possible
1135ᵃ that all men should come to be ambidextrous. The things
which are just by virtue of convention and expediency are
like measures; for wine and corn measures are not everywhere equal, but larger in wholesale and smaller in retail
markets. Similarly, the things which are just not by nature
but by human enactment are not everywhere the same,
since constitutions also are not the same, though there is but
one which is everywhere by nature the best.

5   Of things just and lawful each is related as the universal to its particulars; for the things that are done are many,
but of *them* each is one, since it is universal.

There is a difference between the act of injustice and
what is unjust, and between the act of justice and what is
10 just; for a thing is unjust by nature or by enactment; and
this very thing, when it has been done, is an act of injustice, but before it is done is not yet that but is unjust. So,
too, with an act of justice (though the general term is rather
'just action', and 'act of justice' is applied to the correction
of the act of injustice).

Each of these must later[15] be examined separately with regard to the nature and number of its species and the nature of the things with which it is concerned.

8 Acts just and unjust being as we have described them, a man acts unjustly or justly whenever he does such acts voluntarily; when involuntarily, he acts neither unjustly nor justly except in an incidental way; for he does things which happen to be just or unjust. Whether an act is or is not one of injustice (or of justice) is determined by its voluntariness or involuntariness; for when it is voluntary it is blamed, and at the same time is then an act of injustice; so that there will be things that are unjust but not yet acts of injustice, if voluntariness be not present as well. By the voluntary I mean, as has been said before,[16] any of the things in a man's own power which he does with knowledge, i. e. not in ignorance either of the person acted on or of the instrument used or of the end that will be attained (e. g. whom he is striking, with what, and to what end), each such act being done not incidentally nor under compulsion (e. g. if A takes B's hand and therewith strikes C, B does not act voluntarily; for the act was not in his own power). The person struck may be the striker's father, and the striker may know that it is a man or one of the persons present, but not know that it is his father; a similar distinction may be made in the case of the end, and with regard to the whole action. Therefore that which is done in ignorance, or though not done in ignorance is not in the agent's power, or is done under compulsion, is involuntary (for many natural processes, even we knowingly both perform and experience, none of which is either voluntary or invol-

1135b

---

[15] Possibly a reference to an intended (or now lost) book of the *Politics* on laws.

[16] 1109b35–1111a 24.

untary; e. g. growing old or dying). But in the case of unjust
and just acts alike the injustice or justice may be only incidental; for a man might return a deposit unwillingly and
5 from fear, and then he must not be said either to do what
is just or to act justly, except in an incidental way. Similarly
the man who under compulsion and unwillingly fails to
return the deposit must be said to act unjustly, and to do
what is unjust, only incidentally. Of voluntary acts we do
10 some by choice, others not by choice; by choice those which
we do after deliberation, not by choice those which we do
without previous deliberation. Thus there are three kinds
of injury in transactions between man and man; those done
in ignorance are *mistakes* when the person acted on, the act,
the instrument, or the end that will be attained is other than
the agent supposed; the agent thought either that he was not
hitting any one or that he was not hitting with this missile
or not hitting this person or to this end, but a result followed
15 other than that which he thought likely (e. g. he threw not
with intent to wound but only to prick), or the person hit or
the missile was other than he supposed. Now when (1) the
injury takes place contrary to reasonable expectation, it is a
misadventure. When (2) it is not contrary to reasonable
expectation, but does not imply vice, it is a *mistake* (for a
man makes a mistake when the fault originates in him, but
is the victim of accident when the origin lies outside him).
When (3) he acts with knowledge but not after deliberation,
20 it is an act of *injustice*—e. g. the acts due to anger or to
other passions necessary or natural to man; for when men
do such harmful and mistaken acts they act unjustly, and
the acts are acts of injustice, but this does not imply that
the doers are unjust or wicked; for the injury is not due to
25 vice. But when (4) a man acts from choice, he is an *unjust
man* and a vicious man.

Hence acts proceeding from anger are rightly judged
not to be done of malice aforethought; for it is not the man

who acts in anger but he who enraged him that starts the
mischief. Again, the matter in dispute is not whether the
thing happened or not, but its justice; for it is apparent
injustice that occasions rage. For they do not dispute about
the occurrence of the act—as in commercial transactions 30
where one of the two parties *must* be vicious[17]—unless they
do so owing to forgetfulness; but, agreeing about the fact,
they dispute on which side justice lies (whereas a man who
has deliberately injured another cannot help knowing that
he has done so), so that the one thinks he is being treated
unjustly and the other disagrees.

But if a man harms another by choice, he acts unjustly; 1136ᵃ
and *these* are the acts of injustice which imply that the doer
is an unjust man, provided that the act violates proportion
or equality. Similarly, a man is *just* when he acts justly by
choice; but he *acts justly* if he merely acts voluntarily.

Of involuntary acts some are excusable, others not. For 5
the mistakes which men make not only in ignorance but
also from ignorance are excusable, while those which men
do not from ignorance but (though they do them *in* ignorance) owing to a passion which is neither natural nor such
as man is liable to, are not excusable.

9 Assuming that we have sufficiently defined the suf- 10
fering and doing of injustice, it may be asked (1)
whether the truth is expressed in Euripides' paradoxical words:

'I slew my mother, that's my tale in brief.'
'Were you both willing, or unwilling both?'

Is it truly possible to be willingly treated unjustly, or is all

---

[17] The plaintiff, if he brings a false accusation; the defendant, if he denies
a true one.

15 suffering of injustice on the contrary involuntary, as all
unjust action is voluntary? And is all suffering of injustice of
the latter kind or else all of the former, or is it sometimes
voluntary, sometimes involuntary? So, too, with the case of
being justly treated; all just action is voluntary, so that it is
reasonable that there should be a similar opposition in either
. case—that both being unjustly and being justly treated
20 should be either alike voluntary or alike involuntary. But it
would be thought paradoxical even in the case of being justly
treated, if it were always voluntary; for some are unwillingly
treated justly. (2) One might raise this question also,
whether every one who has suffered what is unjust is being
unjustly treated, or on the other hand it is with suffering as
25 with acting. In action and in passivity alike it is possible to
partake of justice incidentally, and similarly (it is plain) of
injustice; for to do what is unjust is not the same as to act
unjustly, nor to suffer what is unjust as to be treated
unjustly, and similarly in the case of acting justly and being
justly treated; for it is impossible to be unjustly treated if the
30 other does not act unjustly, or justly treated unless he acts
justly. Now if to act unjustly is simply to harm some one
voluntarily, and 'voluntarily' means 'knowing the person
acted on, the instrument, and the manner of one's acting',
and the incontinent man voluntarily harms himself, not only
will he voluntarily be unjustly treated but it will be possible
to treat oneself unjustly. (This also is one of the questions
in doubt, whether a man can treat himself unjustly.) Again,
1136ᵇ a man may voluntarily, owing to incontinence, be harmed
by another who acts voluntarily, so that it would be possible to be voluntarily treated unjustly. Or is our definition
incorrect; must we to 'harming another, with knowledge
both of the person acted on, of the instrument, and of the
manner' add 'contrary to the wish of the person acted on'?
5 Then a man may be voluntarily harmed and voluntarily suffer what is unjust, but no one is voluntarily treated unjustly;

for no one wishes to be unjustly treated, not even the incontinent man. He acts contrary to his wish; for no one wishes for what he does not think to be good, but the incontinent man does do things that he does not think he ought to do. Again one who gives what is his own, as Homer says Glaucus gave Diomede *Armour of gold for brazen, the price of a hundred beeves for nine*,[18] is not unjustly treated; for though to give is in his power, to be unjustly treated is not, but there must be some one to treat him unjustly. It is plain, then, that being unjustly treated is not voluntary.

Of the questions we intended to discuss two still remain for discussion; (3) whether it is the man who has assigned to another more than his share that acts unjustly, or he who has the excessive share, and (4) whether it is possible to treat oneself unjustly. The questions are connected; for if the former alternative is possible and the distributor acts unjustly and not the man who has the excessive share, then if a man assigns more to another than to himself, knowingly and voluntarily, he treats himself unjustly; which is what modest people seem to do, since the virtuous man tends to take less than his share. Or does this statement too need qualification? For (*a*) he perhaps gets more than his share of some other good, e. g. of honour or of intrinsic nobility. (*b*) The question is solved by applying the distinction we applied to unjust action;[19] for he suffers nothing contrary to his own wish, so that he is not unjustly treated as far as this goes, but at most only suffers harm.

It is plain too that the distributor acts unjustly, but not always the man who has the excessive share; for it is not he to whom what is unjust appertains that acts unjustly, but he to whom it appertains to do the unjust act voluntarily, i. e. the person in whom lies the origin of the action, and

18 *Il.* vi. 236.

19 ll. 3–5.

this lies in the distributor, not in the receiver. Again, since
30 the word 'do' is ambiguous, and there is a sense in which
lifeless things, or a hand, or a servant who obeys an order,
may be said to slay, he who gets an excessive share does not
act unjustly, though he 'does' what is unjust.

Again, if the distributor gave his judgement in ignorance, he does not act unjustly in respect of legal justice, and
his judgement is not unjust in this sense, but in a sense it *is*
1137ᵃ unjust (for legal justice and primordial justice are different);
but if with knowledge he judged unjustly, he is himself aiming at an excessive share either of gratitude or of revenge. As
much, then, as if he were to share in the plunder, the man
who has judged unjustly for these reasons has got too much;
the fact that what he gets is different from what he distributes makes no difference, for even if he awards land with
a view to sharing in the plunder he gets not land but money.
5 Men think that acting unjustly is in their power, and
therefore that being just is easy. But it is not; to lie with
one's neighbour's wife, to wound another, to deliver a bribe,
is easy and in our power, but to do these things as a result
of a certain state of character is neither easy nor in our
power. Similarly to know what is just and what is unjust
requires, men think, no great wisdom, because it is not hard
10 to understand the matters dealt with by the laws (though
these are not the things that are just, except incidentally);
but how actions must be done and distributions effected in
order to be just, to know *this* is a greater achievement than
knowing what is good for the health; though even there,
while it is easy to know that honey, wine, hellebore, cautery,
and the use of the knife are so, to know how, to whom, and
15 when these should be applied with a view to producing
health, is no less an achievement than that of being a physician. Again, for this very reason[20] men think that acting

---

[20] i. e. that stated in l. 4 f., that acting unjustly is in our own power.

unjustly is characteristic of the just man no less than of the
unjust, because he would be not less but even more capable of doing each of these unjust acts;[21] for he could lie with
a woman or wound a neighbour; and the brave man could
throw away his shield and turn to flight in this direction or   20
in that. But to play the coward or to act unjustly consists
not in doing these things, except incidentally, but in doing
them as the result of a certain state of character, just as to
practise medicine and healing consists not in applying or
not applying the knife, in using or not using medicines, but
in doing so in a certain way.   25

Just acts occur between people who participate in things
good in themselves and can have too much or too little of
them; for some beings (e. g. presumably the gods) cannot
have too much of them, and to others, those who are incurably bad, not even the smallest share in them is beneficial
but all such goods are harmful, while to others they are
beneficial up to a point; therefore justice is essentially something human.   30

10   Our next subject is equity and the equitable (to
epieikes), and their respective relations to justice
and the just. For on examination they appear to
be neither absolutely the same nor generically different; and
while we sometimes praise what is equitable and the equi-   35
table man (so that we apply the name by way of praise even
to instances of the other virtues, instead of 'good,' meaning
by *epieikesteron* that a thing is better), at other times, when   1137b
we reason it out, it seems strange if the equitable, being
something different from the just, is yet praiseworthy; for
either the just or the equitable is not good, if they are different; or, if both are good, they are the same.

These, then, are pretty much the considerations that   5

21 Cf. ll. 6–8.

give rise to the problem about the equitable; they are all in
a sense correct and not opposed to one another; for the
equitable, though it is better than one kind of justice, yet is
just, and it is not as being a different class of thing that it
is better than the just. The same thing, then, is just and
10 equitable, and while both are good the equitable is superior.
What creates the problem is that the equitable is just, but
not the legally just but a correction of legal justice. The reason is that all law is universal but about some things it is not
possible to make a universal statement which shall be cor-
15 rect. In those cases, then, in which it is necessary to speak
universally, but not possible to do so correctly, the law takes
the usual case, though it is not ignorant of the possibility of
error. And it is none the less correct; for the error is not in
the law nor in the legislator but in the nature of the thing,
since the matter of practical affairs is of this kind from the
20 start. When the law speaks universally, then, and a case
arises on it which is not covered by the universal statement,
then it is right, where the legislator fails us and has erred
by over-simplicity, to correct the omission—to say what the
legislator himself would have said had he been present, and
would have put into his law if he had known. Hence the
25 equitable is just, and better than one kind of justice—not
better than absolute justice but better than the error that
arises from the absoluteness of the statement. And this is
the nature of the equitable, a correction of law where it is
defective owing to its universality. In fact this is the reason
why all things are not determined by law, viz. that about
some things it is impossible to lay down a law, so that a
decree is needed. For when the thing is indefinite the rule
30 also is indefinite, like the leaden rule used in making the
Lesbian moulding; the rule adapts itself to the shape of the
stone and is not rigid, and so too the decree is adapted to
the facts.

It is plain, then, what the equitable is, and that it is just

and is better than one kind of justice. It is evident also from
this who the equitable man is; the man who chooses and 35
does such acts, and is no stickler for his rights in a bad 1138ª
sense but tends to take less than his share though he has the
law on his side, is equitable, and this state of character is
equity, which is a sort of justice and not a different state of
character.

11 Whether a man can treat himself unjustly or
not, is evident from what has been said.[22] For 5
(a) one class of just acts are those acts in accordance with any virtue which are prescribed by the law; e. g.
the law does not expressly permit suicide, and what it does
not expressly permit it forbids. Again, when a man in violation of the law harms another (otherwise than in
retaliation) voluntarily, he acts unjustly, and a voluntary
agent is one who knows both the person he is affecting by
his action and the instrument he is using; and he who
through anger voluntarily stabs himself does this contrary to 10
the right rule of life, and this the law does not allow; therefore he is acting unjustly. But towards whom? Surely
towards the state, not towards himself. For he suffers voluntarily, but no one is voluntarily treated unjustly. This is
also the reason why the state punishes; a certain loss of civil
rights attaches to the man who destroys himself, on the
ground that he is treating the state unjustly.

Further (b) in that sense of 'acting unjustly' in which the
man who 'acts unjustly' is unjust only and not bad all round,
it is not possible to treat oneself unjustly (this is different
from the former sense; the unjust man in one sense of the 15
term is wicked in a particularized way just as the coward is,
not in the sense of being wicked all round, so that his 'unjust
act' does not manifest wickedness in general). For (i) that

[22] Cf. 1129ª 32–b 1, 1136ª 10–1137ª 4.

would imply the possibility of the same thing's having been subtracted from and added to the same thing at the same time; but this is impossible—the just and the unjust always involve more than one person. Further, (ii) unjust action is
20 voluntary and done by choice, and *takes the initiative* (for the man who because he has suffered does the same in return is not thought to act unjustly); but if a man harms himself he suffers and does the same things *at the same time*. Further, (iii) if a man could treat himself unjustly, he could be voluntarily treated unjustly. Besides, (iv) no one acts unjustly without committing particular acts of injustice; but no one
25 can commit adultery with his own wife or housebreaking on his own house or theft on his own property.

In general, the question 'can a man treat himself unjustly?' is solved also by the distinction we applied to the question 'can a man be voluntarily treated unjustly?'[23]

(It is evident too that both are bad, being unjustly treated and acting unjustly; for the one means having less and the other having more than the intermediate amount,
30 which plays the part here that the healthy does in the medical art, and that good condition does in the art of bodily training. But still acting unjustly is the worse, for it involves vice and is blameworthy—involves vice which is either of the complete and unqualified kind or almost so (we must admit the latter alternative, because not all voluntary unjust action
35 implies injustice as a state of character), while being unjustly treated does not involve vice and injustice in oneself. In
1138ᵇ itself, then, being unjustly treated is less bad, but there is nothing to prevent its being incidentally a greater evil. But theory cares nothing for this; it calls pleurisy a more serious mischief than a stumble; yet the latter may become incidentally the more serious, if the fall due to it leads to your being taken prisoner or put to death by the enemy.)

[23] Cf. 1136ᵃ 31–ᵇ5.

Metaphorically and in virtue of a certain resemblance 5
there is a justice, not indeed between a man and himself,
but between certain parts of him; yet not every kind of justice but that of master and servant or that of husband and
wife.24 For these are the ratios in which the part of the soul
that has a rational principle stands to the irrational part; and
it is with a view to these parts that people also think a man
can be unjust to himself, viz. because these parts are liable 10
to suffer something contrary to their respective desires;
there is therefore thought to be a mutual justice between
them as between ruler and ruled.

Let this be taken as our account of justice and the
other, i. e. the other moral, virtues.

BOOK VI

1 Since we have previously said that one ought to
choose that which is intermediate, not the excess
nor the defect,1 and that the intermediate is determined by the dictates of the right rule,2 let us discuss the 20
nature of these dictates. In all the states of character we
have mentioned,3 as in all other matters, there is a mark to
which the man who has the rule looks, and heightens or
relaxes his activity accordingly, and there is a standard
which determines the mean states which we say are intermediate between excess and defect, being in accordance 25
with the right rule. But such a statement, though true, is by

---

24 Cf. 1134b 15–17.

1 1104a 11–27, 1106a 26–1107a 27.

2 1107a 1, Cf. 1103b 31, 1114b 29.

3 In iii 6–v. 11.

no means clear, for not only here but in all other pursuits which are objects of knowledge it is indeed true to say that we must not exert ourselves nor relax our efforts too much nor too little, but to an intermediate extent and as the right rule dictates; but if a man had only this knowledge he

30 would be none the wiser—e. g. we should not know what sort of medicines to apply to our body if some one were to say 'all those which the medical art prescribes, and which agree with the practice of one who possesses the art.' Hence it is necessary with regard to the states of the soul also not only that this true statement should be made, but also that it should be determined what is the right rule and what is the standard that fixes it.

We divided the virtues of the soul and said that some

35 are virtues of character and others of intellect.[4] Now we

1139ᵃ have discussed in detail the moral virtues;[3] with regard to the others let us express our view as follows, beginning with some remarks about the soul. We said before[5] that there are two parts of the soul—that which grasps a rule or rational

5 principle, and the irrational; let us now draw a similar distinction within the part which grasps a rational principle. And let it be assumed that there are two parts which grasp a rational principle—one by which we contemplate the kind of things whose originative causes are invariable, and one by which we contemplate variable things; for where objects differ in kind the part of the soul answering to each of the two is different in kind, since it is in virtue of a certain like-

10 ness and kinship with their objects that they have the knowledge they have. Let one of these parts be called the scientific and the other the calculative; for to deliberate and to calculate are the same thing, but no one deliberates about

---

[4] 1103ᵃ 3–7.

[5] 1102ᵃ 26–8.

the invariable. Therefore the calculative is one part of the faculty which grasps a rational principle. We must, then, learn what is the best state of each of these two parts; for this is the virtue of each.   15

2   The virtue of a thing is relative to its proper work. Now there are three things in the soul which control action and truth—sensation, reason, desire.

Of these sensation originates no action; this is plain from the fact that the lower animals have sensation but no share in action.   20

What affirmation and negation are in thinking, pursuit and avoidance are in desire; so that since moral virtue is a state of character concerned with choice, and choice is deliberate desire, therefore both the reasoning must be true and the desire right, if the choice is to be good, and the latter 25 must pursue just what the former asserts. Now this kind of intellect and of truth is practical; of the intellect which is contemplative, not practical nor productive, the good and the bad state are truth and falsity respectively (for this is the work of everything intellectual); while of the part which 30 is practical and intellectual the good state is truth in agreement with right desire.

The origin of action—its efficient, not its final cause— is choice, and that of choice is desire and reasoning with a view to an end. This is why choice cannot exist either without reason and intellect or without a moral state; for good action and its opposite cannot exist without a combination 35 of intellect and character. Intellect itself, however, moves nothing, but only the intellect which aims at an end and is practical; for this rules the productive intellect as well, since 1139b every one who makes makes for an end, and that which is made is not an end in the unqualified sense (but only an end in a particular relation, and the end of a particular operation)—only that which is *done* is that; for good action is an

end, and desire aims at this. Hence choice is either desiderative reason or ratiocinative desire, and such an origin of
action is a man. (It is to be noted that nothing that is past is
an object of choice, e. g. no one chooses to have sacked
Troy; for no one *deliberates* about the past, but about what
is future and capable of being otherwise, while what is past
is not capable of not having taken place; hence Agathon is
right in saying

For this alone is lacking even to God,
To make undone things that have once been done.)

The work of both the intellectual parts, then, is truth.
Therefore the states that are most strictly those in respect of
which each of these parts will reach truth are the virtues of
the two parts.

3 Let us begin, then, from the beginning, and discuss
these states once more. Let it be assumed that the
states by virtue of which the soul possesses truth
by way of affirmation or denial are five in number, i. e. art,
scientific knowledge, practical wisdom, philosophic wisdom,
intuitive reason; we do not include judgement and opinion
because in these we may be mistaken.

Now what *scientific knowledge* is, if we are to speak
exactly and not follow mere similarities, is plain from what
follows. We all suppose that what we know is not even
capable of being otherwise; of things capable of being otherwise we do not know, when they have passed outside our
observation, whether they exist or not. Therefore the object
of scientific knowledge is of necessity. Therefore it is eternal; for things that are of necessity in the unqualified sense
are all eternal; and things that are eternal are ungenerated
and imperishable. Again, every science is thought to be
capable of being taught, and its object of being learned.

And all teaching starts from what is already known, as we maintain in the *Analytics*[6] also; for it proceeds sometimes through induction and sometimes by syllogism. Now induction is the starting-point which knowledge even of the universal presupposes, while syllogism proceeds *from* universals. There are therefore starting-points from which syllogism proceeds, which are not reached by syllogism; it is therefore by induction that they are acquired. Scientific 30 knowledge is, then, a state of capacity to demonstrate, and has the other limiting characteristics which we specify in the *Analytics*;[7] for it is when a man believes in a certain way and the starting-points are known to him that he has scientific knowledge, since if they are not better known to him than the conclusion, he will have his knowledge only incidentally.

Let this, then, be taken as our account of scientific knowledge.

4 In the variable are included both things made and things done; making and acting are different (for 1140ᵃ their nature we treat even the discussions outside our school as reliable); so that the reasoned state of capacity to act is different from the reasoned state of capacity to 5 make. Hence too they are not included one in the other; for neither is acting making nor is making acting. Now since architecture is an art and is essentially a reasoned state of capacity to make, and there is neither any art that is not such a state nor any such state that is not an art, *art* is identical with a state of capacity to make, involving a true course of reasoning. All art is concerned with coming into 10 being, i. e. with contriving and considering how something may come into being which is capable of either being or not

6 *An. Post.* 71ᵃ 1.

7 Ib. ᵇ 9–23.

being, and whose origin is in the maker and not in the thing
made; for art is concerned neither with things that are, or
come into being, by necessity, nor with things that do so in
accordance with nature (since these have their origin in
15 themselves). Making and acting being different, art must be
a matter of making, not of acting. And in a sense chance
and art are concerned with the same objects; as Agathon
says, 'art loves chance and chance loves art'. Art, then, as
has been said,[8] is a state concerned with making, involving a
20 true course of reasoning, and lack of art on the contrary is
a state concerned with making, involving a false course of
reasoning; both are concerned with the variable.

5 Regarding *practical wisdom* we shall get at the truth
25 by considering who are the persons we credit with
it. Now it is thought to be the mark of a man of
practical wisdom to be able to deliberate well about what is
good and expedient for himself, not in some particular
respect, e. g. about what sorts of thing conduce to health or
to strength, but about what sorts of thing conduce to the
good life in general. This is shown by the fact that we credit
men with practical wisdom in some particular respect when
30 they have calculated well with a view to some good end
which is one of those that are not the object of any art. It
follows that in the general sense also the man who is capable of deliberating has practical wisdom. Now no one
deliberates about things that are invariable, nor about things
that it is impossible for him to do. Therefore, since scientific knowledge involves demonstration, but there is no
demonstration of things whose first principles are variable
35 (for all such things might actually be otherwise), and since it
is impossible to deliberate about things that are of neces-
1140b sity, practical wisdom cannot be scientific knowledge nor

[8] l. 9.

art; not science because that which can be done is capable of
being otherwise, not art because action and making are different kinds of thing. The remaining alternative, then, is
that it is a true and reasoned state of capacity to act with 5
regard to the things that are good or bad for man. For while
making has an end other than itself, action cannot; for good
action itself is its end. It is for this reason that we think Per-
icles and men like him have practical wisdom, viz. because
they can see what is good for themselves and what is good 10
for men in general; we consider that those can do this who
are good at managing households or states. (This is why we
call temperance (*sophrosyne*) by this name; we imply that it
preserves one's practical wisdom (*sodsousa ten phronesin*).
Now what it preserves is a judgement of the kind we have
described. For it it not any and every judgement that pleasant and painful objects destroy and pervert, e. g. the
judgement that the triangle has or has not its angles equal to 15
two right angles, but only judgements about what is to be
done. For the originating causes of the things that are done
consist in the end at which they are aimed; but the man
who has been ruined by pleasure or pain forthwith fails to
see any such originating cause—to see that for the sake of
this or because of this he ought to choose and do whatever
he chooses and does; for vice is destructive of the originating cause of action.)

Practical wisdom, then, must be a reasoned and true
state of capacity to act with regard to human goods. But 20
further, while there is such a thing as excellence in art, there
is no such thing as excellence in practical wisdom; and in
art he who errs willingly is preferable, but in practical wisdom, as in the virtues, he is the reverse. Plainly, then,
practical wisdom is a virtue and not an art. There being two
parts of the soul that can follow a course of reasoning, it 25
must be the virtue of one of the two, i. e. of that part which
forms opinions; for opinion is about the variable and so is

practical wisdom. But yet it is not only a reasoned state; this
is shown by the fact that a state of that sort may be forgot-
30 ten but practical wisdom cannot.

6 Scientific knowledge is judgement about things that
are universal and necessary, and the conclusions of
demonstration, and all scientific knowledge, follow
from first principles (for scientific knowledge involves
apprehension of a rational ground) . This being so, the first
principle from which what is scientifically known follows
cannot be an object of scientific knowledge, of art, or of
35 practical wisdom; for that which can be scientifically known
can be demonstrated, and art and practical wisdom deal
1141ᵃ with things that are variable. Nor are these first principles
the objects of philosophic wisdom, for it is a mark of the
philosopher to have *demonstration* about some things. If,
then, the states of mind by which we have truth and are
never deceived about things invariable or even variable are
scientific knowledge, practical wisdom, philosophic wisdom,
5 and intuitive reason, and it cannot be any of the three (i. e.
practical wisdom, scientific knowledge, or philosophic wisdom), the remaining alternative is that it is *intuitive reason*
that grasps the first principles.

7 *Wisdom* (1) in the arts we ascribe to their most finished exponents, e. g. to Phidias as a sculptor and
10 to Polyclitus as a maker of portrait-statues, and
here we mean nothing by wisdom except excellence in art;
but (2) we think that some people are wise in general, not in
some particular field or in any other limited respect, as
Homer says in the *Margites*,

Him did the gods make neither a digger nor yet a
15   ploughman
Nor wise in anything else.

Therefore wisdom must plainly be the most finished of the forms of knowledge. It follows that the wise man must not only know what follows from the first principles, but must also possess truth about the first principles. Therefore wisdom must be intuitive reason combined with scientific knowledge—scientific knowledge of the highest objects which has received as it were its proper completion.

Of the highest objects, we say; for it would be strange 20 to think that the art of politics, or practical wisdom, is the best knowledge, since man is not the best thing in the world. Now if what is healthy or good is different for men and for fishes, but what is white or straight is always the 25 same, any one would say that what is wise is the same but what is practically wise is different; for it is to that which observes well the various matters concerning itself that one ascribes practical wisdom, and it is to this that one will entrust such matters. This is why we say that some even of the lower animals have practical wisdom, viz. those which are found to have a power of foresight with regard to their own life. It is evident also that philosophic wisdom and the art of politics cannot be the same; for if the state of mind concerned with a man's own interests is to be called philo- 30 sophic wisdom, there will be many philosophic wisdoms; there will not be one concerned with the good of all animals (any more than there is one art of medicine for all existing things), but a different philosophic wisdom about the good of each species.

But if the argument be that man is the best of the animals, this makes no difference; for there are other things 1141ᵇ much more divine in their nature even than man, e. g., most conspicuously, the bodies of which the heavens are framed. From what has been said it is plain, then, that philosophic wisdom is scientific knowledge, combined with intuitive reason, of the things that are highest by nature. This is why we say Anaxagoras, Thales, and men like them have philo-

5 sophic but not practical wisdom, when we see them ignorant of what is to their own advantage, and why we say that
they know things that are remarkable, admirable, difficult,
and divine, but useless; viz. because it is not human goods
that they seek.

Practical wisdom on the other hand is concerned with
things human and things about which it is possible to delib-
10 erate; for we say this is above all the work of the man of
practical wisdom, to deliberate well, but no one deliberates
about things invariable, nor about things which have not an
end, and that a good that can be brought about by action.
The man who is without qualification good at deliberating
is the man who is capable of aiming in accordance with calculation at the best for man of things attainable by action.
15 Nor is practical wisdom concerned with universals only—it
must also recognize the particulars; for it is practical, and
practice is concerned with particulars. This is why some
who do not know, and especially those who have experience, are more practical than others who know; for if a man
knew that light meats are digestible and wholesome, but did
not know which sorts of meat are light, he would not pro-
20 duce health, but the man who knows that chicken is
wholesome is more likely to produce health.

Now practical wisdom is concerned with action; therefore one should have both forms of it, or the latter in
preference to the former. But of practical as of philosophic
wisdom there must be a controlling kind.

8   Political wisdom and practical wisdom are the same
state of mind, but their essence is not the same. Of
the wisdom concerned with the city, the practical
wisdom which plays a controlling part is legislative wisdom,
25 while that which is related to this as particulars to their universal is known by the general name 'political wisdom'; this
has to do with action and deliberation, for a decree is a

thing to be carried out in the form of an individual act. This is why the exponents of this art are alone said to 'take part in politics'; for these alone 'do things' as manual labourers 'do things'.

Practical wisdom also is identified especially with that form of it which is concerned with a man himself—with the individual; and this is known by the general name 'practical wisdom'; of the other kinds one is called household 30 management, another legislation, the third politics, and of the latter one part is called deliberative and the other judicial. Now knowing what is good for oneself will be one kind of knowledge, but it is very different from the other kinds; and the man who knows and concerns himself with his own 1142ª interests is thought to have practical wisdom, while politicians are thought to be busybodies; hence the words of Euripides,

> But how could I be wise, who might at ease,
> Numbered among the army's multitude,
> Have had an equal share? . . .
> For those who aim too high and do too much . . .   5

Those who think thus seek their own good, and consider that one ought to do so. From this opinion, then, has come the view that such men have practical wisdom; yet perhaps one's own good cannot exist without household management, nor without a form of government. Further, how one 10 should order one's own affairs is not clear and needs inquiry.

What has been said is confirmed by the fact that while young men become geometricians and mathematicians and wise in matters like these, it is thought that a young man of practical wisdom cannot be found. The cause is that such wisdom is concerned not only with universals but with particulars, which become familiar from experience, but a young 15 man has no experience, for it is length of time that gives experience; indeed one might ask this question too, why a boy may become a mathematician, but not a philosopher or a physicist. Is it because the objects of mathematics exist by abstraction, while the first principles of these other subjects come from experience, and because young men have no conviction about the latter but merely use the proper language, while the essence of mathematical objects is plain enough to them?

20   Further, error in deliberation may be either about the universal or about the particular; we may fail to know either that all water that weighs heavy is bad, or that this particular water weighs heavy.

That practical wisdom is not scientific knowledge is evident; for it is, as has been said,[9] concerned with the ulti-
25 mate particular fact, since the thing to be done is of this nature. It is opposed, then, to intuitive reason; for intuitive reason is of the limiting premisses, for which no reason can be given, while practical wisdom is concerned with the ultimate particular, which is the object not of scientific knowledge but of perception—not the perception of qualities peculiar to one sense but a perception akin to that by which we perceive that the particular figure before us is a triangle; for in that direction as well as in that of the major premiss there will be a limit. But this is rather perception than prac-
30 tical wisdom, though it is another kind of perception than that of the qualities peculiar to each sense.

9   There is a difference between inquiry and deliberation; for deliberation is inquiry into a particular kind of thing. We must grasp the nature of excellence in deliberation as well—whether it is a form of scientific knowledge, or opinion, or skill in conjecture, or

9 1141^b 14–22.

some other kind of thing. *Scientific knowledge* it is not; for men do not inquire about the things they know about, but 1142^b good deliberation is a kind of deliberation, and he who deliberates inquires and calculates. Nor is it *skill in conjecture*; for this both involves no reasoning and is something that is quick in its operation, while men deliberate a long time, and they say that one should carry out quickly the conclusions of one's deliberation, but should deliberate slowly. Again, 5 *readiness of mind* is different from excellence in deliberation; it is a sort of skill in conjecture. Nor again is excellence in deliberation *opinion* of any sort. But since the man who deliberates badly makes a mistake, while he who deliberates well does so correctly, excellence in deliberation is clearly a kind of correctness, but neither of knowledge nor of opinion; for there is no such thing as correctness of knowledge (since there is no such thing as error of knowledge), and 10 correctness of opinion is truth; and at the same time everything that is an object of opinion is already determined. But again excellence in deliberation involves reasoning. The remaining alternative, then, is that it is *correctness of thinking*; for this is not yet assertion, since, while even opinion is not inquiry but has reached the stage of assertion, the man who is deliberating, whether he does so well or ill, is searching for something and calculating. 15

But excellence in deliberation is a certain correctness of deliberation; hence we must first inquire what deliberation is and what it is about. And, there being more than one kind of correctness, plainly excellence in deliberation is not any and every kind; for (1) the incontinent man and the bad man, if he is clever, will reach as a result of his calculation what he sets before himself, so that he will have deliberated correctly, but he will have got for himself a great evil. Now to have deliberated well is thought to be a good thing; for it is this kind of correctness of deliberation that is excellence 20 in deliberation, viz. that which tends to attain what is good.

But (2) it is possible to attain even good by a false syllogism, and to attain what one ought to do but not by the
right means, the middle term being false; so that this too is
not yet excellence in deliberation—this state in virtue of
25 which one attains what one ought but not by the right
means. Again (3) it is possible to attain it by long deliberation while another man attains it quickly. Therefore in the
former case we have not yet got excellence in deliberation,
which is rightness with regard to the expedient—rightness
in respect both of the end, the manner, and the time. (4)
Further it is possible to have deliberated well either in the
30 unqualified sense or with reference to a particular end.
Excellence in deliberation in the unqualified sense, then, is
that which succeeds with reference to what is the end in the
unqualified sense, and excellence in deliberation in a particular sense is that which succeeds relatively to a particular
end. If, then, it is characteristic of men of practical wisdom
to have deliberated well, excellence in deliberation will be
correctness with regard to what conduces to the end of
which practical wisdom is the true apprehension.

10 Understanding, also, and goodness of understanding, in virtue of which men are said to be
1143ª men of understanding or of good understanding,
are neither entirely the same as opinion or scientific knowledge (for at that rate all men would have been men of
understanding), nor are they one of the particular sciences,
such as medicine, the science of things connected with
5 health, or geometry, the science of spatial magnitudes. For
understanding is neither about things that are always and
are unchangeable, nor about any and every one of the things
that come into being, but about things which may become
subjects of questioning and deliberation. Hence it is about
the same objects as practical wisdom; but understanding
and practical wisdom are not the same. For practical wisdom

issues commands, since its end is what ought to be done or not to be done; but understanding only judges. (Understanding is identical with goodness of understanding, men 10 of understanding with men of good understanding.) Now understanding is neither the having nor the acquiring of practical wisdom; but as learning is called understanding when it means the exercise of the faculty of knowledge, so 'understanding' is applicable to the exercise of the faculty of opinion for the purpose of judging of what some one else says about matters with which practical wisdom is concerned—and of judging soundly; for 'well' and 'soundly' are 15 the same thing. And from this has come the use of the name 'understanding' in virtue of which men are said to be 'of good understanding', viz. from the application of the word to the grasping of scientific truth; for we often call such grasping understanding.

11 What is called judgement, in virtue of which men are said to 'be sympathetic judges' and to 20 'have judgement', is the right discrimination of the equitable. This is shown by the fact that we say the equitable man is above all others a man of sympathetic judgement, and identify equity with sympathetic judgement about certain facts. And sympathetic judgement is judgement which discriminates what is equitable and does so correctly; and correct judgement is that which judges what is true.

Now all the states we have considered converge, as 25 might be expected, to the same point; for when we speak of judgement and understanding and practical wisdom and intuitive reason we credit the same people with possessing judgement and having reached years of reason and with having practical wisdom and understanding. For all these faculties deal with ultimates, i. e. with particulars; and being a man of understanding and of good or sympathetic judge-

30 ment consists in being able to judge about the things with
which practical wisdom is concerned; for the equities are
common to all good men in relation to other men. Now all
things which have to be done are included among particulars or ultimates; for not only must the man of practical
wisdom know particular facts, but understanding and judgement are also concerned with things to be done, and these
are ultimates. And intuitive reason is concerned with the
35 ultimates in both directions; for both the first terms and the
last are objects of intuitive reason and not of argument, and
1143ᵇ the intuitive reason which is presupposed by demonstrations
grasps the unchangeable and first terms, while the intuitive
reason involved in practical reasonings grasps the last and
variable fact, i. e. the minor premiss. For these variable facts
are the starting-points for the apprehension of the end, since
the universals are reached from the particulars; of these
5 therefore we must have perception, and this perception is
intuitive reason.

This is why these states are thought to be natural
endowments—why, while no one is thought to be a philosopher by nature, people are thought to have by nature
judgement, understanding, and intuitive reason. This is
shown by the fact that we think our powers correspond to
our time of life, and that a particular age brings with it intuitive reason and judgement; this implies that nature is the
cause. [Hence intuitive reason is both beginning and end;
10 for demonstrations are from these and about these.] Therefore we ought to attend to the undemonstrated sayings and
opinions of experienced and older people or of people of
practical wisdom not less than to demonstrations; for
because experience has given them an eye they see aright.

We have stated, then, what practical and philosophic
wisdom are, and with what each of them is concerned, and
15 we have said that each is the virtue of a different part of the
soul.

12 Difficulties might be raised as to the utility of these qualities of mind. For (1) philosophic wisdom will contemplate none of the things that will make a man happy (for it is not concerned with any coming into being), and though practical wisdom has *this* 20 merit, for what purpose do we need it? Practical wisdom is the quality of mind concerned with things just and noble and good for man, but these are the things which it is the mark of a good man to do, and we are none the more able to act for knowing them if the virtues are states of *character*, just as we are none the better able to act for knowing the 25 things that are healthy and sound, in the sense not of producing but of issuing from the state of health; for we are none the more able to act for having the art of medicine or of gymnastics. But (2) if we are to say that a man should have practical wisdom not for the sake of knowing moral truths but for the sake of becoming good, practical wisdom 30 will be of no use to those who are good; but again it is of no use to those who have *not* virtue; for it will make no difference whether they have practical wisdom themselves or obey others who have it, and it would be enough for us to do what we do in the case of health; though we wish to become healthy, yet we do not learn the art of medicine. (3) Besides this, it would be thought strange if practical wisdom, being inferior to philosophic wisdom, is to be put in authority over it, as seems to be implied by the fact that the art which produces anything rules and issues commands about that thing.

These, then, are the questions we must discuss; so far 35 we have only stated the difficulties.

(1) Now first let us say that in themselves these states 1144ª must be worthy of choice because they are the virtues of the two parts of the soul respectively, even if neither of them produce anything.

(2) Secondly, they do produce something, not as the art

of medicine produces health, however, but as health produces health;[10] so does philosophic wisdom produce
happiness; for, being a part of virtue entire, by being pos-
5 sessed and by actualizing itself it makes a man happy.

(3) Again, the work of man is achieved only in accordance with practical wisdom as well as with moral virtue;
for virtue makes us aim at the right mark, and practical wisdom makes us take the right means. (Of the fourth part of
10 the soul—the nutritive[11]—there is no such virtue; for there
is nothing which it is in its power to do or not to do.)

(4) With regard to our being none the more able to do
because of our practical wisdom what is noble and just, let
us begin a little further back, starting with the following
principle. As we say that some people who do just acts are
15 not necessarily just, i. e. those who do the acts ordained by
the laws either unwillingly or owing to ignorance or for
some other reason and not for the sake of the acts themselves (though, to be sure, they do what they should and all
the things that the good man ought), so is it, it seems, that
in order to be good one must be in a certain state when one
20 does the several acts, i. e. one must do them as a result of
choice and for the sake of the acts themselves. Now virtue
makes the choice right, but the question of the things which
should naturally be done to carry out our choice belongs not
to virtue but to another faculty. We must devote our attention to these matters and give a clearer statement about
them. There is a faculty which is called cleverness; and this
25 is such as to be able to do the things that tend towards the
mark we have set before ourselves, and to hit it. Now if the
mark be noble, the cleverness is laudable, but if the mark be
bad, the cleverness is mere smartness; hence we call even

[10] i. e. as health, as an inner state, produces the activities which we know as
constituting health.

[11] The other three being the scientific, the calculative, and the desiderative.

men of practical wisdom clever or smart. Practical wisdom is not the faculty, but it does not exist without this faculty. And this eye of the soul acquires its formed state not with- 30 out the aid of virtue, as has been said[12] and is plain; for the syllogisms which deal with acts to be done are things which involve a starting-point, viz. 'since the end, i. e. what is best, is of such and such a nature', whatever it may be (let it for the sake of argument be what we please); and this is not evident except to the good man; for wickedness perverts us and causes us to be deceived about the starting-points of 35 action. Therefore it is evident that it is impossible to be practically wise without being good.

13 We must therefore consider virtue also once more; for virtue too is similarly related; as prac- 1144^b tical wisdom is to cleverness—not the same, but like it—so is natural virtue to virtue in the strict sense. For all men think that each type of character belongs to its pos- sessors in some sense by nature; for from the very moment of birth we are just or fitted for self-control or brave or have 5 the other moral qualities; but yet we seek something else as that which is good in the strict sense—we seek for the pres- ence of such qualities in another way. For both children and brutes have the natural dispositions to these qualities, but without reason these are evidently hurtful. Only we seem to see this much, that, while one may be led astray by them, as 10 a strong body which moves without sight may stumble badly because of its lack of sight, still, if a man once acquires reason, that makes a difference in action; and his state, while still like what it was, will then be virtue in the strict sense. Therefore, as in the part of us which forms opinions there are two types, cleverness and practical wis- dom, so too in the moral part there are two types, natural 15

---

[12] ll. 6–26.

virtue and virtue in the strict sense, and of these the latter involves practical wisdom. This is why some say that all the virtues are forms of practical wisdom, and why Socrates in one respect was on the right track while in another he went astray; in thinking that all the virtues were forms of practical wisdom he was wrong, but in saying they implied
20 practical wisdom he was right. This is confirmed by the fact that even now all men, when they define virtue, after naming the state of character and its objects add 'that (state) which is in accordance with the right rule'; now the right rule is that which is in accordance with practical wisdom. All men, then, seem somehow to divine that this kind of
25 state is virtue, viz. that which is in accordance with practical wisdom. But we must go a little further. For it is not merely the state in accordance with the right rule, but the state that implies the *presence* of the right rule, that is virtue; and practical wisdom is a right rule about such matters. Socrates, then, thought the virtues were rules or rational principles (for he thought they were, all of them, forms of scientific knowledge), while we think they *involve* a rational principle.
30   It is clear, then, from what has been said, that it is not possible to be good in the strict sense without practical wisdom, nor practically wise without moral virtue. But in this way we may also refute the dialectical argument whereby it might be contended that the virtues exist in separation from each other; the same man, it might be said, is not best equipped by nature for all the virtues, so that he will have
35 already acquired one when he has not yet acquired another. This is possible in respect of the natural virtues, but not in
1145ª respect of those in respect of which a man is called without qualification good: for with the presence of the one quality, practical wisdom, will be given all the virtues. And it is plain that, even if it were of no practical value, we should have needed it because it is the virtue of the part of us in question; plain too that the choice will not be right without

practical wisdom any more than without virtue; for the one determines the end and the other makes us do the things that lead to the end.

But again it is not *supreme* over philosophic wisdom, i. e. over the superior part of us, any more than the art of medicine is over health; for it does not use it but provides for its coming into being; it issues orders, then, for its sake, 10 but not to it. Further, to maintain its supremacy would be like saying that the art of politics rules the gods because it issues orders about all the affairs of the state.

BOOK VII

1 Let us now make a fresh beginning and point out 15 that of moral states to be avoided there are three kinds—vice, incontinence, brutishness. The contraries of two of these are evident—one we call virtue, the other continence; to brutishness it would be most fitting to 20 oppose superhuman virtue, a heroic and divine kind of nature, as Homer has represented Priam saying of Hector that he was very good,

> For he seemed not, he,
> The child of a mortal man, but as one that of God's
> seed came.[1]

Therefore if, as they say, men become gods by excess of virtue, of this kind must evidently be the state opposed to the brutish state; for as a brute has no vice or virtue, so neither has a god; his state is higher than virtue, and that 25 of a brute is a different kind of state from vice.

[1] *Il.* xxiv. 258 f.

Now, since it is rarely that a godlike man is found—to use the epithet of the Spartans, who when they admire any one highly call him a 'godlike man'—so too the brutish type is rarely found among men; it is found chiefly among bar-
30 barians, but some brutish qualities are also produced by disease or deformity; and we also call by this evil name those men who go beyond all ordinary standards by reason of vice. Of this kind of disposition, however, we must later make some mention,[2] while we have discussed vice before;[3] we must now discuss incontinence and softness (or effemi-
35 nacy), and continence and endurance; for we must treat each of the two neither as identical with virtue or wicked-
1145b ness, nor as a different genus. We must, as in all other cases, set the observed facts before us and, after first discussing the difficulties, go on to prove, if possible, the truth of all the common opinions about these affections of the mind, or, failing this, of the greater number and the most
5 authoritative; for if we both refute the objections and leave the common opinions undisturbed, we shall have proved the case sufficiently.

Now (1) both continence and endurance are thought to be included among things good and praiseworthy, and both incontinence and softness among things bad and blamewor-
10 thy; and the same man is thought to be continent and ready to abide by the result of his calculations, or incontinent and ready to abandon them. And (2) the incontinent man, knowing that what he does is bad, does it as a result of passion, while the continent man, knowing that his appetites are bad, refuses on account of his rational principle to follow them. (3) The temperate man all men call continent and
15 disposed to endurance, while the continent man some maintain to be always temperate but others do not; and some call

2 Ch. 5.

3 Bks. II–V.

the self-indulgent man incontinent and the incontinent man self-indulgent indiscriminately while others distinguish them. (4) The man of practical wisdom, they sometimes say, cannot be incontinent, while sometimes they say that some who are practically wise and clever are incontinent. Again (5) men are said to be incontinent even with respect to anger, honour, and gain.—These, then, are the things 20 that are said.

2 Now we may ask (1) how a man who judges rightly can behave incontinently. That he should behave so when he has knowledge, some say is impossible; for it would be strange—so Socrates[4] thought—if when knowledge was in a man something else could master it and 25 drag it about like a slave. For *Socrates* was entirely opposed to the view in question, holding that there is no such thing as incontinence; no one, he said, when he judges acts against what he judges best—people act so only by reason of ignorance. Now this view plainly contradicts the observed facts, and we must inquire about what happens to such a man; if he acts by reason of ignorance, what is the manner of his ignorance? For that the man who behaves inconti- 30 nently does not, before he gets into this state, *think* he ought to act so, is evident. But there are *some* who concede certain of Socrates' contentions but not others; that nothing is stronger than knowledge they admit, but not that no one acts contrary to what has seemed to him the better course, and therefore they say that the incontinent man has not knowledge when he is mastered by his pleasures, but opin- ion. But *if* it is opinion and not knowledge, if it is not a 35 strong conviction that resists but a weak one, as in men who 1146ᵃ hesitate, we sympathize with their failure to stand by such convictions against strong appetites; but we do not sympa-

4 Pl. *Prot.* 352 B. C.

thize with wickedness, nor with any of the other blamewor-
5 thy states. Is it then *practical wisdom* whose resistance is
mastered? That is the strongest of all states. But this is
absurd; the same man will be at once practically wise and
incontinent, but *no one* would say that it is the part of a
practically wise man to do willingly the basest acts. Besides,
it has been shown before that the man of practical wisdom
is one who will act[5] (for he is a man concerned with the
individual facts)[6] and who has the other virtues.[7]

(2) Further, if continence involves having strong and
10 bad appetites, the temperate man will not be continent nor
the continent man temperate; for a temperate man will have
neither excessive nor bad appetites. But the continent man
must; for if the appetites are good, the state of character that
15 restrains us from following them is bad, so that not all continence will be good; while if they are weak and not bad,
there is nothing admirable in resisting them, and if they are
weak and bad, there is nothing great in resisting these
either.

(3) Further, if continence makes a man ready to stand
by any and every opinion, it is bad, i. e. if it makes him
stand even by a false opinion; and if incontinence makes a
man apt to abandon any and every opinion, there will be a
good incontinence, of which Sophocles' Neoptolemus in the
20 *Philoctetes*[8] will be an instance; for he is to be praised for
not standing by what Odysseus persuaded him to do,
because he is pained at telling a lie.

(4) Further, the sophistic argument presents a difficulty; the syllogism arising from men's wish to expose

5 1140[b] 4–6.

6 1141[b] 16, 1142[a] 24.

7 1144[b] 30–1145[a] 2.

8 ll. 895–916.

paradoxical results arising from an opponent's view, in order that they may be admired when they succeed, is one that puts us in a difficulty (for thought is bound fast when 25 it will not rest because the conclusion does not satisfy it, and cannot advance because it cannot refute the argument). There is an argument from which it follows that folly coupled with incontinence is virtue; for a man does the opposite of what he judges, owing to incontinence, but judges what is good to be evil and something that he should not do, and in consequence he will do what is good and not what is evil. 30

(5) Further, he who on conviction does and pursues and chooses what is pleasant would be thought to be better than one who does so as a result not of calculation but of incontinence; for he is easier to cure since he may be persuaded to change his mind. But to the incontinent man may be applied the proverb 'when water chokes, what is one to wash it down with?' If he had been persuaded of the rightness of what he does, he would have desisted when he was 35 persuaded to change his mind; but now he acts in spite of 1146^b his being persuaded of something quite different.

(6) Further, if incontinence and continence are concerned with any and every kind of object, who is it that is incontinent in the unqualified sense? No one has all the forms of incontinence, but we say some people are incontinent without qualification. 5

3 Of some such kind are the difficulties that arise; some of these points must be refuted and the others left in possession of the field; for the solution of the difficulty is the discovery of the truth. (1) We must consider first, then, whether incontinent people act know-ingly or not, and in what sense knowingly; then (2) with what sorts of object the incontinent and the continent man may be said to be concerned (i. e. whether with any and every pleasure and pain or with certain determinate kinds), 10

and whether the continent man and the man of endurance
are the same or different; and similarly with regard to the
other matters germane to this inquiry. The starting-point
of our investigation is (a) the question whether the continent man and the incontinent are differentiated by their
15 objects or by their attitude, i. e. whether the incontinent
man is incontinent simply by being concerned with such
and such objects, or, instead, by his attitude, or, instead of
that, by both these things; (b) the second question is whether incontinence and continence are concerned with any
and every object or not. The man who is incontinent in the
unqualified sense is neither concerned with any and every
20 object, but with precisely those with which the self-indulgent man is concerned, nor is he characterized by being
simply related to these (for then his state would be the
same as self-indulgence), but by being related to them in a
certain way. For the one is led on in accordance with his
own choice, thinking that he ought always to pursue the
present pleasure; while the other does not think so, but yet
pursues it.

(1) As for the suggestion that it is true opinion and not
knowledge against which we act incontinently, that makes
25 no difference to the argument; for some people when in a
state of opinion do not hesitate, but think they know
exactly. If, then, the notion is that owing to their weak conviction those who have opinion are more likely to act against
their judgement than those who know, we answer that there
need be no difference between knowledge and opinion in
this respect; for some men are no less convinced of what
30 they think than others of what they know; as is shown by
the case of Heraclitus. But (a), since we use the word 'know'
in two senses (for both the man who has knowledge but is
not using it and he who is using it are said to know), it *will*
make a difference whether, when a man does what he
should not, he has the knowledge but is not exercising it;

or is exercising it; for the latter seems strange, but not the former.

(b) Further, since there are two kinds of premisses, 35 there is nothing to prevent a man's having both premisses 1147ª and acting against his knowledge, provided that he is using only the universal premiss and not the particular; for it is particular acts that have to be done. And there are also two kinds of universal term; one is predicable of the agent, the 5 other of the object; e. g. 'dry food is good for every man', and 'I am a man', or 'such and such food is dry'; but whether 'this food is such and such', of this the incontinent man either has not or is not exercising the knowledge.[9] There will, then, be, firstly, an enormous difference between these manners of knowing, so that to know in one way when we act incontinently would not seem anything strange, while to know in the other way would be extraordinary.

And further (c) the possession of knowledge in another sense than those just named is something that happens to 10 men; for within the case of having knowledge but not using it we see a difference of state, admitting of the possibility of having knowledge in a sense and yet not having it, as in the instance of a man asleep, mad, or drunk. But now this is just the condition of men under the influence of passion; for outbursts of anger and sexual appetites and some other such passions, it is evident, actually alter our bodily condition, 15 and in some men even produce fits of madness. It is plain, then, that incontinent people must be said to be in a similar condition to men asleep, mad, or drunk. The fact that men use the language that flows from knowledge proves

[9] i. e., if I am to be able to deduce from (a) 'dry food is good for all men' that 'this food is good for me', I must have (b) the premiss 'I am a man' and (c) the premisses (i) 'x food is dry', (ii) 'this food is x'. I cannot fail to know (b), and I may know (c i), but if I do not know (c ii), or know it only 'at the back of my mind', I shall not draw the conclusion.

20 nothing; for even men under the influence of these passions utter scientific proofs and verses of Empedocles, and those who have just begun to learn a science can string together its phrases, but do not yet know it; for it has to become part of themselves, and that takes time; so that we must suppose that the use of language by men in an incontinent state means no more than its utterance by actors on the stage.

(d) Again, we may also view the cause as follows with
25 reference to the facts of human nature. The one opinion is universal, the other is concerned with the particular facts, and here we come to something within the sphere of perception; when a single opinion results from the two, the soul must in one type of case[10] affirm the conclusion, while in the case of opinions concerned with production it must immediately act (e. g. if 'everything sweet ought to be tasted', and 'this is sweet', in the sense of being one of the particular
30 sweet things, the man who can act and is not prevented must at the same time actually act accordingly). When, then, the universal opinion is present in us forbidding us to taste, and there is also the opinion that 'everything sweet is pleasant', and that 'this is sweet' (now this is the opinion that is active),[11] and when appetite happens to be present in us, the one opinion bids us avoid the object, but appetite
35 leads us towards it (for it can move each of our bodily parts); so that it turns out that a man behaves incontinently under the influence (in a sense) of a rule and an opinion,
1147b and of one not contrary in itself, but only incidentally—for the appetite is contrary, not the opinion—to the right rule. It also follows that this is the reason why the lower animals
5 are not incontinent, viz. because they have no universal judgement but only imagination and memory of particulars.

The explanation of how the ignorance is dissolved and

[10] i. e. in scientific reasoning.

[11] i. e. determines action (Cf. b10).

the incontinent man regains his knowledge, is the same as in the case of the man drunk or asleep and is not particular to this condition; we must go to the students of natural science for it. Now, the last premiss both being an opinion about a perceptible object, and being what determines our actions, this a man either has not when he is in the state of passion, or has it in the sense in which having knowledge did not mean knowing but only talking, as a drunken man may mutter the verses of Empedocles.[12] And because the last term is not universal nor equally an object of scientific knowledge with the universal term, the position that Socrates sought to establish[13] actually seems to result; for it is not in the presence of what is thought to be knowledge proper that the affection of incontinence arises (nor is it this that is dragged about' as a result of the state of passion), but in that of perceptual knowledge.[14]

This must suffice as our answer to the question of action with and without knowledge, and how it is possible to behave incontinently with knowledge.

4   (2) We must next discuss whether there is any one who is incontinent without qualification, or all men who are incontinent are so in a particular sense, and if there is, with what sort of objects he is concerned. That both continent persons and persons of endurance, and incontinent and soft persons, are concerned with pleasures and pains, is evident.

Now of the things that produce pleasure some are nec-

---

[12] Cf ᵃ10–24.

[13] 1145ᵇ 22–24.

[14] Even before the minor premiss of the practical syllogism has been obscured by passion, the incontinent man has not scientific knowledge in the strict sense, since his minor premiss is not universal but has for its subject a sensible particular, e. g. 'this glass of wine'.

essary, while others are worthy of choice in themselves but
25 admit of excess, the bodily causes of pleasure being necessary (by such I mean both those concerned with food and
those concerned with sexual intercourse, i. e. the bodily
matters with which we defined self-indulgence[15] and temperance as being concerned), while the others are not
necessary but worthy of choice in themselves (e. g. victory,
30 honour, wealth, and good and pleasant things of this sort).
This being so, (*a*) those who go to excess with reference to
the latter, contrary to the right rule which is in themselves,
are not called incontinent simply, but incontinent with the
qualification 'in respect of money, gain, honour or anger',—
not simply incontinent, on the ground that they are
different from incontinent people and are called incontinent
by reason of a resemblance. (Compare the case of Anthro-
35 pos (Man), who won a contest at the Olympic games; in his
1148ª case the general definition of man differed little from the
definition peculiar to *him*, but yet it *was* different.)[16] This is
shown by the fact that incontinence either without qualification or in respect of some particular bodily pleasure is
blamed not only as a fault but as a kind of vice, while none
of the people who are incontinent in these other respects is
so blamed.

But (*b*) of the people who are incontinent with respect to
bodily enjoyments, with which we say the temperate and the
5 self-indulgent man are concerned, he who pursues the
excesses of things pleasant—and shuns those of things
painful, of hunger and thirst and heat and cold and all the
objects of touch and taste—not by choice but contrary to his
choice and his judgement, is called incontinent, not with the
10 qualification 'in respect of this or that', e. g. of anger, but

[15] III. 10.

[16] i. e. the definition appropriate to him was not 'rational animal' but
'rational animal who won the boxing contest at Olympia in 456 B.C.'

just simply. This is confirmed by the fact that men are called 'soft' with regard to these pleasures, but not with regard to any of the others. And for this reason we group together the incontinent and the self-indulgent, the continent and the temperate man—but not any of these other types—because they are concerned somehow with the same pleasures and pains; but though these are concerned with the same objects, they are not similarly related to them, but some of them make a deliberate choice while the others do not.[17]

This is why we should describe as self-indulgent rather the man who without appetite or with but a slight appetite pursues the excesses of pleasure and avoids moderate pains, than the man who does so because of his strong appetites; for what would the former do, if he had in addition a vigorous appetite, and a violent pain at the lack of the 'necessary' objects?

Now of appetites and pleasures some belong to the class of things generically noble and good—for some pleasant things are by nature worthy of choice, while others are contrary to these, and others are intermediate, to adopt our previous distinction[18]—e. g. wealth, gain, victory, honour. And with reference to all objects whether of this or of the intermediate kind men are not blamed for being affected by them, for desiring and loving them, but for doing so in a certain way, i. e. for going to excess. (This is why all those who contrary to the rule either are mastered by or pursue one of the objects which are naturally noble and good, e. g. those who busy themselves more than they ought about honour or about children and parents, [are not wicked]; for these too are goods, and those who busy themselves about them are praised; but yet there is an excess even in them—

[17] i. e. the temperate and the self-indulgent, not the continent and the incontinent.

[18] 1147^b 23–31, where, however, the 'contraries' are not mentioned.

if like Niobe one were to fight even against the gods, or
1148ᵇ were to be as much devoted to one's father as Satyrus nick-
named 'the filial', who was thought to be very silly on this
point.[19]) There is no wickedness, then, with regard to these
objects, for the reason named, viz. because each of them is
by nature a thing worthy of choice for its own sake; yet
excesses in respect of them are bad and to be avoided. Similarly there is no incontinence with regard to them; for
incontinence is not only to be avoided but is also a thing
worthy of blame; but owing to a similarity in the state of
feeling people apply the name incontinence, adding in each
case what it is in respect of, as we may describe as a bad
doctor or a bad actor one whom we should not call bad,
simply. As, then, in this case we do not apply the term
without qualification because each of these conditions is not
10 badness but only analogous to it, so it is clear that in the
other case also that alone must be taken to be incontinence
and continence which is concerned with the same objects as
temperance and self-indulgence, but we apply the term to
anger by virtue of a resemblance; and this is why we say
with a qualification 'incontinent in respect of anger' as we
say 'incontinent in respect of honour, or of gain'.

15   **5** (1) Some things are pleasant by nature, and of these
(*a*) some are so without qualification, and (*b*) others
are so with reference to particular classes either of
animals or of men; while (2) others are not pleasant by
nature, but (*a*) some of them become so by reason of
injuries to the system, and (*b*) others by reason of acquired
habits, and (*c*) others by reason of originally bad natures.
This being so, it is possible with regard to each of the latter

---

[19] Nothing is really known about the Satyrus referred to, but Prof. Burnet's
suggestion that he was a king of Bosporus who deified his father seems
probable.

kinds to discover similar states of character to those recognized with regard to the former; I mean (A) the brutish   20
states,[20] as in the case of the female who, they say, rips open
pregnant women and devours the infants, or of the things in
which some of the tribes about the Black Sea that have gone
savage are said to delight—in raw meat or in human flesh,
or in lending their children to one another to feast upon—or
of the story told of Phalaris.[21]

These states are brutish, but (B) others arise as a result
of disease[22] (or, in some cases, of madness, as with the man
who sacrificed and ate his mother, or with the slave who ate   25
the liver of his fellow), and others are morbid states (C)
resulting from custom,[23] e. g. the habit of plucking out the
hair or of gnawing the nails, or even coals or earth, and in
addition to these paederasty; for these arise in some by
nature and in others, as in those who have been the victims
of lust from childhood, from habit.   30

Now those in whom nature is the cause of such a state
no one would call incontinent, any more than one would
apply the epithet to women because of the passive part they
play in copulation; nor would one apply it to those who are
in a morbid condition as a result of habit. To have these
various types of habit is beyond the limits of vice, as brutishness is too; for a man who has them to master or be   1149ª
mastered by them is not simple [continence or] incontinence
but that which is so by analogy, as the man who is in this
condition in respect of fits of anger is to be called incontinent in respect of that feeling, but not incontinent simply.

For every excessive state whether of folly, of cowardice,

[20] Answering to (2 c).

[21] sc. and the bull. But Cf. 1149ª 14.

[22] Answering to (2 a).

[23] Answering to (2 b).

5 of self-indulgence, or of bad temper, is either brutish or
morbid; the man who is by nature apt to fear everything,
even the squeak of a mouse, is cowardly with a brutish cowardice, while the man who feared a weasel did so in
consequence of disease; and of foolish people those who by
nature are thoughtless and live by their senses alone are
brutish, like some races of the distant barbarians, while
10 those who are so as a result of disease (e. g. of epilepsy) or
of madness are morbid. Of these characteristics it is possible
to have some only at times, and not to be mastered by
them, e. g. Phalaris may have restrained a desire to eat the
flesh of a child or an appetite for unnatural sexual pleasure;
but it is also possible to be mastered, not merely to have the
15 feelings. Thus, as the wickedness which is on the human
level is called wickedness simply, while that which is not is
called wickedness not simply but with the qualification
'brutish' or 'morbid', in the same way it is plain that some
incontinence is brutish and some morbid, while only that
20 which corresponds to *human* self-indulgence is incontinence
simply.

That incontinence and continence, then, are concerned
only with the same objects as self-indulgence and temperance and that what is concerned with other objects is a type
distinct from incontinence, and called incontinence by a
metaphor and not simply, is plain.

6 That incontinence in respect of anger is less disgraceful than that in respect of the appetites is what
25 we will now proceed to see. (1) Anger seems to listen to argument to some extent, but to mishear it, as do
hasty servants who run out before they have heard the
whole of what one says, and then muddle the order, or as
dogs bark if there is but a knock at the door, before look-
30 ing to see if it is a friend; so anger by reason of the warmth
and hastiness of its nature, though it hears, does not hear

an order, and springs to take revenge. For argument or imagination informs us that we have been insulted or slighted, and anger, reasoning as it were that anything like this must be fought against, boils up straightway; while appetite, if argument or perception merely says that an object is pleasant, springs to the enjoyment of it. Therefore anger obeys the argument in a sense, but appetite does not. It is therefore more disgraceful; for the man who is incontinent in respect of anger is in a sense conquered by argument, while the other is conquered by appetite and not by argument.

(2) Further, we pardon people more easily for following natural desires, since we pardon them more easily for following such appetites as are common to all men, and in so far as they are common; now anger and bad temper are more natural than the appetites for excess, i. e. for unnecessary objects. Take for instance the man who defended himself on the charge of striking his father by saying 'yes, but *he* struck *his* father, and *he* struck *his*, and' (pointing to his child) 'this boy will strike *me* when he is a man; it runs in the family'; or the man who when he was being dragged along by his son bade him stop at the doorway, since he himself had dragged his father only as far as that.

(3) Further, those who are more given to plotting against others are more criminal. Now a passionate man is not given to plotting, nor is anger itself—it is open; but the nature of appetite is illustrated by what the poets call Aphrodite, 'guile-weaving daughter of Cyprus', and by Homer's words about her 'embroidered girdle':

> And the whisper of wooing is there,
> Whose subtlety stealeth the wits of the wise, how
>   prudent soe'er.[24]

24 *Il.* xiv. 214, 217.

Therefore if this form of incontinence is more criminal and disgraceful than that in respect of anger, it is both incontinence without qualification and in a sense vice.

(4) Further, no one commits wanton outrage with a
20 feeling of pain, but every one who acts in anger acts with pain, while the man who commits outrage acts with pleasure. If, then, those acts at which it is most just to be angry are more criminal than others, the incontinence which is due to appetite is the more criminal; for there is no wanton outrage involved in anger.

Plainly, then, the incontinence concerned with appetite is more disgraceful than that concerned with anger, and
25 continence and incontinence are concerned with bodily appetites and pleasures; but we must grasp the differences among the latter themselves. For, as has been said at the beginning,[25] some are human and natural both in kind and in magnitude, others are brutish, and others are due to organic injuries and diseases. Only with the first of these
30 are temperance and self-indulgence concerned; this is why we call the lower animals neither temperate nor self-indulgent except by a metaphor, and only if some one race of animals exceeds another as a whole in wantoness, destructiveness, and omnivorous greed; these have no power of choice or calculation, but they *are* departures from the nat-
35 ural norm,[26] as, among men, madmen are. Now brutishness
1150ᵃ is a less evil than vice, though more alarming; for it is not that the better part has been perverted, as in man—they *have* no better part. Thus it is like comparing a lifeless thing with a living in respect of badness; for the badness of that which has no originative source of movement is always less hurtful, and reason is an originative source. Thus it is like

---

[25] 1148ᵇ 15–31.

[26] And therefore cannot be called self-indulgent properly, but *can* be called so by a metaphor.

comparing injustice in the abstract with an unjust man. 5
Each is in some sense worse; for a bad man will do ten
thousand times as much evil as a brute.

7 With regard to the pleasures and pains and
appetites and aversions arising through touch and
taste, to which both self-indulgence and temper- 10
ance were formerly narrowed down,[27] it is possible to be in
such a state as to be defeated even by those of them which
most people master, or to master even those by which most
people are defeated; among these possibilities, those relating
to pleasures are incontinence and continence, those relating
to pains softness and endurance. The state of most people is
intermediate, even if they lean more towards the worse 15
states.

Now, since some pleasures are necessary while others
are not, and are necessary up to a point while the excesses
of them are not, nor the deficiencies, and this is equally true
of appetites and pains, the man who pursues the excesses
of things pleasant, or pursues to excess necessary objects, 20
and does so by choice, for their own sake and not at all for
the sake of any result distinct from them, is self-indulgent;
for such a man is of necessity unlikely to repent, and therefore incurable, since a man who cannot repent cannot be
cured. The man who is deficient in his pursuit of them is
the opposite of self-indulgent; the man who is intermediate
is temperate. Similarly, there is the man who avoids bodily
pains not because he is defeated by them but by choice. (Of
those who do not *choose* such acts, one kind of man is led to 25
them as a result of the pleasure involved, another because
he avoids the pain arising from the appetite, so that these
types differ from one another. Now any one would think
worse of a man if with no appetite or with weak appetite he

[27] III. 10.

were to do something disgraceful, than if he did it under the influence of powerful appetite, and worse of him if he struck a blow not in anger than if he did it in anger; for 30 what would he have done if he *had* been strongly affected? This is why the self-indulgent man is worse than the incontinent.) Of the states named, then,[28] the latter is rather a kind of softness;[29] the former is self-indulgence. While to the incontinent man is opposed the continent, to the soft is opposed the man of endurance; for endurance consists in 35 resisting, while continence consists in conquering, and resisting and conquering are different, as not being beaten is 1150ᵇ different from winning; this is why continence is also more worthy of choice than endurance. Now the man who is defective in respect of resistance to the things which most men both resist and resist successfully is soft and effeminate; for effeminacy too is a kind of softness; such a man trails his cloak to avoid the pain of lifting it, and plays the invalid without thinking himself wretched, though the man he imitates is a wretched man.

5   The case is similar with regard to continence and incontinence. For if a man is defeated by violent and excessive pleasures or pains, there is nothing wonderful in that; indeed we are ready to pardon him if he has resisted, as Theodectes' Philoctetes does when bitten by the snake, or Carcinus' Cer- 10 cyon in the *Alope*, and as people who try to restrain their laughter burst out in a guffaw, as happened to Xenophantus. But it is surprising if a man is defeated by and cannot resist pleasures or pains which most men can hold out against, when this is not due to heredity or disease, like the softness that is hereditary with the kings of the Scythians, or that 15 which distinguishes the female sex from the male.

[28] In ll. 19–25.

[29] Not softness proper, which is non-deliberate avoidance of pain (ll. 13–15).

The lover of amusement, too, is thought to be self-indulgent, but is really soft. For amusement is a relaxation, since it is a rest from work; and the lover of amusement is one of the people who go to excess in this.

Of incontinence one kind is impetuosity, another weakness. For some men after deliberating fail, owing to their emotion, to stand by the conclusions of their deliberation, 20 others because they have not deliberated are led by their emotion; since some men (just as people who first tickle others are not tickled themselves), if they have first perceived and seen what is coming and have first roused themselves and their calculative faculty, are not defeated by their emotion, whether it be pleasant or painful. It is keen and excitable people that suffer especially from the impetu- 25 ous form of incontinence; for the former by reason of their quickness and the latter by reason of the violence of their passions do not await the argument, because they are apt to follow their imagination.

8 The self-indulgent man, as was said,[30] is not apt to repent; for he stands by his choice; but any incontinent man is likely to repent. This is why the 30 position is not as it was expressed in the formulation of the problem,[31] but the self-indulgent man is incurable and the incontinent man curable; for wickedness is like a disease such as dropsy or consumption, while incontinence is like epilepsy; the former is a permanent, the latter an intermittent badness. And generally incontinence and vice are 35 different in kind; vice is unconscious of itself, incontinence is not (of incontinent men themselves, those who become 1151ª temporarily beside themselves are better than those who have the rational principle but do not abide by it, since the

[30] a 21.

[31] 1146ª 31–b 2.

latter are defeated by a weaker passion, and do not act without previous deliberation like the others); for the incontinent man is like the people who get drunk quickly and on little wine, i. e. on less than most people.

Evidently, then, incontinence is not vice (though perhaps it is so in a qualified sense); for incontinence is contrary to choice while vice is in accordance with choice; not but what they are similar in respect of the actions they lead to; as in the saying of Demodocus about the Milesians, 'the Milesians are not without sense, but they do the things that senseless people do', so too incontinent people are not criminal, but they will do criminal acts.

Now, since the incontinent man is apt to pursue, not on conviction, bodily pleasures that are excessive and contrary to the right rule, while the self-indulgent man is convinced because he is the sort of man to pursue them, it is on the contrary the former that is easily persuaded to change his mind, while the latter is not. For virtue and vice respectively preserve and destroy the first principle, and in actions the final cause is the first principle, as the hypotheses[32] are in mathematics; neither in that case is it argument that teaches the first principles, nor is it so here—virtue either natural or produced by habituation is what teaches right opinion about the first principle. Such a man as this, then, is temperate; his contrary is the self-indulgent.

But there is a sort of man who is carried away as a result of passion and contrary to the right rule—a man whom passion masters so that he does not act according to the right rule, but does not master to the extent of making him ready to believe that he ought to pursue such pleasures without reserve; this is the incontinent man, who is better than the self-indulgent man, and not bad without qualifi-

---

[32] i. e. the assumptions of the existence of the primary objects of mathematics, such as the straight line or the unit.

cation; for the best thing in him, the first principle, is preserved. And contrary to him is another kind of man, he who abides by his convictions and is not carried away, at least as a result of passion. It is evident from these considerations that the latter is a good state and the former a bad one.

9 Is the man continent who abides by any and every rule and any and every choice, or the man who abides by the right choice, and is he incontinent 30 who abandons any and every choice and any and every rule, or he who abandons the rule that is not false and the choice that is right; this is how we put it before in our statement of the problem.[33] Or is it incidentally any and every choice but *per se* the true rule and the right choice by which the one 35 abides and the other does not? If any one chooses or pursues this for the sake of that, *per se* he pursues and chooses the latter, but incidentally the former. But when we speak without qualification we mean what is *per se*. Therefore in a sense the one abides by, and the other abandons, any and every opinion; but without qualification, the true opinion.

There are some who are apt to abide by their opinion, who are called strong-headed, viz. those who are hard to 5 persuade in the first instance and are not easily persuaded to change; these have in them something like the continent man, as the prodigal is in a way like the liberal man and the rash man like the confident man; but they are different in many respects. For it is to passion and appetite that the one will not yield, since on occasion the continent man *will* be easy to persuade; but it is to argument that the others refuse to yield, for they do form appetites and many of them are 10 led by their pleasures. Now the people who are strongheaded are the opinionated, the ignorant, and the boorish —the opinionated being influenced by pleasure and pain;

for they delight in the victory they gain if they are not persuaded to change, and are pained if their decisions become
15 null and void as decrees sometimes do; so that they are liker
the incontinent than the continent man.

But there are some who fail to abide by their resolutions, not as a result of incontinence, e. g. Neoptolemus in
Sophocles' *Philoctetes*; yet it was for the sake of pleasure that
he did not stand fast—but a noble pleasure; for telling the
20 truth was noble to him, but he had been persuaded by
Odysseus to tell the lie. For not every one who does anything for the sake of pleasure is either self-indulgent or bad
or incontinent, but he who does it for a disgraceful pleasure.

Since there is also a sort of man who takes less delight
than he should in bodily things, and does not abide by the
rule, he who is intermediate between him and the inconti-
25 nent man is the continent man; for the incontinent man fails
to abide by the rule because he delights too much in them,
and this man because he delights in them too little; while
the continent man abides by the rule and does not change
on either account. Now if continence is good, both the contrary states must be bad, as they actually appear to be; but
30 because the other extreme is seen in few people and seldom,
as temperance is thought to be contrary only to self-indulgence, so is continence to incontinence.

Since many names are applied analogically, it is by
analogy that we have come to speak of the 'continence' of
the temperate man; for both the continent man and the
35 temperate man are such as to do nothing contrary to the
1152ᵃ rule for the sake of the bodily pleasures, but the former has
and the latter has not bad appetites, and the latter is such as
not to feel pleasure contrary to the rule, while the former is
such as to feel pleasure but not to be led by it. And the
incontinent and the self-indulgent man are also like another;
5 they are different, but both pursue bodily pleasures—the

latter, however, also thinking that he ought to do so, while
the former does not think this.

10

Nor can the same man have practical wisdom
and be incontinent; for it has been shown[34] that
a man is at the same time practically wise, and
good in respect of character. Further, a man has practical
wisdom not by knowing only but by being able to act; but
the incontinent man is unable to act—there is, however,
nothing to prevent a *clever* man from being incontinent; 10
this is why it is sometimes actually thought that some people have practical wisdom but are incontinent, viz. because
cleverness and practical wisdom differ in the way we have
described in our first discussions,[35] and are near together in
respect of their reasoning, but differ in respect of their
purpose—nor yet is the incontinent man like the man who
knows and is contemplating a truth, but like the man who 15
is asleep or drunk. And he acts willingly (for he acts in a
sense with knowledge both of what he does and of the end
to which he does it), but is not wicked, since his purpose
is good; so that he is half-wicked. And he is not a criminal; for he does not act of malice aforethought; of the two
types of incontinent man the one does not abide by the
conclusions of his deliberation, while the excitable man 20
does not deliberate at all. And thus the incontinent man
is like a city which passes all the right decrees and has
good laws, but makes no use of them, as in Anaxandrides'
jesting remark,

'The city willed it, that cares nought for laws';

34 1144^a 11–^{b} 32.

35 1144^a 23–^{b} 4.

but the wicked man is like a city that uses its laws, but has wicked laws to use.

25   Now incontinence and continence are concerned with that which is in excess of the state characteristic of most men; for the continent man abides by his resolutions more and the incontinent man less than most men can.

Of the forms of incontinence, that of excitable people is more curable than that of those who deliberate but do not abide by their decisions, and those who are incontinent through habituation are more curable than those in whom
30 incontinence is innate; for it is easier to change a habit than to change one's nature; even habit is hard to change just because it is like nature, as Evenus says:

> I say that habit's but long practice, friend,
> And this becomes men's nature in the end.

We have now stated what continence, incontinence,
35 endurance, and softness are, and how these states are related to each other.

1152ᵇ   **11**   The study of pleasure and pain belongs to the province of the political philosopher; for he is the architect of the end, with a view to which we call one thing bad and another good without qualification. Further, it is one of our necessary tasks to consider them;
5 for not only did we lay it down that moral virtue and vice are concerned with pains and pleasures,[36] but most people say that happiness involves pleasure; this is why the blessed man is called by a name derived from a word meaning enjoyment.[37]

Now (I) some people think that no pleasure is a good,

[36] 1104ᵇ 8–1105ᵃ 13.

[37] *makarios* from *mala chairein!*

either in itself or incidentally, since the good and pleasure
are not the same; (2) others think that some pleasures are
good but that most are bad. (3) Again there is a third view,   10
that even if all pleasures are goods, yet the best thing in the
world cannot be pleasure. (1) The reasons given for the
view that pleasure is not a good at all are (a) that every
pleasure is a perceptible process to a natural state, and that
no process is of the same kind as its end, e. g. no process
of building of the same kind as a house. (b) A temperate   15
man avoids pleasures. (c) A man of practical wisdom pursues what is free from pain, not what is pleasant. (d) The
pleasures are a hindrance to thought, and the more so the
more one delights in them, e. g. in sexual pleasure; for no
one could think of anything while absorbed in this. (e)
There is no art of pleasure; but every good is the product of
some art. (f) Children and the brutes pursue pleasures. (2)
The reasons for the view that not all pleasures are good are   20
that (a) there are pleasures that are actually base and objects
of reproach, and (b) there are harmful pleasures; for some
pleasant things are unhealthy. (3) The reason for the view
that the best thing in the world is not pleasure is that pleasure is not an end but a process.

12 These are pretty much the things that are said.
That it does not follow from these grounds that   25
pleasure is not a good, or even the chief good, is
plain from the following considerations. (A)[38] (a) First, since
that which is good may be so in either of two senses (one
thing good simply and another good for a particular person), natural constitutions and states of being, and therefore
also the corresponding movements and processes, will be
correspondingly divisible. Of those which are thought to be
bad some will be bad if taken without qualification but not

[38] (A) is the answer to (1a) and (3).

bad for a particular person, but worthy of his choice, and
30 some will not be worthy of choice even for a particular person, but only at a particular time and for a short period,
though not without qualification; while others are not even
pleasures, but seem to be so, viz. all those which involve
pain and whose end is curative, e. g. the processes that go
on in sick persons.

(b) Further, one kind of good being activity and another
being state, the processes that restore us to our natural state
35 are only incidentally pleasant; for that matter the activity at
work in the appetites for them is the activity of so much of
our state and nature as has remained unimpaired; for there
1153ᵃ are actually pleasures that involve *no* pain or appetite (e. g.
those of contemplation), the nature in such a case not being
defective at all. That the others are incidental is indicated
by the fact that men do not enjoy the same pleasant objects
when their nature is in its settled state as they do when it
is being replenished, but in the former case they enjoy the
things that are pleasant without qualification, in the latter
the contraries of these as well; for then they enjoy even
5 sharp and bitter things, none of which is pleasant either by
nature or without qualification The states they produce,
therefore, are not pleasures naturally or without qualification; for as pleasant things differ, so do the pleasures arising
from them.

(c) Again, it is not necessary that there should be something else better than pleasure, as some say the end is better
10 than the process; for pleasures are not processes nor do they
all involve process—they are activities and ends; nor do
they arise when we are becoming something, but when we
are exercising some faculty; and not all pleasures have an
end different from themselves, but only the pleasures of
persons who are being led to the perfecting of their nature.
This is why it is not right to say that pleasure is percepti-
15 ble process, but it should rather be called activity of the

natural state, and instead of 'perceptible' 'unimpeded'. It is thought by *some* people to be process just because they think it is in the strict sense *good*; for they think that activity is process, which it is not.

(B)[39] The view that pleasures are bad because some pleasant things are unhealthy is like saying that healthy things are bad because some healthy things are bad for money-making; both are bad in the respect mentioned, but they are not *bad* for *that* reason—indeed, thinking itself is sometimes injurious to health.

Neither practical wisdom nor any state of being is impeded by the pleasure arising from it; it is foreign pleasures that impede, for the pleasures arising from thinking and learning will make us think and learn all the more.

(C)[40] The fact that no pleasure is the product of any art arises naturally enough; there is no art of any other activity either, but only of the corresponding faculty; though for that matter the arts of the perfumer and the cook are thought to be arts of pleasure.

(D)[41]The arguments based on the grounds that the temperate man avoids pleasure and that the man of practical wisdom pursues the painless life, and that children and the brutes pursue pleasure, are all refuted by the same consideration. We have pointed out[42] in what sense pleasures are good without qualification and in what sense some are not good; now both the brutes and children pursue pleasures of the latter kind (and the man of practical wisdom pursues tranquil freedom from that kind), viz. those which imply appetite and pain, i. e. the bodily pleasures (for it is these

[39] Answer to (2 *b*) and (1 *d*).

[40] Answer to (1 *e*).

[41] Answer to (1 *b*), (1 *c*), (1 *f*).

[42] 1152b 26–1153a 7.

that are of this nature) and the excesses of them, in respect
of which the self-indulgent man is self-indulgent. This is
35 why the temperate man avoids these pleasures; for even he
has pleasures of his own.

1153ᵇ **13** But further (E) it is agreed that pain is bad and
to be avoided; for some pain is without qualification bad, and other pain is bad because it is in
some respect an impediment to us. Now the contrary of that
which is to be avoided, *qua* something to be avoided and
bad, is good. Pleasure, then, is necessarily a good. For the
answer of Speusippus, that pleasure is contrary both to pain
5 and to good, as the greater is contrary both to the less and
to the equal, is not successful; since he would not say that
pleasure is essentially just a species of evil.

And (F)[43] if certain pleasures are bad, that does not prevent the chief good from being some pleasure, just as the
chief good may be some form of knowledge though certain
kinds of knowledge are bad. Perhaps it is even necessary, if
10 each disposition has unimpeded activities, that, whether the
activity (if unimpeded) of all our dispositions or that of some
one of them is happiness, this should be the thing most worthy of our choice; and this activity is pleasure. Thus the
chief good would be some pleasure, though most pleasures
might perhaps be bad without qualification. And for this
reason all men think that the happy life is pleasant and
weave pleasure into their ideal of happiness—and reasonably
15 too; for no activity is perfect when it is impeded, and happiness is a perfect thing, this is why the happy man needs
the goods of the body and external goods, i. e. those of fortune, viz. in order that he may not be impeded in these
ways. Those who say that the victim on the rack or the man
who falls into great misfortunes is happy if he is good, are,

[43] Answer to (2 *a*).

whether they mean to or not, talking nonsense. Now because 20
we need fortune as well as other things, some people think
good fortune the same thing as happiness; but it is not that,
for even good fortune itself when in excess is an impediment, and perhaps should then be no longer called good
fortune; for its limit is fixed by reference to happiness.

And indeed the fact that all things, both brutes and 25
men, pursue pleasure is an indication of its being somehow
the chief good:

No voice is wholly lost that many peoples . . .

But since no one nature or state either is or is thought the
best for all, neither do all pursue the same pleasure; yet all 30
pursue pleasure. And perhaps they actually pursue not the
pleasure they think they pursue nor that which they would
say they pursue, but the same pleasure; for all things have
by nature something divine in them. But the bodily pleasures
have appropriated the name both because we oftenest steer
our course for them and because all men share in them; thus
because they alone are familiar, men think there are no others 35

It is evident also that if pleasure, i. e. the activity of our 1154ᵃ
faculties, is not a good, it will not be the case that the happy
man lives a pleasant life; for to what end should he need
pleasure, if it is not a good but the happy man may even
live a painful life? For pain is neither an evil nor a good, if 5
pleasure is not; why then should he avoid it? Therefore, too,
the life of the good man will not be pleasanter than that of
any one else, if his activities are not more pleasant.

14
(G)⁴⁴ With regard to the bodily pleasures, those
who say that *some* pleasures are very much to be
chosen, viz. the noble pleasures, but not the 10

⁴⁴ Answer to (2a).

bodily pleasures, i. e. those with which the self-indulgent man is concerned, must consider why, then, the contrary things are bad. For the contrary of bad is good. Are the necessary pleasures good in the sense in which even that which is not bad is good? Or are they good up to a point? Is it that where you have states and processes of which there cannot be too much, there cannot be too much of the corresponding pleasure, and that where there can be too much
15 of the one there can be too much of the other also? Now there can be too much of bodily goods, and the bad man is bad by virtue of pursuing the excess, not by virtue of pursuing the necessary pleasures (for *all* men enjoy in some way or other both dainty foods and wines and sexual intercourse, but not all men do so as they ought). The contrary is the case with pain; for he does not avoid the excess of it,
20 he avoids it altogether; and this is peculiar to him, for the alternative to excess of pleasure is not pain, except to the man who pursues this excess.

Since we should state not only the truth, but also the cause of error—for this contributes towards producing conviction, since when a reasonable explanation is given of why the false view appears true, this tends to produce belief in
25 the true view—therefore we must state why the bodily pleasures appear the more worthy of choice. (*a*) Firstly, then, it is because they expel pain; owing to the excesses of pain that men experience, they pursue excessive and in general bodily pleasure as being a cure for the pain. Now curative
30 agencies produce intense feeling—which is the reason why they are pursued—because they show up against the contrary pain. (Indeed pleasure is thought not to be good for these two reasons, as has been said,[45] viz. that (*a*) some of them are activities belonging to a bad nature—either congenital, as in the case of a brute, or due to habit, i. e. those

[45] 1152^b 26–33.

of bad men; while (β) others are meant to cure a defective
nature, and it is better to be in a healthy state than to be
getting into it, but these arise during the process of being 1154ᵇ
made perfect and are therefore only incidentally good.) (b)
Further, they are pursued because of their violence by those
who cannot enjoy other pleasures. (At all events they go out
of their way to manufacture thirsts somehow for themselves.
When these are harmless, the practice is irreproachable;
when they are hurtful, it is bad.) For they have nothing else
to enjoy, and, besides, a neutral state is painful to many 5
people because of their nature. For the animal nature is
always in travail, as the students of natural science also testify, saying that sight and hearing are painful; but we have
become used to this, as they maintain. Similarly, while, in
youth, people are, owing to the growth that is going on, in a
situation like that of drunken men, and youth is pleasant,⁴⁶
on the other hand people of excitable nature⁴⁷ always need 10
relief; for even their body is ever in torment owing to its
special composition, and they are always under the influence of violent desire; but pain is driven out both by the
contrary pleasure, and by any chance pleasure if it be
strong; and for these reasons they become self-indulgent
and bad. But the pleasures that do not involve pains do not 15
admit of excess; and these are among the things pleasant by
nature and not incidentally. By things pleasant incidentally
I mean those that act as cures (for because as a result people
are cured, through some action of the part that remains
healthy, for this reason the process is thought pleasant); by
things naturally pleasant I mean those that stimulate the
action of the healthy nature.

There is no one thing that is always pleasant, because 20

---

⁴⁶ i. e. the growth or replenishment that is going on produces exhilaration
and pleasure.

⁴⁷ Lit., melancholic people, those characterized by an excess of black bile.

our nature is not simple but there is another element in us as well, inasmuch as we are perishable creatures, so that if the one element does something, this is unnatural to the other nature, and when the two elements are evenly balanced, what is done seems neither painful nor pleasant; for
25 if the nature of anything were simple, the same action would always be most pleasant to it. This is why God always enjoys a single and simple pleasure; for there is not only an activity of movement but an activity of immobility, and pleasure is found more in rest than in movement. But 'change in all things is sweet', as the poet says, because of some vice; for as it is the vicious man that is changeable, so
30 the nature that needs change is vicious; for it is not simple nor good.

We have now discussed continence and incontinence, and pleasure and pain, both what each is and in what sense some of them are good and others bad; it remains to speak of friendship.

BOOK VIII

1155ª 1 After what we have said, a discussion of friendship would naturally follow, since it is a virtue or
5 implies virtue, and is besides most necessary with a view to living. For without friends no one would choose to live, though he had all other goods; even rich men and those in possession of office and of dominating power are thought to need friends most of all; for what is the use of such prosperity without the opportunity of beneficence, which is exercised chiefly and in its most laudable form towards
10 friends? Or how can prosperity be guarded and preserved without friends? The greater it is, the more exposed is it to risk. And in poverty and in other misfortunes men think

friends are the only refuge. It helps the young, too, to keep
from error; it aids older people by ministering to their needs
and supplementing the activities that are failing from weakness; those in the prime of life it stimulates to noble 15
actions—'two going together'[1]—for with friends men are
more able both to think and to act. Again, parent seems by
nature to feel it for offspring and offspring for parent, not
only among men but among birds and among most animals;
it is felt mutually by members of the same race, and espe- 20
cially by men, whence we praise lovers of their fellowmen.
We may see even in our travels how near and dear every
man is to every other. Friendship seems too to hold states
together, and lawgivers to care more for it than for justice;
for unanimity seems to be something like friendship, and
this they aim at most of all, and expel faction as their worst
enemy; and when men are friends they have no need of jus- 25
tice, while when they are just they need friendship as well,
and the truest form of justice is thought to be a friendly
quality.

But it is not only necessary but also noble; for we praise
those who love their friends, and it is thought to be a fine
thing to have many friends; and again we think it is the 30
same people that are good men and are friends.

Not a few things about friendship are matters of debate.
Some define it as a kind of likeness and say like people are
friends, whence come the sayings 'like to like', 'birds of a
feather flock together', and so on; others on the contrary 35
say 'two of a trade never agree'. On this very question they 1155b
inquire for deeper and more physical causes, Euripides saying that 'parched earth loves the rain, and stately heaven
when filled with rain loves to fall to earth', and Heraclitus
that 'it is what opposes that helps' and 'from different tones
comes the fairest tune' and 'all things are produced through 5

[1] *Il.* x. 224.

strife'; while Empedocles, as well as others, expresses the opposite view that like aims at like. The physical problems we may leave alone (for they do not belong to the present inquiry); let us examine those which are human and involve character and feeling, e. g. whether friendship can arise
10 between any two people or people cannot be friends if they are wicked, and whether there is one species of friendship or more than one. Those who think there is only one because it admits of degrees have relied on an inadequate indication; for even things different in species admit of degree. We
15 have discussed this matter previously.

2 The kinds of friendship may perhaps be cleared up if we first come to know the object of love. For not everything seems to be loved but only the lovable, and this is good, pleasant, or useful; but it would seem to be that by which some good or pleasure is produced that is useful, so that it is the good and the useful that are lovable
20 as ends. Do men love, then, *the* good, or what is good for *them*? These sometimes clash. So too with regard to the pleasant. Now it is thought that each loves what is good for himself, and that the good is without qualification lovable, and what is good for each man is lovable for him; but each
25 man loves not what is good for him but what seems good. This however will make no difference; we shall just have to say that this is 'that which seems lovable'. Now there are three grounds on which people love; of the love of lifeless objects we do not use the word 'friendship'; for it is not mutual love, nor is there a wishing of good to the other (for
30 it would surely be ridiculous to wish wine well; if one wishes anything for it, it is that it may keep, so that one may have it oneself); but to a friend we say we ought to wish what is good for his sake. But to those who thus wish good we ascribe only goodwill, if the wish is not recipro-cated; goodwill when it *is* reciprocal being friendship. Or

must we add 'when it is recognized'? For many people have 35
goodwill to those whom they have not seen but judge to be 1156ᵃ
good or useful; and one of these might return this feeling.
These people seem to bear goodwill to each other; but how
could one call them friends when they do not know their
mutual feelings? To be friends, then, they must be mutually
recognized as bearing goodwill and wishing well to each 5
other for one of the aforesaid reasons.

3 Now these reasons differ from each other in kind;
so, therefore, do the corresponding forms of love
and friendship. There are therefore three kinds of
friendship, equal in number to the things that are lovable;
for with respect to each there is a mutual and recognized
love, and those who love each other wish well to each other
in that respect in which they love one another. Now those 10
who love each other for their utility do not love each other
for themselves but in virtue of some good which they get
from each other. So too with those who love for the sake of
pleasure; it is not for their character that men love ready-
witted people, but because they find them pleasant. Therefore
those who love for the sake of utility love for the sake of 15
what is good for *themselves*, and those who love for the sake
of pleasure do so for the sake of what is pleasant to *themselves*, and not in so far as the other is the person loved but
in so far as he is useful or pleasant. And thus these friendships are only incidental; for it is not as being the man he
is that the loved person is loved, but as providing some
good or pleasure. Such friendships, then, are easily dis- 20
solved, if the parties do not remain like themselves; for if
the one party is no longer pleasant or useful the other ceases
to love him.

Now the useful is not permanent but is always changing. Thus when the motive of the friendship is done away,
the friendship is dissolved, inasmuch as it existed only for

25 the ends in question. This kind of friendship seems to exist
chiefly between old people (for at that age people pursue
not the pleasant but the useful) and, of those who are in
their prime or young, between those who pursue utility.
And such people do not live much with each other either;
for sometimes they do not even find each other pleasant;
therefore they do not need such companionship unless they
are useful to each other; for they are pleasant to each other
only in so far as they rouse in each other hopes of some-
30 thing good to come. Among such friendships people also
class the friendship of host and guest. On the other hand
the friendship of young people seems to aim at pleasure; for
they live under the guidance of emotion, and pursue above
all what is pleasant to themselves and what is immediately
before them; but with increasing age their pleasures become
different. This is why they quickly become friends and
35 quickly cease to be so; their friendship changes with the
object that is found pleasant, and such pleasure alters
quickly.

1156^b   Young people are amorous too; for the greater part of
the friendship of love depends on emotion and aims at pleasure; this is why they fall in love and quickly fall out of
love, changing often within a single day. But these people
do wish to spend their days and lives together; for it is thus
5 that they attain the purpose of their friendship.

Perfect friendship is the friendship of men who are
good, and alike in virtue; for these wish well alike to each
other qua good, and they are good in themselves. Now those
who wish well to their friends for their sake are most truly
10 friends; for they do this by reason of their own nature and
not incidentally; therefore their friendship lasts as long as
they are good—and goodness is an enduring thing. And
each is good without qualification and to his friend, for the
good are both good without qualification and useful to each
15 other. So too they are pleasant; for the good are pleasant

both without qualification and to each other, since to each
his own activities and others like them are pleasurable, and
the actions of the good *are* the same or like. And such a
friendship is as might be expected permanent, since there
meet in it all the qualities that friends should have. For all
friendship is for the sake of good or of pleasure—good or
pleasure either in the abstract or such as will be enjoyed by 20
him who has the friendly feeling—and is based on a certain
resemblance; and to a friendship of good men all the qualities we have named belong in virtue of the nature of the
friends themselves; for in the case of this kind of friendship
the other qualities also[2] are alike in both friends, and that
which is good without qualification is also without qualification pleasant, and these are the most lovable qualities.
Love and friendship therefore are found most and in their
best form between such men.

But it is natural that such friendships should be infre-
quent; for such men are rare. Further, such friendship
requires time and familiarity; as the proverb says, men can- 25
not know each other till they have 'eaten salt together'; nor
can they admit each other to friendship or be friends till
each has been found lovable and been trusted by each.
Those who quickly show the marks of friendship to each
other wish to be friends, but are not friends unless they 30
both are lovable and know the fact; for a wish for friendship may arise quickly, but friendship does not.

4 This kind of friendship, then, is perfect both in
respect of duration and in all other respects, and in
it each gets from each in all respects the same as, or
something like what, he gives; which is what ought to hap- 35
pen between friends. Friendship for the sake of pleasure 1157ª

[2] i. e. absolute pleasantness, relative goodness, and relative pleasantness,
as well as absolute goodness.

bears a resemblance to this kind; for good people *too* are pleasant to each other. So too does friendship for the sake of utility, for the good are also useful to each other. Among men of these inferior sorts too, friendships are most perma-
5 nent when the friends get the same thing from each other (e. g. pleasure), and not only that but also from the same source, as happens between ready-witted people, not as happens between lover and beloved. For these do not take pleasure in the same things, but the one in seeing the beloved and the other in receiving attentions from his lover; and when the bloom of youth is passing the friendship sometimes passes too (for the one finds no pleasure in the
10 sight of the other, and the other gets no attentions from the first); but many lovers on the other hand are constant, if familiarity has led them to love each other's characters, these being alike. But those who exchange not pleasure but utility in their amour are both less truly friends and less
15 constant. Those who are friends for the sake of utility part when the advantage is at an end; for they were lovers not of each other but of profit.

For the sake of pleasure or utility, then, even bad men may be friends of each other, or good men of bad, or one who is neither good nor bad may be a friend to any sort of person, but for their own sake clearly only good men can be friends; for bad men do not delight in each other unless some advantage come of the relation.

20 The friendship of the good too and this alone is proof against slander; for it is not easy to trust any one's talk about a man who has long been tested by oneself; and it is among good men that trust and the feeling that 'he would never wrong me' and all the other things that are demanded in true friendship are found. In the other kinds of friendship, however, there is nothing to prevent these evils arising.

25 For men apply the name of friends even to those whose motive is utility, in which sense states are said to be friendly

(for the alliances of states seem to aim at advantage), and
to those who love each other for the sake of pleasure, in
which sense children are called friends. Therefore we too
ought perhaps to call such people friends, and say that there   30
are several kinds of friendship—firstly and in the proper
sense that of good men *qua* good, and by analogy the other
kinds; for it is in virtue of something good and something
akin to what is found in true friendship that they are friends,
since even the pleasant is good for the lovers of pleasure. But
these two kinds of friendship are not often united, nor do
the same people become friends for the sake of utility and of
pleasure; for things that are only incidentally connected are   35
not often coupled together.

Friendship being divided into these kinds, bad men will
be friends for the sake of pleasure or of utility, being in this   1157^b
respect like each other, but good men will be friends for
their own sake, i. e. in virtue of their goodness. These, then,
are friends without qualification; the others are friends incidentally and through a resemblance to these.

5   As in regard to the virtues some men are called
good in respect of a state of character, others in   5
respect of an activity, so too in the case of friendship; for those who live together delight in each other and
confer benefits on each other, but those who are asleep or
locally separated are not performing, but are disposed to
perform, the activities of friendship; distance does not break
off the friendship absolutely, but only the activity of it. But   10
if the absence is lasting, it seems actually to make men forget their friendship; hence the saying 'out of sight, out of
mind'. Neither old people nor sour people seem to make
friends easily; for there is little that is pleasant in them, and
no one can spend his days with one whose company is   15
painful, or not pleasant, since nature seems above all to
avoid the painful and to aim at the pleasant. Those, how-

ever, who approve of each other but do not live together seem to be well-disposed rather than actual friends. For there is nothing so characteristic of friends as living together 20 (since while it is people who are in need that desire benefits, even those who are supremely happy desire to spend their days together; for solitude suits such people least of all); but people cannot live together if they are not pleasant and do not enjoy the same things, as friends who are companions seem to do.

The truest friendship, then, is that of the good, as we 25 have frequently said;[3] for that which is without qualification good or pleasant seems to be lovable and desirable, and for each person that which is good or pleasant to him; and the good man is lovable and desirable to the good man for both these reasons. Now it looks as if love were a feeling, friend- 30 ship a state of character; for love may be felt just as much towards lifeless things, but mutual love involves choice and choice springs from a state of character; and men wish well to those whom they love, for their sake, not as a result of feeling but as a result of a state of character. And in loving a friend men love what is good for themselves; for the good man in becoming a friend becomes a good to his friend. 35 Each, then, both loves what is good for himself, and makes an equal return in goodwill and in pleasantness; for friendship is said to be equality, and both of these are found most in the friendship of the good.

1158ª 6 Between sour and elderly people friendship arises less readily, inasmuch as they are less good-tempered and enjoy companionship less; for these are thought to be the greatest marks of friendship and most 5 productive of it. This is why, while young men become friends quickly, old men do not; it is because men do not

[3] 1156ᵇ 7, 23, 33, 1157ª 30, ᵇ4.

become friends with those in whom they do not delight; and similarly sour people do not quickly make friends either. But such men may bear goodwill to each other; for they wish one another well and aid one another in need; but they are hardly *friends* because they do not spend their days together nor delight in each other, and these are thought the greatest marks of friendship.

One cannot be a friend to many people in the sense of having friendship of the perfect type with them, just as one cannot be in love with many people at once (for love is a sort of excess of feeling, and it is the nature of such only to be felt towards one person); and it is not easy for many people at the same time to please the same person very greatly, or perhaps even to be good in his eyes. One must, too, acquire some experience of the other person and become familiar with him, and that is very hard. But with a view to utility or pleasure it is possible that many people should please one; for many people are useful or pleasant, and these services take little time.

Of these two kinds that which is for the sake of pleasure is the more like friendship, when both parties get the same things from each other and delight in each other or in the same things, as in the friendships of the young; for generosity is more found in such friendships. Friendship based on utility is for the commercially minded. People who are supremely happy, too, have no need of useful friends, but do need pleasant friends: for they wish to live with *some one* and, though they can endure for a short time what is painful, no one could put up with it continuously, nor even with the Good itself if it were painful to him; this is why they look out for friends who are pleasant. Perhaps they should look out for friends who, being pleasant, are also good, and good for them, too; for so they will have all the characteristics that friends should have.

People in positions of authority seem to have friends

who fall into distinct classes; some people are useful to them and others are pleasant, but the same people are rarely both; for they seek neither those whose pleasantness is accompa-
30 nied by virtue nor those whose utility is with a view to noble objects, but in their desire for pleasure they seek for ready-witted people, and their other friends they choose as being clever at doing what they are told, and these charac- teristics are rarely combined. Now we have said that the *good* man *is* at the same time pleasant and useful;[4] but such a man does not become the friend of one who surpasses him in station, unless he is surpassed also in virtue; if this is not
35 so, he does not establish equality by being proportionally exceeded in both respects. But people who surpass him in both respects are not so easy to find.

However that may be, the aforesaid friendships involve
1158b equality; for the friends get the same things from one another and wish the same things for one another, or exchange one thing for another, e. g. pleasure for utility; we have said,[5] however, that they are both less truly friendships and less permanent. But it is from their likeness and their
5 unlikeness to the same thing that they are thought both to be and not to be friendships. It is by their likeness to the friendship of virtue that they seem to be friendships (for one of them involves pleasure and the other utility, and these characteristics belong to the friendship of virtue as well); while it is because the friendship of virtue is proof against slander and permanent, while these quickly change (besides differing from the former in many other respects),
10 that they appear *not* to be friendships; i. e. it is because of their unlikeness to the friendship of virtue.

[4] 1156b 13–15, 1157a 1–3.

[5] 1156a 16–24, 1157a 20–33.

7 But there is another kind of friendship, viz. that which involves an inequality between the parties, e. g. that of father to son and in general of elder to younger, that of man to wife and in general that of ruler to subject. And these friendships differ also from each other; 15 for it is not the same that exists between parents and children and between rulers and subjects, nor is even that of father to son the same as that of son to father, nor that of husband to wife the same as that of wife to husband. For the virtue and the function of each of these is different, and so are the reasons for which they love; the love and the 20 friendship are therefore different also. Each party, then, neither gets the same from the other, nor ought to seek it; but when children render to parents what they ought to render to those who brought them into the world, and parents render what they should to their children, the friendship of such persons will be abiding and excellent. In all friendships implying inequality the love also should be proportional, i. e. 25 the better should be more loved than he loves, and so should the more useful, and similarly in each of the other cases; for when the love is in proportion to the merit of the parties, then in a sense arises equality, which is certainly held to be characteristic of friendship.

But equality does not seem to take the same form in acts justice and in friendship; for in acts of justice what is 30 equal in the primary sense is that which is in proportion to merit, while quantitative equality is secondary, but in friendship quantitative equality is primary and proportion to merit secondary. This becomes clear if there is a great interval in respect of virtue or vice or wealth or anything else between the parties; for then they are no longer friends, and do not even expect to be so. And this is most manifest 35 in the case of the gods; for they surpass us most decisively in all good things. But it is clear also in the case of kings; 1159^a for with them, too, men who are much their inferiors do not

expect to be friends; nor do men of no account expect to be
friends with the best or wisest men. In such cases it is not
possible to define exactly up to what point friends can
5 remain friends; for much can be taken away and friendship
remain, but when one party is removed to a great distance,
as God is, the possibility of friendship ceases. This is in fact
the origin of the question whether friends really wish for
their friends the greatest goods, e. g. that of being gods;
since in that case their friends will no longer be friends to
them, and therefore will not be good things for them (for
friends *are* good things). The answer is that if we were
right in saying that friend wishes good to friend for his
10 sake,[6] his friend must remain the sort of being he is, whatever that may be; therefore it is for him only so long as he
remains a man that he will wish the greatest goods. But perhaps not *all* the greatest goods; for it is for himself most of
all that each man wishes what is good.

8 Most people seem, owing to ambition, to wish to
be loved rather than to love; which is why most
men love flattery; for the flatterer is a friend in an
inferior position, or pretends to be such and to love more
15 than he is loved; and being loved seems to be akin to being
honoured, and this is what most people aim at. But it seems
to be not for its own sake that people choose honour, but
incidentally. For most people enjoy being honoured by those
in positions of authority because of their hopes (for they
20 think that if they want anything they will get it from them;
and therefore they delight in honour as a token of favour to
come); while those who desire honour from good men, and
men who know, are aiming at confirming their own opinion
of themselves; they delight in honour, therefore, because
they believe in their own goodness on the strength of the

[6] 1155[b] 31.

judgement of those who speak about them. In being loved, on the other hand, people delight for its own sake; whence it would seem to be better than being honoured, and friend- 25 ship to be desirable in itself. But it seems to lie in loving rather than in being loved, as is indicated by the delight mothers take in loving; for some mothers hand over their children to be brought up, and so long as they know their fate they love them and do not seek to be loved in return 30 (if they cannot have both), but seem to be satisfied if they see them prospering; and they themselves love their children even if these owing to their ignorance give them nothing of a mother's due. Now since friendship depends more on loving, and it is those who love their friends that are praised, loving seems to be the characteristic virtue of friends, so that it is only those in whom this is found in due 35 measure that are lasting friends, and only their friendship that endures.

It is in this way more than any other that even unequals can be friends; they can be equalized. Now equality and 1159b likeness are friendship, and especially the likeness of those who are like in virtue; for being steadfast in themselves they hold fast to each other, and neither ask nor give base ser- 5 vices, but (one may say) even prevent them; for it is characteristic of good men neither to go wrong themselves nor to let their friends do so. But wicked men have no steadfastness (for they do not remain even like to themselves), but become friends for a short time because they delight in each other's wickedness. Friends who are useful 10 or pleasant last longer; i. e. as long as they provide each other with enjoyments or advantages. Friendship for utility's sake seems to be that which most easily exists between contraries, e. g. between poor and rich, between ignorant and learned; for what a man actually lacks he aims at, and one gives something else in return. But under this head, too, 15 we might bring lover and beloved, beautiful and ugly. This

is why lovers sometimes seem ridiculous, when they demand to be loved as they love; if they are equally lovable their claim can perhaps be justified, but when they have nothing lovable about them it is ridiculous. Perhaps, how-
20 ever, contrary does not even aim at contrary by its own nature, but only incidentally, the desire being for what is intermediate; for that is what is good, e. g. it is good for the dry not to become wet[7] but to come to the intermediate state, and similarly with the hot and in all other cases. These subjects we may dismiss; for they are indeed some-what foreign to our inquiry.

25   9   Friendship and justice seem, as we have said at the outset of our discussion,[8] to be concerned with the same objects and exhibited between the same persons. For in every community there is thought to be some form of justice, and friendship too; at least men address as friends their fellow-voyagers and fellow-soldiers, and so too those associated with them in any other kind of community. And the extent of their association is the extent of their friend-
30 ship, as it is the extent to which justice exists between them. And the proverb 'what friends have is common property' expresses the truth; for friendship depends on community. Now brothers and comrades have all things in common, but the others to whom we have referred have definite things in common—some more things, others fewer; for of friend-
35 ships, too, some are more and others less truly friendships.
1160a And the claims of justice differ too; the duties of parents to children and those of brothers to each other are not the same nor those of comrades and those of fellow-citizens, and so, too, with the other kinds of friendship. There is a difference, therefore, also between the acts that are unjust

[7] Cf. 1155b 3.

[8] 1155a 22–28.

towards each of these classes of associates, and the injustice
increases by being exhibited towards those who are friends
in a fuller sense; e. g. it is a more terrible thing to defraud
a comrade than a fellow-citizen, more terrible not to help a   5
brother than a stranger, and more terrible to wound a father
than any one else. And the demands of justice also seem to
increase with the intensity of the friendship, which implies
that friendship and justice exist between the same persons
and have an equal extension.

Now all forms of community are like parts of the political community; for men journey together with a view to
some particular advantage, and to provide something that   10
they need for the purposes of life; and it is for the sake of
advantage that the political community too seems both to
have come together originally and to endure, for this is what
legislators aim at, and they call just that which is to the
common advantage. Now the other communities aim at
advantage bit by bit, e. g. sailors at what is advantageous on
a voyage with a view to making money or something of the   15
kind, fellow-soldiers at what is advantageous in war, whether
it is wealth or victory or the taking of a city that they seek,
and members of tribes and demes act similarly [Some communities seem to arise for the sake of pleasure, viz. religious
guilds and social clubs; for these exist respectively for the
sake of offering sacrifice and of companionship. But all these   20
seem to fall under the political community; for it aims not
at present advantage but at what is advantageous for life as a
whole], offering sacrifices and arranging gatherings for the
purpose, and assigning honours to the gods, and providing
pleasant relaxations for themselves. For the ancient sacrifices
and gatherings seem to take place after the harvest as a sort   25
of firstfruits, because it was at these seasons that people had
most leisure. All the communities, then, seem to be parts of
the political community; and the particular kinds of friendship will correspond to the particular kinds of community.   30

10 There are three kinds of constitution, and an equal number of deviation-forms—perversions, as it were, of them. The constitutions are monarchy, aristocracy, and thirdly that which is based on a property qualification, which it seems appropriate to call timocratic, though most people are wont to call it polity.

35 The best of these is monarchy, the worst timocracy. The deviation from monarchy is tyranny; for both are forms of

1160^b one-man rule, but there is the greatest difference between them; the tyrant looks to his own advantage, the king to that of his subjects. For a man is not a king unless he is sufficient to himself and excels his subjects in all good things; and such a man needs nothing further; therefore he will not

5 look to his own interests but to those of his subjects; for a king who is not like that would be a mere titular king. Now tyranny is the very contrary of this; the tyrant pursues his own good. And it is clearer in the case of tyranny that it is the worst deviation-form;[9] but it is the contrary of the best that is worst.[10] Monarchy passes over into tyranny; for

10 tyranny is the evil form of one-man rule and the bad king becomes a tyrant. Aristocracy passes over into oligarchy by the badness of the rulers, who distribute contrary to equity what belongs to the city—all or most of the good things to

15 themselves, and office always to the same people, paying most regard to wealth; thus the rulers are few and are bad men instead of the most worthy. Timocracy passes over into democracy; for these are coterminous, since it is the ideal even of timocracy to be the rule of the majority, and all who have the property qualification count as equal. Democracy

20 is the least bad of the deviations; for in its case the form of constitution is but a slight deviation. These then are the

---

[9] Than it is that monarchy is the best genuine form (^a 35).

[10] Therefore monarchy must be the best.

changes to which constitutions are most subject; for these are the smallest and easiest transitions.

One may find resemblances to the constitutions and, as it were, patterns of them even in households. For the association of a father with his sons bears the form of monarchy, 25 since the father cares for his children; and this is why Homer calls Zeus 'father'; it is the ideal of monarchy to be paternal rule. But among the Persians the rule of the father is tyrannical; they use their sons as slaves. Tyrannical too is the rule of a master over slaves; for it is the advantage of the master that is brought about in it. Now this seems to 30 be a correct form of government, but the Persian type is perverted; for the modes of rule appropriate to different relations are diverse. The association of man and wife seems to be aristocratic; for the man rules in accordance with his worth, and in those matters in which a man should rule, but the matters that befit a woman he hands over to her. If the 35 man rules in everything the relation passes over into oligarchy; for in doing so he is not acting in accordance with their respective worth, and not ruling in virtue of his superiority. Sometimes, however, women rule, because they are 1161ᵃ heiresses; so their rule is not in virtue of excellence but due to wealth and power, as in oligarchies. The association of brothers is like timocracy; for they are equal, except in so 5 far as they differ in age; hence if they differ *much* in age, the friendship is no longer of the fraternal type. Democracy is found chiefly in masterless dwellings (for here every one is on an equality), and in those in which the ruler is weak and every one has license to do as he pleases.

11 Each of the constitutions may be seen to involve 10 friendship just in so far as it involves justice. The friendship between a king and his subjects depends on an excess of benefits conferred; for he confers

benefits on his subjects if being a good man he cares for
them with a view to their well-being, as a shepherd does for
15 his sheep (whence Homer called Agamemnon 'shepherd of
the peoples'). Such too is the friendship of a father, though
this exceeds the other in the greatness of the benefits conferred; for he is responsible for the existence of his children,
which is thought the greatest good, and for their nurture
and upbringing. These things are ascribed to ancestors as
well. Further, by nature a father tends to rule over his sons,
ancestors over descendants, a king over his subjects. These
friendships imply superiority of one party over the other,
20 which is why ancestors are honoured. The justice therefore
that exists between persons so related is not the same on
both sides but is in every case proportioned to merit; for
that is true of the friendship as well. The friendship of man
and wife, again, is the same that is found in an aristocracy;
for it is in accordance with virtue—the better gets more of
what is good, and each gets what befits him; and so, too,
with the justice in these relations. The friendship of brothers is like that of comrades; for they are equal and of like
25 age, and such persons are for the most part like in their feelings and their character. Like this, too, is the friendship
appropriate to timocratic government; for in such a constitution the ideal is for the citizens to be equal and fair;
therefore rule is taken in turn, and on equal terms; and the
friendship appropriate here will correspond.

But in the deviation-forms, as justice hardly exists, so
30 too does friendship. It exists least in the worst form; in
tyranny there is little or no friendship. For where there is
nothing common to ruler and ruled, there is not friendship
either, since there is not justice; e. g. between craftsman and
35 tool, soul and body, master and slave; the latter in each case
1161ᵇ is benefited by that which uses it, but there is no friendship
nor justice towards lifeless things. But neither is there friendship towards a horse or an ox, nor to a slave *qua* slave. For

there is nothing common to the two parties; the slave is a living tool and the tool a lifeless slave. *Qua* slave then, one cannot be friends with him. But *qua* man one can; for there seems to be some justice between any man and any other who can share in a system of law or be a party to an agreement; therefore there can also be friendship with him in so far as he is a man. Therefore while in tyrannies friendship and justice hardly exist, in democracies they exist more fully; for where the citizens are equal they have much in common.

12 Every form of friendship, then, involves association, as has been said.[11] One might, however, mark off from the rest both the friendship of kindred and that of comrades. Those of fellow-citizens, fellow-tribesmen, fellow voyagers, and the like are more like mere friendships of association; for they seem to rest on a sort of compact. With them we might class the friendship of host and guest.

The friendship of kinsmen itself, while it seems to be of many kinds, appears to depend in every case on parental friendship; for parents love their children as being a part of themselves, and children their parents as being something originating from them. Now (1) parents know their offspring better than their children know that they are their children, and (2) the originator feels his offspring to be his own more than the offspring do their begetter; for the product belongs to the producer (e. g. a tooth or hair or anything else to him whose it is), but the producer does not belong to the product, or belongs in a less degree. And (3) the length of time produces the same result; parents love their children as soon as these are born, but children love their parents only after time has elapsed and they have acquired understanding or the power of discrimination by the senses. From

11 1159ᵇ 29–32.

these considerations it is also plain why mothers love more
than fathers do. Parents, then, love their children as themselves (for their issue are by virtue of their separate
existence a sort of other selves), while children love their
parents as being born of them, and brothers love each other
30 as being born of the same parents; for their identity with
them makes them identical with each other (which is the
reason why people talk of 'the same blood', 'the same stock',
and so on). They are, therefore, in a sense the same thing,
though in separate individuals. Two things that contribute
greatly to friendship are a common upbringing and similar-
35 ity of age; for two of an age take to each other', and people
brought up together tend to be comrades; whence the
1162ᵃ friendship of brothers is akin to that of comrades. And
cousins and other kinsmen are bound up together by derivation from brothers, viz. by being derived from the same
parents. They come to be closer together or farther apart by
virtue of the nearness or distance of the original ancestor.

The friendship of children to parents, and of men to
5 gods, is a relation to them as to something good and superior; for they have conferred the greatest benefits, since they
are the causes of their being and of their nourishment, and
of their education from their birth; and this kind of friendship possesses pleasantness and utility also, more than that
of strangers, inasmuch as their life is lived more in common. The friendship of brothers has the characteristics
10 found in that of comrades (and especially when these are
good), and in general between people who are like each
other, inasmuch as they belong more to each other and start
with a love for each other from their very birth, and inasmuch as those born of the same parents and brought up
together and similarly educated are more akin in character;
and the test of time has been applied most fully and con-
vincingly in their case.

Between other kinsmen friendly relations are found in

due proportion. Between man and wife friendship seems to 15
exist by nature; for man is naturally inclined to form cou-
ples even more than to form cities, inasmuch as the
household is earlier and more necessary than the city, and
reproduction is more common to man with the animals.
With the other animals the union extends only to this point,
but human beings live together not only for the sake of
reproduction but also for the various purposes of life; for 20
from the start the functions are divided, and those of man
and woman are different; so they help each other by throwing their peculiar gifts into the common stock. It is for these
reasons that both utility and pleasure seem to be found in 25
this kind of friendship. But this friendship may be based
also on virtue, if the parties are good; for each has its own
virtue and they will delight in the fact. And children seem
to be a bond of union (which is the reason why childless
people part more easily); for children are a good common
to both and what is common holds them together.

How man and wife and in general friend and friend
ought mutually to behave seems to be the same question as
how it is just for them to behave; for a man does not seem 30
to have the same duties to a friend, a stranger, a comrade,
and a schoolfellow.

13 There are three kinds of friendship, as we said
at the outset of our inquiry,[12] and in respect of
each some are friends on an equality and others 35
by virtue of a superiority (for not only can equally good
men become friends but 'a better man can make friends 1162^b
with a worse, and similarly in friendships of pleasure or
utility the friends may be equal or unequal in the benefits
they confer). This being so, equals must effect the required
equalization on a basis of equality in love and in all other

[12] 1156^a 7.

respects, while unequals must render what is in proportion
to their superiority or inferiority.

Complaints and reproaches arise either only or chiefly
5 in the friendship of utility, and this is only to be expected.
For those who are friends on the ground of virtue are anxious to do well by each other (since that is a mark of virtue
and of friendship), and between men who are emulating
each other in this there cannot be complaints or quarrels;
no one is offended by a man who loves him and does well
by him—if he is a person of nice feeling he takes his
10 revenge by doing well by the other. And the man who
excels the other in the services he renders will not complain
of his friend, since he gets what he aims at; for each man
desires what is good. Nor do complaints arise much even in
friendships of pleasure; for both get at the same time what
they desire, if they enjoy spending their time together; and
15 even a man who complained of another for *not* affording
him pleasure would seem ridiculous since it is in his power
not to spend his days with him.

But the friendship of utility is full of complaints; for as
they use each other for their own interests they always want
to get the better of the bargain, and think they have got less
than they should, and blame their partners because they do
20 not get all they 'want and deserve'; and those who do well
by others cannot help them as much as those whom they
benefit want.

Now it seems that, as justice is of two kinds, one
unwritten and the other legal, one kind of friendship of utility is moral and the other legal. And so complaints arise
most of all when men do not dissolve the relation in the
25 spirit of the same type of friendship in which they contracted it. The *legal* type is that which is on fixed terms; its
purely commercial variety is on the basis of immediate payment, while the more liberal variety allows time but
stipulates for a definite *quid pro quo*. In this variety the debt

is clear and not ambiguous, but in the postponement it contains an element of friendliness, and so some states do not 30
allow suits arising out of such agreements, but think men
who have bargained on a basis of credit ought to accept the
consequences. The *moral* type is not on fixed terms; it
makes a gift, or does whatever it does, as to a friend, but
one expects to receive as much or more, as having not given
but lent; and if a man is worse off when the relation is dissolved than he was when it was contracted he will complain. 35
This happens because all or most men, while they wish for
what is noble, choose what is advantageous; now it is noble
to do well by another without a view to repayment, but it
is the receiving of benefits that is advantageous.

Therefore if we can we should return the equivalent of 1163ᵃ
what we have received (for we must not make a man our
friend against his will; we must recognize that we were mistaken at the first and took a benefit from a person we should
not have taken it from—since it was not from a friend, nor
from one who did it just for the sake of acting so—and we
must settle up just as if we had been benefited on fixed 5
terms). Indeed, one would agree to repay if one could (if one
could not, even the giver would not have expected one to do
so); therefore if it is possible we must repay. But at the outset we must consider the man by whom we are being
benefited and on what terms he is acting, in order that we
may accept the benefit on these terms, or else decline it.

It is disputable whether we ought to measure a service
by its utility to the receiver and make the return with a view 10
to that, or by the benevolence of the giver. For those who
have received say they have received from their benefactors
what meant little to the latter and what they might have got
from others—minimizing the service; while the givers, on
the contrary, say it was the biggest thing they had, and
what could not have been got from others, and that it was
given in times of danger or similar need. Now if the friend- 15

ship is one that aims at *utility*, surely the advantage to the receiver is the measure. For it is he that asks for the service, and the other man helps him on the assumption that he will receive the equivalent; so the assistance has been precisely as great as the advantage to the receiver, and therefore he must return as much as he has received, or
20 even more (for that would be nobler). In friendships based on *virtue* on the other hand, complaints do not arise, but the purpose of the doer is a sort of measure; for in purpose lies the essential element of virtue and character.

14 Differences arise also in friendships based on superiority; for each expects to get more out of
25 them, but when this happens the friendship is dissolved. Not only does the better man think he ought to get more, since more should be assigned to a good man, but the more useful similarly expects this; they say a useless man should not get as much as they should, since it becomes an act of public service and not a friendship if the proceeds of the friendship do not answer to the worth of the
30 benefits conferred. For they think that, as in a commercial partnership those who put more in get more out, so it should be in friendship. But the man who is in a state of need and inferiority makes the opposite claim; they think it is the part of a good friend to help those who are in need; what, they say, is the use of being the friend of a good man
35 or a powerful man, if one is to get nothing out of it?

At all events it seems that each party is justified in his
1163b claim, and that each should get more out of the friendship than the other—not more of the same thing, however, but the superior more honour and the inferior more gain; for honour is the prize of virtue and of beneficence, while gain is the assistance required by inferiority.

It seems to be so in constitutional arrangements also;
5 the man who contributes nothing good to the common stock

is not honoured; for what belongs to the public is given to the man who benefits the public, and honour does belong to the public. It is not possible to get wealth from the common stock and at the same time honour. For no one puts 10 up with the smaller share in *all* things; therefore to the man who loses in wealth they assign honour and to the man who is willing to be paid, wealth, since the proportion to merit equalizes the parties and preserves the friendship, as we have said.[13]

This then is also the way in which we should associate with unequals; the man who is benefited in respect of wealth or virtue must give honour in return, repaying what he can. For friendship asks a man to do what he can, not what is proportional to the merits of the case; since that 15 cannot always be done, e. g. in honours paid to the gods or to parents; for no one could ever return to them the equivalent of what he gets, but the man who serves them to the utmost of his power is thought to be a good man.

This is why it would not seem open to a man to disown his father (though a father may disown his son; being 20 in debt, he should repay, but there is nothing by doing which a son will have done the equivalent of what he has received, so that he is always in debt. But creditors can remit a debt; and a father can therefore do so too. At the same time it is thought that presumably no one would repudiate a son who was not far gone in wickedness; for apart from the natural friendship of father and son it is human nature not to reject a son's assistance. But the son, if he *is* 25 wicked, will naturally avoid aiding his father, or not be zealous about it; for most people wish to get benefits, but avoid doing them, as a thing unprofitable.—So much for these questions.

---

13 1162ª 34–b4, Cf. 1158b 27, 1159ª 35–b 3.

BOOK IX

1   In all friendships between dissimilars it is, as we have said,[1] proportion that equalizes the parties and preserves the friendship; e. g. in the political form of friendship the shoemaker gets a return for his shoes in proportion to his worth, and the weaver and all other craftsmen do the same. Now here a common measure has been provided in the form of money, and therefore everything is referred to this and measured by this; but in the friendship of lovers sometimes the lover complains that his excess of love is not met by love in return (though perhaps there is nothing lovable about him), while often the beloved complains that the lover who formerly promised everything now performs nothing. Such incidents happen when the lover loves the beloved for the sake of pleasure while the beloved loves the lover for the sake of utility, and they do not both possess the qualities expected of them. If these be the objects of the friendship it is dissolved when they do not get the things that formed the motives of their love; for each did not love the other person himself but the qualities he had, and these were not enduring; that is why the friendships also are transient. But the love of characters, as has been said, endures because it is self-dependent.[2] Differences arise when what they get is something different and not what they desire; for it is like getting nothing at all when we do not get what we aim at; compare the story of the person who made promises to a lyre-player, promising him the more, the better he sang, but in the morning, when the

---

[1] This has not been said precisely of friendship between dissimilars, but Cf. 1132^b 31–33, 1158^b 27, 1159^a 35–^{b} 3, 1162^a 34–^{b} 4, 1163^b 11.

[2] 1156^b 9–12.

other demanded the fulfilment of his promises, said that he had given pleasure[3] for pleasure. Now if this had been what each wanted, all would have been well; but if the one wanted enjoyment but the other gain, and the one has what he wants while the other has not, the terms of the association will not have been properly fulfilled; for what each in fact wants is what he attends to, and it is for the sake of that that he will give what he has.

But who is to fix the worth of the service; he who makes the sacrifice or he who has got the advantage? At any rate the other seems to leave it to him. This is what they say Protagoras used to do;[4] whenever he taught anything whatsoever, he bade the learner assess the value of the knowledge, and accepted the amount so fixed. But in such matters some men approve of the saying 'let a man have his fixed reward'.

Those who get the money first and then do none of the things they said they would, owing to the extravagance of their promises, naturally find themselves the objects of complaint; for they do not fulfil what they agreed to. The sophists are perhaps compelled to do this because no one would give money for the things they *do* know. These people then, if they do not do what they have been paid for, are naturally made the objects of complaint.

But where there is *no* contract of service, those who give up something for the sake of the other party cannot (as we have said[5]) be complained of (for that is the nature of the friendship of virtue), and the return to them must be made on the basis of their purpose (for it is purpose that is the characteristic thing in a friend and in virtue). And so too, it

---

[3] i. e. the pleasure of expectation.

[4] Cf. Pl. *Prot.* 328 B, C.

[5] 1162[b] 6–13.

seems, should one make a return to those with whom one has studied philosophy; for their worth cannot be measured against money, and they can get no honour which will bal-
5 ance their services, but still it is perhaps enough, as it is with the gods and with one's parents, to give them what one can.

If the gift was not of this sort, but was made with a view to a return, it is no doubt preferable that the return made should be one that seems fair to both parties, but if this can- not be achieved, it would seem not only necessary that the
10 person who gets the first service should fix the reward, but also just; for if the other gets in return the equivalent of the advantage the beneficiary has received, or the price he would have paid for the pleasure, he will have got what is fair as from the other.

We see this happening too with things put up for sale, and in some places there are laws providing that no actions shall arise out of voluntary contracts, on the assumption that
15 one should settle with a person to whom one has given credit, in the spirit in which one bargained with him. The law holds that it is more just that the person to whom credit was given should fix the terms than that the person who gave a credit should do so. For most things are not assessed at the same value by those who have them and those who want them; each class values highly what is its own and what
20 it is offering; yet the return is made on the terms fixed by the receiver. But no doubt the receiver should assess a thing not at what it seems worth when he has it, but at what he assessed it at before he had it.

2 A further problem is set by such questions as, whether one should in all things give the preference to one's father and obey him, or whether when one
25 is ill one should trust a doctor, and when one has to elect a general should elect a man of military skill; and similarly whether one should render a service by preference to a

friend or to a good man, and should show gratitude to a benefactor or oblige a friend, if one cannot do both.

All such questions are hard, are they not, to decide with precision? For they admit of many variations of all sorts in respect both of the magnitude of the service and of its nobility and necessity. But that we should not give the preference in all things to the same person is plain enough; and we must for the most part return benefits rather than oblige friends, as we must pay back a loan to a creditor rather than make one to a friend. But perhaps even this is not always true; e. g. should a man who has been ransomed out of the hands of brigands ransom his ransomer in return, whoever he may be (or pay him if he has not been captured but demands payment), or should he ransom his father? It would seem that he should ransom his father in preference even to himself. As we have said,[6] then, generally the debt should be paid, but if the gift is exceedingly noble or exceedingly necessary, one should defer to these considerations. For sometimes it is not even fair to return the equivalent of what one has received, when the one man has done a service to one whom he knows to be good, while the other makes a return to one whom he believes to be bad. For that matter, one should sometimes not lend in return to one who has lent to oneself; for the one person lent to a good man, expecting to recover his loan, while the other has no hope of recovering from one who is believed to be bad. Therefore if the facts really are so, the demand is not fair; and if they are not, but people think they are, they would be held to be doing nothing strange in refusing. As we have often pointed out,[7] then, discussions about feelings and actions have just as much definiteness as their subject-matter.

[6] 1164^b 31–1165^a 2.

[7] 1094^b 11–27, 1098^a 26–29, 1103^b 34–1104^a 5.

That we should not make the same return to everyone, nor give a father the preference in everything, as one does
15 not sacrifice everything to Zeus,[8] is plain enough; but since we ought to render different things to parents, brothers, comrades, and benefactors, we ought to render to each class what is appropriate and becoming. And this is what people seem in fact to do; to marriages they invite their kinsfolk; for these have a part in the family and therefore in the doings that affect the family; and at funerals also they think
20 that kinsfolk, before all others, should meet, for the same reason. And it would be thought that in the matter of food we should help our parents before all others, since we owe our own nourishment to them, and it is more honourable to help in this respect the authors of our being even before ourselves; and honour too one should give to one's parents as one does to the gods, but not any and every honour; for
25 that matter one should not give the same honour to one's father and one's mother, nor again should one give them the honour due to a philosopher or to a general, but the honour due to a father, or again to a mother. To all older persons, too, one should give honour appropriate to their age, by rising to receive them and finding seats for them and so on; while to comrades and brothers one should allow
30 freedom of speech and common use of all things. To kinsmen, too, and fellow-tribesmen and fellow-citizens and to every other class one should always try to assign what is appropriate, and to compare the claims of each class with respect to nearness of relation and to virtue or usefulness. The comparison is easier when the persons belong to the same class, and more laborious when they are different. Yet
35 we must not on *that* account shrink from the task, but decide the question as best we can.

[8] Cf. 1134[b] 18–24.

3 Another question that arises is whether friendships should or should not be broken off when the other party does not remain the same. Perhaps we may 1165^b say that there is nothing strange in breaking off a friendship based on utility or pleasure, when our friends no longer have these attributes. For it was of these attributes that we were the friends; and when these have failed it is reasonable to love no longer. But one might complain of another if, 5 when he loved us for our usefulness or pleasantness, he pretended to love us for our character. For, as we said at the outset,[9] most differences arise between friends when they are not friends in the spirit in which they think they are. So when a man has deceived himself and has thought he was being loved for his character, when the other person was doing nothing of the kind, he must blame himself; but 10 when he has been deceived by the pretences of the other person, it is just that he should complain against his deceiver; he will complain with more justice than one does against people who counterfeit the currency, inasmuch as the wrongdoing is concerned with something more valuable.

But if one accepts another man as good, and he turns out badly and is seen to do so, must one still love him? Surely it is impossible, since not everything can be loved, but only what is good. What is evil neither can nor should 15 be loved; for it is not one's duty to be a lover of evil, nor to become like what is bad; and we have said[10] that like is dear to like. Must the friendship, then, be forthwith broken off? Or is this not so in all cases, but only when one's friends are incurable in their wickedness? If they are capable of being reformed one should rather come to the assistance of their character or their property, inasmuch as this is bet- 20 ter and more characteristic of friendship. But a man who

9 1162^b 23-25.

10 1156^b 19-21, 1159^b 1.

breaks off such a friendship would seem to be doing nothing strange; for it was not to a man of this sort that he was
a friend; when his friend has changed, therefore, and he is
unable to save him, he gives him up.

But if one friend remained the same while the other
became better and far outstripped him in virtue, should the
25 latter treat the former as a friend? Surely he cannot. When
the interval is great this becomes most plain, e. g. in the
case of childish friendships; if one friend remained a child
in intellect while the other became a fully developed man,
how could they be friends when they neither approved of
the same things nor delighted in and were pained by the
same things? For not even with regard to each other will
their tastes agree, and without this (as we saw 11) they can-
30 not be friends; for they cannot live together. But we have
discussed these matters.12

Should he, then, behave no otherwise towards him than
he would if he had never been his friend? Surely he should
keep a remembrance of their former intimacy, and as we
think we ought to oblige friends rather than strangers, so to
35 those who have been our friends we ought to make some
allowance for our former friendship, when the breach has
not been due to excess of wickedness.

1166ª   **4**   Friendly relations with one's neighbours, and the
marks by which friendships are defined, seem to
have proceeded from a man's relations to himself.
For (1) we define a friend as one who wishes and does what
is good, or seems so, for the sake of his friend, or (2) as one
who wishes his friend to exist and live, for his sake; which
5 mothers do to their children, and friends do who have come
into conflict. And (3) others define him as one who lives

11 1157ᵇ 22–24.

12 ib. 17–24, 1158ᵇ 33–35.

with and (4) has the same tastes as another, or (5) one who grieves and rejoices with his friend; and this too is found in mothers most of all. It is by some one of these characteristics that friendship too is defined.

Now each of these is true of the good man's relation to himself (and of all other men in so far as they think them- 10 selves good; virtue and the good man seem, as has been said,[13] to be the measure of every class of things). For[14] his opinions are harmonious, and he desires the same things with all his soul; and therefore[15] he wishes for himself what is good and what seems so, and does it (for it is characteristic of the good man to work out the good), and does so for his 15 own sake (for he does it for the sake of the intellectual element in him, which is thought to be the man himself); and[16] he wishes himself to live and be preserved, and especially the element by virtue of which he thinks. For existence is good to the virtuous man, and each man wishes himself what is good, while no one chooses to possess the whole world if he 20 has first to become some one else (for that matter, even now God possesses the good[17]); he wishes for this only on condition of being whatever he is; and the element that thinks would seem to be the individual man, or to be so more than any other element in him. And[18] such a man wishes to live with himself; for he does so with pleasure, since the memories of his past acts are delightful and his hopes for the 25

---

[13] 1113ª 22–33, Cf. 1099ª 13.

[14] (4) above.

[15] (1) above.

[16] (2) above.

[17] *sc.* but as no one gains by God's now having the good, he would not gain if a new person which was no longer himself were to possess it. Cf. 1159ª 5–11.

[18] (3) above.

future are good, and therefore pleasant. His mind is well
stored too with subjects of contemplation. And[19] he grieves
and rejoices, more than any other, with himself; for the same
thing is always painful, and the same thing always pleasant,
and not one thing at one time and another at another; he
has, so to speak nothing to repent of.

Therefore, since each of these characteristics belongs to
30 the good man in relation to himself, and he is related to his
friend as to himself (for his friend is another self), friendship
too is thought to be one of these attributes, and those who
have these attributes to be friends. Whether there is or is not
friendship between a man and himself is a question we may
35 dismiss for the present;[20] there would seem to be friendship in
1166[b] so far as he is two or more, to judge from the aforementioned
attributes of friendship, and from the fact that the extreme
of friendship is likened to one's love for oneself.

But the attributes named seem to belong even to the
majority of men, poor creatures though they may be. Are
we to say then that in so far as they are satisfied with them-
5 selves and think they are good, they share in these attributes?
Certainly no one who is thoroughly bad and impious has
these attributes, or even seems to do so. They hardly belong
even to inferior people; for they[21] are at variance with themselves, and have appetites for some things and rational
desires for others. This is true, for instance, of incontinent
people; for they choose, instead of the things they them-
10 selves think good, things that are pleasant but hurtful; while
others again, through cowardice and laziness, shrink from
doing what they think best for themselves. And[22] those who

[19] (5) above.

[20] Cf. 1168[a] 28–1169[b] 2.

[21] (4) above.

[22] (2) above.

have done many terrible deeds and are hated for their wickedness even shrink from life and destroy themselves. And[23] wicked men seek for people with whom to spend their days, and shun themselves; for they remember many a grievous deed, and anticipate others like them, when they are by themselves, but when they are with others they forget. And[24] having nothing lovable in them they have no feeling of love to themselves. Therefore[25] also such men do not rejoice or grieve with themselves; for their soul is rent by faction, and one element in it by reason of its wickedness grieves when it abstains from certain acts, while the other part is pleased, and one draws them this way and the other that, as if they were pulling them in pieces. If a man cannot at the same time be pained and pleased, at all events after a short time he is pained *because* he was pleased, and he could have wished that these things had not been pleasant to him; for bad men are laden with repentance.

Therefore the bad man does not seem to be amicably disposed even to himself, because there is nothing in him to love; so that if to be thus is the height of wretchedness, we should strain every nerve to avoid wickedness and should endeavour to be good; for so and only so can one be either friendly to oneself or a friend to another.

5 Goodwill is a friendly sort of relation, but is not *identical* with friendship; for one may have goodwill both towards people whom one does not know, and with out their knowing it, but not friendship. This has indeed been said already.[26] But goodwill is not even friendly

[23] (3) above.

[24] (1) above.

[25] (5) above.

[26] 1155^b 32–1156^a 5.

feeling. For it does not involve intensity or desire, whereas these accompany friendly feeling; and friendly feeling implies intimacy while goodwill may arise of a sudden, as 35 it does towards competitors in a contest; we come to feel 1167a goodwill for them and to share in their wishes, but we would not *do* anything with them, for, as we said, we feel goodwill suddenly and love them only superficially.

Goodwill seems, then, to be a beginning of friendship, as the pleasure of the eye is the beginning of love. For no one loves if he has not first been delighted by the form of 5 the beloved, but he who delights in the form of another does not, for all that, love him, but only does so when he also longs for him when absent and craves for his presence; so too it is not possible for people to be friends if they have not come to feel goodwill for each other, but those who feel goodwill are not for all that friends; for they only *wish* well to those for whom they feel goodwill, and would not do anything with them nor take trouble for them. And so one 10 might by an extension of the term friendship say that goodwill is inactive friendship, though when it is prolonged and reaches the point of intimacy it becomes friendship—not the friendship based on utility nor that based on pleasure; for goodwill too does not arise on those terms. The man who has received a benefit bestows goodwill in return for what has been done to him, but in doing so is only doing what is just; while he who wishes some one to prosper because 15 he hopes for enrichment through him seems to have goodwill not to him but rather to himself, just as a man is not a friend to another if he cherishes him for the sake of some use to be made of him. In general, goodwill arises on account of some excellence and worth, when one man seems to another beautiful or brave or something of the sort, as 20 we pointed out in the case of competitors in a contest.

6 Unanimity also seems to be a friendly relation. For this reason it is not identity of opinion; for that might occur even with people who do not know each other; nor do we say that people who have the same views on any and every subject are unanimous, e. g. those 25 who agree about the heavenly bodies (for unanimity about these is not a friendly relation), but we do say that a city is unanimous when men have the same opinion about what is to their interest, and choose the same actions, and do what they have resolved in common. It is about things to be done, therefore, that people are said to be unanimous, and, among these, about matters of consequence and in which it is possible for both or all parties to get what they want; e. g. a city is unanimous when all its citizens think that the 30 offices in it should be elective, or that they should form an alliance with Sparta, or that Pittacus should be their ruler— at a time when he himself was also willing to rule. But when each of two people wishes himself to have the thing in question, like the captains in the *Phoenissae*,[27] they are in a state 35 of faction; for it is not unanimity when each of two parties thinks of the same thing, whatever that may be, but only when they think of the same thing in the same hands, e. g. when both the common people and those of the better class 1167b wish the best men to rule; for thus and thus alone do all get what they aim at. Unanimity seems, then, to be political friendship, as indeed it is commonly said to be; for it is concerned with things that are to our interest and have an influence on our life.

Now such unanimity is found among good men; for 5 they are unanimous both in themselves and with one another, being, so to say, of one mind (for the wishes of such men are constant and not at the mercy of opposing currents like a strait of the sea), and they wish for what is

[27] Eteocles and Polynices (Eur. *Phoen.* 588 ff.).

just and what is advantageous, and these are the objects of their common endeavour as well. But bad men cannot be unanimous except to a small extent, any more than they can
10 be friends, since they aim at getting more than their share of advantages, while in labour and public service they fall short of their share; and each man wishing for advantage to himself criticizes his neighbour and stands in his way; for if people do not watch it carefully the common weal is soon destroyed. The result is that they are in a state of faction,
15 putting compulsion on each other but unwilling themselves to do what is just.

7 Benefactors are thought to love those they have benefited, more than those who have been well treated love those that have treated them well, and this is discussed as though it were paradoxical. Most people think it is because the latter are in the position of debtors and the former of creditors; and therefore as, in the
20 case of loans, debtors wish their creditors did not exist, while creditors actually take care of the safety of their debtors, so it is thought that benefactors wish the objects of their action to exist since they will then get their grati-
25 tude, while the beneficiaries take no interest in making this return. Epicharmus would perhaps declare that they say this because they 'look at things on their bad side', but it is quite like human nature; for most people are forgetful, and are more anxious to be well treated than to treat others well. But the cause would seem to be more deeply rooted in the nature of things; the case of those who have lent money is not even analogous. For they have no friendly feeling to
30 their debtors, but only a wish that they may be kept safe with a view to what is to be got from them; while those who have done a service to others feel friendship and love for those they have served even if these are not of any use to them and never will be. This is what happens with crafts-

men too; every man loves his own handiwork better than 35
he would be loved by it if it came alive; and this happens
perhaps most of all with poets; for they have an excessive 1168ᵃ
love for their own poems, doting on them as if they were
their children. This is what the position of benefactors is
like; for that which they have treated well is their handiwork, and therefore they love this more than the handiwork
does its maker. The cause of this is that existence is to all 5
men a thing to be chosen and loved, and that we exist by
virtue of activity (i. e. by living and acting), and that the
handiwork is in a sense, the producer in activity; he loves
his handiwork, therefore, because he loves existence. And
this is rooted in the nature of things; for what he is in
potentiality, his handiwork manifests in activity.

At the same time to the benefactor that is noble which
depends on his action, so that he delights in the object of
his action, whereas to the patient there is nothing noble in 10
the agent, but at most something advantageous, and this is
less pleasant and lovable. What is pleasant is the activity of
the present, the hope of the future, the memory of the past;
but most pleasant is that which depends on activity, and
similarly this is most lovable. Now for a man who has made
something his work remains (for the noble is lasting), but 15
for the person acted on the utility passes away. And the
memory of noble things is pleasant, but that of useful things
is not likely to be pleasant, or is less so; though the reverse
seems true of expectation.

Further, love is like activity, being loved like passivity;
and loving and its concomitants are attributes of those who
are the more active.[28]   20

Again, all men love more what they have won by
labour; e. g. those who have made their money love it more
than those who have inherited it; and to be well treated

[28] i. e. benefactors.

seems to involve no labour, while to treat others well is a
25 laborious task. These are the reasons, too, why mothers are
fonder of their children than fathers; bringing them into the
world costs them more pains, and they know better that the
children are their own. This last point, too, would seem to
apply to benefactors.

8 The question is also debated, whether a man
should love himself most, or some one else. People
criticize those who love themselves most, and call
30 them self-lovers, using this as an epithet of disgrace, and a
bad man seems to do everything for his own sake, and the
more so the more wicked he is—and so men reproach him,
for instance, with doing nothing of his own accord—while
the good man acts for honour's sake, and the more so the
better he is, and acts for his friend's sake, and sacrifices his
own interest.

35   But the facts clash with these arguments, and this is not
1168ᵇ surprising. For men say that one ought to love best one's
best friend, and a man's best friend is one who wishes well
to the object of his wish for his sake, even if no one is to
know of it; and these attributes are found most of all in a
man's attitude towards himself, and so are all the other
5 attributes by which a friend is defined; for, as we have
said,²⁹ it is from this relation that all the characteristics of
friendship have extended to our neighbours. All the
proverbs, too, agree with this, e. g. 'a single soul', and 'what
friends have is common property', and 'friendship is equality', and 'charity begins at home'; for all these marks will
be found most in a man's relation to himself; he is his own
best friend and therefore ought to love himself best. It is
10 therefore a reasonable question, which of the two views we
should follow; for both are plausible.

²⁹ Ch. 4.

Perhaps we ought to mark off such arguments from each other and determine how far and in what respects each view is right. Now if we grasp the sense in which each school uses the phrase 'lover of self', the truth may become 15 evident. Those who use the term as one of reproach ascribe self-love to people who assign to themselves the greater share of wealth, honours, and bodily pleasures; for these are what most people desire, and busy themselves about as though they were the best of all things, which is the reason, too, why they become objects of competition. So those who are grasping with regard to these things gratify their 20 appetites and in general their feelings and the irrational element of the soul; and most men are of this nature (which is the reason why the epithet has come to be used as it is— it takes its meaning from the prevailing type of self-love, which is a bad one); it is just, therefore, that men who are lovers of self in this way are reproached for being so. That it is those who give themselves the preference in regard to objects of this sort that most people usually call lovers of self is plain; for if a man were always anxious that he him- 25 self, above all things, should act justly, temperately, or in accordance with any other of the virtues, and in general were always to try to secure for himself the honourable course, no one will call such a man a lover of self or blame him.

But such a man would seem more than the other a lover of self; at all events he assigns to himself the things that are noblest and best, and gratifies the most authorita- tive element in himself and in all things obeys this; and just 30 as a city or any other systematic whole is most properly identified with the most authoritative element in it, so is a man; and therefore the man who loves this and gratifies it is most of all a lover of self. Besides, a man is said to have or not to have self-control according as his reason has or has not the control, on the assumption that this is the man him- self; and the things men have done on a rational principle 35

1169^a are thought most properly their own acts and voluntary acts. That this is the man himself, then, or is so more than anything else, is plain, and also that the good man loves most this part of him. Whence it follows that he is most truly a lover of self, of another type than that which is a matter of reproach, and as different from that as living according to a rational principle is from living as passion
5 dictates, and desiring what is noble from desiring what seems advantageous. Those, then, who busy themselves in an exceptional degree with noble actions all men approve and praise; and if *all* were to strive towards what is noble and strain every nerve to do the noblest deeds, everything would be as it should be for the common weal, and every
10 one would secure for himself the goods that are greatest, since virtue is the greatest of goods.

Therefore the good man should be a lover of self (for he will both himself profit by doing noble acts, and will benefit his fellows), but the wicked man should not; for he will hurt both himself and his neighbours, following as he
15 does evil passions. For the wicked man, what he does clashes with what he ought to do, but what the good man ought to do he does; for reason in each of its possessors chooses what is best for itself, and the good man obeys his reason. It is true of the good man too that he does many acts for the sake of his friends and his country, and if nec-
20 essary dies for them; for he will throw away both wealth and honours and in general the goods that are objects of competition, gaining for himself nobility; since he would prefer a short period of intense pleasure to a long one of mild enjoyment, a twelve-month of noble life to many years
25 of humdrum existence, and one great and noble action to many trivial ones. Now those who die for others doubtless attain this result; it is therefore a great prize that they choose for themselves. They will throw away wealth too on condition that their friends will gain more; for while a man's

friend gains wealth he himself achieves nobility; he is therefore assigning the greater good to himself. The same too is 30
true of honour and office; all these things he will sacrifice to
his friend; for this is noble and laudable for himself. Rightly
then is he thought to be good, since he chooses nobility
before all else. But he may even give up actions to his
friend; it may be nobler to become the cause of his friend's
acting than to act himself. In all the actions, therefore, that 35
men are praised for, the good man is seen to assign to himself the greater share in what is noble. In this sense, then, as
has been said, a man should be a lover of self; but in the 1169ᵇ
sense in which most men are so, he ought not.

9 It is also disputed whether the happy man will
need friends or not. It is said that those who are
supremely happy and self-sufficient have no need 5
of friends; for they have the things that are good, and therefore being self-sufficient they need nothing further, while a
friend, being another self, furnishes what a man cannot provide by his own effort; whence the saying 'when fortune is
kind, what need of friends?' But it seems strange, when one
assigns all good things to the happy man, not to assign 10
friends, who are thought the greatest of external goods. And
if it is more characteristic of a friend to do well by another
than to be well done by, and to confer benefits is characteristic of the good man and of virtue, and it is nobler to do
well by friends than by strangers, the good man will need
people to do well by. This is why the question is asked 15
whether we need friends more in prosperity or in adversity,
on the assumption that not only does a man in adversity
need people to confer benefits on him, but also those who
are prospering need people to do well by. Surely it is
strange, too, to make the supremely happy man a solitary;
for no one would choose the whole world on condition of
being alone, since man is a political creature and one whose

nature is to live with others. Therefore even the happy man
lives with others; for he has the things that are by nature
20 good. And plainly it is better to spend his days with friends
and good men than with strangers or any chance persons.
Therefore the happy man needs friends.

What then is it that the first school means, and in what
respect is it right? Is it that most men identify friends with
useful people? Of such friends indeed the supremely happy
man will have no need, since he already has the things that
25 are good; nor will he need those whom one makes one's
friends because of their pleasantness, or he will need them
only to a small extent (for his life, being pleasant, has no
need of adventitious pleasure); and because he does not
need *such* friends he is thought not to need friends.

But that is surely not true. For we have said at the outset[30] that happiness is an activity; and activity plainly comes
into being and is not present at the start like a piece of
30 property. If (1) happiness lies in living and being active, and
the good man's activity is virtuous and pleasant in itself, as
we have said at the outset,[31] and (2) a thing's being one's
own is one of the attributes that make it pleasant, and (3)
we can contemplate our neighbours better than ourselves
and their actions better than our own, and if the actions of
35 virtuous men who are their friends are pleasant to good men
1170ᵃ (since these have both the attributes that are naturally pleasant[32])—if this be so, the supremely happy man will need
friends of this sort, since his purpose is to contemplate worthy actions and actions that are his own, and the actions of
a good man who is his friend have both these qualities.

Further, men think that the happy man ought to live

[30] 1098ᵃ 16, ᵇ31–1099ᵃ 7.

[31] 1099ᵃ 14, 21.

[32] i. e. the attribute of goodness and that of being their own.

pleasantly. Now if he were a solitary, life would be hard for
him; for by oneself it is not easy to be continuously active; 5
but with others and towards others it is easier. With others
therefore his activity will be more continuous, and it is in
itself pleasant, as it ought to be for the man who is
supremely happy; for a good man *qua* good delights in virtuous actions and is vexed at vicious ones, as a musical man
enjoys beautiful tunes but is pained at bad ones. A certain 10
training in virtue arises also from the company of the good,
as Theognis has said before us.

If we look deeper into the nature of things, a virtuous
friend seems to be naturally desirable for a virtuous man.
For that which is good by nature, we have said,[33] is for the
virtuous man good and pleasant in itself. Now life is defined 15
in the case of animals by the power of perception, in that
of man by the power of perception or thought; and a power
is defined by reference to the corresponding activity, which
is the essential thing; therefore life seems to be essentially
the act of perceiving or thinking. And life is among the
things that are good and pleasant in themselves, since it is 20
determinate and the determinate is of the nature of the
good; and that which is good by nature is also good for the
virtuous man (which is the reason why life seems pleasant
to all men); but we must not apply this to a wicked and cor-
rupt life nor to a life spent in pain; for such a life is
indeterminate, as are its attributes. The nature of pain will 25
become plainer in what follows.[34] But if life itself is good
and pleasant (which it seems to be, from the very fact that
all men desire it, and particularly those who are good and
supremely happy; for to such men life is most desirable, and
their existence is the most supremely happy); and if he who

[33] 1099ᵃ 7–11, 1113ᵃ 25–33.

[34] x. 1–5.

sees perceives that he sees, and he who hears, that he hears,
30 and he who walks, that he walks, and in the case of all other
activities similarly there is something which perceives that
we are active, so that if we perceive, we perceive that we
perceive, and if we think, that we think; and if to perceive
that we perceive or think is to perceive that we exist (for
1170ᵇ existence was defined as perceiving or thinking); and if perceiving that one lives is in itself one of the things that are
pleasant (for life is by nature good, and to perceive what is
good present in oneself is pleasant); and if life is desirable,
and particularly so for good men, because to them existence
5 is good and pleasant (for they are pleased at the consciousness of the presence in them of what is in itself good); and
if as the virtuous man is to himself, he is to his friend also
(for his friend is another self):—if all this be true, as his
own being is desirable for each man, so, or almost so, is that
of his friend. Now his being was seen to be desirable
10 because he perceived his own goodness, and such perception
is pleasant in itself. He needs, therefore, to be conscious of
the existence of his friend as well, and this will be realized
in their living together and sharing in discussion and
thought; for this is what living together would seem to
mean in the case of man, and not, as in the case of cattle,
feeding in the same place.

If, then, being is in itself desirable for the supremely
15 happy man (since it is by its nature good and pleasant), and
that of his friend is very much the same, a friend will be
one of the things that are desirable. Now that which is
desirable for him he must have, or he will be deficient in
this respect. The man who is to be happy will therefore
need virtuous friends.

20 **10** Should we, then, make as many friends as possible, or—as in the case of hospitality it is thought
to be suitable advice, that one should be 'neither

a man of many guests nor a man with none'—will that apply to friendship as well; should a man neither be friendless nor have an excessive number of friends?

To friends made with a view to *utility* this saying would seem thoroughly applicable; for to do services to many people in return is a laborious task and life is not long enough for its performance. Therefore friends in excess of those 25 who are sufficient for our own life are superfluous and hindrances to the noble life; so that we have no need of them. Of friends made with a view to *pleasure*, also, few are enough, as a little seasoning in food is enough.

But as regards *good* friends, should we have as many as possible, or is there a limit to the number of one's friends, as there is to the size of a city? You cannot make a city of 30 ten men, and if there are a hundred thousand it is a city no longer. But the proper number is presumably not a single number, but anything that falls between certain fixed points. So for friends too there is a fixed number—perhaps 1171ᵃ the largest number with whom one can live together (for that, we found,[35] is thought to be very characteristic of friendship); and that one cannot live with many people and divide oneself up among them is plain. Further, they too must be friends of one another, if they are all to spend their days together; and it is a hard business for this condition to be fulfilled with a large number. It is found difficult, too, to 5 rejoice and to grieve in an intimate way with many people, for it may likely happen that one has at once to be happy with one friend and to mourn with another. Presumably, then, it is well not to seek to have as many friends as possible, but as many as are enough for the purpose of living together; for it would seem actually impossible to be a great friend to many people. This is why one cannot love several 10 people; love is ideally a sort of excess of friendship, and that

35 1157ᵇ 19, 1158ᵃ 3, 10.

can only be felt towards one person; therefore great friendship too can only be felt towards a few people. This seems
to be confirmed in practice; for we do not find many people who are friends in the comradely way of friendship, and
the famous friendships of this sort are always between two
15 people. Those who have many friends and mix intimately
with them all are thought to be no one's friend, except in
the way proper to fellow-citizens, and such people are also
called obsequious. In the way proper to fellow-citizens,
indeed, it is possible to be the friend of many and yet not be
obsequious but a genuinely good man; but one cannot have
with many people the friendship based on virtue and on the
20 character of our friends themselves, and we must be content if we find even a few such.

11   Do we need friends more in good fortune or in
bad? They are sought after in both; for while
men in adversity need help, in prosperity they
need people to live with and to make the objects of their
beneficence; for they wish to do well by others. Friendship,
25 then, is more necessary in bad fortune, and so it is useful
friends that one wants in this case; but it is more noble in
good fortune, and so we also seek for good men as our
friends, since it is more desirable to confer benefits on these
and to live with these. For the very presence of friends is
30 pleasant both in good fortune and also in bad, since grief is
lightened when friends sorrow with us. Hence one might
ask whether they share as it were our burden, or—without
that happening—their presence by its pleasantness, and the
thought of their grieving with us, make our pain less.
Whether it is for these reasons or for some other that our
grief is lightened, is a question that may be dismissed; at all
events what we have described appears to take place.

But their presence seems to contain a mixture of vari-
35 ous factors. The very seeing of one's friends is pleasant,

especially if one is in adversity, and becomes a safeguard 1171ᵇ
against grief (for a friend tends to comfort us both by the
sight of him and by his words, if he is tactful, since he
knows our character and the things that please or pain us); 5
but to see him pained at our misfortunes is painful; for
every one shuns being a cause of pain to his friends. For
this reason people of a manly nature guard against making
their friends grieve with them, and, unless he be exception-
ally insensible to pain, such a man cannot stand the pain
that ensues for his friends, and in general does not admit
fellow-mourners because he is not himself given to mourn- 10
ing; but women and womanly men enjoy sympathisers in
their grief, and love them as friends and companions in sorrow. But in all things one obviously ought to imitate the
better type of person.

On the other hand, the presence of friends in our *prosperity* implies both a pleasant passing of our time and the
pleasant thought of their pleasure at our own good fortune.
For this cause it would seem that we ought to summon our 15
friends readily to share our good fortunes (for the benefi-
cent character is a noble one), but summon them to our bad
fortunes with hesitation; for we ought to give them as little
a share as possible in our evils—whence the saying 'enough
is *my* misfortune'. We should summon friends to us most of
all when they are likely by suffering a few inconveniences to
do us a great service.

Conversely, it is fitting to go unasked and readily to the
aid of those in adversity (for it is characteristic of a friend to 20
render services, and especially to those who are in need and
have not demanded them; such action is nobler and pleasanter for both persons); but when our friends are prosperous
we should join readily in their activities (for they need
friends for these too), but be tardy in coming forward to be
the objects of their kindness; for it is not noble to be keen to
receive benefits. Still, we must no doubt avoid getting the

25 reputation of kill-joys by repulsing them; for that sometimes happens.

The presence of friends, then, seems desirable in all circumstances.

12

Does it not follow, then, that, as for lovers the sight of the beloved is the thing they love most, 30 and they prefer this sense to the others because on it love depends most for its being and for its origin, so for friends the most desirable thing is living together? For friendship is a partnership, and as a man is to himself, so is he to his friend; now in his own case the consciousness of his being is desirable, and therefore is the consciousness 35 of his friend's being, and the activity of this consciousness is 1172ᵃ produced when they live together, so that it is natural that they aim at this. And whatever existence means for each class of men, whatever it is for whose sake they value life, in *that* they wish to occupy themselves with their friends; and so some drink together, others dice together, others join in athletic exercises and hunting, or in the study of philoso- 5 phy, each class spending their days together in whatever they love most in life; for since they wish to live with their friends, they do and share in those things which give them the sense of living together. Thus the friendship of bad men turns out an evil thing (for because of their instability they 10 unite in bad pursuits, and besides they become evil by becoming like each other), while the friendship of good men is good, being augmented by their companionship; and they are thought to become better too by their activities and by improving each other; for from each other they take the mould of the characteristics they approve—whence the saying 'noble deeds from noble men'.—So much, then, for 15 friendship; our next task must be to discuss pleasure.

BOOK X

1 After these matters we ought perhaps next to discuss pleasure. For it is thought to be most
intimately connected with our human nature,
which is the reason why in educating the young we steer 20
them by the rudders of pleasure and pain; it is thought, too,
that to enjoy the things we ought and to hate the things we
ought has the greatest bearing on virtue of character. For
these things extend right through life, with a weight and
power of their own in respect both to virtue and to the 25
happy life, since men choose what is pleasant and avoid
what is painful; and such things, it will be thought, we
should least of all omit to discuss, especially since they
admit of much dispute. For some[1] say pleasure is the good,
while others,[2] on the contrary, say it is thoroughly bad—
some no doubt being persuaded that the facts are so, and
others thinking it has a better effect on our life to exhibit 30
pleasure as a bad thing even if it is not; for most people
(they think) incline towards it and are the slaves of their
pleasures, for which reason they ought to lead them in the
opposite direction, since thus they will reach the middle
state. But surely this is not correct. For arguments about
matters concerned with feelings and actions are less reliable 35
than facts: and so when they clash with the facts of perception they are despised, and discredit the truth as well; if a 1172ᵇ
man who runs down pleasure is once seen to be aiming at it,
his inclining towards it is thought to imply that it is all worthy of being aimed at; for most people are not good at
drawing distinctions. True arguments seem, then, most use-

[1] The school of Eudoxus. Cf. ᵇ9. Aristippus is perhaps also referred to.

[2] The school of Speusippus, Cf. 1153ᵇ 5.

5 ful, not only with a view to knowledge, but with a view to
life also; for since they harmonize with the facts they are
believed, and so they stimulate those who understand them
to live according to them.—Enough of such questions; let
us proceed to review the opinions that have been expressed
about pleasure.

2   Eudoxus thought pleasure was the good because he
10   saw all things, both rational and irrational, aiming
at it, and because in all things that which is the
object of choice is what is excellent, and that which is most
the object of choice the greatest good; thus the fact that all
things moved towards the same object indicated that this
was for all things the chief good (for each thing, he argued,
finds its own good, as it finds its own nourishment); and
15 that which is good for all things and at which all aim was
the good. His arguments were credited more because of the
excellence of his character than for their own sake; he was
thought to be remarkably self-controlled, and therefore it
was thought that he was not saying what he did say as a
friend of pleasure, but that the facts really were so. He
believed that the same conclusion followed no less plainly
from a study of the contrary of pleasure; pain was in itself
an object of aversion to all things, and therefore its contrary
20 must be similarly an object of choice. And again that is
most an object of choice which we choose not because or for
the sake of something else, and pleasure is admittedly of
this nature; for no one asks to what end he is pleased, thus
implying that pleasure is in itself an object of choice. Further, he argued that pleasure when added to any good, e. g.
to just or temperate action, makes it more worthy of choice,
25 and that it is only by itself that the good can be increased.
This argument seems to show it to be one of the goods,
and no more a good than any other; for every good is more
worthy of choice along with another good than taken alone.

And so it is by an argument of this kind that Plato[3] proves the good *not* to be pleasure; he argues that the pleasant life is more desirable with wisdom than without, and that if the mixture is better, pleasure is not the good; for the good cannot become more desirable by the addition of anything to it. Now it is clear that nothing else, any more than pleasure, can be the good if it is made more desirable by the addition of any of the things that are good in themselves. What, then, is there that satisfies this criterion, which at the same time we can participate in? It is something of this sort that we are looking for.

Those who object that that at which all things aim is not necessarily good are, we may surmise, talking nonsense. For we say that that which every one thinks really is so; and the man who attacks this belief will hardly have anything more credible to maintain instead. If it is senseless creatures that desire the things in question, there might be something in what they say; but if intelligent creatures do so as well, what sense can there be in this view? But perhaps even in inferior creatures there is some natural good stronger than themselves which aims at their proper good.

Nor does the argument about the contrary of pleasure seem to be correct. They say that if pain is an evil it does not follow that pleasure is a good; for evil is opposed to evil and at the same time both are opposed to the neutral state—which is correct enough but does not apply to the things in question. For if both pleasure and pain belonged to the class of evils they ought both to be objects of aversion, while if they belonged to the class of neutrals neither should be an object of aversion or they should both be equally so; but in fact people evidently avoid the one as evil and choose the other as good; that then must be the nature of the opposition between them.

[3] *Phil.* 60 B–E.

3 Nor again, if pleasure is not a quality, does it follow that it is not a good; for the activities of virtue are not qualities either, nor is happiness.

15 They say,[4] however, that the good is determinate, while pleasure is indeterminate, because it admits of degrees. Now if it is from the feeling of pleasure that they judge thus, the same will be true of justice and the other virtues, in respect of which we plainly say that people of a certain character 20 are so more or less, and act more or less in accordance with these virtues; for people may be more just or brave, and it is possible also to act justly or temperately more or less. But if their judgement is based on the various pleasures, surely they are not stating the real cause,[5] if in fact some pleasures are unmixed and others mixed. Again, just as health admits 25 of degrees without being indeterminate, why should not pleasure? The same proportion is not found in all things, nor a single proportion always in the same thing, but it may be relaxed and yet persist up to a point, and it may differ in degree. The case of pleasure also may therefore be of this kind.

Again, they assume[6] that the good is perfect while 30 movements and comings into being are imperfect, and try to exhibit pleasure as being a movement and a coming into being. But they do not seem to be right even in saying that it is a movement. For speed and slowness are thought to be proper to every movement, and if a movement, e. g. that of the heavens, has not speed or slowness in itself, it has it in relation to something else; but of pleasure neither of these things is true. For while we may *become* pleased quickly as 1173ᵇ we may become angry quickly, we *cannot be* pleased quickly,

---

[4] Ib. 24 E–25 A, 31 A.

[5] *sc.*, of the badness of (some) pleasures.

[6] Pl. *Phil.* 53 C–54 D.

not even in relation to some one else, while we *can* walk, or grow, or the like, quickly. While, then, we can change quickly or slowly into a state of pleasure, we cannot quickly exhibit the activity of pleasure, i. e. be pleased. Again, how can it be a coming into being? It is not thought that any chance thing can come out of any chance thing, but that a thing is dissolved into that out of which it comes into being; 5 and pain would be the destruction of that of which pleasure is the coming into being.

They say, too,[7] that pain is the lack of that which is according to nature, and pleasure is replenishment. But these experiences are bodily. If then pleasure is replenishment with that which is according to nature, that which feels pleasure will be that in which the replenishment takes place, i. e. the body; but that is not thought to be the case; 10 therefore the replenishment is not pleasure, though one would be pleased when replenishment was taking place, just as one would be pained if one was being operated on.[8] This opinion seems to be based on the pains and pleasures connected with nutrition; on the fact that when people have been short of food and have felt pain beforehand they are pleased by the replenishment. But this does not happen with all pleasures; for the pleasures of learning and, among 15 the sensuous pleasures, those of smell, and also many sounds and sights, and memories and hopes, do not presuppose pain. Of what then will these be the coming into being? There has not been lack of anything of which they could be the supplying anew.

In reply to those who bring forward the disgraceful pleasures one may say that these are not pleasant; if things 20 are pleasant to people of vicious constitution, we must not

[7] Ib. 31 E–32 B, 42 C, D.

[8] The point being that the being replenished no more *is* pleasure than the being operated on *is* pain. For the instance, Cf. Pl. *Tim.* 65 B.

suppose that they are also pleasant to others than these, just as we do not reason so about the things that are wholesome or sweet or bitter to sick people, or ascribe whiteness to the things that seem white to those suffering from a disease of the eye. Or one might answer thus—that the 25 pleasures are desirable, but not from *these* sources, as wealth is desirable, but not as the reward of betrayal, and health, but not at the cost of eating anything and everything. Or perhaps pleasures differ in kind; for those derived from noble sources are different from those derived from base sources, and one cannot get the pleasure of the just 30 man without being just, nor that of the musical man without being musical, and so on.

The fact, too, that a friend is different from a flatterer seems to make it plain that pleasure is not a good or that pleasures are different in kind; for the one is thought to consort with us with a view to the good, the other with a view to our pleasure, and the one is reproached for his conduct while the other is praised on the ground that he consorts with us for different ends. And no one would 1174ª choose to live with the intellect of a child throughout his life, however much he were to be pleased at the things that children are pleased at, nor to get enjoyment by doing some most disgraceful deed, though he were never to feel any pain in consequence. And there are many things we should 5 be keen about even if they brought no pleasure, e. g. seeing, remembering, knowing, possessing the virtues. If pleasures necessarily do accompany these, that makes no odds; we should choose these even if no pleasure resulted. It seems to be clear, then, that neither is pleasure the good nor is all 10 pleasure desirable, and that some pleasures are desirable in themselves being different in kind or in their sources from the others. So much for the things that are said about pleasure and pain.

4 What pleasure is, or what kind of thing it is, will become plainer if we take up the question again from the beginning. Seeing seems to be at any 15 moment complete, for it does not lack anything which coming into being later will complete its form; and pleasure also seems to be of this nature. For it is a whole, and at no time can one find a pleasure whose form will be completed if the pleasure lasts longer. For this reason, too, it is not a movement. For every movement (e. g. that of building) takes time and is for the sake of an end, and is complete when it 20 has made what it aims at. It is complete, therefore, only in the whole time or at that final moment. In their parts and during the time they occupy, all movements are incomplete, and are different in kind from the whole movement and from each other. For the fitting together of the stones is different from the fluting of the column, and these are both different from the making of the temple; and the making of 25 the temple is complete (for it lacks nothing with a view to the end proposed), but the making of the base or of the triglyph is incomplete; for each is the making of only a part. They differ in kind, then, and it is not possible to find at any and every time a movement complete in form, but if at all, only in the whole time. So, too, in the case of walking and all other movements. For if locomotion is a movement 30 from here to there, it, too, has differences in kind—flying, walking, leaping, and so on. And not only so, but in walking itself there are such differences; for the whence and whither are not the same in the whole racecourse and in a part of it, nor in one part and in another, nor is it the same 1174b thing to traverse this line and that; for one traverses not only a line but one which is in a place, and this one is in a different place from that. We have discussed movement with precision in another work,[9] but it seems that it is not

_____
[9] *Phys.* vi–viii.

complete at any and every time, but that the many movements are incomplete and different in kind, since the
5 whence and whither give them their form. But of pleasure
the form is complete at any and every time. Plainly, then,
pleasure and movement must be different from each other,
and pleasure must be one of the things that are whole and
complete. This would seem to be the case, too, from the
fact that it is not possible to move otherwise than in time,
but it *is* possible to be pleased; for that which takes place
in a moment is a whole.

From these considerations it is clear, too, that these
thinkers are not right in saying there is a movement or a
coming into being *of* pleasure. For these cannot be ascribed
10 to all things, but only to those that are divisible and not
wholes; there is no coming into being of seeing nor of a
point nor of a unit, nor is any of these a movement or coming into being; therefore there is no movement or coming
into being of pleasure either; for it is a whole.

Since every sense is active in relation to its object, and a
15 sense which is in good condition acts perfectly in relation
to the most beautiful of its objects (for perfect activity
seems to be ideally of this nature; whether we say that *it* is
active, or the organ in which it resides, may be assumed to
be immaterial), it follows that in the case of each sense the
best activity is that of the best-conditioned organ in relation to the finest of its objects. And this activity will be the
most complete and pleasant. For, while there is pleasure in
20 respect of any sense, and in respect of thought and contemplation no less, the most complete is pleasantest, and that of
a well-conditioned organ in relation to the worthiest of its
objects is the most complete; and the pleasure completes the
activity. But the pleasure does not complete it in the same
way as the combination of object and sense, both good, just
25 as health and the doctor are not in the same way the cause
of a man's being healthy. (That pleasure is produced in

respect to each sense is plain; for we speak of sights and
sounds as pleasant. It is also plain that it arises most of all
when both the sense is at its best and it is active in reference
to an object which corresponds; when both object and per-
ceiver are of the best there will always be pleasure, since the 30
requisite agent and patient are both present.) Pleasure completes the activity not as the corresponding permanent state
does, by its immanence, but as an end which supervenes as
the bloom of youth does on those in the flower of their age.
So long, then, as both the intelligible or sensible object and
the discriminating or contemplative faculty are as they
should be, the pleasure will be involved in the activity; for
when both the passive and the active factor are unchanged 1175ᵃ
and are related to each other in the same way, the same
result naturally follows.

How, then, is it that no one is continuously pleased? Is
it that we grow weary? Certainly all human things are incapable of continuous activity. Therefore pleasure also is not
continuous; for it accompanies activity. Some things delight 5
us when they are new, but later do so less, for the same reason; for at first the mind is in a state of stimulation and
intensely active about them, as people are with respect to
their vision when they look hard at a thing, but afterwards
our activity is not of this kind, but has grown relaxed; for
which reason the pleasure also is dulled.

One might think that all men desire pleasure because 10
they all aim at life; life is an activity, and each man is active
about those things and with those faculties that he loves
most; e. g. the musician is active with his hearing in reference to tunes, the student with his mind in reference to 15
theoretical questions, and so on in each case; now pleasure
completes the activities, and therefore life, which they
desire. It is with good reason, then, that they aim at pleasure too, since for every one it completes life, which is
desirable. But whether we choose life for the sake of plea-

sure or pleasure for the sake of life is a question we may
20 dismiss for the present. For they seem to be bound up
together and not to admit of separation, since without activity pleasure does not arise, and every activity is completed
by the attendant pleasure.

5 For this reason pleasures seem, too, to differ in
kind. For things different in kind are, we think,
completed by different things (we see this to be
25 true both of natural objects and of things produced by art,
e. g. animals, trees, a painting, a sculpture, a house, an
implement); and, similarly, we think that activities differing in kind are completed by things differing in kind. Now
the activities of thought differ from those of the senses, and
both differ among themselves, in kind; so, therefore, do the
pleasures that complete them.

This may be seen, too, from the fact that each of the
pleasures is bound up with the activity it completes. For an
30 activity is intensified by its proper pleasure, since each class
of things is better judged of and brought to precision by
those who engage in the activity with pleasure; e. g. it is
those who enjoy geometrical thinking that become geometers and grasp the various propositions better, and,
similarly, those who are fond of music or of building, and
35 so on, make progress in their proper function by enjoying it;
so the pleasures intensify the activities, and what intensifies
a thing is proper to it, but things different in kind have
properties different in kind.

1175ᵇ   This will be even more apparent from the fact that
activities are hindered by pleasures arising from other
sources. For people who are fond of playing the flute are
incapable of attending to arguments if they overhear some
5 one playing the flute, since they enjoy flute-playing more
than the activity in hand; so the pleasure connected with
flute-playing destroys the activity concerned with argument.

This happens, similarly, in all other cases, when one is active about two things at once; the more pleasant activity drives out the other, and if it is much more pleasant does so all the more, so that one even ceases from the other. This is why when we enjoy anything very much we do not throw 10 ourselves into anything else, and do one thing only when we are not much pleased by another; e. g. in the theatre the people who eat sweets do so most when the actors are poor. Now since activities are made precise and more enduring and better by their proper pleasure, and injured by alien pleasures, evidently the two kinds of pleasure are far apart. 15 For alien pleasures do pretty much what proper pains do, since activities are destroyed by their proper pains; e. g. if a man finds writing or doing sums unpleasant and painful, he does not write, or does not do sums, because the activity is painful. So an activity suffers contrary effects from its 20 proper pleasures and pains, i. e. from those that supervene on it in virtue of its own nature. And alien pleasures have been stated to do much the same as pain; they destroy the activity, only not to the same degree.

Now since activities differ in respect of goodness and badness, and some are worthy to be chosen, others to be avoided, and others neutral, so, too, are the pleasures; for 25 to each activity there is a proper pleasure. The pleasure proper to a worthy activity is good and that proper to an unworthy activity bad; just as the appetites for noble objects are laudable, those for base objects culpable. But the pleasures involved in activities are more proper to them than the 30 desires; for the latter are separated both in time and in nature, while the former are close to the activities, and so hard to distinguish from them that it admits of dispute whether the activity is not the same as the pleasure. (Still, pleasure does not seem to *be* thought or perception—that would be strange; but because they are not found apart they appear to some people the same.) As activities are different, 35

then, so are the corresponding pleasures. Now sight is supe-
1176ᵃ rior to touch in purity, and hearing and smell to taste; the
pleasures, therefore, are similarly superior, and those of
thought superior to these, and within each of the two kinds
some are superior to others.

Each animal is thought to have a proper pleasure, as it
has a proper function; viz. that which corresponds to its
activity. If we survey them species by species, too, this will
5 be evident; horse, dog, and man have different pleasures, as
Heraclitus says 'asses would prefer sweepings to gold'; for
food is pleasanter than gold to asses. So the pleasures of
creatures different in kind differ in kind, and it is plausible
to suppose that those of a single species do not differ. But
10 they vary to no small extent, in the case of men at least; the
same things delight some people and pain others, and are
painful and odious to some, and pleasant to and liked by
others. This happens, too, in the case of sweet things; the
same things do not seem sweet to a man in a fever and a
healthy man—nor hot to a weak man and one in good con-
15 dition. The same happens in other cases. But in all such
matters that which appears to the good man is thought to
be really so. If this is correct, as it seems to be, and virtue
and the good man as such are the measure of each thing,
those also will be pleasures which appear so to him, and
those things pleasant which he enjoys. If the things he finds
20 tiresome seem pleasant to some one, that is nothing surprising; for men may be ruined and spoilt in many ways; but
the things are not pleasant, but only pleasant to these people and to people in this condition. Those which are
admittedly disgraceful plainly should not be said to be pleasures, except to a perverted taste; but of those that are
thought to be good what kind of pleasure or what pleasure
25 should be said to be that proper to man? Is it not plain from
the corresponding activities? The pleasures follow these.
Whether, then, the perfect and supremely happy man has

one or more activities, the pleasures that perfect these will be said in the strict sense to be pleasures proper to man, and the rest will be so in a secondary and fractional way, as are the activities.

6 Now that we have spoken of the virtues, the forms 30 of friendship, and the varieties of pleasure, what remains is to discuss in outline the nature of happiness, since this is what we state the end of human nature to be. Our discussion will be the more concise if we first sum up what we have said already. We said,[10] then, that it is not a disposition; for if it were it might belong to some one who was asleep throughout his life, living the life of a 35 plant, or, again, to some one who was suffering the greatest 1176b misfortunes. If these implications are unacceptable, and we must rather class happiness as an activity, as we have said before,[11] and if some activities are necessary, and desirable for the sake of something else, while others are so in themselves, evidently happiness must be placed among those desirable in themselves, not among those desirable for the 5 sake of something else; for happiness does not lack anything, but is self-sufficient. Now those activities are desirable in themselves from which nothing is sought beyond the activity. And of this nature virtuous actions are thought to be; for to do noble and good deeds is a thing desirable for its own sake.

Pleasant amusements also are thought to be of this nature; we choose them not for the sake of other things; for we are injured rather than benefited by them, since we are led to neglect our bodies and our property. But most of the 10 people who are deemed happy take refuge in such pastimes, which is the reason why those who are ready-witted at them

are highly esteemed at the courts of tyrants; they make
themselves pleasant companions in the tyrants' favourite
15 pursuits, and that is the sort of man they want. Now these
things are thought to be of the nature of happiness because
people in despotic positions spend their leisure in them, but
perhaps such people prove nothing; for virtue and reason,
from which good activities flow, do not depend on despotic
position; nor, if these people, who have never tasted pure
and generous pleasure, take refuge in the bodily pleasures,
20 should these for that reason be thought more desirable; for
boys, too, think the things that are valued among themselves
are the best. It is to be expected, then, that, as different
things seem valuable to boys and to men, so they should to
bad men and to good. Now, as we have often maintained,[12]
25 those things are both valuable and pleasant which are such
to the good man; and to each man the activity in accordance
with his own disposition is most desirable, and, therefore,
to the good man that which is in accordance with virtue.
Happiness, therefore, does not lie in amusement; it would,
indeed, be strange if the end were amusement, and one were
30 to take trouble and suffer hardship all one's life in order to
amuse oneself. For, in a word, everything that we choose
we choose for the sake of something else—except happiness,
which is an end. Now to exert oneself and work for the sake
of amusement seems silly and utterly childish. But to amuse
oneself in order that one may exert oneself, as Anacharsis
puts it, seems right; for amusement is a sort of relaxation,
35 and we need relaxation because we cannot work continuously. Relaxation, then, is not an end; for it is taken for the
sake of activity.

The happy life is thought to be virtuous; now a vir-
1177ª tuous life requires exertion, and does not consist in
amusement. And we say that serious things are better than

[12] 1099ª 13, 1113ª 22–33, 1166ª 12, 1170ª 14–16, 1176ª 15–22.

laughable things and those connected with amusement, and that the activity of the better of any two things—whether it be two elements of our being or two men—is the more serious; but the activity of the better is *ipso facto* superior and 5 more of the nature of happiness. And any chance person— even a slave—can enjoy the bodily pleasures no less than the best man; but no one assigns to a slave a share in happiness—unless he assigns to him also a share in human life. 10 For happiness does not lie in such occupations, but, as we have said before,[13] in virtuous activities.

7 If happiness is activity in accordance with virtue, it is reasonable that it should be in accordance with the highest virtue; and this will be that of the best thing in us. Whether it be reason or something else that is this element which is thought to be our natural ruler and 15 guide and to take thought of things noble and divine, whether it be itself also divine or only the most divine element in us, the activity of this in accordance with its proper virtue will be perfect happiness. That this activity is contemplative we have already said.[14]

Now this would seem to be in agreement both with what we said before[15] and with the truth. For, firstly, this 20 activity is the best (since not only is reason the best thing in us, but the objects of reason are the best of knowable objects); and, secondly, it is the most continuous, since we can contemplate truth more continuously than we can do anything. And we think happiness has pleasure mingled with it, but the activity of philosophic wisdom is admittedly the pleasantest of virtuous activities; at all events the pursuit of 25

[13] 1098ᵃ 16, 1176ᵃ 35–ᵇ9.

[14] This has not been said, but Cf. 1095ᵇ 14–1096ᵃ 5, 1141ᵃ 18–ᵇ 3, 1143ᵇ 33–1144ᵃ 6, 1145ᵃ 6–11.

[15] 1097ᵃ 25–ᵇ 21, 1099ᵃ 7–21, 1173ᵇ 15–19, 1174ᵇ 20–23, 1175ᵇ 36–1176ᵃ 3.

it is thought to offer pleasures marvellous for their purity
and their enduringness, and it is to be expected that those
who know will pass their time more pleasantly than those
who inquire. And the self-sufficiency that is spoken of must
belong most to the contemplative activity. For while a
philosopher, as well as a just man or one possessing any
30 other virtue, needs the necessaries of life, when they are sufficiently equipped with things of that sort the just man needs
people towards whom and with whom he shall act justly,
and the temperate man, the brave man, and each of the others is in the same case, but the philosopher, even when by
himself, can contemplate truth, and the better the wiser he
is; he can perhaps do so better if he has fellow-workers, but
1177ᵇ still he is the most self-sufficient. And this activity alone
would seem to be loved for its own sake; for nothing arises
from it apart from the contemplating, while from practical
activities we gain more or less apart from the action. And
5 happiness is thought to depend on leisure; for we are busy
that we may have leisure, and make war that we may live in
peace. Now the activity of the practical virtues is exhibited
in political or military affairs, but the actions concerned with
these seem to be unleisurely. Warlike actions are completely
so (for no one chooses to be at war, or provokes war, for the
10 sake of being at war; any one would seem absolutely mur-
derous if he were to make enemies of his friends in order to
bring about battle and slaughter); but the action of the
statesman is also unleisurely, and—apart from the political
action itself—aims at despotic power and honours, or at all
events happiness, for him and his fellow citizens—a happi-
15 ness different from political action, and evidently sought as
being different. So if among virtuous actions political and
military actions are distinguished by nobility and greatness,
and these are unleisurely and aim at an end and are not
desirable for their own sake, but the activity of reason, which
is contemplative, seems both to be superior in serious worth

and to aim at no end beyond itself, and to have its pleasure proper to itself (and this augments the activity), and the self- 20 sufficiency, leisureliness, unweariedness (so far as this is possible for man), and all the other attributes ascribed to the supremely happy man are evidently those connected with this activity, it follows that this will be the complete happiness of man, if it be allowed a complete term of life (for none of the attributes of happiness is *in*complete). 25

But such a life would be too high for man; for it is not in so far as he is man that he will live so, but in so far as something divine is present in him; and by so much as this is superior to our composite nature is its activity superior to that which is the exercise of the other kind of virtue. If reason is divine, then, in comparison with man, the life according to it is divine in comparison with human life. But 30 we must not follow those who advise us, being men, to think of human things, and, being mortal, of mortal things, but must, so far as we can, make ourselves immortal, and strain every nerve to live in accordance with the best thing in us; for even if it be small in bulk, much more does it in 1178ᵃ power and worth surpass everything. This would seem, too, to be each man himself, since it is the authoritative and better part of him. It would be strange, then, if he were to choose not the life of his self but that of something else. And what we said before¹⁶ will apply now; that which is proper to each thing is by nature best and most pleasant for 5 each thing; for man, therefore, the life according to reason is best and pleasantest, since reason more than anything else *is* man. This life therefore is also the happiest.

8 But in a secondary degree the life in accordance with the other kind of virtue is happy; for the activities in accordance with this befit our human 10

---

¹⁶ 1169ᵇ 33, 1176ᵇ 26.

estate. Just and brave acts, and other virtuous acts, we do in
relation to each other, observing our respective duties with
regard to contracts and services and all manner of actions
and with regard to passions; and all of these seem to be typ-
15 ically human. Some of them seem even to arise from the
body, and virtue of character to be in many ways bound up
with the passions. Practical wisdom, too, is linked to virtue
of character, and this to practical wisdom, since the principles of practical wisdom are in accordance with the moral
virtues and rightness in morals is in accordance with practical wisdom. Being connected with the passions also, the
moral virtues must belong to our composite nature; and the
20 virtues of our composite nature are human; so, therefore, are
the life and the happiness which correspond to these. The
excellence of the reason is a thing apart; we must be content
to say this much about it, for to describe it precisely is a
task greater than our purpose requires. It would seem, how-
25 ever, also to need external equipment but little, or less than
moral virtue does. Grant that both need the necessaries, and
do so equally, even if the statesman's work is the more concerned with the body and things of that sort; for there will
be little difference there; but in what they need for the exercise of their activities there will be much difference. The
liberal man will need money for the doing of his liberal
30 deeds, and the just man too will need it for the returning of
services (for wishes are hard to discern, and even people
who are not just pretend to wish to act justly); and the
brave man will need power if he is to accomplish any of the
acts that correspond to his virtue, and the temperate man
will need opportunity; for how else is either he or any of the
others to be recognized? It is debated, too, whether the will
35 or the deed is more essential to virtue, which is assumed to
1178b involve both; it is surely clear that its perfection involves
both; but for deeds many things are needed, and more, the
greater and nobler the deeds are. But the man who is con-

templating the truth needs no such thing, at least with a
view to the exercise of his activity; indeed they are, one may
say, even hindrances, at all events to his contemplation; but
in so far as he is a man and lives with a number of people,
he chooses to do virtuous acts; he will therefore need such
aids to living a human life.

But that perfect happiness is a contemplative activity
will appear from the following consideration as well. We
assume the gods to be above all other beings blessed and
happy; but what sort of actions must we assign to them?
Acts of justice? Will not the gods seem absurd if they make
contracts and return deposits, and so on? Acts of a brave
man, then, confronting dangers and running risks because it
is noble to do so? Or liberal acts? To whom will they give?
It will be strange if they are really to have money or anything of the kind. And what would their temperate acts be?
Is not such praise tasteless, since they have no bad appetites?
If we were to run through them all, the circumstances of
action would be found trivial and unworthy of gods. Still,
every one supposes that they *live* and therefore that they are
active; we cannot suppose them to sleep like Endymion.
Now if you take away from a living being action, and still
more production, what is left but contemplation? Therefore
the activity of God, which surpasses all others in blessedness, must be contemplative; and of human activities,
therefore, that which is most akin to this must be most of
the nature of happiness.

This is indicated, too, by the fact that the other animals
have no share in happiness, being completely deprived of
such activity. For while the whole life of the gods is blessed,
and that of men too in so far as some likeness of such activity belongs to them, none of the other animals is happy,
since they in no way share in contemplation. Happiness
extends, then, just so far as contemplation does, and those to
whom contemplation more fully belongs are more truly

happy, not as a mere concomitant but in virtue of the con-
30 templation; for this is in itself precious. Happiness, therefore, must be some form of contemplation.

But, being a man, one will also need external prosper-
ity; for our nature is not self-sufficient for the purpose of contemplation, but our body also must be healthy and must
35 have food and other attention. Still, we must not think that
1179a the man who is to be happy will need many things or great things, merely because he cannot be supremely happy without external goods; for self-sufficiency and action do not involve excess, and we can do noble acts without ruling
5 earth and sea; for even with moderate advantages one can act virtuously (this is manifest enough; for private persons are thought to do worthy acts no less than despots—indeed even more); and it is enough that we should have so much as that; for the life of the man who is active in accordance with virtue will be happy. Solon, too, was perhaps sketching
10 well the happy man when he described him as moderately furnished with externals but as having done (as Solon thought) the noblest acts, and lived temperately; for one can with but moderate possessions do what one ought. Anaxagoras also seems to have supposed the happy man not to be rich nor a despot, when he said that he would not be surprised if the happy man were to seem to most people a
15 strange person; for they judge by externals, since these are all they perceive. The opinions of the wise seem, then, to harmonize with our arguments. But while even such things carry some conviction, the truth in practical matters is dis-
20 cerned from the facts of life; for these are the decisive factor. We must therefore survey what we have already said, bringing it to the test of the facts of life, and if it har-
monizes with the facts we must accept it, but if it clashes with them we must suppose it to be mere theory. Now he who exercises his reason and cultivates it seems to be both in the best state of mind and most dear to the gods. For if

the gods have any care for human affairs, as they are 25
thought to have, it would be reasonable both that they
should delight in that which was best and most akin to
them (i. e. reason) and that they should reward those who
love and honour this most, as caring for the things that are
dear to them and acting both rightly and nobly. And that
all these attributes belong most of all to the philosopher is 30
manifest. He, therefore, is the dearest to the gods. And he
who is that will presumably be also the happiest; so that in
this way too the philosopher will more than any other be
happy.

9 If these matters and the virtues, and also friendship
and pleasure, have been dealt with sufficiently in
outline, are we to suppose that our programme has 35
reached its end? Surely, as the saying goes, where there are
things to be done the end is not to survey and recognize the 1179b
various things, but rather to do them; with regard to virtue,
then, it is not enough to know, but we must try to have and
use it, or try any other way there may be of becoming good.
Now if arguments were in themselves enough to make men
good, they would justly, as Theognis says, have won very 5
great rewards, and such rewards should have been provided;
but as things are, while they seem to have power to encourage and stimulate the generous-minded among our youth,
and to make a character which is gently born, and a true
lover of what is noble, ready to be possessed by virtue, they 10
are not able to encourage the many to nobility and goodness. For these do not by nature obey the sense of shame,
but only fear, and do not abstain from bad acts because of
their baseness but through fear of punishment; living by
passion they pursue their own pleasures and the means to
them, and avoid the opposite pains, and have not even a 15
conception of what is noble and truly pleasant, since they
have never tasted it. What argument would remould such

people? It is hard, if not impossible, to remove by argument the traits that have long since been incorporated in the character; and perhaps we must be content if, when all the influences by which we are thought to become good are present, we get some tincture of virtue.

20 Now some think that we are made good by nature, others by habituation, others by teaching. Nature's part evidently does not depend on us, but as a result of some divine causes is present in those who are truly fortunate; while argument and teaching, we may suspect, are not powerful with all men, but the soul of the student must first have 25 been cultivated by means of habits for noble joy and noble hatred, like earth which is to nourish the seed. For he who lives as passion directs will not hear argument that dissuades him, nor understand it if he does; and how can we persuade one in such a state to change his ways? And in general passion seems to yield not to argument but to force. The character, then, must somehow be there already with a kin-30 ship to virtue, loving what is noble and hating what is base.

But it is difficult to get from youth up a right training for virtue if one has not been brought up under right laws; for to live temperately and hardily is not pleasant to most people, especially when they are young. For this reason 35 their nurture and occupations should be fixed by law; for they will not be painful when they have become customary. 1180ᵃ But it is surely not enough that when they are young they should get the right nurture and attention; since they must, even when they are grown up, practise and be habituated to them, we shall need laws for this as well, and generally speaking to cover the whole of life; for most people obey necessity rather then argument, and punishments rather than the sense of what is noble.

This is why some think[17] that legislators ought to stim-

17 Pl. *Laws* 722 D ff.

ulate men to virtue and urge them forward by the motive 5
of the noble, on the assumption that those who have been
well advanced by the formation of habits will attend to such
influences; and that punishments and penalties should be
imposed on those who disobey and are of inferior nature,
while the incurably bad should be completely banished.[18] A
good man (they think), since he lives with his mind fixed
on what is noble, will submit to argument, while a bad man,
whose desire is for pleasure, is corrected by pain like a beast 10
of burden. This is, too, why they say the pains inflicted
should be those that are most opposed to the pleasures such
men love.

However that may be, if (as we have said)[19] the man
who is to be good must be well trained and habituated, and 15
go on to spend his time in worthy occupations and neither
willingly nor unwillingly do bad actions, and if this can be
brought about if men live in accordance with a sort of reason and right order, provided this has force—if this be so,
the paternal command indeed has not the required force or
compulsive power (nor in general has the command of one 20
man, unless he be a king or something similar), but the law
has compulsive power, while it is at the same time a rule
proceeding from a sort of practical wisdom and reason. And
while people hate *men* who oppose their impulses, even if
they oppose them rightly, the law in its ordaining of what is
good is not burdensome.

In the Spartan state alone, or almost alone, the legisla- 25
tor seems to have paid attention to questions of nurture and
occupations; in most states such matters have been neglected, and each man lives as he pleases, Cyclops-fashion,
'to his own wife and children dealing law'.[20] Now it is best

[18] Pl. *Prot.* 325 A.

[19] 1179[b] 31–1180[a] 5.

[20] *Od.* ix. 114 f.

30 that there should be a public and proper care for such matters; but if they are neglected by the community it would
seem right for each man to help his children and friends
towards virtue, and that they should have the power, or at
least the will, to do this.

It would seem from what has been said that he can do
this better if he makes himself capable of legislating. For
public control is plainly effected by laws, and good control
35 by good laws; whether written or unwritten would seem to
1180ᵇ make no difference, nor whether they are laws providing for
the education of individuals or of groups—any more than
it does in the case of music or gymnastics and other such
pursuits. For as in cities laws and prevailing types of character have force, so in households do the injunctions and the
5 habits of the father, and these have even more because of
the tie of blood and the benefits he confers; for the children
start with a natural affection and disposition to obey. Further, private education has an advantage over public, as
private medical treatment has; for while in general rest and
abstinence from food are good for a man in a fever, for a
10 particular man they may not be; and a boxer presumably
does not prescribe the same style of fighting to all his
pupils. It would seem, then, that the detail is worked out
with more precision if the control is private; for each person
is more likely to get what suits his case.

But the details can be best looked after, one by one, by
a doctor or gymnastic instructor or any one else who has the
general knowledge of what is good for every one or for people of a certain kind (for the sciences both are said to be,
15 and are, concerned with what is universal); not but what
some particular detail may perhaps be well looked after by
an unscientific person, if he has studied accurately in the
light of experience what happens in each case, just as some
people seem to be their own best doctors, though they could

give no help to any one else. None the less, it will perhaps be agreed that if a man does wish to become master of an 20 art or science he must go to the universal, and come to know it as well as possible; for, as we have said, it is with this that the sciences are concerned.

And surely he who wants to make men, whether many or few, better by his care must try to become capable of legislating, if it is through laws that we can become good. For to get any one whatever—any one who is put before us— 25 into the right condition is not for the first chance comer; if any one can do it, it is the man who knows, just as in medicine and all other matters which give scope for care and prudence.

Must we not, then, next examine whence or how one can learn how to legislate? Is it, as in all other cases, from statesmen? Certainly it was thought to be a part of statesmanship.[21] Or is a difference apparent between statesmanship and the 30 other sciences and arts? In the others the same people are found offering to teach the arts and practising them, e. g. doctors or painters; but while the sophists profess to teach politics, it is practised not by any of them but by the politi- 35 cians, who would seem to do so by dint of a certain skill 1181a and experience rather than of thought; for they are not found either writing or speaking about such matters (though it were a nobler occupation perhaps than composing speeches for the law-courts and the assembly), nor again are they found to have made statesmen of their own sons or any 5 other of their friends. But it was to be expected that they should if they could; for there is nothing better than such a skill that they could have left to their cities, or could prefer to have for themselves, or, therefore, for those dearest to them. Still, experience seems to contribute not a little; else

[21] 1141b 24.

10 they could not have become politicians by familiarity with
politics; and so it seems that those who aim at knowing
about the art of politics need experience as well.

But those of the sophists who profess the art seem to be
very far from teaching it. For, to put the matter generally,
they do not even know what kind of thing it is nor what
kinds of things it is about; otherwise they would not have
15 classed it as identical with rhetoric or even inferior to it,[22]
nor have thought it easy to legislate by collecting the laws
that are thought well of;[23] they say it is possible to select the
best laws, as though even the selection did not demand intelligence and as though right judgement were not the greatest
thing, as in matters of music. For while people experienced
20 in any department judge rightly the works produced in it,
and understand by what means or how they are achieved,
and what harmonizes with what, the inexperienced must be
content if they do not fail to see whether the work has been
well or ill made—as in the case of painting. Now laws are
as it were the 'works' of the political art; how then can one
1181ᵇ learn from them to be a legislator, or judge which are best?
Even medical men do not seem to be made by a study of
text-books. Yet people try, at any rate, to state not only the
treatments, but also how particular classes of people can be
5 cured and should be treated—distinguishing the various
habits of body; but while this seems useful to experienced
people, to the inexperienced it is valueless. Surely, then,
while collections of laws, and of constitutions also, may be
serviceable to those who can study them and judge what is
good or bad and what enactments suit what circumstances,
10 those who go through such collections without a practised
faculty will not have right judgement (unless it be as a spon-

22 Isoc. *Antid.* § 80.

23 Ib. §§ 82, 83.

taneous gift of nature), though they may perhaps become more intelligent in such matters.

Now our predecessors have left the subject of legislation to us unexamined; it is perhaps best, therefore, that we should ourselves study it, and in general study the question of the constitution, in order to complete to the best of our 15 ability our philosophy of human nature. First, then, if anything has been said well in detail by earlier thinkers, let us try to review it; then in the light of the constitutions we have collected let us study what sorts of influence preserve and destroy states, and what sorts preserve or destroy the particular kinds of constitution, and to what causes it is due that some are well and others ill administered. When these 20 have been studied we shall perhaps be more likely to see with a comprehensive view, which constitution is best, and how each must be ordered, and what laws and customs it must use, if it is to be at its best.[24] Let us make a beginning of our discussion.

[24] 1181[b] 12–23 is a programme for the *Politics*, agreeing to a large extent with the existing contents of that work.

POLITICS

INTRODUCTION

Since every community is established with a view to some good, the investigation of political problems takes its peculiar turn in the philosophy of Aristotle from his undertaking to treat the communities of men in terms of the natural bases of human association and the varieties of ends obtainable by association. He stresses the differences that distinguish the qualifications of statesman, king, householder, and master, which Plato had argued were the same, and his demonstration that the state is "natural, "since it is essential to living well, is based on analysis of its parts—the family, the household, and village—which are likewise "natural, "since they are essential to mere living.

There is therefore a basic pluralism and dynamism in the political analyses of Aristotle, for there are as many kinds of states as there are characteristics in men and their situations affecting human relations or the purposes that may be sought in association. They may be classified under three main heads, since a "constitution," as Aristotle uses the term, is an arrangement of magistracies and is therefore identical with governments, which are of three main kinds—monarchy, aristocracy, and polity—dependent on whether the supreme authority is exercised by one, or the few, or the many. These three forms of government may be differentiated in turn into many subspecies, or they may be distinguished from three perversions—tyranny, oligarchy, and extreme democracy—dependent on whether their aim is the common welfare or private interest. When the kinds of states treated under these six heads are compared, the criteria of what is "best "may be sought in four different senses: (1) the best in the abstract (and then political problems are conceived largely in terms of the education and improvement of citizens as a means of improving political institutions and their functioning), (2) the best under particular circumstances (and then political problems are conceived in terms of fitting political institutions and their operations to the limitations and predicaments of a state), (3) the best in general (and then political problems are conceived in terms of balances of powers and functions for the resolution of problems and the conduct of political affairs), and (4) the best in the modification or preservation of the original forms of government (and then political problems are conceived in terms of the prevention or furtherance of revolutions).

In Book I of the *Politics,* the natural foundation of the state is sought in the analysis of its parts. In Book III, the basic principles and fundamental distinctions of political science are set up. In those two books the chief possibilities of political action are determined and prefigured. For the state is defined in terms of the citizen and the citizen in terms of his participation in the functions of government. This definition, Aristotle recognizes, is best adapted to a democracy, and he therefore uses the generic term "polity" (which is also translated "constitution ") to designate the good form of democratic government. The functions of citizenship, however, require abilities and virtues in the citizen, and the proper exercise of those functions depends on equality and justice in the state, and Aristotle is therefore fond of repeating his observation that the good citizen will be the same as the good man only in the perfect state The constitution of a state depends on who the citizens are and on what they may be educated to become, but it may also be formulated in terms of the general interplay of functions of government (and modern constitutional thinking has profited by the tradition of thought in which Aristotle's differentiation of the legislative, executive, and judicial functions has been elaborated) or in terms of the revolutions by which real or alleged inequalities and injustices are to be remedied (and Machiavelli found many of his devices in Aristotle's treatment of power and persuasion).

There is no simple relation between ethics, which is part of political science, and political science conceived as the study of the state, for the state influences the education and formation of its citizens and the character of its citizens determines the constitution of the state. Nor is there a simple relation between politics and the theoretic sciences, for knowledge affects the conditions of citizens and states, and states influence the development of science; nor indeed between politics and the arts, since the same interdependence is found there. But politics is itself a "science," in need of a scientific method, which some men, notably the sophists, have confused with rhetoric; and legislation is an "art," which sophists have separated from its subject matter by studying collections of laws as if a physician could be made by the study of medical textbooks. The controlling consideration in all these variabilities of political determination is that all states are established on a kind of equality and justice, and that politics is a practical, not a theoretic, science, whose end is not to acquire knowledge of what virtue is but to make men good.

POLITICS

CONTENTS

BOOK I

Chapters 1, 2. Definition and structure of the State.

1. The state is the highest form of community and aims at the highest good. How it differs from other communities will appear if we examine the parts of which it is composed.

2. It consists of villages which consist of households. The household is founded upon the two relations of male and female, of master and slave; it exists to satisfy man's daily needs. The village, a wider community, satisfies a wider range of needs. The state aims at satisfying all the needs of men. Men form states to secure a bare subsistence; but the ultimate object of the state is the good life. The naturalness of the state is proved by the faculty of speech in man. In the order of Nature the state precedes the household and the individual. It is founded on a natural impulse, that towards political association.

Chapters 3-13. Household economy. The Slave.
Property. Children and Wives.

3. Let us discuss the household, since the state is composed of households.

4. First as to slavery. The slave is a piece of property which is animate, and useful for action rather than for production.

5. Slavery is natural; in every department of the natural universe we find the relation of ruler and subject. There are human beings who, without possessing reason, understand it. These are natural slaves.

6. But we find persons in slavery who are not natural slaves. Hence slavery itself is condemned by some; but they are wrong. The natural slave benefits by subjection to a master.

7. The art of ruling slaves differs from that of ruling free men but calls for no detailed description; any one who is a natural master can acquire it for himself.

8. As to property and the modes of acquiring it. This subject concerns us in so far as property is an indispensable substratum to the household.

9. But we do not need that form of finance which accumulates wealth for its own sake. This is unnatural finance. It has been made possible by the invention of coined money. It accumulates money by means of exchange. Natural and unnatural finance are often treated as though they were the same, but differ in their aims;

10. Also in their subject-matter; for natural finance is only concerned with the fruits of the earth and animals.

11. Natural finance is necessary to the householder; he must therefore know about live stock, agriculture, possibly about the exchange of the products of the earth, such as wood and minerals, for money. Special treatises on finance exist, and the subject should be specially studied by statesmen.

12. Lastly, we must discuss and distinguish the relations of husband to wife, of father to child.

13. In household management persons call for more attention than things; free persons for more than slaves. Slaves are only capable of an inferior kind of virtue. Socrates was wrong in denying that there are several kinds of virtue. Still the slave must be trained in virtue. The education of the free man will be subsequently discussed.

BOOK III

Chapters 1-5. *The Citizen, civic virtue, and the civic body.*

1. How are we to define a citizen? He is more than a mere denizen; private rights do not make a citizen. He is ordinarily one who possesses political power; who sits on juries and in the assembly. But it is hard to find a definition which applies to all so-called citizens. To define him as the son of citizen parents is futile.

2. Some say that his civic rights must have been justly

acquired. But he is a citizen who has political power, however acquired.

3. Similarly the state is defined by reference to the distribution of political power; when the mode of distribution is
changed a new state comes into existence.

4. The good citizen may not be a good man; the good citizen is one who does good service to his state, and this state
may be bad in principle. In a constitutional state the good
citizen knows both how to rule and how to obey. The
good man is one who is fitted to rule. But the citizen in a
constitutional state learns to rule by obeying orders.
Therefore citizenship in such a state is a moral training.

5. Mechanics will not be citizens in the best state. Extreme
democracies, and some oligarchies, neglect this rule. But
circumstances oblige them to do this. They have no choice.

*Chapters 6-13. The Classification of Constitutions;
Democracy and Oligarchy; Kingship.*

6. The aims of the state are two: to satisfy man's social
instinct, and to fit him for the good life. Political rule differs from that over slaves in aiming primarily at the good
of those who are ruled.

7. Constitutions are bad or good according as the common
welfare is, or is not, their aim. Of good Constitutions there
are three: Monarchy, Aristocracy and Polity. Of bad there
are also three: Tyranny, Oligarchy, Extreme Democracy.
The bad are perversions of the good.

8. Democracies and Oligarchies are not made by the numerical proportion of the rulers to the ruled. Democracy is the
rule of the poor, oligarchy is that of the rich.

9. Democrats take Equality for their motto; oligarchs believe
that political rights should be unequal and proportionate
to wealth. But both sides miss the true object of the state,
which is virtue. Those who do most to promote virtue
deserve the greatest share of power.

10. On the same principle, Justice is not the will of the majority or of the wealthier, but that course of action which the
moral aim of the state requires.

11. But are the Many or the Few likely to be the better rulers?

It would be unreasonable to give the highest offices to the Many. But they have a faculty of criticism which fits them for deliberative and judicial power. The good critic need not be an expert; experts are sometimes bad judges. Moreover, the Many have a greater stake in the city than the Few. But the governing body, whether Few or Many, must be held in check by the laws.

12. On what principle should political power be distributed? Granted that equals deserve equal shares; who are these equals? Obviously those who are equally able to be of service to the state.

13. Hence there is something in the claims advanced by the wealthy, the free born, the noble, the highly gifted. But no one of these classes should be allowed to rule the rest. A state should consist of men who are equal, or nearly so, in wealth, in birth, in moral and intellectual excellence. The principle which underlies Ostracism is plausible. But in the ideal state, if a pre-eminent individual be found, he should be made a king.

Chapters 14-18. The Forms of Monarchy.

14. Of Monarchy there are five kinds, (1) the Spartan, (2) the Barbarian, (3) the elective dictatorship, (4) the Heroic, (5) Absolute Kingship.

15. The last of these forms might appear the best polity to some; that is, if the king acts as the embodiment of law. For he will dispense from the law in the spirit of the law. But this power would be less abused if reserved for the Many. Monarchy arose to meet the needs of primitive society; it is now obsolete and on various grounds objectionable.

16. It tends to become hereditary; it subjects equals to the rule of an equal. The individual monarch may be misled by his passions, and no single man can attend to all the duties of government.

17. One case alone can be imagined in which Absolute Kingship would be just.

18. Let us consider the origin and nature of the best polity, now that we have agreed not to call Absolute Kingship the best.

POLITICA

Politics

Translated by Benjamin Jowett

BOOK I

1 Every state is a community of some kind, and every community is established with a view to some good; for mankind always act in order to obtain that which they think good. But, if all communities aim at some good, the state or political community, which is the highest of all, and which embraces all the rest, aims at good in a greater degree than any other, and at the highest good. 1252ª

5

Some people think[1] that the qualifications of a statesman, king, householder, and master are the same, and that they differ, not in kind, but only in the number of their subjects. For example, the ruler over a few is called a master; over more, the manager of a household; over a still larger number, a statesman or king, as if there were no difference between a great household and a small state. The distinction which is made between the king and the statesman is as follows: When the government is personal, the ruler is a king; when, according to the rules of the political science, the citizens rule and are ruled in turn, then he is called a statesman. 10

15

[1] Cf. Plato, *Politicus,* 258 E–259 D.

But all this is a mistake; for governments differ in kind, as will be evident to any one who considers the matter according to the method[2] which has hitherto guided us. As 20 in other departments of science, so in politics, the compound should always be resolved into the simple elements or least parts of the whole. We must therefore look at the elements of which the state is composed, in order that we may see in what the different kinds of rule differ from one another, and whether any scientific result can be attained about each one of them.

2 He who thus considers things in their first growth and origin, whether a state or anything else, will 25 obtain the clearest view of them. In the first place there must be a union of those who cannot exist without each other; namely, of male and female, that the race may continue (and this is a union which is formed, not of deliberate purpose, but because, in common with other animals 30 and with plants, mankind have a natural desire to leave behind them an image of themselves), and of natural ruler and subject, that both may be preserved. For that which can foresee by the exercise of mind is by nature intended to be lord and master, and that which can with its body give effect to such foresight is a subject, and by nature a slave; 1252b hence master and slave have the same interest. Now nature has distinguished between the female and the slave. For she is not niggardly, like the smith who fashions the Delphian knife for many uses; she makes each thing for a single use, and every instrument is best made when intended for one 5 and not for many uses. But among barbarians no distinction is made between women and slaves, because there is no natural ruler among them: they are a community of slaves, male and female. Wherefore the poets say—

2 Cf. 1256a 2.

'It is meet that Hellenes should rule over barbarians';

as if they thought that the barbarian and the slave were by
nature one.

Out of these two relationships between man and woman,
master and slave, the first thing to arise is the family, and 10
Hesiod is right when he says—

'First house and wife and an ox for the plough',

for the ox is the poor man's slave. The family is the association established by nature for the supply of men's everyday
wants, and the members of it are called by Charondas 'companions of the cupboard', and by Epimenides the Cretan,
'companions of the manger.' But when several families are
united, and the association aims at something more than the 15
supply of daily needs, the first society to be formed is the
village. And the most natural form of the village appears to
be that of a colony from the family, composed of the children and grandchildren, who are said to be 'suckled with 20
the same milk'. And this is the reason why Hellenic states
were originally governed by kings; because the Hellenes
were under royal rule before they came together, as the barbarians still are. Every family is ruled by the eldest, and
therefore in the colonies of the family the kingly form of
government prevailed because they were of the same blood.
As Homer says:[3]

'Each one gives law to his children and to his wives.'

For they lived dispersedly, as was the manner in ancient
times. Wherefore men say that the Gods have a king,
because they themselves either are or were in ancient times

[3] *Od*. ix. 114, quoted by Plato, *Laws*, iii. 680 B, and in *N. Eth*. x. 1180ᵃ 28.

25 under the rule of a king. For they imagine, not only the forms of the Gods, but their ways of life to be like their own.

When several villages are united in a single complete community, large enough to be nearly or quite self-sufficing, the state comes into existence, originating in the bare needs of life, and continuing in existence for the sake of a 30 good life. And therefore, if the earlier forms of society are natural, so is the state, for it is the end of them, and the nature of a thing is its end. For what each thing is when fully developed, we call its nature, whether we are speaking of a man, a horse, or a family. Besides, the final cause and end of a thing is the best, and to be self-sufficing is the end 1253ᵃ and the best.

Hence it is evident that the state is a creation of nature, and that man is by nature a political animal. And he who by nature and not by mere accident is without a state, is either a bad man or above humanity; he is like the

'Tribeless, lawless, heartless one,'

whom Homer[4] denounces—the natural outcast is forthwith a lover of war; he may be compared to an isolated piece at draughts.

Now, that man is more of a political animal than bees or any other gregarious animals is evident. Nature, as we often say, makes nothing in vain,[5] and man is the only animal whom she has endowed with the gift of speech.[6] And 10 whereas mere voice is but an indication of pleasure or pain, and is therefore found in other animals (for their nature attains to the perception of pleasure and pain and the intimation of them to one another, and no further), the power

[4] *Il.* ix. 63.

[5] Cf. 1256ᵇ 20.

[6] Cf. vii. 1332ᵇ 5.

of speech is intended to set forth the expedient and inexpedient, and therefore likewise the just and the unjust. And it is a characteristic of man that he alone has any sense of good and evil, of just and unjust, and the like, and the association of living beings who have this sense makes a family and a state.

Further, the state is by nature clearly prior to the family and to the individual, since the whole is of necessity prior to to the part; for example, if the whole body be destroyed, there will be no foot or hand, except in an equivocal sense, as we might speak of a stone hand; for when destroyed the hand will be no better than that. But things are defined by their working and power; and we ought not to say that they are the same when they no longer have their proper quality, but only that they have the same name. The proof that the state is a creation of nature and prior to the individual is that the individual, when isolated, is not self-sufficing; and therefore he is like a part in relation to the whole. But he who is unable to live in society, or who has no need because he is sufficient for himself, must be either a beast or a god: he is no part of a state. A social instinct is implanted in all men by nature, and yet he who first founded the state was the greatest of benefactors. For man, when perfected, is the best of animals, but, when separated from law and justice, he is the worst of all; since armed injustice is the more dangerous, and he is equipped at birth with arms, meant to be used by intelligence and virtue, which he may use for the worst ends. Wherefore, if he have not virtue, he is the most unholy and the most savage of animals, and the most full of lust and gluttony. But justice is the bond of men in states, for the administration of justice, which is the determination of what is just,[7] is the principle of order in political society.

---

[7] Cf. *N. Eth.* v. 1134ᵃ 31.

3 Seeing then that the state is made up of households, before speaking of the state we must speak
1253b of the management of the household. The parts of
household management correspond to the persons who
compose the household, and a complete household consists
of slaves and freemen. Now we should begin by examining
5 everything in its fewest possible elements; and the first and
fewest possible parts of a family are master and slave, husband and wife, father and children. We have therefore to
consider what each of these three relations is and ought to
10 be:—I mean the relation of master and servant, the marriage
relation (the conjunction of man and wife has no name of its
own), and thirdly, the procreative relation (this also has no
proper name). And there is another element of a household,
the so-called art of getting wealth, which, according to
some, is identical with household management, according
to others, a principal part of it; the nature of this art will
also have to be considered by us.

15   Let us first speak of master and slave, looking to the
needs of practical life and also seeking to attain some better
theory of their relation than exists at present. For some are
of opinion that the rule of a master is a science, and that the
management of a household, and the mastership of slaves,
20 and the political and royal rule, as I was saying at the outset,[8] are all the same. Others affirm that the rule of a master
over slaves is contrary to nature, and that the distinction
between slave and freeman exists by law only, and not by
nature; and being an interference with nature is therefore
unjust.

4 Property is a part of the household, and the art of
acquiring property is a part of the art of managing
the household; for no man can live well, or indeed

[8] Plato in *Pol.* 258 E–259 D, referred to already in 1252ª 7–16.

live at all, unless he be provided with necessaries. And as in 25
the arts which have a definite sphere the workers must have
their own proper instruments for the accomplishment of
their work, so it is in the management of a household. Now
instruments are of various sorts; some are living, others lifeless; in the rudder, the pilot of a ship has a lifeless, in the
look-out man, a living instrument; for in the arts the servant is a kind of instrument. Thus, too, a possession is an
instrument for maintaining life. And so, in the arrangement 30
of the family, a slave is a living possession, and property a
number of such instruments; and the servant is himself an
instrument which takes precedence of all other instruments.
For if every instrument could accomplish its own work,
obeying or anticipating the will of others, like the statues of
Daedalus, or the tripods of Hephaestus, which, says the 35
poet,[9]

'of their own accord entered the assembly of the Gods';

if, in like manner, the shuttle would weave and the plectrum
touch the lyre without a hand to guide them, chief workmen would not want servants, nor masters slaves. Here,
however, another distinction must be drawn; the instru- 1254ᵃ
ments commonly so called are instruments of production,
whilst a possession is an instrument of action. The shuttle,
for example, is not only of use; but something else is made
by it, whereas of a garment or of a bed there is only the use.
Further, as production and action are different in kind, and
both require instruments, the instruments which they 5
employ must likewise differ in kind. But life is action and
not production, and therefore the slave is the minister of
action. Again, a possession is spoken of as a part is spoken
of; for the part is not only a part of something else, but

[9] Hom. *Il.* xviii. 376.

10 wholly belongs to it; and this is also true of a possession.
The master is only the master of the slave; he does not
belong to him, whereas the slave is not only the slave of his
master, but wholly belongs to him. Hence we see what is
the nature and office of a slave; he who is by nature not his
15 own but another's man, is by nature a slave; and he may be
said to be another's man who, being a human being, is also
a possession. And a possession may be defined as an instrument of action, separable from the possessor.

5 But is there any one thus intended by nature to be
a slave, and for whom such a condition is expedient
and right, or rather is not all slavery a violation of
nature?
20   There is no difficulty in answering this question, on
grounds both of reason and of fact. For that some should
rule and others be ruled is a thing not only necessary, but
expedient; from the hour of their birth, some are marked
out for subjection, others for rule.
       And there are many kinds both of rulers and subjects
25 (and that rule is the better which is exercised over better
subjects—for example, to rule over men is better than to rule
over wild beasts; for the work is better which is executed by
better workmen, and where one man rules and another is
ruled, they may be said to have a work); for in all things
which form a composite whole and which are made up of
30 parts, whether continuous or discrete, a distinction between
the ruling and the subject element comes to light. Such a
duality exists in living creatures, but not in them only; it
originates in the constitution of the universe; even in things
which have no life there is a ruling principle, as in a musical mode. But we are wandering from the subject. We will
therefore restrict ourselves to the living creature, which, in
35 the first place, consists of soul and body: and of these two,
the one is by nature the ruler, and the other the subject. But

then we must look for the intentions of nature in things
which retain their nature, and not in things which are corrupted. And therefore we must study the man who is in the
most perfect state both of body and soul, for in him we shall
see the true relation of the two; although in bad or corrupted 1254^b
natures the body will often appear to rule over the soul,
because they are in an evil and unnatural condition. At all
events we may firstly observe in living creatures both a
despotical and a constitutional rule; for the soul rules the
body with a despotical rule, whereas the intellect rules the
appetites with a constitutional and royal rule. And it is clear 5
that the rule of the soul over the body, and of the mind and
the rational element over the passionate, is natural and expedient; whereas the equality of the two or the rule of the
inferior is always hurtful. The same holds good of animals in
relation to men; for tame animals have a better nature than 10
wild, and all tame animals are better off when they are ruled
by man; for then they are preserved. Again, the male is by
nature superior, and the female inferior; and the one rules,
and the other is ruled; this principle, of necessity, extends
to all mankind. Where then there is such a difference as that 15
between soul and body, or between men and animals (as in
the case of those whose business is to use their body, and
who can do nothing better), the lower sort are by nature
slaves, and it is better for them as for all inferiors that they
should be under the rule of a master. For he who can be,
and therefore is, another's, and he who participates in rational principle enough to apprehend, but not to have, such a 20
principle, is a slave by nature. Whereas the lower animals
cannot even apprehend a principle; they obey their instincts.
And indeed the use made of slaves and of tame animals is
not very different; for both with their bodies minister to the
needs of life. Nature would like to distinguish between the 25
bodies of freemen and slaves, making the one strong for
servile labour, the other upright, and although useless for

30 such services, useful for political life in the arts both of war
and peace. But the opposite often happens—that some have
the souls and others have the bodies of freemen. And doubtless if men differed from one another in the mere forms of
their bodies as much as the statues of the Gods do from
35 men, all would acknowledge that the inferior class should be
slaves of the superior. And if this is true of the body, how
much more just that a similar distinction should exist in the
soul? but the beauty of the body is seen, whereas the beauty
1255ª of the soul is not seen. It is clear, then, that some men are by
nature free, and others slaves, and that for these latter slavery is both expedient and right.

6 But that those who take the opposite view have in
a certain way right on their side, may be easily seen.
For the words slavery and slave are used in two
5 senses. There is a slave or slavery by law as well as by
nature. The law of which I speak is a sort of convention—
the law by which whatever is taken in war is supposed to
belong to the victors. But this right many jurists impeach, as
they would an orator who brought forward an unconstitu-
tional measure: they detest the notion that, because one man
has the power of doing violence and is superior in brute
10 strength, another shall be his slave and subject. Even among
philosophers there is a difference of opinion. The origin of
the dispute, and what makes the views invade each other's
territory, is as follows: in some sense virtue, when furnished
with means, has actually the greatest power of exercising
force: and as superior power is only found where there is
superior excellence of some kind, power seems to imply
virtue, and the dispute to be simply one about justice (for it
15 is due to one party identifying justice with goodwill,[10] while

[10] i. e. mutual goodwill, which is held to be incompatible with the relation
of master and slave.

the other identifies it with the mere rule of the stronger). If these views are thus set out separately, the other views[11] have no force or plausibility against the view that the supe- 20 rior in virtue ought to rule, or be master. Others, clinging, as they think, simply to a principle of justice (for law and custom are a sort of justice), assume that slavery in accordance with the custom of war is justified by law, but at the same moment they deny this. For what if the cause of the war be unjust? And again, no one would ever say that he is 25 a slave who is unworthy to be a slave. Were this the case, men of the highest rank would be slaves and the children of slaves if they or their parents chance to have been taken captive and sold. Wherefore Hellenes do not like to call Hellenes slaves, but confine the term to barbarians. Yet, in using this language, they really mean the natural slave of 30 whom we spoke at first;[12] for it must be admitted that some are slaves everywhere, others nowhere. The same principle applies to nobility. Hellenes regard themselves as noble everywhere, and not only in their own country, but they 35 deem the barbarians noble only when at home, thereby implying that there are two sorts of nobility and freedom, the one absolute, the other relative. The Helen of Theodectes says:

> 'Who would presume to call me servant who am on
>   both sides sprung from the stem of the Gods?'

What does this mean but that they distinguish freedom and slavery, noble and humble birth, by the two principles of 40

[11] i. e. those stated in ll. 5–12, that the stronger always has, and that he never has, a right to enslave the weaker. Aristotle finds that these views cannot maintain themselves against his intermediate view, that the superior in *virtue* should rule.

[12] Chap. 5.

1255^b good and evil? They think that as men and animals beget men and animals, so from good men a good man springs. But this is what nature, though she may intend it, cannot always accomplish.

5 We see then that there is some foundation for this difference of opinion, and that all are not either slaves by nature or freemen by nature, and also that there is in some cases a marked distinction between the two classes, rendering it expedient and right for the one to be slaves and the others to be masters: the one practising obedience, the others exercising the authority and lordship which nature intended them to have. The abuse of this authority is injurious to both; for the interests of part and whole,[13] of body and soul, are the same, and the slave is a part of the master, a living but separated part of his bodily frame. Hence, where the relation of master and slave between them is natural they are friends and have a common interest, but where it rests merely on law and force the reverse is true.

7 The previous remarks are quite enough to show that the rule of a master is not a constitutional rule, and that all the different kinds of rule are not, as some affirm, the same with each other.[14] For there is one rule exercised over subjects who are by nature free, another over subjects who are by nature slaves. The rule of a household is a monarchy for every house is under one head: whereas constitutional rule is a government of freemen and 20 equals. The master is not called a master because he has science,[15] but because he is of a certain character, and the same remark applies to the slave and the freeman. Still there may

---

[13] Cp. 1254^a 8.

[14] Plato, *Polit*. 258 E–259 D, referred to already in 1252^a 7–16, 1253^b 18–20.

[15] *Polit*. 259 C, 293 C.

be a science for the master and a science for the slave. The
science of the slave would be such as the man of Syracuse
taught, who made money by instructing slaves in their ordinary duties. And such a knowledge may be carried further, 25
so as to include cookery and similar menial arts. For some
duties are of the more necessary, others of the more honourable sort; as the proverb says, 'slave before slave, master
before master'. But all such branches of knowledge are
servile. There is likewise a science of the master, which 30
teaches the use of slaves; for the master as such is concerned, not with the acquisition, but with the use of them.
Yet this so-called science is not anything great or wonderful; for the master need only know how to order that which
the slave must know how to execute. Hence those who are
in a position which places them above toil have stewards 35
who attend to their households while they occupy themselves with philosophy or with politics. But the art of
acquiring slaves, I mean of justly acquiring them, differs
both from the art of the master and the art of the slave,
being a species of hunting or war.[16] Enough of the distinction between master and slave.   40

8 Let us now inquire into property generally, and into
the art of getting wealth, in accordance with our 1256ª
usual method,[17] for a slave has been shown[18] to be
a part of property. The first question is whether the art of
getting wealth is the same with the art of managing a household or a part of it, or instrumental to it; and if the last,
whether in the way that the art of making shuttles is instrumental to the art of weaving, or in the way that the casting

[16] Cp. vii. 1333ᵇ 38.

[17] Of understanding the whole by the part, Cp. 1252ª 17.

[18] Chap. 4.

5 of bronze is instrumental to the art of the statuary, for they
are not instrumental in the same way, but the one provides
tools and the other material; and by material I mean the
10 substratum out of which any work is made; thus wool is the
material of the weaver, bronze of the statuary. Now it is easy
to see that the art of household management is not identical
with the art of getting wealth, for the one uses the material
which the other provides. For the art which uses household
stores can be no other than the art of household management. There is, however, a doubt whether the art of getting
wealth is a part of household management or a distinct art.
15 If the getter of wealth has to consider whence wealth and
property can be procured, but there are many sorts of property and riches, then are husbandry, and the care and
provision of food in general, parts of the wealth-getting art
or distinct arts? Again, there are many sorts of food, and
20 therefore there are many kinds of lives both of animals and
men; they must all have food, and the differences in their
food have made differences in their ways of life. For of
beasts, some are gregarious, others are solitary; they live in
the way which is best adapted to sustain them; accordingly
25 as they are carnivorous or herbivorous or omnivorous: and
their habits are determined for them by nature in such a
manner that they may obtain with greater facility the food of
their choice. But, as different species have different tastes,
the same things are not naturally pleasant to all of them; and
30 therefore the lives of carnivorous or herbivorous animals further differ among themselves. In the lives of men too there
is a great difference. The laziest are shepherds, who lead an
idle life, and get their subsistence without trouble from tame
animals; their flocks having to wander from place to place in
35 search of pasture, they are compelled to follow them, culti-
vating a sort of living farm. Others support themselves by
hunting, which is of different kinds. Some, for example, are
brigands, others, who dwell near lakes or marshes or rivers

or a sea in which there are fish, are fishermen, and others
live by the pursuit of birds or wild beasts. The greater number obtain a living from the cultivated fruits of the soil. Such 40
are the modes of subsistence which prevail among those
whose industry springs up of itself, and whose food is not 1256b
acquired by exchange and retail trade—there is the shepherd, the husbandman, the brigand, the fisherman, the
hunter. Some gain a comfortable maintenance out of two
employments, eking out the deficiencies of one of them by
another: thus the life of a shepherd may be combined with 5
that of a brigand, the life of a farmer with that of a hunter.
Other modes of life are similarly combined in any way
which the needs of men may require. Property, in the sense
of a bare livelihood, seems to be given by nature herself to
all, both when they are first born, and when they are grown
up. For some animals bring forth, together with their off- 10
spring, so much food as will last until they are able to
supply themselves; of this the vermiparous or oviparous animals are an instance; and the viviparous animals have up to
a certain time a supply of food for their young in themselves, which is called milk. In like manner we may infer
that, after the birth of animals, plants exist for their sake, 15
and that the other animals exist for the sake of man, the
tame for use and food, the wild, if not all, at least the greater
part of them, for food, and for the provision of clothing and
various instruments. Now if nature makes nothing incomplete, and nothing in vain, the inference must be that she 20
has made all animals for the sake of man. And so, in one
point of view, the art of war is a natural art of acquisition,
for the art of acquisition includes hunting, an art which we
ought to practise against wild beasts, and against men who,
though intended by nature to be governed, will not submit; 25
for war of such a kind is naturally just.[19]

19 Cf. 1255b 38, 1333b 38.

Of the art of acquisition then there is one kind which by nature is a part of the management of a household, in so far as the art of household management must either find ready to hand, or itself provide, such things necessary to
30 life, and useful for the community of the family or state, as can be stored. They are the elements of true riches; for the amount of property which is needed for a good life is not unlimited, although Solon in one of his poems says that

'No bound to riches has been fixed for man'.

But there is a boundary fixed, just as there is in the other arts; for the instruments of any art are never unlimited,
35 either in number or size, and riches may be defined as a number of instruments to be used in a household or in a state. And so we see that there is a natural art of acquisition which is practised by managers of households and by statesmen, and what is the reason of this.

9 There is another variety of the art of acquisition
40 which is commonly and rightly called an art of wealth-getting, and has in fact suggested the notion
1257ᵃ that riches and property have no limit. Being nearly connected with the preceding, it is often identified with it. But though they are not very different, neither are they the same. The kind already described is given by nature, the other is gained by experience and art.

Let us begin our discussion of the question with the
5 following considerations:

Of everything which we possess there are two uses: both belong to the thing as such, but not in the same manner, for one is the proper, and the other the improper or secondary use of it. For example, a shoe is used for wear
10 and is used for exchange; both are uses of the shoe. He who gives a shoe in exchange for money or food to him who

wants one, does indeed use the shoe as a shoe, but this is
not its proper or primary purpose, for a shoe is not made
to be an object of barter. The same may be said of all possessions, for the art of exchange extends to all of them, and 15
it arises at first from what is natural, from the circumstance
that some have too little, others too much. Hence we may
infer that retail trade is not a natural part of the art of getting wealth; had it been so, men would have ceased to
exchange when they had enough. In the first community,
indeed, which is the family, this art is obviously of no use, 20
but it begins to be useful when the society increases. For
the members of the family originally had all things in common; later, when the family divided into parts, the parts
shared in many things, and different parts in different
things, which they had to give in exchange for what they
wanted, a kind of barter which is still practised among bar- 25
barous nations who exchange with one another the
necessaries of life and nothing more; giving and receiving
wine, for example, in exchange for corn, and the like. This
sort of barter is not part of the wealth-getting art and is not
contrary to nature, but is needed for the satisfaction of 30
men's natural wants. The other or more complex form of
exchange grew, as might have been inferred, out of the sim-
pler. When the inhabitants of one country became more
dependent on those of another, and they imported what
they needed, and exported what they had too much of,
money necessarily came into use. For the various necessaries 35
of life are not easily carried about, and hence men agreed
to employ in their dealings with each other something
which was intrinsically useful and easily applicable to the
purposes of life, for example, iron, silver, and the like. Of
this the value was at first measured simply by size and
weight, but in process of time they put a stamp upon it, to 40
save the trouble of weighing and to mark the value.

When the use of coin had once been discovered, out of 1257^b

the barter of necessary articles arose the other art of wealth-
getting, namely, retail trade; which was at first probably a
simple matter, but became more complicated as soon as
men learned by experience whence and by what exchanges
5 the greatest profit might be made. Originating in the use of
coin, the art of getting wealth is generally thought to be
chiefly concerned with it, and to be the art which produces
riches and wealth; having to consider how they may be
accumulated. Indeed, riches is assumed by many to be only
a quantity of coin, because the arts of getting wealth and
10 retail trade are concerned with coin. Others maintain that
coined money is a mere sham, a thing not natural, but conventional only, because, if the users substitute another
commodity for it, it is worthless, and because it is not useful as a means to any of the necessities of life, and, indeed,
he who is rich in coin may often be in want of necessary
food. But how can that be wealth of which a man may have
15 a great abundance and yet perish with hunger, like Midas in
the fable, whose insatiable prayer turned everything that
was set before him into gold?

Hence men seek after a better notion of riches and of
the art of getting wealth than the mere acquisition of coin,
and they are right. For natural riches and the natural art of
wealth-getting are a different thing; in their true form they
20 are part of the management of a household; whereas retail
trade is the art of producing wealth, not in every way, but
by exchange. And it is thought to be concerned with coin;
for coin is the unit of exchange and the measure or limit of
it. And there is no bound to the riches which spring from
this art of wealth-getting.[20] As in the art of medicine there is
25 no limit to the pursuit of health, and as in the other arts
there is no limit to the pursuit of their several ends, for they
aim at accomplishing their ends to the uttermost (but of the

[20] Cf. 1256[b] 32.

means there is a limit, for the end is always the limit), so,
too, in this art of wealth-getting there is no limit of the end,
which is riches of the spurious kind, and the acquisition of
wealth. But the art of wealth-getting which consists in 30
household management, on the other hand, has a limit; the
unlimited acquisition of wealth is not its business. And,
therefore, in one point of view, all riches must have a limit;
nevertheless, as a matter of fact, we find the opposite to be
the case; for all getters of wealth increase their hoard of coin
without limit. The source of the confusion is the near connexion between the two kinds of wealth-getting; in either,
the instrument is the same, although the use is different, 35
and so they pass into one another; for each is a use of the
same property, but with a difference: accumulation is the
end in the one case, but there is a further end in the other.
Hence some persons are led to believe that getting wealth
is the object of household management, and the whole idea
of their lives is that they ought either to increase their
money without limit, or at any rate not to lose it. The ori- 40
gin of this disposition in men is that they are intent upon
living only, and not upon living well; and, as their desires
are unlimited, they also desire that the means of gratifying 1258ª
them should be without limit. Those who do aim at a good
life seek the means of obtaining bodily pleasures; and, since 5
the enjoyment of these appears to depend on property, they
are absorbed in getting wealth: and so there arises the second species of wealth-getting. For, as their enjoyment is in
excess, they seek an art which produces the excess of enjoyment; and, if they are not able to supply their pleasures by
the art of getting wealth, they try other arts, using in turn
every faculty in a manner contrary to nature. The quality of 10
courage, for example, is not intended to make wealth, but to
inspire confidence; neither is this the aim of the general's
or of the physician's art; but the one aims at victory and the
other at health. Nevertheless, some men turn every quality

or art into a means of getting wealth; this they conceive to be the end, and to the promotion of the end they think all things must contribute.

Thus, then, we have considered the art of wealth-get-
15 ting which is unnecessary, and why men want it; and also the necessary art of wealth-getting, which we have seen to be different from the other, and to be a natural part of the art of managing a household, concerned with the provision of food, not, however, like the former kind, unlimited, but having a limit.

10 And we have found the answer to our original question,[21] Whether the art of getting wealth is
20 the business of the manager of a household and of the statesman or not their business?—viz. that wealth is presupposed by them. For as political science does not make men, but takes them from nature and uses them, so too nature provides them with earth or sea or the like as a source of food. At this stage begins the duty of the man-
25 ager of a household, who has to order the things which nature supplies;—he may be compared to the weaver who has not to make but to use wool, and to know, too, what sort of wool is good and serviceable or bad and unservice-able. Were this otherwise, it would be difficult to see why the art of getting wealth is a part of the management of a household and the art of medicine not; for surely the mem-
30 bers of a household must have health just as they must have life or any other necessary. The answer is that as from one point of view the master of the house and the ruler of the state have to consider about health, from another point of view not they but the physician; so in one way the art of household management, in another way the subordinate art, has to consider about wealth. But, strictly speaking, as I

[21] 1256ᵃ 3.

have already said, the means of life must be provided
beforehand by nature; for the business of nature is to fur- 35
nish food to that which is born, and the food of the
offspring is always what remains over of that from which it
is produced.[22] Wherefore the art of getting wealth out of
fruits and animals is always natural.

There are two sorts of wealth-getting, as I have said[23];
one is a part of household management, the other is retail
trade: the former necessary and honourable, while that
which consists in exchange is justly censured; for it is 40
unnatural, and a mode by which men gain from one 1258b
another. The most hated sort, and with the greatest reason,
is usury, which makes a gain out of money itself, and not
from the natural object of it. For money was intended to be
used in exchange, but not to increase at interest. And this
term interest,[24] which means the birth of money from 5
money, is applied to the breeding of money because the offspring resembles the parent. Wherefore of all modes of
getting wealth this is the most unnatural.

11

Enough has been said about the theory of wealth-
getting; we will now proceed to the practical part.
The discussion of such matters is not unworthy 10
of philosophy, but to be engaged in them practically is illiberal and irksome. The useful parts of wealth-getting are,
first, the knowledge of live-stock—which are most profitable,
and where, and how—as, for example, what sort of horses or
sheep or oxen or any other animals are most likely to give
a return. A man ought to know which of these pay better 15
than others, and which pay best in particular places, for

---

[22] Cf. 1256b 10.

[23] 1256a 15–1258a 18.

[24] *tokos*, lit. 'offspring'.

some do better in one place and some in another. Secondly, husbandry, which may be either tillage or planting, and the keeping of bees and of fish, or fowl, or of any animals which may be useful to man. These are the divisions of the true or
20 proper art of wealth-getting and come first. Of the other, which consists in exchange, the first and most important division is commerce (of which there are three kinds—the provision of a ship, the conveyance of goods, exposure for sale—these again differing as they are safer or more profitable), the second is usury, the third, service for hire—of
25 this, one kind is employed in the mechanical arts, the other in unskilled and bodily labour. There is still a third sort of wealth-getting intermediate between this and the first or natural mode which is partly natural, but is also concerned with exchange, viz. the industries that make their profit from the earth, and from things growing from the earth
30 which, although they bear no fruit, are nevertheless profitable; for example, the cutting of timber and all mining. The art of mining, by which minerals are obtained, itself has many branches, for there are various kinds of things dug out of the earth. Of the several divisions of wealth-getting I now speak generally; a minute consideration of them might be useful in practice, but it would be tiresome to dwell upon them at greater length now.

35   Those occupations are most truly arts in which there is the least element of chance; they are the meanest in which the body is most deteriorated, the most servile in which there is the greatest use of the body, and the most illiberal in which there is the least need of excellence.

Works have been written upon these subjects by vari-
40 ous persons; for example, by Chares the Parian, and
1259a Apollodorus the Lemnian, who have treated of Tillage and Planting, while others have treated of other branches; any one who cares for such matters may refer to their writings. It would be well also to collect the scattered stories of the

ways in which individuals have succeeded in amassing a fortune; for all this is useful to persons who value the art of 5
getting wealth. There is the anecdote of Thales the Mile-
sian and his financial device, which involves a principle of
universal application, but is attributed to him on account of
his reputation for wisdom. He was reproached for his
poverty, which was supposed to show that philosophy was 10
of no use. According to the story, he knew by his skill in
the stars while it was yet winter that there would be a great
harvest of olives in the coming year; so, having a little
money, he gave deposits for the use of all the olive-presses
in Chios and Miletus, which he hired at a low price because
no one bid against him. When the harvest-time came, and
many were wanted all at once and of a sudden, he let them 15
out at any rate which he pleased, and made a quantity of
money. Thus he showed the world that philosophers can
easily be rich if they like, but that their ambition is of
another sort. He is supposed to have given a striking proof
of his wisdom, but, as I was saying, his device for getting 20
wealth is of universal application, and is nothing but the
creation of a monopoly. It is an art often practised by cities
when they are in want of money; they make a monopoly of
provisions.

There was a man of Sicily, who, having money depos-
ited with him, bought up all the iron from the iron mines;
afterwards, when the merchants from their various markets 25
came to buy, he was the only seller, and without much
increasing the price he gained 200 per cent. Which when
Dionysius heard, he told him that he might take away his
money, but that he must not remain at Syracuse, for he
thought that the man had discovered a way of making 30
money which was injurious to his own interests. He made
the same discovery as Thales; they both contrived to create
a monopoly for themselves. And statesmen as well ought to
know these things; for a state is often as much in want of

money and of such devices for obtaining it as a household,
or even more so; hence some public men devote themselves
35 entirely to finance.

12 Of household management we have seen[25] that
there are three parts—one is the rule of a master over slaves, which has been discussed
already,[26] another of a father, and the third of a husband. A
husband and father, we saw, rules over wife and children,
40 both free, but the rule differs, the rule over his children
being a royal, over his wife a constitutional rule. For
although there may be exceptions to the order of nature, the
1259b male is by nature fitter for command than the female, just
as the elder and full-grown is superior to the younger and
more immature. But in most constitutional states the cit-
5 izens rule and are ruled by turns, for the idea of a
constitutional state implies that the natures of the citizens
are equal, and do not differ at all.[27] Nevertheless, when one
rules and the other is ruled we endeavour to create a difference of outward forms and names and titles of respect,
which may be illustrated by the saying of Amasis about his
foot-pan.[28] The relation of the male to the female is of this
kind, but there the inequality is permanent. The rule of a
10 father over his children is royal, for he rules by virtue both
of love and of the respect due to age, exercising a kind of
royal power. And therefore Homer has appropriately called
Zeus 'father of Gods and men', because he is the king of
them all. For a king is the natural superior of his subjects,

[25] 1253b 3–11.

[26] 1 1253b 14–1255b 39.

[27] Cf. ii. 1261a 39, iii. 1288a 12.

[28] Herod. ii. 172.

but he should be of the same kin or kind with them, and
such is the relation of elder and younger, of father and son. 15

13 Thus it is clear that household management
attends more to men than to the acquisition of
inanimate things, and to human excellence more
than to the excellence of property which we call wealth, and 20
to the virtue of freemen more than to the virtue of slaves. A
question may indeed be raised, whether there is any excellence at all in a slave beyond and higher than merely
instrumental and ministerial qualities—whether he can have
the virtues of temperance, courage, justice, and the like; or
whether slaves possess only bodily and ministerial qualities. 25
And, whichever way we answer the question, a difficulty
arises; for, if they have virtue, in what will they differ from
freemen? On the other hand, since they are men and share
in rational principle, it seems absurd to say that they have
no virtue. A similar question may be raised about women
and children, whether they too have virtues: ought a woman 30
to be temperate and brave and just, and is a child to be
called temperate, and intemperate, or not? So in general we
may ask about the natural ruler, and the natural subject,
whether they have the same or different virtues. For if a
noble nature is equally required in both, why should one of 35
them always rule, and the other always be ruled? Nor can
we say that this is a question of degree, for the difference
between ruler and subject is a difference of kind, which the
difference of more and less never is. Yet how strange is the
supposition that the one ought, and that the other ought
not, to have virtue! For if the ruler is intemperate and 40
unjust, how can he rule well? if the subject, how can he 1260ᵃ
obey well? If he be licentious and cowardly, he will certainly
not do his duty. It is evident, therefore, that both of them
must have a share of virtue, but varying as natural subjects

5 also vary among themselves. Here the very constitution of the soul has shown us the way; in it one part naturally rules, and the other is subject, and the virtue of the ruler we maintain to be different from that of the subject;—the one being the virtue of the rational, and the other of the irrational part. Now, it is obvious that the same principle applies generally, and therefore almost all things rule and are ruled according to nature. But the kind of rule differs;— the freeman rules over the slave after another manner from
10 that in which the male rules over the female, or the man over the child; although the parts of the soul are present in all of them, they are present in different degrees. For the slave has no deliberative faculty at all; the woman has, but
15 it is without authority, and the child has, but it is immature. So it must necessarily be supposed to be with the moral virtues also; all should partake of them, but only in such manner and degree as is required by each for the fulfillment of his duty. Hence the ruler ought to have moral virtue in perfection, for his function, taken absolutely, demands a master artificer, and rational principle is such an
20 artificer; the subjects, on the other hand, require only that measure of virtue which is proper to each of them. Clearly, then, moral virtue belongs to all of them; but the temperance of a man and of a woman, or the courage and justice of a man and of a woman, are not, as Socrates maintained,[29] the same; the courage of a man is shown in commanding, of
25 a woman in obeying. And this holds of all other virtues, as will be more clearly seen if we look at them in detail, for those who say generally that virtue consists in a good disposition of the soul, or in doing rightly, or the like, only deceive themselves. Far better than such definitions is their mode of speaking, who, like Gorgias,[30] enumerate the

[29] Plato, *Meno*, 72 A–73 C.

[30] *Meno*, 71 E–72 A.

virtues. All classes must be deemed to have their special
attributes; as the poet says of women,

'Silence is a woman's glory',   30

but this is not equally the glory of man. The child is imperfect, and therefore obviously his virtue is not relative to
himself alone, but to the perfect man and to his teacher, and
in like manner the virtue of the slave is relative to a master. Now we determined[31] that a slave is useful for the wants
of life, and therefore he will obviously require only so much
virtue as will prevent him from failing in his duty through   35
cowardice or lack of self-control. Some one will ask whether,
if what we are saying is true, virtue will not be required also
in the artisans, for they often fail in their work through the
lack of self-control? But is there not a great difference in the
two cases? For the slave shares in his master's life; the artisan is less closely connected with him, and only attains   40
excellence in proportion as he becomes a slave. The meaner
sort of mechanic has a special and separate slavery; and
whereas the slave exists by nature, not so the shoemaker or   1260b
other artisan. It is manifest, then, that the master ought to
be the source of such excellence in the slave, and not a mere
possessor of the art of mastership which trains the slave in
his duties.[32] Wherefore they are mistaken who forbid us to   5
converse with slaves and say that we should employ command only,[33] for slaves stand even more in need of
admonition than children.

So much for this subject; the relations of husband and
wife, parent and child, their several virtues, what in their

---

[31] 1254b 16–39. Cf. 1259b 25 sq.

[32] Cf. 1255b 23, 31–35.

[33] Plato, *Laws*, vi. 777 E.

intercourse with one another is good, and what is evil, and
10 how we may pursue the good and escape the evil, will have to
be discussed when we speak of the different forms of government.[34] For, inasmuch as every family is a part of a state,
and these relationships are the parts of a family, and the
virtue of the part must have regard to the virtue of the whole,
women and children must be trained by education with an
15 eye to the constitution,[35] if the virtues of either of them are
supposed to make any difference in the virtues of the state.
And they must make a difference: for the children grow up to
be citizens, and half the free persons in a state are women.[36]

Of these matters, enough has been said; of what remains,
20 let us speak at another time. Regarding, then, our present
inquiry as complete, we will make a new beginning. And,
first, let us examine the various theories of a perfect state.

BOOK III

1274ᵇ

1 He who would inquire into the essence and
attributes of various kinds of governments must
first of all determine 'What is a state?' At present
35 this is a disputed question. Some say that the state has done
a certain act; others, no, not the state,[1] but the oligarchy or
the tyrant. And the legislator or statesman is concerned
entirely with the state; a constitution or government being
an arrangement of the inhabitants of a state. But a state is
40 composite, like any other whole made up of many parts,—

---

[34] The question is not actually discussed in the *Politics*.

[35] Cf. v. 1310ᵃ 12–36, viii. 1337ᵃ 11–18.

[36] Plato, *Laws*, vi. 781 A.

[1] Cf. 1276ᵃ 8.

these are the citizens, who compose it. It is evident, there- 1275ᵃ
fore, that we must begin by asking, Who is the citizen, and
what is the meaning of the term? For here again there may
be a difference of opinion. He who is a citizen in a democracy will often not be a citizen in an oligarchy. Leaving out 5
of consideration those who have been made citizens, or who
have obtained the name of citizen in any other accidental
manner, we may say, first, that a citizen is not a citizen
because he lives in a certain place, for resident aliens and
slaves share in the place; nor is he a citizen who has no legal
right except that of suing and being sued; for this right may 10
be enjoyed under the provisions of a treaty. Nay, resident
aliens in many places do not possess even such rights completely, for they are obliged to have a patron, so that they
do but imperfectly participate in citizenship, and we call
them citizens only in a qualified sense, as we might apply
the term to children who are too young to be on the regis- 15
ter, or to old men who have been relieved from state duties.
Of these we do not say quite simply that they are citizens,
but add in the one case that they are not of age, and in the
other, that they are past the age, or something of that sort; 20
the precise expression is immaterial, for our meaning is
clear. Similar difficulties to those which I have mentioned
may be raised and answered about deprived citizens and
about exiles. But the citizen whom we are seeking to define
is a citizen in the strictest sense, against whom no such
exception can be taken, and his special characteristic is that
he shares in the administration of justice, and in offices.
Now of offices some are discontinuous, and the same persons are not allowed to hold them twice, or can only hold
them after a fixed interval; others have no limit of time—for 25
example, the office of dicast or ecclesiast.² It may, indeed, be

---

² 'Dicast' = juryman and judge in one: 'ecclesiast' = member of the eccle-
sia or assembly of the citizens.

argued that these are not magistrates at all, and that their functions give them no share in the government. But surely it is ridiculous to say that those who have the supreme power do not govern. Let us not dwell further upon this, which is a purely verbal question; what we want is a com-

30 mon term including both dicast and ecclesiast. Let us, for the sake of distinction, call it 'indefinite office', and we will assume that those who share in such office are citizens. This is the most comprehensive definition of a citizen, and best suits all those who are generally so called.

But we must not forget that things of which the under-

35 lying principles differ in kind, one of them being first, another second, another third, have, when regarded in this relation, nothing, or hardly anything, worth mentioning in common. Now we see that governments differ in kind, and that some of them are prior and that others are posterior; those which are faulty or perverted are necessarily posterior

1275ᵇ to those which are perfect. (What we mean by perversion will be hereafter explained.[3]) The citizen then of necessity differs under each form of government; and our definition is

5 best adapted to the citizen of a democracy; but not necessarily to other states. For in some states the people are not acknowledged, nor have they any regular assembly, but only extraordinary ones; and suits are distributed by sections among the magistrates. At Lacedaemon, for instance, the Ephors determine suits about contracts, which they dis-

10 tribute among themselves, while the elders are judges of homicide, and other causes are decided by other magistrates. A similar principle prevails at Carthage;[4] there certain magistrates decide all causes. We may, indeed, modify our definition of the citizen so as to include these states. In them it is the holder of a definite, not of an indefinite

[3] Cf. 1279ᵃ 19.

[4] Cf. ii 1273ᵃ 19.

office, who legislates and judges, and to some or all such 15
holders of definite offices is reserved the right of deliberating or judging about some things or about all things. The
conception of the citizen now begins to clear up.

He who has the power to take part in the deliberative or
judicial administration of any state is said by us to be a citizen of that state; and, speaking generally, a state is a body 20
of citizens sufficing for the purposes of life.

2 But in practice a citizen is defined to be one of
whom both the parents are citizens; others insist on
going further back; say to two or three or more 25
ancestors. This is a short and practical definition; but there
are some who raise the further question: How this third or
fourth ancestor came to be a citizen? Gorgias of Leontini,
partly because he was in a difficulty, partly in irony, said—
'Mortars are what is made by the mortar-makers, and the
citizens of Larissa are those who are made by the magistrates;[5] for it is their trade to make Larissaeans.' Yet the 30
question is really simple, for, if according to the definition
just given they shared in the government, they were citizens. This is a better definition than the other. For the
words, 'born of a father or mother who is a citizen', cannot
possibly apply to the first inhabitants or founders of a state.

There is a greater difficulty in the case of those who
have been made citizens after a revolution, as by Cleisthenes 35
at Athens after the expulsion of the tyrants, for he enrolled
in tribes many metics, both strangers and slaves. The doubt
in these cases is, not who is, but whether he who is ought to 1276ᵃ
be a citizen; and there will still be a further doubt, whether
he who ought not to be a citizen, is one in fact, for what
ought not to be is what is false. Now, there are some who

---

[5] An untranslatable play upon the word *demiourgos*, which means either 'a
magistrate' or 'an artisan'.

hold office, and yet ought not to hold office, whom we describe as ruling, but ruling unjustly. And the citizen was defined[6] by the fact of his holding some kind of rule or 5 office—he who holds a judicial or legislative office fulfils our definition of a citizen. It is evident, therefore, that the citizens about whom the doubt has arisen must be called citizens.

3 Whether they ought to be so or not is a question which is bound up with the previous inquiry.[7] For a parallel question is raised respecting the state, whether a certain act is or is not an act of the state; for example, in the transition from an oligarchy or a tyranny to 10 a democracy. In such cases persons refuse to fulfil their contracts or any other obligations, on the ground that the tyrant, and not the state, contracted them; they argue that some constitutions are established by force, and not for the sake of the common good. But this would apply equally to 15 democracies, for they too may be founded on violence, and then the acts of the democracy will be neither more nor less acts of the state in question than those of an oligarchy or of a tyranny. This question runs up into another:—on what principle shall we ever say that the state is the same, or different? It would be a very superficial view which considered only the place and the inhabitants (for the soil and the population may be separated, and some of the inhabitants may 20 live in one place and some in another). This, however, is not a very serious difficulty; we need only remark that the word 'state' is ambiguous.[8]

It is further asked: When are men, living in the same

6 1275a 22 sqq.

7 Cf. 1274b 34.

8 i. e. *Polis* means both 'state' and 'city'.

place, to be regarded as a single city—what is the limit? 25
Certainly not the wall of the city, for you might surround
all Peloponnesus with a wall. Like this, we may say, is
Babylon,[9] and every city that has the compass of a nation
rather than a city; Babylon, they say, had been taken for
three days before some part of the inhabitants became aware
of the fact. This difficulty may, however, with advantage 30
be deferred[10] to another occasion; the statesman has to consider the size of the state, and whether it should consist of
more than one nation or not.

Again, shall we say that while the race of inhabitants,
as well as their place of abode, remain the same, the city is 35
also the same, although the citizens are always dying and
being born, as we call rivers and fountains the same,
although the water is always flowing away and coming
again? Or shall we say that the generations of men, like the
rivers, are the same, but that the state changes? For, since 40
the state is a partnership, and is a partnership of citizens in 1276^b
a constitution, when the form of the government changes,
and becomes different, then it may be supposed that the
state is no longer the same, just as a tragic differs from a
comic chorus, although the members of both may be iden- 5
tical. And in this manner we speak of every union or
composition of elements as different when the form of their
composition alters; for example, a scale containing the same
sounds is said to be different, accordingly as the Dorian or
the Phrygian mode is employed. And if this is true it is evi- 10
dent that the sameness of the state consists chiefly in the
sameness of the constitution, and it may be called or not
called by the same name, whether the inhabitants are the

[9] Cf. ii. 1265^a 14.

[10] The size of the state is discussed in vii. 1326^a 8–1327^a 3; the question
whether it should consist of more than one nation is barely touched upon,
in v. 1303^a 25–^{b} 3.

same or entirely different. It is quite another question,
15 whether a state ought or ought not to fulfil engagements
when the form of government changes.

4 There is a point nearly allied to the preceding:
Whether the virtue of a good man and a good citizen is the same or not.[11] But, before entering on
20 this discussion, we must certainly first obtain some general
notion of the virtue of the citizen. Like the sailor, the citizen
is a member of a community. Now, sailors have different
functions, for one of them is a rower, another a pilot, and a
third a look-out man, a fourth is described by some similar
25 term; and while the precise definition of each individual's
virtue applies exclusively to him, there is, at the same time,
a common definition applicable to them all. For they have
all of them a common object, which is safety in navigation.
Similarly, one citizen differs from another, but the salvation
of the community is the common business of them all. This
30 community is the constitution; the virtue of the citizen must
therefore be relative to the constitution of which he is a
member. If, then, there are many forms of government, it is
evident that there is not one single virtue of the good citizen
which is perfect virtue. But we say that the good man is he
who has one single virtue which is perfect virtue. Hence it is
evident that the good citizen need not of necessity possess
35 the virtue which makes a good man.

The same question may also be approached by another
road, from a consideration of the best constitution. If the
state cannot be entirely composed of good men, and yet
40 each citizen is expected to do his own business well, and
1277ᵃ must therefore have virtue, still, inasmuch as all the citizens
cannot be alike, the virtue of the citizen and of the good
man cannot coincide. All must have the virtue of the good

---

[11] Cf. *N. Eth.* v. 1130ᵇ 28.

citizen—thus, and thus only, can the state be perfect; but they will not have the virtue of a good man, unless we assume that in the good state all the citizens must be good.

Again, the state, as composed of unlikes, may be com- 5 pared to the living being: as the first elements into which a living being is resolved are soul and body, as soul is made up of rational principle and appetite, the family of husband and wife, property of master and slave, so of all these, as well as other dissimilar elements, the state is composed; and, therefore, the virtue of all the citizens cannot possibly 10 be the same, any more than the excellence of the leader of a chorus is the same as that of the performer who stands by his side. I have said enough to show why the two kinds of virtue cannot be absolutely and always the same.

But will there then be no case in which the virtue of the good citizen and the virtue of the good man coincide? To 15 this we answer that the good ruler is a good and wise man, and that he who would be a statesman must be a wise man. And some persons say that even the education of the ruler should be of a special kind; for are not the children of kings instructed in riding and military exercises? As Euripides says:

'No subtle arts for me, but what the state requires.'

As though there were a special education needed by a ruler. If then the virtue of a good ruler is the same as that of a good man, and we assume further that the subject is a citi- 20 zen as well as the ruler, the virtue of the good citizen and the virtue of the good man cannot be absolutely the same, although in some cases they may; for the virtue of a ruler differs from that of a citizen. It was the sense of this differ- ence which made Jason say that 'he felt hungry when he was not a tyrant', meaning that he could not endure to live in a private station. But, on the other hand, it may be

25 argued that men are praised for knowing both how to rule
and how to obey, and he is said to be a citizen of approved
virtue who is able to do both. Now if we suppose the virtue
of a good man to be that which rules, and the virtue of the
citizen to include ruling and obeying, it cannot be said that
they are equally worthy of praise. Since, then, it is some-
30 times thought that the ruler and the ruled must learn
different things and not the same, but that the citizen must
know and share in them both, the inference is obvious.
There is, indeed, the rule of a master, which is concerned
with menial offices[12]—the master need not know how to
perform these, but may employ others in the execution of
35 them: the other would be degrading, and by the other I
mean the power actually to do menial duties, which vary
much in character and are executed by various classes of
slaves, such, for example, as handicraftsmen, who, as their
name signifies, live by the labour of their hands:—under
1277b these the mechanic is included. Hence in ancient times, and
among some nations, the working classes had no share in
the government—a privilege which they only acquired
under the extreme democracy. Certainly the good man and
the statesman and the good citizen ought not to learn the
crafts of inferiors except for their own occasional use;[13] if
5 they habitually practise them, there will cease to be a distinction between master and slave.

    This is not the rule of which we are speaking; but there
is a rule of another kind, which is exercised over freemen
and equals by birth—a constitutional rule, which the ruler
10 must learn by obeying, as he would learn the duties of a
general of cavalry by being under the orders of a general of
cavalry, or the duties of a general of infantry by being under

[12] Cf. i. 1255b 20–37.

[13] Cf. viii. 1337b 15.

the orders of a general of infantry, and by having had the command of a regiment and of a company. It has been well said that 'he who has never learned to obey cannot be a good commander'. The two are not the same, but the good citizen ought to be capable of both; he should know how to govern like a freeman, and how to obey like a freeman— 15 these are the virtues of a citizen. And, although the temperance and justice of a ruler are distinct from those of a subject, the virtue of a good man will include both; for the virtue of the good man who is free and also a subject, e. g. his justice, will not be one but will comprise distinct kinds, the one qualifying him to rule, the other to obey, and differing as the temperance and courage of men and women 20 differ.[14] For a man would be thought a coward if he had no more courage than a courageous woman, and a woman would be thought loquacious if she imposed no more restraint on her conversation than the good man; and indeed their part in the management of the household is different, for the duty of the one is to acquire, and of the other to pre- 25 serve. Practical wisdom only is characteristic of the ruler:[15] it would seem that all other virtues must equally belong to ruler and subject. The virtue of the subject is certainly not wisdom, but only true opinion; he may be compared to the maker of the flute, while his master is the flute-player or user of the flute.[16]

From these considerations may be gathered the answer 30 to the question, whether the virtue of the good man is the same as that of the good citizen, or different, and how far the same, and how far different.[17]

[14] Cf. i. 1260^a 20.

[15] Cf. *Rep.* iv. 428.

[16] Cf. *Rep.* x. 601 D, E.

[17] Cf. 1278^a 40, 1288^a 39, iv. 1293^b 5, vii. 1333^a 11.

35 **5** There still remains one more question about the citizen: Is he only a true citizen who has a share of office, or is the mechanic to be included? If they who hold no office are to be deemed citizens, not every citizen can have this virtue of ruling and obeying; for this man is a citizen. And if none of the lower class are citizens, in which part of the state are they to be placed? For they are

1278ª not resident aliens, and they are not foreigners. May we not reply, that as far as this objection goes there is no more absurdity in excluding them than in excluding slaves and freedmen from any of the above-mentioned classes? It must be admitted that we cannot consider all those to be citizens who are necessary to the existence of the state; for example, children are not citizens equally with grown-up men, who

5 are citizens absolutely, but children, not being grown up, are only citizens on a certain assumption.[18] Nay, in ancient times, and among some nations, the artisan class *were* slaves or foreigners, and therefore the majority of them are so now. The best form of state will not admit them to citizenship; but if they are admitted, then our definition of the virtue of a citizen will not apply to every citizen, nor to every free man as such, but only to those who are freed from necessary

10 services. The necessary people are either slaves who minister to the wants of individuals, or mechanics and labourers who are the servants of the community. These reflections carried a little further will explain their position; and indeed what has been said already[19] is of itself, when understood, explanation enough.

Since there are many forms of government there must

15 be many varieties of citizens, and especially of citizens who are subjects; so that under some governments the mechanic and the labourer will be citizens, but not in others, as, for

[18] *sc.* that they grow up to be men.

[19] 1275ª 38 sqq.

example, in aristocracy or the so-called government of the best (if there be such an one), in which honours are given according to virtue and merit; for no man can practise 20 virtue who is living the life of a mechanic or labourer. In oligarchies the qualification for office is high, and therefore no labourer can ever be a citizen; but a mechanic may, for an actual majority of them are rich. At Thebes[20] there was a law that no man could hold office who had not retired from 25 business for ten years. But in many states the law goes to the length of admitting aliens; for in some democracies a man is a citizen though his mother only be a citizen; and a similar principle is applied to illegitimate children; the law is relaxed when there is a dearth of population. But when the number of citizens increases, first the children of a male 30 or a female slave are excluded; then those whose mothers only are citizens; and at last the right of citizenship is confined to those whose fathers and mothers are both citizens.

Hence, as is evident, there are different kinds of citizens; and he is a citizen in the highest sense who shares in 35 the honours of the state. Compare Homer's words 'like some dishonoured stranger';[21] he who is excluded from the honours of the state is no better than an alien. But when this exclusion is concealed, then the object is that the privileged class may deceive their fellow inhabitants.

As to the question whether the virtue of the good man is the same as that of the good citizen, the considerations 40 already adduced prove that in some states the good man and 1278b the good citizen are the same, and in others different. When they are the same it is not every citizen who is a good man, but only the statesman and those who have or may have, 5 alone or in conjunction with others, the conduct of public affairs.

[20] Cf. vi. 1321ᵃ 28.

[21] Achilles complains of Agamemnon's so treating him, *Il.* ix 648, xvi. 59.

6 Having determined these questions, we have next to consider whether there is only one form of government or many, and if many, what they are, and how many, and what are the differences between them.

10   A constitution is the arrangement of magistracies in a state,[22] especially of the highest of all. The government is everywhere sovereign in the state, and the constitution is in fact the government. For example, in democracies the people are supreme, but in oligarchies, the few; and, therefore, we say that these two forms of government also are different: and so in other cases.

15   First, let us consider what is the purpose of a state, and how many forms of government there are by which human society is regulated. We have already said, in the first part of this treatise,[23] when discussing household management 20 and the rule of a master, that man is by nature a political animal. And therefore, men, even when they do not require one another's help, desire to live together; not but that they are also brought together by their common interests in proportion as they severally attain to any measure of well-being. This is certainly the chief end, both of individuals 25 and of states. And also for the sake of mere life (in which there is possibly some noble element so long as the evils of existence do not greatly overbalance the good) mankind meet together and maintain the political community. And we all see that men cling to life even at the cost of enduring great misfortune, seeming to find in life a natural sweetness and happiness.

30   There is no difficulty in distinguishing the various kinds of authority; they have been often defined already in discussions outside the school. The rule of a master,

[22] Cf. 1274[b] 38, iv. 1289[a] 15.

[23] Cf. i. 1253[a] 2.

although the slave by nature and the master by nature have
in reality the same interests, is nevertheless exercised pri- 35
marily with a view to the interest of the master, but
accidentally considers the slave, since, if the slave perish,
the rule of the master perishes with him. On the other
hand, the government of a wife and children and of a
household, which we have called household management,
is exercised in the first instance for the good of the governed
or for the common good of both parties, but essentially for 40
the good of the governed, as we see to be the case in
medicine, gymnastic, and the arts in general, which are only 1279a
accidentally concerned with the good of the artists themselves.[24] For there is no reason why the trainer may not
sometimes practise gymnastics, and the helmsman is always
one of the crew. The trainer or the helmsman considers the
good of those committed to his care. But, when he is one
of the persons taken care of, he accidentally participates in 5
the advantage, for the helmsman is also a sailor, and the
trainer becomes one of those in training. And so in politics:
when the state is framed upon the principle of equality and
likeness, the citizens think that they ought to hold office by
turns. Formerly, as is natural, every one would take his turn 10
of service; and then again, somebody else would look after
his interest, just as he, while in office, had looked after
theirs.[25] But nowadays, for the sake of the advantage which
is to be gained from the public revenues and from office,
men want to be always in office. One might imagine that
the rulers, being sickly, were only kept in health while they
continued in office; in that case we may be sure that they 15
would be hunting after places. The conclusion is evident:
that governments which have a regard to the common inter-

---

[24] Cf. Pl. *Rep.* i. 341 D.

[25] Cf. ii. 1261a 37–b 6

est are constituted in accordance with strict principles of
justice, and are therefore true forms; but those which regard
20 only the interest of the rulers are all defective and perverted
forms, for they are despotic, whereas a state is a community of freemen.

7 Having determined these points, we have next to
consider how many forms of government there are,
and what they are; and in the first place what are
the true forms, for when they are determined the perver-
25 sions of them will at once be apparent. The words
constitution and government have the same meaning, and
the government, which is the supreme authority in states,
must be in the hands of one, or of a few, or of the many.
The true forms of government, therefore, are those in which
the one, or the few, or the many, govern with a view to the
30 common interest; but governments which rule with a view
to the private interest, whether of the one, or of the few, or
of the many, are perversions.[26] For the members of a state, if
they are truly citizens, ought to participate in its advantages.
Of forms of government in which one rules, we call that
which regards the common interests, kingship or royalty;
35 that in which more than one, but not many, rule, aristocracy; and it is so called, either because the rulers are the
best men, or because they have at heart the best interests of
the state and of the citizens. But when the citizens at large
administer the state for the common interest, the government is called by the generic name—a constitution. And
40 there is a reason for this use of language. One man or a few
1279b may excel in virtue; but as the number increases it becomes
more difficult for them to attain perfection in every kind of
virtue, though they may in military virtue, for this is found
in the masses. Hence in a constitutional government the

[26] Cf. *N. Eth.* viii. 10.

fighting-men have the supreme power, and those who possess arms are the citizens.

Of the above-mentioned forms, the perversions are as
follows:—of royalty, tyranny; of aristocracy, oligarchy; of 5
constitutional government, democracy. For tyranny is a
kind of monarchy which has in view the interest of the
monarch only; oligarchy has in view the interest of the
wealthy; democracy, of the needy: none of them the com- 10
mon good of all.

8 But there are difficulties about these forms of government, and it will therefore be necessary to state
a little more at length the nature of each of them.
For he who would make a philosophical study of the various sciences, and does not regard practice only, ought not to 15
overlook or omit anything, but to set forth the truth in
every particular. Tyranny, as I was saying, is monarchy
exercising the rule of a master over the political society; oligarchy is when men of property have the government in
their hands; democracy, the opposite, when the indigent,
and not the men of property, are the rulers. And here arises
the first of our difficulties, and it relates to the distinction 20
just drawn. For democracy is said to be the government of
the many. But what if the many are men of property and
have the power in their hands? In like manner oligarchy is
said to be the government of the few; but what if the poor
are fewer than the rich, and have the power in their hands 25
because they are stronger? In these cases the distinction
which we have drawn between these different forms of government would no longer hold good.

Suppose, once more, that we add wealth to the few and
poverty to the many, and name the governments accordingly—an oligarchy is said to be that in which the few and
the wealthy, and a democracy that in which the many and 30
the poor are the rulers—there will still be a difficulty. For,

if the only forms of government are the ones already mentioned, how shall we describe those other governments also
just mentioned by us, in which the rich are the more numerous and the poor are the fewer, and both govern in their
respective states?

35   The argument seems to show that, whether in oligarchies or in democracies, the number of the governing
body, whether the greater number, as in a democracy, or the
smaller number, as in an oligarchy, is an accident due to the
fact that the rich everywhere are few, and the poor numerous. But if so, there is a misapprehension of the causes of
the difference between them. For the real difference between
40 democracy and oligarchy is poverty and wealth. Wherever
1280ᵃ men rule by reason of their wealth, whether they be few or
many, that is an oligarchy, and where the poor rule, that is
a democracy. But as a fact the rich are few and the poor
many; for few are well-to-do, whereas freedom is enjoyed by
all, and wealth and freedom are the grounds on which the oli-
5   garchical and democratical parties respectively claim power
in the state.

9   Let us begin by considering the common defini-
     tions of oligarchy and democracy, and what is
     justice oligarchical and democratical. For all men
10 cling to justice of some kind, but their conceptions are
imperfect and they do not express the whole idea. For
example, justice is thought by them to be, and is, equality,
not, however, for all, but only for equals. And inequality is
thought to be, and is, justice; neither is this for all, but only
for unequals. When the persons are omitted, then men
judge erroneously. The reason is that they are passing
15 judgement on themselves, and most people are bad judges
in their own case. And whereas justice implies a relation to
persons as well as to things, and a just distribution, as I

have already said in the *Ethics*,[27] implies the same ratio
between the persons and between the things, they agree
about the equality of the things, but dispute about the
equality of the persons, chiefly for the reason which I have 20
just given—because they are bad judges in their own affairs;
and secondly, because both the parties to the argument are
speaking of a limited and partial justice, but imagine themselves to be speaking of absolute justice. For the one party,
if they are unequal in one respect, for example wealth, consider themselves to be unequal in all; and the other party,
if they are equal in one respect, for example free birth, consider themselves to be equal in all. But they leave out the 25
capital point. For if men met and associated out of regard to
wealth only, their share in the state would be proportioned
to their property, and the oligarchical doctrine would then
seem to carry the day. It would not be just that he who paid
one mina should have the same share of a hundred minae,
whether of the principal or of the profits, as he who paid
the remaining ninety-nine. But a state exists for the sake of 30
a good life, and not for the sake of life only: if life only were
the object, slaves and brute animals might form a state, but
they cannot, for they have no share in happiness or in a life 35
of free choice. Nor does a state exist for the sake of alliance
and security from injustice, nor yet for the sake of exchange
and mutual intercourse; for then the Tyrrhenians and the
Carthaginians, and all who have commercial treaties with
one another,[28] would be the citizens of one state. True, they
have agreements about imports, and engagements that 40
they will do no wrong to one another, and written articles 1280[b]
of alliance. But there are no magistracies common to the
contracting parties who will enforce their engagements; dif-

[27] v. 1131[a] 15.

[28] Cf. 1275[a] 10.

ferent states have each their own magistracies. Nor does one
state take care that the citizens of the other are such as they
ought to be, nor see that those who come under the terms of
the treaty do no wrong or wickedness at all, but only that
5 they do no injustice to one another. Whereas, those who
care for good government take into consideration virtue and
vice in states. Whence it may be further inferred that virtue
must be the care of a state which is truly so called, and not
merely enjoys the name: for without this end the community becomes a mere alliance which differs only in place
from alliances of which the members live apart; and law is
10 only a convention, 'a surety to one another of justice,' as the
sophist Lycophron says, and has no real power to make the
citizens good and just.

This is obvious; for suppose distinct places, such as
Corinth and Megara, to be brought together so that their
walls touched, still they would not be one city, not even if
15 the citizens had the right to intermarry, which is one of the
rights peculiarly characteristic of states. Again, if men dwelt
at a distance from one another, but not so far off as to have
no intercourse, and there were laws among them that they
should not wrong each other in their exchanges, neither
20 would this be a state. Let us suppose that one man is a carpenter, another a husbandman, another a shoemaker, and so
on, and that their number is ten thousand: nevertheless, if
they have nothing in common but exchange, alliance, and the
25 like, that would not constitute a state. Why is this? Surely
not because they are at a distance from one another: for even
supposing that such a community were to meet in one place,
but that each man had a house of his own, which was in a
manner his state, and that they made alliance with one
another, but only against evil-doers; still an accurate thinker
30 would not deem this to be a state, if their intercourse with
one another was of the same character after as before their
union. It is clear then that a state is not a mere society, hav-

ing a common place, established for the prevention of mutual
crime and for the sake of exchange.[29] These are conditions
without which a state cannot exist; but all of them together
do not constitute a state, which is a community of families
and aggregations of families in well-being, for the sake of a
perfect and self-sufficing life. Such a community can only be   35
established among those who live in the same place and
intermarry. Hence arise in cities family connexions, brother-
hoods, common sacrifices, amusements which draw men
together. But these are created by friendship, for the will to
live together is friendship. The end of the state is the good
life, and these are the means towards it. And the state is the   40
union of families and villages in a perfect and self-sufficing
life, by which we mean a happy and honourable life.[30]   1281ª

Our conclusion, then, is that political society exists for
the sake of noble actions, and not of mere companionship.
Hence they who contribute most to such a society have a
greater share in it than those who have the same or a greater   5
freedom or nobility of birth but are inferior to them in
political virtue; or than those who exceed them in wealth
but are surpassed by them in virtue.

From what has been said it will be clearly seen that all
the partisans of different forms of government speak of a
part of justice only.   10

10 There is also a doubt as to what is to be the
supreme power in the state:—Is it the multitude? Or the wealthy? Or the good? Or the one
best man? Or a tyrant? Any of these alternatives seems to
involve disagreeable consequences. If the poor, for example,
because they are more in number, divide among themselves
the property of the rich—is not this unjust? No, by heaven

[29] Cf. *Protag.* 322 B.

[30] Cf. 1252ᵇ 27; *N. Eth.* i. 1097ᵇ 6.

15 (will be the reply), for the supreme authority justly willed it. But if this is not injustice, pray what is? Again, when in the first division all has been taken, and the majority divide anew the property of the minority, is it not evident, if this goes on, that they will ruin the state? Yet surely, virtue is not the ruin of those who possess her, nor is justice destructive of a state; and therefore this law of confiscation clearly cannot

20 be just. If it were, all the acts of a tyrant must of necessity be just; for he only coerces other men by superior power, just as the multitude coerce the rich. But is it just then that the few

25 and the wealthy should be the rulers? And what if they, in like manner, rob and plunder the people—is this just? If so, the other case will likewise be just. But there can be no doubt that all these things are wrong and unjust.

Then ought the good to rule and have supreme power?

30 But in that case everybody else, being excluded from power, will be dishonoured. For the offices of a state are posts of honour; and if one set of men always hold them, the rest must be deprived of them. Then will it be well that the one best man should rule? Nay, that is still more oligarchical, for the number of those who are dishonoured is thereby increased. Some one may say that it is bad in any case for

35 a man, subject as he is to all the accidents of human passion, to have the supreme power, rather than the law. But what if the law itself be democratical or oligarchical, how will that help us out of our difficulties?[31] Not at all; the same consequences[32] will follow.

11 Most of these questions may be reserved for another occasion.[33] The principle that the multitude ought to be supreme rather than the few

[31] Cf. 1282^b 6.

[32] Cf. ll. 11–34.

[33] cc. 12–17, iv., vi.

best is one that is maintained, and, though not free from
difficulty, yet seems to contain an element of truth. For the 1281^b
many, of whom each individual is but an ordinary person,
when they meet together may very likely be better than the
few good, if regarded not individually but collectively, just
as a feast to which many contribute is better than a dinner
provided out of a single purse. For each individual among
the many has a share of virtue and prudence, and when they 5
meet together, they become in a manner one man, who has
many feet, and hands, and senses; that is a figure of their
mind and disposition. Hence the many are better judges
than a single man of music and poetry; for some understand
one part, and some another, and among them they under- 10
stand the whole. There is a similar combination of qualities
in good men, who differ from any individual of the many,
as the beautiful are said to differ from those who are not
beautiful, and works of art from realities, because in them
the scattered elements are combined, although, if taken separately, the eye of one person or some other feature in
another person would be fairer than in the picture. Whether 15
this principle can apply to every democracy, and to all bodies of men, is not clear. Or rather, by heaven, in some cases
it is impossible of application; for the argument would
equally hold about brutes; and wherein, it will be asked, do
some men differ from brutes? But there may be bodies of 20
men about whom our statement is nevertheless true. And if
so, the difficulty which has been already raised,[34] and also
another which is akin to it—viz. what power should be
assigned to the mass of freemen and citizens, who are not
rich and have no personal merit—are both solved. There is 25
still a danger in allowing them to share the great offices of
state, for their folly will lead them into error, and their dis-
honesty into crime. But there is a danger also in not letting

[34] c. 10.

them share, for a state in which many poor men are
30 excluded from office will necessarily be full of enemies. The
only way of escape is to assign to them some deliberative
and judicial functions. For this reason Solon[35] and certain
other legislators give them the power of electing to offices,
and of calling the magistrates to account, but they do not
allow them to hold office singly. When they meet together
35 their perceptions are quite good enough, and combined with
the better class they are useful to the state (just as impure
food when mixed with what is pure sometimes makes the
entire mass more wholesome than a small quantity of the
pure would be), but each individual, left to himself, forms
an imperfect judgement. On the other hand, the popular
form of government involves certain difficulties. In the first
40 place, it might be objected that he who can judge of the
healing of a sick man would be one who could himself heal
his disease, and make him whole—that is, in other words,
1282[a] the physician; and so in all professions and arts. As, then,
the physician ought to be called to account by physicians, so
ought men in general to be called to account by their peers.
But physicians are of three kinds:—there is the ordinary
practitioner, and there is the physician of the higher class,
and thirdly the intelligent man who has studied the art: in
all arts there is such a class; and we attribute the power of
5 judging to them quite as much as to professors of the art.
Secondly, does not the same principle apply to elections?
For a right election can only be made by those who have
knowledge; those who know geometry, for example, will
choose a geometrician rightly, and those who know how to
steer, a pilot; and, even if there be some occupations and
10 arts in which private persons share in the ability to choose,
they certainly cannot choose better than those who know.
So that, according to this argument, neither the election of

[35] Cf. ii. 1274[a] 15.

magistrates, nor the calling of them to account, should be entrusted to the many. Yet possibly these objections are to a great extent met by our old answer,[36] that if the people are not utterly degraded, although individually they may be worse judges than those who have special knowledge—as a body they are as good or better. Moreover, there are some arts whose products are not judged of solely, or best, by the artists themselves, namely those arts whose products are recognized even by those who do not possess the art; for example, the knowledge of the house is not limited to the builder only; the user, or, in other words, the master, of the house will even be a better judge than the builder, just as the pilot will judge better of a rudder than the carpenter, and the guest will judge better of a feast than the cook.

This difficulty seems now to be sufficiently answered, but there is another akin to it. That inferior persons should have authority in greater matters than the good would appear to be a strange thing, yet the election and calling to account of the magistrates is the greatest of all. And these, as I was saying,[37] are functions which in some states are assigned to the people, for the assembly is supreme in all such matters. Yet persons of any age, and having but a small property qualification, sit in the assembly and deliberate and judge, although for the great officers of state, such as treasurers and generals, a high qualification is required. This difficulty may be solved in the same manner as the preceding, and the present practice of democracies may be really defensible. For the power does not reside in the dicast, or senator, or ecclesiast, but in the court, and the senate, and the assembly, of which individual senators, or ecclesiasts, or dicasts, are only parts or members. And for this reason the many may claim to have a higher authority

[36] 1281ᵃ 40–ᵇ 21.

[37] 1281ᵇ 32.

than the few; for the people, and the senate, and the courts
40 consist of many persons, and their property collectively is
greater than the property of one or of a few individuals
holding great offices. But enough of this.

1282ᵇ   The discussion of the first question[38] shows nothing so
clearly as that laws, when good, should be supreme; and
that the magistrate or magistrates should regulate those
5 matters only on which the laws are unable to speak with
precision owing to the difficulty of any general principle
embracing all particulars.[39] But what are good laws has not
yet been clearly explained; the old difficulty remains.[40] The
goodness or badness, justice or injustice, of laws varies of
10 necessity with the constitutions of states. This, however, is
clear, that the laws must be adapted to the constitutions.
But if so, true forms of government will of necessity have
just laws, and perverted forms of government will have
unjust laws.

15   **12** In all sciences and arts the end is a good, and
the greatest good and in the highest degree a
good in the most authoritative of all[41]—this is
the political science of which the good is justice, in other
words, the common interest. All men think justice to be a
sort of equality; and to a certain extent[42] they agree in the
20 philosophical distinctions which have been laid down by us
about Ethics.[43] For they admit that justice is a thing and has

[38] c. 10.

[39] Cf. *N. Eth.* v. 1137ᵇ 19.

[40] Cf. 1281ᵃ 36.

[41] Cf. i. 1252ᵃ 2; *N. Eth.* i. 1094ᵃ 1.

[42] Cf. 1280ᵃ 9.

[43] Cf. *N. Eth.* v. 3.

a relation to persons, and that equals ought to have equality.
But there still remains a question: equality or inequality of
what? here is a difficulty which calls for political speculation. For very likely some persons will say that offices of
state ought to be unequally distributed according to superior
excellence, in whatever respect, of the citizen, although
there is no other difference between him and the rest of the   25
community; for that those who differ in any one respect
have different rights and claims. But, surely, if this is true,
the complexion or height of a man, or any other advantage,
will be a reason for his obtaining a greater share of political   30
rights. The error here lies upon the surface, and may be
illustrated from the other arts and sciences. When a number
of flute-players are equal in their art, there is no reason why
those of them who are better born should have better flutes
given to them; for they will not play any better on the flute,
and the superior instrument should be reserved for him who
is the superior artist. If what I am saying is still obscure, it
will be made clearer as we proceed. For if there were a
superior flute-player who was far inferior in birth and   35
beauty, although either of these may be a greater good than
the art of flute-playing, and may excel flute-playing in a
greater ratio than he excels the others in his art, still he   40
ought to have the best flutes given to him, unless the
advantages of wealth and birth contribute to excellence in   1283ᵃ
flute-playing, which they do not. Moreover, upon this principle any good may be compared with any other. For if a
given height may be measured against wealth and against
freedom, height in general may be so measured. Thus if A   5
excels in height more than B in virtue, even if virtue in general excels height still more, all goods will be commensurable;
for if a certain amount is better than some other, it is clear
that some other will be equal. But since no such comparison
can be made, it is evident that there is good reason why in   10
politics men do not ground their claim to office on every

sort of inequality any more than in the arts. For if some be
slow, and others swift, that is no reason why the one should
have little and the others much; it is in gymnastic contests
that such excellence is rewarded. Whereas the rival claims
15 of candidates for office can only be based on the possession
of elements which enter into the composition of a state. And
therefore the noble, or freeborn, or rich, may with good reason claim office; for holders of offices must be freemen and
tax-payers: a state can be no more composed entirely of
poor men than entirely of slaves. But if wealth and freedom
are necessary elements, justice and valour are equally so;[44]
20 for without the former qualities a state cannot exist at all,
without the latter not well.

13 If the existence of the state is alone to be considered, then it would seem that all, or some at
25 least, of these claims are just; but, if we take into
account a good life, then, as I have already said,[45] education
and virtue have superior claims. As, however, those who are
equal in one thing ought not to have an equal share in all,
nor those who are unequal in one thing to have an unequal
share in all, it is certain that all forms of government which
rest on either of these principles are perversions. All men
30 have a claim in a certain sense, as I have already admitted,[46]
but all have not an absolute claim. The rich claim because
they have a greater share in the land, and land is the common element of the state; also they are generally more
trustworthy in contracts. The free claim under the same title
as the noble; for they are nearly akin. For the noble are citizens in a truer sense than the ignoble, and good birth is

[44] Cf. iv. 1291ᵃ 19–33.

[45] Cf. 1281ᵃ 4

[46] 1280ᵃ 9 sqq.

always valued in a man's own home and country.[47] Another 35
reason is, that those who are sprung from better ancestors
are likely to be better men, for nobility is excellence of race.
Virtue, too, may be truly said to have a claim, for justice has
been acknowledged by us to be a social[48] virtue, and it
implies all others.[49] Again, the many may urge their claim 40
against the few; for, when taken collectively, and compared
with the few, they are stronger and richer and better. But, 1283b
what if the good, the rich, the noble, and the other classes
who make up a state, are all living together in the same city,
will there, or will there not, be any doubt who shall rule?—
No doubt at all in determining who ought to rule in each of
the above-mentioned forms of government. For states are 5
characterized by differences in their governing bodies—one
of them has a government of the rich, another of the virtuous, and so on. But a difficulty arises when all these
elements coexist. How are we to decide? Suppose the virtuous to be very few in number: may we consider their 10
numbers in relation to their duties, and ask whether they are
enough to administer the state, or so many as will make up a
state? Objections may be urged against all the aspirants to
political power. For those who found their claims on wealth 15
or family might be thought to have no basis of justice; on
this principle, if any one person were richer than all the rest,
it is clear that he ought to be ruler of them. In like manner
he who is very distinguished by his birth ought to have the
superiority over all those who claim on the ground that they
are freeborn. In an aristocracy, or government of the best, a 20
like difficulty occurs about virtue; for if one citizen be better than the other members of the government, however

[47] Cf. i. 1255ª 32.

[48] Cf. i. 1253ª 37.

[49] Cf. N. Eth. v. 1129b 25.

good they may be, he too, upon the same principle of justice, should rule over them. And if the people are to be supreme because they are stronger than the few, then if one man, or 25 more than one, but not a majority, is stronger than the many, they ought to rule, and not the many.

All these considerations appear to show that none of the principles on which men claim to rule and to hold all other men in subjection to them are strictly right. To those who 30 claim to be masters of the government on the ground of their virtue or their wealth, the many might fairly answer that they themselves are often better and richer than the few—I do not say individually, but collectively. And another ingenious objection which is sometimes put forward 35 may be met in a similar manner. Some persons doubt whether the legislator who desires to make the justest laws ought to legislate with a view to the good of the higher classes or of the many, when the case which we have men- 40 tioned occurs.[50] Now what is just or right is to be interpreted in the sense of 'what is equal'; and that which is right in the sense of being equal is to be considered with reference to the advantage of the state, and the common good of the cit- izens. And a citizen is one who shares in governing and being governed. He differs under different forms of govern- 1284ᵃ ment, but in the best state he is one who is able and willing to be governed and to govern with a view to the life of virtue.

If, however, there be some one person, or more than one, although not enough to make up the full complement of a state, whose virtue is so pre-eminent that the virtues 5 or the political capacity of all the rest admit of no compari- son with his or theirs, he or they can be no longer regarded as part of a state; for justice will not be done to the superior, if he is reckoned only as the equal of those who are so far

[50] i. e. when the many collectively are better than the few.

inferior to him in virtue and in political capacity. Such an
one may truly be deemed a God among men. Hence we see 10
that legislation is necessarily concerned only with those who
are equal in birth and in capacity; and that for men of pre-
eminent virtue there is no law—they are themselves a law.
Any one would be ridiculous who attempted to make laws
for them: they would probably retort what, in the fable of 15
Antisthenes, the lions said to the hares,[51] when in the council of the beasts the latter began haranguing and claiming
equality for all. And for this reason democratic states have
instituted ostracism; equality is above all things their aim, 20
and therefore they ostracized and banished from the city for
a time those who seemed to predominate too much through
their wealth, or the number of their friends, or through any
other political influence. Mythology tells us that the Ar-
gonauts left Heracles behind for a similar reason; the ship
Argo would not take him because she feared that he would 25
have been too much for the rest of the crew. Wherefore
those who denounce tyranny and blame the counsel which
Periander gave to Thrasybulus cannot be held altogether
just in their censure. The story is that Periander, when the
herald was sent to ask counsel of him, said nothing, but
only cut off the tallest ears of corn till he had brought the 30
field to a level. The herald did not know the meaning of the
action, but came and reported what he had seen to Thrasybulus, who understood that he was to cut off the principal
men in the state;[52] and this is a policy not only expedient 35
for tyrants or in practice confined to them, but equally necessary in oligarchies and democracies. Ostracism[53] is a
measure of the same kind, which acts by disabling and ban-

[51] i. e. 'where are your claws and teeth?'

[52] Cf. v. 1311ª 20.

[53] Cf. v. 1302ᵇ 18.

ishing the most prominent citizens. Great powers do the
same to whole cities and nations, as the Athenians did to
40 the Samians, Chians, and Lesbians; no sooner had they
obtained a firm grasp of the empire, than they humbled
1284b their allies contrary to treaty; and the Persian king has
repeatedly crushed the Medes, Babylonians, and other
nations, when their spirt has been stirred by the recollec-
tion of their former greatness.

The problem is a universal one, and equally concerns
all forms of government, true as well as false; for, although
5 perverted forms with a view to their own interests may
adopt this policy, those which seek the common interest do
so likewise. The same thing may be observed in the arts and
sciences;[54] for the painter will not allow the figure to have a
foot which, however beautiful, is not in proportion, nor will
10 the ship-builder allow the stern or any other part of the vessel to be unduly large, any more than the chorus-master will
allow any one who sings louder or better than all the rest
to sing in the choir. Monarchs, too, may practise compul-
15 sion and still live in harmony with their cities, if their own
government is for the interest of the state. Hence where
there is an acknowledged superiority the argument in favour
of ostracism is based upon a kind of political justice. It
would certainly be better that the legislator should from the
first so order his state as to have no need of such a remedy.
But if the need arises, the next best thing is that he should
endeavour to correct the evil by this or some similar mea-
20 sure. The principle, however, has not been fairly applied in
states; for, instead of looking to the good of their own constitution, they have used ostracism for factious purposes. It
is true that under perverted forms of government, and from
their special point of view, such a measure is just and expe-
25 dient, but it is also clear that it is not absolutely just. In the

[54] Cf. v. 1302b 34, 1309b 21; vii. 1326a 35; *Rep.* iv. 420.

perfect state there would be great doubts about the use of it, not when applied to excess in strength, wealth, popularity, or the like, but when used against some one who is pre-eminent in virtue—what is to be done with him? Mankind will not say that such an one is to be expelled and exiled; on the other hand, he ought not to be a subject—that would be as 30 if mankind should claim to rule over Zeus, dividing his offices among them. The only alternative is that all should joyfully obey such a ruler, according to what seems to be the order of nature, and that men like him should be kings in their state for life.

14 The preceding discussion, by a natural transition, leads to the consideration of loyalty, which 35 we admit to be one of the true forms of government. Let us see whether in order to be well governed a state or country should be under the rule of a king or under some other form of government; and whether monarchy, although good for some, may not be bad for others. But 40 first we must determine whether there is one species of royalty or many. It is easy to see that there are many, and that 1285a the manner of government is not the same in all of them.

Of royalties according to law, (1) the Lacedaemonian is thought to answer best to the true pattern; but there the royal power is not absolute, except when the kings go on an expedition, and then they take the command. Matters of 5 religion are likewise committed to them. The kingly office is in truth a kind of generalship, irresponsible and perpetual. The king has not the power of life and death, except in a specified case, as for instance, in ancient times, he had it when upon a campaign, by right of force. This custom is described in Homer. For Agamemnon is patient when he is 10 attacked in the assembly, but when the army goes out to battle he has the power even of life and death. Does he not say?—'When I find a man skulking apart from the battle, nothing shall save him from the dogs and vultures, for in my hands is death.'[55]

15   This, then, is one form of royalty—a generalship for life: and of such royalties some are hereditary and others elective.

(2) There is another sort of monarchy not uncommon among the barbarians, which nearly resembles tyranny. But

20 this is both legal and hereditary. For barbarians, being more servile in character than Hellenes, and Asiatics than Europeans, do not rebel against a despotic government. Such royalties have the nature of tyrannies because the people are by nature slaves;[56] but there is no danger of their being overthrown, for they are hereditary and legal. Wherefore

25 also their guards are such as a king and not such as a tyrant would employ, that is to say, they are composed of citizens, whereas the guards of tyrants are mercenaries.[57] For kings rule according to law over voluntary subjects, but tyrants over involuntary; and the one are guarded by their fellow-citizens, the others are guarded against them.

30   These are two forms of monarchy, and there was a third (3) which existed in ancient Hellas, called an Aesymnetia or dictatorship. This may be defined generally as an elective tyranny, which, like the barbarian monarchy, is legal, but differs from it in not being hereditary. Sometimes

35 the office was held for life, sometimes for a term of years, or until certain duties had been performed. For example, the Mytilenaeans elected Pittacus leader against the exiles, who were headed by Antimenides and Alcaeus the poet. And Alcaeus himself shows in one of his banquet odes that they chose Pittacus tyrant, for he reproaches his fellow-citizens

[55] *Il.* ii. 391–393. The last clause is not found in our Homer.

[56] Cf. i. 1252^b 7.

[57] Cf. v. 1311^a 7.

for 'having made the low-born Pittacus tyrant of the spirit-
less and ill-fated city, with one voice shouting his praises'.   1285^b

These forms of government have always had the character of tyrannies, because they possess despotic power; but
inasmuch as they are elective and acquiesced in by their
subjects, they are kingly.

(4) There is a fourth species of kingly rule—that of the
heroic times—which was hereditary and legal, and was exercised over willing subjects. For the first chiefs were 5
benefactors of the people[58] in arts or arms; they either gathered them into a community, or procured land for them;
and thus they became kings of voluntary subjects, and their
power was inherited by their descendants. They took the
command in war and presided over the sacrifices, except 10
those which required a priest. They also decided causes
either with or without an oath; and when they swore, the
form of the oath was the stretching out of their sceptre. In
ancient times their power extended continuously to all
things whatsoever, in city and country, as well as in foreign 15
parts; but at a later date they relinquished several of these
privileges, and others the people took from them, until in
some states nothing was left to them but the sacrifices; and
where they retained more of the reality they had only the
right of leadership in war beyond the border.

These, then, are the four kinds of royalty. First the
monarchy of the heroic ages; this was exercised over volun- 20
tary subjects, but limited to certain functions; the king was
a general and a judge, and had the control of religion. The
second is that of the barbarians, which is an hereditary
despotic government in accordance with law. A third is the
power of the so-called Aesymnete or Dictator; this is an
elective tyranny. The fourth is the Lacedaemonian, which is 25
in fact a generalship, hereditary and perpetual. These four

---

[58] Cf. v. 1310^b 10.

forms differ from one another in the manner which I have described.

(5) There is a fifth form of kingly rule in which one has the disposal of all, just as each nation or each state has the
30 disposal of public matters; this form corresponds to the control of a household. For as household management is the kingly rule of a house, so kingly rule is the household management of a city, or of a nation, or of many nations.

15

Of these forms we need only consider two, the Lacedaemonian and the absolute royalty; for
35 most of the others lie in a region between them, having less power than the last, and more than the first. Thus the inquiry is reduced to two points: first, is it advantageous to the state that there should be a perpetual general, and if so, should the office be confined to one family, or
1286ᵃ open to the citizens in turn? Secondly, is it well that a single man should have the supreme power in all things? The first question falls under the head of laws rather than of constitutions; for perpetual generalship might equally exist under any form of government, so that this matter may be dismissed for the present.[59] The other kind of royalty is a sort
5 of constitution; this we have now to consider, and briefly to run over the difficulties involved in it. We will begin by inquiring whether it is more advantageous to be ruled by the best man or by the best laws.[60]

The advocates of royalty maintain that the laws speak
10 only in general terms, and cannot provide for circumstances; and that for any science to abide by written rules is absurd. In Egypt the physician is allowed to alter his treatment after the fourth day, but if sooner, he takes the risk. Hence it is
15 clear that a government acting according to written laws is

[59] It is not discussed later.

[60] Cf. Plato, *Polit.* 294 A–295 C.

plainly not the best. Yet surely the ruler cannot dispense with the general principle which exists in law; and that is a better ruler which is free from passion than that in which it is innate. Whereas the law is passionless, passion must ever sway the heart of man. Yes, it may be replied, but then 20 on the other hand an individual will be better able to deliberate in particular cases

The best man, then, must legislate, and laws must be passed, but these laws will have no authority when they miss the mark, though in all other cases retaining their 25 authority. But when the law cannot determine a point at all, or not well, should the one best man or should all decide? According to our present practice assemblies meet, sit in judgement, deliberate, and decide, and their judgements all relate to individual cases. Now any member of the assembly, taken separately, is certainly inferior to the wise man. But the state is made up of many individuals. And as a feast to which all the guests contribute is better than a banquet furnished by a single man,[61] so a multitude is a better judge 30 of many things than any individual.

Again, the many are more incorruptible than the few; they are like the greater quantity of water which is less easily corrupted than a little. The individual is liable to be overcome by anger or by some other passion, and then his 35 judgement is necessarily perverted; but it is hardly to be supposed that a great number of persons would all get into a passion and go wrong at the same moment. Let us assume that they are the freemen, and that they never act in violation of the law, but fill up the gaps which the law is obliged to leave. Or, if such virtue is scarcely attainable by the multitude, we need only suppose that the majority are good men and good citizens, and ask which will be the more 40 incorruptible one good ruler, or the many who are all good? 1286b

---

[61] Cf. 1281ᵃ 42.

Will not the many? But, you will say, there may be parties among them, whereas the one man is not divided against himself. To which we may answer that their character is as
5 good as his. If we call the rule of many men, who are all of them good, aristocracy, and the rule of one man royalty, then aristocracy will be better for states than royalty, whether the government is supported by force or not,[62] provided only that a number of men equal in virtue can be found.

The first governments were kingships, probably for this reason, because of old, when cities were small, men of emi-
10 nent virtue were few. Further, they were made kings because they were benefactors,[63] and benefits can only be bestowed by good men. But when many persons equal in merit arose, no longer enduring the pre-eminence of one, they desired to have a commonwealth, and set up a constitution. The ruling class soon deteriorated and enriched themselves out of the public treasury; riches became the
15 path to honour, and so oligarchies naturally grew up. These passed into tyrannies and tyrannies into democracies; for love of gain in the ruling classes was always tending to diminish their number, and so to strengthen the masses, who in the end set upon their masters and established
20 democracies. Since cities have increased in size, no other form of government appears to be any longer even easy to establish.[64]

Even supposing the principle to be maintained that kingly power is the best thing for states, how about the family of the king? Are his children to succeed him? If they are no better than anybody else, that will be mischievous.

[62] Cf. l. 27.

[63] Cf. 1285^b 6.

[64] Cf. iv. 1293^a 1, 1297^b 22.

But, says the lover of royalty, the king, though he might, 25
will not hand on his power to his children. That, however,
is hardly to be expected, and is too much to ask of human
nature. There is also a difficulty about the force which he
is to employ; should a king have guards about him by
whose aid he may be able to coerce the refractory? if not,
how will he administer his kingdom? Even if he be the law- 30
ful sovereign who does nothing arbitrarily or contrary to
law, still he must have some force wherewith to maintain
the law. In the case of a limited monarchy there is not much
difficulty in answering this question; the king must have 35
such force as will be more than a match for one or more
individuals, but not so great as that of the people. The
ancients observe this principle when they have guards to
any one whom they appointed dictator or tyrant. Thus,
when Dionysius asked the Syracusans to allow him guards,
somebody advised that they should give him only such a 40
number.

16 At this place in the discussion there impends the
inquiry respecting the king who acts solely 1287ᵃ
according to his own will; he has now to be considered. The so-called limited monarchy, or kingship
according to law, as I have already remarked,⁶⁵ is not a distinct form of government, for under all governments, as, for
example, in a democracy or aristocracy, there may be a gen- 5
eral holding office for life, and one person is often made
supreme over the administration of a state. A magistracy of
this kind exists at Epidamnus,⁶⁶ and also at Opus, but in
the latter city has a more limited power. Now, absolute 10
monarchy, or the arbitrary rule of a sovereign over all the

⁶⁵ 1286ᵃ 2.

⁶⁶ Cf. v. 1301ᵇ 21.

citizens, in a city which consists of equals, is thought by
some to be quite contrary to nature; it is argued that those
who are by nature equals must have the same natural right
and worth, and that for unequals to have an equal share, or
15 for equals to have an unequal share, in the offices of state, is
as bad as for different bodily constitutions to have the same
food and clothing. Wherefore it is thought to be just that
among equals every one be ruled as well as rule, and therefore that all should have their turn. We thus arrive at law;
for an order of succession implies law. And the rule of the
20 law, it is argued, is preferable to that of any individual. On
the same principle, even if it be better for certain individuals to govern, they should be made only guardians and
ministers of the law. For magistrates there must be—this is
admitted; but then men say that to give authority to any
one man when all are equal is unjust. Nay, there may
indeed be cases which the law seems unable to determine,
25 but in such cases can a man? Nay, it will be replied, the law
trains officers for this express purpose, and appoints them
to determine matters which are left undecided by it, to the
best of their judgement. Further, it permits them to make
any amendment of the existing laws which experience suggests. Therefore he who bids the law rule may be deemed to
30 bid God and Reason alone rule, but he who bids man rule
adds an element of the beast; for desire is a wild beast, and
passion perverts the minds of rulers, even when they are the
best of men. The law is reason unaffected by desire. We are
told[67] that a patient should call in a physician; he will not
get better if he is doctored out of a book. But the parallel
35 of the arts is clearly not in point; for the physician does
nothing contrary to rule from motives of friendship; he only
cures a patient and takes a fee; whereas magistrates do many
things from spite and partiality. And, indeed, if a man sus-

[67] Cf. 1286ᵃ 12–14, *Polit.* 296 B.

pected the physician of being in league with his enemies to
destroy him for a bribe, he would rather have recourse to 40
the book. But certainly physicians, when they are sick, call
in other physicians, and training-masters, when they are in 1287b
training, other training-masters, as if they could not judge
truly about their own case and might be influenced by their
feelings. Hence it is evident that in seeking for justice men
seek for the mean or neutral,[68] for the law is the mean. 5
Again, customary laws have more weight, and relate to
more important matters, than written laws, and a man may
be a safer ruler than the written law, but not safer than the
customary law.

Again, it is by no means easy for one man to superin-
tend many things; he will have to appoint a number of
subordinates, and what difference does it make whether
these subordinates always existed or were appointed by him 10
because he needed them? If, as I said before,[69] the good man
has a right to rule because he is better, still two good men
are better than one: this is the old saying—

'two going together',[70]

and the prayer of Agamemnon—

'would that I had ten such counsellors!'[71]

And at this day there are magistrates, for example judges,
who have authority to decide some matters which the law 15
is unable to determine, since no one doubts that the law

[68] Cf. *N. Eth.* v. 1132a 22.

[69] 1283b 21, 1284b 32.

[70] *Il.* x. 224.

[71] *Il.* ii. 372.

would command and decide in the best manner whatever it could. But some things can, and other things cannot, be
20 comprehended under the law, and this is the origin of the vexed question whether the best law or the best man should rule. For matters of detail about which men deliberate cannot be included in legislation. Nor does any one deny that the decision of such matters must be left to man, but it is argued that there should be many judges, and not one only.
25 For every ruler who has been trained by the law judges well; and it would surely seem strange that a person should see better with two eyes, or hear better with two ears, or act better with two hands or feet, than many with many; indeed, it is already the practice of kings to make to themselves many eyes and ears and hands and feet. For they
30 make colleagues of those who are the friends of themselves and their governments. They must be friends of the monarch and of his government; if not his friends, they will not do what he wants; but friendship implies likeness and equality; and, therefore, if he thinks that his friends ought to rule, he must think that those who are equal to himself
35 and like himself ought to rule equally with himself. These are the principal controversies relating to monarchy.

17 But may not all this be true in some cases and not in others? for there is by nature both a justice and an advantage appropriate to the rule of a master, another to kingly rule, another to constitutional rule; but there is none naturally appropriate to tyranny, or to any other perverted form of government; for these come into being contrary to nature. Now, to judge at least from
40 what has been said, it is manifest that, where men are alike
1288a and equal, it is neither expedient nor just that one man should be lord of all, whether there are laws, or whether there are no laws, but he himself is in the place of law. Neither should a good man be lord over good men, nor a bad

man over bad; nor, even if he excels in virtue, should he
have a right to rule, unless in a particular case, at which I
have already hinted, and to which I will once more recur.[72] 5
But first of all, I must determine what natures are suited for
government by a king, and what for an aristocracy, and
what for a constitutional government.

A people who are by nature capable of producing a race
superior in the virtue needed for political rule are fitted for
kingly government; and a people submitting to be ruled as 10
freemen by men whose virtue renders them capable of political command are adapted for an aristocracy: while the
people who are suited for constitutional freedom are those
among whom there naturally exists a warlike multitude[73]
able to rule and to obey in turn by a law which gives office
to the well-to-do according to their desert. But when a 15
whole family, or some individual, happens to be so pre-eminent in virtue as to surpass all others, then it is just that
they should be the royal family and supreme over all, or
that this one citizen should be king of the whole nation.
For, as I said before,[74] to give them authority is not only 20
agreeable to that ground of right which the founders of all
states, whether aristocratical, or oligarchical, or again democratical, are accustomed to put forward (for these all
recognize the claim of excellence, although not the same 25
excellence), but accords with the principle already laid
down. For surely it would not be right to kill, or ostracize,
or exile such a person, or require that he should take his
turn in being governed. The whole is naturally superior to
the part, and he who has this pre-eminence is in the relation
of a whole to a part. But if so, the only alternative is that

[72] 1284ª 3, and 1288ª 15.

[73] Cf. 1279ᵇ 2.

[74] 1283ᵇ 20, 1284ª 3–17, ᵇ25.

he should have the supreme power, and that mankind
30 should obey him, not in turn, but always. These are the
conclusions at which we arrive respecting royalty and its
various forms, and this is the answer to the question,
whether it is or is not advantageous to states, and to which,
and how.

18 We maintain[75] that the true forms of govern-
35 ment are three, and that the best must be that
which is administered by the best, and in which
there is one man, or a whole family, or many persons,
excelling all the others together in virtue, and both rulers
and subjects are fitted, the one to rule, the others to be
ruled, in such a manner as to attain the most eligible life.
We showed at the commencement of our inquiry[76] that the
virtue of the good man is necessarily the same as the virtue
of the citizen of the perfect state. Clearly then in the same
40 manner, and by the same means through which a man
becomes truly good, he will frame a state that is to be ruled
1288b by an aristocracy or by a king, and the same education and
the same habits will be found to make a good man and a
man fit to be a statesman or king.

Having arrived at these conclusions, we must proceed
to speak of the perfect state, and describe how it comes into
5 being and is established.

[75] Cf. 1279ª 22–b4.
[76] cc. 4, 5.

RHETORIC
AND POETIC

INTRODUCTION

Rhetoric is closely allied to logic, for it is the counterpart of dialectic, in Aristotle's analysis, and it has not infrequently been used by his successors to suggest improvements or substitutions for logical devices. It has a moral and political dimension, and the Sophists, as Aristotle views their practices, confused it with the art of politics. It is finally a verbal art, the development of which, both before Aristotle's analyses and since, has been closely associated with the interpretation of poetry. Consistent with his differentiations among the arts and sciences, Aristotle separates the arts of rhetoric and poetic.

Rhetoric like dialectic is limited to *no* specific subject matter, but may be used *in any* consideration, and it is by that fact opposed to the method of science and limited to questions on which variation of opinion is possible. Aristotle emphasized the consideration of arguments, which are the form and essence of persuasion and which had been neglected by the previous writers on the art of rhetoric. There are three modes of persuasion available to a speaker: the use of his character to make his speech credible, the excitation of desired emotions in the audience, and proof or apparent proof. Rhetoric is therefore defined as the faculty or power of observing *in any* given case the available means of persuasion. It is the audience, however, which determines the means: the kinds of oratory—political or deliberative, forensic or legal, and epideictic or display—are determined by consideration of kinds of audience; the character which will be effective in the speaker depends on the susceptibility of audiences; and questions of rhetorical style and arrangement are in large part questions of appropriateness to the various kinds of oratory.

Poetic, too, treats of an art which employs words, and the end of that art is, as in all arts, the basic consideration; but the end is found, not in the peculiarities of audiences, but in the proper pleasure of the varieties of poetry. Poetry is defined in terms of imitation, not persuasion, and the consideration of the historical development of tragedy *and* the examination of particular tragedies elucidate the definition of tragedy in accordance with which the plot is the form or soul of tragedy. When, finally, tragedy is compared with other forms of poetry, and particularly with the epic in the last four chapters of the *Poetics* as it has come to us, the kinds of poetry are not distinguished in terms of audiences but in terms of a comparison of values achieved and a distinction of devices employed.

Like other Greek philosophers, Aristotle was fond of comparing the arts and the sciences. Whereas Socrates used the likeness of the physician, the pilot, the shepherd and the cobbler, to demonstrate that virtue is knowledge, that philosophers should be kings, and that statesmen are supreme poets, Aristotle used the analogy of the arts to distinguish them as poetic or productive sciences from the practical and theoretic sciences. Art is like virtue in its mode of acquisition and destruction, for both are produced by performing the same actions which they will in turn cause and both are destroyed by the same causes that produced them, but they differ from each other in that virtues are judged by the state of character from which the action is produced and arts are judged by the quality of the objects produced by the action. Art is like nature in its objects and the manner in which artificial and natural objects are produced, for Aristotle is fond of repeating the observation that the objects of art are produced as nature would have produced them, and that in the processes of production and the objects produced, art imitates nature. But nature is a cause of motion internal to the thing moved, while art is an external cause employed by the artist to impose on matter a form first conceived in his mind, and artificial objects are not natures or substances and therefore have no strict definitions comparable to those discovered in physics for natural objects.

DE POETICA

CONTENTS

22. The characteristics of the language of poetry.

(C) Rules for the construction of an epic.

23. It must preserve unity of action.
24. Points of resemblance and of difference between epic poetry and tragedy.

(D) 25. Possible criticisms of an epic or tragedy, and the answers to them.

(E) 26. Tragedy artistically superior to epic poetry.

DE POETICA

Poetics

Translated by Ingram Bywater

1   Our subject being Poetry, I propose to speak not only of the art in general but also of its species and their respective capacities; of the structure of plot required for a good poem; of the number and nature of the constituent parts of a poem; and likewise of any other matters in the same line of inquiry. Let us follow the natural order and begin with the primary facts.

    Epic poetry and Tragedy, as also Comedy, Dithyrambic poetry, and most flute-playing and lyre-playing, are all, viewed as a whole, modes of imitation. But at the same time they differ from one another in three ways, either by a difference of kind in their means, or by differences in the objects, or in the manner of their imitations.

    I. Just as colour and form are used as means by some, who (whether by art or constant practice) imitate and portray many things by their aid, and the voice is used by others; so also in the above-mentioned group of arts, the means with them as a whole are rhythm, language, and harmony—used, however, either singly or in certain combinations. A combination of harmony and rhythm alone is the means in flute-playing and lyre-playing, and any other arts there may be of the same description, e. g. imitative piping. Rhythm alone, without harmony, is the means in the dancer's imitations; for even he, by the rhythms of his attitudes, may represent men's characters, as well as what they do and suffer. There is further an art which imitates by

language alone, without harmony, in prose or in verse, and
if in verse, either in some one or in a plurality of metres.
1447ᵇ This form of imitation is to this day without name. We
have no common name for a mime of Sophron or Xenar-
10 chus and a Socratic Conversation; and we should still be
without one even if the imitation in the two instances were
in trimeters or elegiacs or some other kind of verse—though
it is the way with people to tack on 'poet' to the name of a
metre, and talk of elegiac-poets and epic-poets, thinking
that they call them poets not by reason of the imitative
15 nature of their work, but indiscriminately by reason of the
metre they write in. Even if a theory of medicine or physical philosophy be put forth in a metrical form, it is usual
to describe the writer in this way; Homer and Empedocles,
however, have really nothing in common apart from their
metre; so that, if the one is to be called a poet, the other
20 should be termed a physicist rather than a poet. We should be
in the same position also, if the imitation in these instances
were in all the metres, like the *Centaur* (a rhapsody in a
medley of all metres) of Chaeremon; and Chaeremon one
has to recognize as a poet. So much, then, as to these arts.
25 There are, lastly, certain other arts, which combine all the
means enumerated, rhythm, melody, and verse, e. g. Dithy-
rambic and Nomic poetry, Tragedy and Comedy; with this
difference, however, that the three kinds of means are in
some of them all employed together, and in others brought
in separately, one after the other. These elements of difference in the above arts I term the means of their imitation.

1448ᵃ   2   II. The objects the imitator represents are actions,
with agents who are necessarily either good men or
bad—the diversities of human character being
nearly always derivative from this primary distinction, since
the line between virtue and vice is one dividing the whole of
mankind. It follows, therefore, that the agents represented

must be either above our own level of goodness, or beneath
it, or just such as we are; in the same way as, with the 5
painters, the personages of Polygnotus are better than we
are, those of Pauson worse, and those of Dionysius just like
ourselves. It is clear that each of the above-mentioned arts
will admit of these differences, and that it will become a
separate art by representing objects with this point of difference. Even in dancing, flute-playing, and lyre-playing
such diversities are possible; and they are also possible in 10
the nameless art that uses language, prose or verse without
harmony, as its means; Homer's personages, for instance,
are better than we are; Cleophon's are on our own level; and
those of Hegemon of Thasos, the first writer of parodies,
and Nicochares, the author of the *Diliad*, are beneath it. 15
The same is true of the Dithyramb and the Nome: the personages may be presented in them with the difference
exemplified in the . . . of . . . and Argas, and in the
Cyclopses of Timotheus and Philoxenus. This difference it
is that distinguishes Tragedy and Comedy also; the one
would make its personages worse, and the other better, than
the men of the present day.

3 III. A third difference in these arts is in the manner
in which each kind of object is represented. Given 20
both the same means and the same kind of object
for imitation one may either (1) speak at one moment in
narrative and at another in an assumed character, as Homer
does; or (2) one may remain the same throughout, without
any such change; or (3) the imitators may represent the
whole story dramatically, as though they were actually
doing the things described.

As we said at the beginning, therefore, the differences
in the imitation of these arts come under three heads, their
means, their objects, and their manner.

So that as an imitator Sophocles will be on one side

25 akin to Homer, both portraying good men; and on another
to Aristophanes, since both present their personages as acting and doing. This in fact, according to some, is the reason
for plays being termed dramas, because in a play the personages act the story. Hence too both Tragedy and Comedy
30 are claimed by the Dorians as their discoveries; Comedy by
the Megarians—by those in Greece as having arisen when
Megara became a democracy, and by the Sicilian Megarians on the ground that the poet Epicharmus was of their
country, and a good deal earlier than Chionides and
Magnes; even Tragedy also is claimed by certain of the
Peloponnesian Dorians. In support of this claim they point
to the words 'comedy' and 'drama'. Their word for the out-
35 lying hamlets, they say, is *comae*, whereas Athenians call
them *demes*—thus assuming that comedians got the name
not from their *comoe* or revels, but from their strolling from
hamlet to hamlet, lack of appreciation keeping them out of
1448^b the city. Their word also for 'to act', they say, is *dran*,
whereas Athenians use *prattein*.

So much, then, as to the number and nature of the
points of difference in the imitation of these arts.

4 It is clear that the general origin of poetry was due
to two causes, each of them part of human nature.
5 Imitation is natural to man from childhood, one of
his advantages over the lower animals being this, that he is
the most imitative creature in the world, and learns at first
by imitation. And it is also natural for all to delight in
works of imitation. The truth of this second point is shown
10 by experience: though the objects themselves may be
painful to see, we delight to view the most realistic repre-
sentations of them in art, the forms for example of the
lowest animals and of dead bodies. The explanation is to be
found in a further fact: to be learning something is the
greatest of pleasures not only to the philosopher but also to

the rest of mankind, however small their capacity for it; the 15
reason of the delight in seeing the picture is that one is at
the same time learning—gathering the meaning of things,
e. g. that the man there is so-and-so; for if one has not seen
the thing before, one's pleasure will not be in the picture as
an imitation of it, but will be due to the execution or 20
colouring or some similar cause. Imitation, then, being natural to us—as also the sense of harmony and rhythm, the
metres being obviously species of rhythms—it was through
their original aptitude, and by a series of improvements for
the most part gradual on their first efforts, that they created
poetry out of their improvisations.

Poetry, however, soon broke up into two kinds according to the differences of character in the individual poets; 25
for the graver among them would represent noble actions,
and those of noble personages; and the meaner sort the
actions of the ignoble. The latter class produced invectives
at first, just as others did hymns and panegyrics. We know
of no such poem by any of the pre-Homeric poets, though
there were probably many such writers among them;
instances, however, may be found from Homer downwards,
e. g. his *Margites*, and the similar poems of others. In this 30
poetry of invective its natural fitness brought an iambic
metre into use; hence our present term 'iambic', because it
was the metre of their 'iambs' or invectives against one
another. The result was that the old poets became some of
them writers of heroic and others of iambic verse. Homer's
position, however, is peculiar: just as he was in the serious
style the poet of poets, standing alone not only through the 35
literary excellence, but also through the dramatic character
of his imitations, so too he was the first to outline for us the
general forms of Comedy by producing not a dramatic
invective, but a dramatic picture of the Ridiculous; his *Margites* in fact stands in the same relation to our comedies as
the *Iliad* and *Odyssey* to our tragedies. As soon, however, 1449a

as Tragedy and Comedy appeared in the field, those naturally drawn to the one line of poetry became writers of
5 comedies instead of iambs, and those naturally drawn to the
other, writers of tragedies instead of epics, because these
new modes of art were grander and of more esteem than the
old.

If it be asked whether Tragedy is now all that it need
be in its formative elements, to consider that, and decide it
theoretically and in relation to the theatres, is a matter for
another inquiry.

10   It certainly began in improvisations—as did also Comedy; the one originating with the authors of the Dithyramb,
the other with those of the phallic songs, which still survive
as institutions in many of our cities. And its advance after
that was little by little, through their improving on whatever
they had before them at each stage. It was in fact only after
a long series of changes that the movement of Tragedy
15 stopped on its attaining to its natural form. (1) The number of actors was first increased to two by Aeschylus, who
curtailed the business of the Chorus, and made the dialogue, or spoken portion, take the leading part in the play.
(2) A third actor and scenery were due to Sophocles. (3)
Tragedy acquired also its magnitude. Discarding short sto-
20 ries and a ludicrous diction, through its passing out of its
satyric stage, it assumed, though only at a late point in its
progress, a tone of dignity; and its metre changed then from
trochaic to iambic. The reason for their original use of the
trochaic tetrameter was that their poetry was satyric and
more connected with dancing than it now is. As soon, however, as a spoken part came in, nature herself found the
appropriate metre. The iambic, we know, is the most speak-
25 able of metres, as is shown by the fact that we very often
fall into it in conversation, whereas we rarely talk hexame-
ters, and only when we depart from the speaking tone of
voice. (4) Another change was a plurality of episodes or

acts. As for the remaining matters, the superadded embellishments and the account of their introduction, these must be taken as said, as it would probably be a long piece of work to go through the details.   30

5 As for Comedy, it is (as has been observed[1] an imitation of men worse than the average; worse, however, not as regards any and every sort of fault, but only as regards one particular kind, the Ridiculous, which is a species of the Ugly. The Ridiculous may be defined as a mistake or deformity not productive of pain or 35 harm to others; the mask, for instance, that excites laughter, is something ugly and distorted without causing pain.

Though the successive changes in Tragedy and their authors are not unknown, we cannot say the same of Comedy; its early stages passed unnoticed, because it was not as yet taken up in a serious way. It was only at a late point in 1449ᵇ its progress that a chorus of comedians was officially granted by the archon; they used to be mere volunteers. It had also already certain definite forms at the time when the record of those termed comic poets begins. Who it was who supplied it with masks, or prologues, or a plurality of actors and the like, has remained unknown. The invented Fable, or Plot, however, originated in Sicily with Epicharmus and 5 Phormis; of Athenian poets Crates was the first to drop the Comedy of invective and frame stories of a general and non-personal nature, in other words, Fables or Plots.

Epic poetry, then, has been seen to agree with Tragedy to this extent, that of being an imitation of serious subjects in a grand kind of verse. It differs from it, however, (1) in 10 that it is in one kind of verse and in narrative form; and (2) in its length—which is due to its action having no fixed limit of time, whereas Tragedy endeavours to keep as far as

[1] 1448ᵃ 17; 1448ᵇ 37.

possible within a single circuit of the sun, or something near
that. This, I say, is another point of difference between
15 them, though at first the practice in this respect was just the
same in tragedies as in epic poems. They differ also (3) in
their constituents, some being common to both and others
peculiar to Tragedy—hence a judge of good and bad in
Tragedy is a judge of that in epic poetry also. All the parts
of an epic are included in Tragedy; but those of Tragedy
are not all of them to be found in the Epic.

20 **6** Reserving hexameter poetry and Comedy for consideration hereafter,[2] let us proceed now to the
discussion of Tragedy; before doing so, however,
we must gather up the definition resulting from what has
25 been said. A tragedy, then, is the imitation of an action that
is serious and also, as having magnitude, complete in itself;
in language with pleasurable accessories, each kind brought
in separately in the parts of the work; in a dramatic, not in
a narrative form; with incidents arousing pity and fear,
wherewith to accomplish its catharsis of such emotions.
Here by 'language with pleasurable accessories' I mean that
30 with rhythm and harmony or song superadded; and by 'the
kinds separately' I mean that some portions are worked out
with verse only, and others in turn with song.

   I. As they act the stories, it follows that in the first
place the Spectacle (or stage-appearance of the actors) must
be some part of the whole; and in the second Melody and
Diction, these two being the means of their imitation. Here
35 by 'Diction' I mean merely this, the composition of the
verses; and by 'Melody', what is too completely understood
to require explanation. But further: the subject represented
also is an action; and the action involves agents, who must

[2] For hexameter poetry cf. chap 23 f.; comedy was treated of in the lost
Second Book.

necessarily have their distinctive qualities both of character
and thought, since it is from these that we ascribe certain 1450ᵃ
qualities to their actions. There are in the natural order of
things, therefore, two causes, Thought and Character, of
their actions, and consequently of their success or failure in
their lives. Now the action (that which was done) is represented in the play by the Fable or Plot. The Fable, in our
present sense of the term, is simply this, the combination
of the incidents, or things done in the story; whereas Character is what makes us ascribe certain moral qualities to the 5
agents; and Thought is shown in all they say when proving
a particular point or, it may be, enunciating a general truth.
There are six parts consequently of every tragedy, as a
whole (that is) of such or such quality, viz. a Fable or Plot,
Characters, Diction, Thought, Spectacle, and Melody; two
of them arising from the means, one from the manner, and
three from the objects of the dramatic imitation; and there is 10
nothing else besides these six. Of these, its formative elements, then, not a few of the dramatists have made due use,
as every play, one may say, admits of Spectacle, Character,
Fable, Diction, Melody, and Thought.

II. The most important of the six is the combination of
the incidents of the story. Tragedy is essentially an imita- 15
tion not of persons but of action and life, of happiness and
misery. All human happiness or misery takes the form of
action; the end for which we live is a certain kind of activity, not a quality. Character gives us qualities, but it is in
our actions—what we do—that we are happy or the reverse.
In a play accordingly they do not act in order to portray the
Characters; they include the Characters for the sake of the 20
action. So that it is the action in it, i. e. its Fable or Plot,
that is the end and purpose of the tragedy; and the end is
everywhere the chief thing. Besides this, a tragedy is impossible without action, but there may be one without Character.
The tragedies of most of the moderns are characterless—a

25 defect common among poets of all kinds, and with its counterpart in painting in Zeuxis as compared with Polygnotus;
for whereas the latter is strong in character, the work of
Zeuxis is devoid of it. And again: one may string together
a series of characteristic speeches of the utmost finish as
regards Diction and Thought, and yet fail to produce the
30 true tragic effect; but one will have much better success
with a tragedy which, however inferior in these respects, has
a Plot, a combination of incidents, in it. And again: the
most powerful elements of attraction in Tragedy, the
Peripeties and Discoveries, are parts of the Plot. A further
35 proof is in the fact that beginners succeed earlier with the
Diction and Characters than with the construction of a
story; and the same may be said of nearly all the early
dramatists. We maintain, therefore, that the first essential,
the life and soul, so to speak, of Tragedy is the Plot; and
that the Characters come second—compare the parallel in
1450b painting, where the most beautiful colours laid on without
order will not give one the same pleasure as a simple black-
and-white sketch of a portrait. We maintain that Tragedy is
primarily an imitation of action, and that it is mainly for the
sake of the action that it imitates the personal agents. Third
comes the element of Thought, i. e. the power of saying
5 whatever can be said, or what is appropriate to the occasion.
This is what, in the speeches in Tragedy, falls under the
arts of Politics and Rhetoric; for the older poets make their
personages discourse like statesmen, and the modern like
rhetoricians. One must not confuse it with Character. Character in a play is that which reveals the moral purpose of
the agents, i. e. the sort of thing they seek or avoid, where
that is not obvious—hence there is no room for Character in
a speech on a purely indifferent subject. Thought, on the
10 other hand, is shown in all they say when proving or
disproving some particular point, or enunciating some
universal proposition. Fourth among the literary elements is

the Diction of the personages, i. e., as before explained,[3] the expression of their thoughts in words, which is practically the same thing with verse as with prose. As for the two 15 remaining parts, the Melody is the greatest of the pleasurable accessories of Tragedy. The Spectacle, though an attraction, is the least artistic of all the parts, and has least to do with the art of poetry. The tragic effect is quite possible without a public performance and actors; and besides, the getting-up of the Spectacle is more a matter for the costumier than the poet. 20

7 Having thus distinguished the parts, let us now consider the proper construction of the Fable or Plot, as that is at once the first and the most important thing in Tragedy. We have laid it down that a tragedy is an imitation of an action that is complete in itself, as a whole of some magnitude; for a whole may be of no magni- 25 tude to speak of. Now a whole is that which has beginning, middle, and end. A beginning is that which is not itself necessarily after anything else, and which has naturally something else after it; an end is that which is naturally after 30 something itself, either as its necessary or usual consequent, and with nothing else after it; and a middle, that which is by nature after one thing and has also another after it. A well-constructed Plot, therefore, cannot either begin or end at any point one likes; beginning and end in it must be of the forms just described. Again: to be beautiful, a living creature, and every whole made up of parts, must not only 35 present a certain order in its arrangement of parts, but also be of a certain definite magnitude. Beauty is a matter of size and order, and therefore impossible either (1) in a very minute creature, since our perception becomes indistinct as it approaches instantaneity; or (2) in a creature of vast size—

---

[3] 1449b 34.

one, say, 1,000 miles long—as in that case, instead of the
1451ᵃ object being seen all at once, the unity and wholeness of it
is lost to the beholder. Just in the same way, then, as a beautiful whole made up of parts, or a beautiful living creature,
must be of some size, but a size to be taken in by the eye,
5 so a story or Plot must be of some length, but of a length to
be taken in by the memory. As for the limit of its length, so
far as that is relative to public performances and spectators,
it does not fall within the theory of poetry. If they had to
perform a hundred tragedies, they would be timed by water-
clocks, as they are said to have been at one period. The
10 limit, however, set by the actual nature of the thing is this:
the longer the story, consistently with its being comprehen-
sible as a whole, the finer it is by reason of its magnitude. As
a rough general formula, 'a length which allows of the hero
passing by a series of probable or necessary stages from misfortune to happiness, or from happiness to misfortune', may
15 suffice as a limit for the magnitude of the story.

8 The Unity of a Plot does not consist, as some suppose, in its having one man as its subject. An
infinity of things befall that one man, some of
which it is impossible to reduce to unity; and in like manner
there are many actions of one man which cannot be made to
form one action. One sees, therefore, the mistake of all the
20 poets who have written a *Heracleid,* a *Theseid,* or similar
poems; they suppose that, because Heracles was one man,
the story also of Heracles must be one story. Homer, however, evidently understood this point quite well, whether by
art or instinct, just in the same way as he excels the rest in
every other respect. In writing an *Odyssey,* he did not make
25 the poem cover all that ever befell his hero—it befell him,
for instance, to get wounded on Parnassus and also to feign
madness at the time of the call to arms, but the two incidents had no necessary or probable connexion with one

another—instead of doing that, he took as the subject of the
Odyssey, as also of the *Iliad,* an action with a Unity of the   30
kind we are describing. The truth is that, just as in the
other imitative arts one imitation is always of one thing, so
in poetry the story, as an imitation of action, must represent one action, a complete whole, with its several incidents
so closely connected that the transposal or withdrawal of
any one of them will disjoin and dislocate the whole. For
that which makes no perceptible difference by its presence
or absence is no real part of the whole.   35

9 From what we have said it will be seen that the
poet's function is to describe, not the thing that has
happened, but a kind of thing that might happen,
i. e. what is possible as being probable or necessary. The distinction between historian and poet is not in the one writing   1451ᵇ
prose and the other verse—you might put the work of
Herodotus into verse, and it would still be a species of history; it consists really in this, that the one describes the thing
that has been, and the other a kind of thing that might be.   5
Hence poetry is something more philosophic and of graver
import than history, since its statements are of the nature
rather of universals, whereas those of history are singulars.
By a universal statement I mean one as to what such or such
a kind of man will probably or necessarily say or do—which
is the aim of poetry, though it affixes proper names to the   10
characters; by a singular statement, one as to what, say,
Alcibiades did or had done to him. In Comedy this has
become clear by this time; it is only when their plot is
already made up of probable incidents that they give it a
basis of proper names, choosing for the purpose any names
that may occur to them, instead of writing like the old   15
iambic poets about particular persons. In Tragedy, however,
they still adhere to the historic names; and for this reason:
what convinces is the possible; now whereas we are not yet

sure as to the possibility of that which has not happened,
that which has happened is manifestly possible, else it would
not have come to pass. Nevertheless even in Tragedy there
20 are some plays with but one or two known names in them,
the rest being inventions; and there are some without a single known name, e. g. Agathon's *Antheus*, in which both
incidents and names are of the poet's invention; and it is no
less delightful on that account. So that one must not aim at a
25 rigid adherence to the traditional stories on which tragedies
are based. It would be absurd, in fact, to do so, as even the
known stories are only known to a few, though they are a
delight none the less to all.

It is evident from the above that the poet must be more
the poet of his stories or Plots than of his verses, inasmuch
as he is a poet by virtue of the imitative element in his work,
and it is actions that he imitates. And if he should come to
30 take a subject from actual history, he is none the less a poet
for that; since some historic occurrences may very well be in
the probable and possible order of things; and it is in that
aspect of them that he is their poet.

Of simple Plots and actions the episodic are the worst.
I call a Plot episodic when there is neither probability nor
35 necessity in the sequence of its episodes. Actions of this sort
bad poets construct through their own fault, and good ones
on account of the players. His work being for public performance, a good poet often stretches out a Plot beyond its
capabilities, and is thus obliged to twist the sequence of incident.

1452ᵃ   Tragedy, however, is an imitation not only of a complete action, but also of incidents arousing pity and fear.
Such incidents have the very greatest effect on the mind
when they occur unexpectedly and at the same time in consequence of one another; there is more of the marvellous in
5 them then than if they happened of themselves or by mere
chance. Even matters of chance seem most marvellous if

there is an appearance of design as it were in them; as for instance the statue of Mitys at Argos killed the author of Mitys' death by falling down on him when a looker-on at a public spectacle; for incidents like that we think to be not without a meaning. A Plot, therefore, of this sort is neces- 10 sarily finer than others.

10 Plots are either simple or complex, since the actions they represent are naturally of this twofold description. The action, proceeding in the way defined, as one continuous whole, I call simple, when the change in the hero's fortunes takes place without Peripety 15 or Discovery; and complex, when it involves one or the other, or both. These should each of them arise out of the structure of the Plot itself, so as to be the consequence, necessary or probable, of the antecedents. There is a great difference between a thing happening *propter hoc* and *post hoc*.   20

11 A Peripety is the change of the kind described from one state of things within the play to its opposite, and that too in the way we are saying, in the probable or necessary sequence of events; as it is for instance in *Oedipus:* here the opposite state of things is pro- 25 duced by the Messenger, who, coming to gladden Oedipus and to remove his fears as to his mother, reveals the secret of his birth.[4] And in *Lynceus*,[5] just as he is being led off for execution, with Danaus at his side to put him to death, the incidents preceding this bring it about that he is saved and Danaus put to death. A Discovery is, as the very word 30 implies, a change from ignorance to knowledge, and thus to either love or hate, in the personages marked for good or evil fortune. The finest form of Discovery is one attended

[4] *O.T.* 911–1085.

[5] By Theodectes.

by Peripeties, like that which goes with the Discovery in
Oedipus. There are no doubt other forms of it; what we
have said may happen in a way in reference to inanimate
35 things, even things of a very casual kind; and it is also possible to discover whether some one has done or not done
something. But the form most directly connected with the
Plot and the action of the piece is the first-mentioned. This,
1452ᵇ with a Peripety, will arouse either pity or fear—actions of
that nature being what Tragedy is assumed to represent;
and it will also serve to bring about the happy or unhappy
ending. The Discovery, then, being of persons, it may be
that of one party only to the other, the latter being already
5 known; or both the parties may have to discover themselves.
Iphigenia, for instance, was discovered to Orestes by sending the letter;⁶ and another Discovery was required to reveal
him to Iphigenia.

Two parts of the Plot, then, Peripety and Discovery, are
10 on matters of this sort. A third part is Suffering; which we
may define as an action of a destructive or painful nature,
such as murders on the stage, tortures, woundings, and the
like. The other two have been already explained.

15 **12** The parts of Tragedy to be treated as formative
elements in the whole were mentioned in a
previous Chapter.⁷ From the point of view, how-
ever, of its quantity. i. e. the separate sections into which it
is divided, a tragedy has the following parts: Prologue,
Episode, Exode, and a choral portion, distinguished into
Parode and Stasimon; these two are common to all tragedies,
20 whereas songs from the stage and *Commoe* are only found in
some. The Prologue is all that precedes the Parode of the
chorus; an Episode all that comes in between two whole

⁶ *Iph. Taur.* 727 ff.
⁷ Ch. 6

choral songs; the Exode all that follows after the last choral song. In the choral portion the Parode is the whole first statement of the chorus; a Stasimon, a song of the chorus without anapaests or trochees; a *Commos*, a lamentation sung by chorus and actor in concert. The parts of Tragedy to be 25 used as formative elements in the whole we have already mentioned; the above are its parts from the point of view of its quantity, or the separate sections into which it is divided.

13 The next points after what we have said above will be these: (1) What is the poet to aim at, and what is he to avoid, in constructing his Plots? and (2) What are the conditions on which the tragic effect depends?

We assume that, for the finest form of Tragedy, the 30 Plot must be not simple but complex; and further, that it must imitate actions arousing fear and pity, since that is the distinctive function of this kind of imitation. It follows, therefore, that there are three forms of Plot to be avoided. (1) A good man must not be seen passing from happiness to misery, or (2) a bad man from misery to happiness. The 35 first situation is not fear-inspiring or piteous, but simply odious to us. The second is the most untragic that can be; it has no one of the requisites of Tragedy; it does not appeal either to the human feeling in us, or to our pity, or to our fears. Nor, on the other hand, should (3) an extremely bad 1453a man be seen falling from happiness into misery. Such a story may arouse the human feeling in us, but it will not move us to either pity or fear; pity is occasioned by unde- 5 served misfortune, and fear by that of one like ourselves; so that there will be nothing either piteous or fear-inspiring in the situation. There remains, then, the intermediate kind of personage, a man not pre-eminently virtuous and just, whose misfortune, however, is brought upon him not by vice and depravity but by some error of judgement, of the

number of those in the enjoyment of great reputation and
10 prosperity; e. g. Oedipus, Thyestes, and the men of note of
similar families. The perfect Plot, accordingly, must have a
single, and not (as some tell us) a double issue; the change
in the hero's fortunes must be not from misery to happiness, but on the contrary from happiness to misery; and the
cause of it must lie not in any depravity, but in some great
15 error on his part; the man himself being either such as we
have described, or better, not worse, than that. Fact also
confirms our theory. Though the poets began by accepting
any tragic story that came to hand, in these days the finest
tragedies are always on the story of some few houses, on
20 that of Alcmeon, Oedipus, Orestes, Meleager, Thyestes,
Telephus, or any others that may have been involved, as
either agents or sufferers, in some deed of horror. The theoretically best tragedy, then, has a Plot of this description.
The critics, therefore, are wrong who blame Euripides for
taking this line in his tragedies, and giving many of them
25 an unhappy ending. It is, as we have said, the right line to
take. The best proof is this: on the stage, and in the public
performances, such plays, properly worked out, are seen to
be the most truly tragic; and Euripides, even if his execution be faulty in every other point, is seen to be nevertheless
the most tragic certainly of the dramatists. After this comes
30 the construction of Plot which some rank first, one with a
double story (like the *Odyssey*) and an opposite issue for the
good and the bad personages. It is ranked as first only
through the weakness of the audiences; the poets merely follow their public, writing as its wishes dictate. But the
35 pleasure here is not that of Tragedy. It belongs rather to
Comedy, where the bitterest enemies in the piece (e. g.
Orestes and Aegisthus) walk off good friends at the end,
with no slaying of any one by any one.

14

The tragic fear and pity may be aroused by the Spectacle; but they may also be aroused by the 1453^b very structure and incidents of the play—which is the better way and shows the better poet. The Plot in fact should be so framed that, even without seeing the things 5 take place, he who simply hears the account of them shall be filled with horror and pity at the incidents; which is just the effect that the mere recital of the story in *Oedipus* would have on one. To produce this same effect by means of the Spectacle is less artistic, and requires extraneous aid. Those, however, who make use of the Spectacle to put before us that which is merely monstrous and not productive of fear, 10 are wholly out of touch with Tragedy; not every kind of pleasure should be required of a tragedy, but only its own proper pleasure.

The tragic pleasure is that of pity and fear, and the poet has to produce it by a work of imitation; it is clear, there-fore, that the causes should be included in the incidents of his story. Let us see, then, what kinds of incident strike one 15 as horrible, or rather as piteous. In a deed of this description the parties must necessarily be either friends, or enemies, or indifferent to one another. Now when enemy does it on enemy, there is nothing to move us to pity either in his doing or in his meditating the deed, except so far as the actual pain of the sufferer is concerned; and the same is true when the parties are indifferent to one another. Whenever the tragic deed, however, is done within the family—when 20 murder or the like is done or meditated by brother on brother, by son on father, by mother on son, or son on mother—these are the situations the poet should seek after. The traditional stories, accordingly, must be kept as they are, e. g. the murder of Clytaemnestra by Orestes and of Eriphyle by Alcmeon. At the same time even with these 25 there is something left to the poet himself; it is for him to devise the right way of treating them. Let us explain more

clearly what we mean by 'the right way'. The deed of horror may be done by the doer knowingly and consciously, as in the old poets, and in Medea's murder of her children in
30 Euripides.[8] Or he may do it, but in ignorance of his relationship, and discover that afterwards, as does the Oedipus in Sophocles. Here the deed is outside the play; but it may be within it, like the act of the Alcmeon in Astydamas, or that of the Telegonus in *Ulysses Wounded*.[9] A third possi-
35 bility is for one meditating some deadly injury to another, in ignorance of his relationship, to make the discovery in time to draw back. These exhaust the possibilities, since the deed must necessarily be either done or not done, and either knowingly or unknowingly.

The worst situation is when the personage is with full knowledge on the point of doing the deed, and leaves it undone. It is odious and also (through the absence of suffering) untragic; hence it is that no one is made to act thus
1454a except in some few instances, e. g. Haemon and Creon in *Antigone*.[10] Next after this comes the actual perpetration of the deed meditated. A better situation than that, however, is for the deed to be done in ignorance, and the relationship discovered afterwards, since there is nothing odious in it, and the Discovery will serve to astound us. But the best of
5 all is the last; what we have in *Cresphontes*,[11] for example, where Merope, on the point of slaying her son, recognizes him in time; in *Iphigenia*, where sister and brother are in a like position; and in *Helle*,[12] where the son recognizes his mother, when on the point of giving her up to her enemy.

[8] *Med.* 1236.

[9] Perhaps by Sophocles.

[10] l. 1231.

[11] By Euripides.

[12] Authorship unknown.

This will explain why our tragedies are restricted (as we said just now)[13] to such a small number of families. It was accident rather than art that led the poets in quest of sub- 10 jects to embody this kind of incident in their Plots. They are still obliged, accordingly, to have recourse to the families in which such horrors have occurred.

On the construction of the Plot, and the kind of Plot required for Tragedy, enough has now been said. 15

15 In the Characters there are four points to aim at. First and foremost, that they shall be good. There will be an element of character in the play, if (as has been observed)[14] what a personage says or does reveals a certain moral purpose; and a good element of character, if the purpose so revealed is good. Such good- ness is possible in every type of personage, even in a 20 woman or a slave, though the one is perhaps an inferior, and the other a wholly worthless being. The second point is to make them appropriate. The Character before us may be, say, manly; but it is not appropriate in a female Char- acter to be manly, or clever. The third is to make them like the reality, which is not the same as their being good and 25 appropriate, in our sense of the term. The fourth is to make them consistent and the same throughout; even if inconsistency be part of the man before one for imitation as presenting that form of character, he should still be con- sistently inconsistent. We have an instance of baseness of character, not required for the story, in the Menelaus in *Orestes*; of the incongruous and unbefitting in the lamen- 30 tation of Ulysses in *Scylla*,[15] and in the (clever) speech of

[13] 1453ᵃ 19.

[14] 1450ᵇ 8.

[15] A dithyramb by Timotheus.

Melanippe;[16] and of inconsistency in *Iphigenia at Aulis*,[17]
where Iphigenia the suppliant is utterly unlike the later
Iphigenia. The right thing, however, is in the Characters
35 just as in the incidents of the play to endeavour always after
the necessary or the probable; so that whenever such-and-
such a personage says or does such-and-such a thing, it
shall be the necessary or probable outcome of his character;
and whenever this incident follows on that, it shall be either
the necessary or the probable consequence of it. From this
1454ᵇ one sees (to digress for a moment) that the Dénouement
also should arise out of the plot itself, and not depend on
stage-artifice, as in *Medea*,[18] or in the (arrested) departure of
the Greeks in the *Iliad*.[19] The artifice must be reserved for
5 matters outside the play—for past events beyond human
knowledge, or events yet to come, which require to be fore-
told or announced; since it is the privilege of the Gods to
know everything. There should be nothing improbable
among the actual incidents. If it be unavoidable, however, it
should be outside the tragedy, like the improbability in the
Oedipus of Sophocles. But to return to the Characters. As
Tragedy is an imitation of personages better than the ordi-
10 nary man, we in our way should follow the example of good
portrait-painters, who reproduce the distinctive features of a
man, and at the same time, without losing the likeness,
make him handsomer than he is. The poet in like manner,
in portraying men quick or slow to anger, or with similar
infirmities of character, must know how to represent them
as such, and at the same time as good men, as Agathon and
Homer respectively have represented Achilles.

[16] (Euripides).

[17] ll. 1211 ff., 1368 ff.

[18] l. 1317.

[19] ii. 155.

All these rules one must keep in mind throughout, and, 15
further, those also for such points of stage-effect as directly
depend on the art of the poet, since in these too one may
often make mistakes. Enough, however, has been said on
the subject of our published writings.[20]

16 Discovery in general has been explained already.[21] As for the species of Discovery, the first 20
to be noted is (1) the least artistic form of it, of
which the poets make the most use of through mere lack of
invention, Discovery by signs or marks. Of these some are
congenital, like the 'lance-head which the Earth-born have
on them',[22] or 'stars', such as Carcinus brings in his
Thyestes; others acquired after birth—these latter being
either marks on the body, e. g. scars, or external tokens, like
necklaces, or (to take another sort of instance) the ark in the 25
Discovery in *Tyro*.[23] Even these, however, admit of two
uses, a better and a worse; the scar of Ulysses is an instance;
the Discovery of him through it is made in one way by the
nurse[24] and in another by the swineherds.[25] A Discovery
using signs as a means of assurance is less artistic, as indeed
are all such as imply reflection; whereas one bringing them
in all of a sudden, as in the *Bath-story*,[26] is of a better order. 30
Next after these are (2) Discoveries made directly by the
poet; which are inartistic for that very reason; e. g. Orestes'

[20] In the lost dialogue *On Poets*.

[21] 1452[a] 29.

[22] Authorship unknown.

[23] By Euripides.

[24] *Od.* xix. 386–475.

[25] *Od.* xxi. 205–25.

[26] *Od.* xix. 392.

Discovery of himself in *Iphigenia*: whereas his sister reveals
who she is by the letter,[27] Orestes is made to say himself
35 what the poet rather than the story demands.[28] This, therefore, is not far removed from the first-mentioned fault, since
he might have presented certain tokens as well. Another
instance is the 'shuttle's voice' in the *Tereus* of Sophocles.
(3) A third species is Discovery through memory, from a
man's consciousness being awakened by something seen.
1455ª Thus in *The Cyprioe* of Dicaeogenes, the sight of the picture
makes the man burst into tears; and in the *Tale of Alci-
nous*,[29] hearing the harper Ulysses is reminded of the past
and weeps; the Discovery of them being the result. (4) A
fourth kind is Discovery through reasoning; e. g. in *The
Choephoroe*;[30] 'One like me is here; there is no one like me
5 but Orestes; he, therefore, must be here.' Or that which
Polyidus the Sophist suggested for *Iphigenia;* since it was
natural for Orestes to reflect: 'My sister was sacrificed, and
I am to be sacrificed like her.' Or that in the *Tydeus* of
Theodectes: 'I came to find a son, and am to die myself.'
10 Or that in *The Phinidae*:[31] on seeing the place the women
inferred their fate, that they were to die there, since they
had also been exposed there. (5) There is, too, a composite
Discovery arising from bad reasoning on the side of the
other party. An instance of it is in *Ulysses the False Messenger*:[31] he said he should know the bow—which he had not
15 seen; but to suppose from that that he would know it again
(as though he had once seen it) was bad reasoning. (6) The
best of all Discoveries, however, is that arising from the

---

[27] *Iph. Taur.* 727 ff.

[28] Ib., 800 ff.

[29] *Od.* viii. 521 ff. (Cf. viii. 83 ff.).

[30] ll. 168–234.

[31] Authorship unknown.

incidents themselves, when the great surprise comes about
through a probable incident, like that in the *Oedipus* of
Sophocles; and also in *Iphigenia*;[32] for it was not improbable that she should wish to have a letter taken home. These
last are the only Discoveries independent of the artifice of
signs and necklaces. Next after them come Discoveries 20
through reasoning.

17 At the time when he is constructing his Plots,
and engaged on the Diction in which they are
worked out, the poet should remember (1) to put
the actual scenes as far as possible before his eyes. In this 25
way, seeing everything with the vividness of an eye-witness
as it were, he will devise what is appropriate, and be least
likely to overlook incongruities. This is shown by what was
censured in Carcinus, the return of Amphiaraus from the
sanctuary; it would have passed unnoticed, if it had not been
actually seen by the audience; but on the stage his play
failed, the incongruity of the incident offending the spectators. (2) As far as may be, too, the poet should even act his
story with the very gestures of his personages. Given the 30
same natural qualifications, he who feels the emotions to be
described will be the most convincing; distress and anger, for
instance, are portrayed most truthfully by one who is feeling
them at the moment. Hence it is that poetry demands a man
with a special gift for it, or else one with a touch of madness
in him; the former can easily assume the required mood, and
the latter may be actually beside himself with emotion. (3)
His story, again, whether already made or of his own making, he should first simplify and reduce to a universal form, 1455^b
before proceeding to lengthen it out by the insertion of
episodes. The following will show how the universal element
in *Iphigenia*, for instance, may be viewed: A certain maiden

32 *Iph. Taur.* 582

having been offered in sacrifice, and spirited away from her
5 sacrifices into another land, where the custom was to sacrifice all strangers to the Goddess, she was made there the
priestess of this rite. Long after that the brother of the
priestess happened to come; the fact, however, of the oracle
having for a certain reason bidden him go thither, and his
object in going, are outside the Plot of the play. On his coming he was arrested, and about to be sacrificed, when he
10 revealed who he was—either as Euripides puts it, or (as suggested by Polyidus) by the not improbable exclamation, 'So
I too am doomed to be sacrificed, as my sister was', and the
disclosure led to his salvation. This done, the next thing,
after the proper names have been fixed as a basis for the
story, is to work in episodes or accessory incidents. One
must mind, however, that the episodes are appropriate, like
15 the fit of madness[33] in Orestes, which led to his arrest, and
the purifying,[34] which brought about his salvation. In plays,
then, the episodes are short; in epic poetry they serve to
lengthen out the poem. The argument of the *Odyssey* is not
a long one. A certain man has been abroad many years;
Poseidon is ever on the watch for him, and he is all alone.
20 Matters at home too have come to this, that his substance is
being wasted and his son's death plotted by suitors to his
wife. Then he arrives there himself after his grievous sufferings; reveals himself, and falls on his enemies; and the end is
his salvation and their death. This being all that is proper
to the *Odyssey*, everything else in it is episode.

18 (4) There is a further point to be borne in mind.
Every tragedy is in part Complication and in
part Dénouement; the incidents before the opening scene, and often certain also of those within the play,

[33] *Iph. Taur.* 281 ff.

[34] Ib., 1163 ff.

forming the Complication; and the rest the Dénouement. 25
By Complication I mean all from the beginning of the story
to the point just before the change in the hero's fortunes;
by Dénouement, all from the beginning of the change to
the end. In the *Lynceus* of Theodectes, for instance, the
Complication includes, together with the presupposed 30
incidents, the seizure of the child and that in turn of the
parents; and the Dénouement all from the indictment for 1456ᵃ7
the murder to the end. Now it is right, when one speaks of
a tragedy as the same or not the same as another, to do so
on the ground before all else of their Plot, i. e. as having
the same or not the same Complication and Dénouement.
Yet there are many dramatists who, after a good Complication, fail in the Dénouement. But it is necessary for both
points of construction to be always duly mastered. (5) There
are four distinct species of Tragedy—that being the number 1455ᵇ32
of the constituents also that have been mentioned:[35] first,
the complex Tragedy, which is all Peripety and Discovery;
second, the Tragedy of suffering, e. g. the *Ajaxes* and *Ixions*;
third, the Tragedy of character, e. g. *The Phthiotides*[36] and
Peleus.[37] The fourth constituent is that of 'Spectacle', exem- 1456ᵃ
plified in *The Phorcides*,[38] in *Prometheus*,[39] and in all plays
with the scene laid in the nether world. The poet's aim,
then, should be to combine every element of interest, if possible, or else the more important and the major part of
them. This is now especially necessary owing to the unfair
criticism to which the poet is subjected in these days. Just 5
because there have been poets before him strong in the sev-

[35] This does not agree with anything actually said before.

[36] By Sophocles.

[37] Probably Sophocles' *Peleus* is incorrect.

[38] By Aeschylus.

[39] Probably a satiric drama by Aeschylus.

eral species of tragedy, the critics now expect the one man
to surpass that which was the strong point of each one of
his predecessors. (6) One should also remember what has
been said more than once,[40] and not write a tragedy on an
epic body of incident (i. e one with a plurality of stories in
it), by attempting to dramatize, for instance, the entire story
of the *Iliad*. In the epic owing to its scale every part is
treated at proper length; with a drama, however, on the
same story the result is very disappointing. This is shown
by the fact that all who have dramatized the fall of Ilium in
its entirety, and not part by part, like Euripides, of the
whole of the Niobe story, instead of a portion, like Aeschylus, either fail utterly or have but ill success on the stage; for
that and that alone was enough to ruin even a play by
Agathon. Yet in their Peripeties, as also in their simple
plots, the poets I mean show wonderful skill in aiming at
the kind of effect they desire—a tragic situation that arouses
the human feeling in one, like the clever villain (e. g. Sisy-
phus) deceived, or the brave wrongdoer worsted. This is
probable, however, only in Agathon's sense, when he speaks
of the probability of even improbabilities coming to pass.
(7) The Chorus too should be regarded as one of the actors;
it should be an integral part of the whole, and take a share
in the action—that which it has in Sophocles, rather than
in Euripides. With the later poets, however, the songs in a
play of theirs have no more to do with the Plot of that than
of any other tragedy. Hence it is that they are now singing
intercalary pieces, a practice first introduced by Agathon.
And yet what real difference is there between singing such
intercalary pieces, and attempting to fit in a speech, or even
a whole act, from one play into another?

[40] A loose reference to 1449[b] 12, 1455[b] 15.

19
The Plot and Characters having been discussed, it remains to consider the Diction and Thought. As for the Thought, we may assume what is 35 said of it in our Art of Rhetoric,[41] as it belongs more properly to that department of inquiry. The Thought of the personages is shown in everything to be effected by their language—in every effort to prove or disprove, to arouse emotion (pity, fear, anger, and the like), or to maximize or 1456b minimize things. It is clear, also, that their mental procedure must be on the same lines in their actions likewise, whenever they wish them to arouse pity or horror, or to 5 have a look of importance or probability. The only difference is that with the act the impression has to be made without explanation; whereas with the spoken word it has to be produced by the speaker, and result from his language. What, indeed, would be the good of the speaker, if things appeared in the required light even apart from anything he says?

As regards the Diction, one subject for inquiry under this head is the turns given to the language when spoken; e. g. the difference between command and prayer, simple 10 statement and threat, question and answer, and so forth. The theory of such matters, however, belongs to Elocution and the professors of that art. Whether the poet knows these things or not, his art as a poet is never seriously criti- 15 cized on that account. What fault can one see in Homer's 'Sing of the wrath, Goddess'?—which Protagoras has criticized as being a command where a prayer was meant, since to bid one do or not do, he tells us, is a command. Let us pass over this, then, as appertaining to another art, and not to that of poetry.

[41] Cf. especially *Rhet.* 1356a 1.

20 The Diction viewed as a whole is made up of the following parts: the Letter (or ultimate element), the Syllable, the Conjunction, the Article, the Noun, the Verb, the Case, and the Speech. (1) The Letter is an indivisible sound of a particular kind, one that may become a factor in an intelligible sound. Indivisible sounds are uttered by the brutes also, but no one of these is a Letter in our sense of the term. These elementary sounds are either vowels, semi-vowels, or mutes. A vowel is a Letter having an audible sound without the addition of another Letter. A semi-vowel, one having an audible sound by the addition of another Letter; e. g. S and R. A mute, one having no sound at all by itself, but becoming audible by an addition, that of one of the Letters which have a sound of some sort of their own; e. g. G and D. The Letters differ in various ways: as produced by different conformations or in different regions of the mouth; as aspirated, not aspirated, or sometimes one and sometimes the other; as long, short, or of variable quantity; and further as having an acute, grave, or intermediate accent. The details of these matters we must leave to the metricians. (2) A Syllable is a nonsignificant composite sound, made up of a mute and a Letter having a sound (a vowel or semi-vowel); for GR, without an A, is just as much a Syllable as GRA, with an A. The various forms of the Syllable also belong to the theory of metre. (3) A Conjunction is (*a*) a non-significant sound which, when one significant sound is formable out of several, neither hinders nor aids the union, and which, if the Speech thus formed stands by itself (apart from other Speeches), must not be inserted at the beginning of it; e. g. μέν, δή, τοι, δέ. Or (*b*) a non-significant sound capable of combining two or more significant sounds into one; e. g. ἀμφί, περί &c. (4) An Article is a non-significant sound marking the beginning, end, or dividing-point of a Speech, its natural place being either at the extremities or in

the middle. (5) A Noun or name is a composite significant 10
sound not involving the idea of time, with parts which have
no significance by themselves in it. It is to be remembered
that in a compound we do not think of the parts as having
a significance also by themselves; in the name 'Theodorus',
for instance, the δῶρον means nothing to us. (6) A Verb is
a composite significant sound involving the idea of time,
with parts which (just as in the Noun) have no significance
by themselves in it. Whereas the word 'man' or 'white' 15
does not imply *when*, 'walks' and 'has walked,' involve in
addition to the idea of walking that of time present or time
past. (7) A Case of a Noun or Verb is when the word
means 'of' or 'to' a thing, and so forth, or for one or many 20
(e. g. 'man' and 'men'); or it may consist merely in the
mode of utterance, e. g. in question, command, &c.
'Walked?' and 'Walk!' are Cases of the verb 'to walk' of
this last kind. (8) A Speech is a composite significant
sound, some of the parts of which have a certain significance by themselves. It may be observed that a Speech is 25
not always made up of Noun and Verb; it may be without a
Verb, like the definition of man; but it will always have
some part with a certain significance by itself. In the Speech
'Cleon walks', 'Cleon' is an instance of such a part. A
Speech is said to be one in two ways, either as signifying
one thing, or as a union of several Speeches made into one
by conjunction. Thus the *Iliad* is one Speech by conjunc- 30
tion of several; and the definition of man is one through its
signifying one thing.

21 Nouns are of two kinds, either (1) simple, i. e.
made of non-significant parts like the word γῆ,
or (2) double; in the latter case the word may be
made up either of a significant and a non-significant part (a
distinction which disappears in the compound), or of two
significant parts. It is possible also to have triple, quadruple, 35

or higher compounds, like most of our amplified names;
e. g. 'Hermocaïcoxanthus' and the like.

1457^b   Whatever its structure, a Noun must always be either
(1) the ordinary word for the thing, or (2) a strange word, or
(3) a metaphor, or (4) an ornamental word, or (5) a coined
word, or (6) a word lengthened out, or (7) curtailed, or (8)
altered in form. By the ordinary word I mean that in general
use in a country; and by a strange word, one in use elsewhere. So that the same word may obviously be at once
5 strange and ordinary, though not in reference to the same
people; σίγυνον, for instance, is an ordinary word in
Cyprus, and a strange word with us. Metaphor consists in
giving the thing a name that belongs to something else; the
transference being either from genus to species, or from
species to genus, or from species to species, or on grounds
10 of analogy. That from genus to species is exemplified in
'Here stands my ship';[42] for lying at anchor is the 'standing' of a particular kind of thing. That from species to
genus in 'Truly ten thousand good deeds has Ulysses
wrought',[43] where 'ten thousand', which is a particular large
number, is put in place of the generic 'a large number'.
That from species to species in 'Drawing the life with the
15 bronze',[44] and in 'Severing with the enduring bronze';[44]
where the poet uses 'draw' in the sense of 'sever' and
'sever' in that of 'draw', both words meaning to 'take away'
something. That from analogy is possible whenever there
are four terms so related that the second (B) is to the first
(A), as the fourth (D) to the third (C); for one may then
metaphorically put D in lieu of B, and B in lieu of D. Now
and then, too, they qualify the metaphor by adding on to it

---

[42] *Od.* i. 185, xxiv. 308.

[43] *Il.* ii. 272.

[44] Empedocles.

that to which the word it supplants is relative. Thus a cup 20
(B) is in relation to Dionysus (A) what a shield (D) is to
Ares (C). The cup accordingly will be metaphorically
described as the 'shield of *Dionysus*' (D + A), and the shield
as the 'cup of *Ares*'[45] (B + C). Or to take another instance:
As old age (D) is to life (C), so is evening (B) to day (A).
One will accordingly describe evening (B) as the 'old age *of
the day*' (D + A)—or by the Empedoclean equivalent; and
old age (D) as the 'evening'[46] or 'sunset *of life*'[47] (B + C). It
may be that some of the terms thus related have no special 25
name of their own, but for all that they will be metaphorically described in just the same way. Thus to cast forth
seed-corn is called 'sowing'; but to cast forth its flame, as
said of the sun, has no special name. This nameless act (B),
however, stands in just the same relation to its object, sun-
light (A), as sowing (D) to the seed-corn (C). Hence the
expression in the poet, 'sowing around a god-created
flame'[48] (D + A). There is also another form of qualified 30
metaphor. Having given the thing the alien name, one may
by a negative addition deny of it one of the attributes naturally associated with its new name. An instance of this
would be to call the shield not the 'cup of *Ares*', as in the
former case, but a 'cup *that holds no wine*' . . . A coined
word is a name which, being quite unknown among a people, is given by the poet himself; e. g. (for there are some
words that seem to be of this origin) ἔρνυγς for horns, and
ἀρητήρ for priest.[49] A word is said to be lengthened out,
when it has a short vowel made long, or an extra syllable 35

---

[45] Timotheus.

[46] Alexis.

[47] Pl., *Laws* 770 A.

[48] Authorship unknown.

[49] *Il.* i. 11.

1458ᵃ   inserted; e. g. πόληος for πόλεως, Πηληιάδεω for Πηλείδου.
It is said to be curtailed, when it has lost a part; e. g. κρῖ,
5   δῶ, and ὄψ in μία γίνεται ἀμφοτέρων ὄψ.⁵⁰ It is an altered
word, when part is left as it was and part is of the poet's
making; e. g. δεξιτερόν for δεξιόν, in δεξιτερὸν κατὰ
μαζόν.⁵¹

The Nouns themselves (to whatever class they may
belong) are either masculines, feminines, or intermediates
(neuter). All ending in Ν, Ρ, Σ, or in the two compounds of
10   this last, Ψ and Ξ, are masculines. All ending in the invariably long vowels, Η and Ω, and in Α among the vowels that
may be long, are feminines. So that there is an equal number of masculine and feminine terminations, as Ψ and Ξ are
the same as Σ, and need not be counted. There is no Noun,
15   however, ending in a mute or in either of the two short
vowels, Ε and Ο. Only three (μέλι, κόμμι, πέπερι) end in
Ι and five in Υ. The intermediates, or neuters, end in the
variable vowels or in Ν, Ρ, Σ.

22

The perfection of Diction is for it to be at once
clear and not mean. The clearest indeed is that
20   made up of the ordinary words for things, but
it is mean, as is shown by the poetry of Cleophon and
Sthenelus. On the other hand the Diction becomes distinguished and non-prosaic by the use of unfamiliar terms, i. e.
strange words, metaphors, lengthened forms, and everything
that deviates from the ordinary modes of speech.—But a
25   whole statement in such terms will be either a riddle or a
barbarism, a riddle, if made up of metaphors, a barbarism,
if made up of strange words. The very nature indeed of a
riddle is this, to describe a fact in an impossible combination of words (which cannot be done with the real names

⁵⁰ Empedocles.

⁵¹ Il. v. 393.

for things, but can be with their metaphorical substitutes);
e. g. 'I saw a man glue brass on another with fire',[52] and the 30
like. The corresponding use of strange words results in a
barbarism. —A certain admixture, accordingly, of unfamiliar terms is necessary. These, the strange word, the
metaphor, the ornamental equivalent, &c., will save the language from seeming mean and prosaic, while the ordinary
words in it will secure the requisite clearness. What helps 1458ᵇ
most, however, to render the Diction at once clear and non-
prosaic is the use of the lengthened, curtailed, and altered
forms of words Their deviation from the ordinary words
will, by making the language unlike that in general use, give
it a non-prosaic appearance; and their having much in common with the words in general use will give it the quality 5
of clearness. It is not right, then, to condemn these modes
of speech, and ridicule the poet for using them, as some
have done; e. g. the elder Euclid, who said it was easy to
make poetry if one were to be allowed to lengthen the words
in the statement itself as much as one likes—a procedure he
caricatured by reading Ἐπιχάρην εἶδον Μαραθῶνάδε βαδί- 10
ζοντα, and οὐκ ἂν γ' ἐράμενος τὸν ἐκείνου ἐλλέβορον as
verses. A too apparent use of these licences has certainly a
ludicrous effect, but they are not alone in that; the rule of
moderation applies to all the constituents of the poetic
vocabulary; even with metaphors, strange words, and the
rest, the effect will be the same, if one uses them improperly
and with a view to provoking laughter. The proper use of
them is a very different thing. To realize the difference one 15
should take an epic verse and see how it reads when the
normal words are introduced. The same should be done too
with the strange word, the metaphor, and the rest; for one
has only to put the ordinary words in their place to see the
truth of what we are saying. The same iambic, for instance,

52 Cleobulina.

is found in Aeschylus and Euripides, and as it stands in the
former it is a poor line; whereas Euripides, by the change of
20 a single word, the substitution of a strange for what is by
usage the ordinary word, has made it seem a fine one.
Aeschylus having said in his *Philoctetes*:

φαγέδαινα ἥ μου σάρκας ἐσθίει ποδός

Euripides has merely altered the ἐσθίει here into ηοινᾶται.
Or suppose

25   νῦν δέ μ᾽ ἐὼν ὀλίγος τε καὶ οὐτιδανὸς καὶ ἀειδής[53]

to be altered, by the substitution of the ordinary words, into

νῦν δέ μ᾽ ἐὼν μικρός τε καὶ ἀσθενικὸς καὶ ἀειδής.

Or the line

δίφρον ἀεικέλιον καταθεὶς ὀλίγην τε τράπεζαν[54]

into

30   δίφρον μοχθηρὸν καταθεὶς μικράν τε τράπεζαν.

Or ἠιόνες βοόωσιν[55] into ἠιόνες κράζουσιν. Add to this
that Ariphrades used to ridicule the tragedians for introduc-
ing expressions unknown in the language of common life,
δωμάτων ἄπο (for ἀπὸ δωμάτων), σέθεν, ἐγὼ δέ νιν,[56]

53 *Od.* ix. 515.

54 *Od.* xx. 259.

55 *Il.* xvii. 265.

56 Soph., *O. C.*, 986.

'Αχιλλέως πέρι (for περὶ 'Αχιλλέως) and the like. The mere
fact of their not being in ordinary speech gives the Diction 1459ᵃ
a non-prosaic character; but Ariphrades was unaware of
that. It is a great thing, indeed, to make a proper use of
these poetical forms, as also of compounds and strange
words. But the greatest thing by far is to be a master of
metaphor. It is the one thing that cannot be learnt from 5
others; and it is also a sign of genius, since a good metaphor
implies an intuitive perception of the similarity in dissimilars.

Of the kinds of words we have enumerated it may be
observed that compounds are most in place in the dithyramb, strange words in heroic, and metaphors in iambic 10
poetry. Heroic poetry, indeed, may avail itself of them all.
But in iambic verse, which models itself as far as possible
on the spoken language, only those kinds of words are in
place which are allowable also in an oration, i. e. the ordinary word, the metaphor, and the ornamental equivalent.

Let this then, suffice as an account of Tragedy, the art 15
imitating by means of action on the stage.

23

As for the poetry which merely narrates, or imitates by means of versified language (without
action), it is evident that it has several points in
common with Tragedy.

I. The construction of its stories should clearly be like
that in a drama; they should be based on a single action,
one that is a complete whole in itself, with a beginning,
middle, and end, so as to enable the work to produce its 20
own proper pleasure with all the organic unity of a living
creature. Nor should one suppose that there is anything like
them in our usual histories. A history has to deal not with
one action, but with one period and all that happened in
that to one or more persons, however disconnected the several events may have been. Just as two events may take 25

place at the same time, e. g. the sea-fight off Salamis and the battle with the Carthaginians in Sicily, without converging to the same end, so too of two consecutive events one may sometimes come after the other with no one end as their common issue. Nevertheless most of our epic poets, one may say, ignore the distinction.

30   Herein, then, to repeat what we have said before,[57] we have a further proof of Homer's marvellous superiority to the rest. He did not attempt to deal even with the Trojan war in its entirety, though it was a whole with a definite beginning and end—through a feeling apparently that it was
35 too long a story to be taken in in one view, or if not that, too complicated from the variety of incident in it. As it is, he has singled out one section of the whole; many of the other incidents, however, he brings in as episodes, using the Catalogue of the Ships, for instance, and other episodes to relieve the uniformity of his narrative. As for the other epic poets, they treat of one man, or one period; or else of an
1459b action which, although one, has a multiplicity of parts in it. This last is what the authors of the Cypria[58] and Little Iliad[58] have done. And the result is that, whereas the Iliad or Odyssey supplies materials for only one, or at most two tragedies, the Cypria does that for several and the Little Iliad for more than eight: for an Adjudgment of Arms, a
5 Philoctetes, a Neoptolemus, a Eurypylus, a Ulysses as Beggar, a Laconian Women, a Fall of Ilium, and a Departure of the Fleet; as also a Sinon, and a Women of Troy.

[57] 1451a 23 ff.

[58] Authorship unknown.

24 II. Besides this, Epic poetry must divide into the same species as Tragedy; it must be either simple or complex, a story of character or one of suffering. Its parts, too, with the exception of Song and Spectacle, must be the same, as it requires Peripeties, Dis- coveries, and scenes of suffering just like Tragedy. Lastly, the Thought and Diction in it must be good in their way. All these elements appear in Homer first; and he has made due use of them. His two poems are each examples of con- struction, the *Iliad* simple and a story of suffering, the *Odyssey* complex (there is Discovery throughout it) and a story of character. And they are more than this, since in Diction and Thought too they surpass all other poems.

There is, however, a difference in the Epic as compared with Tragedy, (1) in its length, and (2) in its metre. (1) As to its length, the limit already suggested[59] will suffice: it must be possible for the beginning and end of the work to be taken in in one view—a condition which will be fulfilled if the poem be shorter than the old epics, and about as long as the series of tragedies offered for one hearing. For the extension of its length epic poetry has a special advantage, of which it makes large use. In a play one cannot represent an action with a number of parts going on simultaneously; one is limited to the part on the stage and connected with the actors. Whereas in epic poetry the narrative form makes it possible for one to describe a number of simultaneous incidents; and these, if germane to the subject, increase the body of the poem. This then is a gain to the Epic, tending to give it grandeur, and also variety of interest and room for episodes of diverse kinds. Uniformity of incident by the satiety it soon creates is apt to ruin tragedies on the stage. (2) As for its metre, the heroic has been assigned it from experience; were any one to attempt a narrative poem in

---

[59] 1451ᵃ 3.

some one, or in several, of the other metres, the incongruity
of the thing would be apparent. The heroic in fact is the
gravest and weightiest of metres—which is what makes it
35 more tolerant than the rest of strange words and metaphors,
that also being a point in which the narrative form of poetry
goes beyond all others. The iambic and trochaic, on the
1460ᵃ other hand, are metres of movement, the one representing
that of life and action, the other that of the dance. Still more
unnatural would it appear, if one were to write an epic in a
medley of metres, as Chaeremon did.[60] Hence it is that no
one has ever written a long story in any but heroic verse;
nature herself, as we have said,[61] teaches us to select the
metre appropriate to such a story.

5   Homer, admirable as he is in every other respect, is
especially so in this, that he alone among epic poets is not
unaware of the part to be played by the poet himself in the
poem. The poet should say very little *in propria persona*, as
he is no imitator when doing that. Whereas the other poets
are perpetually coming forward in person, and say but little,
and that only here and there, as imitators, Homer after a
10 brief preface brings in forthwith a man, a woman, or some
other Character—no one of them characterless, but each
with distinctive characteristics.

The marvellous is certainly required in Tragedy. The
Epic, however, affords more opening for the improbable,
the chief factor in the marvellous, because in it the agents
15 are not visibly before one. The scene of the pursuit of Hector would be ridiculous on the stage—the Greeks halting
instead of pursuing him, and Achilles shaking his head to
stop them;[62] but in the poem the absurdity is overlooked.

[60] *Centaur.* cf. 1447ᵇ 21.

[61] 1449ᵃ 24

[62] *Il.* xxii. 205.

The marvellous, however, is a cause of pleasure, as is shown
by the fact that we all tell a story with additions, in the
belief that we are doing our hearers a pleasure.

Homer more than any other has taught the rest of us
the art of framing lies in the right way. I mean the use of   20
paralogism. Whenever, if *A* is or happens, a consequent, *B*,
is or happens, men's notion is that, if the *B* is, the *A* also
is—but that is a false conclusion. Accordingly, if *A* is
untrue, but there is something else, *B*, that on the assumption of its truth follows as its consequent, the right thing
then is to add on the *B*. Just because we know the truth of
the consequent, we are in our own minds led on to the erroneous inference of the truth of the antecedent. Here is an   25
instance, from the *Bath-story* in the *Odyssey*.[63]

A likely impossibility is always preferable to an unconvincing possibility. The story should never be made up of
improbable incidents; there should be nothing of the sort in
it. If, however, such incidents are unavoidable, they should
be outside the piece, like the hero's ignorance in *Oedipus* of   30
the circumstances of Laius' death; not within it, like the
report of the Pythian games in *Electra*,[64] or the man's having
come to Mysia from Tegea without uttering a word on the
way, in *The Mysians*.[65] So that it is ridiculous to say that
one's Plot would have been spoilt without them, since it is
fundamentally wrong to make up such Plots. If the poet has
taken such a Plot, however, and one sees that he might have
put it in a more probable form, he is guilty of absurdity as   35
well as a fault of art. Even in the *Odyssey* the improbabilities in the setting-ashore of Ulysses[66] would be clearly

[63] xix. 164–260.

[64] Soph. *El.* 660 ff.

[65] Probably by Aeschylus.

[66] xiii. 116 ff.

1460ᵇ intolerable in the hands of an inferior poet. As it is, the poet
conceals them, his other excellences veiling their absurdity.
Elaborate Diction, however, is required only in places where
there is no action, and no Character or Thought to be
5 revealed. Where there is Character or Thought, on the other
hand, an over-ornate Diction tends to obscure them.

25 As regards Problems and their Solutions, one
may see the number and nature of the assumptions on which they proceed by viewing the
matter in the following way. (1) The poet being an imitator just like the painter or other maker of likenesses, he
must necessarily in all instances represent things in one or
10 other of three aspects, either as they were or are, or as they
are said or thought to be or to have been, or as they ought
to be. (2) All this he does in language, with an admixture, it
may be, of strange words and metaphors, as also of the various modified forms of words, since the use of these is
conceded in poetry. (3) It is to be remembered, too, that there
is not the same kind of correctness in poetry as in politics, or
indeed any other art. There is, however, within the limits of
15 poetry itself a possibility of two kinds of error, the one
directly, the other only accidentally connected with the art. If
the poet meant to describe the thing correctly, and failed
through lack of power of expression, his art itself is at fault.
But if it was through his having meant to describe it in
some incorrect way (e. g. to make the horse in movement
have both right legs thrown forward) that the technical error
(one in a matter of, say, medicine or some other special sci-
20 ence), or impossibilities of whatever kind they may be, have
got into his description, his error in that case is not in the
essentials of the poetic art. These, therefore, must be the
premisses of the Solutions in answer to the criticisms
involved in the Problems.

I. As to the criticisms relating to the poet's art itself.

Any impossibilities there may be in his descriptions of things are faults. But from another point of view they are justifiable, if they serve the end of poetry itself—if (to 25 assume what we have said of that end)[67] they make the effect of either that very portion of the work or some other portion more astounding. The Pursuit of Hector is an instance in point. If, however, the poetic end might have been as well or better attained without sacrifice of technical correctness in such matters, the impossibility is not to be justified, since the description should be, if it can, entirely free from error. One may ask, too, whether the error is in a 30 matter directly or only accidentally connected with the poetic art; since it is a lesser error in an artist not to know, for instance, that the hind has no horns, than to produce an unrecognizable picture of one.

II. If the poet's description be criticized as not true to fact, one may urge perhaps that the object ought to be as described—an answer like that of Sophocles, who said that he drew men as they ought to be, and Euripides as they 35 were. If the description, however, be neither true nor of the thing as it ought to be, the answer must be then, that it is in accordance with opinion. The tales about Gods, for instance, may be as wrong as Xenophanes thinks, neither true nor the better thing to say; but they are certainly in accordance with opinion. Of other statements in poetry one 1461a may perhaps say, not that they are better than the truth, but that the fact was so at the time; e. g. the description of the arms: 'their spears stood upright, butt-end upon the ground';[68] for that was the usual way of fixing them then, as it is still with the Illyrians. As for the question whether something said or done in a poem is morally right or not, in dealing with that one should consider not only the intrinsic 5

[67] 1452ª 4, 1454ª 4, 1455ª 17, 1460ª 11.

[68] *Il.* x. 152.

quality of the actual word or deed, but also the person who says or does it, the person to whom he says or does it, the time, the means, and the motive of the agent—whether he does it to attain a greater good, or to avoid a greater evil.

III. Other criticisms one must meet by considering a
10 language of the poet: (1) by the assumption of a strange word in a passage like οὐρῆας μὲν πρῶτον,[69] where by οὐρῆας Homer may perhaps mean not mules but sentinels. And in saying of Dolon, ὅς ῥ' ἦ τοι εἶδος μὲν ἔην κακός,[70] his meaning may perhaps be, not that Dolon's body was deformed, but that his face was ugly, as εὐειδής is the Cre-
15 tan word for handsome-faced. So, too, ζωρότερον δὲ κέραιε[71] may mean not 'mix the wine stronger', as though for topers, but 'mix it quicker', (2) Other expressions in Homer may be explained as metaphorical; e. g. in ἄλλοι μέν ῥα θεοί τε καὶ ἀνέρες εὗδον<ἅπαντες>παννύχιοι,[72] as compared with what he tells us at the same time, ἦ τοι ὅτ' ἐς πεδίον τὸ Τρωικὸν ἀθρήσειεν, αὐλῶν συρίγγων †τε ὁμαδόν†,[73] the word ἅπαντες, 'all', is metaphorically put for 'many', since 'all' is a species of 'many'. So also his οἴη δ'
20 ἄμμορος[74] is metaphorical, the best known standing 'alone'. (3) A change, as Hippias of Thasos suggested, in the mode of reading a word will solve the difficulty in δίδομεν δέ οἱ,[75] and in τὸ μὲν οὗ καταπύθεται ὄμβρῳ.[76] (4) Other difficul-

[69] Il. i. 50.

[70] Il. x. 316.

[71] Il. ix. 202.

[72] Cf. Il. x. 1, ii. 1.

[73] Il. x. 11–13.

[74] Il. xviii. 489 = Od. v. 275.

[75] Cf. Soph. El. 166[b] 1; Il. ii. 15.

[76] Il. xxiii. 327.

ties may be solved by another punctuation; e. g. in Empedocles, αἶψα δὲ θνήτ᾽ ἐφύοντο, τὰ πρὶν μάθον ἀθάνατα 25
ζωρά τε πρὶν κέκρητο. Or (5) by the assumption of an
equivocal term, as in παρῴχηκεν δὲ πλέω νύξ,[77] where
πλέω is equivocal. Or (6) by an appeal to the custom of language. Wine-and-water we call 'wine'; and it is on the same
principle that Homer speaks of a κνημὶς νεοτεύκτου κασ-
σιτέροιο[78] a 'greave of new-wrought *tin*'. A worker in iron
we call a 'brazier'; and it is on the same principle that
Ganymede is described as the '*wine*-server' of Zeus,[79]
though the Gods do not drink wine. This latter, however, 30
may be an instance of metaphor. But whenever also a word
seems to imply some contradiction, it is necessary to reflect
how many ways there may be of understanding it in the
passage in question; e. g. in Homer's τῇ ῥ᾽ ἔσχετο χάλκεον
ἔγχος[80] one should consider the possible senses of 'was
stopped there'—whether by taking it in this sense or in that
one will best avoid the fault of which Glaucon speaks: 35
'They start with some improbable presumption; and hav- 1461ᵇ
ing so decreed it themselves, proceed to draw inferences,
and censure the poet as though he had actually said whatever they happen to believe, if his statement conflicts with
their own notion of things.' This is how Homer's silence
about Icarius has been treated. Starting with the notion of
his having been a Lacedaemonian, the critics think it
strange for Telemachus not to have met him when he went 5
to Lacedaemon. Whereas the fact may have been as the
Cephallenians say, that the wife of Ulysses was of a Cephal-
lenian family, and that her father's name was Icadius, not

[77] *Il.* x. 251.

[78] *Il.* xxi. 592.

[79] *Il.* xx. 234.

[80] *Il.* xx. 267.

Icarius. So that it is probably a mistake of the critics that has given rise to the Problem.

Speaking generally, one has to justify (1) the Impossible by reference to the requirements of poetry, or to the
10 better, or to opinion. For the purposes of poetry a convincing impossibility is preferable to an unconvincing possibility; and if men such as Zeuxis depicted be impossible, the answer is that it is better they should be like that, as the artist ought to improve on his model. (2) The Improbable one has to justify either by showing it to be in accordance with opinion, or by urging that at times it is not improbable;
15 for there is a probability of things happening also against probability. (3) The contradictions found in the poet's language one should first test as one does an opponent's confutation in a dialectical argument, so as to see whether he means the same thing, in the same relation, and in the same sense, before admitting that he has contradicted either something he has said himself or what a man of sound sense assumes as true. But there is no possible apology for improbability of Plot or depravity of character, when they
20 are not necessary and no use is made of them, like the improbability in the appearance of Aegeus in *Medea*[81] and the baseness of Menelaus in *Orestes*.

The objections, then, of critics start with faults of five kinds: the-allegation is always that something is either (1) impossible, (2) improbable, (3) corrupting, (4) contradictory, or (5) against technical correctness. The answers to
25 these objections must be sought under one or other of the above-mentioned heads, which are twelve in number.

26 The question may be raised whether the epic or the tragic is the higher forrn of imitation. It may be argued that, if the less vulgar is the higher,

[81] l. 663.

and the less vulgar is always that which addresses the better public, an art addressing any and every one is of a very
vulgar order. It is a belief that their public cannot see the
meaning, unless they add something themselves, that causes 30
the perpetual movements of the performers—bad flute-players, for instance, rolling about, if quoit-throwing is to be
represented, and pulling at the conductor, if Scylla is the
subject of the piece. Tragedy, then, is said to be an art of
this order —to be in fact just what the later actors were in
the eyes of their predecessors; for Mynniscus used to call
Callippides 'the ape', because he thought he so overacted 35
his parts; and a similar view was taken of Pindarus also. All 1462ᵃ
Tragedy, however, is said to stand to the Epic as the newer
to the older school of actors. The one, accordingly, is said to
address a cultivated audience, which does not need the
accompaniment of gesture; the other, an uncultivated one.
If, therefore, Tragedy is a vulgar art, it must clearly be 5
lower than the Epic.

The answer to this is twofold. In the first place, one
may urge (1) that the censure does not touch the art of the
dramatic poet, but only that of his interpreter; for it is quite
possible to overdo the gesturing even in an epic recital, as
did Sosistratus, and in a singing contest, as did Mnasitheus
of Opus. (2) That one should not condemn all movement,
unless one means to condemn even the dance, but only that
of ignoble people—which is the point of the criticism passed
on Callippides and in the present day on others, that their 10
women are not like gentlewomen. (3) That Tragedy may
produce its effect even without movement or action in just
the same way as Epic poetry; for from the mere reading of a
play its quality may be seen. So that, if it be superior in all
other respects, this element of inferiority is no necessary
part of it.

In the second place, one must remember (1) that
Tragedy has everything that the Epic has (even the epic

metre being admissible), together with a not inconsiderable
15 addition in the shape of the Music (a very real factor in the
pleasure of the drama) and the Spectacle. (2) That its reality
of presentation is felt in the play as read, as well as in the
play as acted. (3) That the tragic imitation requires less
space for the attainment of its end; which is a great advan-
1462ᵇ tage, since the more concentrated effect is more pleasurable
than one with a large admixture of time to dilute it—consider the *Oedipus* of Sophocles, for instance, and the effect
of expanding it into the number of lines of the *Iliad*. (4)
That there is less unity in the imitation of the epic poets,
as is proved by the fact that any one work of theirs supplies
matter for several tragedies; the result being that, if they
5 take what is really a single story, it seems curt when briefly
told, and thin and waterish when on the scale of length
usual with their verse. In saying that there is less unity in
an epic, I mean an epic made up of a plurality of actions,
in the same way as the *Iliad* and *Odyssey* have many such
10 parts, each one of them in itself of some magnitude; yet the
structure of the two Homeric poems is as perfect as can be,
and the action in them is as nearly as possible one action. If,
then, Tragedy is superior in these respects, and also, besides
these, in its poetic effect (since the two forms of poetry
should give us, not any or every pleasure, but the very special kind we have mentioned), it is clear that, as attaining
15 the poetic effect better than the Epic, it will be the higher
form of art.

So much for Tragedy and Epic poetry—for these two
arts in general and their species; the number and nature of
their constituent parts; the causes of success and failure in
them; the Objections of the critics, and the Solutions in
answer to them.

A NOTE ON THE TYPE

The principal text of this Modern Library edition
was composed in a digitized version of
Horley Old Style, a typeface issued by
the English type foundry Monotype in 1925.
It has such distinctive features
as lightly cupped serifs and an oblique horizontal bar
on the lowercase "e."